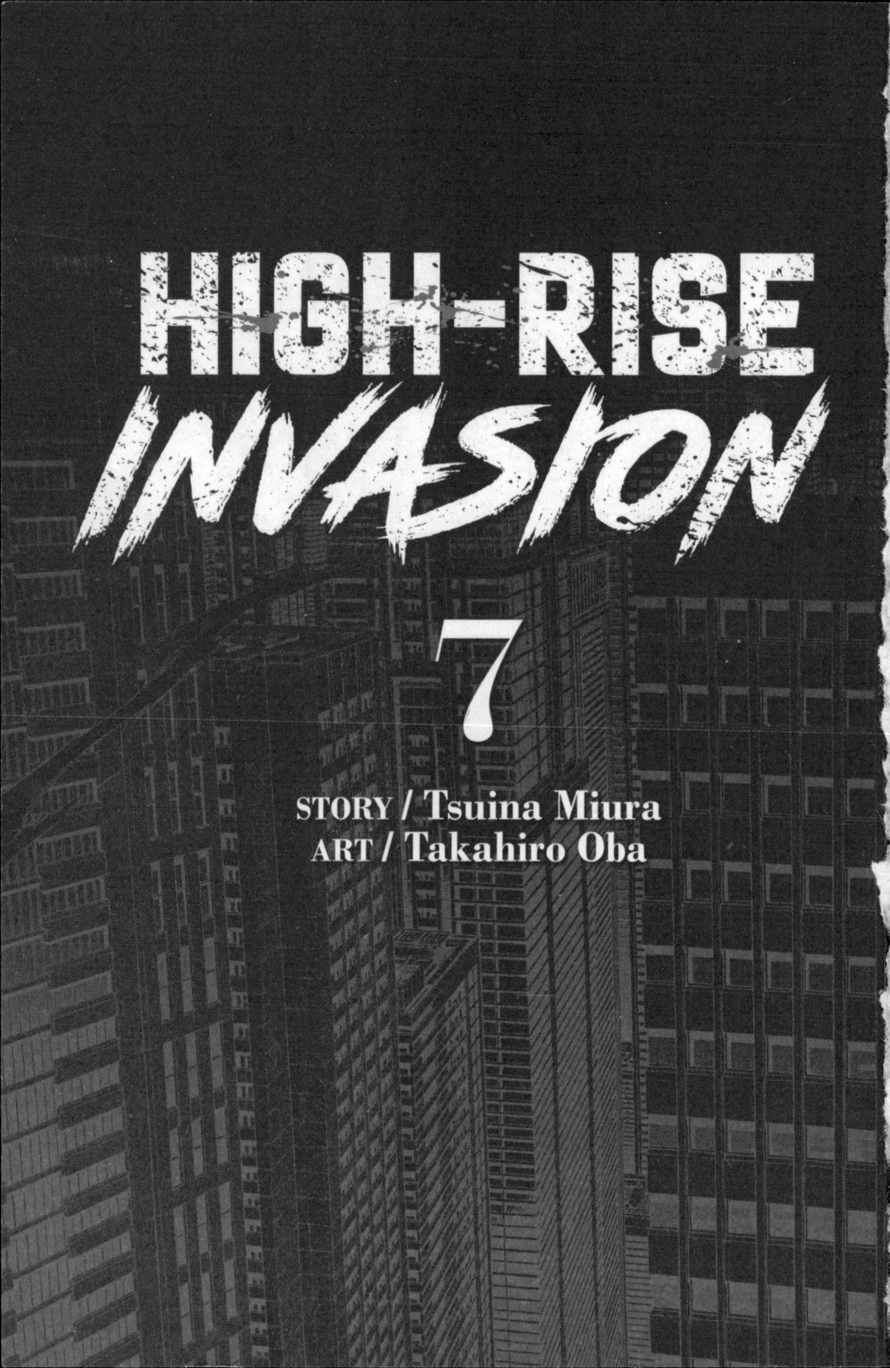
HIGH-RISE
INVASION
7
STORY / Tsuina Miura
ART / Takahiro Oba

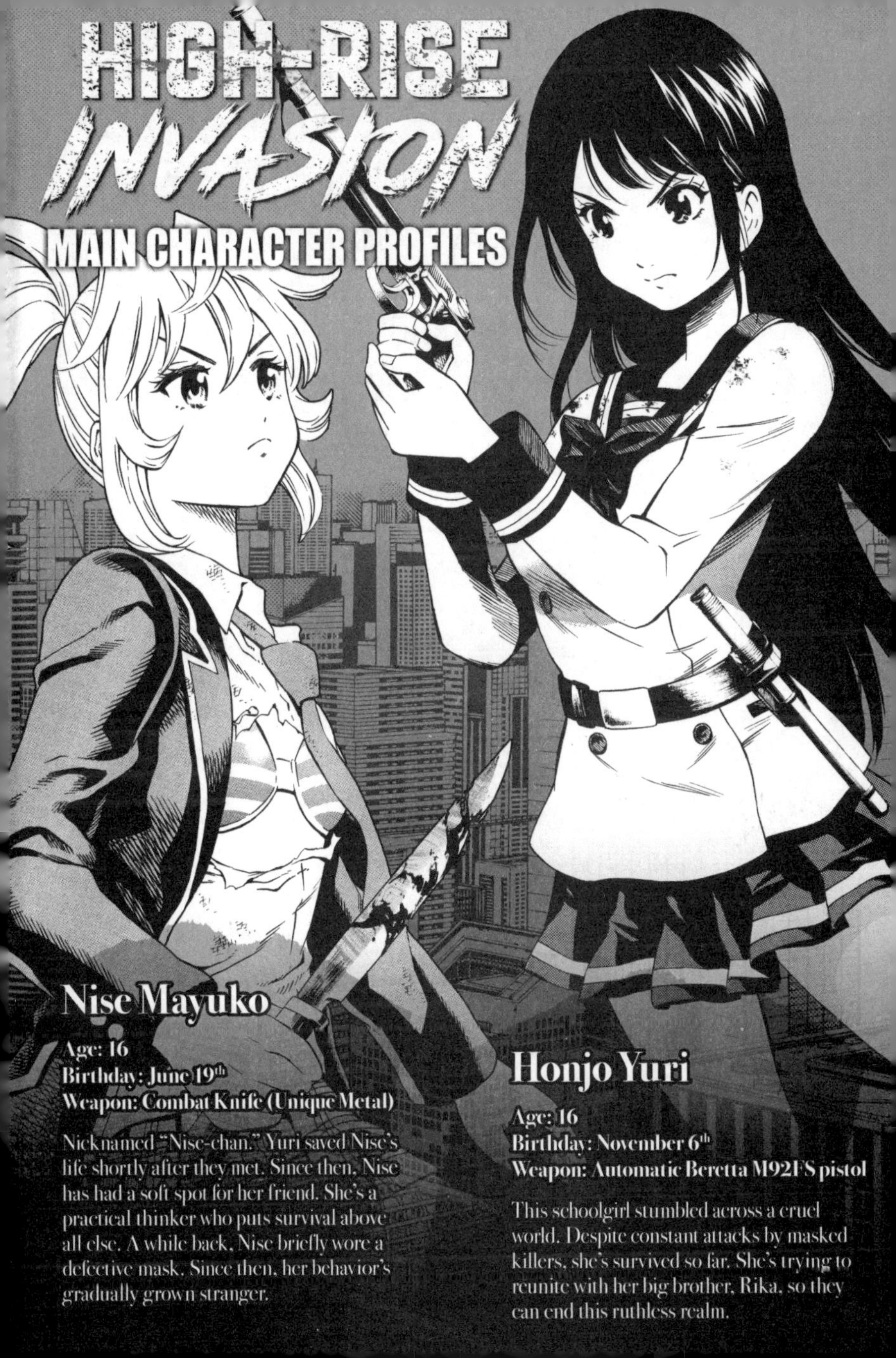

HIGH-RISE INVASION

MAIN CHARACTER PROFILES

Nise Mayuko

Age: 16
Birthday: June 19th
Weapon: Combat Knife (Unique Metal)

Nicknamed "Nise-chan." Yuri saved Nise's life shortly after they met. Since then, Nise has had a soft spot for her friend. She's a practical thinker who puts survival above all else. A while back, Nise briefly wore a defective mask. Since then, her behavior's gradually grown stranger.

Honjo Yuri

Age: 16
Birthday: November 6th
Weapon: Automatic Beretta M92FS pistol

This schoolgirl stumbled across a cruel world. Despite constant attacks by masked killers, she's survived so far. She's trying to reunite with her big brother, Rika, so they can end this ruthless realm.

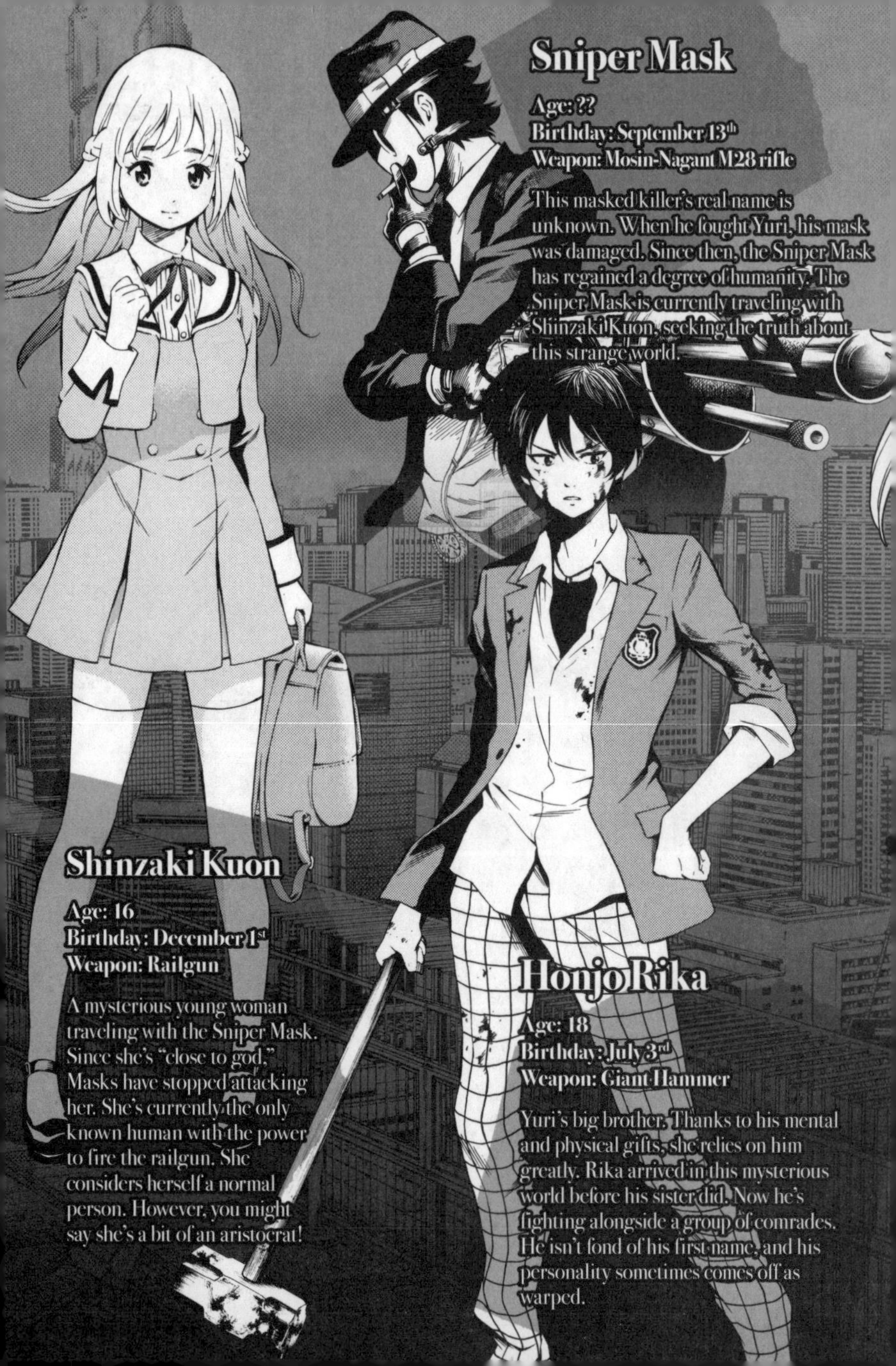
Sniper Mask
Age: ??
Birthday: September 13th
Weapon: Mosin-Nagant M28 rifle
This masked killer's real name is unknown. When he fought Yuri, his mask was damaged. Since then, the Sniper Mask has regained a degree of humanity. The Sniper Mask is currently traveling with Shinzaki Kuon, seeking the truth about this strange world.
Shinzaki Kuon
Age: 16
Birthday: December 1st
Weapon: Railgun
A mysterious young woman traveling with the Sniper Mask. Since she's "close to god," Masks have stopped attacking her. She's currently the only known human with the power to fire the railgun. She considers herself a normal person. However, you might say she's a bit of an aristocrat!
Honjo Rika
Age: 18
Birthday: July 3rd
Weapon: Giant Hammer
Yuri's big brother. Thanks to his mental and physical gifts, she relies on him greatly. Rika arrived in this mysterious world before his sister did. Now he's fighting alongside a group of comrades. He isn't fond of his first name, and his personality sometimes comes off as warped.

HIGH-RISE INVASION 7

CONTENTS

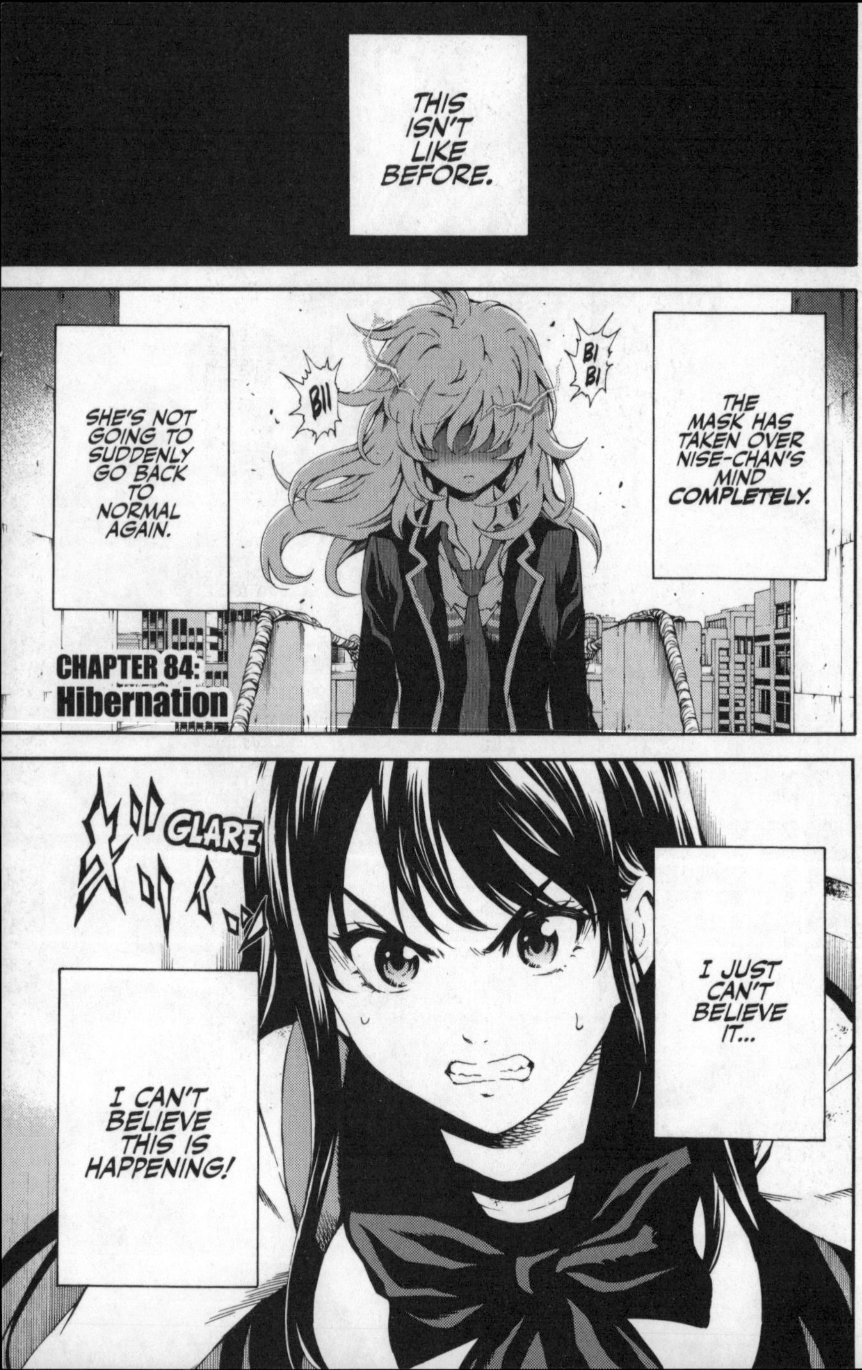
THIS ISN'T LIKE BEFORE.
THE MASK HAS TAKEN OVER NISE-CHAN'S MIND COMPLETELY.
BI BI
BII
SHE'S NOT GOING TO SUDDENLY GO BACK TO NORMAL AGAIN.
CHAPTER 84: Hibernation
GLARE
I JUST CAN'T BELIEVE IT...
I CAN'T BELIEVE THIS IS HAPPENING!

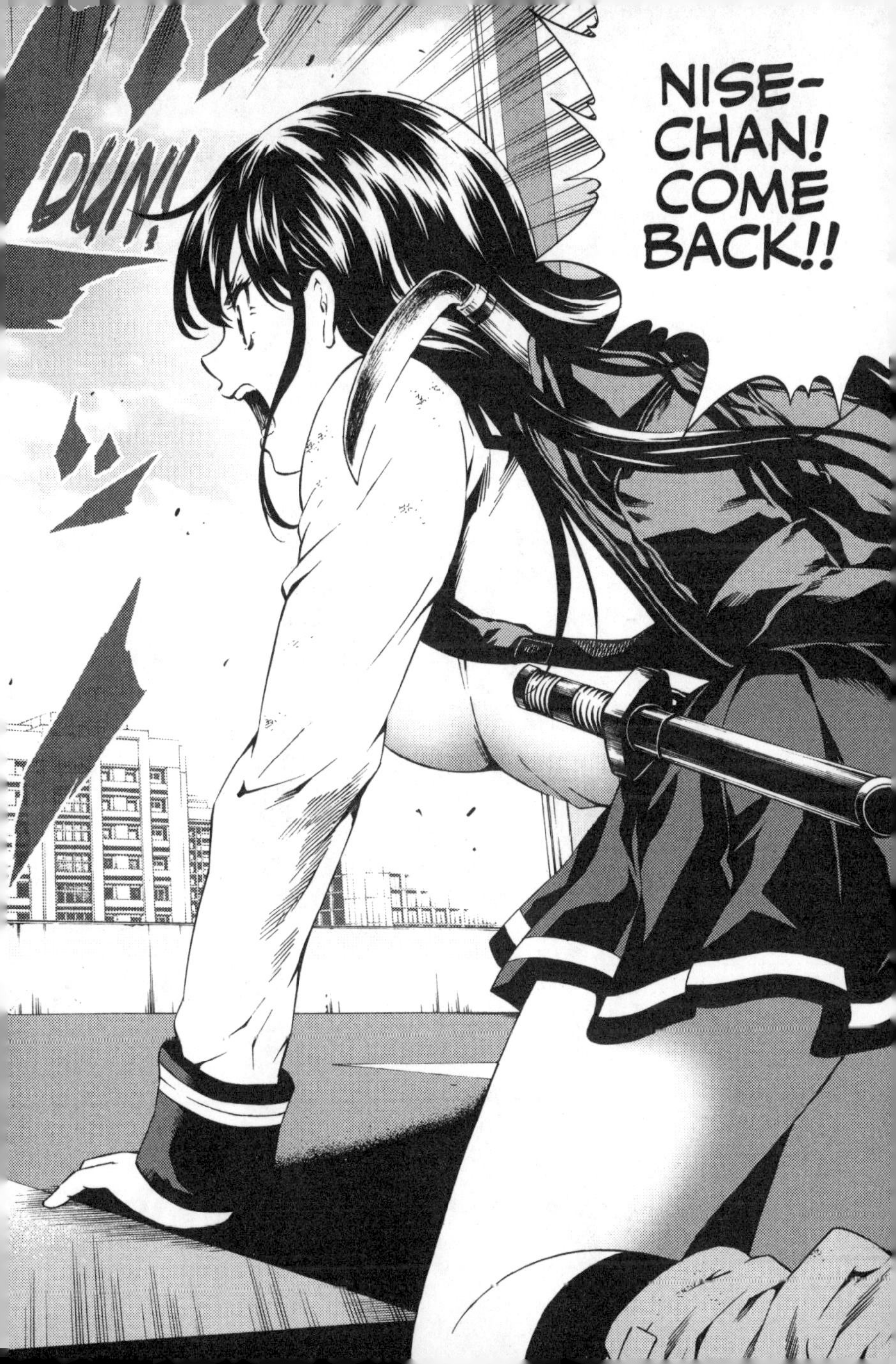
NISE-CHAN! COME BACK!!
DUN!

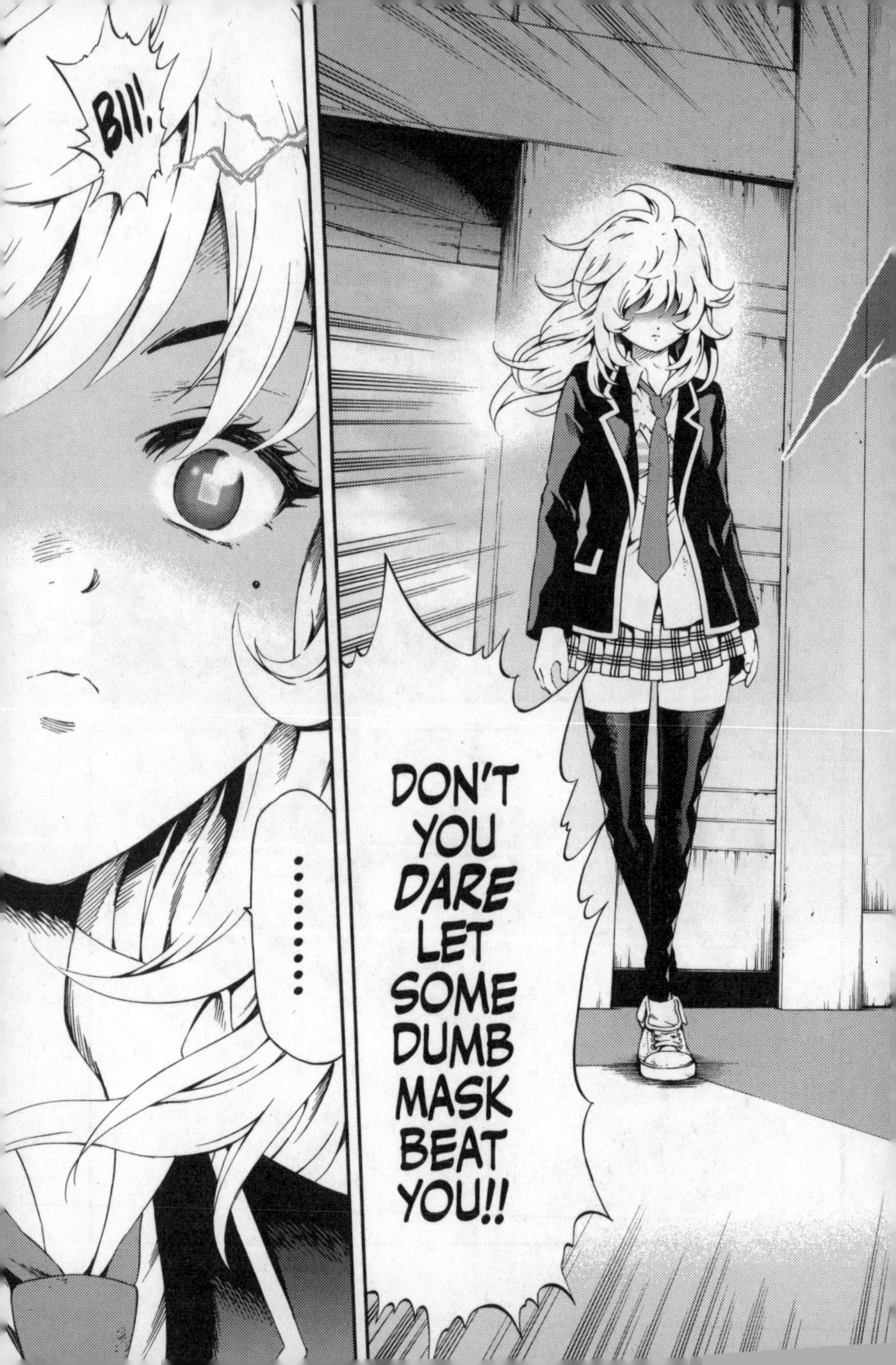
DON'T YOU DARE LET SOME DUMB MASK BEAT YOU!!
BII!
......

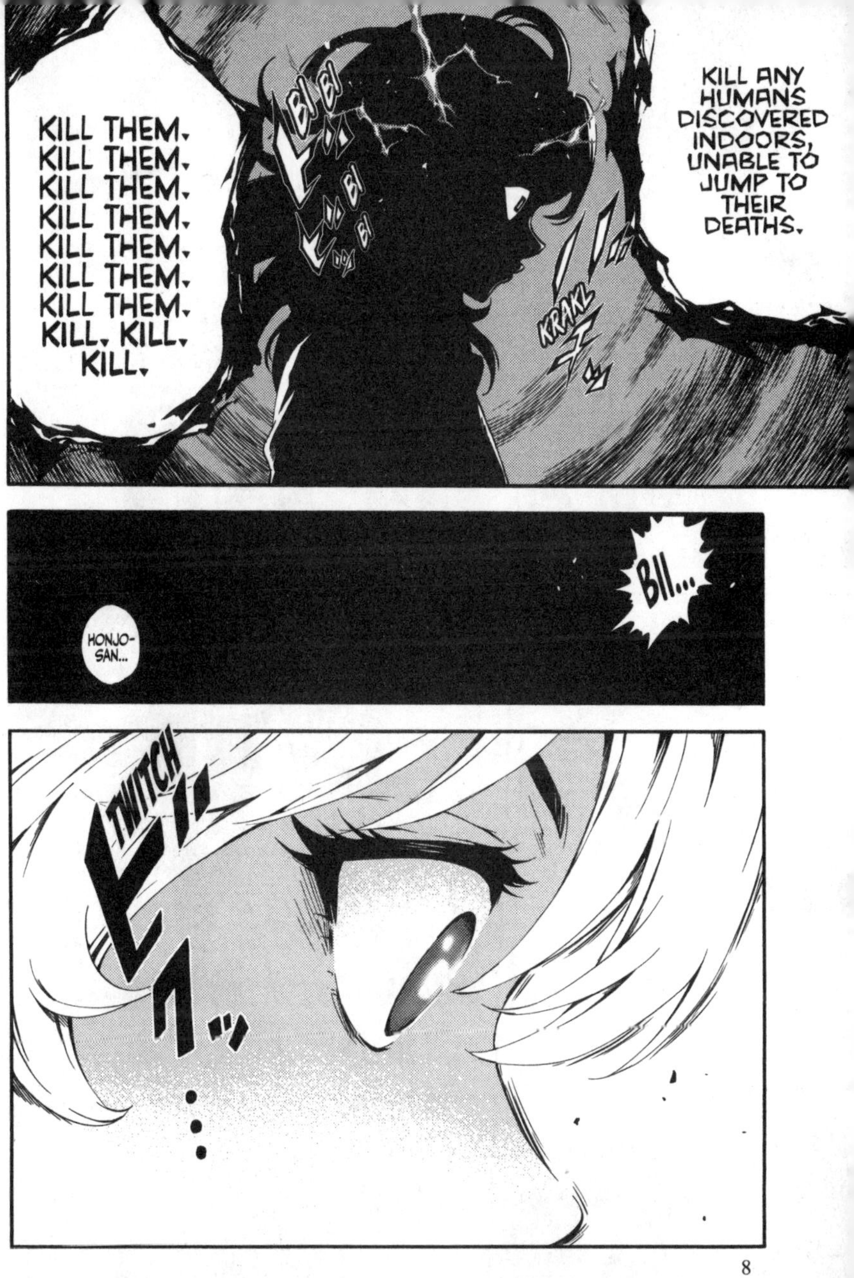
KILL ANY HUMANS DISCOVERED INDOORS, UNABLE TO JUMP TO THEIR DEATHS.
KRAKL
BI BI
BI
BI
KILL THEM. KILL THEM. KILL THEM. KILL THEM. KILL THEM. KILL THEM. KILL THEM. KILL. KILL. KILL.
BII...
HONJO-SAN...
TWITCH
...

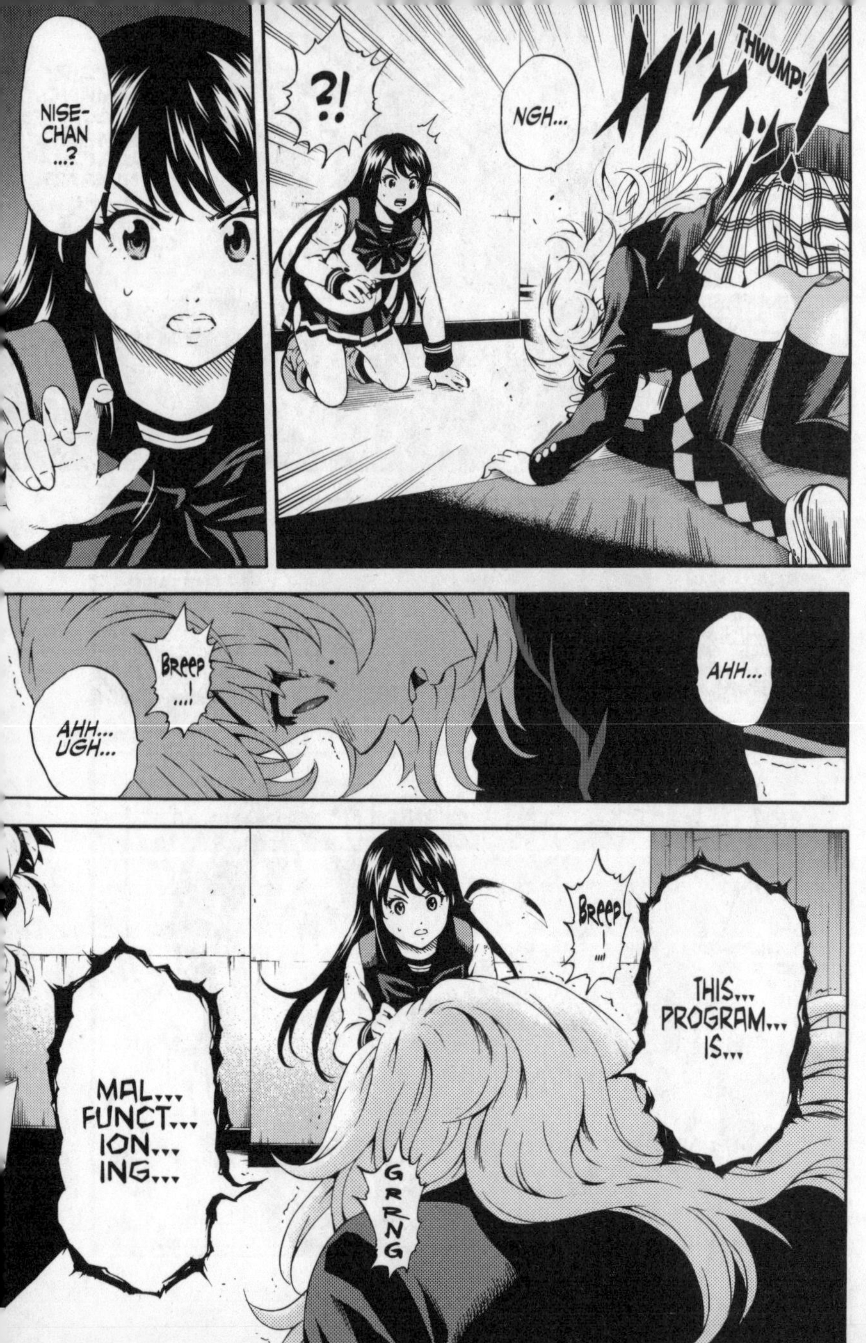
THWUMP!
NGH...
?!
NISE-CHAN ...?
AHH...
Breep ...!
AHH... UGH...
Breep ...!
THIS... PROGRAM... IS...
MAL... FUNCT... ION... ING...
GRRNG

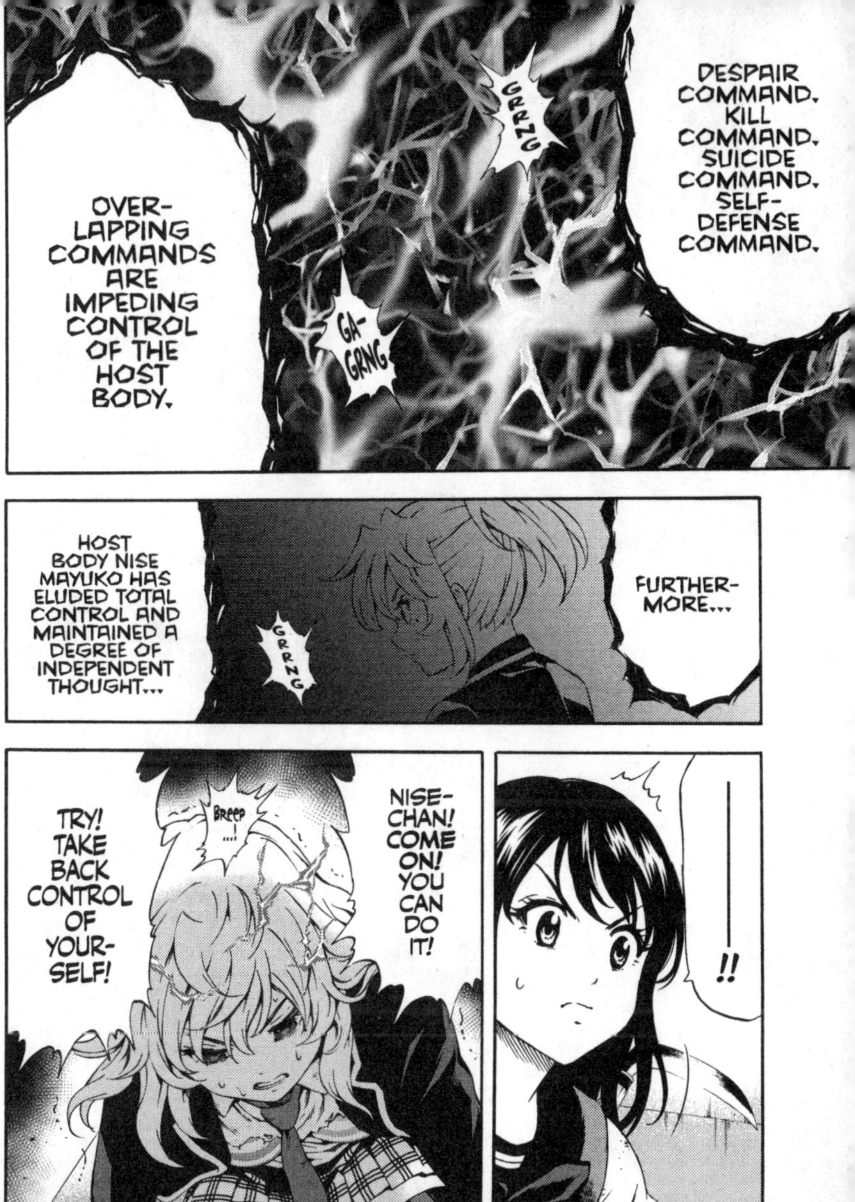
DESPAIR COMMAND. KILL COMMAND. SUICIDE COMMAND. SELF-DEFENSE COMMAND.
GRRNG
GA-GRNG
OVER-LAPPING COMMANDS ARE IMPEDING CONTROL OF THE HOST BODY.
FURTHER-MORE...
GRRNG
HOST BODY NISE MAYUKO HAS ELUDED TOTAL CONTROL AND MAINTAINED A DEGREE OF INDEPENDENT THOUGHT...
!!
NISE-CHAN! COME ON! YOU CAN DO IT!
Breep ...!
TRY! TAKE BACK CONTROL OF YOURSELF!

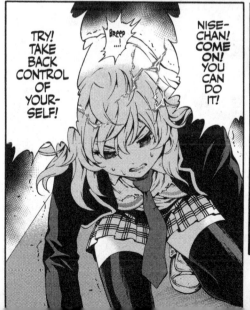

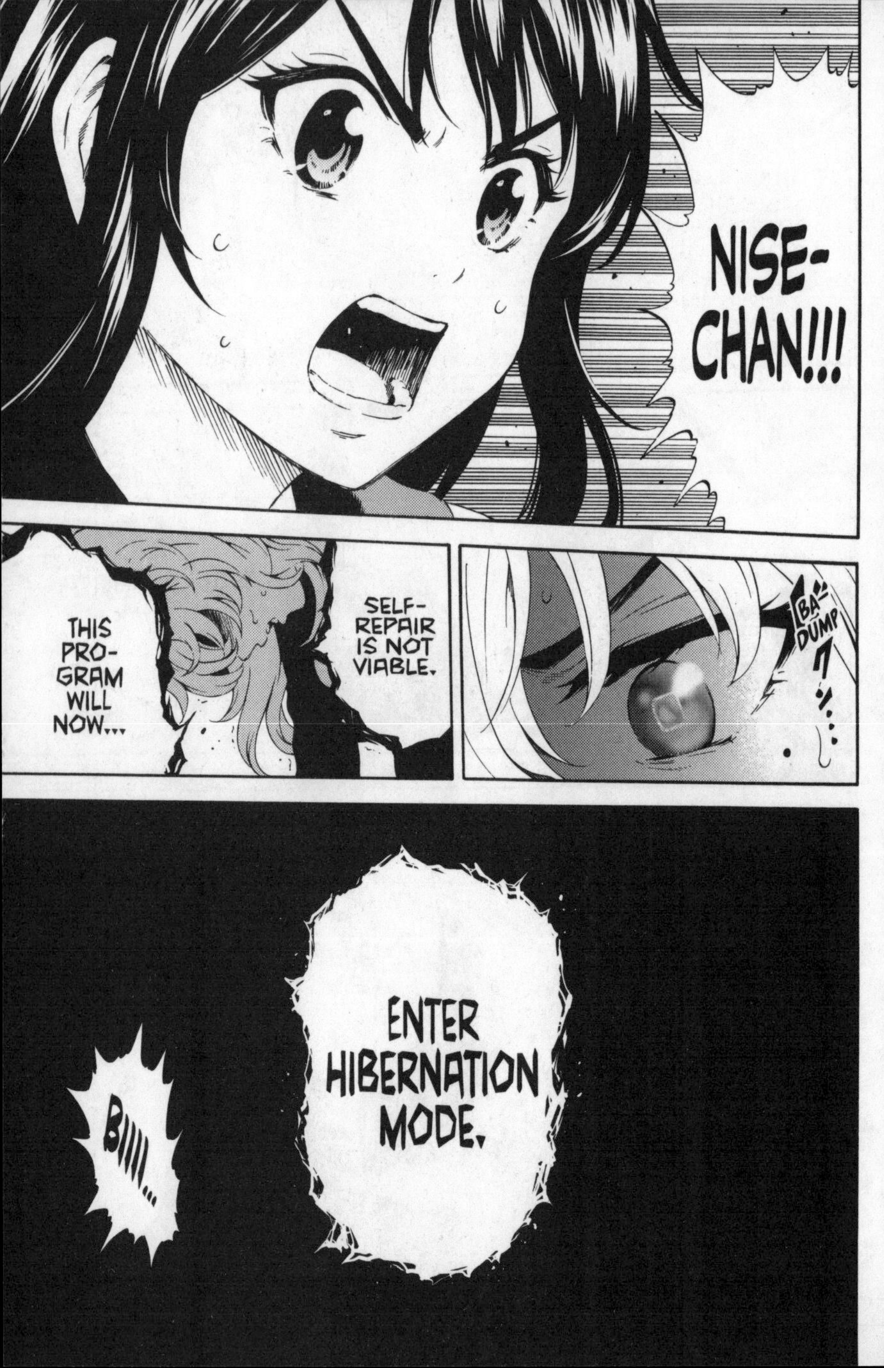
NISE-CHAN!!!
BA-DUMP
SELF-REPAIR IS NOT VIABLE.
THIS PROGRAM WILL NOW...
ENTER HIBERNATION MODE.
BIIII...

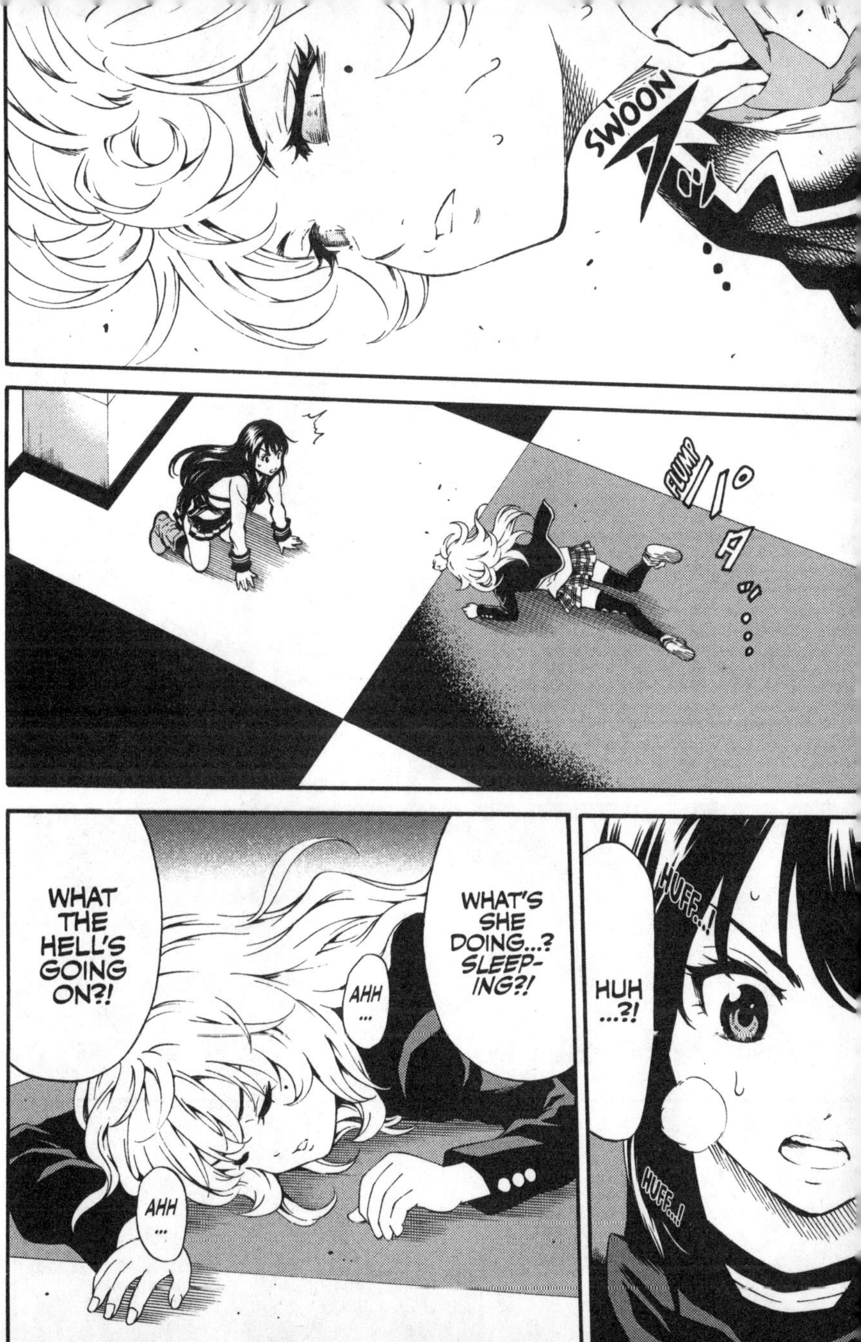
SWOON
FLUMP
HUFF..!
HUH ...?!
HUFF..!
WHAT'S SHE DOING...? SLEEPING?!
AHH ...
WHAT THE HELL'S GOING ON?!
AHH ...

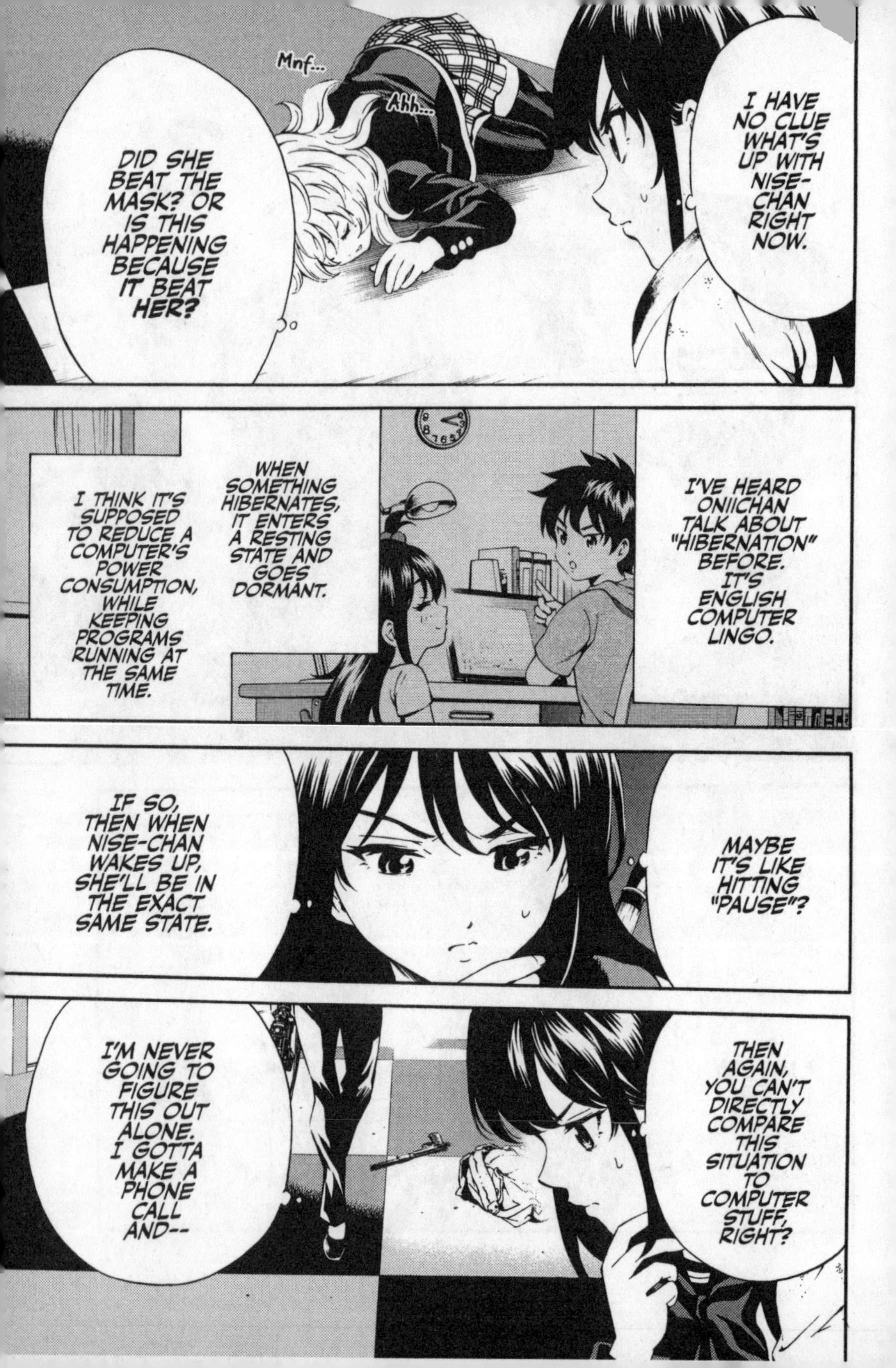
I HAVE NO CLUE WHAT'S UP WITH NISE-CHAN RIGHT NOW.
Mnf...
Ahh...
DID SHE BEAT THE MASK? OR IS THIS HAPPENING BECAUSE IT BEAT HER?
I'VE HEARD ONIICHAN TALK ABOUT "HIBERNATION" BEFORE. IT'S ENGLISH COMPUTER LINGO.
WHEN SOMETHING HIBERNATES, IT ENTERS A RESTING STATE AND GOES DORMANT.
I THINK IT'S SUPPOSED TO REDUCE A COMPUTER'S POWER CONSUMPTION, WHILE KEEPING PROGRAMS RUNNING AT THE SAME TIME.
MAYBE IT'S LIKE HITTING "PAUSE"?
IF SO, THEN WHEN NISE-CHAN WAKES UP, SHE'LL BE IN THE EXACT SAME STATE.
THEN AGAIN, YOU CAN'T DIRECTLY COMPARE THIS SITUATION TO COMPUTER STUFF, RIGHT?
I'M NEVER GOING TO FIGURE THIS OUT ALONE. I GOTTA MAKE A PHONE CALL AND--

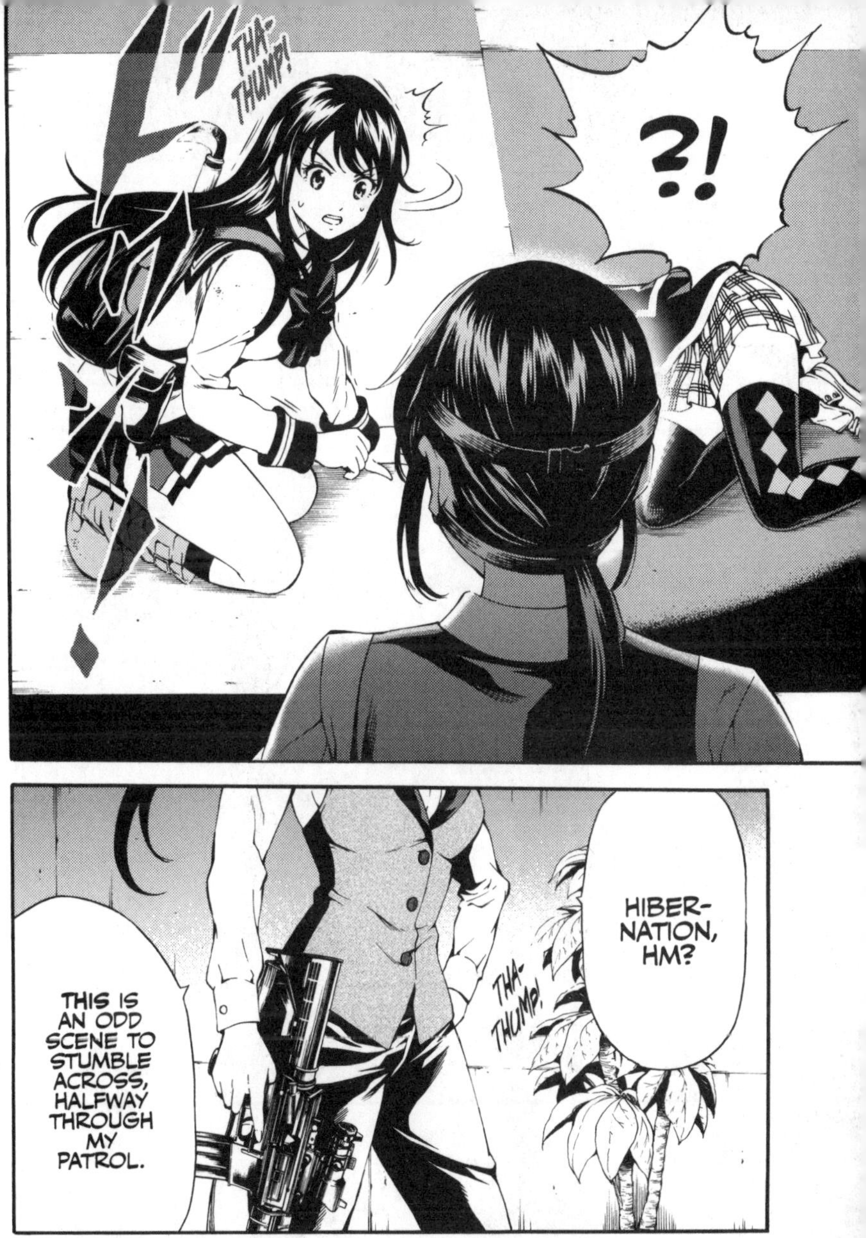
?!
THA-THUMP!
HIBER-NATION, HM?
THA-THUMP!
THIS IS AN ODD SCENE TO STUMBLE ACROSS, HALFWAY THROUGH MY PATROL.

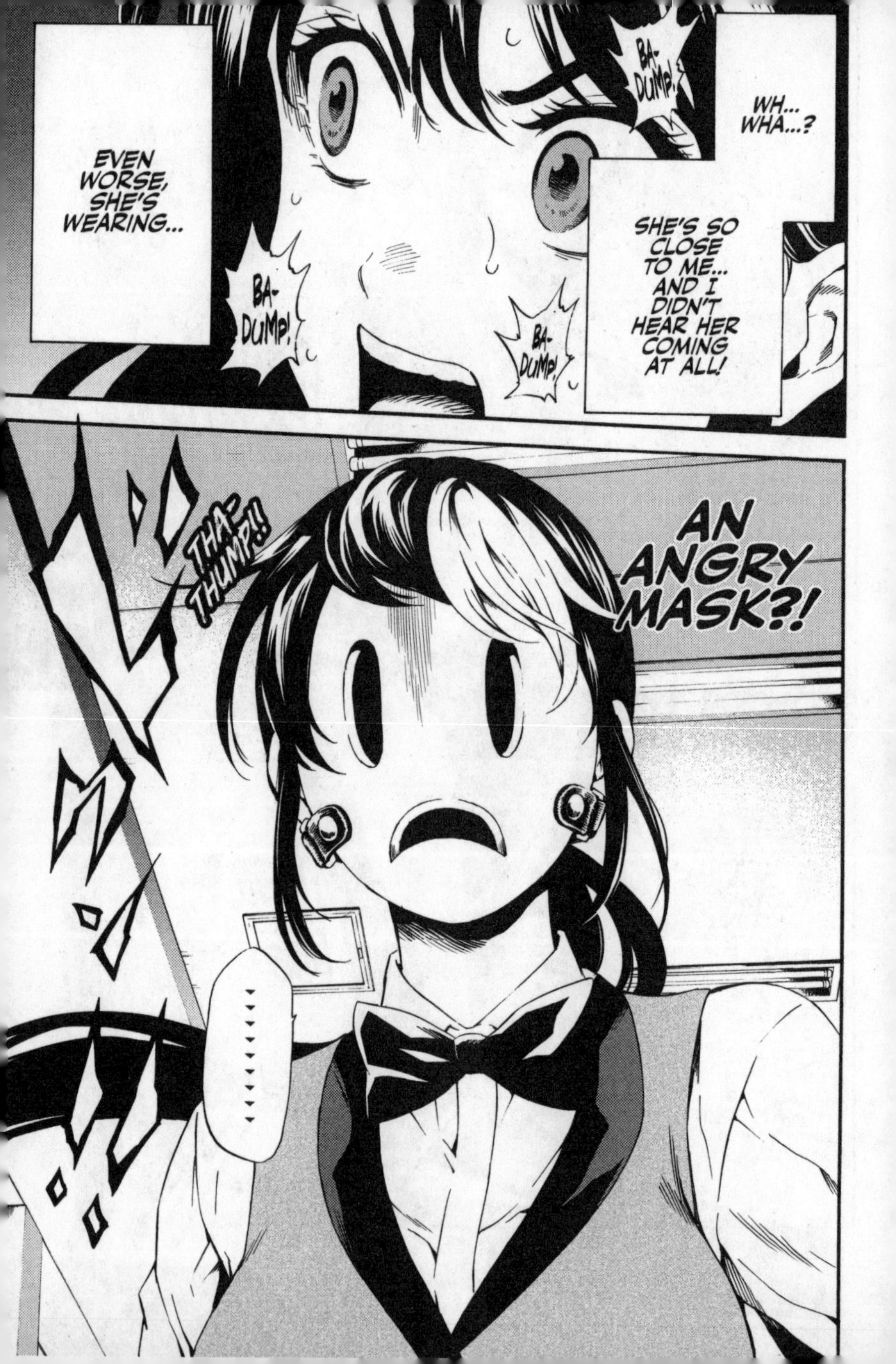
WH... WHA...?
BA-DUMP!
SHE'S SO CLOSE TO ME... AND I DIDN'T HEAR HER COMING AT ALL!
BA-DUMP!
BA-DUMP!
EVEN WORSE, SHE'S WEARING...
AN ANGRY MASK?!
THA-THUMP!!

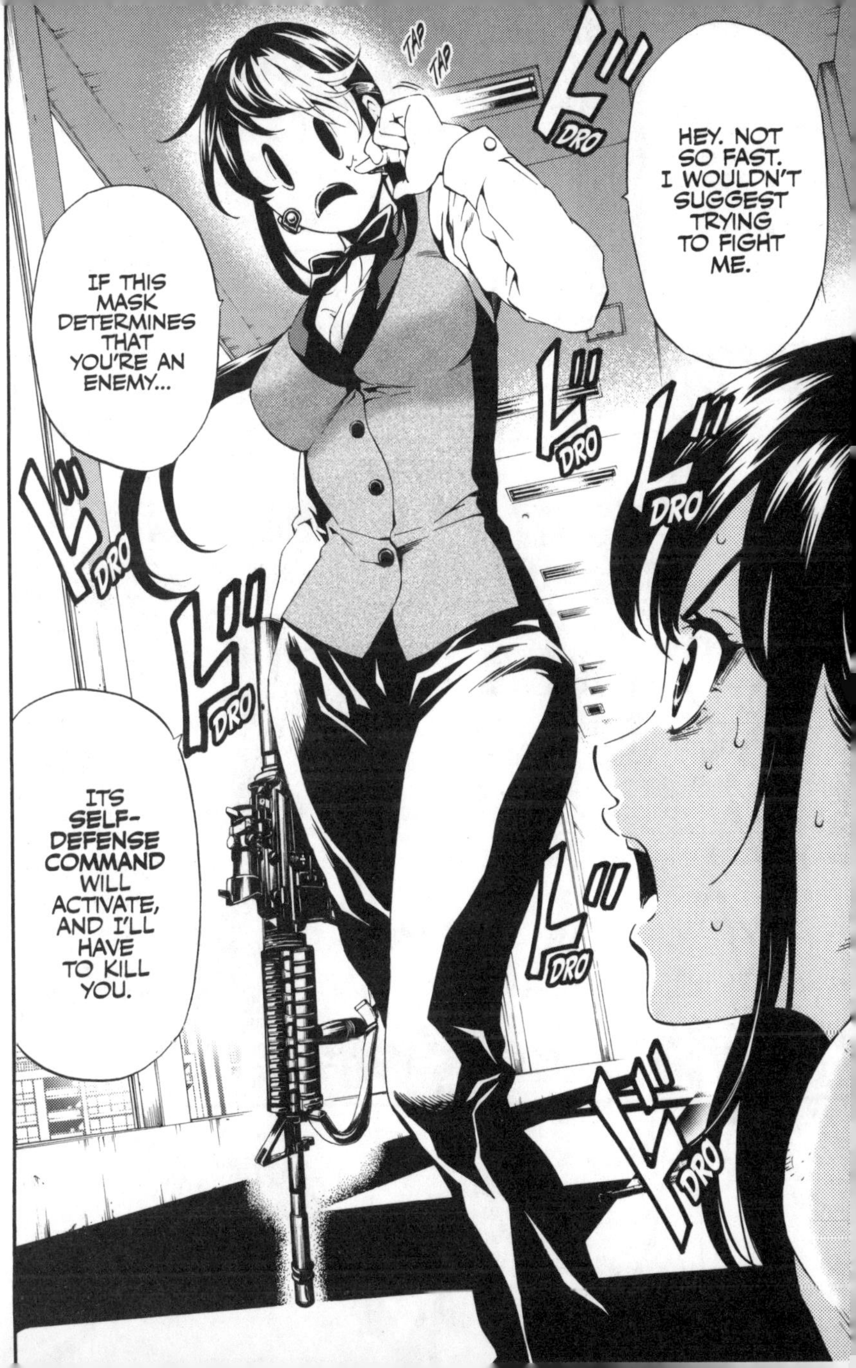

DRO
TAP
TAP
HEY. NOT SO FAST. I WOULDN'T SUGGEST TRYING TO FIGHT ME.
IF THIS MASK DETERMINES THAT YOU'RE AN ENEMY...
DRO
DRO
DRO
DRO
ITS SELF-DEFENSE COMMAND WILL ACTIVATE, AND I'LL HAVE TO KILL YOU.
DRO
DRO

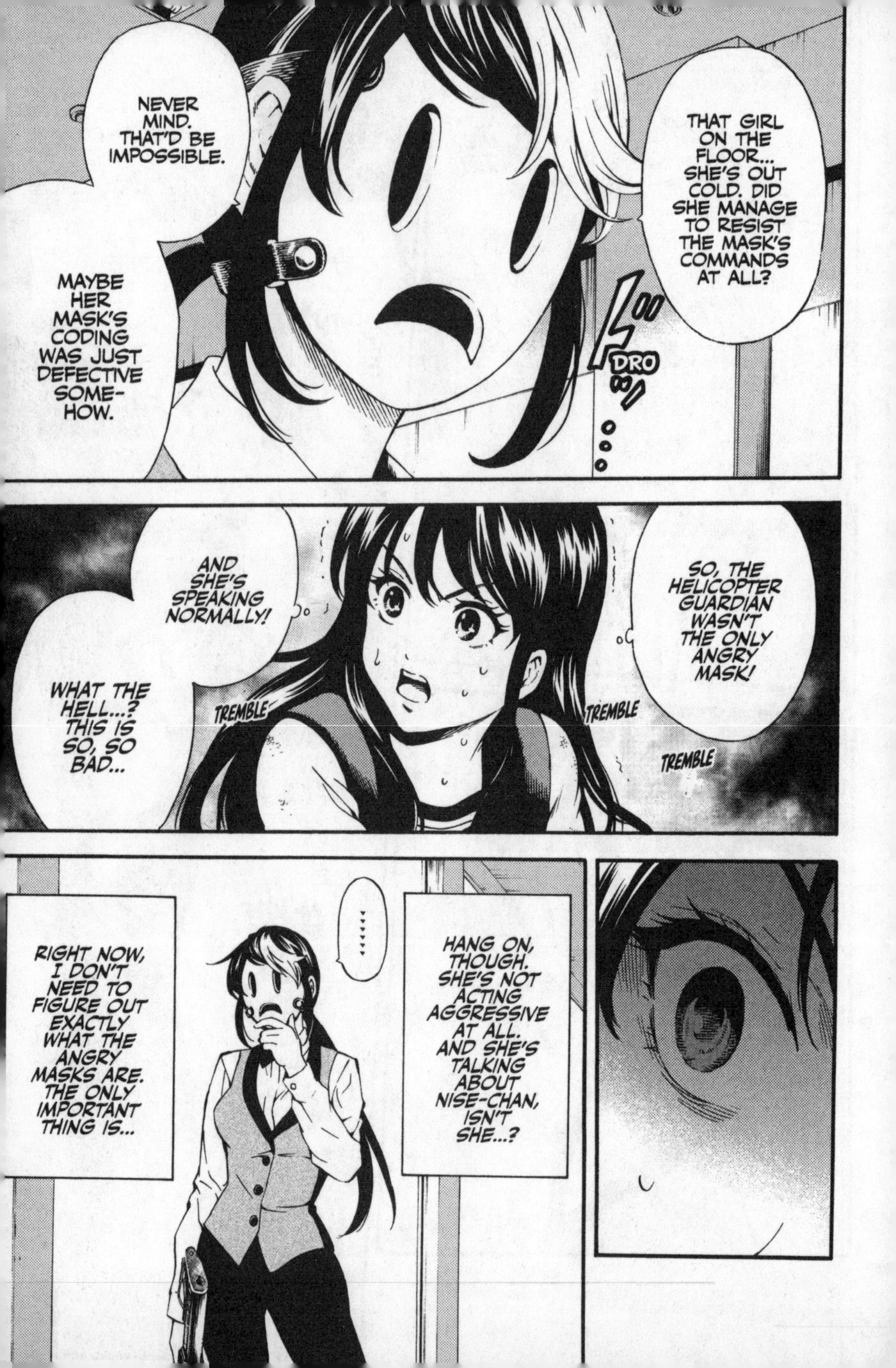
THAT GIRL ON THE FLOOR... SHE'S OUT COLD. DID SHE MANAGE TO RESIST THE MASK'S COMMANDS AT ALL?
DRO
NEVER MIND. THAT'D BE IMPOSSIBLE.
MAYBE HER MASK'S CODING WAS JUST DEFECTIVE SOME-HOW.
SO, THE HELICOPTER GUARDIAN WASN'T THE ONLY ANGRY MASK!
TREMBLE
TREMBLE
AND SHE'S SPEAKING NORMALLY!
TREMBLE
WHAT THE HELL...? THIS IS SO, SO BAD...
HANG ON, THOUGH. SHE'S NOT ACTING AGGRESSIVE AT ALL. AND SHE'S TALKING ABOUT NISE-CHAN, ISN'T SHE...?
......
RIGHT NOW, I DON'T NEED TO FIGURE OUT EXACTLY WHAT THE ANGRY MASKS ARE. THE ONLY IMPORTANT THING IS...

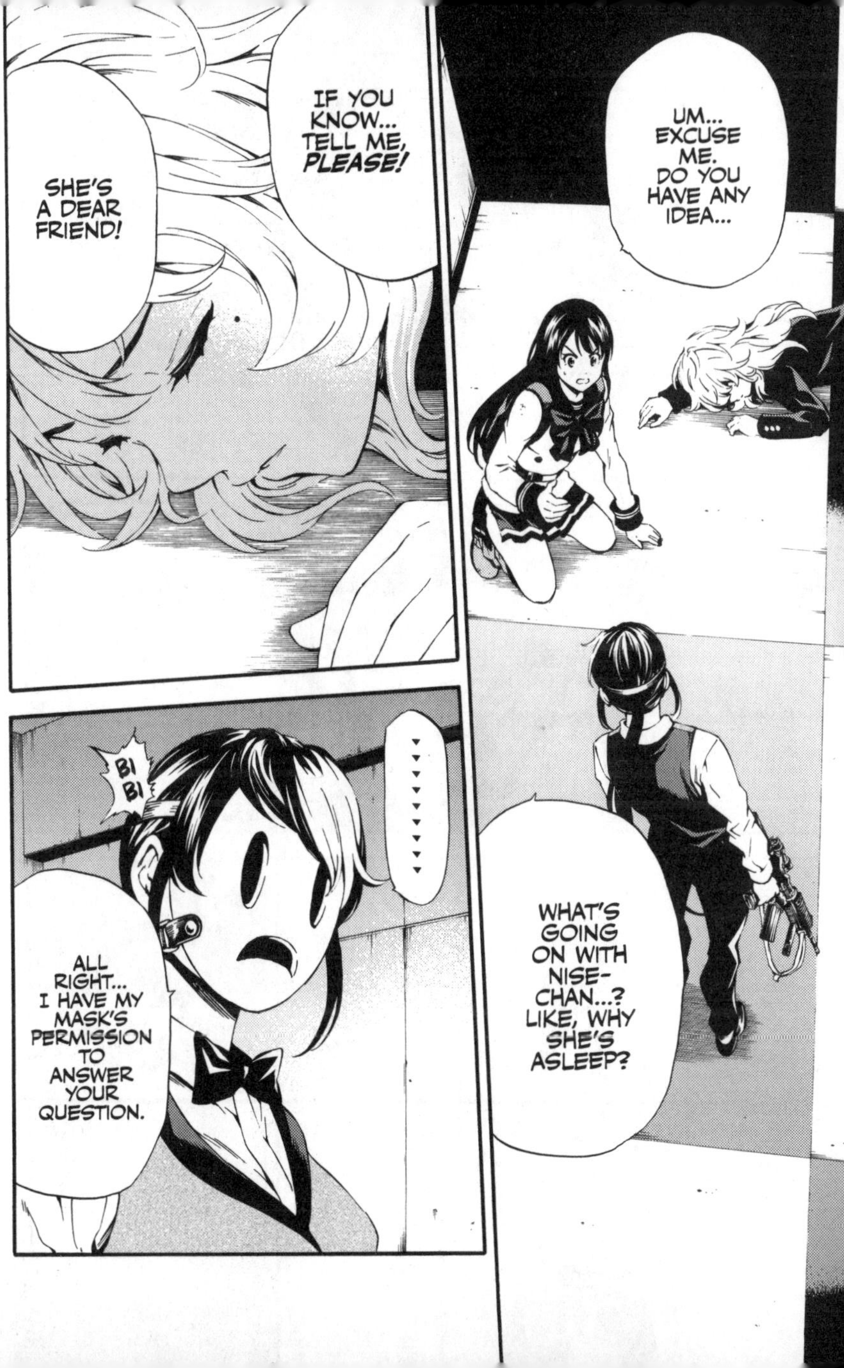
UM... EXCUSE ME. DO YOU HAVE ANY IDEA...
IF YOU KNOW... TELL ME, *PLEASE!*
SHE'S A DEAR FRIEND!
WHAT'S GOING ON WITH NISE-CHAN...? LIKE, WHY SHE'S ASLEEP?
BI BI
ALL RIGHT... I HAVE MY MASK'S PERMISSION TO ANSWER YOUR QUESTION.

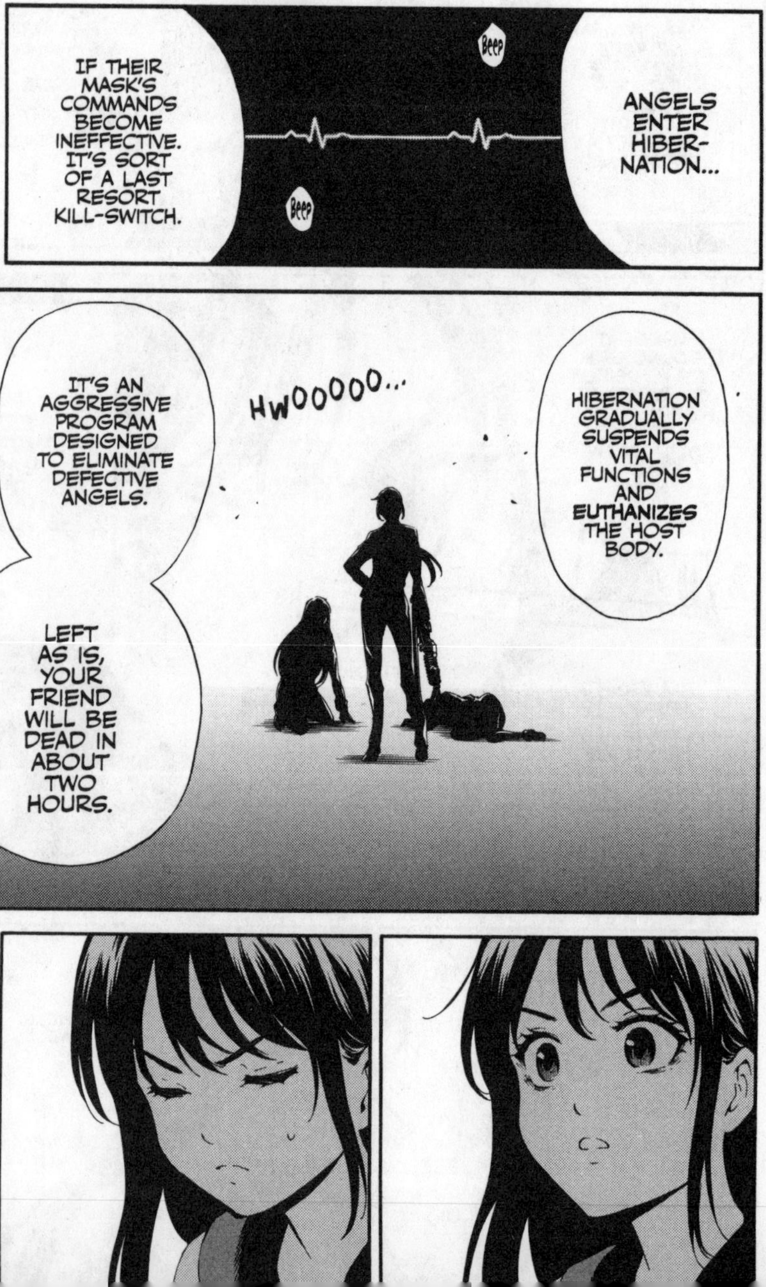
ANGELS ENTER HIBER-NATION...
Beep
IF THEIR MASK'S COMMANDS BECOME INEFFECTIVE. IT'S SORT OF A LAST RESORT KILL-SWITCH.
Beep
HIBERNATION GRADUALLY SUSPENDS VITAL FUNCTIONS AND EUTHANIZES THE HOST BODY.
HWOOOOO...
IT'S AN AGGRESSIVE PROGRAM DESIGNED TO ELIMINATE DEFECTIVE ANGELS.
LEFT AS IS, YOUR FRIEND WILL BE DEAD IN ABOUT TWO HOURS.

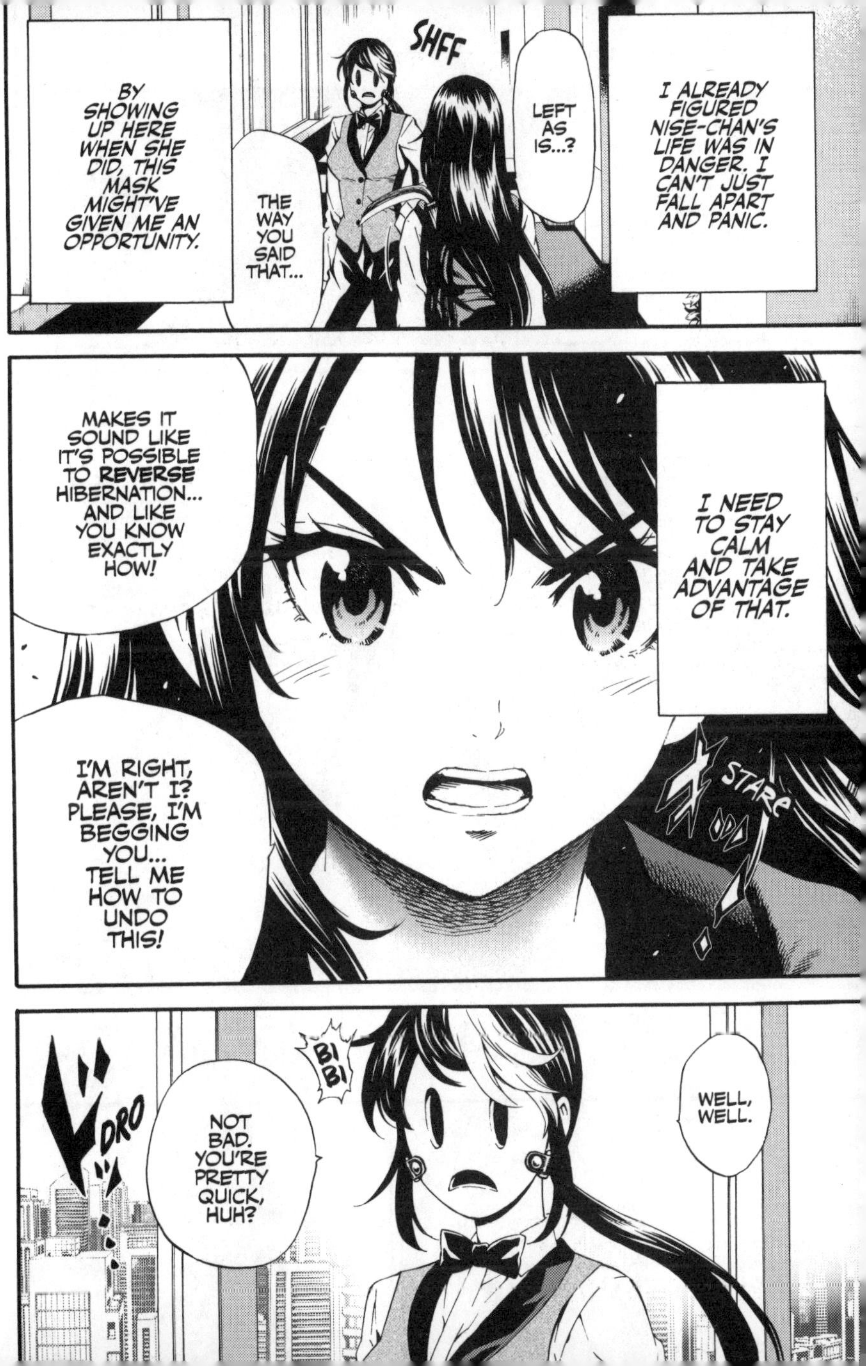
I ALREADY FIGURED NISE-CHAN'S LIFE WAS IN DANGER. I CAN'T JUST FALL APART AND PANIC.
LEFT AS IS...?
SHFF
THE WAY YOU SAID THAT...
BY SHOWING UP HERE WHEN SHE DID, THIS MASK MIGHT'VE GIVEN ME AN OPPORTUNITY.
I NEED TO STAY CALM AND TAKE ADVANTAGE OF THAT.
STARE
MAKES IT SOUND LIKE IT'S POSSIBLE TO **REVERSE** HIBERNATION... AND LIKE YOU KNOW EXACTLY HOW!
I'M RIGHT, AREN'T I? PLEASE, I'M BEGGING YOU... TELL ME HOW TO UNDO THIS!
WELL, WELL.
BI BI
NOT BAD. YOU'RE PRETTY QUICK, HUH?
DRO

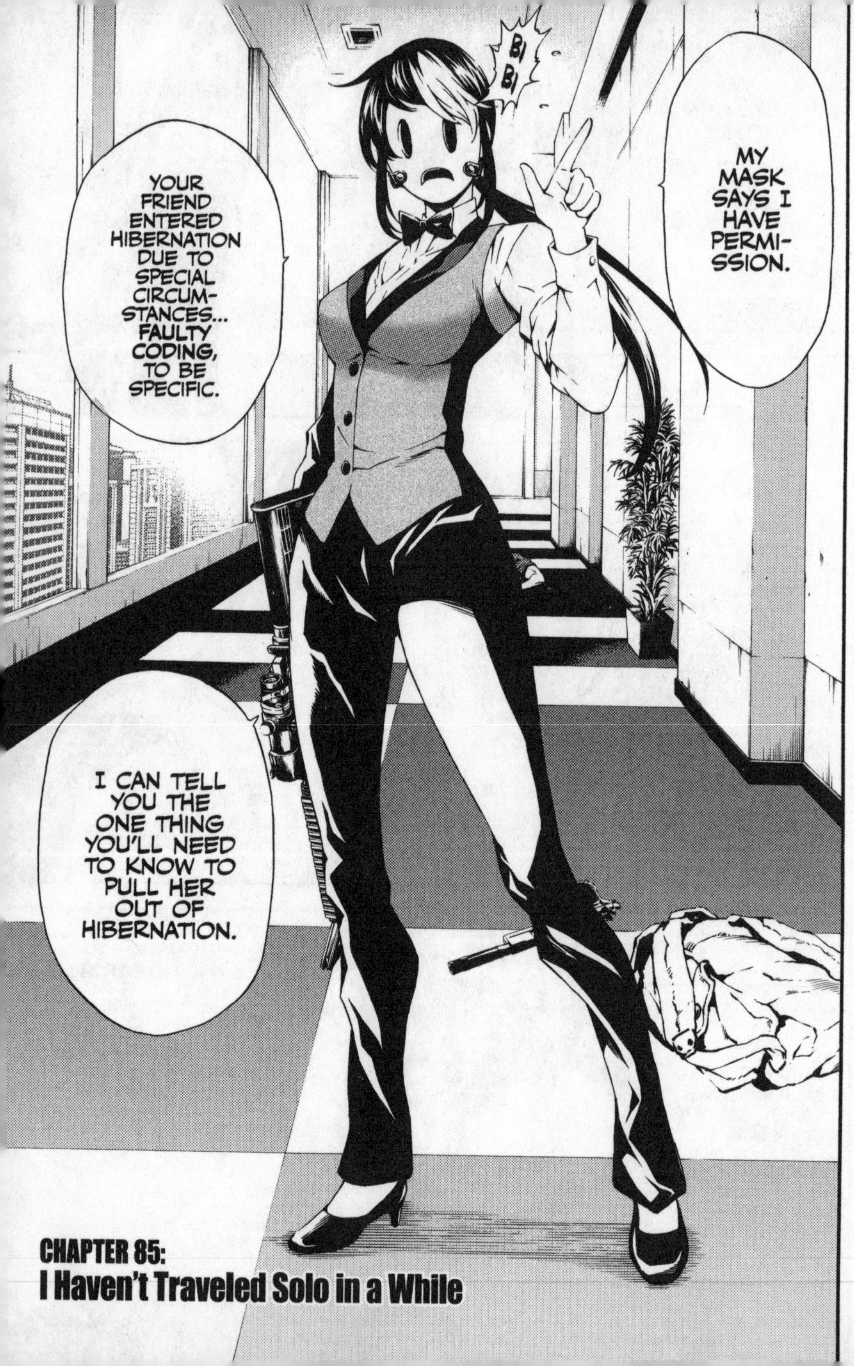
MY MASK SAYS I HAVE PERMISSION.
BI BI
YOUR FRIEND ENTERED HIBERNATION DUE TO SPECIAL CIRCUMSTANCES... FAULTY CODING, TO BE SPECIFIC.
I CAN TELL YOU THE ONE THING YOU'LL NEED TO KNOW TO PULL HER OUT OF HIBERNATION.

CHAPTER 85:
I Haven't Traveled Solo in a While

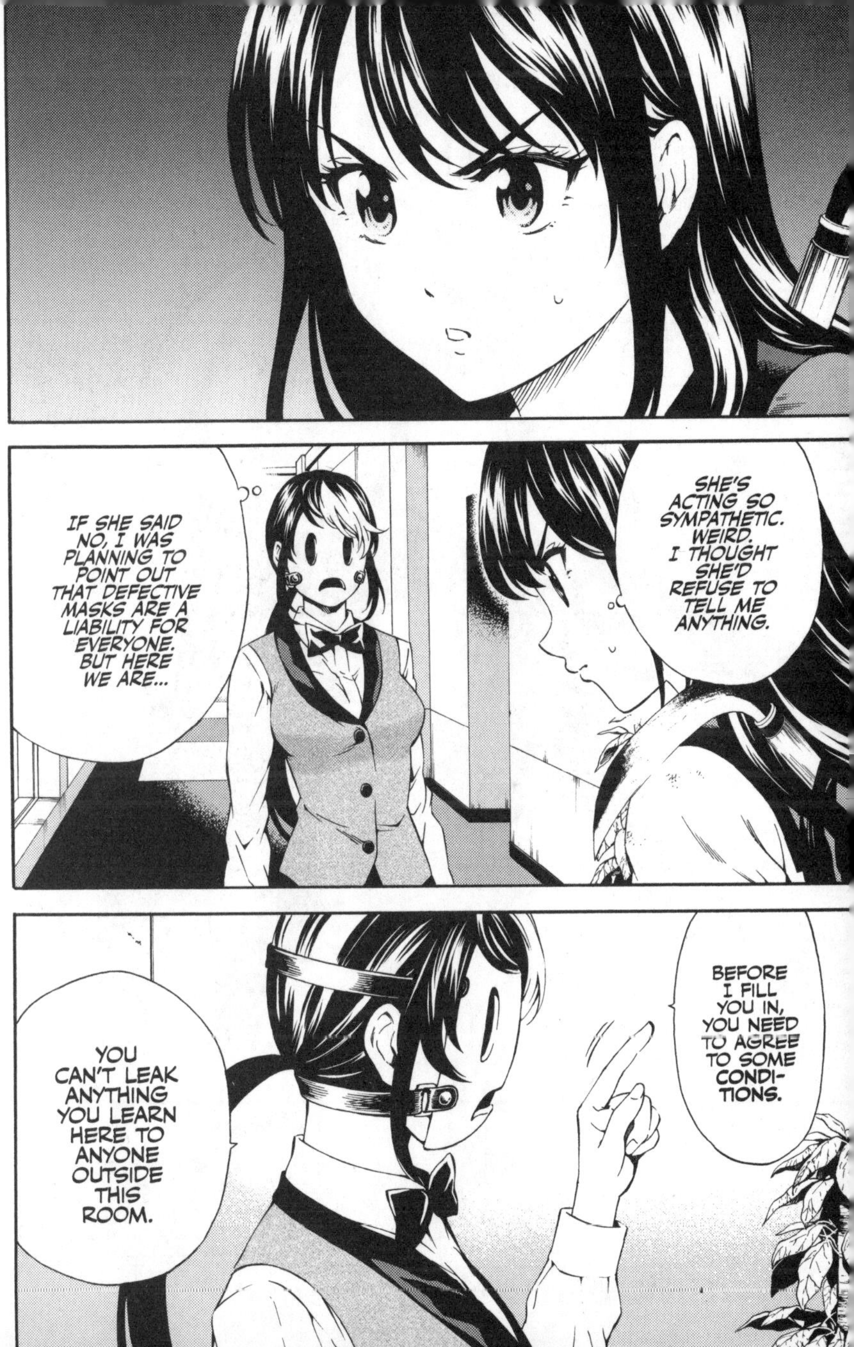
SHE'S ACTING SO SYMPATHETIC. WEIRD. I THOUGHT SHE'D REFUSE TO TELL ME ANYTHING.
IF SHE SAID NO, I WAS PLANNING TO POINT OUT THAT DEFECTIVE MASKS ARE A LIABILITY FOR EVERYONE. BUT HERE WE ARE...
BEFORE I FILL YOU IN, YOU NEED TO AGREE TO SOME CONDI-TIONS.
YOU CAN'T LEAK ANYTHING YOU LEARN HERE TO ANYONE OUTSIDE THIS ROOM.

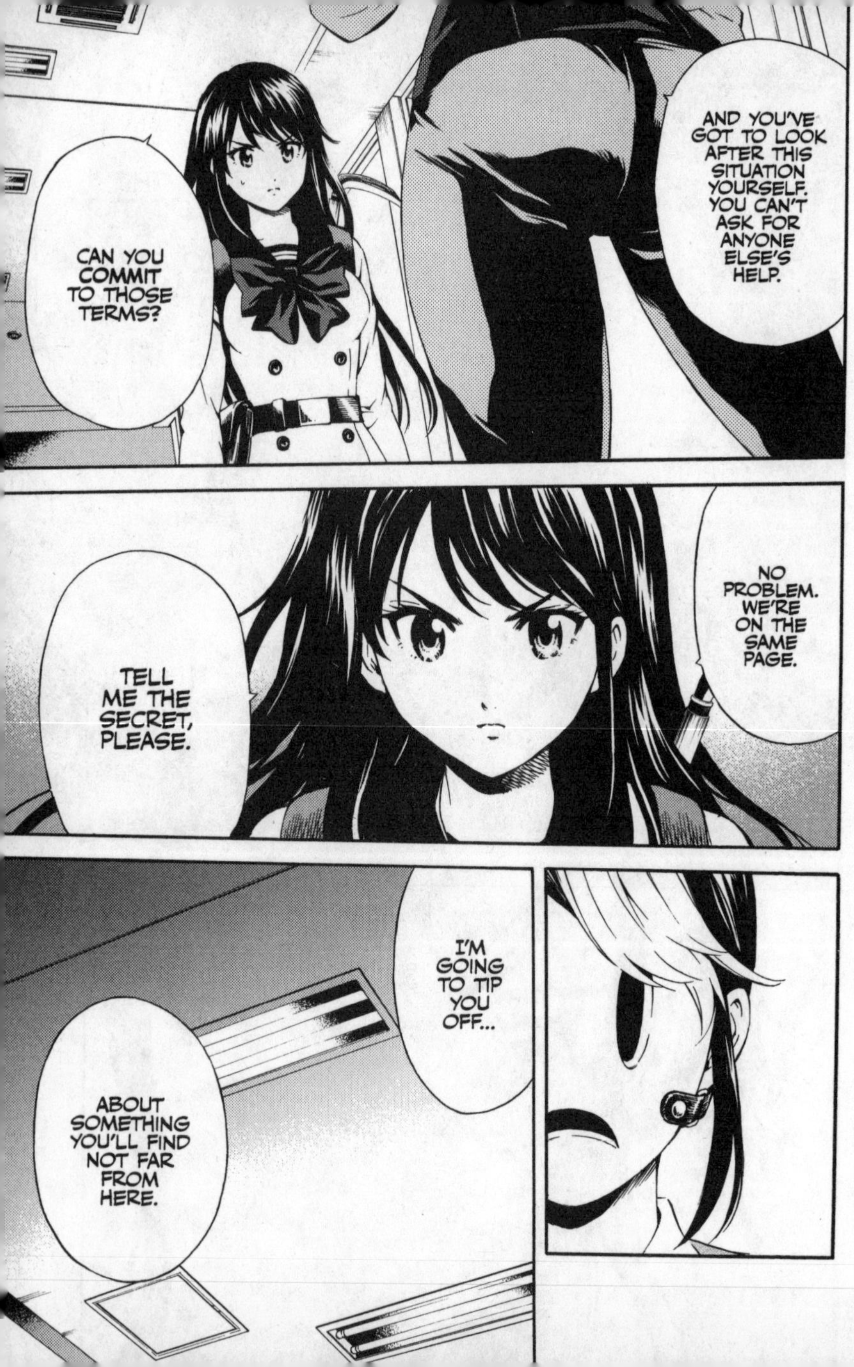
AND YOU'VE GOT TO LOOK AFTER THIS SITUATION YOURSELF. YOU CAN'T ASK FOR ANYONE ELSE'S HELP.
CAN YOU COMMIT TO THOSE TERMS?
NO PROBLEM. WE'RE ON THE SAME PAGE.
TELL ME THE SECRET, PLEASE.
I'M GOING TO TIP YOU OFF...
ABOUT SOMETHING YOU'LL FIND NOT FAR FROM HERE.

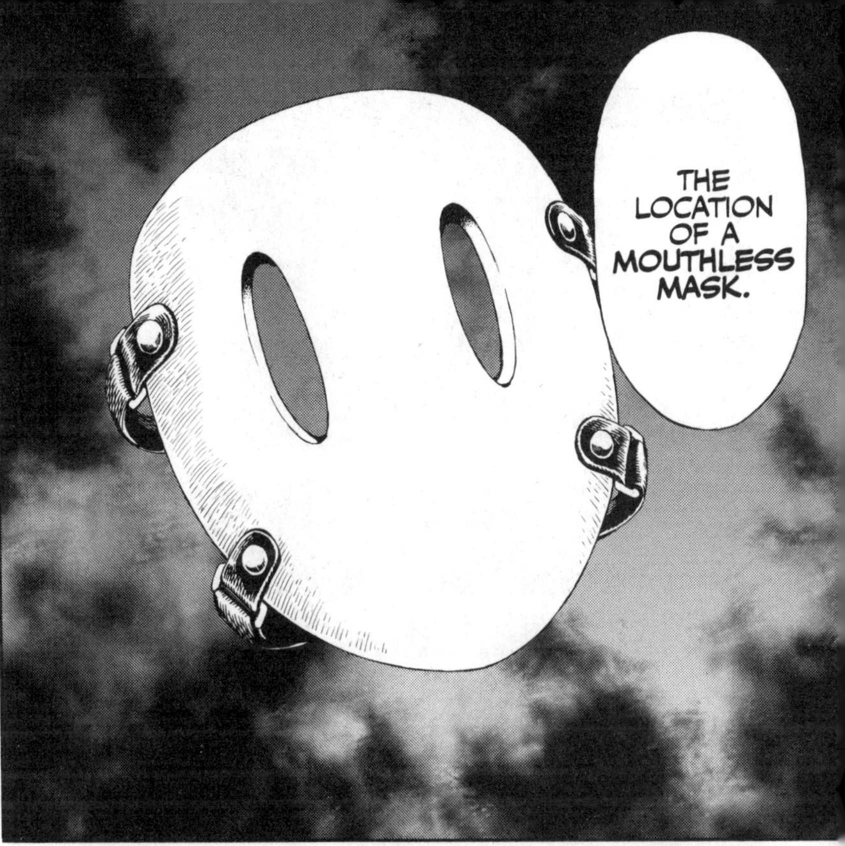
THE LOCATION OF A MOUTHLESS MASK.

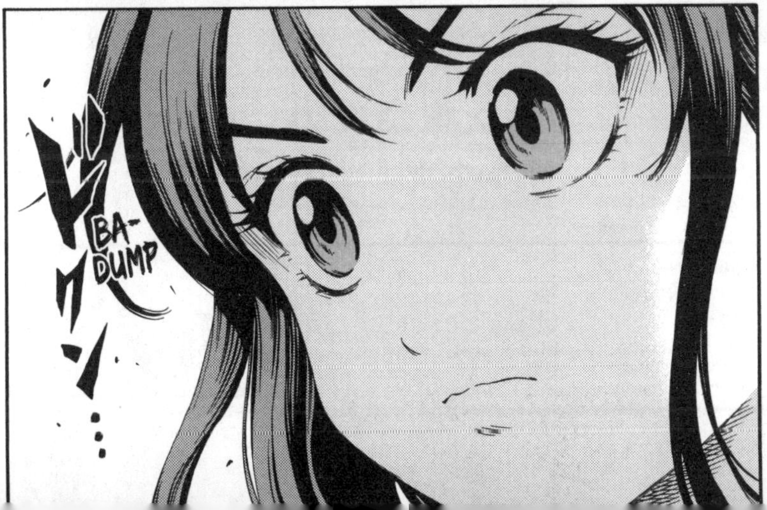
BA-DUMP

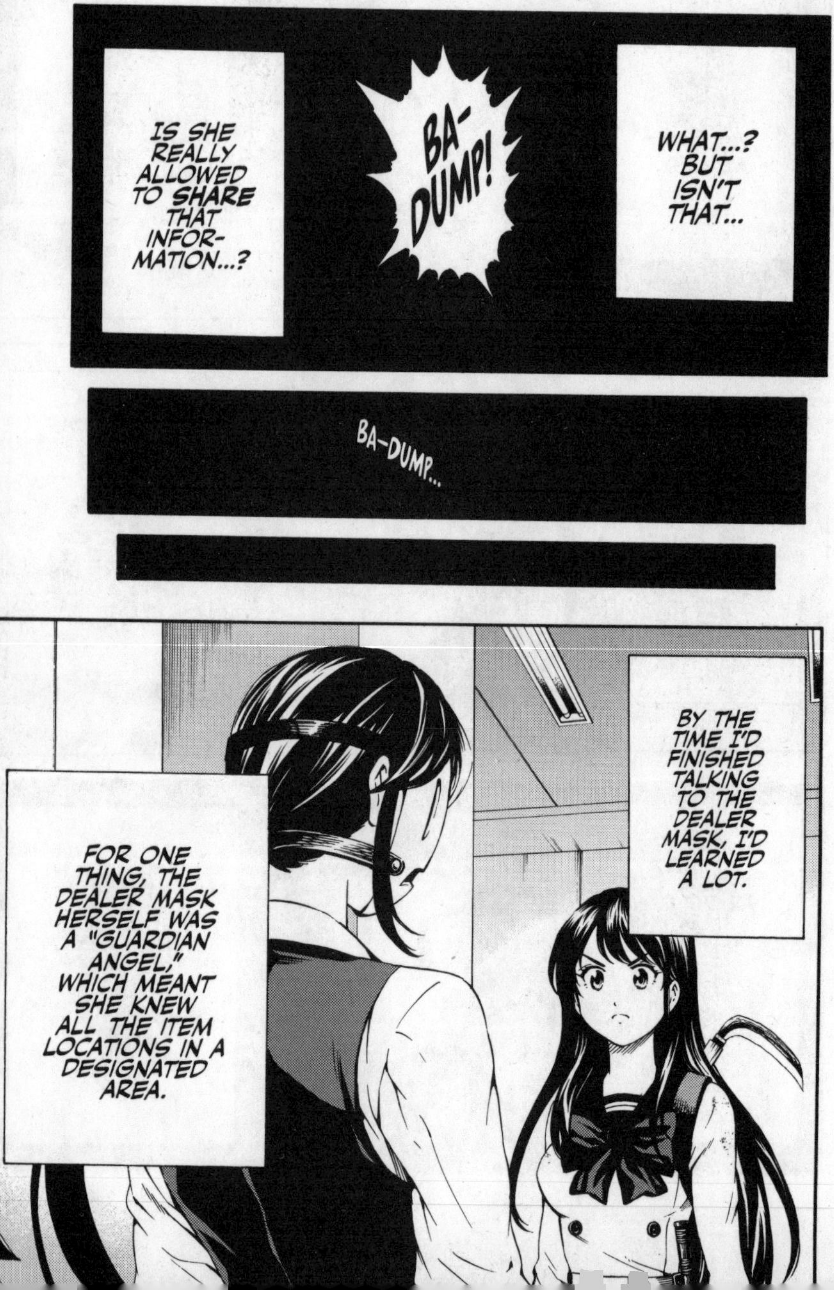
WHAT...? BUT ISN'T THAT...
BA-DUMP!
IS SHE REALLY ALLOWED TO SHARE THAT INFORMATION...?
BA-DUMP...
BY THE TIME I'D FINISHED TALKING TO THE DEALER MASK, I'D LEARNED A LOT.
FOR ONE THING, THE DEALER MASK HERSELF WAS A "GUARDIAN ANGEL," WHICH MEANT SHE KNEW ALL THE ITEM LOCATIONS IN A DESIGNATED AREA.

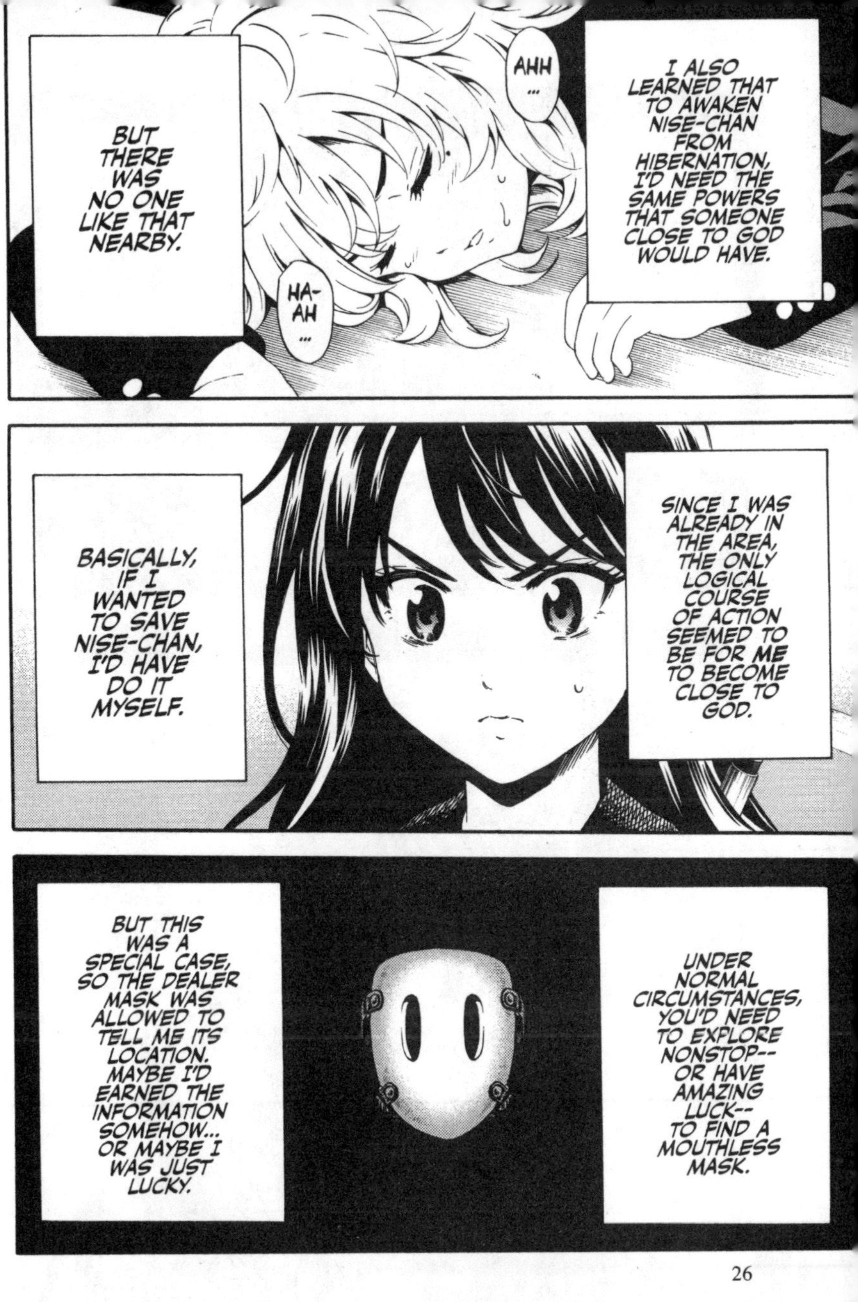

I ALSO LEARNED THAT TO AWAKEN NISE-CHAN FROM HIBERNATION, I'D NEED THE SAME POWERS THAT SOMEONE CLOSE TO GOD WOULD HAVE.
AHH ...
HA-AH ...
BUT THERE WAS NO ONE LIKE THAT NEARBY.
SINCE I WAS ALREADY IN THE AREA, THE ONLY LOGICAL COURSE OF ACTION SEEMED TO BE FOR ME TO BECOME CLOSE TO GOD.
BASICALLY, IF I WANTED TO SAVE NISE-CHAN, I'D HAVE DO IT MYSELF.
UNDER NORMAL CIRCUMSTANCES, YOU'D NEED TO EXPLORE NONSTOP-- OR HAVE AMAZING LUCK-- TO FIND A MOUTHLESS MASK.
BUT THIS WAS A SPECIAL CASE, SO THE DEALER MASK WAS ALLOWED TO TELL ME ITS LOCATION. MAYBE I'D EARNED THE INFORMATION SOMEHOW... OR MAYBE I WAS JUST LUCKY.

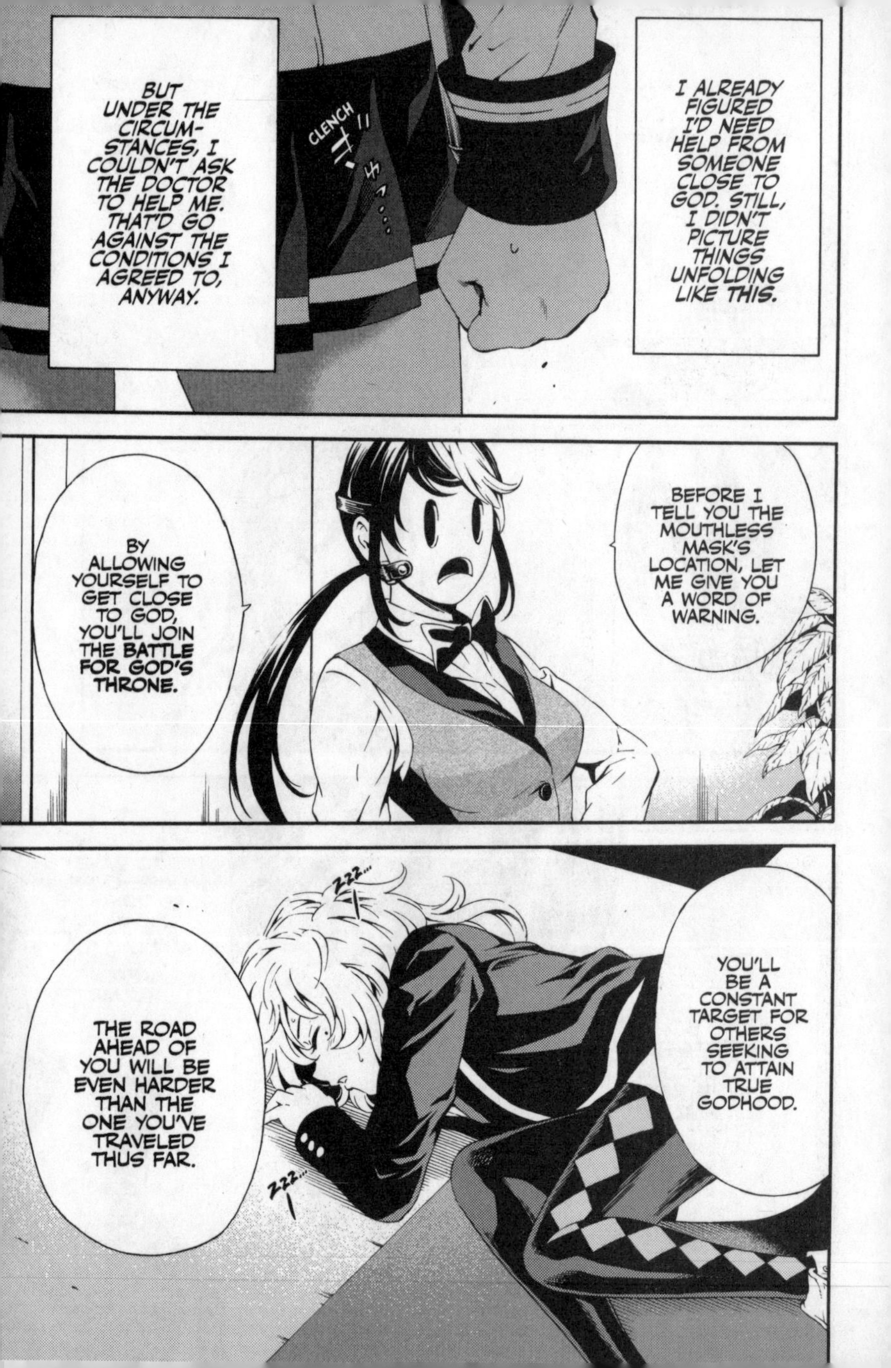
I ALREADY FIGURED I'D NEED HELP FROM SOMEONE CLOSE TO GOD. STILL, I DIDN'T PICTURE THINGS UNFOLDING LIKE THIS.
CLENCH
BUT UNDER THE CIRCUM-STANCES, I COULDN'T ASK THE DOCTOR TO HELP ME. THAT'D GO AGAINST THE CONDITIONS I AGREED TO, ANYWAY.
BEFORE I TELL YOU THE MOUTHLESS MASK'S LOCATION, LET ME GIVE YOU A WORD OF WARNING.
BY ALLOWING YOURSELF TO GET CLOSE TO GOD, YOU'LL JOIN THE BATTLE FOR GOD'S THRONE.
YOU'LL BE A CONSTANT TARGET FOR OTHERS SEEKING TO ATTAIN TRUE GODHOOD.
ZZZ...
THE ROAD AHEAD OF YOU WILL BE EVEN HARDER THAN THE ONE YOU'VE TRAVELED THUS FAR.
ZZZ...

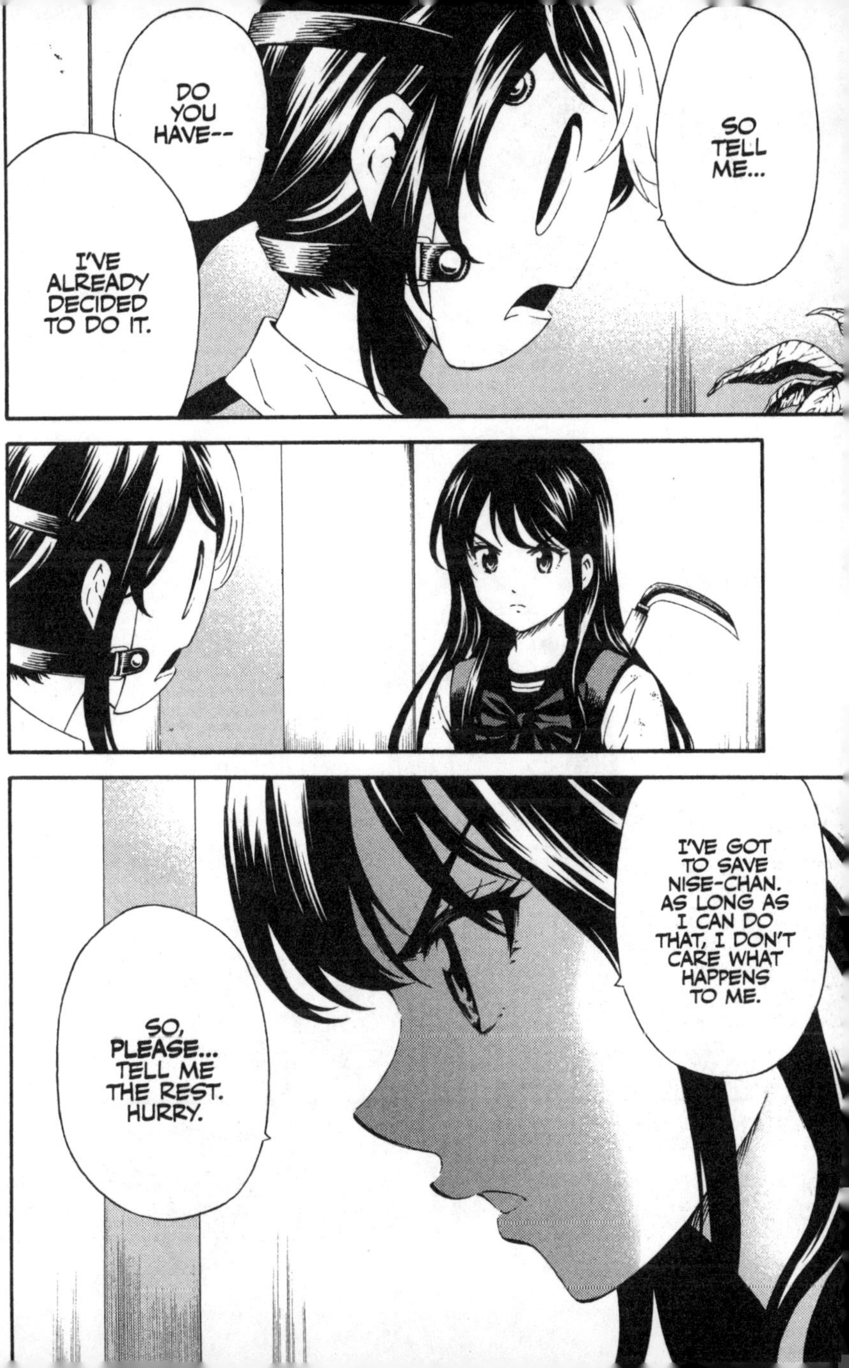
SO TELL ME...
DO YOU HAVE--
I'VE ALREADY DECIDED TO DO IT.
I'VE GOT TO SAVE NISE-CHAN. AS LONG AS I CAN DO THAT, I DON'T CARE WHAT HAPPENS TO ME.
SO, PLEASE... TELL ME THE REST. HURRY.

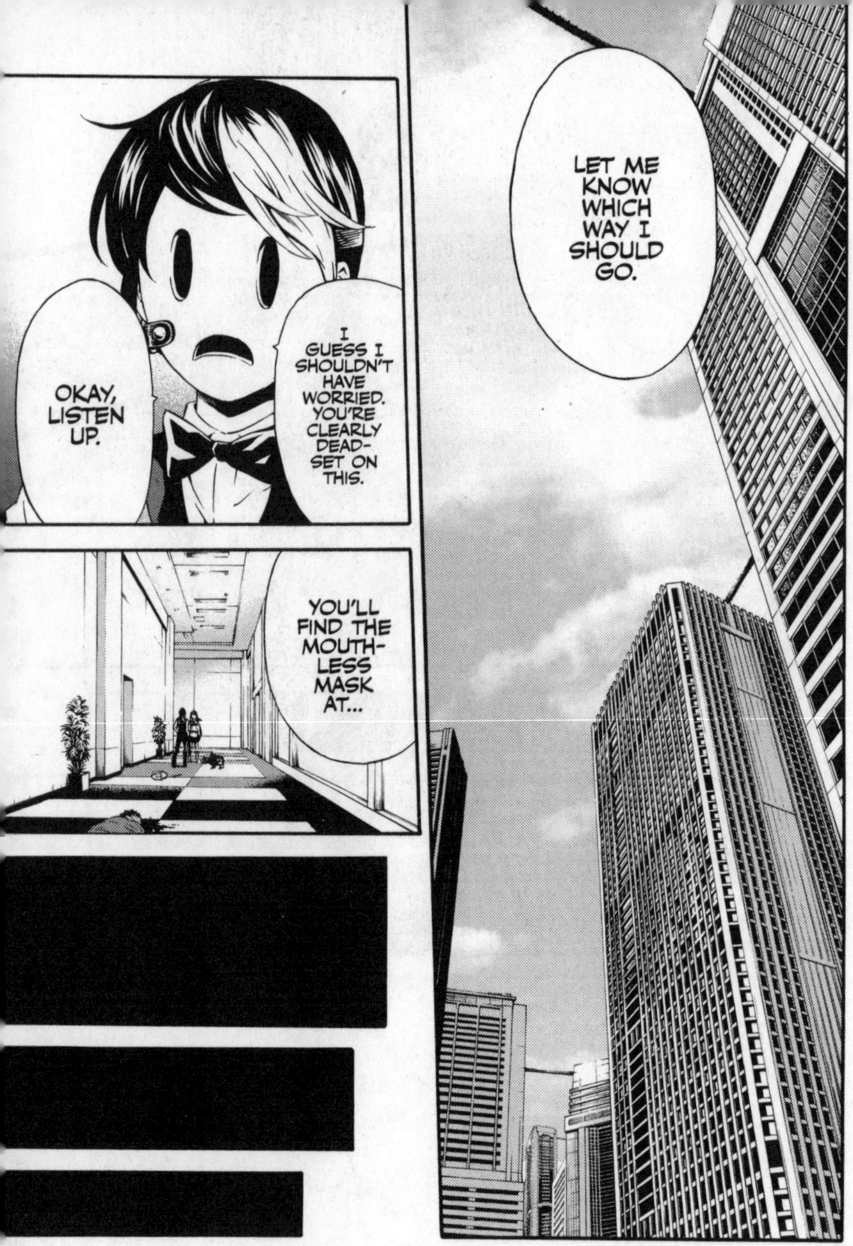
LET ME KNOW WHICH WAY I SHOULD GO.
I GUESS I SHOULDN'T HAVE WORRIED. YOU'RE CLEARLY DEAD-SET ON THIS.
OKAY, LISTEN UP.
YOU'LL FIND THE MOUTH-LESS MASK AT...

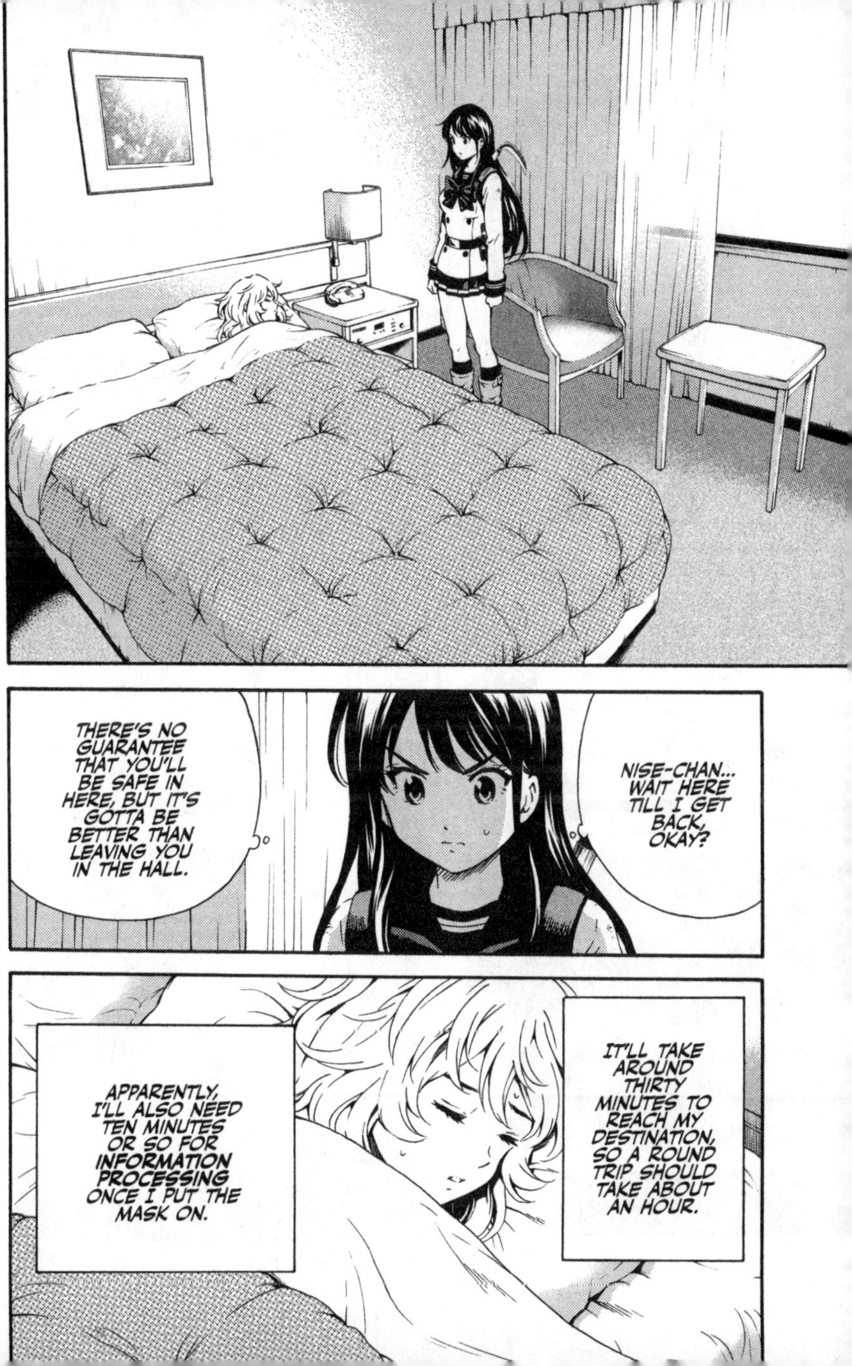
NISE-CHAN... WAIT HERE TILL I GET BACK, OKAY?
THERE'S NO GUARANTEE THAT YOU'LL BE SAFE IN HERE, BUT IT'S GOTTA BE BETTER THAN LEAVING YOU IN THE HALL.
IT'LL TAKE AROUND THIRTY MINUTES TO REACH MY DESTINATION, SO A ROUND TRIP SHOULD TAKE ABOUT AN HOUR.
APPARENTLY, I'LL ALSO NEED TEN MINUTES OR SO FOR **INFORMATION PROCESSING** ONCE I PUT THE MASK ON.

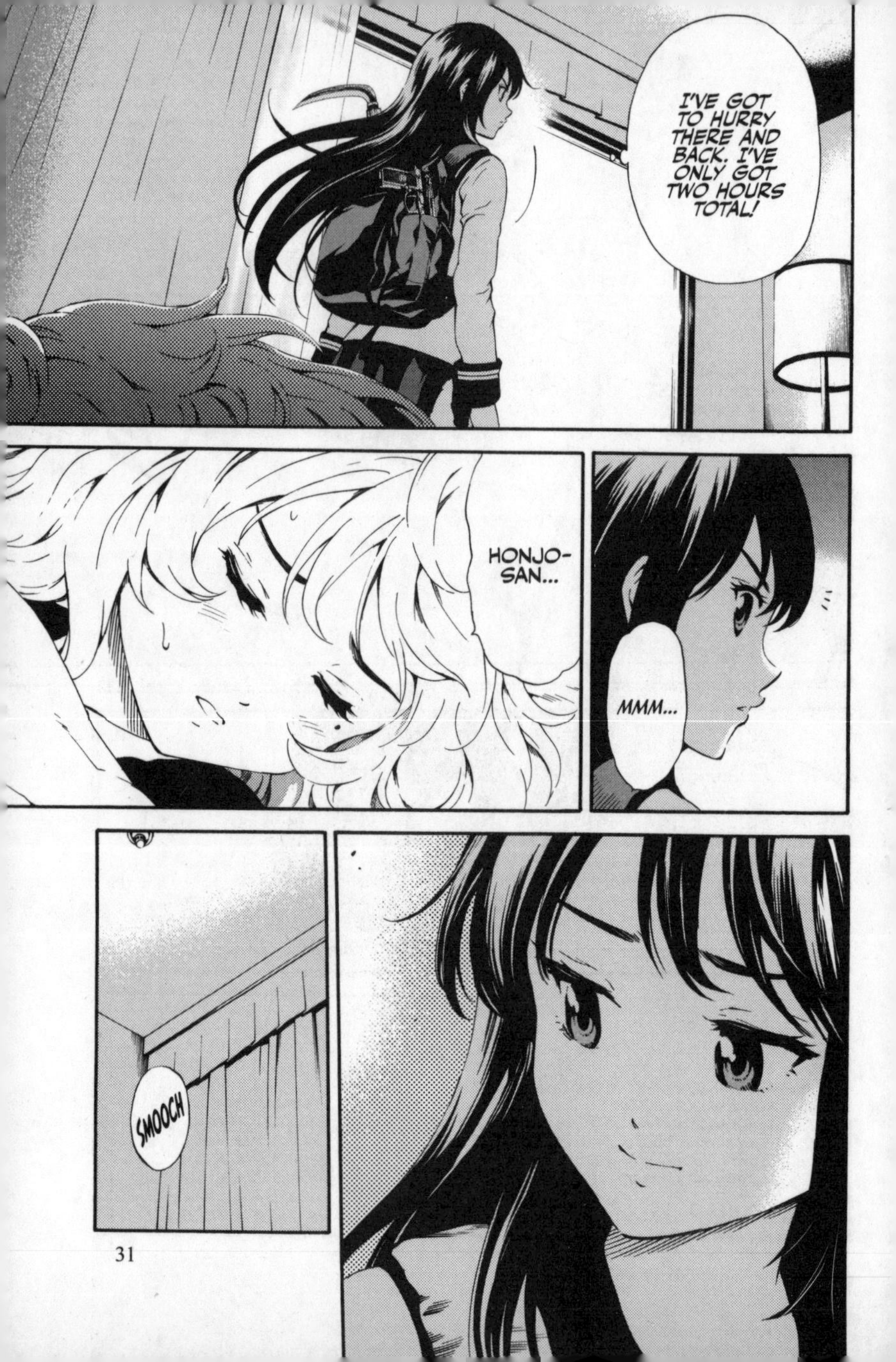
I'VE GOT TO HURRY THERE AND BACK. I'VE ONLY GOT TWO HOURS TOTAL!
MMM...
HONJO-SAN...
SMOOCH

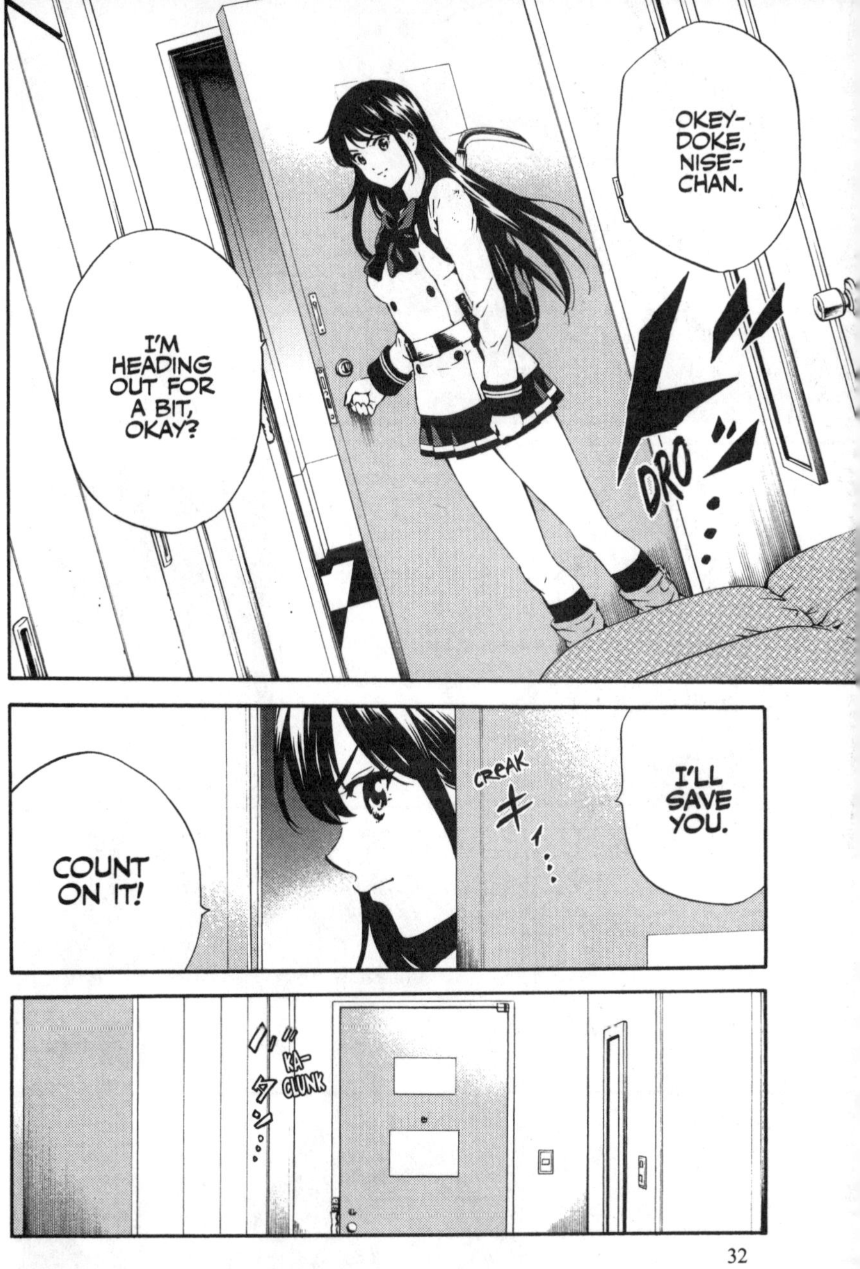
OKEY-DOKE, NISE-CHAN.
DRO...
I'M HEADING OUT FOR A BIT, OKAY?
I'LL SAVE YOU.
CREAK
COUNT ON IT!
KA-CLUNK

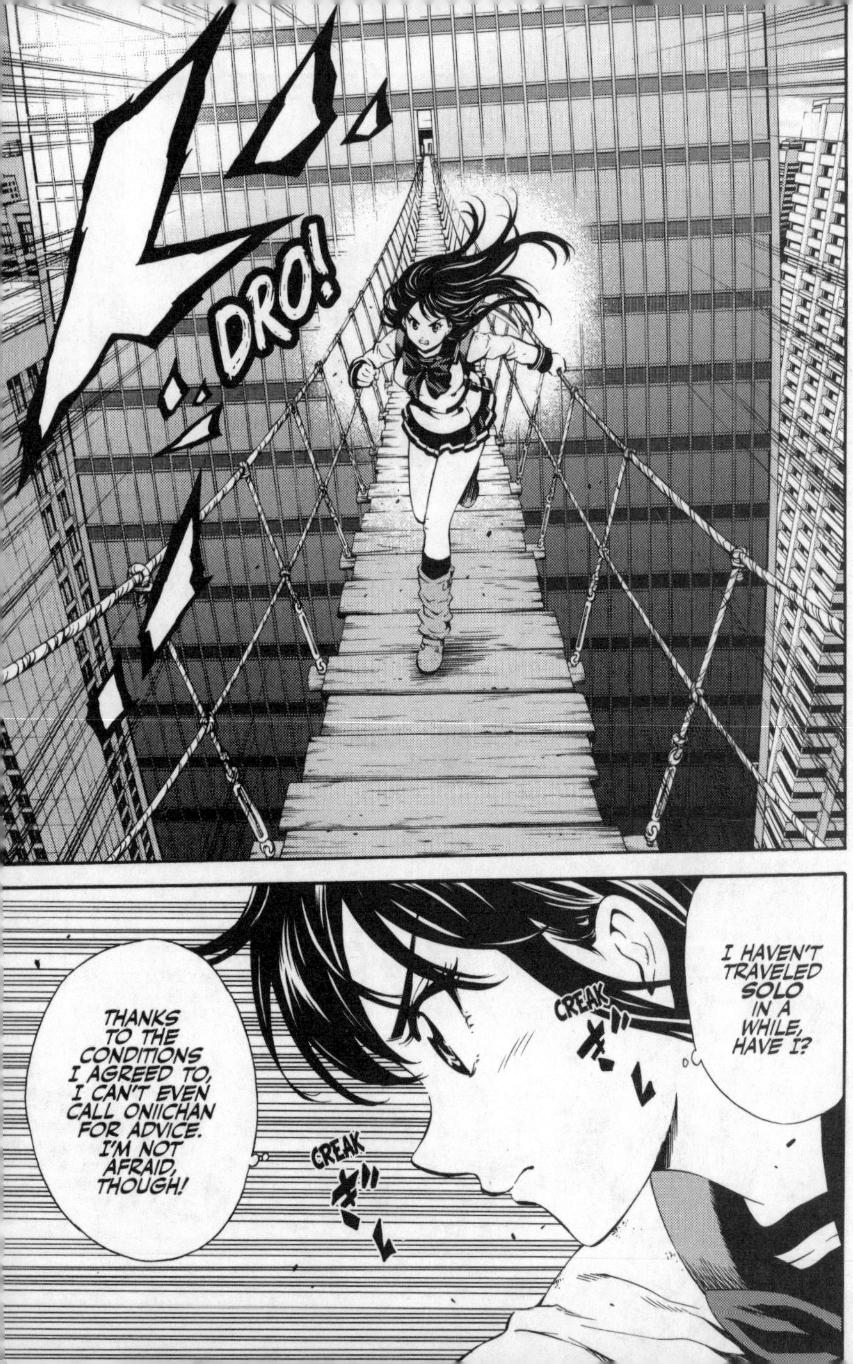
DRO!
I HAVEN'T TRAVELED SOLO IN A WHILE, HAVE I?
CREAK
THANKS TO THE CONDITIONS I AGREED TO, I CAN'T EVEN CALL ONIICHAN FOR ADVICE. I'M NOT AFRAID, THOUGH!
CREAK

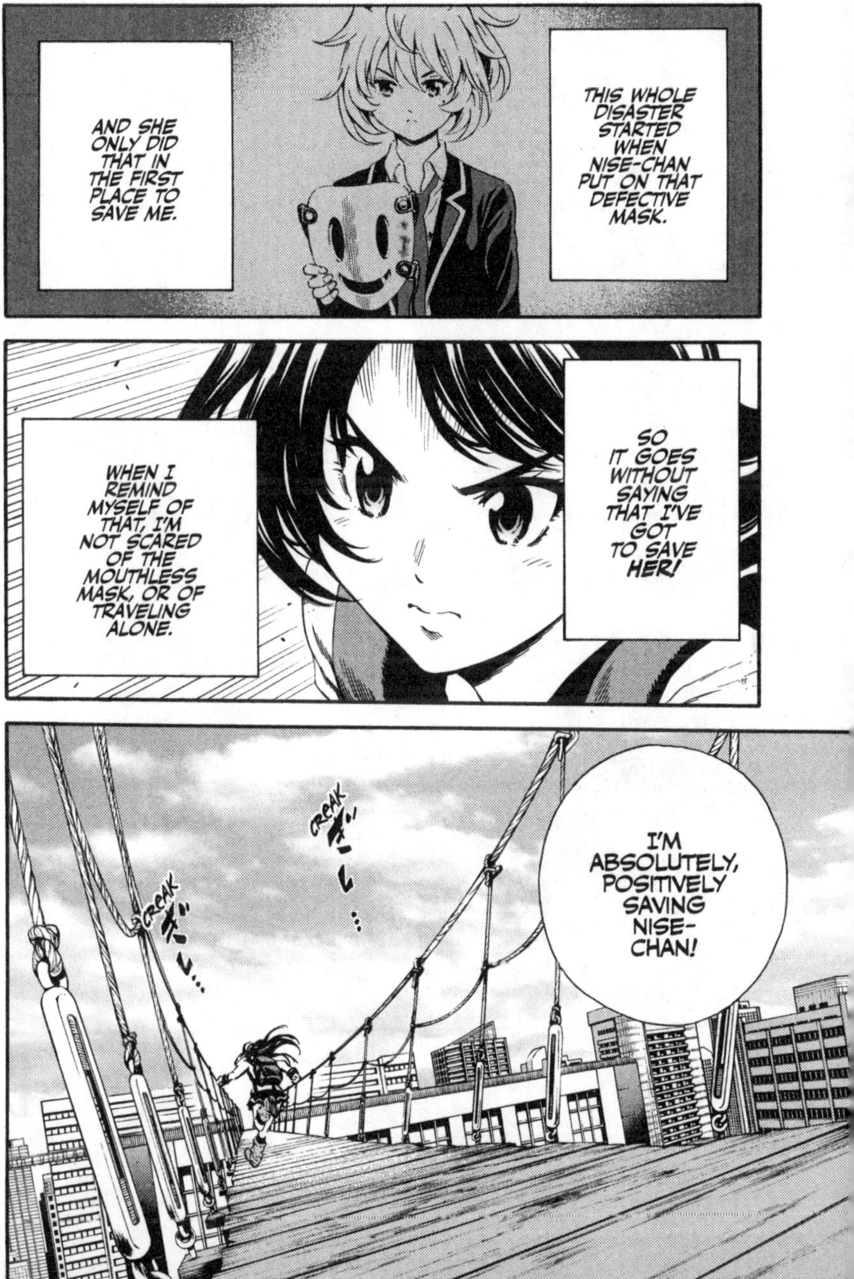
THIS WHOLE DISASTER STARTED WHEN NISE-CHAN PUT ON THAT DEFECTIVE MASK.
AND SHE ONLY DID THAT IN THE FIRST PLACE TO SAVE ME.
SO IT GOES WITHOUT SAYING THAT I'VE GOT TO SAVE HER!
WHEN I REMIND MYSELF OF THAT, I'M NOT SCARED OF THE MOUTHLESS MASK, OR OF TRAVELING ALONE.
I'M ABSOLUTELY, POSITIVELY SAVING NISE-CHAN!
CREAK
CREAK

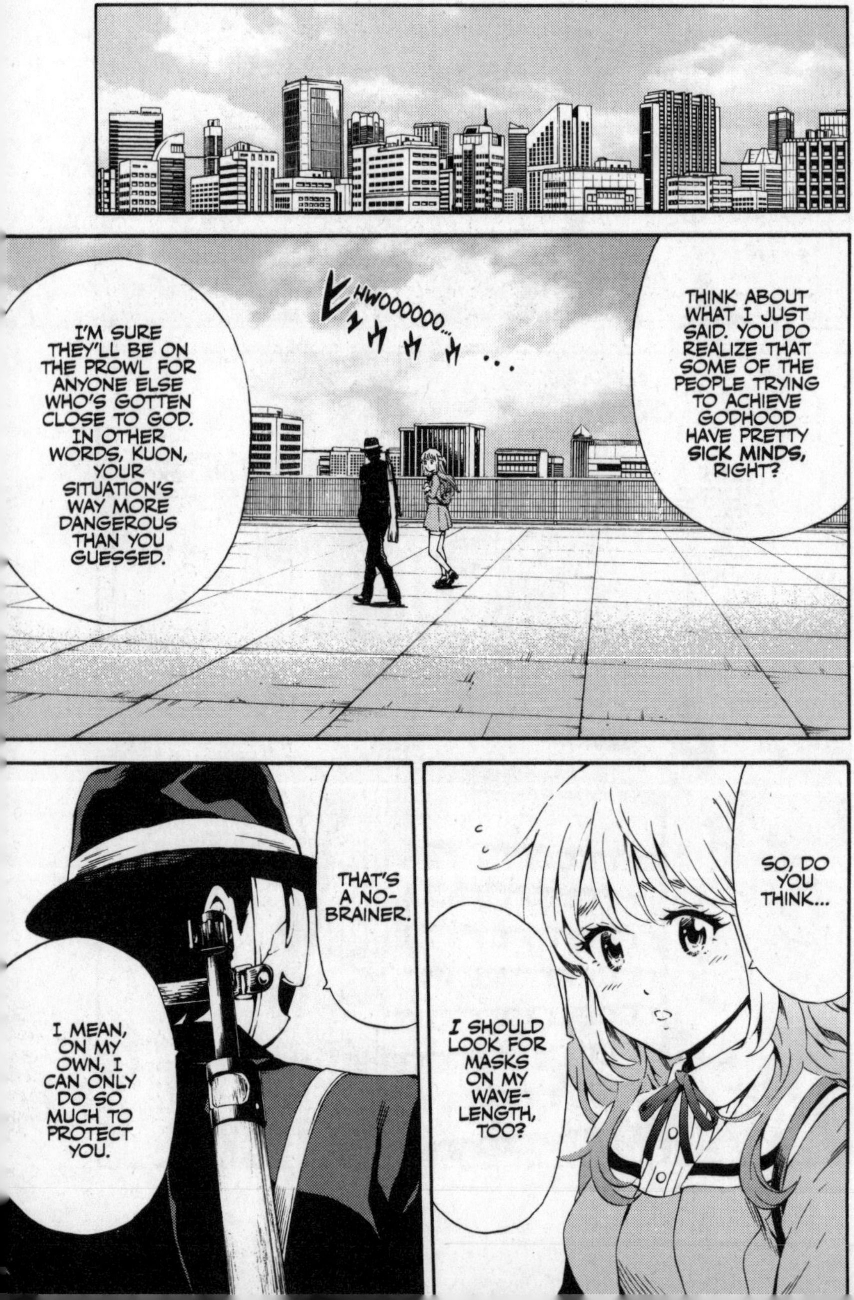
THINK ABOUT WHAT I JUST SAID. YOU DO REALIZE THAT SOME OF THE PEOPLE TRYING TO ACHIEVE GODHOOD HAVE PRETTY SICK MINDS, RIGHT?
HWOOOOOO...
I'M SURE THEY'LL BE ON THE PROWL FOR ANYONE ELSE WHO'S GOTTEN CLOSE TO GOD. IN OTHER WORDS, KUON, YOUR SITUATION'S WAY MORE DANGEROUS THAN YOU GUESSED.
SO, DO YOU THINK...
I SHOULD LOOK FOR MASKS ON MY WAVE-LENGTH, TOO?
THAT'S A NO-BRAINER.
I MEAN, ON MY OWN, I CAN ONLY DO SO MUCH TO PROTECT YOU.

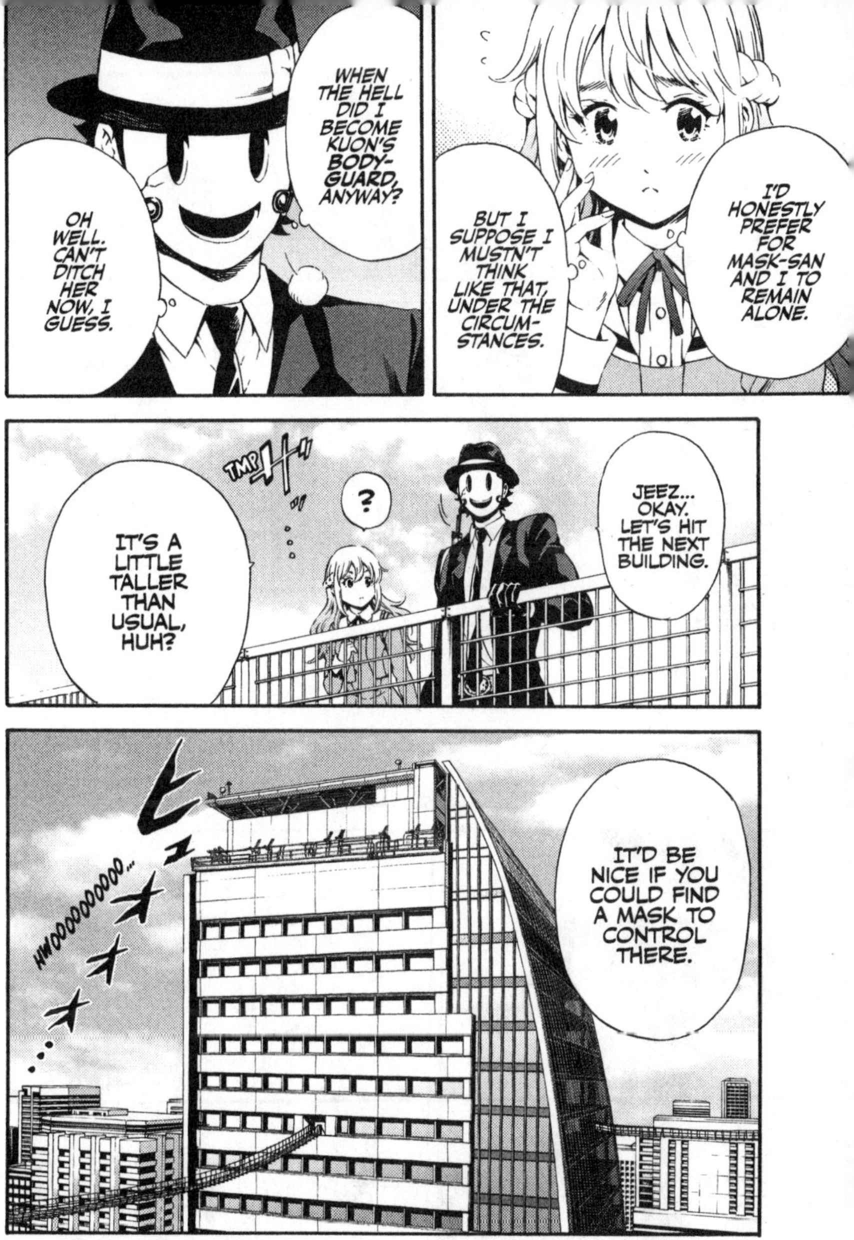
I'D HONESTLY PREFER FOR MASK-SAN AND I TO REMAIN ALONE.
BUT I SUPPOSE I MUSTN'T THINK LIKE THAT, UNDER THE CIRCUMSTANCES.
WHEN THE HELL DID I BECOME KUON'S BODY-GUARD, ANYWAY?
OH WELL. CAN'T DITCH HER NOW, I GUESS.
JEEZ... OKAY. LET'S HIT THE NEXT BUILDING.
?
TMP
IT'S A LITTLE TALLER THAN USUAL, HUH?
IT'D BE NICE IF YOU COULD FIND A MASK TO CONTROL THERE.
HWOOOOOOOOOO...

Why is it so hard to draw an
Angry Mask's mouth...?!

HIGH-RISE INVASION

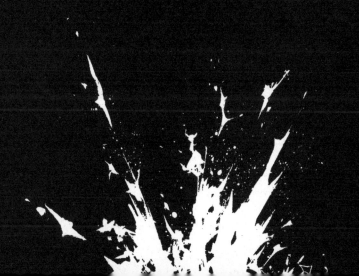

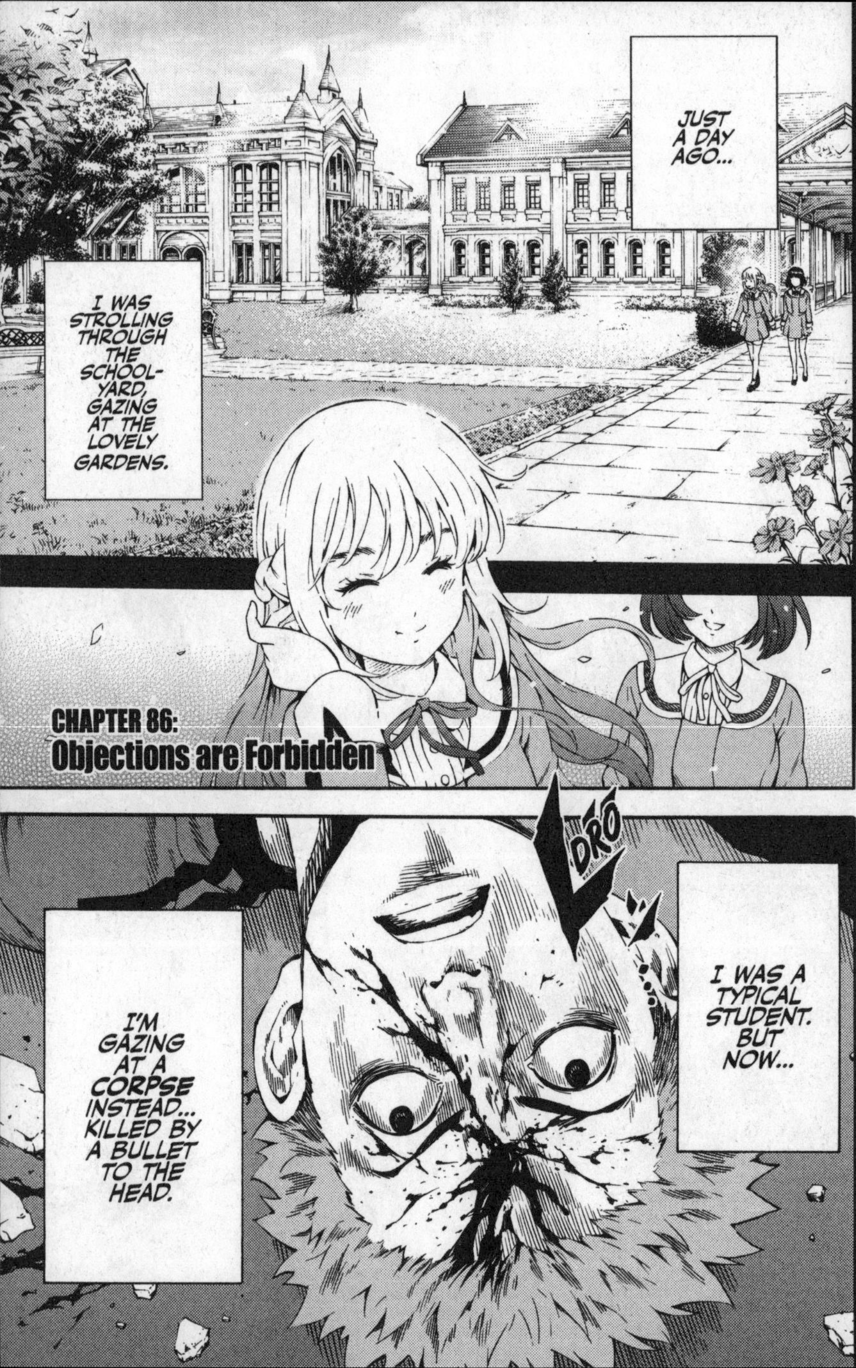
JUST A DAY AGO...
I WAS STROLLING THROUGH THE SCHOOL-YARD, GAZING AT THE LOVELY GARDENS.
CHAPTER 86:
Objections are Forbidden
I WAS A TYPICAL STUDENT. BUT NOW...
DRO
I'M GAZING AT A CORPSE INSTEAD... KILLED BY A BULLET TO THE HEAD.

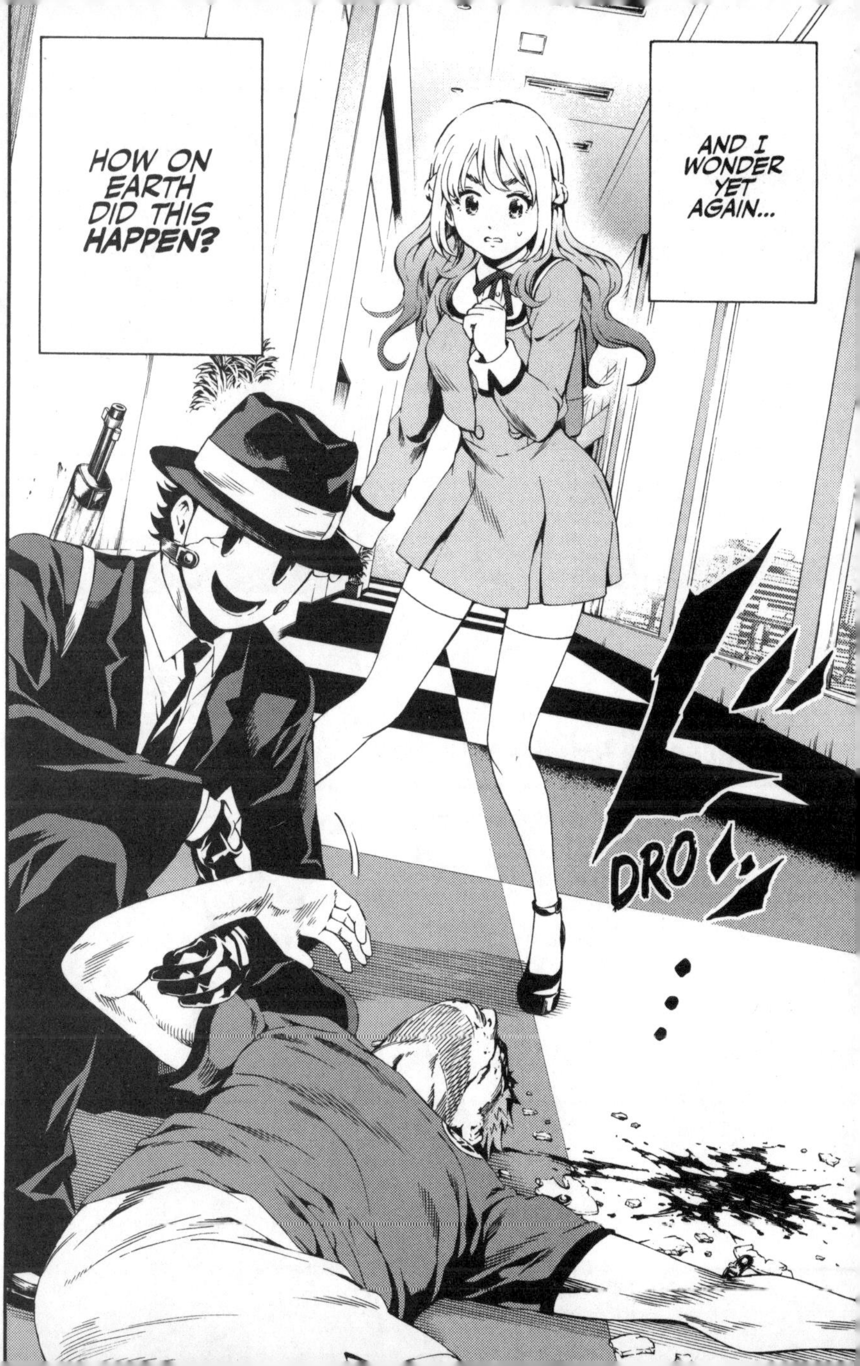
AND I WONDER YET AGAIN...
HOW ON EARTH DID THIS HAPPEN?
DRO

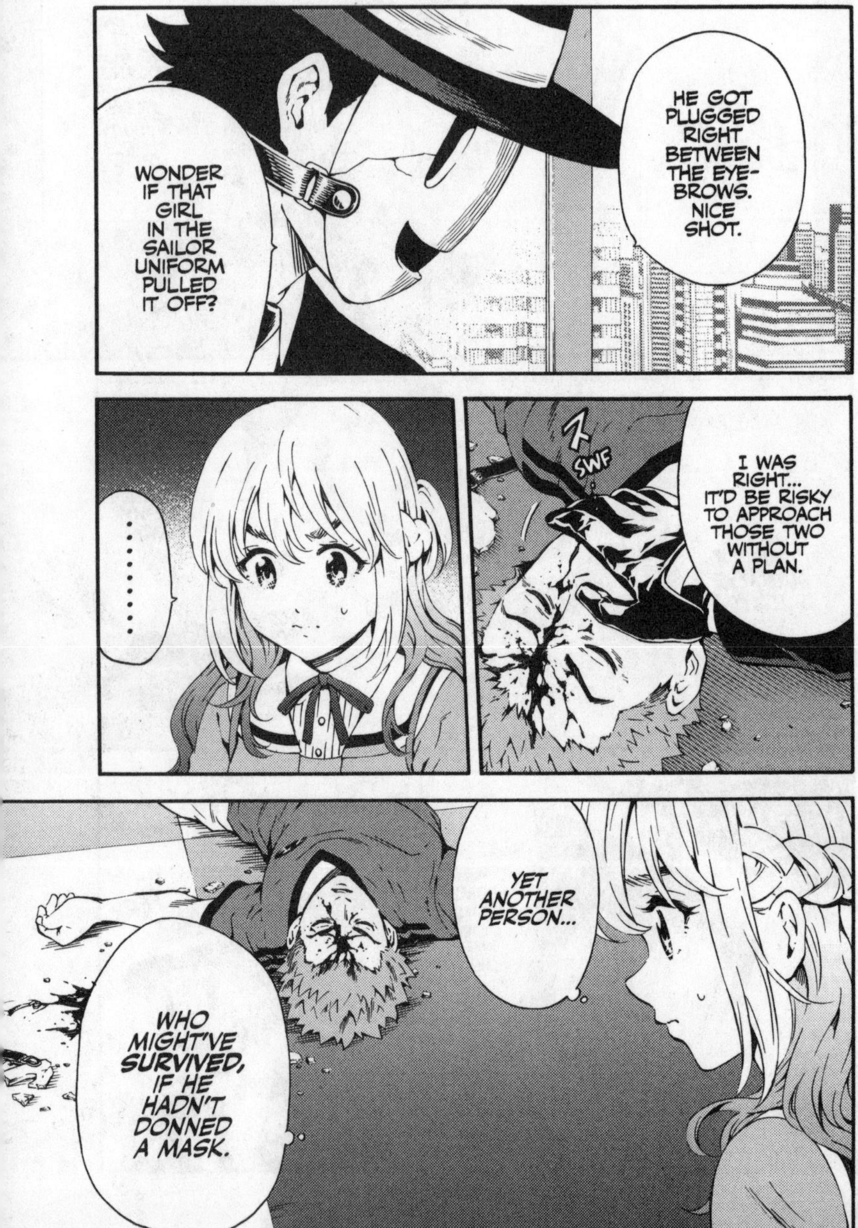
HE GOT PLUGGED RIGHT BETWEEN THE EYE-BROWS. NICE SHOT.
WONDER IF THAT GIRL IN THE SAILOR UNIFORM PULLED IT OFF?
ス
SWF
I WAS RIGHT... IT'D BE RISKY TO APPROACH THOSE TWO WITHOUT A PLAN.
......
YET ANOTHER PERSON...
WHO MIGHT'VE SURVIVED, IF HE HADN'T DONNED A MASK.

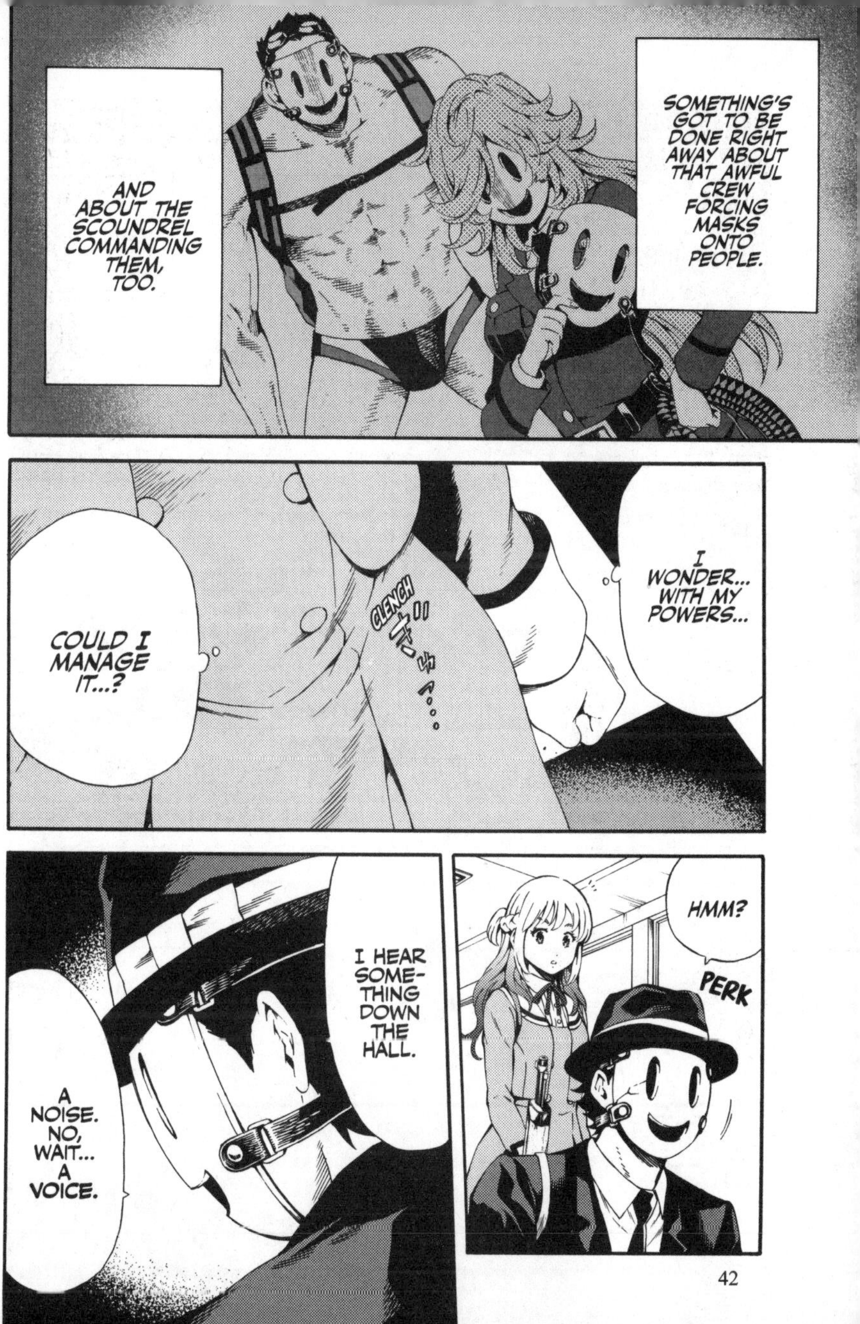

SOMETHING'S GOT TO BE DONE RIGHT AWAY ABOUT THAT AWFUL CREW FORCING MASKS ONTO PEOPLE.
AND ABOUT THE SCOUNDREL COMMANDING THEM, TOO.
I WONDER... WITH MY POWERS...
CLENCH
COULD I MANAGE IT...?
HMM?
PERK
I HEAR SOME-THING DOWN THE HALL.
A NOISE. NO, WAIT... A VOICE.

SOMEONE MOANING...?
NNH...
MMH...
NUUUH...

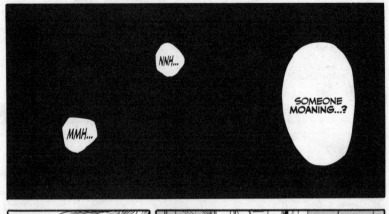

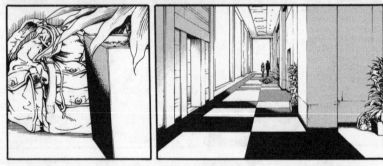

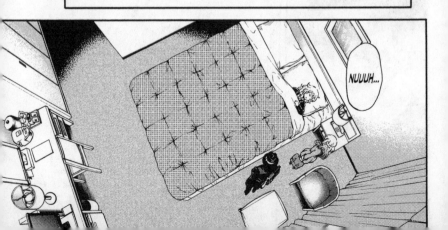

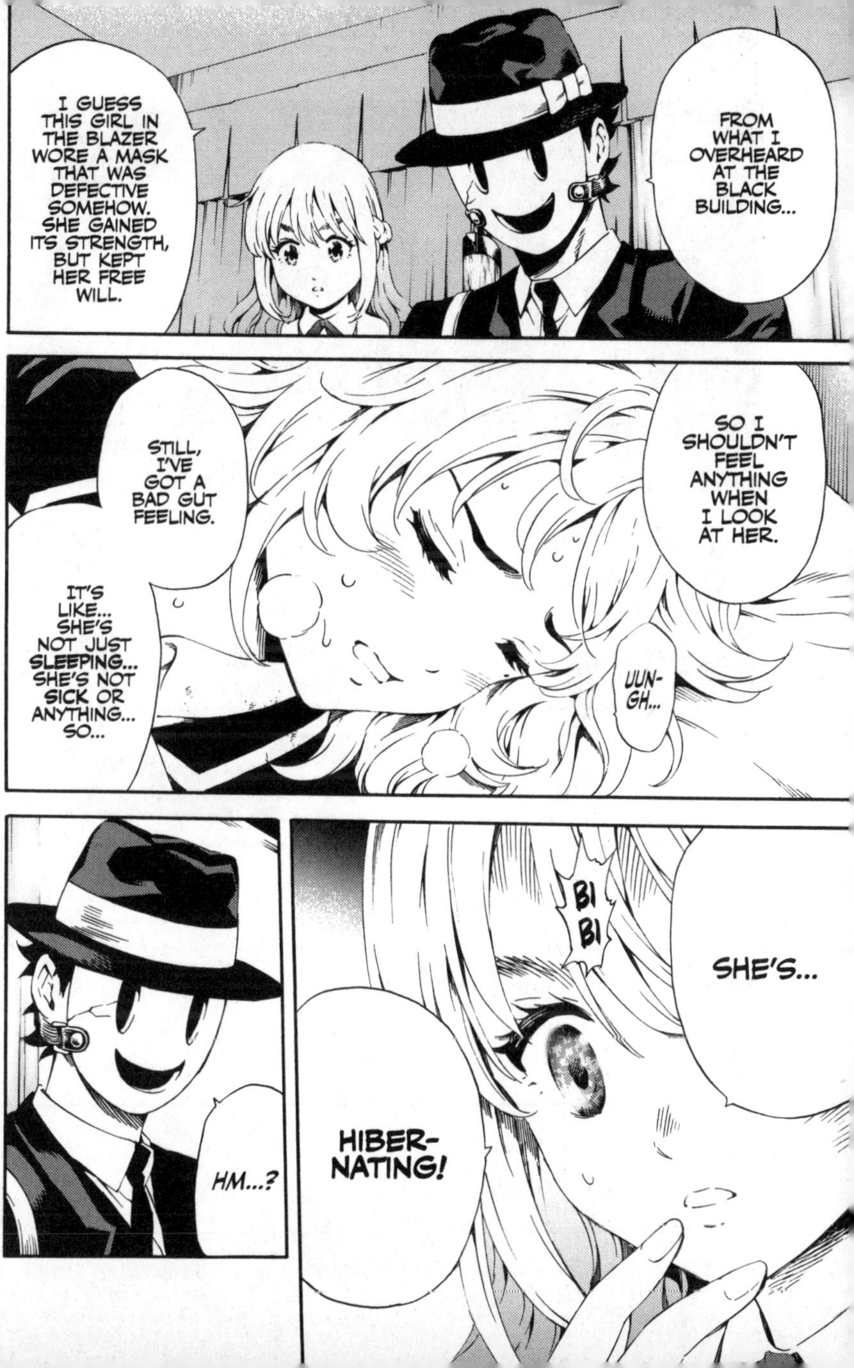
FROM WHAT I OVERHEARD AT THE BLACK BUILDING...
I GUESS THIS GIRL IN THE BLAZER WORE A MASK THAT WAS DEFECTIVE SOMEHOW. SHE GAINED ITS STRENGTH, BUT KEPT HER FREE WILL.
SO I SHOULDN'T FEEL ANYTHING WHEN I LOOK AT HER.
UUN-GH...
STILL, I'VE GOT A BAD GUT FEELING.
IT'S LIKE... SHE'S NOT JUST SLEEPING... SHE'S NOT SICK OR ANYTHING... SO...
SHE'S...
BI BI
HIBER-NATING!
HM...?

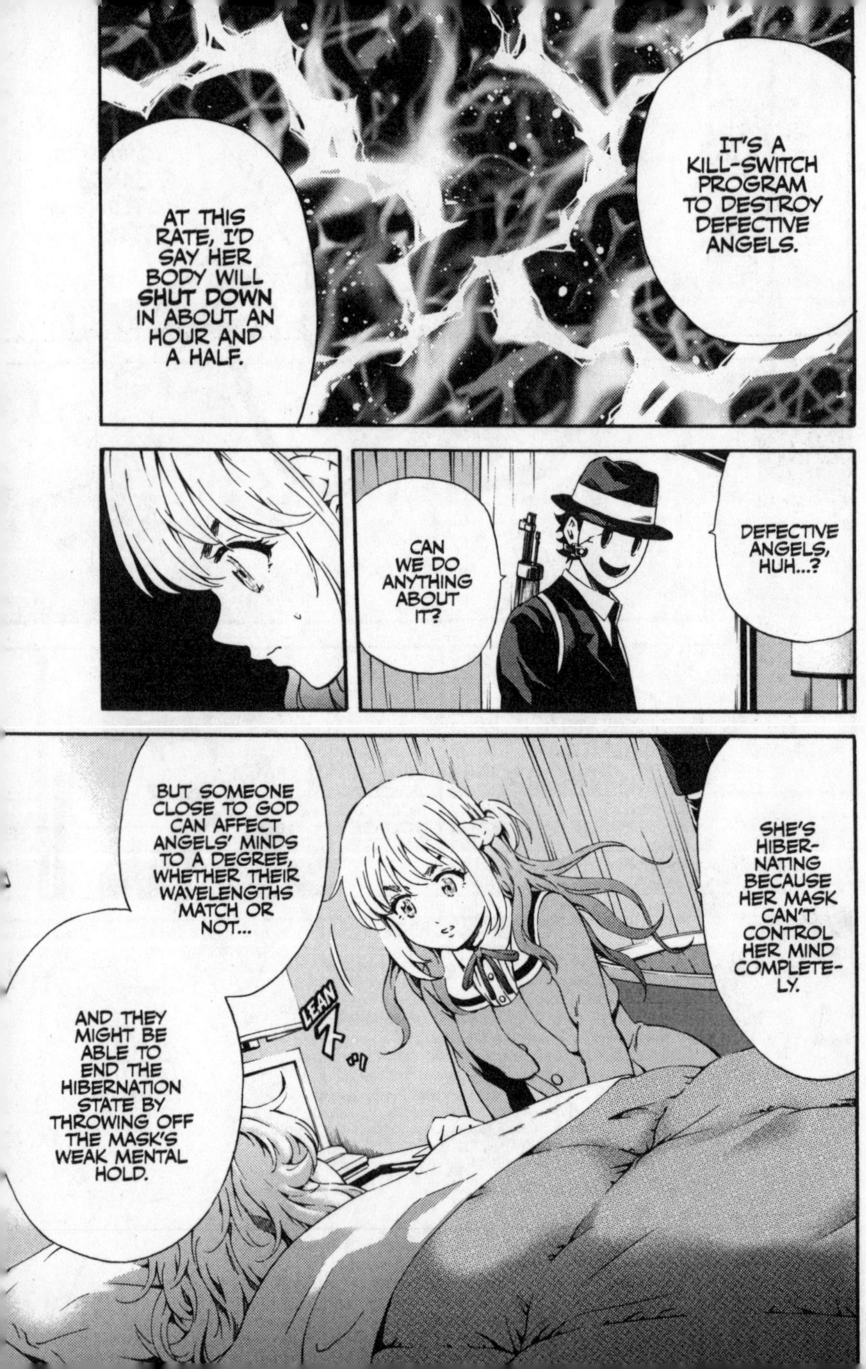
IT'S A KILL-SWITCH PROGRAM TO DESTROY DEFECTIVE ANGELS.
AT THIS RATE, I'D SAY HER BODY WILL SHUT DOWN IN ABOUT AN HOUR AND A HALF.
DEFECTIVE ANGELS, HUH...?
CAN WE DO ANYTHING ABOUT IT?
SHE'S HIBER-NATING BECAUSE HER MASK CAN'T CONTROL HER MIND COMPLETE-LY.
BUT SOMEONE CLOSE TO GOD CAN AFFECT ANGELS' MINDS TO A DEGREE, WHETHER THEIR WAVELENGTHS MATCH OR NOT...
LEAN
AND THEY MIGHT BE ABLE TO END THE HIBERNATION STATE BY THROWING OFF THE MASK'S WEAK MENTAL HOLD.

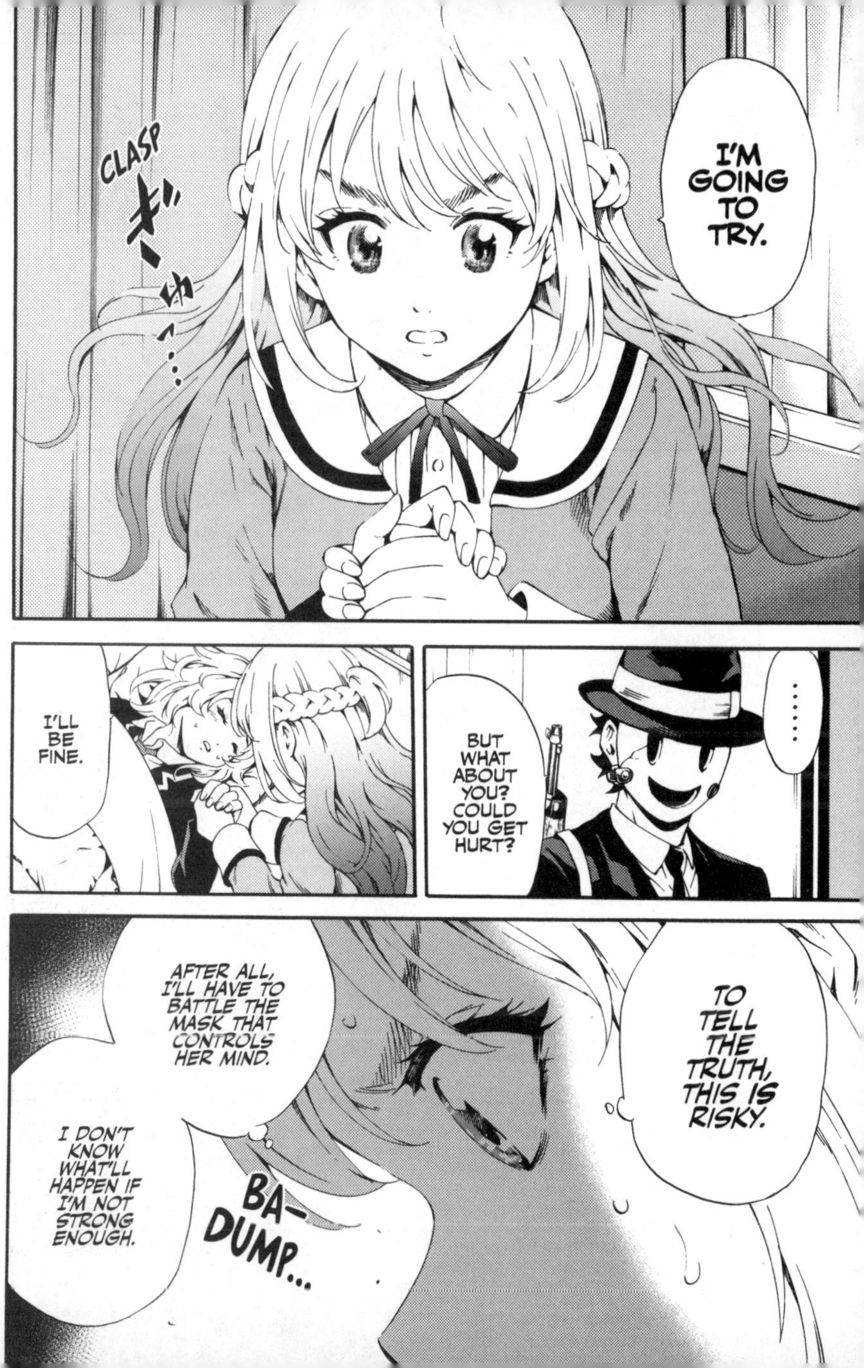
I'M GOING TO TRY.
CLASP
ぎゅ…
……
BUT WHAT ABOUT YOU? COULD YOU GET HURT?
I'LL BE FINE.
TO TELL THE TRUTH, THIS IS RISKY.
AFTER ALL, I'LL HAVE TO BATTLE THE MASK THAT CONTROLS HER MIND.
BA-DUMP...
I DON'T KNOW WHAT'LL HAPPEN IF I'M NOT STRONG ENOUGH.

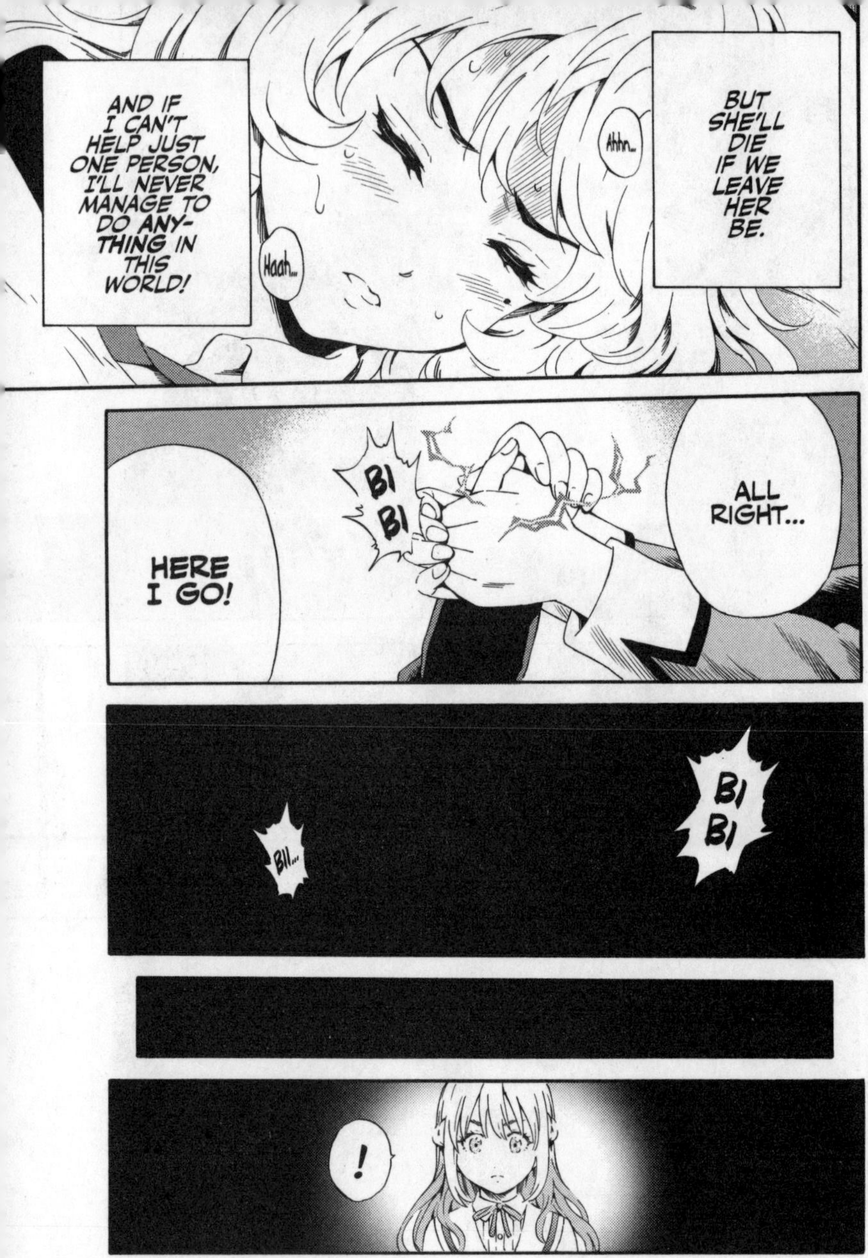
BUT SHE'LL DIE IF WE LEAVE HER BE.
Ahhn...
Haah...
AND IF I CAN'T HELP JUST ONE PERSON, I'LL NEVER MANAGE TO DO ANYTHING IN THIS WORLD!
ALL RIGHT...
BI BI
HERE I GO!
BI BI
BII...
!

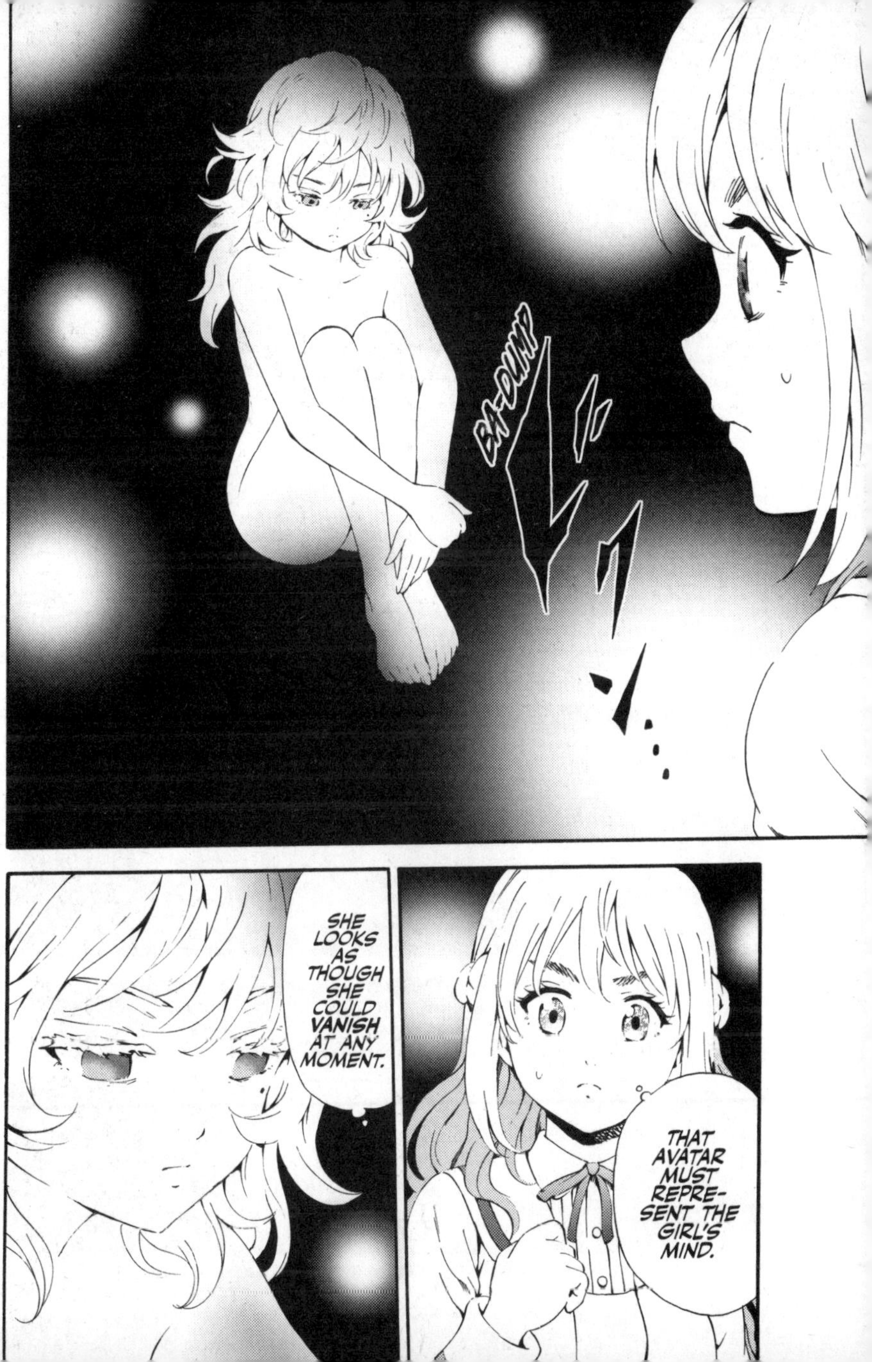
BA-DUMP
THAT AVATAR MUST REPRE-SENT THE GIRL'S MIND.
SHE LOOKS AS THOUGH SHE COULD VANISH AT ANY MOMENT.

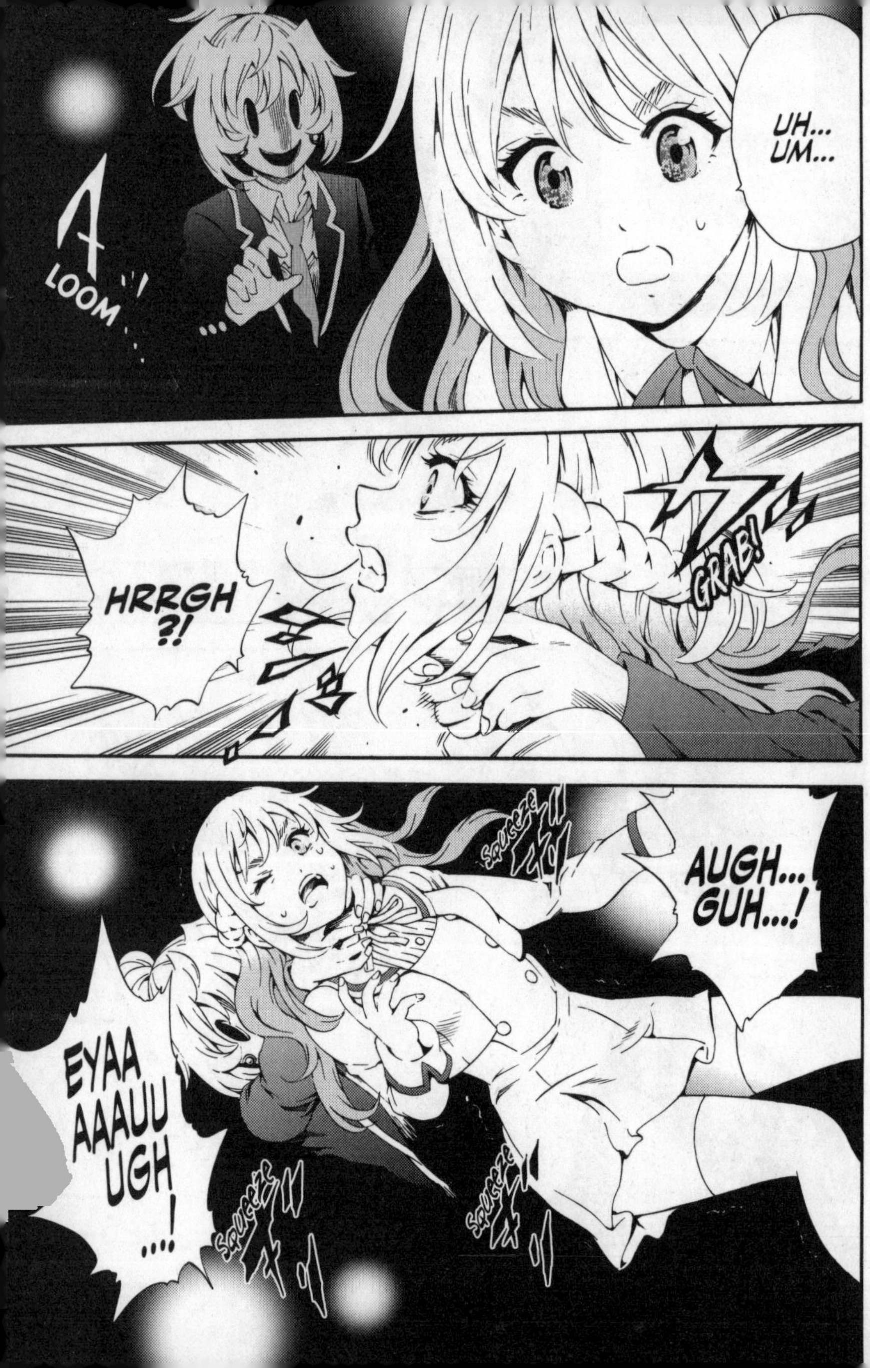

UH... UM...
A LOOM...!
GRAB!
HRRGH ?!
AUGH... GUH...!
Squeeze
EYAAAAAUUUGH ...!
Squeeze
Squeeze

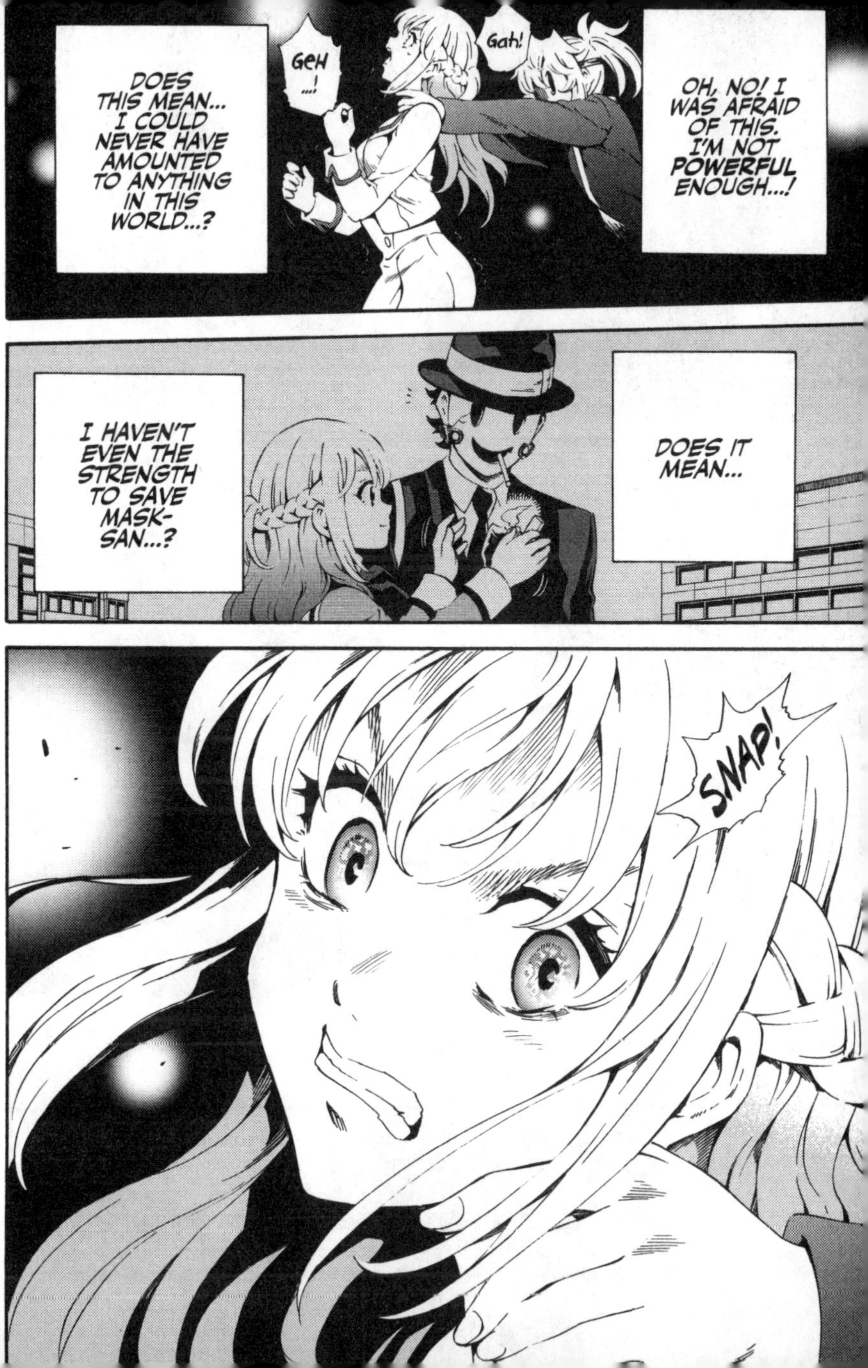
OH, NO! I WAS AFRAID OF THIS. I'M NOT POWERFUL ENOUGH...!
Gah!
GEH ...!
DOES THIS MEAN... I COULD NEVER HAVE AMOUNTED TO ANYTHING IN THIS WORLD...?
DOES IT MEAN...
I HAVEN'T EVEN THE STRENGTH TO SAVE MASK-SAN...?
SNAP!

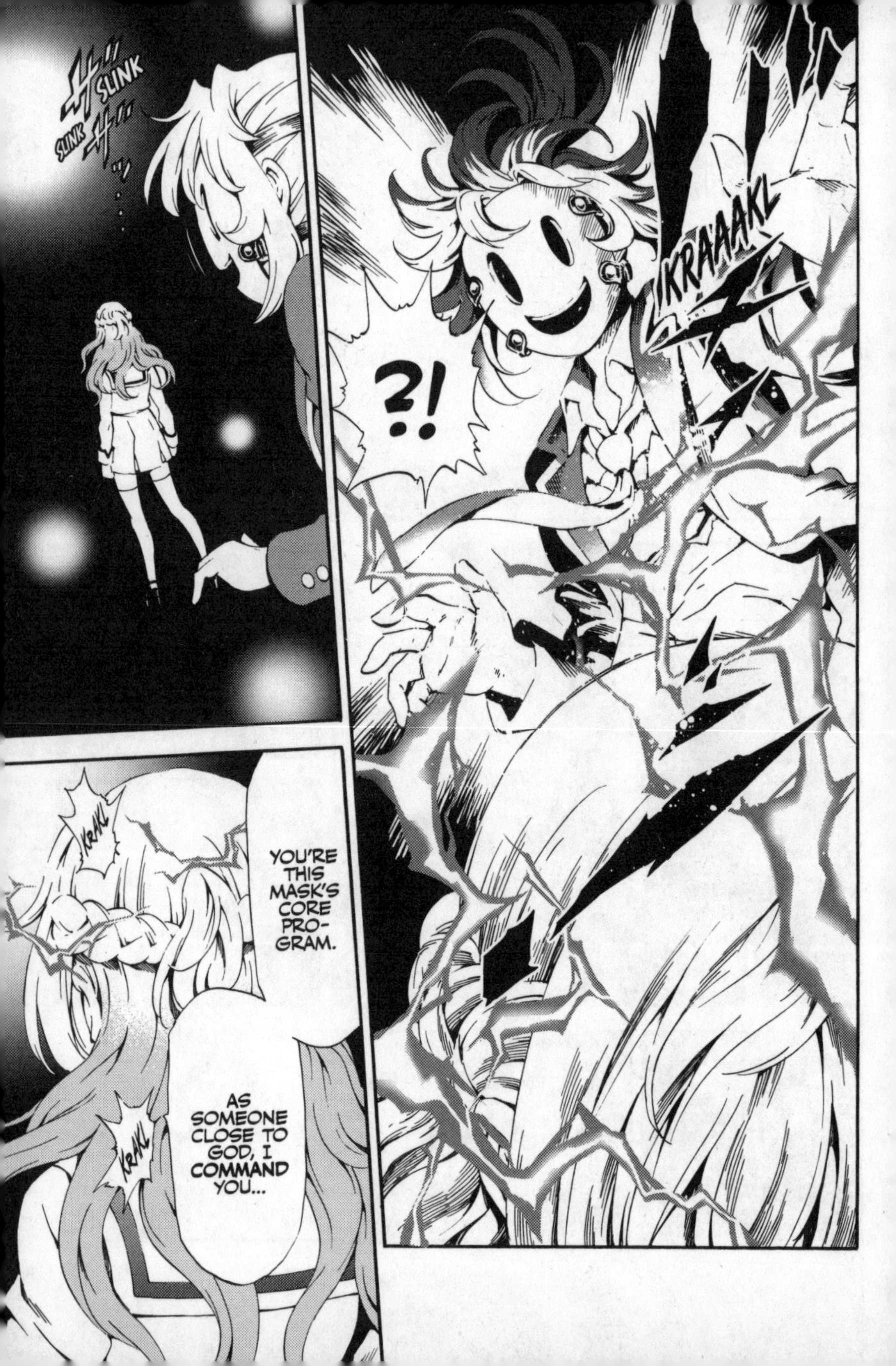
KRAAAKL
?!
SLINK
SLINK
YOU'RE THIS MASK'S CORE PROGRAM.
KRAKL
AS SOMEONE CLOSE TO GOD, I COMMAND YOU...
KRAKL

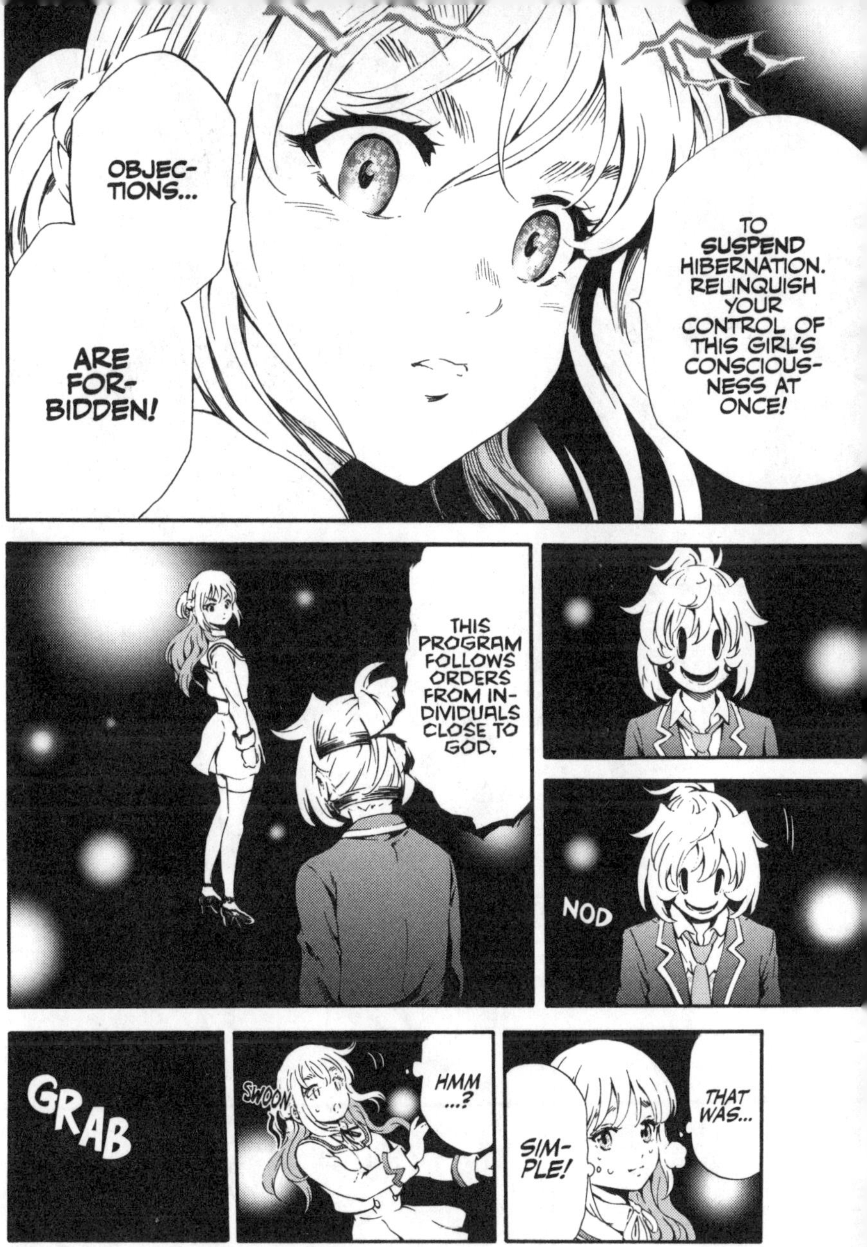
TO SUSPEND HIBERNATION. RELINQUISH YOUR CONTROL OF THIS GIRL'S CONSCIOUS-NESS AT ONCE!
OBJEC-TIONS...
ARE FOR-BIDDEN!
NOD
THIS PROGRAM FOLLOWS ORDERS FROM IN-DIVIDUALS CLOSE TO GOD.
THAT WAS...
SIM-PLE!
HMM ...?
SWOON
GRAB

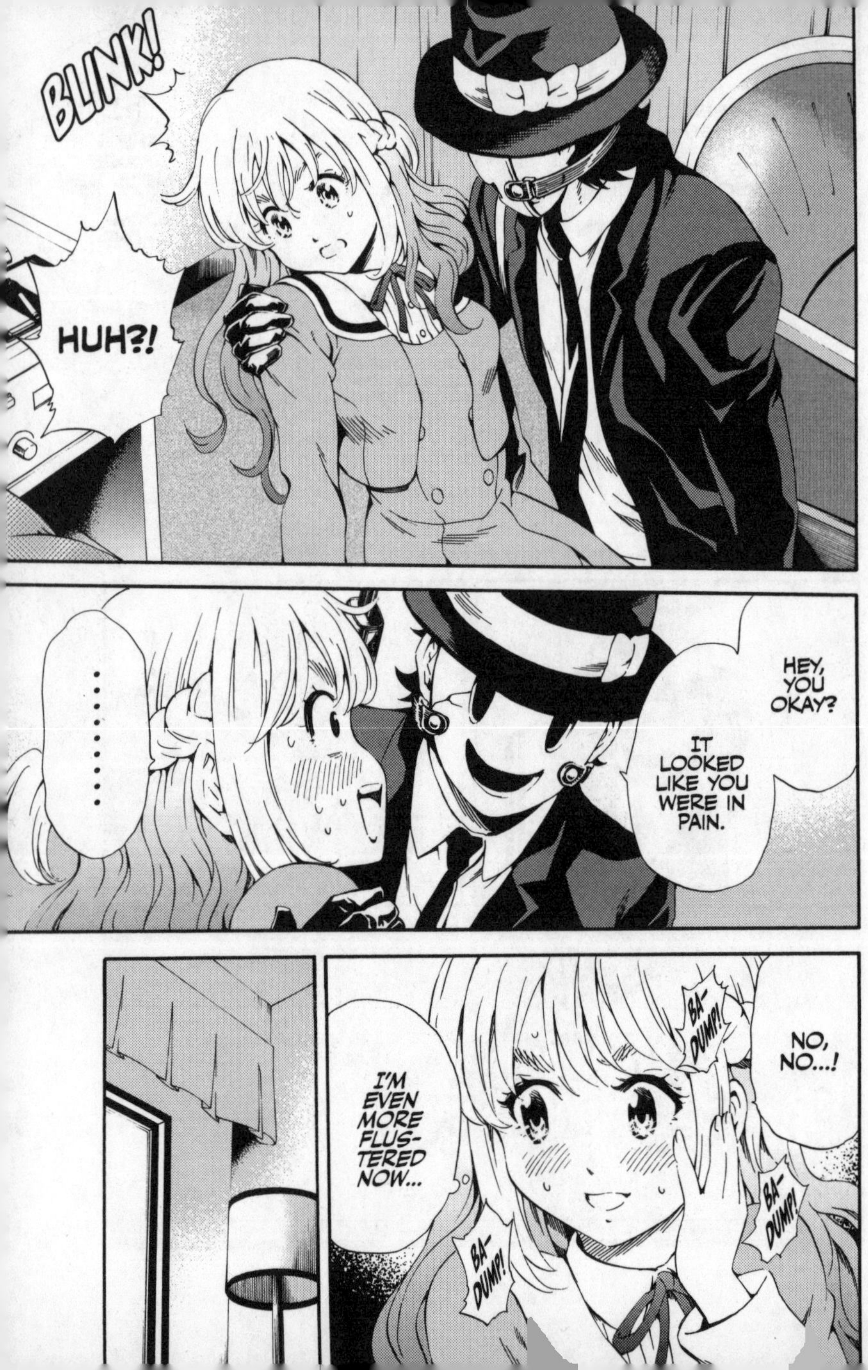
BLINK!
HUH?!
HEY, YOU OKAY?
IT LOOKED LIKE YOU WERE IN PAIN.
....
NO, NO...!
BA-DUMP!
BA-DUMP!
BA-DUMP!
I'M EVEN MORE FLUS-TERED NOW...

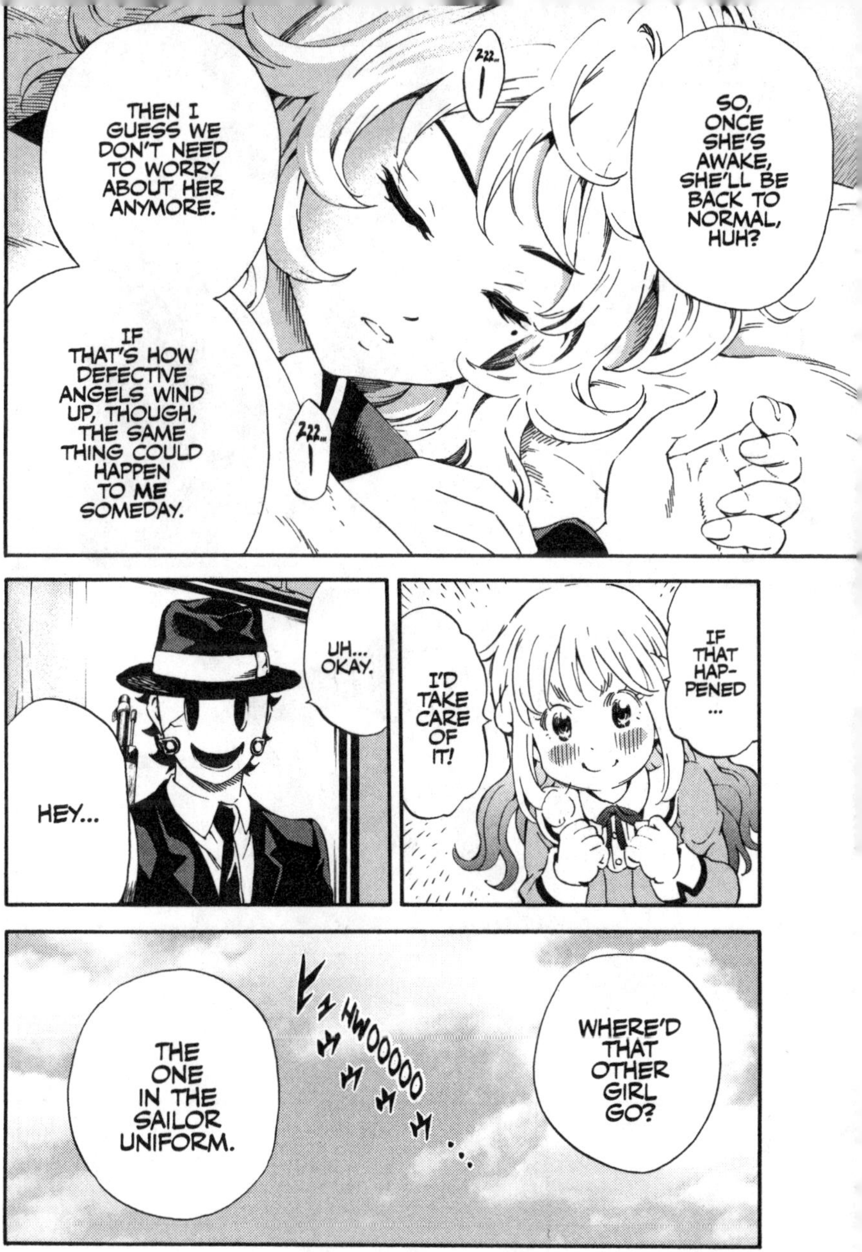

ZZZ...
SO, ONCE SHE'S AWAKE, SHE'LL BE BACK TO NORMAL, HUH?
THEN I GUESS WE DON'T NEED TO WORRY ABOUT HER ANYMORE.
ZZZ...
IF THAT'S HOW DEFECTIVE ANGELS WIND UP, THOUGH, THE SAME THING COULD HAPPEN TO ME SOMEDAY.
IF THAT HAP-PENED...
I'D TAKE CARE OF IT!
UH... OKAY.
HEY...
WHERE'D THAT OTHER GIRL GO?
HWOOOOO...
THE ONE IN THE SAILOR UNIFORM.

CHAPTER 87: The Final Test

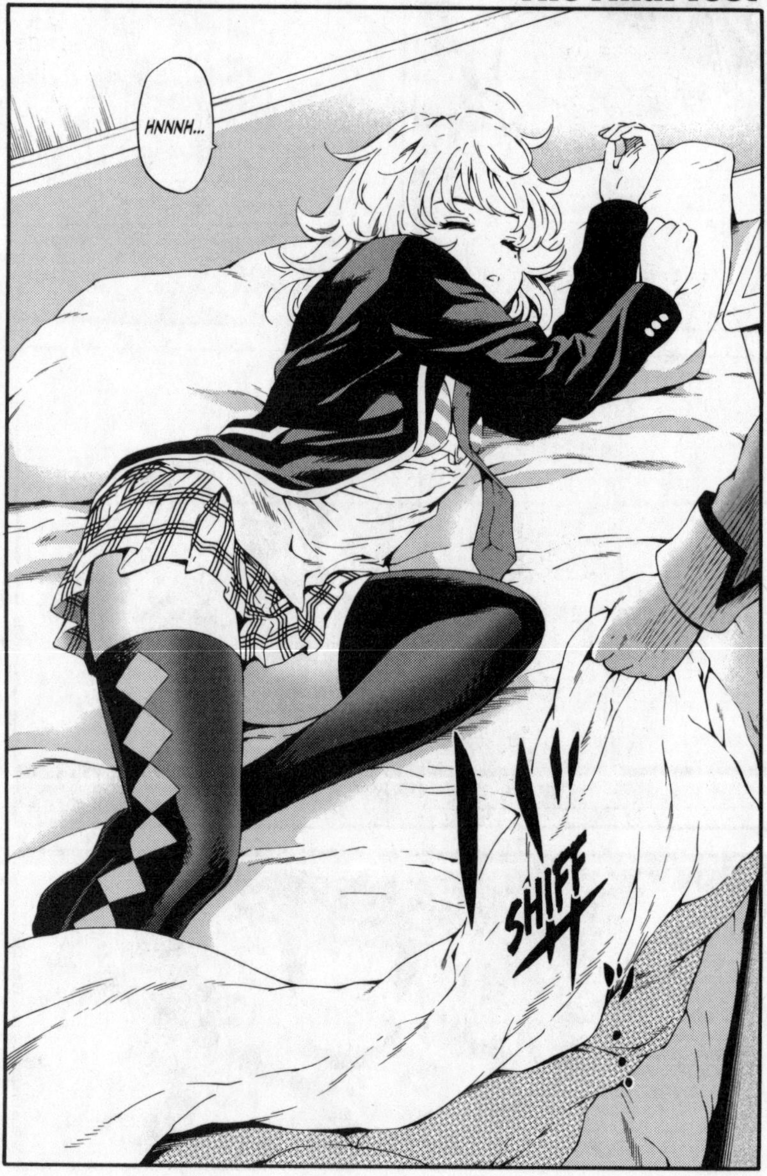
HNNNH...
SHIFF

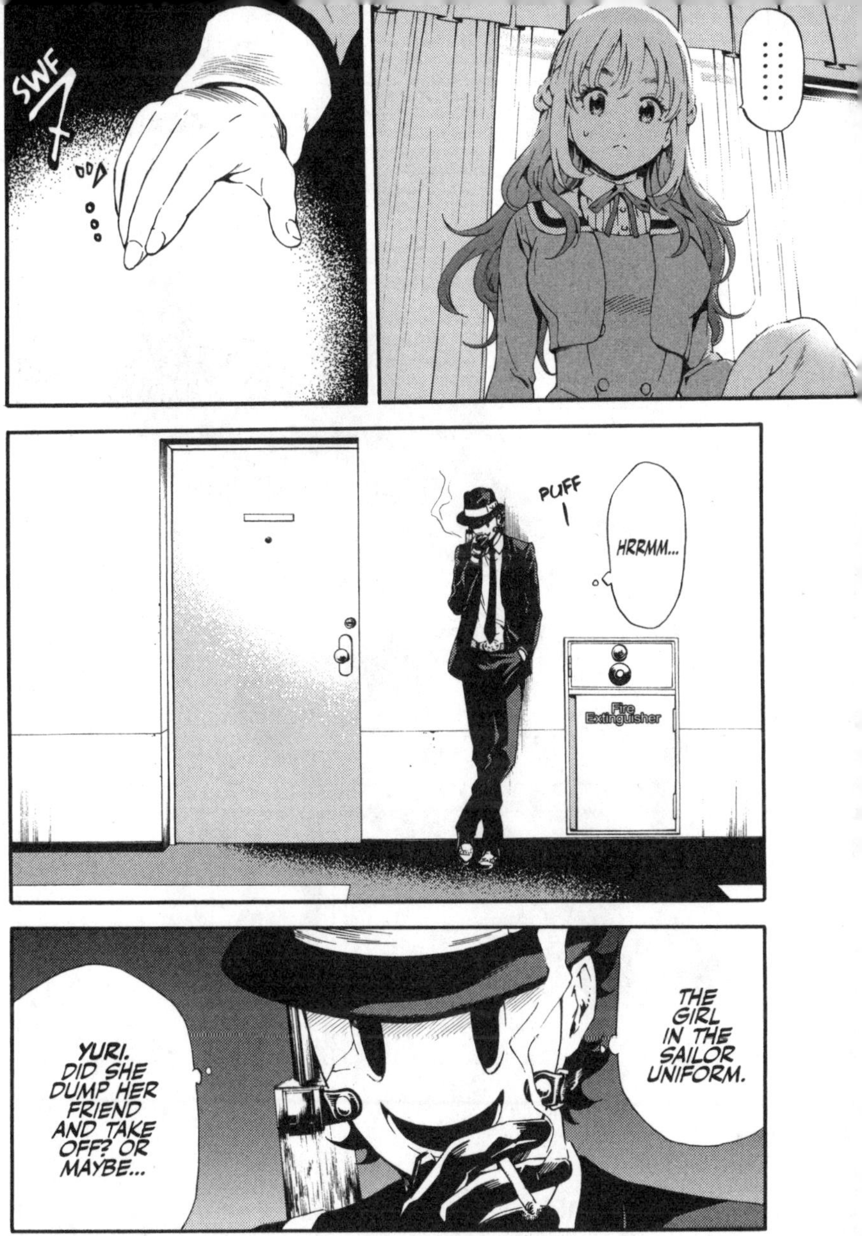
......
SWF
PUFF
HRRMM...
THE GIRL IN THE SAILOR UNIFORM.
YURI. DID SHE DUMP HER FRIEND AND TAKE OFF? OR MAYBE...

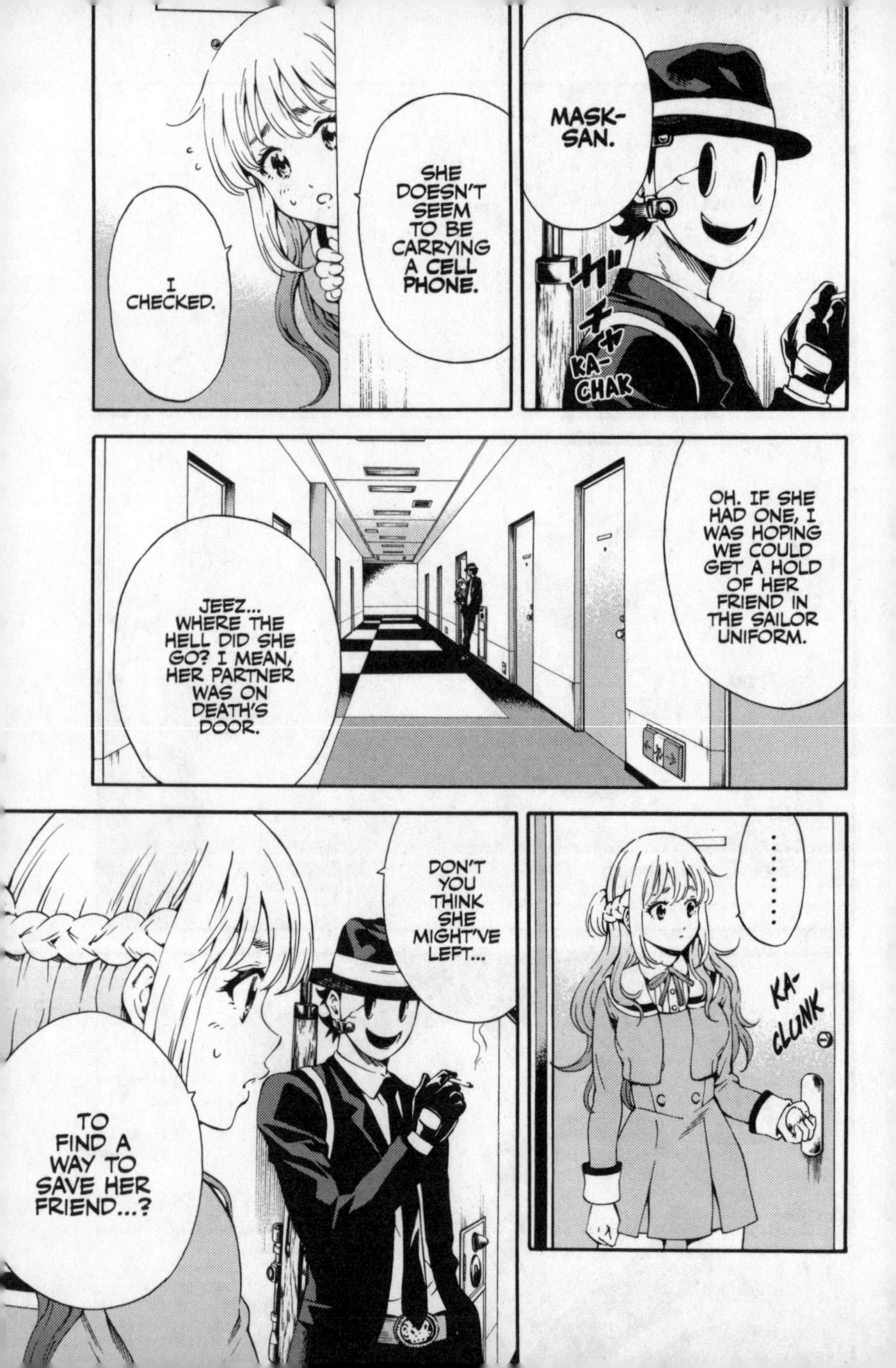
MASK-SAN.
ガチャ
KA-CHAK
SHE DOESN'T SEEM TO BE CARRYING A CELL PHONE.
I CHECKED.
OH. IF SHE HAD ONE, I WAS HOPING WE COULD GET A HOLD OF HER FRIEND IN THE SAILOR UNIFORM.
JEEZ... WHERE THE HELL DID SHE GO? I MEAN, HER PARTNER WAS ON DEATH'S DOOR.
......
KA-CLUNK
DON'T YOU THINK SHE MIGHT'VE LEFT...
TO FIND A WAY TO SAVE HER FRIEND...?

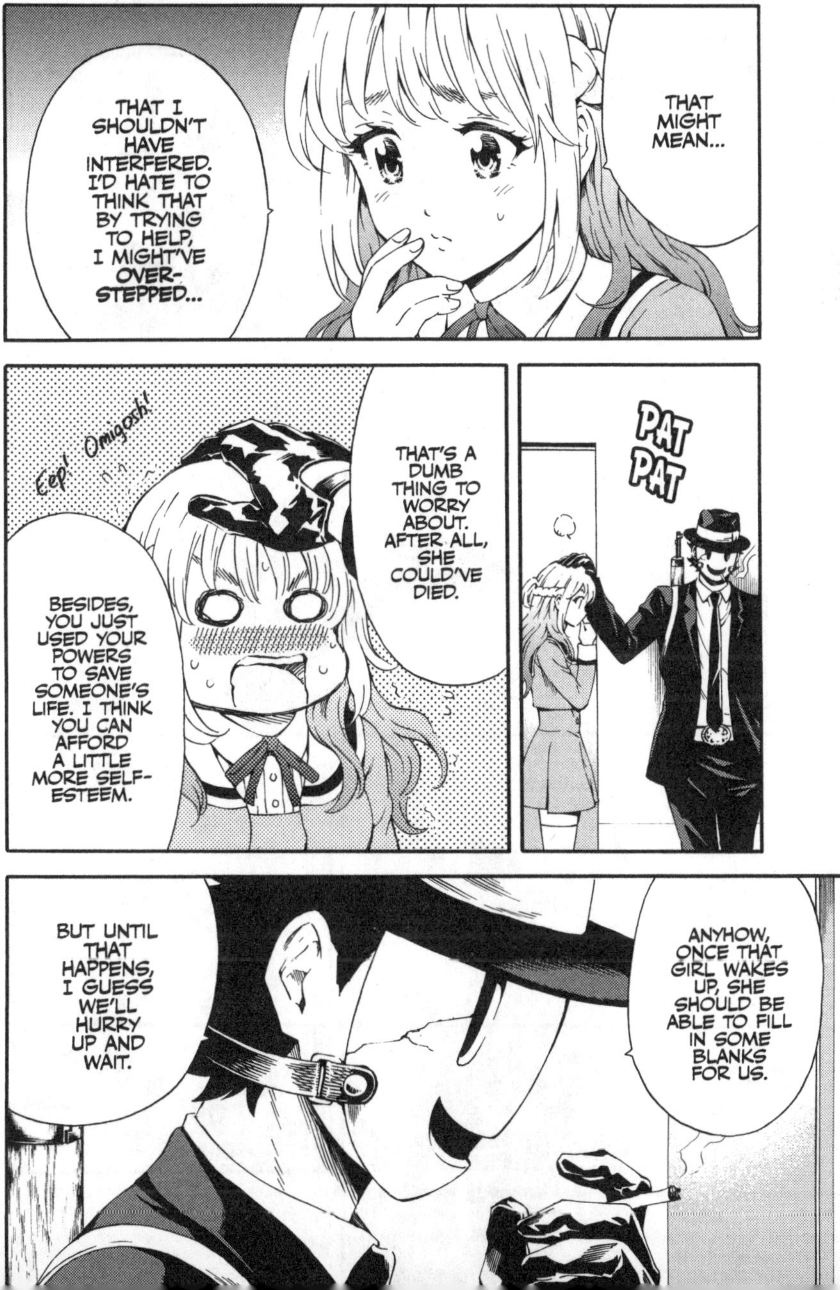
THAT MIGHT MEAN...
THAT I SHOULDN'T HAVE INTERFERED. I'D HATE TO THINK THAT BY TRYING TO HELP, I MIGHT'VE OVER-STEPPED...
PAT PAT
THAT'S A DUMB THING TO WORRY ABOUT. AFTER ALL, SHE COULD'VE DIED.
Eep! Omigosh!
BESIDES, YOU JUST USED YOUR POWERS TO SAVE SOMEONE'S LIFE. I THINK YOU CAN AFFORD A LITTLE MORE SELF-ESTEEM.
ANYHOW, ONCE THAT GIRL WAKES UP, SHE SHOULD BE ABLE TO FILL IN SOME BLANKS FOR US.
BUT UNTIL THAT HAPPENS, I GUESS WE'LL HURRY UP AND WAIT.

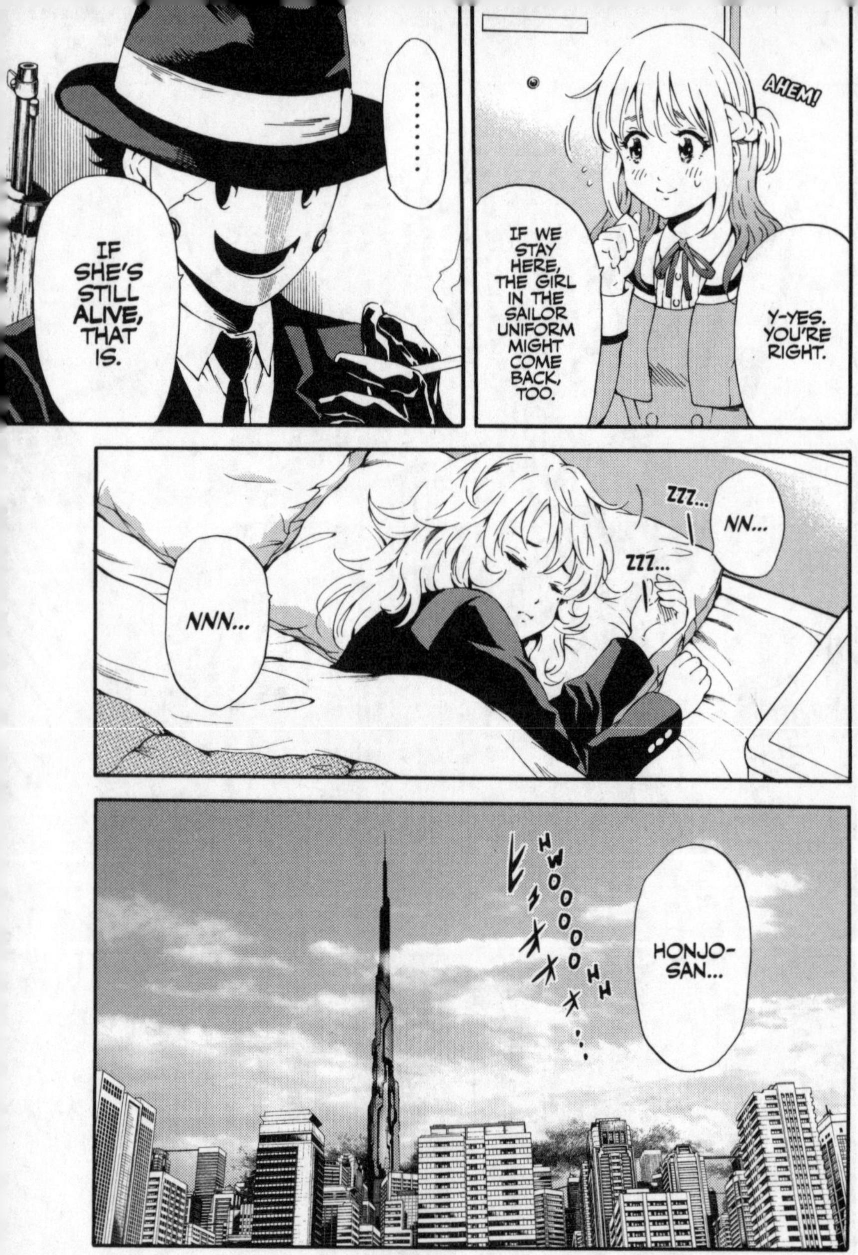
AHEM!
Y-YES. YOU'RE RIGHT.
IF WE STAY HERE, THE GIRL IN THE SAILOR UNIFORM MIGHT COME BACK, TOO.
......
IF SHE'S STILL ALIVE, THAT IS.
ZZZ...
NN...
ZZZ...
NNN...
HONJO-SAN...
HWOOOOOHH...

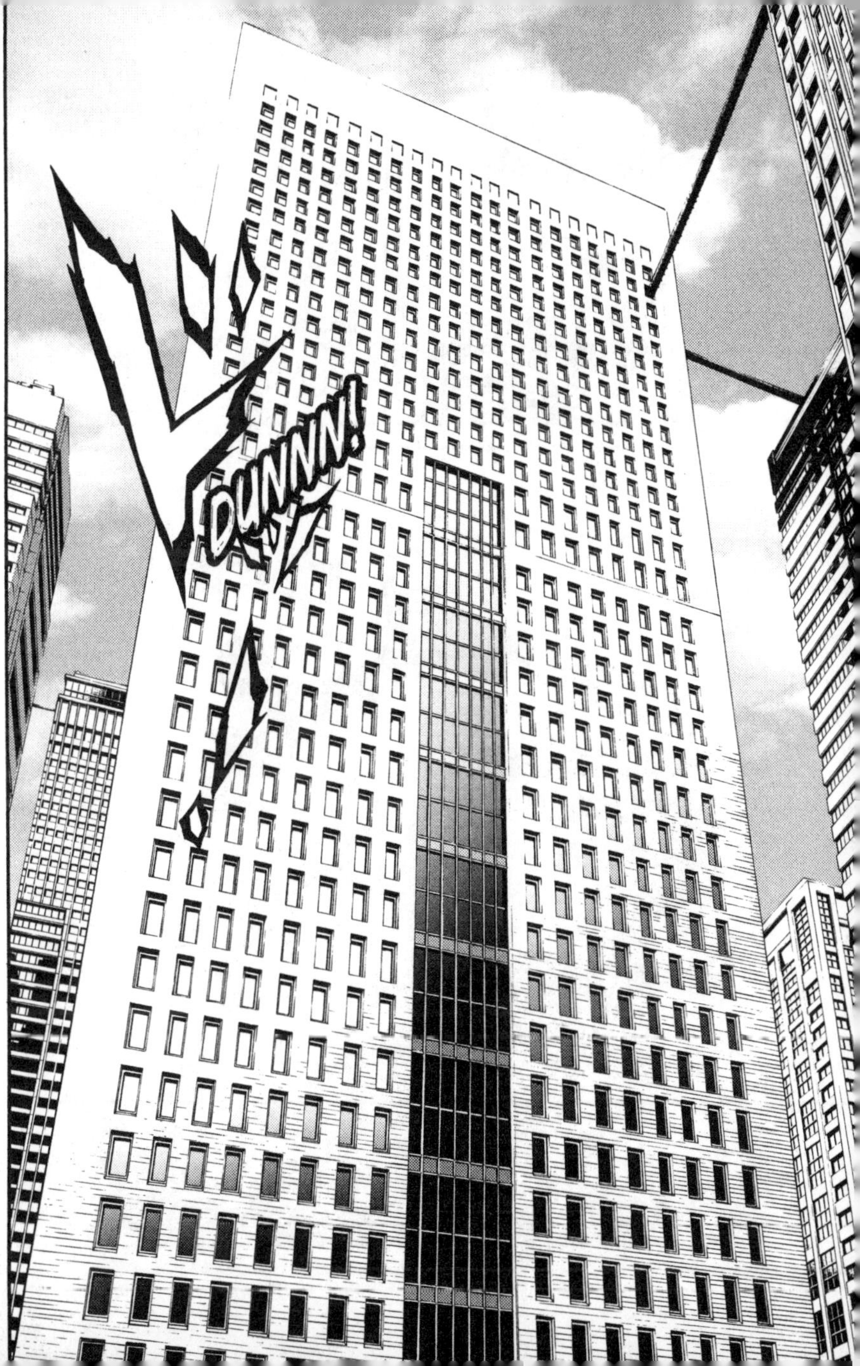
DUNNN!

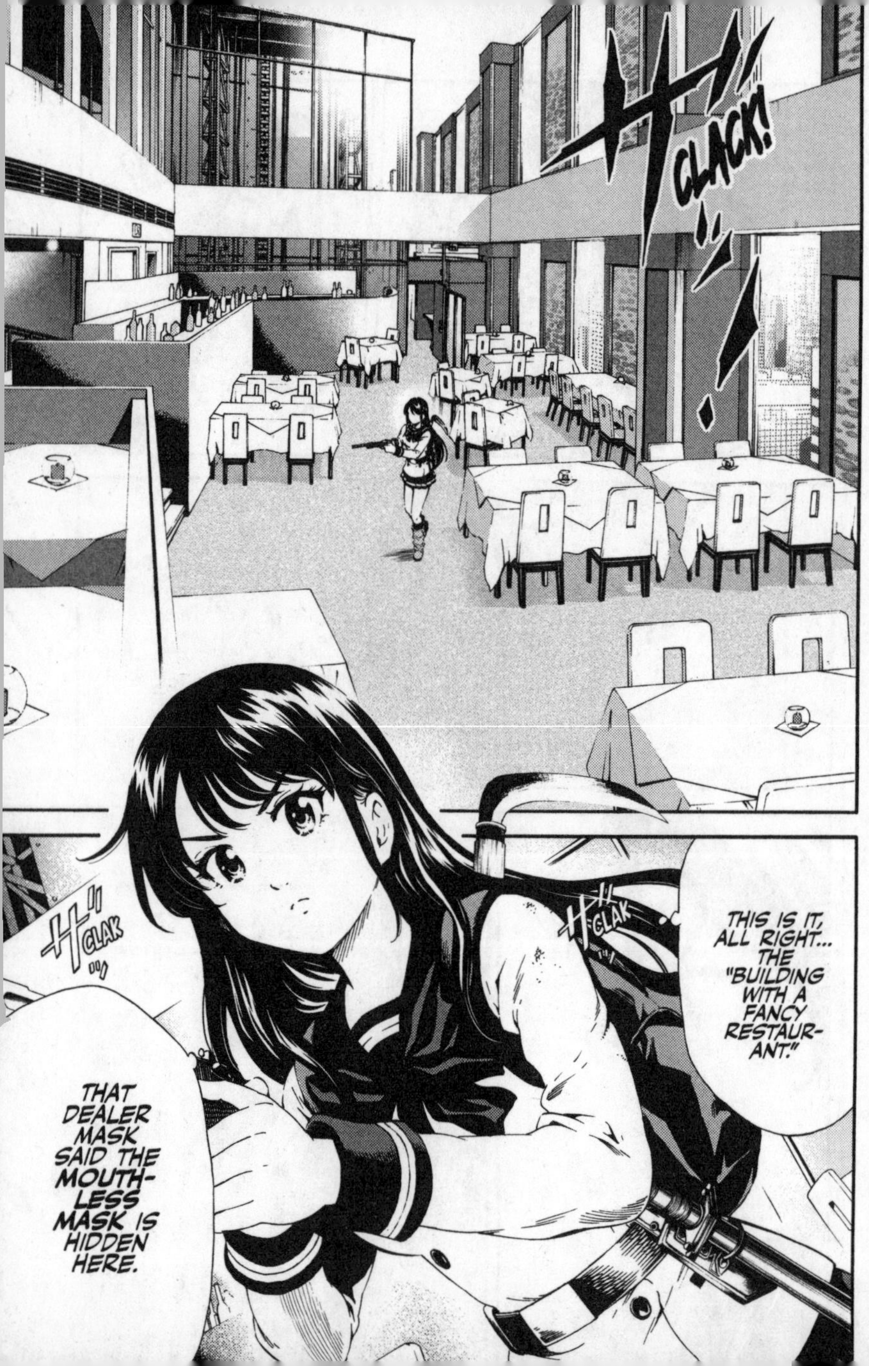
CLACK!
CLAK
THIS IS IT, ALL RIGHT... THE "BUILDING WITH A FANCY RESTAUR-ANT."
CLAK
THAT DEALER MASK SAID THE MOUTH-LESS MASK IS HIDDEN HERE.

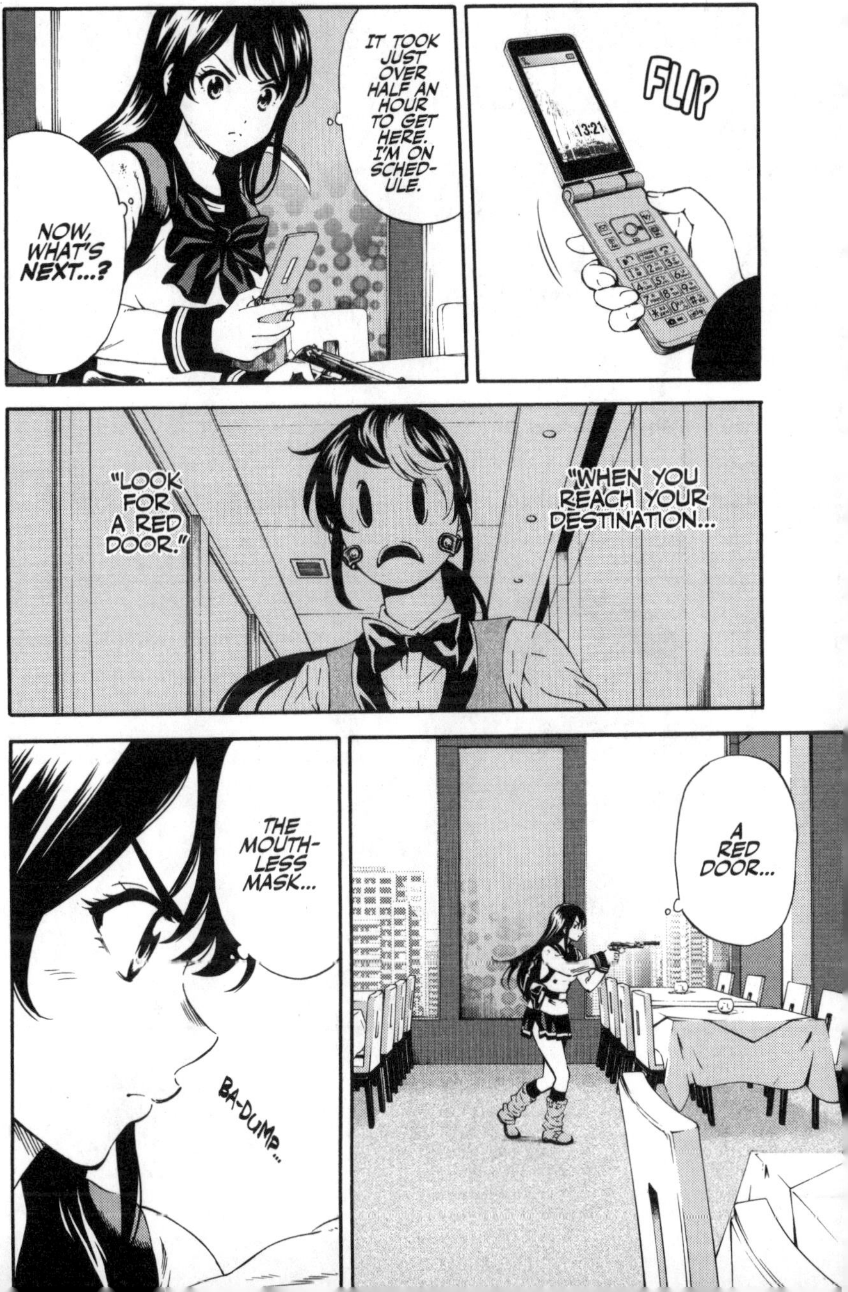
FLIP
IT TOOK JUST OVER HALF AN HOUR TO GET HERE. I'M ON SCHEDULE.
NOW, WHAT'S NEXT...?
"WHEN YOU REACH YOUR DESTINATION...
"LOOK FOR A RED DOOR."
A RED DOOR...
THE MOUTHLESS MASK...
BA-DUMP...

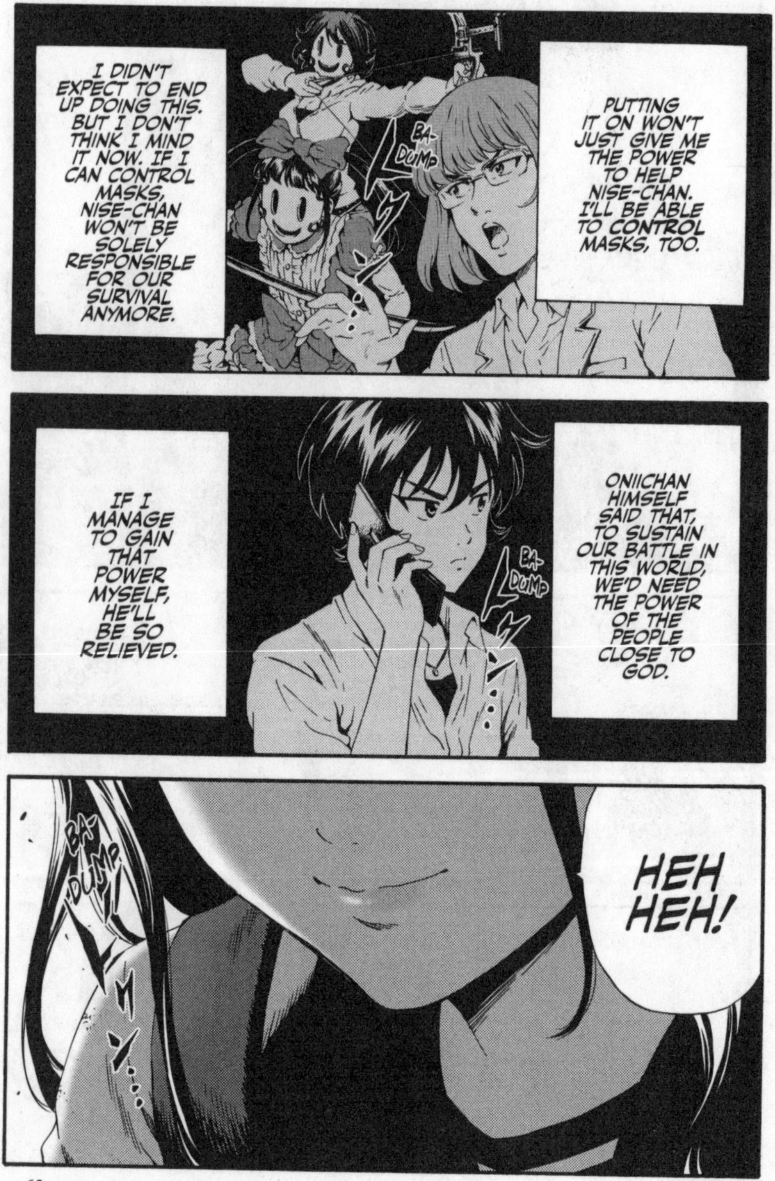

PUTTING IT ON WON'T JUST GIVE ME THE POWER TO HELP NISE-CHAN. I'LL BE ABLE TO CONTROL MASKS, TOO.
BA-DUMP
I DIDN'T EXPECT TO END UP DOING THIS. BUT I DON'T THINK I MIND IT NOW. IF I CAN CONTROL MASKS, NISE-CHAN WON'T BE SOLELY RESPONSIBLE FOR OUR SURVIVAL ANYMORE.
ONIICHAN HIMSELF SAID THAT, TO SUSTAIN OUR BATTLE IN THIS WORLD, WE'D NEED THE POWER OF THE PEOPLE CLOSE TO GOD.
BA-DUMP
IF I MANAGE TO GAIN THAT POWER MYSELF, HE'LL BE SO RELIEVED.
HEH HEH!
BA-DUMP

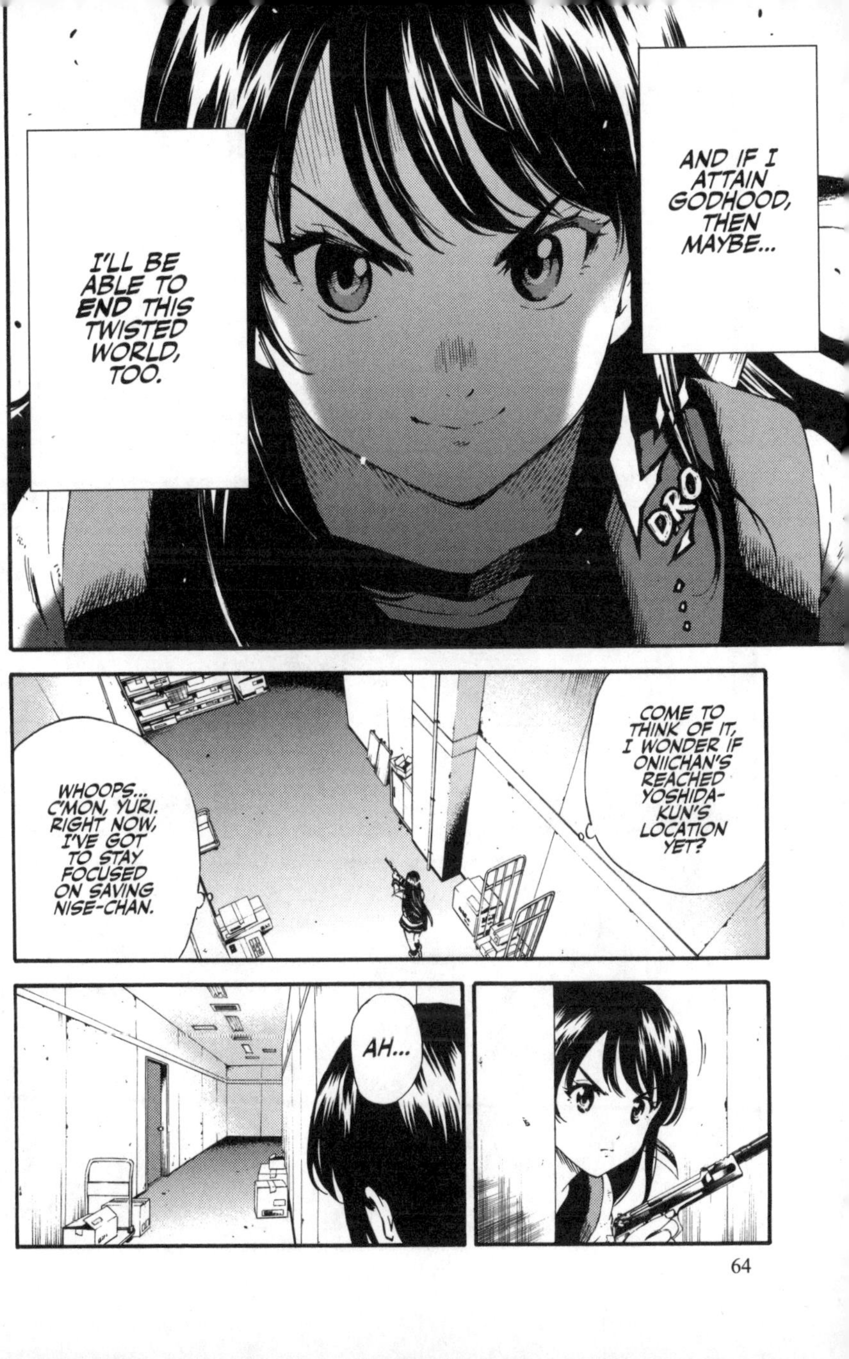
AND IF I ATTAIN GODHOOD, THEN MAYBE...
I'LL BE ABLE TO END THIS TWISTED WORLD, TOO.
DRO
COME TO THINK OF IT, I WONDER IF ONIICHAN'S REACHED YOSHIDA-KUN'S LOCATION YET?
WHOOPS... C'MON, YURI. RIGHT NOW, I'VE GOT TO STAY FOCUSED ON SAVING NISE-CHAN.
AH...

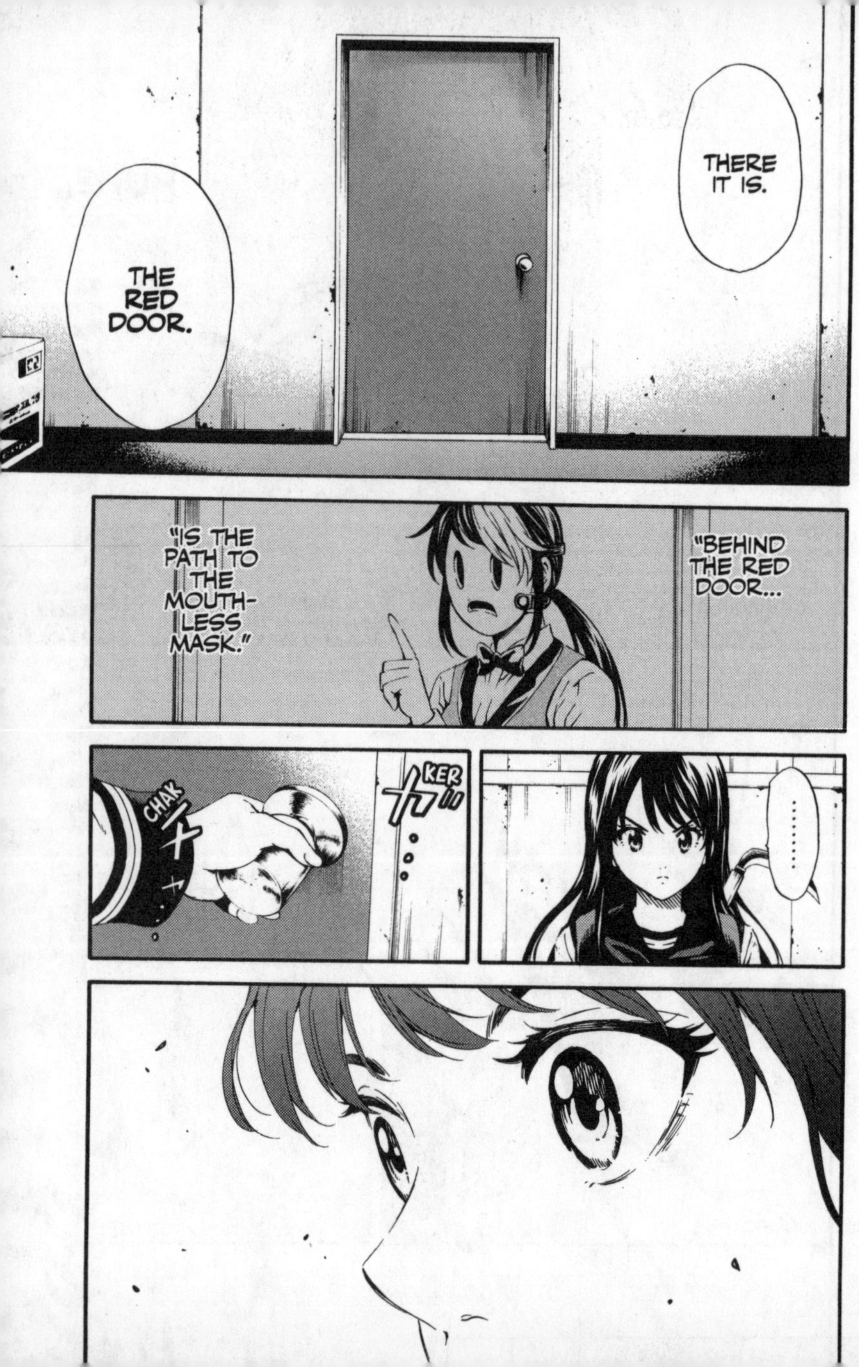
THERE IT IS.
THE RED DOOR.
"BEHIND THE RED DOOR...
"IS THE PATH TO THE MOUTH-LESS MASK."
......
KER
CHAK

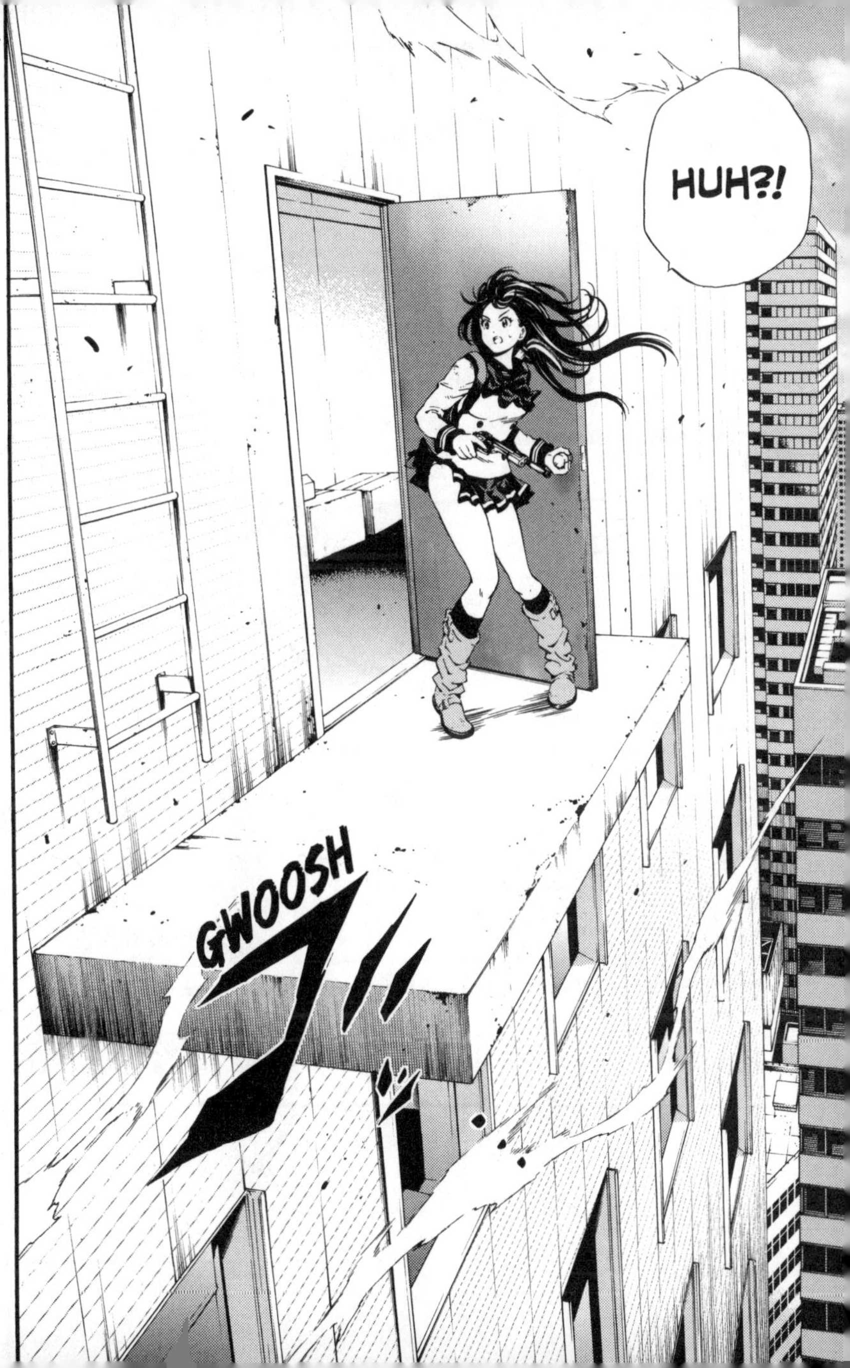
HUH?!
GWOOSH

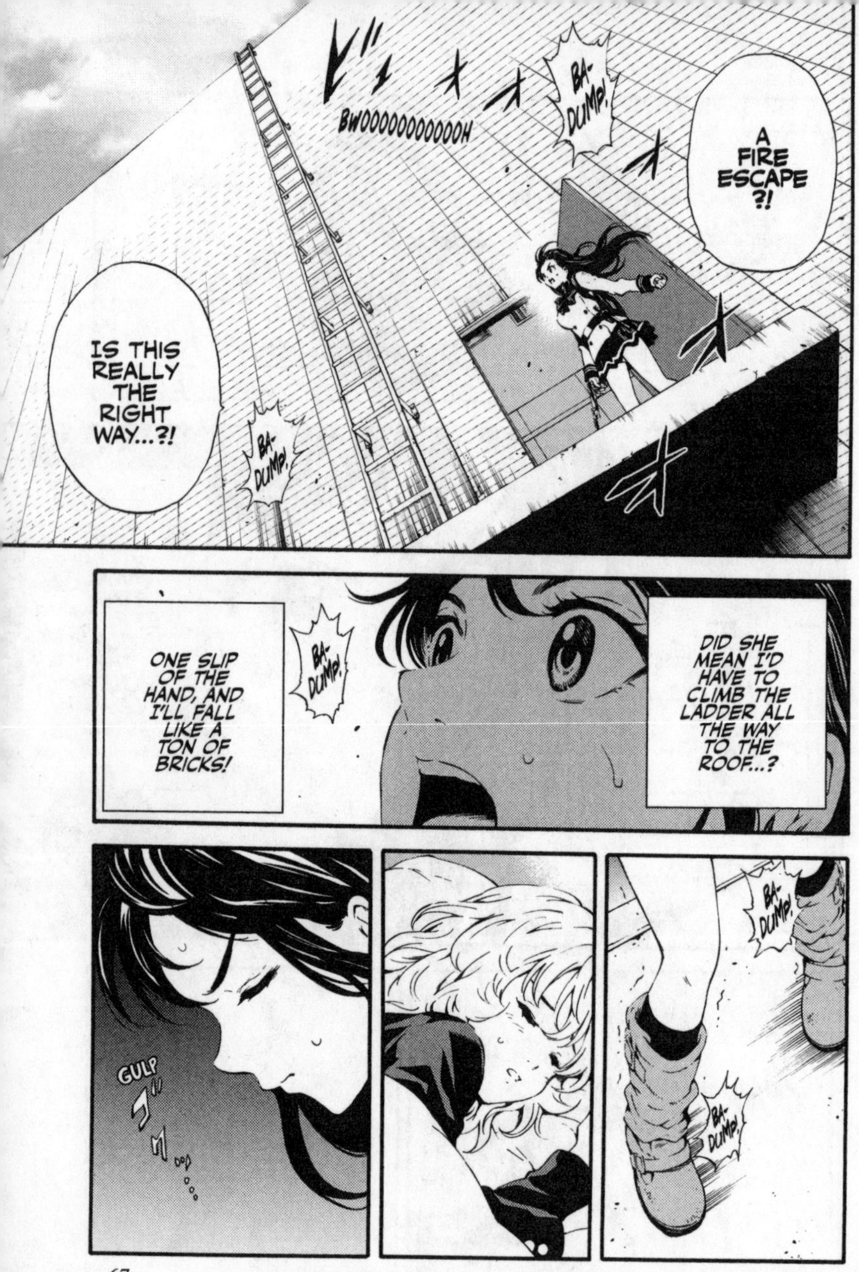
A FIRE ESCAPE ?!
BA-DUMP!
BWOOOOOOOOOOOH
IS THIS REALLY THE RIGHT WAY...?!
BA-DUMP!
DID SHE MEAN I'D HAVE TO CLIMB THE LADDER ALL THE WAY TO THE ROOF...?
BA-DUMP!
ONE SLIP OF THE HAND, AND I'LL FALL LIKE A TON OF BRICKS!
BA-DUMP!
BA-DUMP!
GULP

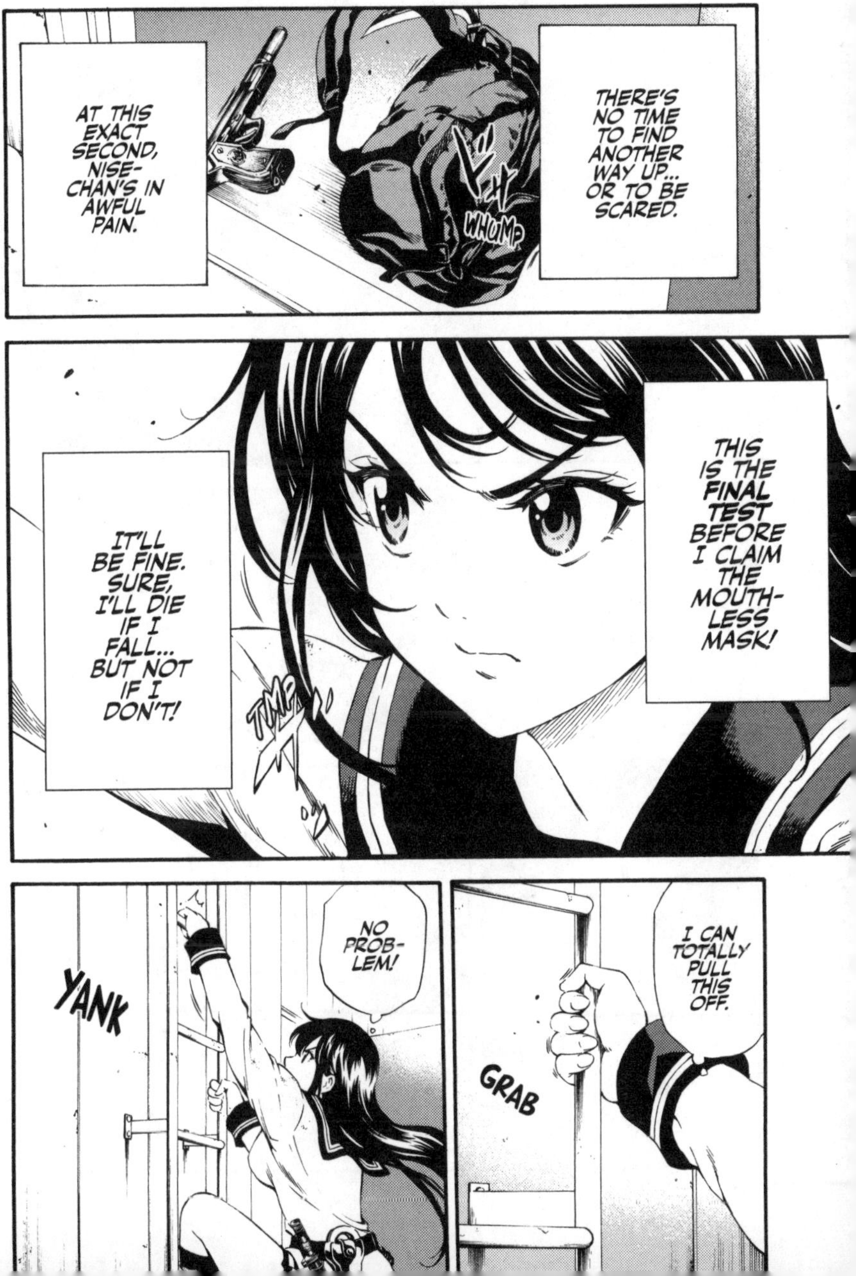
THERE'S NO TIME TO FIND ANOTHER WAY UP... OR TO BE SCARED.
WHUMP
AT THIS EXACT SECOND, NISE-CHAN'S IN AWFUL PAIN.
THIS IS THE FINAL TEST BEFORE I CLAIM THE MOUTH-LESS MASK!
IT'LL BE FINE. SURE, I'LL DIE IF I FALL... BUT NOT IF I DON'T!
TMP
I CAN TOTALLY PULL THIS OFF.
GRAB
NO PROB-LEM!
YANK

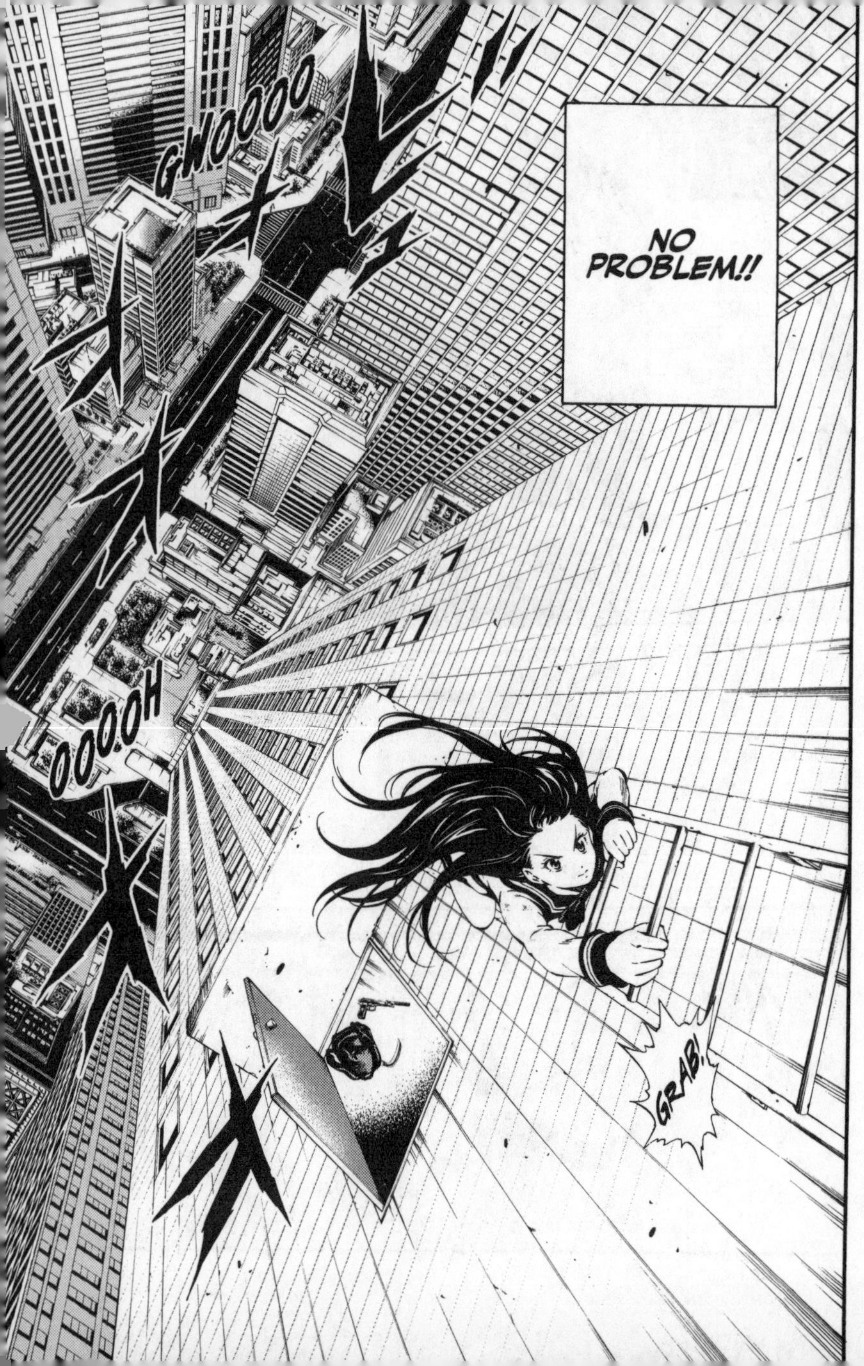
NO PROBLEM!!
GWOOOO
OOOOH
GRAB!

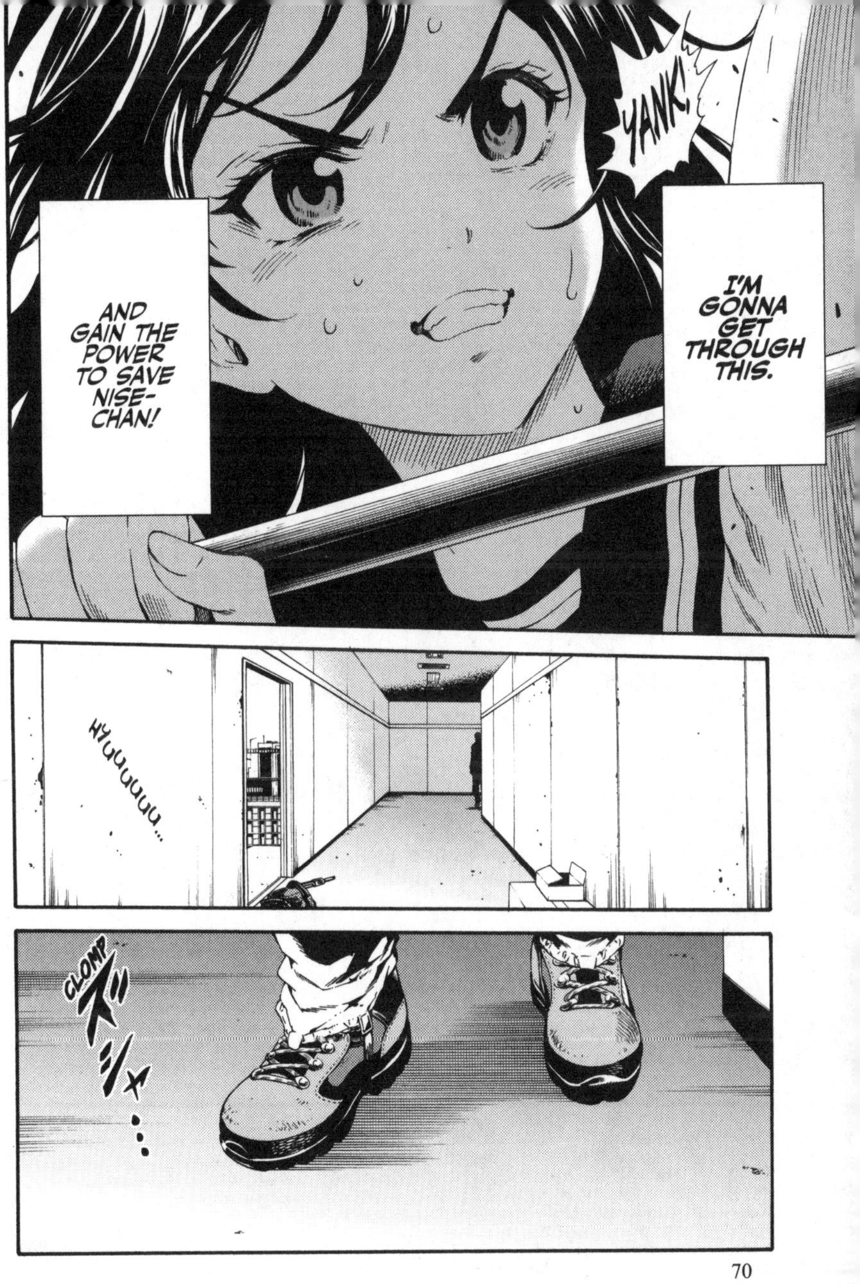
YANK!
I'M GONNA GET THROUGH THIS.
AND GAIN THE POWER TO SAVE NISE-CHAN!
HYUUUUUU...
CLOMP

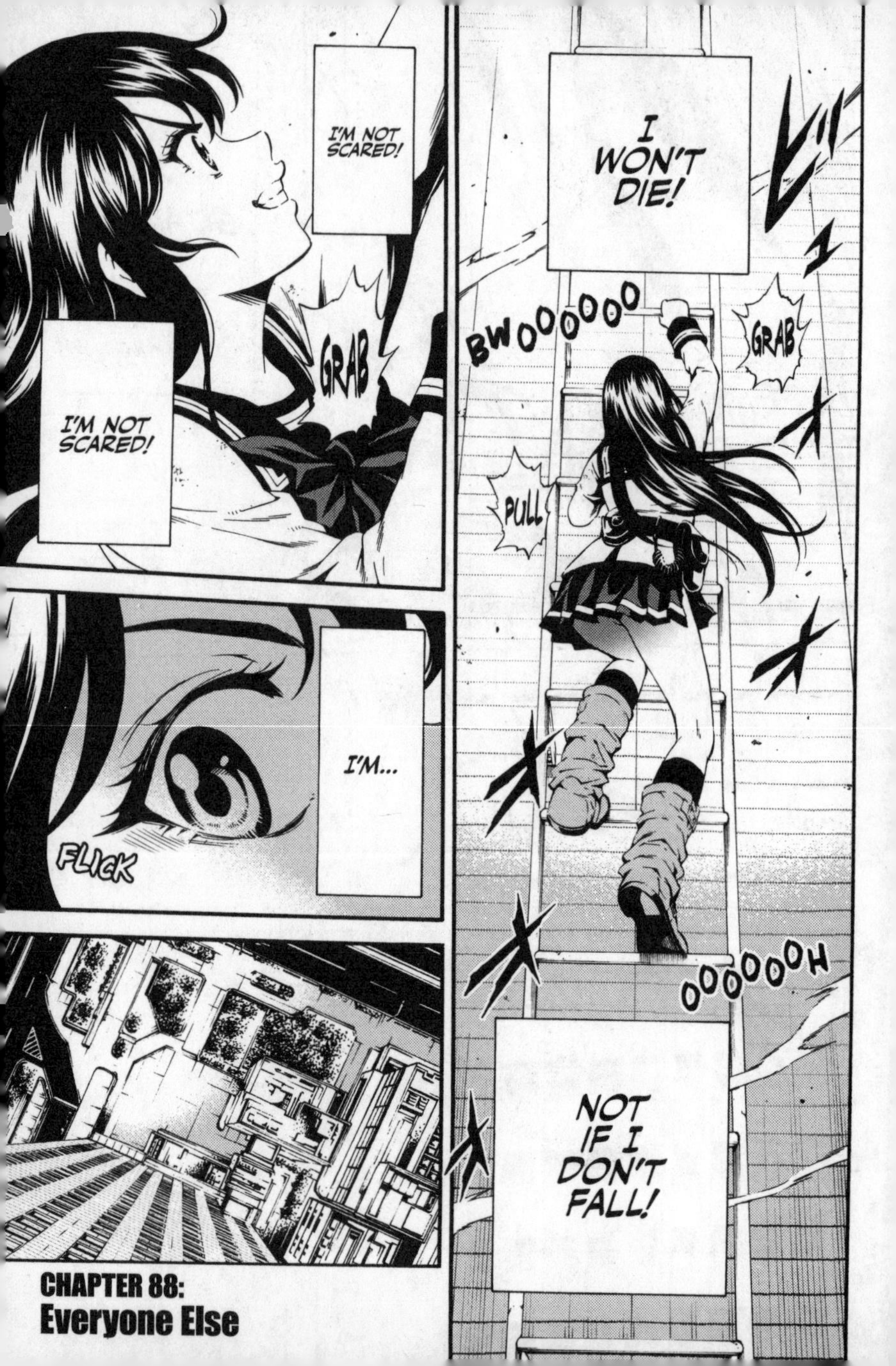
I WON'T DIE!
BWOOOOOO
GRAB
PULL
OOOOOOH
NOT IF I DON'T FALL!
I'M NOT SCARED!
GRAB
I'M NOT SCARED!
I'M...
FLICK

CHAPTER 88:
Everyone Else

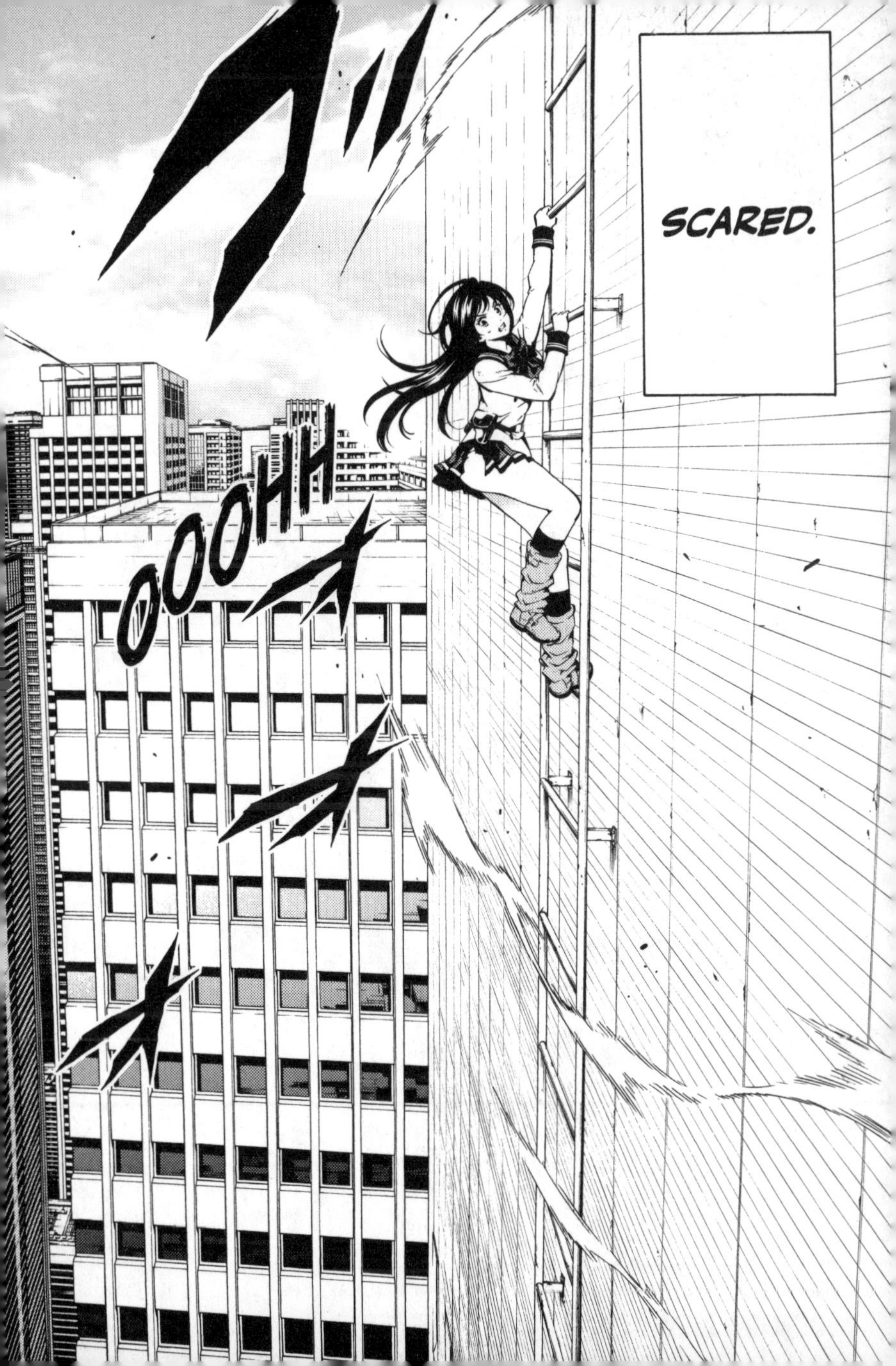
SCARED.
OOOHH

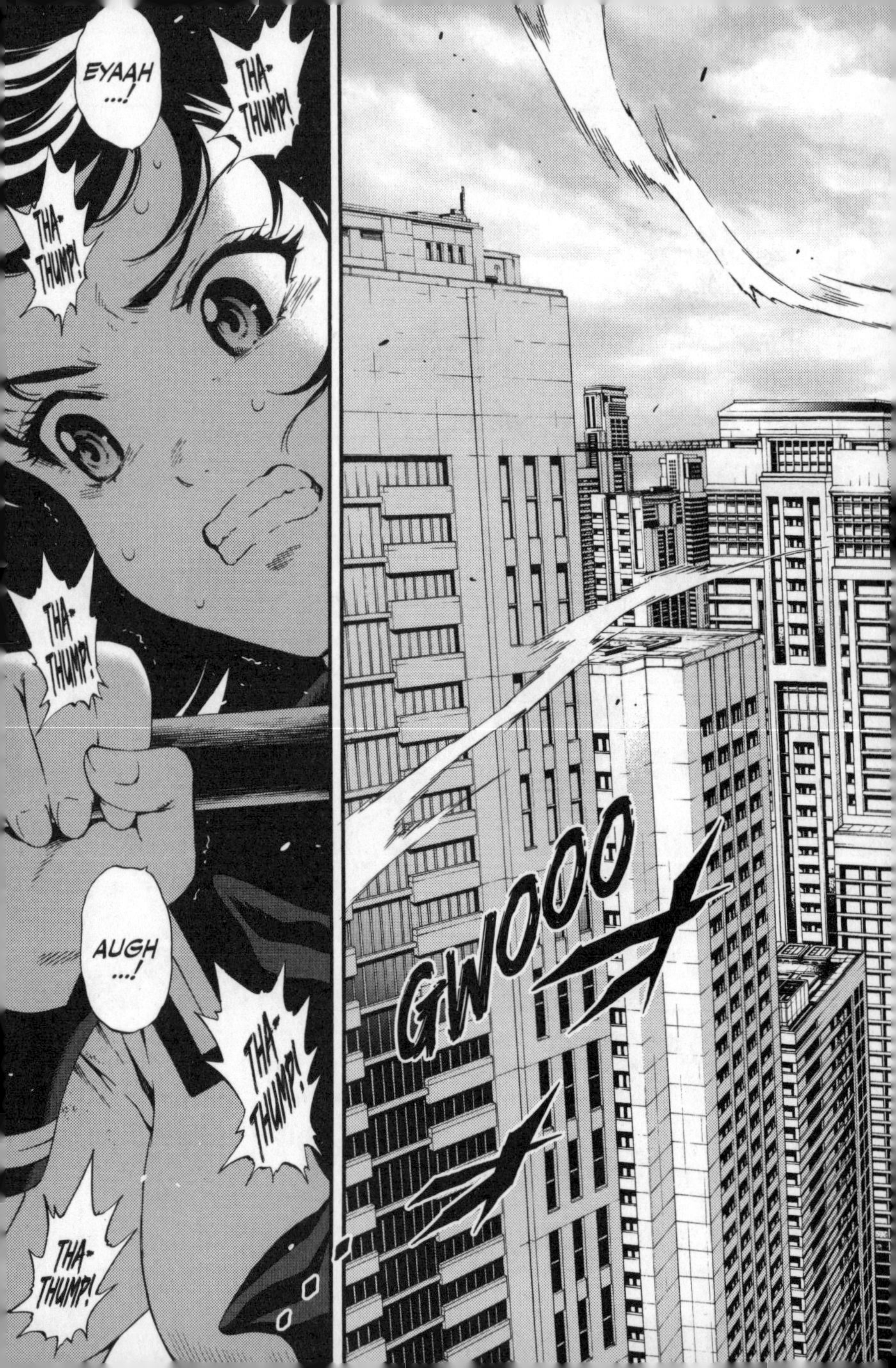
GWOOO
THA-THUMP!
EYAAH ...!
THA-THUMP!
THA-THUMP!
AUGH ...!
THA-THUMP!
THA-THUMP!

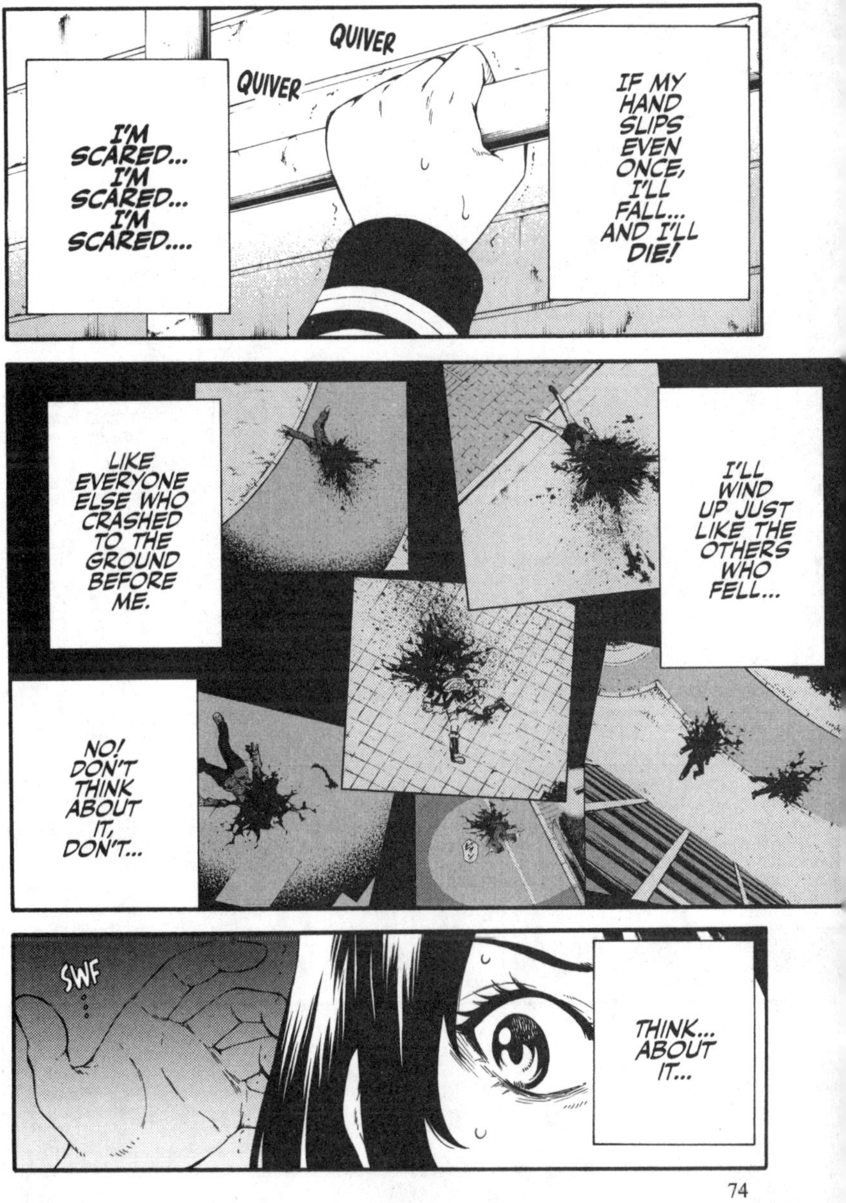
IF MY HAND SLIPS EVEN ONCE, I'LL FALL... AND I'LL DIE!
QUIVER
QUIVER
I'M SCARED... I'M SCARED... I'M SCARED....
I'LL WIND UP JUST LIKE THE OTHERS WHO FELL...
LIKE EVERYONE ELSE WHO CRASHED TO THE GROUND BEFORE ME.
NO! DON'T THINK ABOUT IT, DON'T...
THINK... ABOUT IT...
SWF

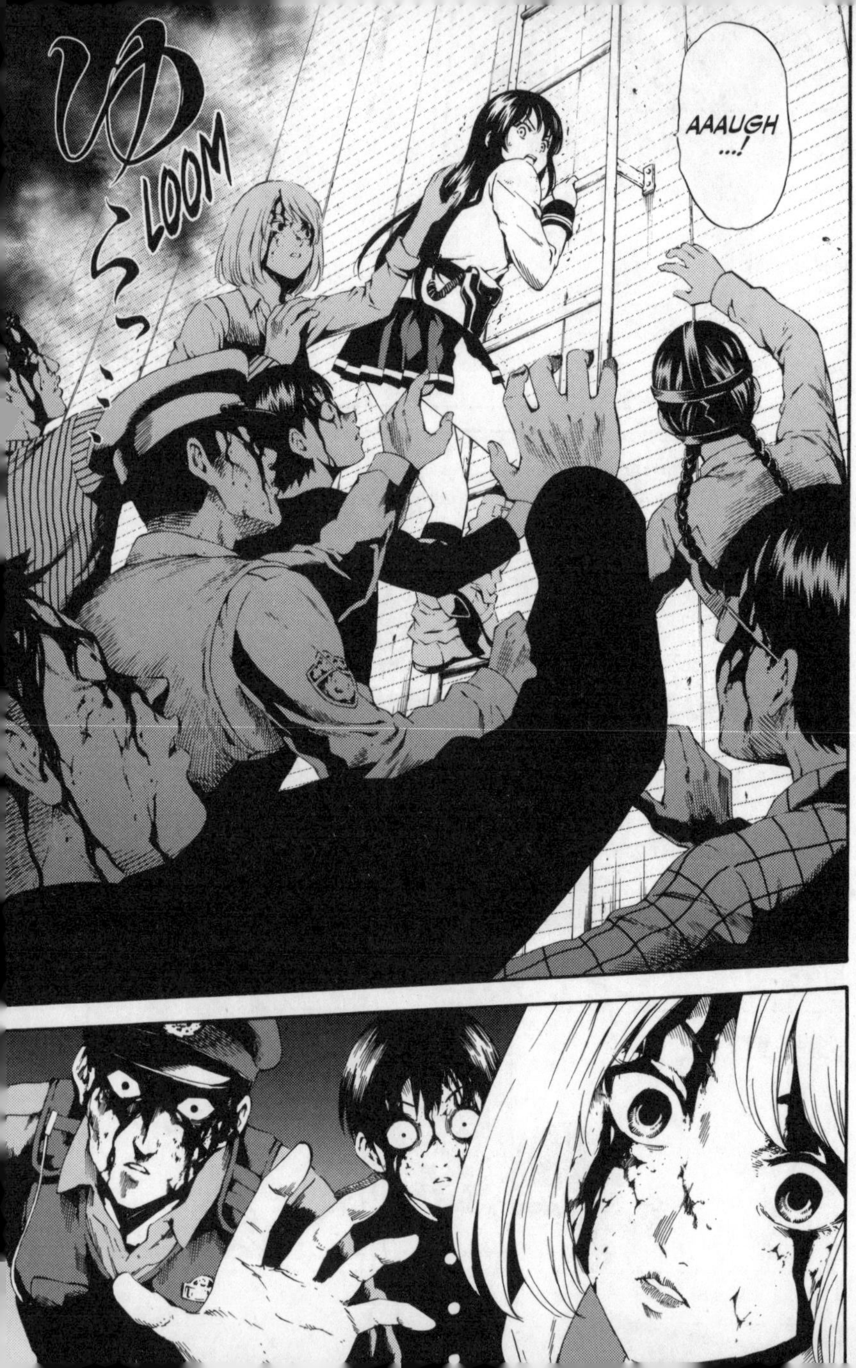
AAAUGH ...!
ゆら
LOOM

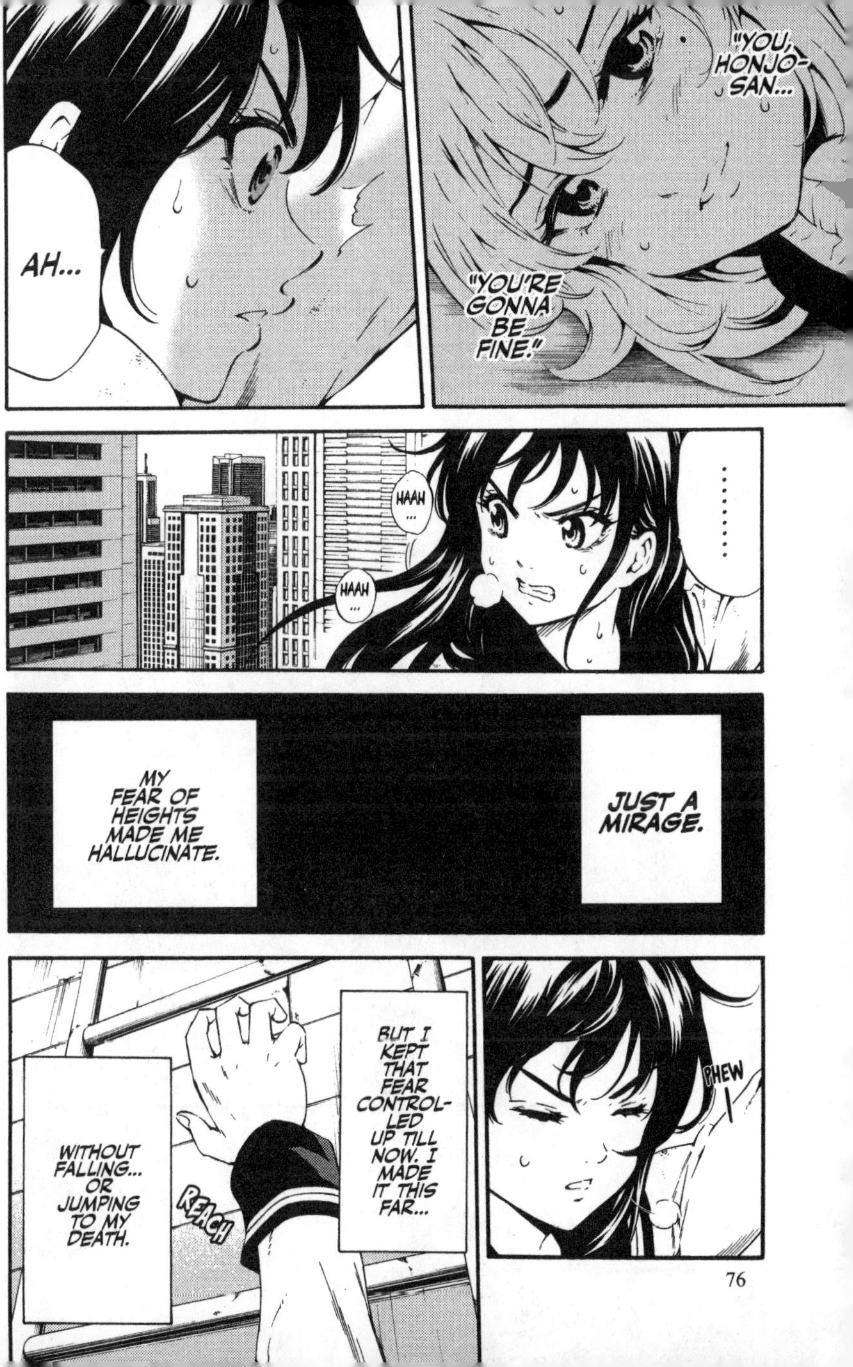
"YOU, HONJO-SAN...
"YOU'RE GONNA BE FINE."
AH...
......
HAAH...
HAAH...
JUST A MIRAGE.
MY FEAR OF HEIGHTS MADE ME HALLUCINATE.
PHEW
BUT I KEPT THAT FEAR CONTROL-LED UP TILL NOW. I MADE IT THIS FAR...
WITHOUT FALLING... OR JUMPING TO MY DEATH.
REACH

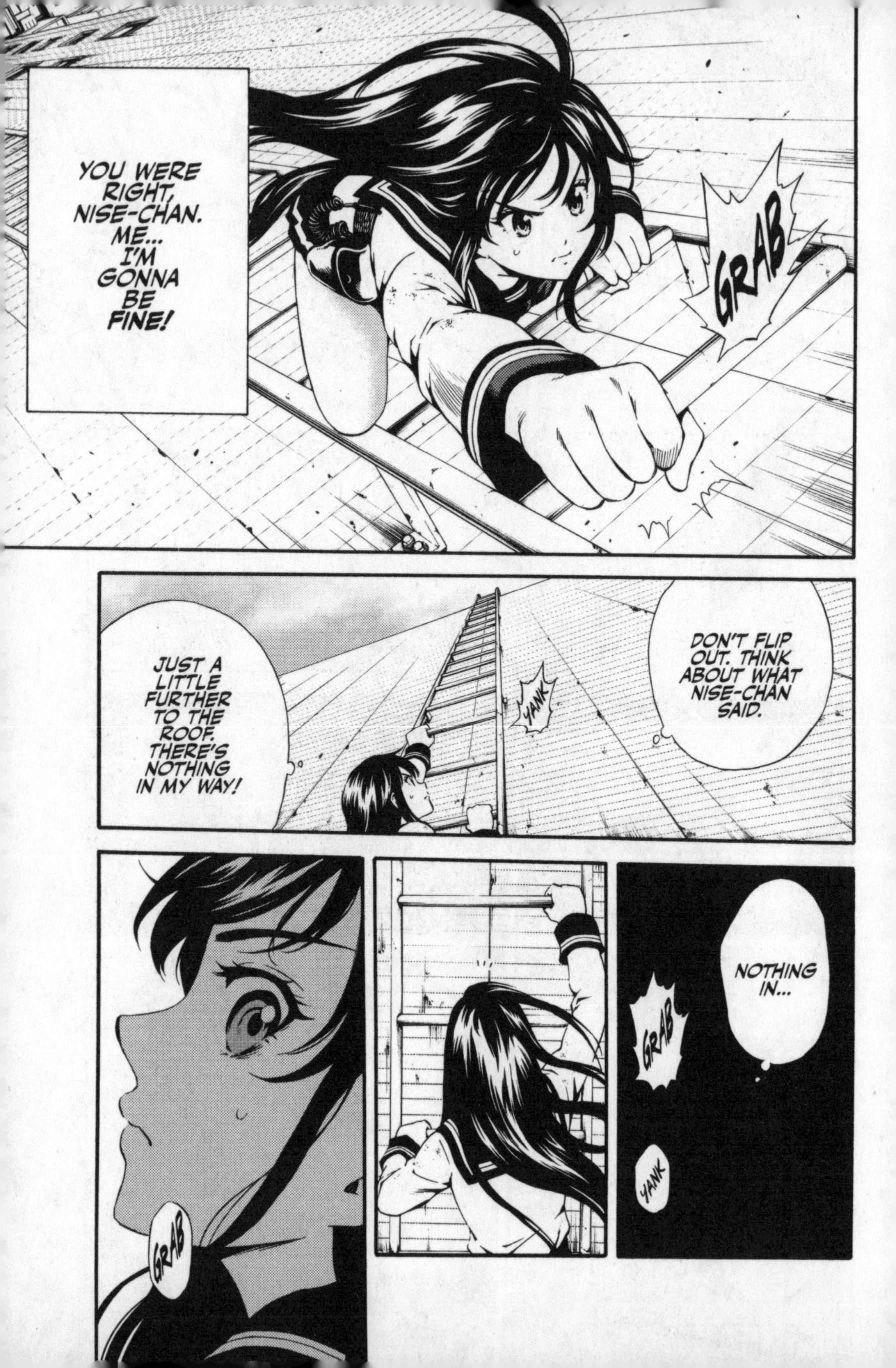
YOU WERE RIGHT, NISE-CHAN. ME... I'M GONNA BE FINE!
GRAB
DON'T FLIP OUT. THINK ABOUT WHAT NISE-CHAN SAID.
YANK
JUST A LITTLE FURTHER TO THE ROOF. THERE'S NOTHING IN MY WAY!
NOTHING IN...
GRAB
YANK
GRAB

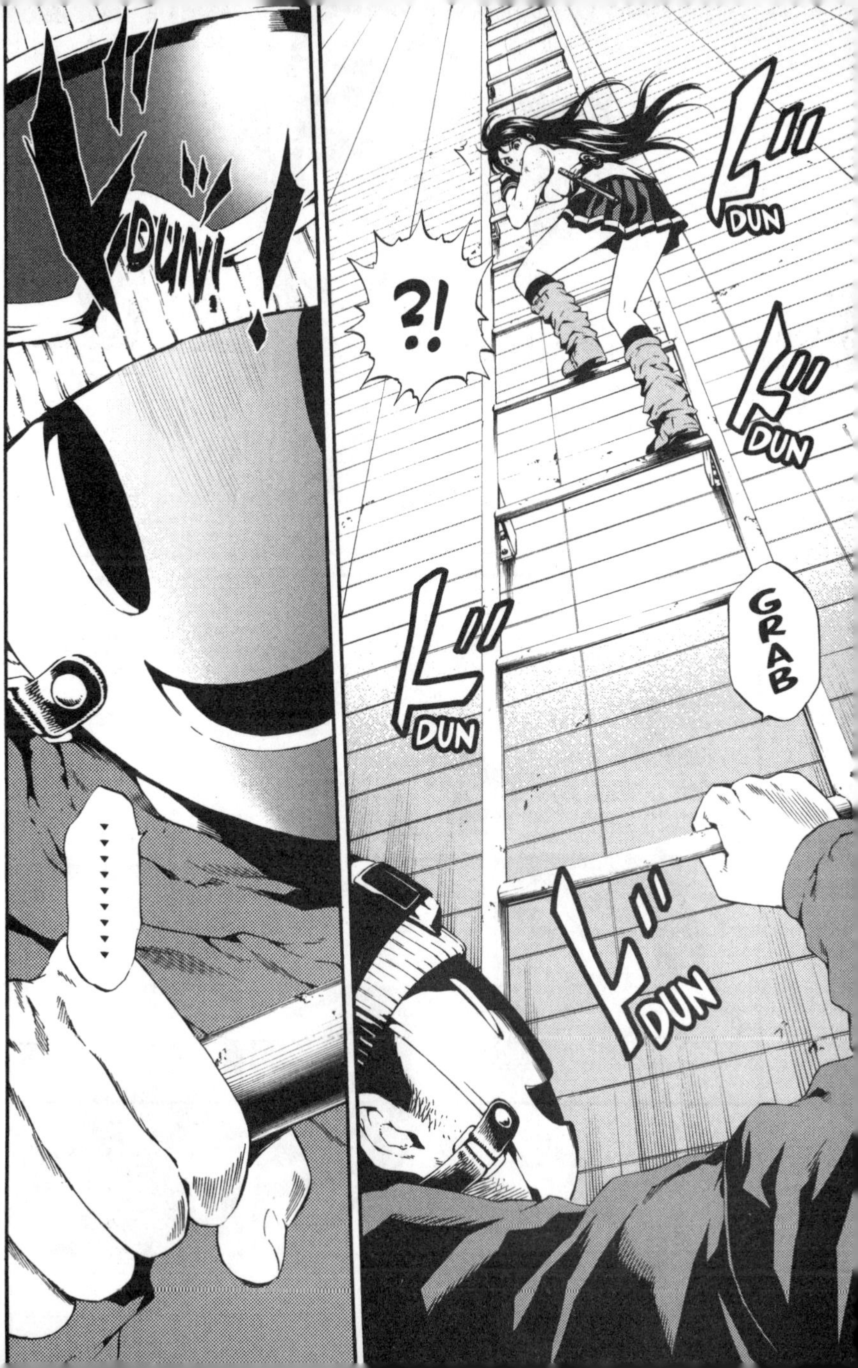
DUN
DUN
?!
GRAB
DUN
DUN
DUN!
……

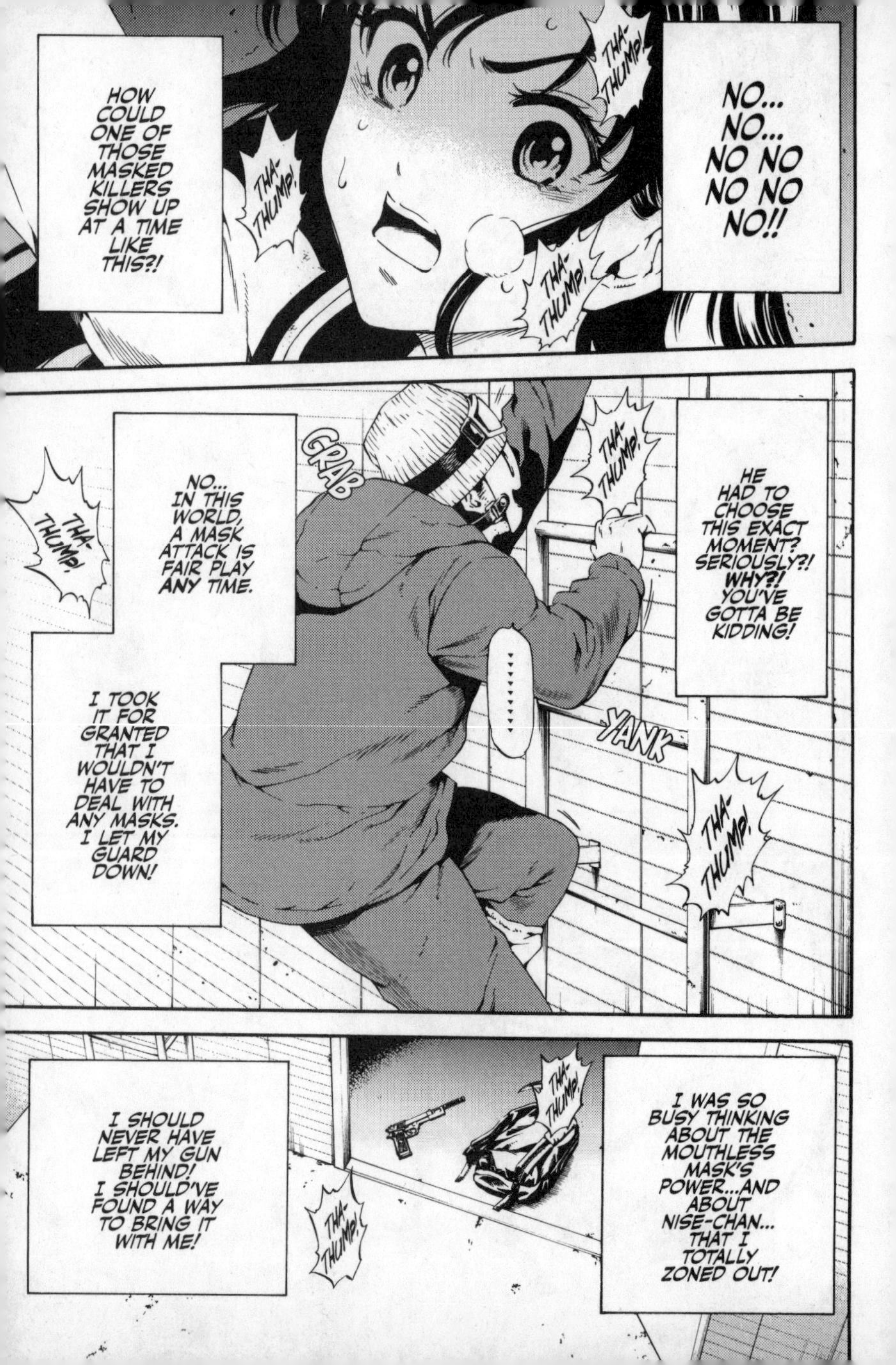
NO... NO... NO NO NO NO NO!!
THA-THUMP!
THA-THUMP!
THA-THUMP!
HOW COULD ONE OF THOSE MASKED KILLERS SHOW UP AT A TIME LIKE THIS?!
HE HAD TO CHOOSE THIS EXACT MOMENT? SERIOUSLY?! WHY?! YOU'VE GOTTA BE KIDDING!
THA-THUMP!
GRAB
NO... IN THIS WORLD, A MASK ATTACK IS FAIR PLAY ANY TIME.
THA-THUMP!
YANK
THA-THUMP!
I TOOK IT FOR GRANTED THAT I WOULDN'T HAVE TO DEAL WITH ANY MASKS. I LET MY GUARD DOWN!
I WAS SO BUSY THINKING ABOUT THE MOUTHLESS MASK'S POWER...AND ABOUT NISE-CHAN... THAT I TOTALLY ZONED OUT!
THA-THUMP!
THA-THUMP!
I SHOULD NEVER HAVE LEFT MY GUN BEHIND! I SHOULD'VE FOUND A WAY TO BRING IT WITH ME!

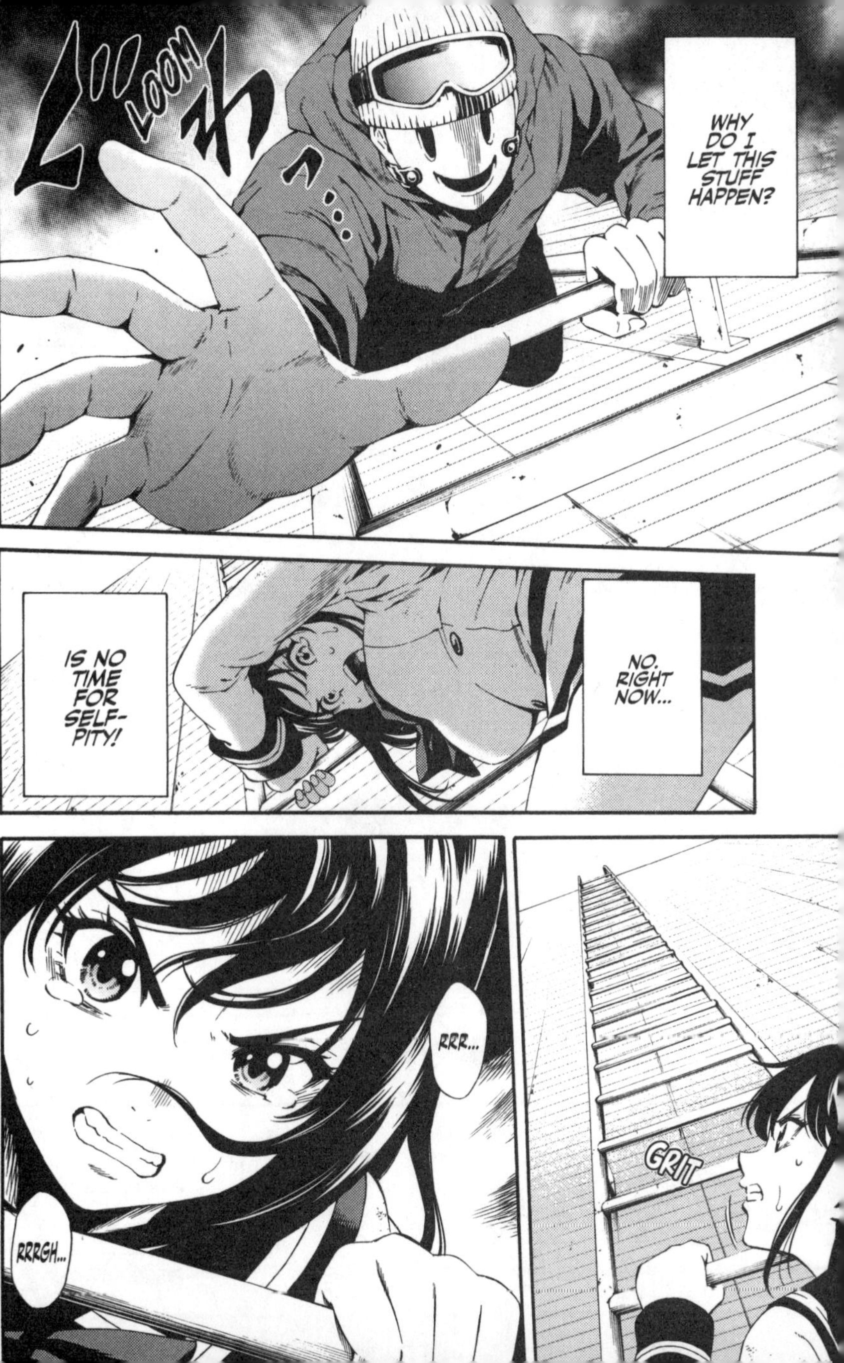
LOOM
WHY DO I LET THIS STUFF HAPPEN?
NO. RIGHT NOW...
IS NO TIME FOR SELF-PITY!
GRIT
RRR...
RRRGH...

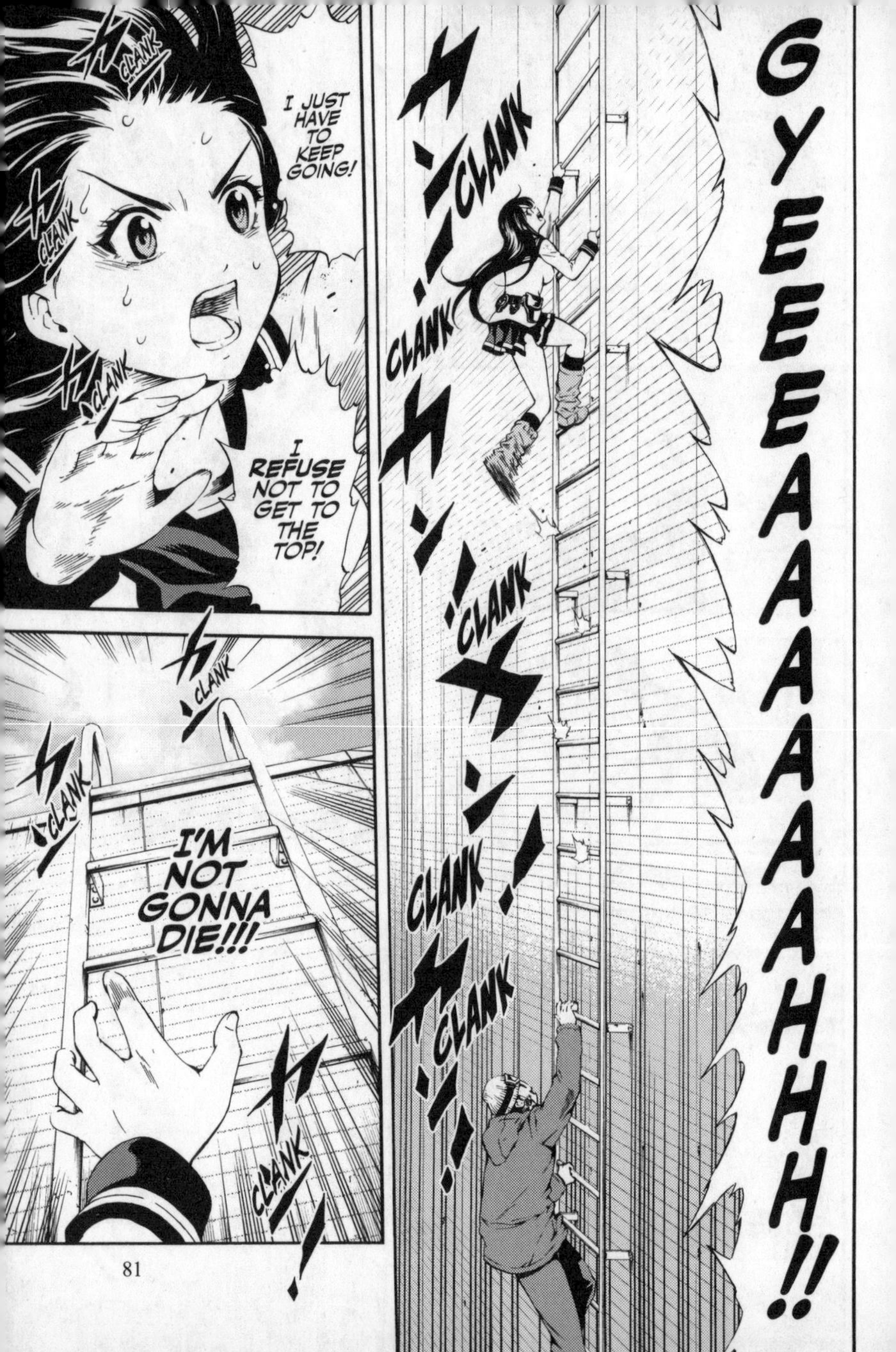
GYEEEAAAAAAHHH!!
CLANK
CLANK
CLANK
CLANK
CLANK
CLANK
CLANK
CLANK
I JUST HAVE TO KEEP GOING!
CLANK
I REFUSE NOT TO GET TO THE TOP!
CLANK
CLANK
I'M NOT GONNA DIE!!!
CLANK

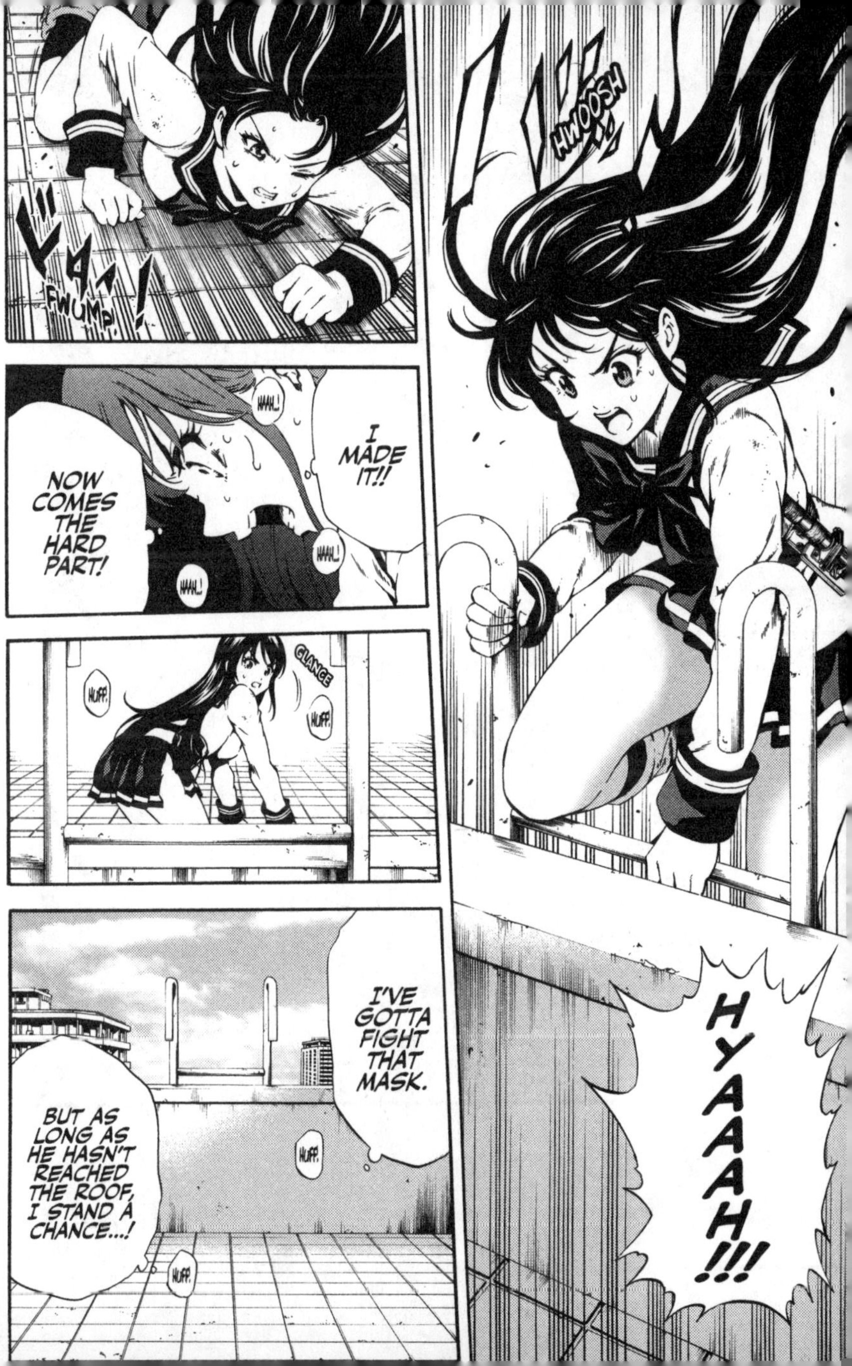
HWOOSH
HYAAAAH!!!
FWUMP!
HAAH..!
I MADE IT!!
NOW COMES THE HARD PART!
HAAH..!
HAAH..!
GLANCE
HUFF.
HUFF.
I'VE GOTTA FIGHT THAT MASK.
BUT AS LONG AS HE HASN'T REACHED THE ROOF, I STAND A CHANCE...!
HUFF.
HUFF.

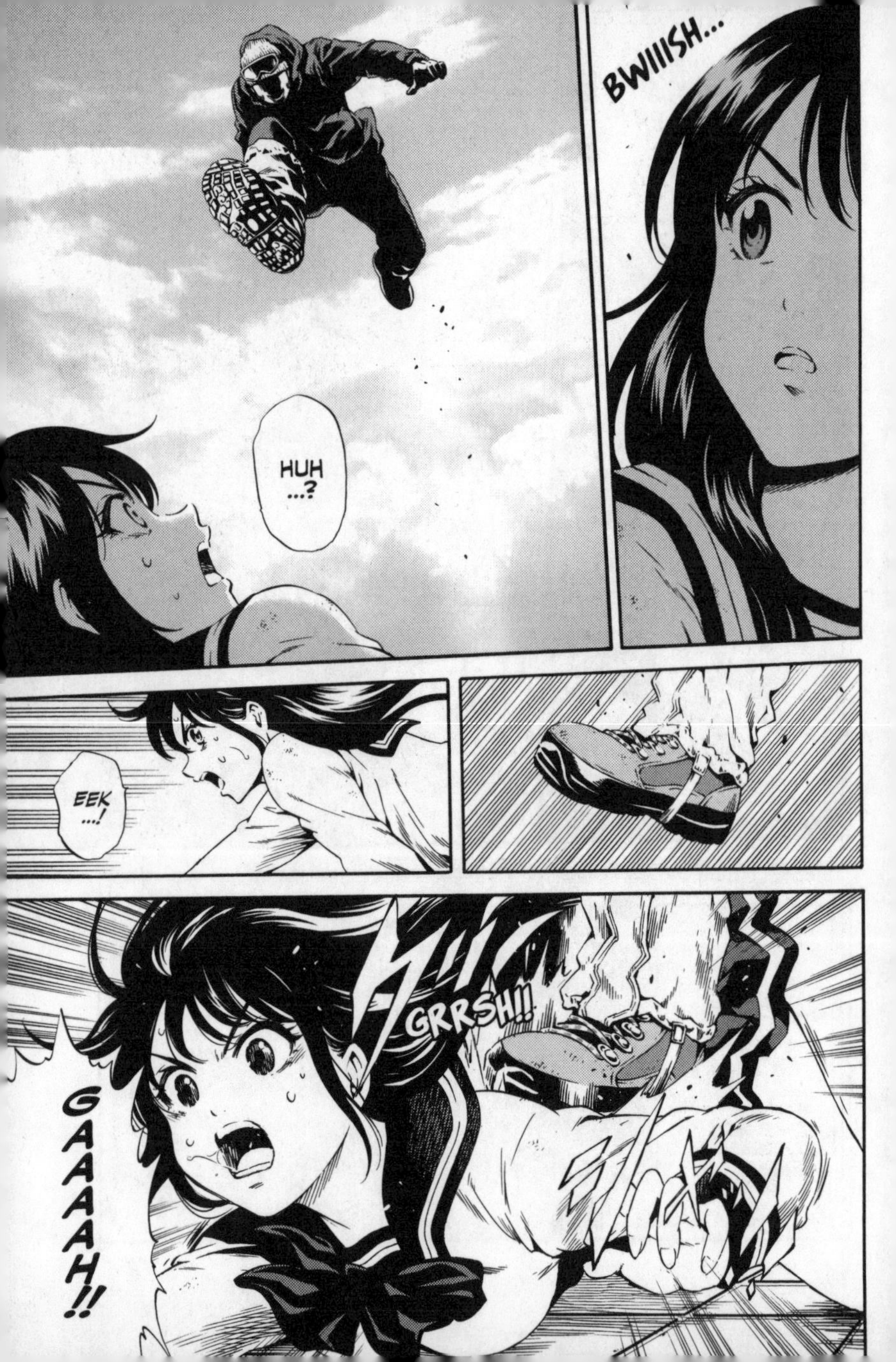
BWIIISH...
HUH ...?
EEK ...!
GRRSH!!
GAAAAH!!

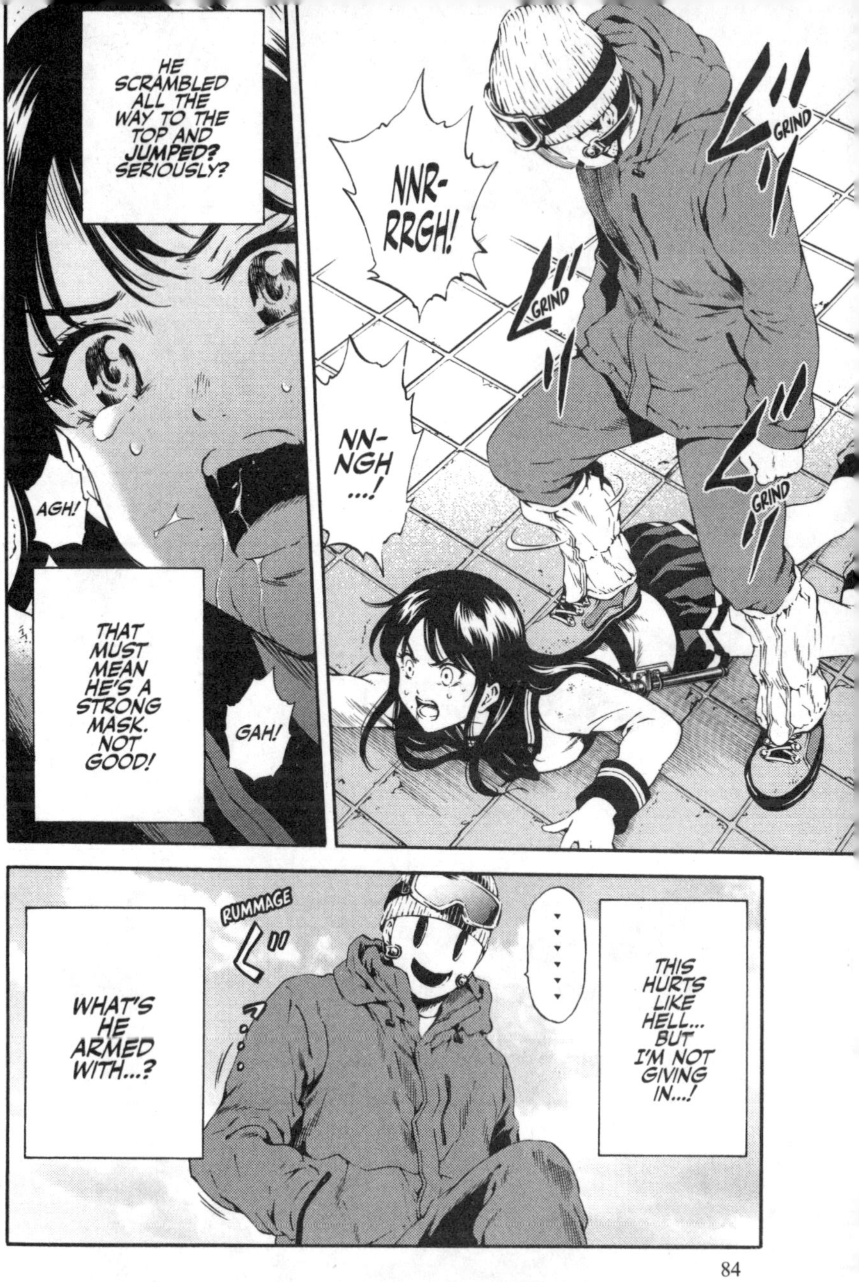
GRIND
NNR-RRGH!
GRIND
GRIND
NN-NGH...!
HE SCRAMBLED ALL THE WAY TO THE TOP AND JUMPED? SERIOUSLY?
AGH!
THAT MUST MEAN HE'S A STRONG MASK. NOT GOOD!
GAH!
THIS HURTS LIKE HELL... BUT I'M NOT GIVING IN...!
......
RUMMAGE
WHAT'S HE ARMED WITH...?

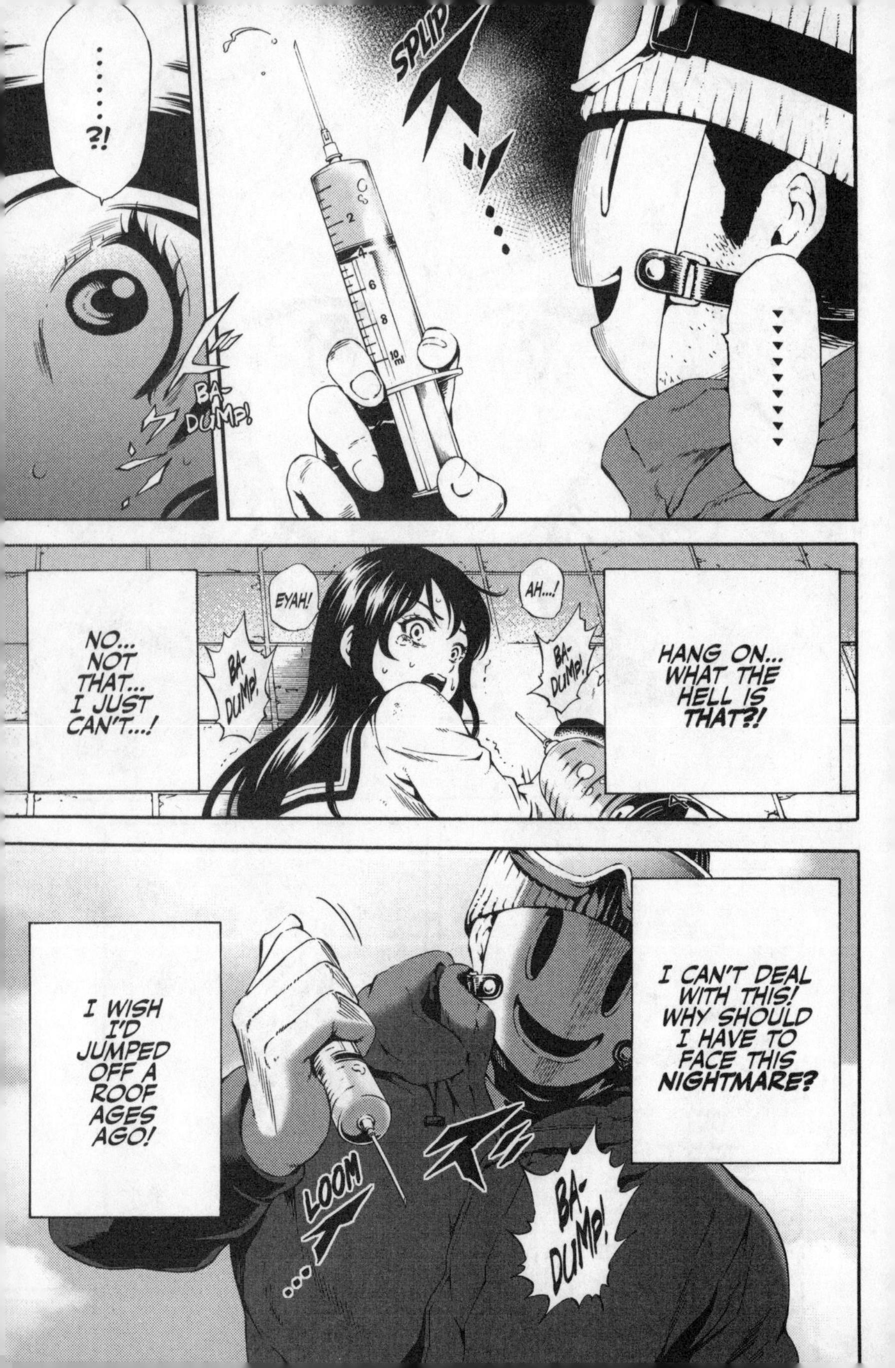

SPLIP
▼▼▼▼▼▼▼▼▼
......?!
BA-DUMP!
HANG ON... WHAT THE HELL IS THAT?!
AH...!
BA-DUMP!
EYAH!
BA-DUMP!
NO... NOT THAT... I JUST CAN'T...!
I CAN'T DEAL WITH THIS! WHY SHOULD I HAVE TO FACE THIS NIGHTMARE?
BA-DUMP!
LOOM
I WISH I'D JUMPED OFF A ROOF AGES AGO!

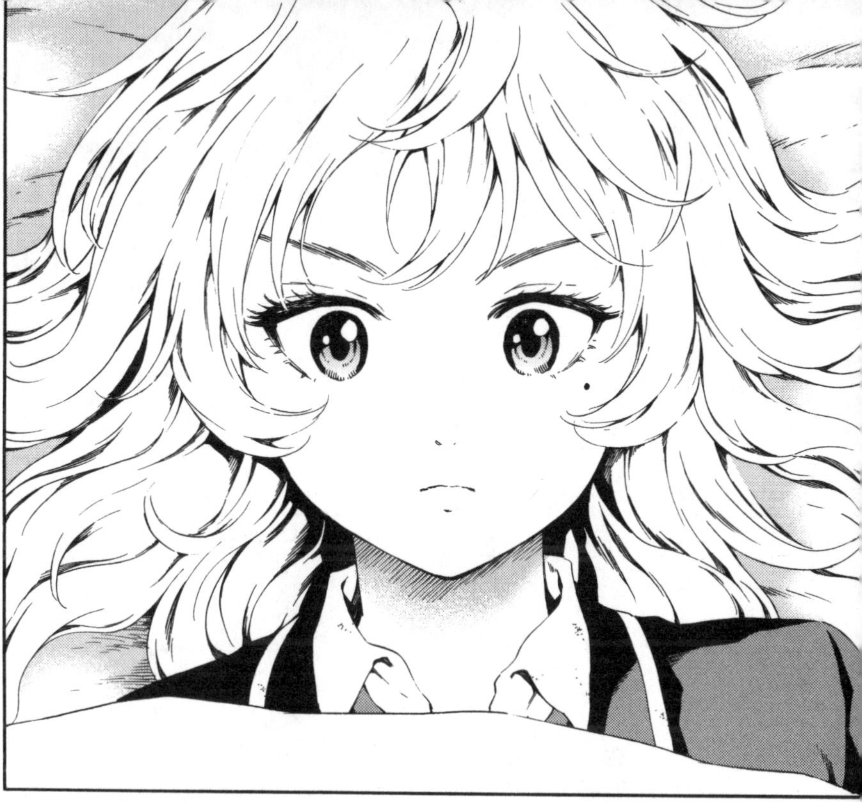

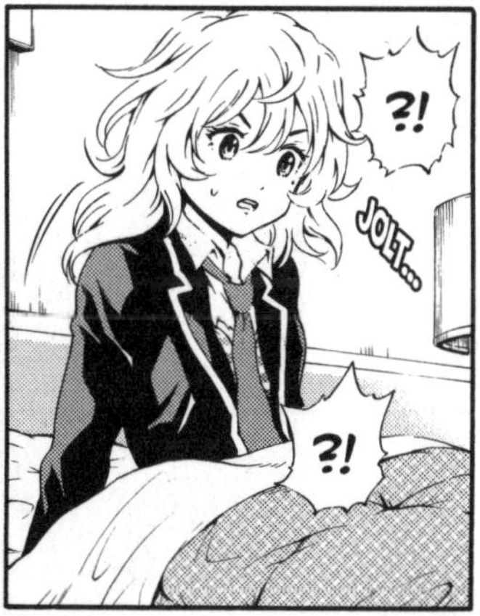
?!
JOLT...
?!

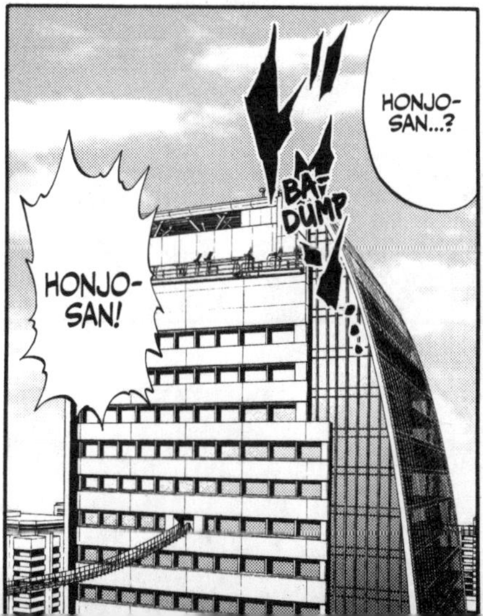
HONJO-SAN...?
BA-DUMP
HONJO-SAN!

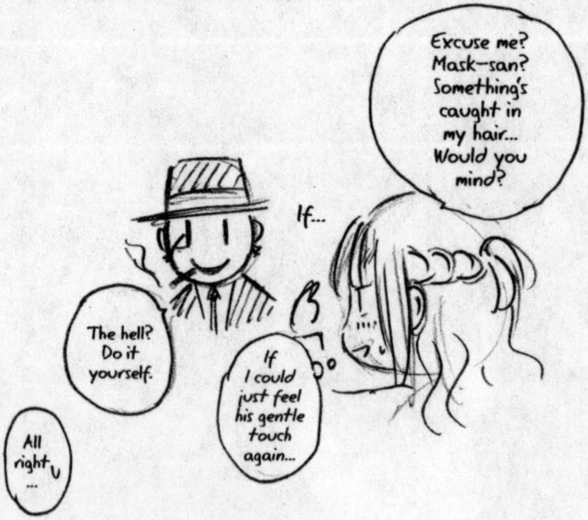
Excuse me? Mask-san? Something's caught in my hair... Would you mind?
If...
The hell? Do it yourself.
If I could just feel his gentle touch again...
All right♡ ...

HIGH-RISE INVASION

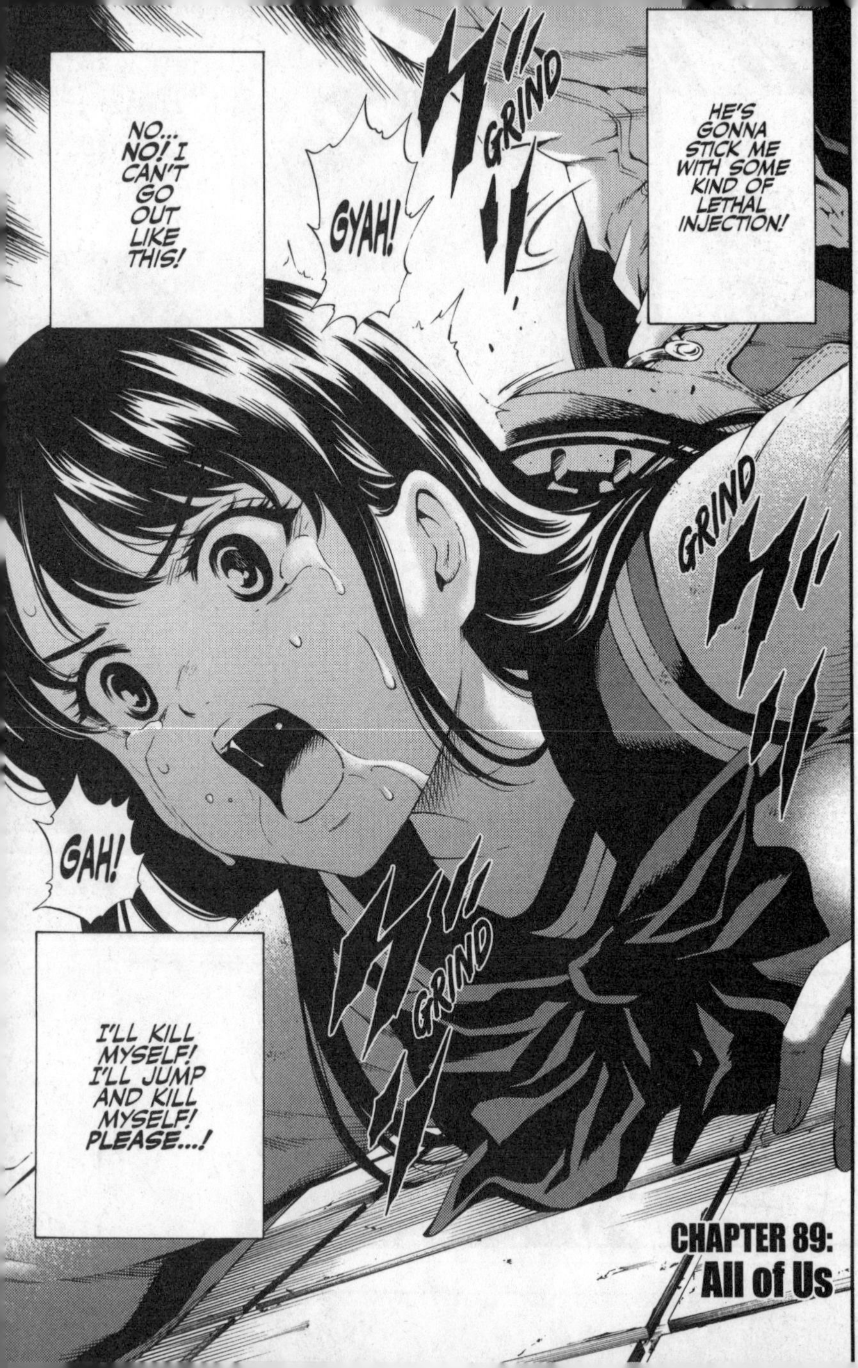
HE'S GONNA STICK ME WITH SOME KIND OF LETHAL INJECTION!
GRIND
GYAH!
NO... NO! I CAN'T GO OUT LIKE THIS!
GRIND
GAH!
GRIND
I'LL KILL MYSELF! I'LL JUMP AND KILL MYSELF! PLEASE...!

CHAPTER 89: All of Us

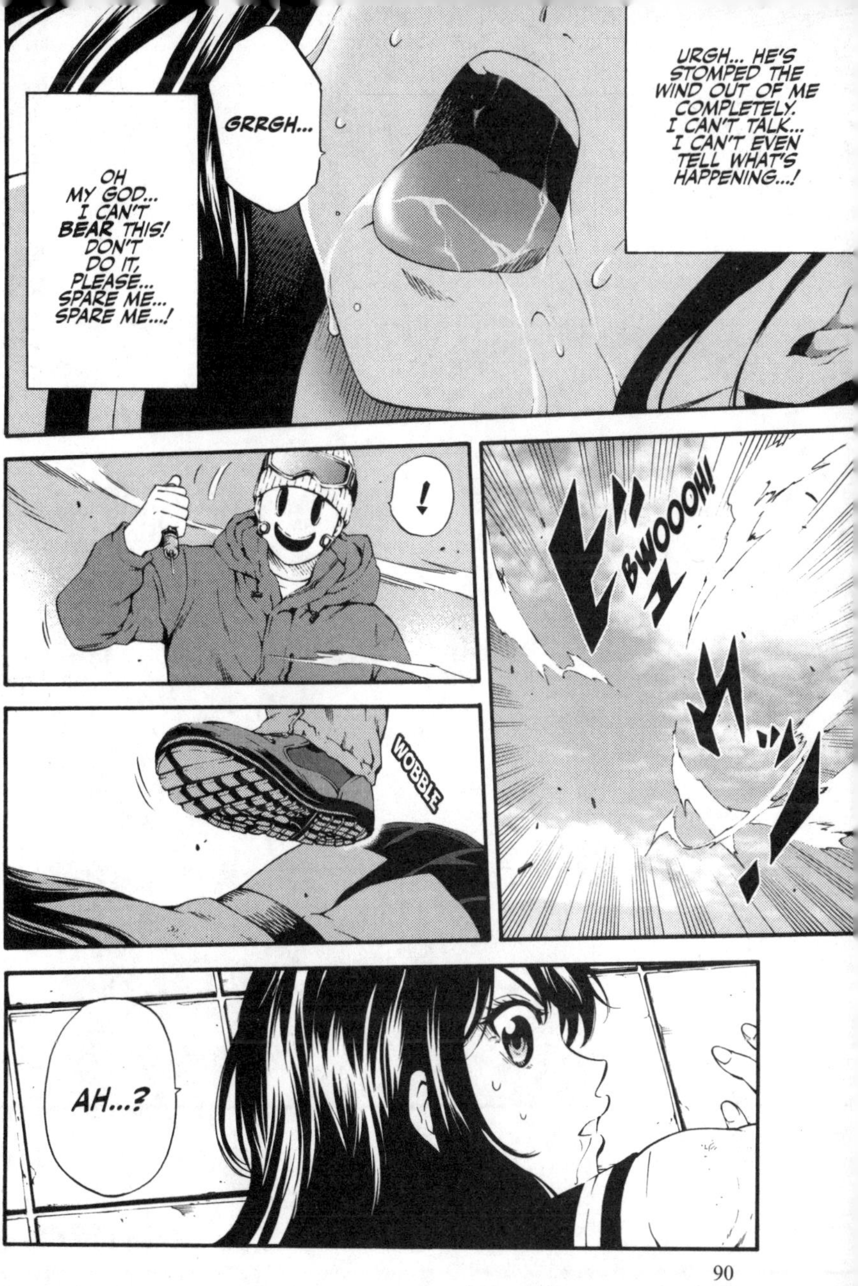
URGH... HE'S STOMPED THE WIND OUT OF ME COMPLETELY. I CAN'T TALK... I CAN'T EVEN TELL WHAT'S HAPPENING...!
GRRGH...
OH MY GOD... I CAN'T BEAR THIS! DON'T DO IT, PLEASE... SPARE ME... SPARE ME...!
BWOOOH!
!
WOBBLE
AH...?

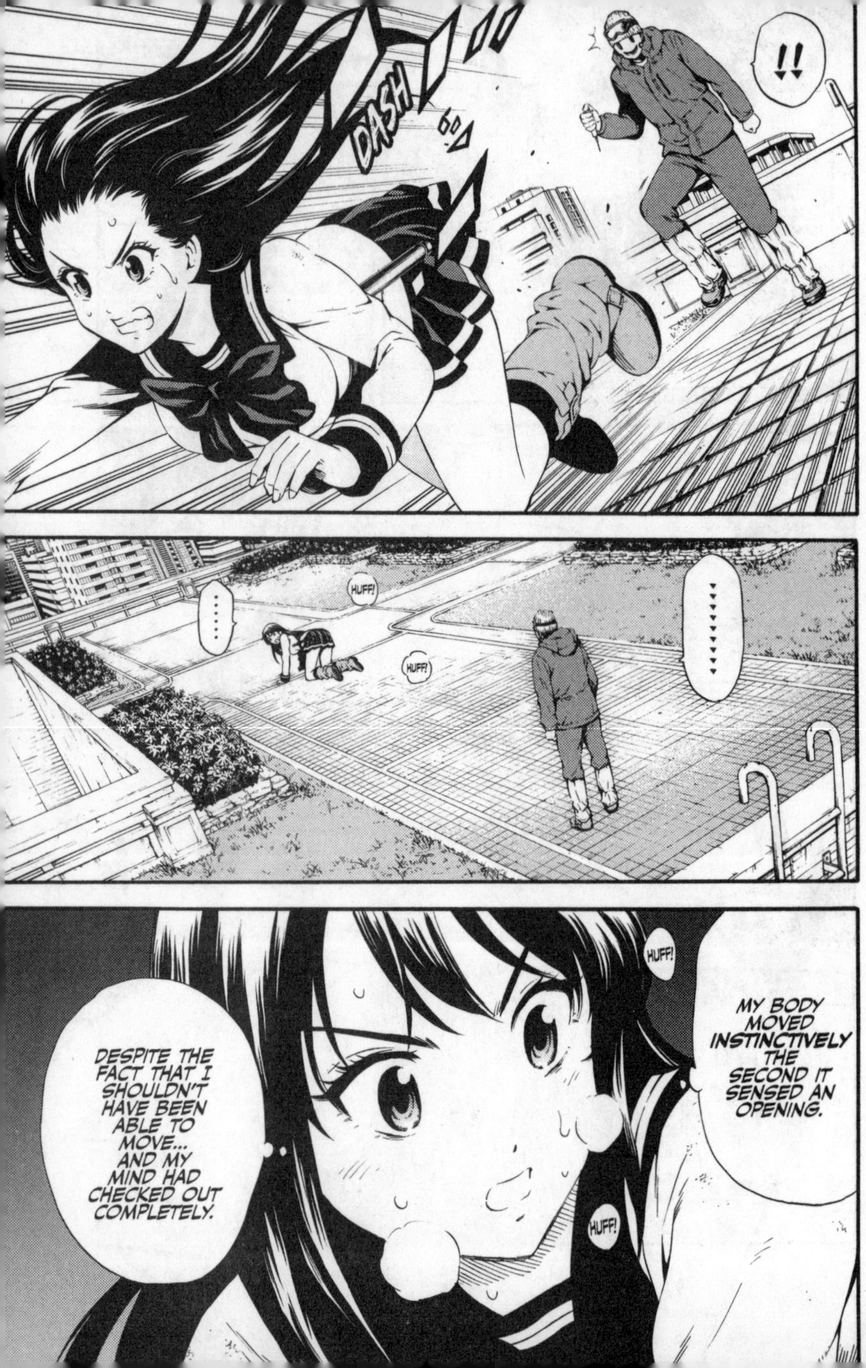
!!
DASH
HUFF!
......
HUFF!
HUFF!
MY BODY MOVED INSTINCTIVELY THE SECOND IT SENSED AN OPENING.
DESPITE THE FACT THAT I SHOULDN'T HAVE BEEN ABLE TO MOVE... AND MY MIND HAD CHECKED OUT COMPLETELY.
HUFF!

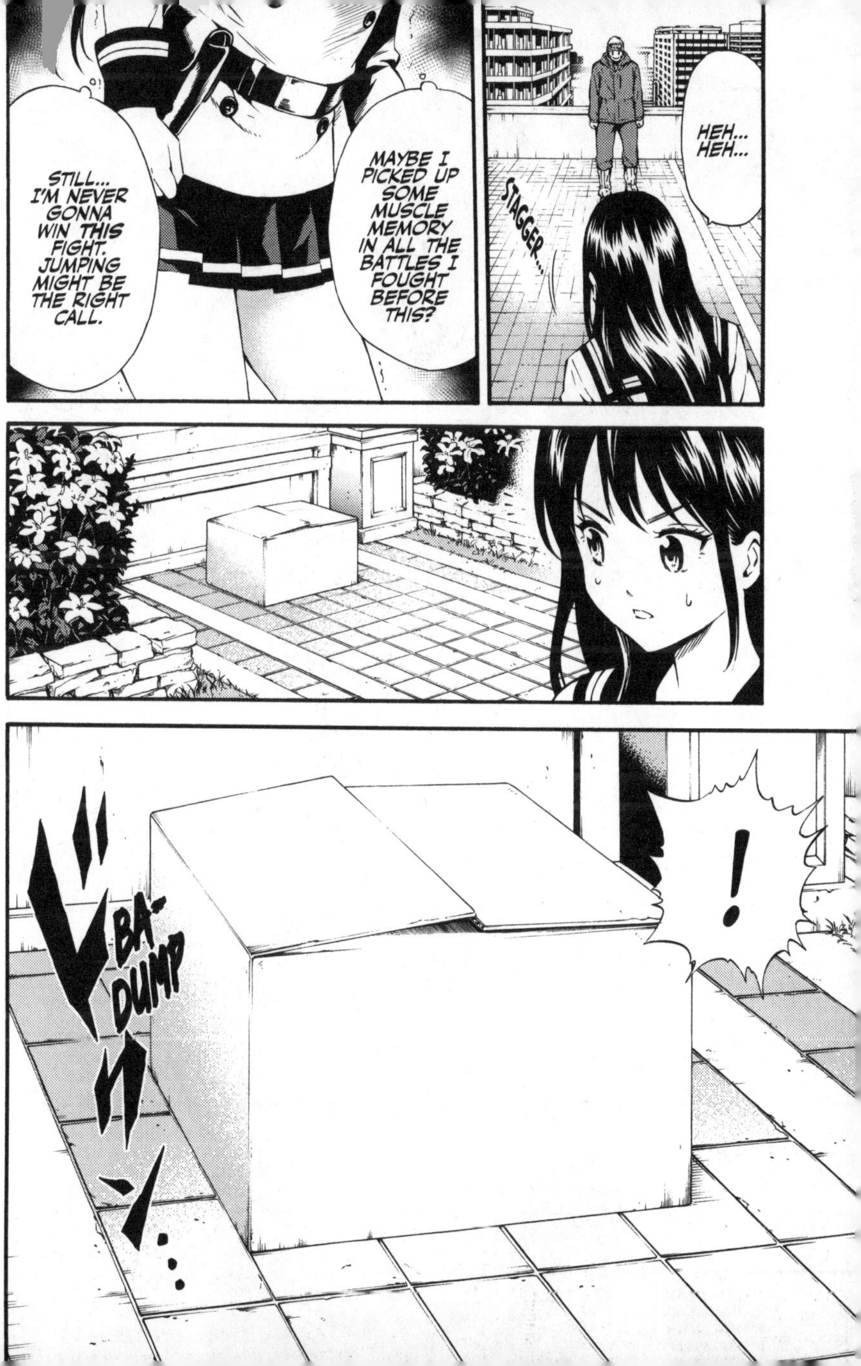
HEH... HEH...
STAGGER...
MAYBE I PICKED UP SOME MUSCLE MEMORY IN ALL THE BATTLES I FOUGHT BEFORE THIS?
STILL... I'M NEVER GONNA WIN THIS FIGHT. JUMPING MIGHT BE THE RIGHT CALL.
!
BA-DUMP

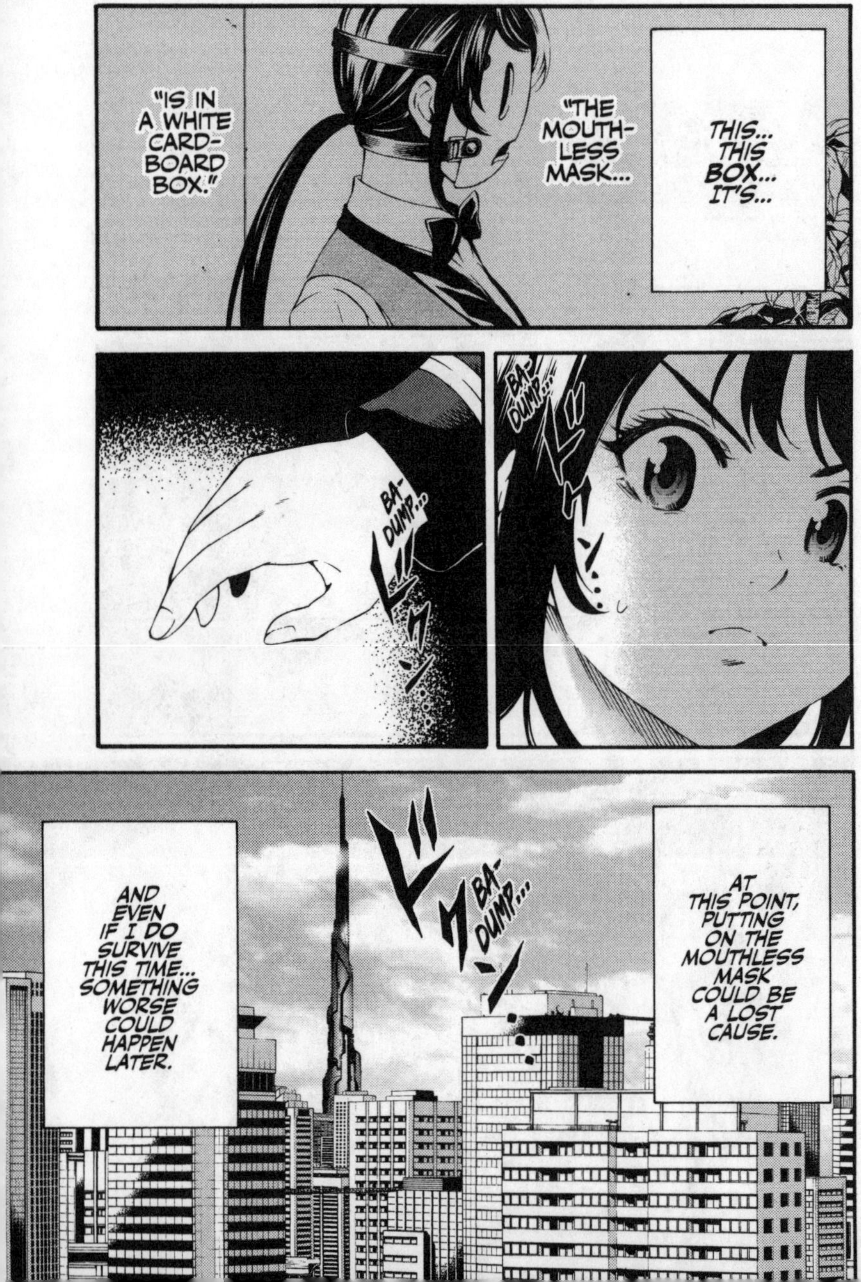
THIS... THIS BOX... IT'S...
"THE MOUTH-LESS MASK...
"IS IN A WHITE CARD-BOARD BOX."
BA-DUMP...
BA-DUMP...
AT THIS POINT, PUTTING ON THE MOUTHLESS MASK COULD BE A LOST CAUSE.
BA-DUMP...
AND EVEN IF I DO SURVIVE THIS TIME... SOMETHING WORSE COULD HAPPEN LATER.

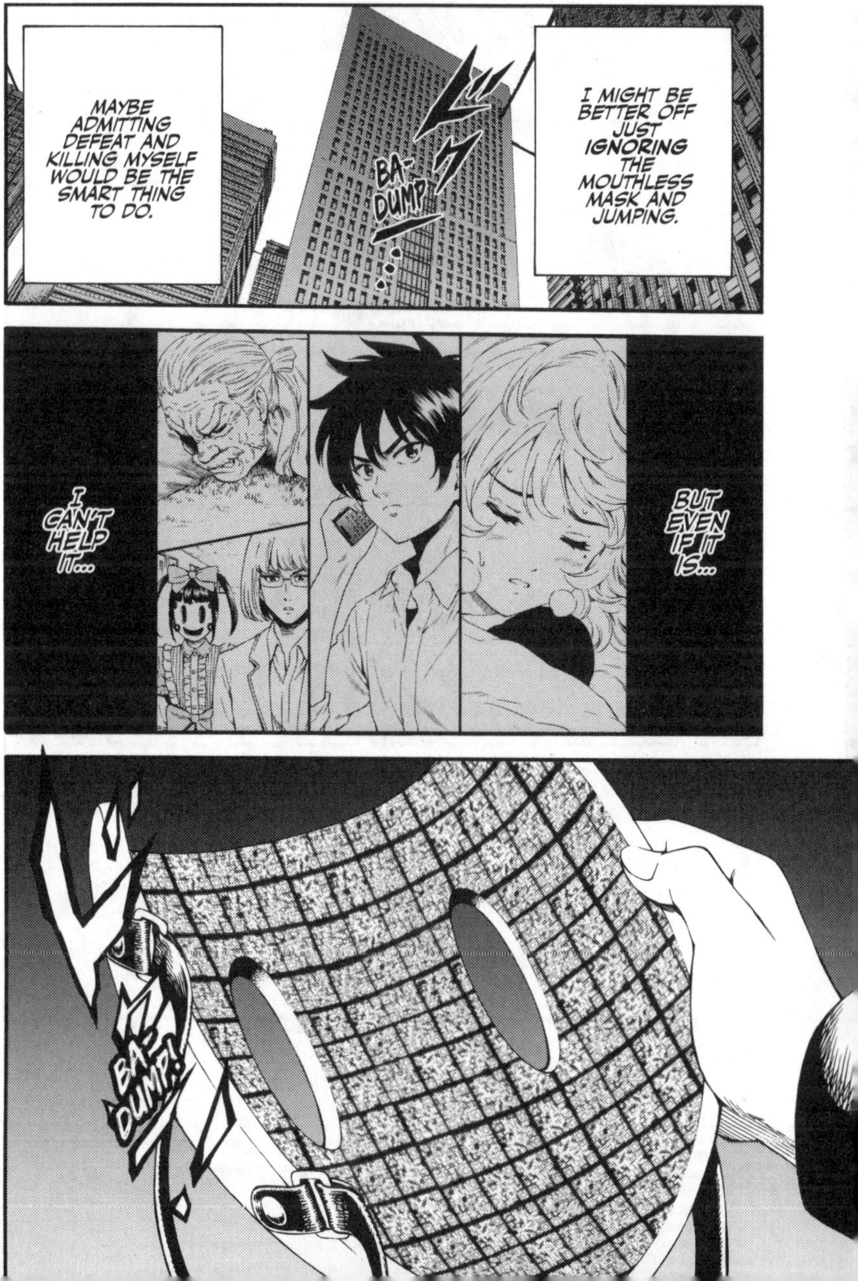
I MIGHT BE BETTER OFF JUST **IGNORING** THE MOUTHLESS MASK AND JUMPING.
BA-DUMP
MAYBE ADMITTING DEFEAT AND KILLING MYSELF WOULD BE THE SMART THING TO DO.
BUT EVEN IF IT IS...
I CAN'T HELP IT...
BA-DUMP!

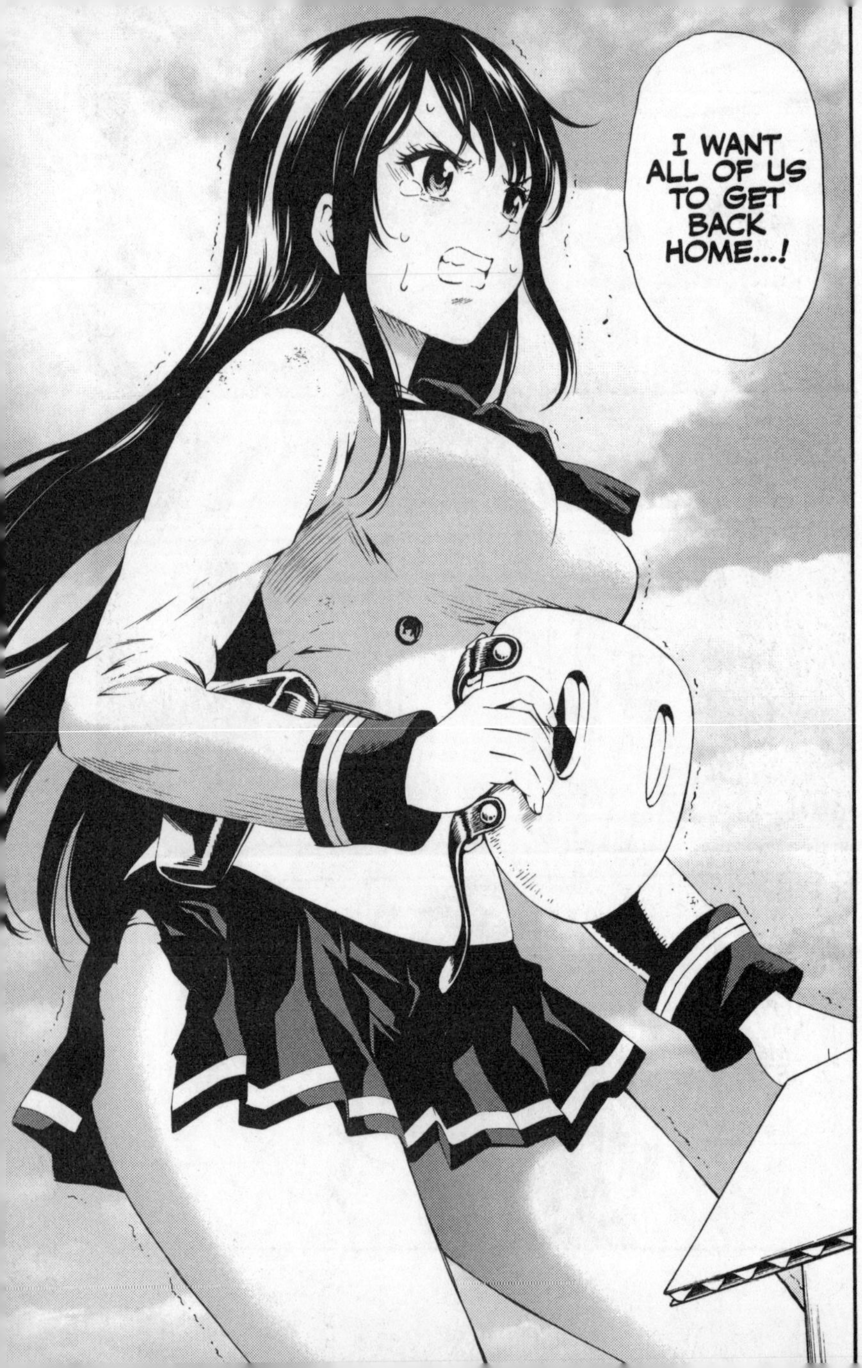
I WANT ALL OF US TO GET BACK HOME...!

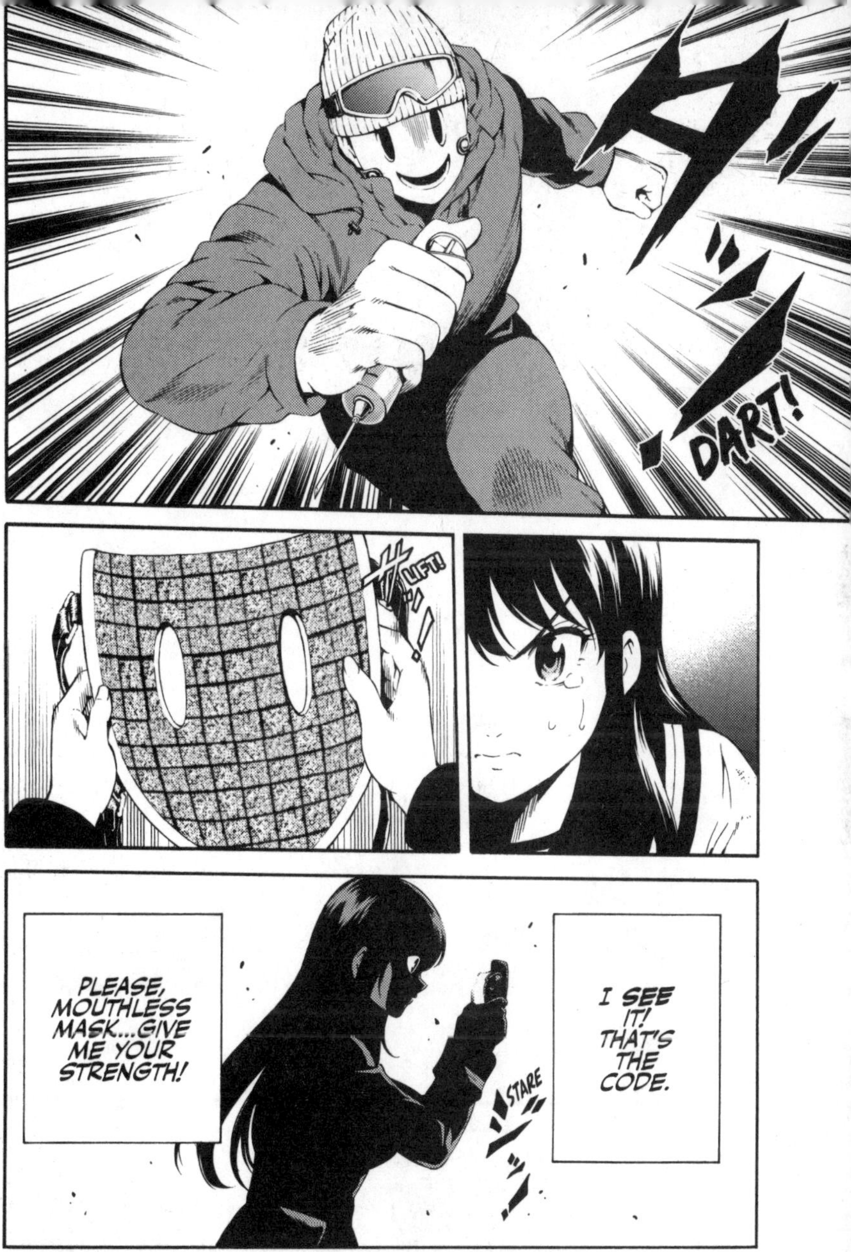

DART!
LIFT!
I SEE IT! THAT'S THE CODE.
STARE
PLEASE, MOUTHLESS MASK...GIVE ME YOUR STRENGTH!

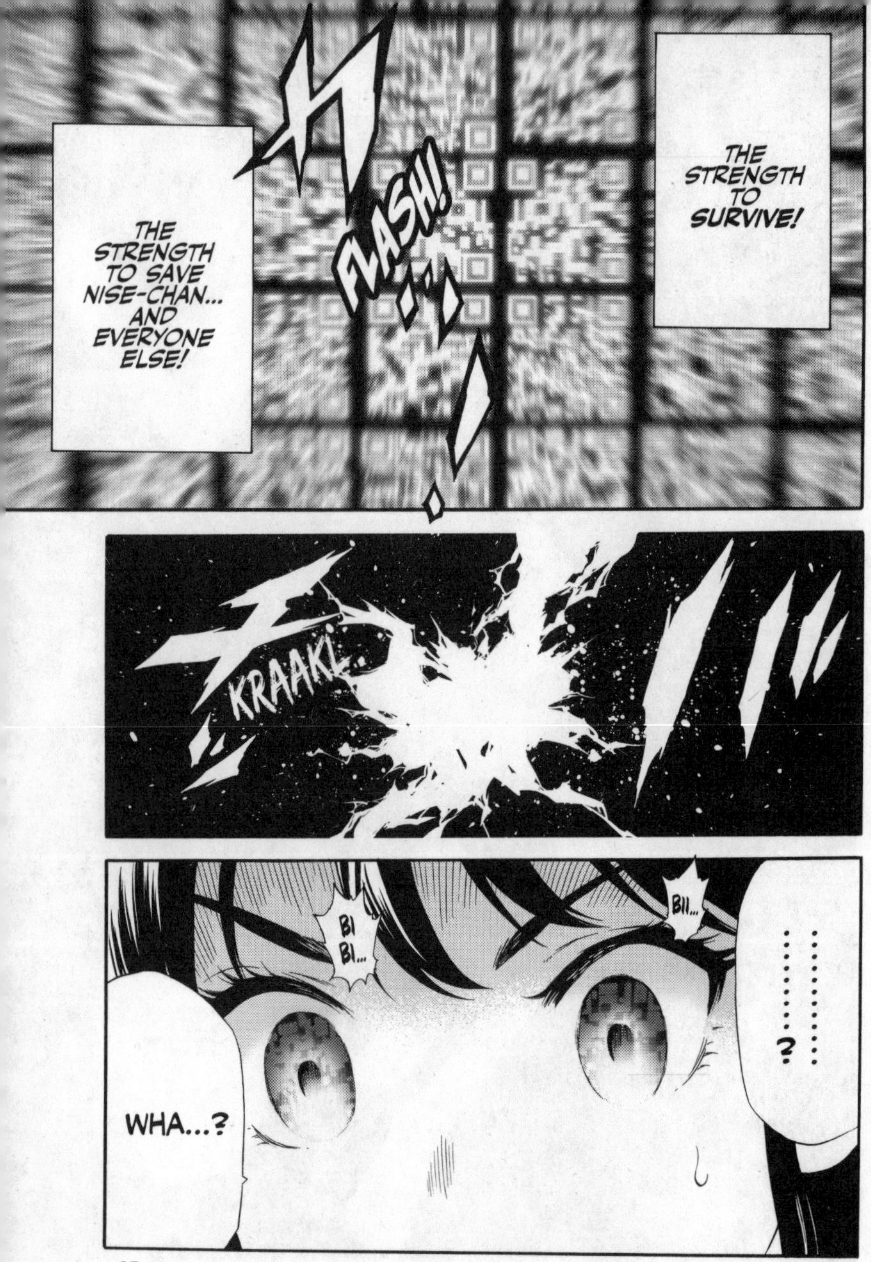
THE STRENGTH TO SURVIVE!
FLASH!
THE STRENGTH TO SAVE NISE-CHAN... AND EVERYONE ELSE!
KRAAK!
......?
BII...
BI BI...
WHA...?

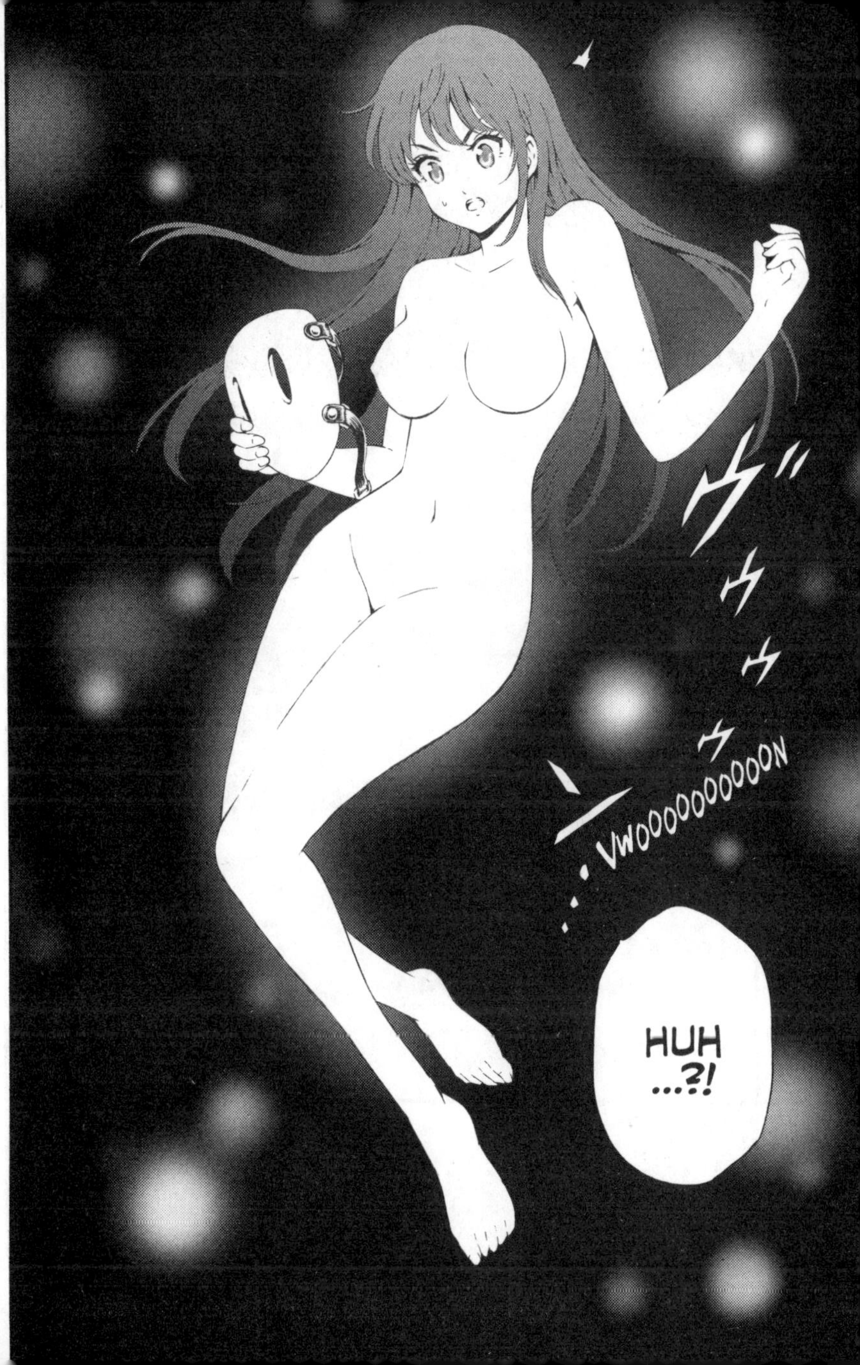
ヴゥゥゥゥン
VWOOOOOOOOOON
HUH ...?!

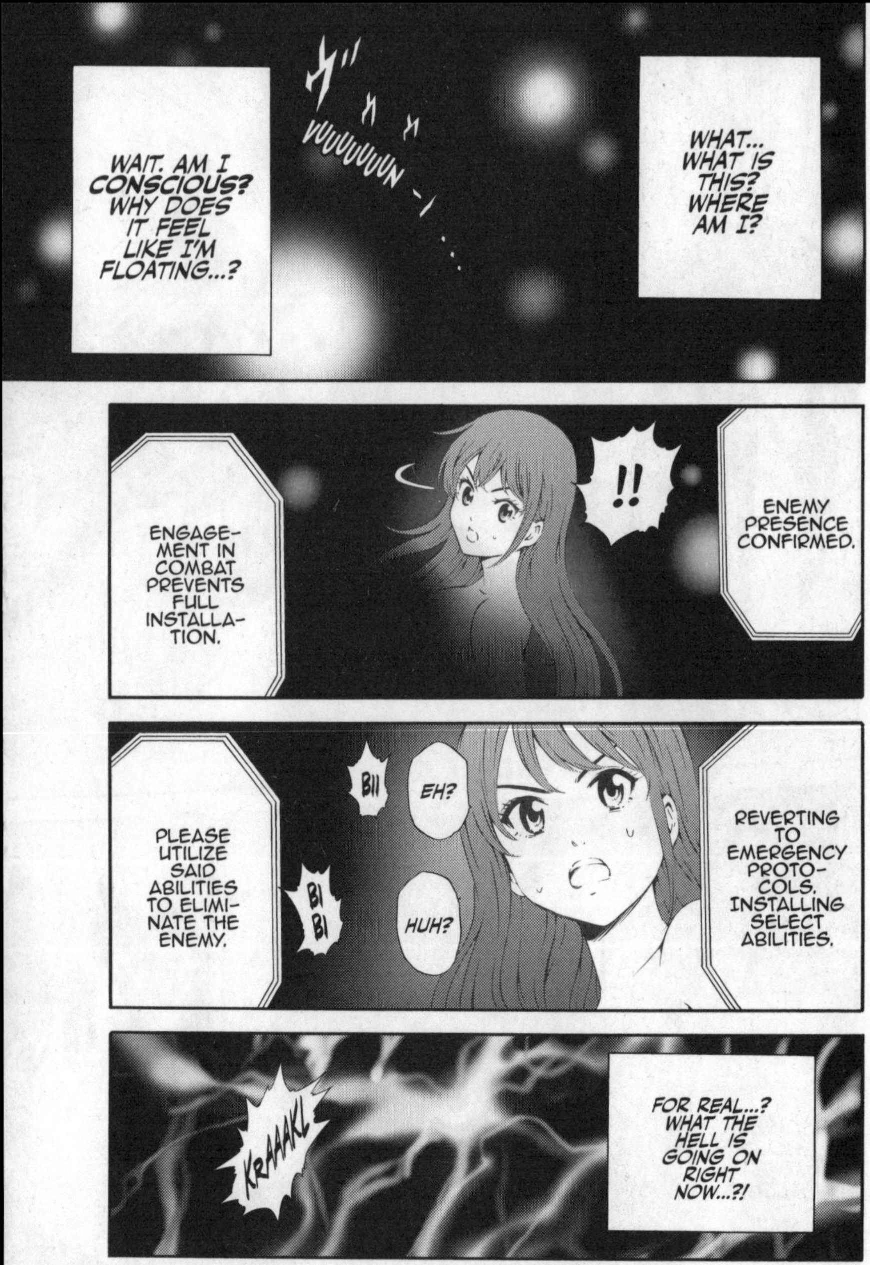
WHAT... WHAT IS THIS? WHERE AM I?
VUUUUUUUN
WAIT. AM I CONSCIOUS? WHY DOES IT FEEL LIKE I'M FLOATING...?
ENEMY PRESENCE CONFIRMED.
!!
ENGAGEMENT IN COMBAT PREVENTS FULL INSTALLATION.
REVERTING TO EMERGENCY PROTOCOLS. INSTALLING SELECT ABILITIES.
EH?
BII
HUH?
BI BI
PLEASE UTILIZE SAID ABILITIES TO ELIMINATE THE ENEMY.
FOR REAL...? WHAT THE HELL IS GOING ON RIGHT NOW...?!
KRAAAKL

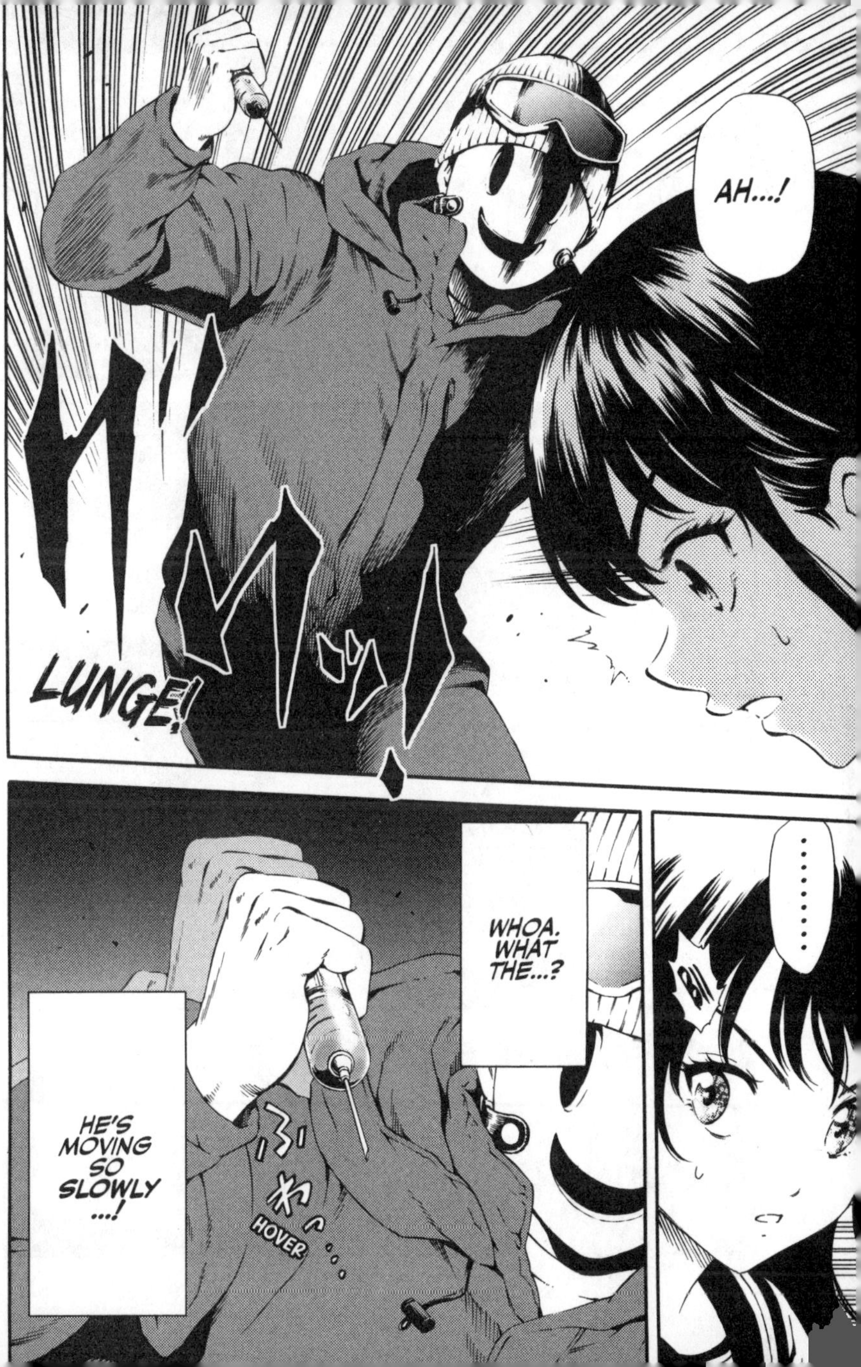
AH...!
LUNGE!
....
WHOA. WHAT THE...?
HE'S MOVING SO SLOWLY ...!
HOVER

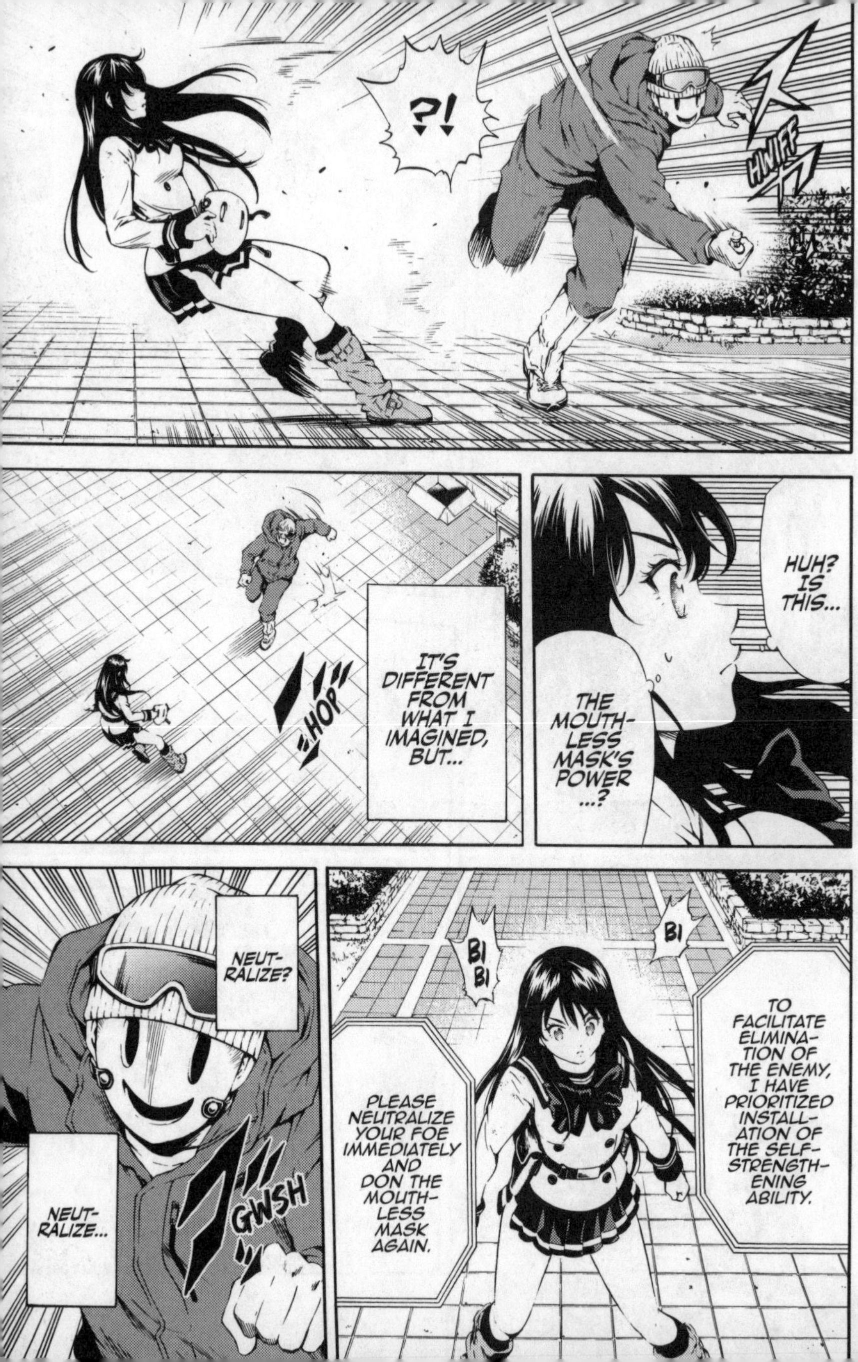
HWIFF
?!
HUH? IS THIS...
THE MOUTH-LESS MASK'S POWER ...?
IT'S DIFFERENT FROM WHAT I IMAGINED, BUT...
HOP
BI
BI BI
TO FACILITATE ELIMINA-TION OF THE ENEMY, I HAVE PRIORITIZED INSTALL-ATION OF THE SELF-STRENGTH-ENING ABILITY.
PLEASE NEUTRALIZE YOUR FOE IMMEDIATELY AND DON THE MOUTH-LESS MASK AGAIN.
NEUT-RALIZE?
GWSH
NEUT-RALIZE...

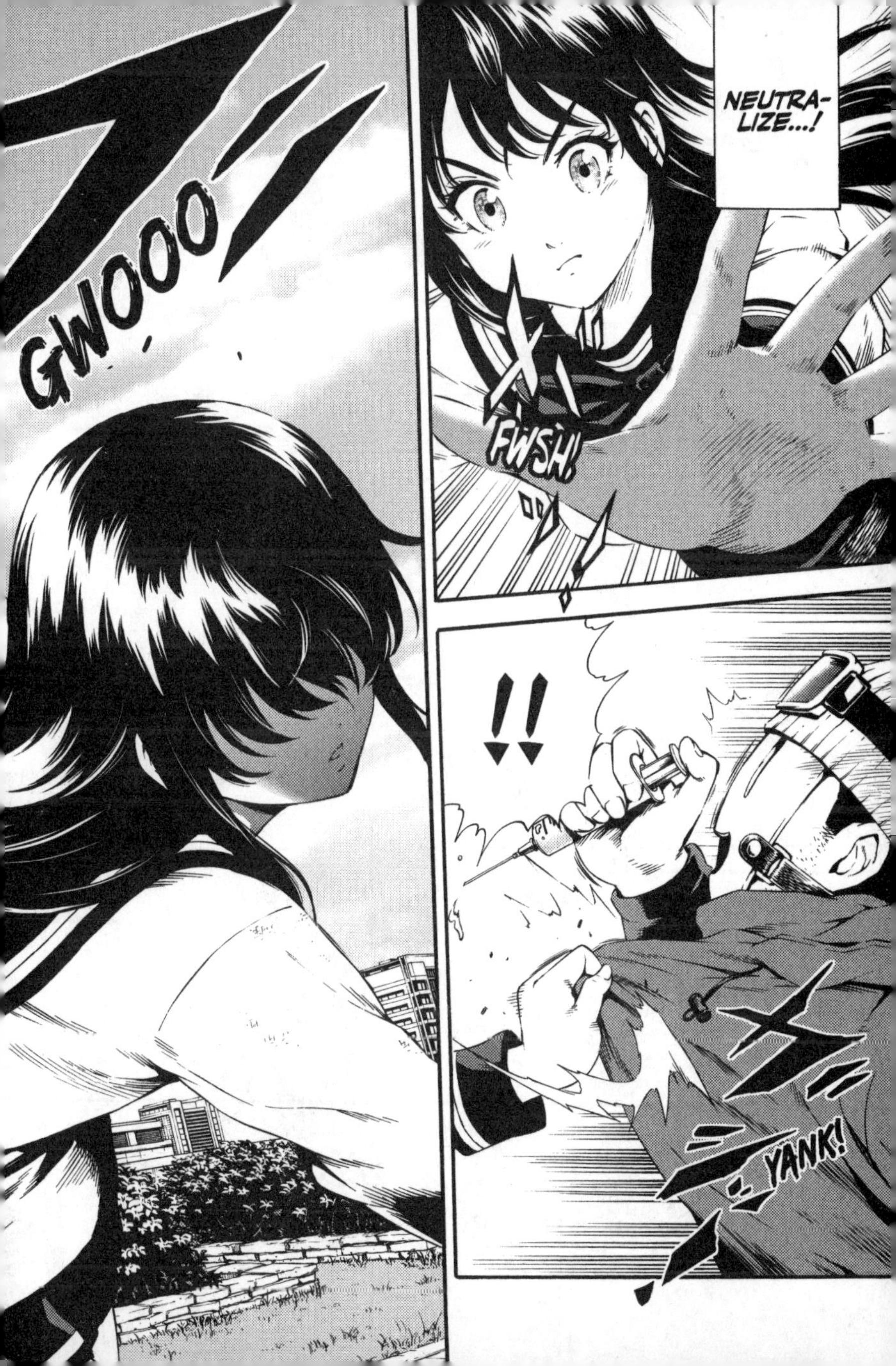
NEUTRA-
LIZE...!
FWSH!
!!
YANK!
GWOOO

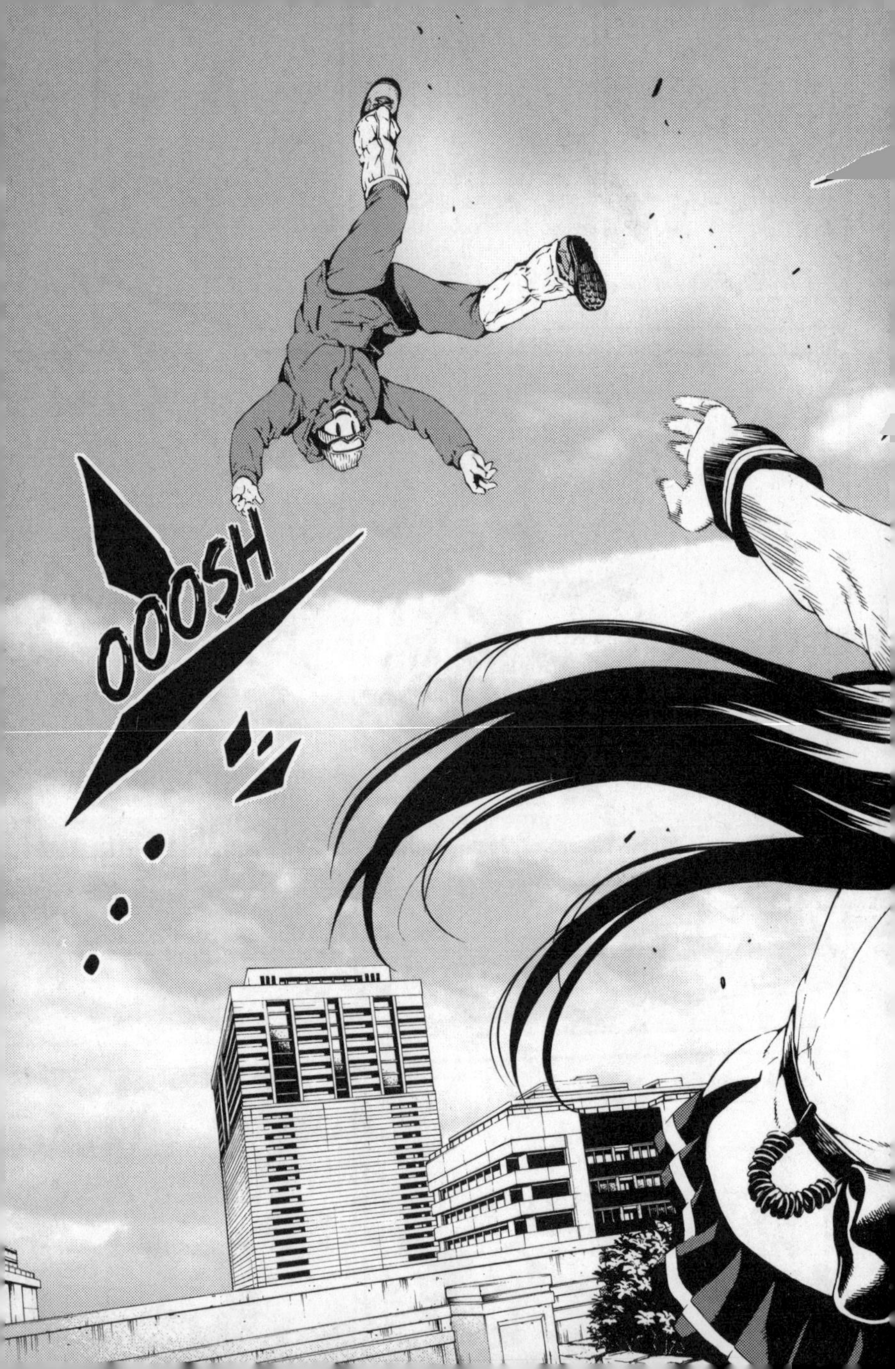
OOOSH

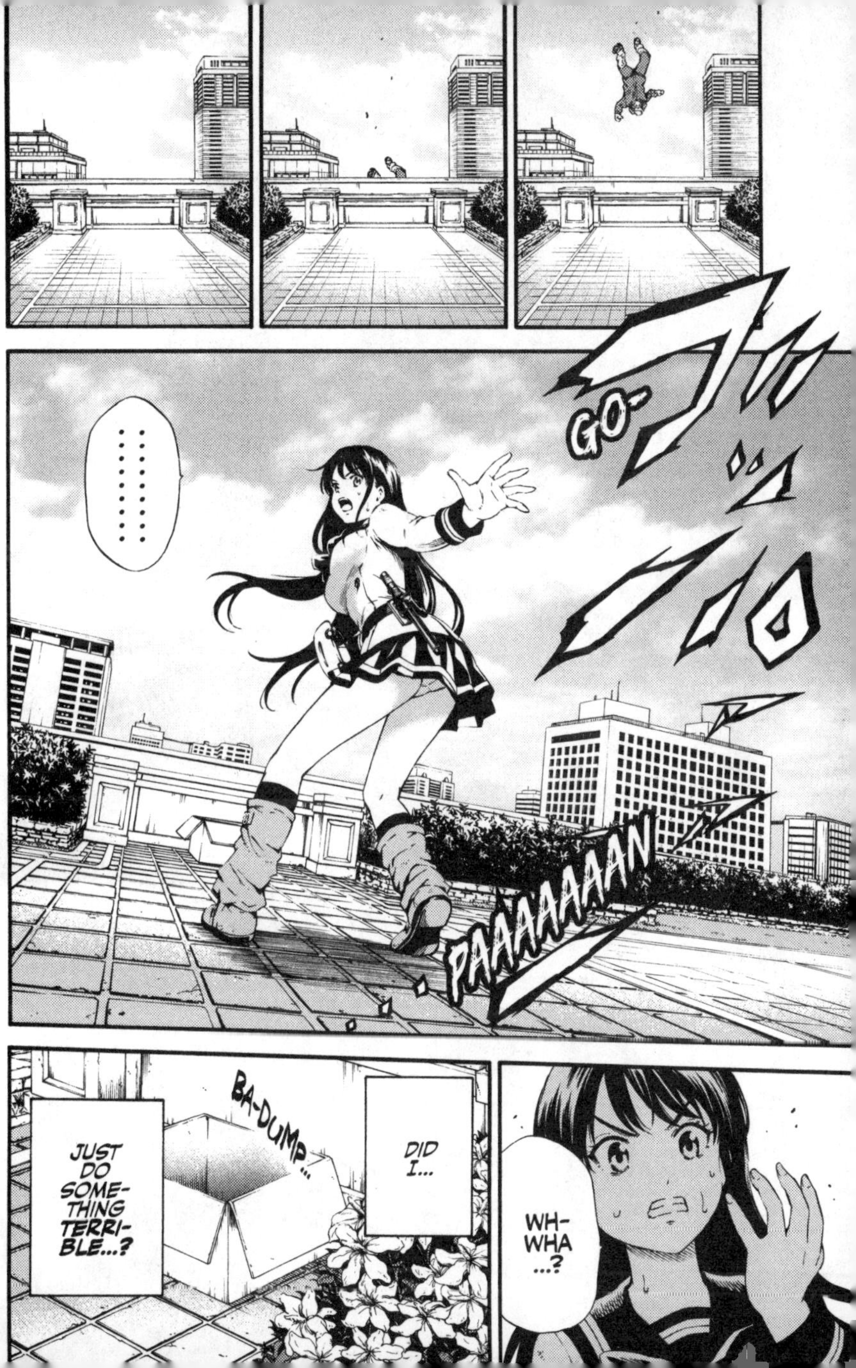
GO-
......
PAAAAAAAN
WH-WHA...?
DID I...
BA-DUMP...
JUST DO SOMETHING TERRIBLE...?

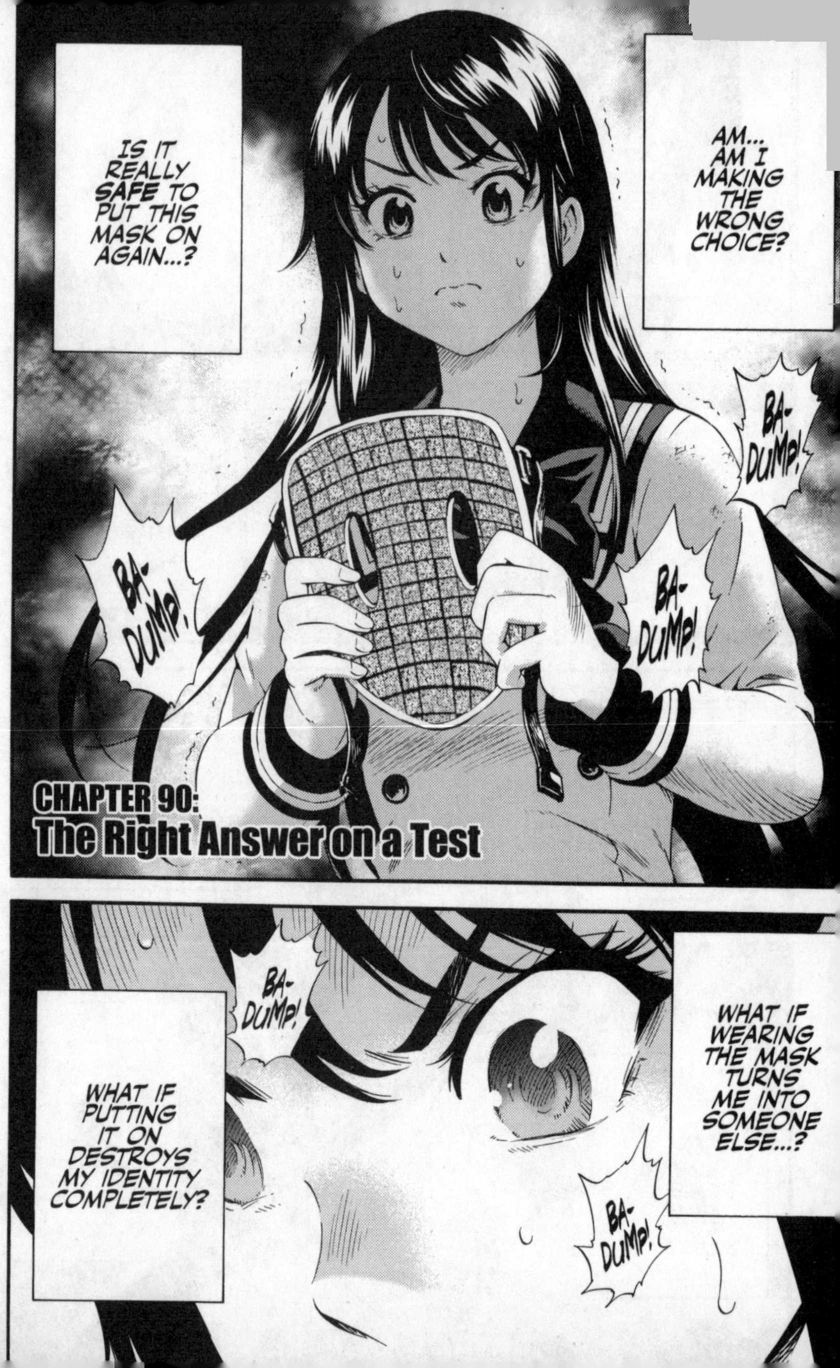
AM... AM I MAKING THE WRONG CHOICE?
IS IT REALLY SAFE TO PUT THIS MASK ON AGAIN...?
BA-DUMP!
BA-DUMP!
BA-DUMP!
CHAPTER 90:
The Right Answer on a Test
WHAT IF WEARING THE MASK TURNS ME INTO SOMEONE ELSE...?
BA-DUMP!
WHAT IF PUTTING IT ON DESTROYS MY IDENTITY COMPLETELY?
BA-DUMP!

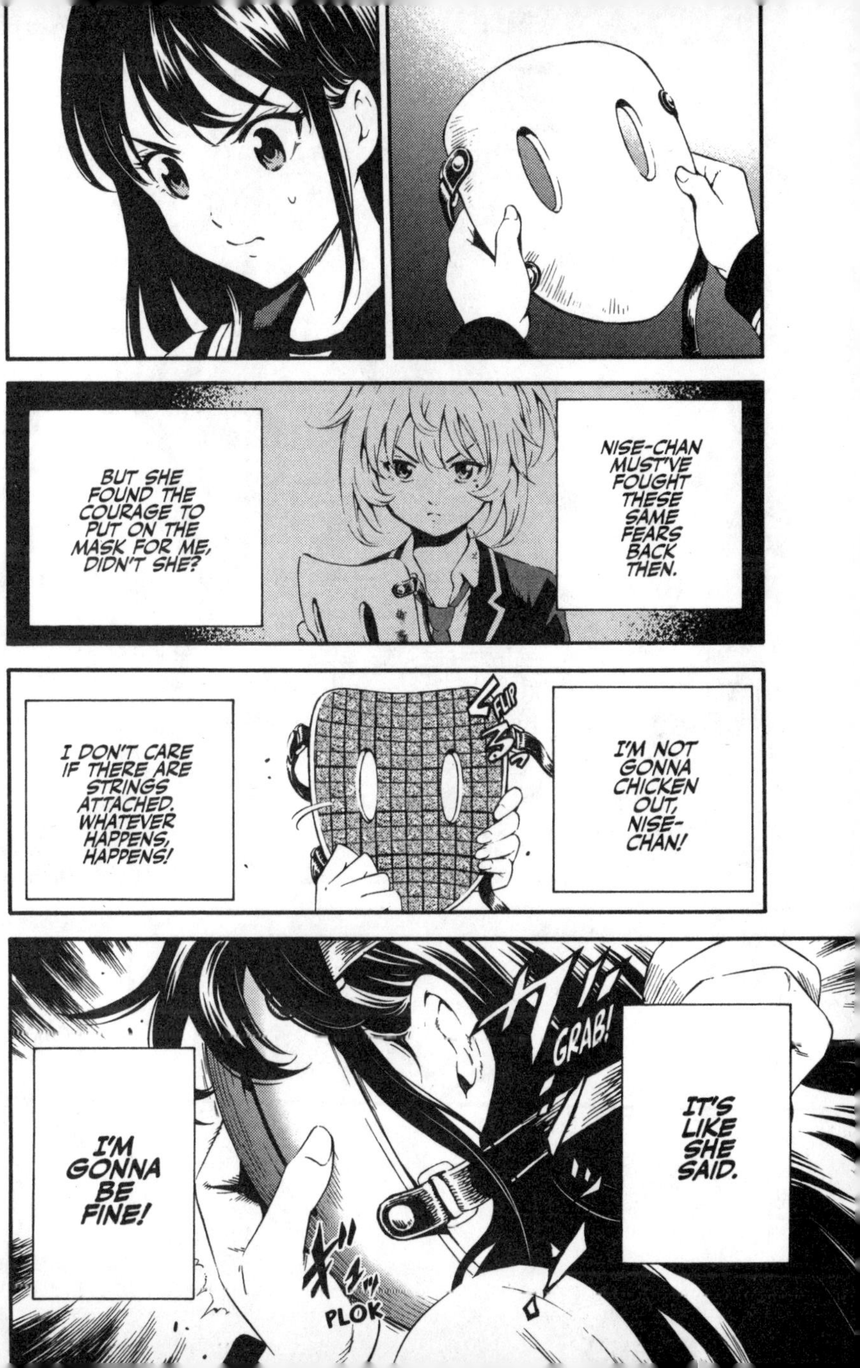
NISE-CHAN MUST'VE FOUGHT THESE SAME FEARS BACK THEN.
BUT SHE FOUND THE COURAGE TO PUT ON THE MASK FOR ME, DIDN'T SHE?
FLIP
I'M NOT GONNA CHICKEN OUT, NISE-CHAN!
I DON'T CARE IF THERE ARE STRINGS ATTACHED. WHATEVER HAPPENS, HAPPENS!
GRAB!
IT'S LIKE SHE SAID.
I'M GONNA BE FINE!
PLOK

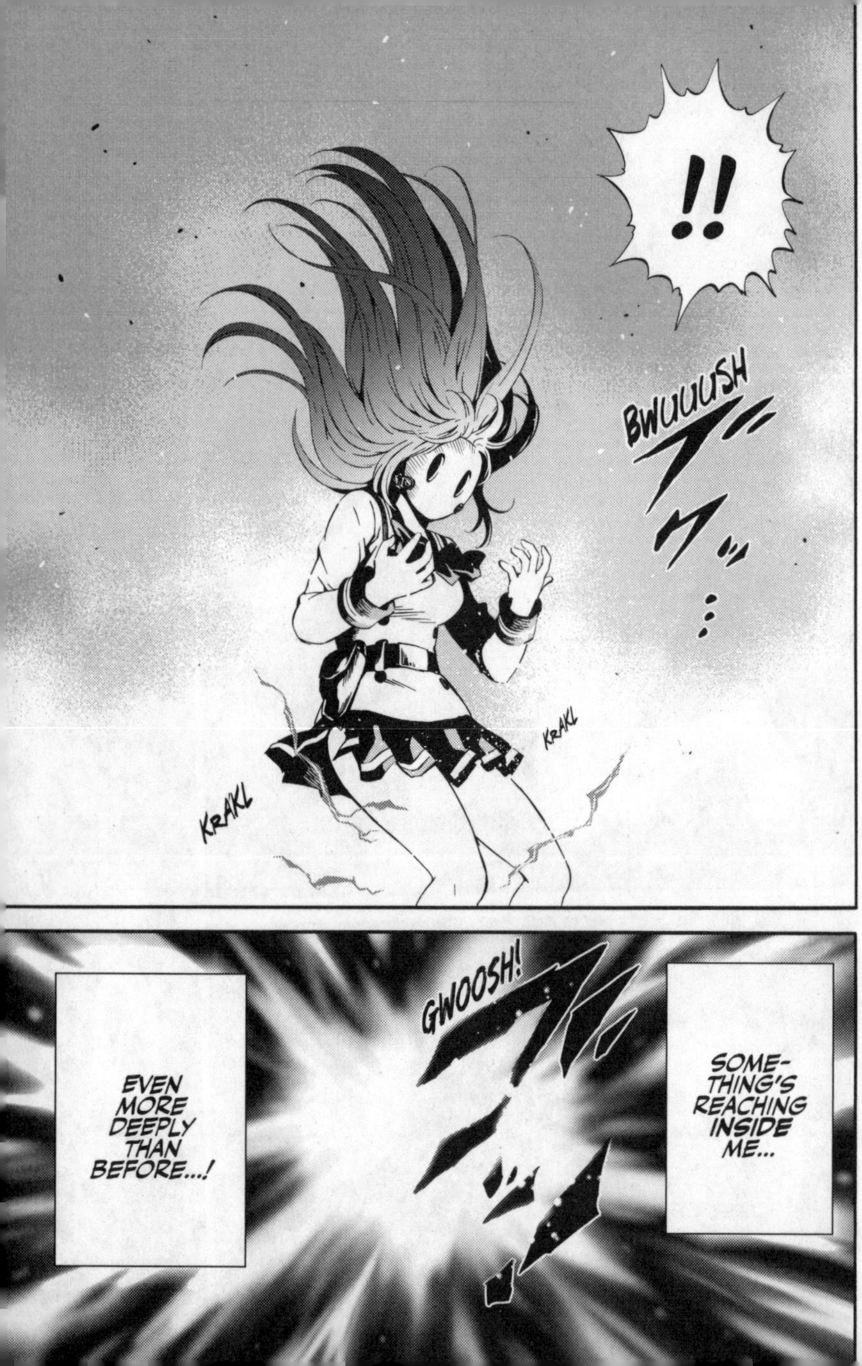
!!
BWUUUSH
KRAKL
KRAKL
SOME-THING'S REACHING INSIDE ME...
GWOOSH!
EVEN MORE DEEPLY THAN BEFORE...!

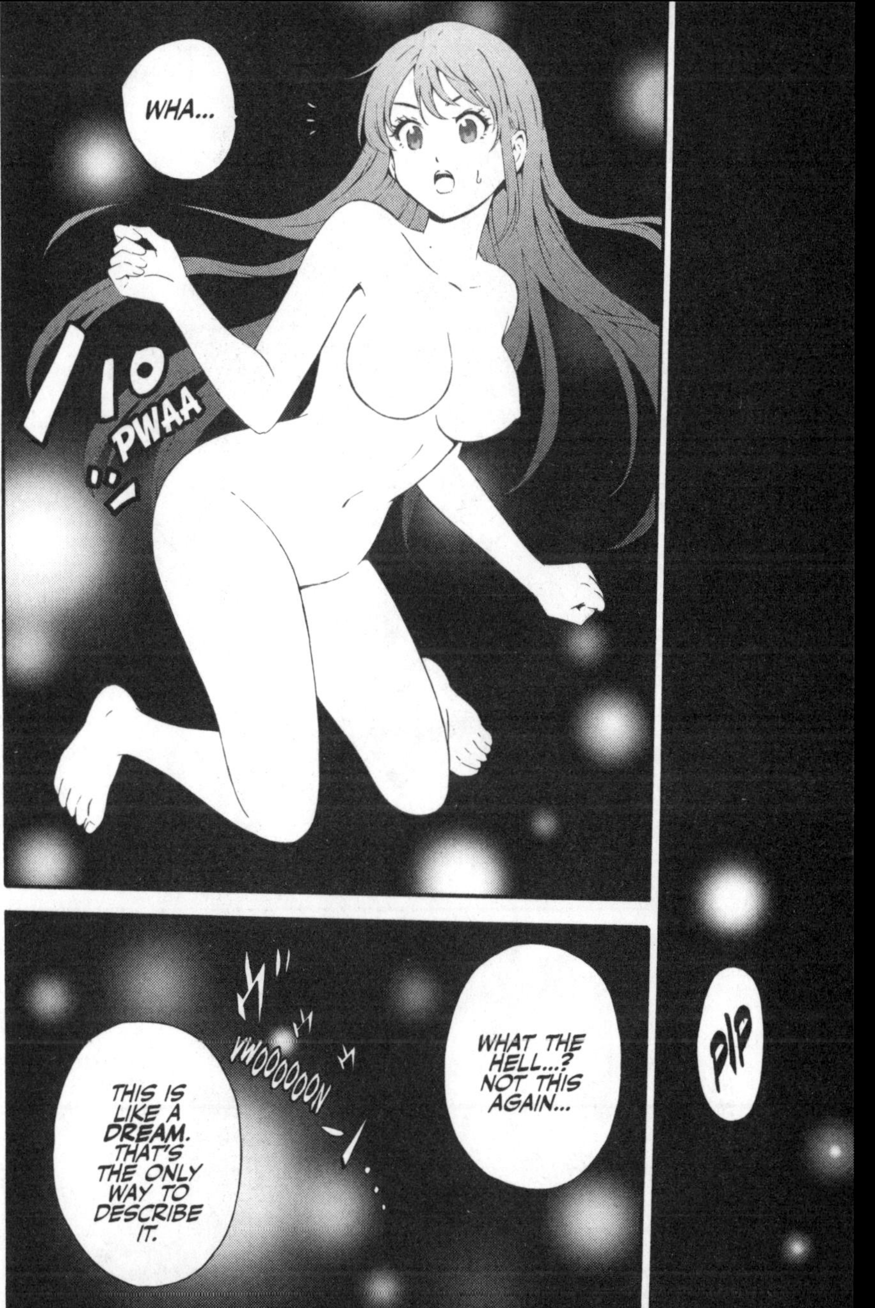
PIP
WHA...
PWAA
WHAT THE HELL...? NOT THIS AGAIN...
VWOOOOOOON
THIS IS LIKE A DREAM. THAT'S THE ONLY WAY TO DESCRIBE IT.

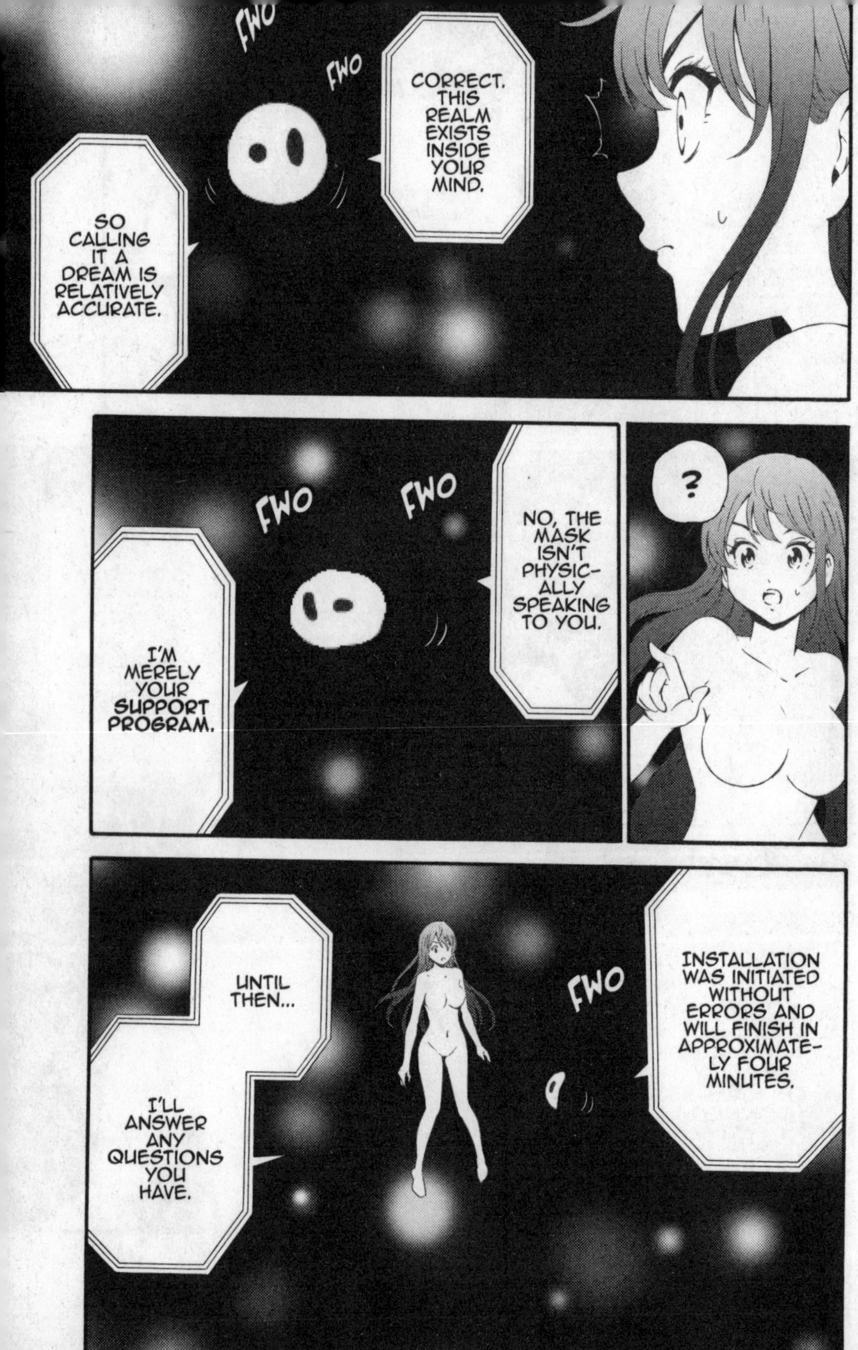
FWO
FWO
CORRECT. THIS REALM EXISTS INSIDE YOUR MIND.
SO CALLING IT A DREAM IS RELATIVELY ACCURATE.
?
NO, THE MASK ISN'T PHYSIC-ALLY SPEAKING TO YOU.
FWO
FWO
I'M MERELY YOUR SUPPORT PROGRAM.
INSTALLATION WAS INITIATED WITHOUT ERRORS AND WILL FINISH IN APPROXIMATE-LY FOUR MINUTES.
FWO
UNTIL THEN...
I'LL ANSWER ANY QUESTIONS YOU HAVE.

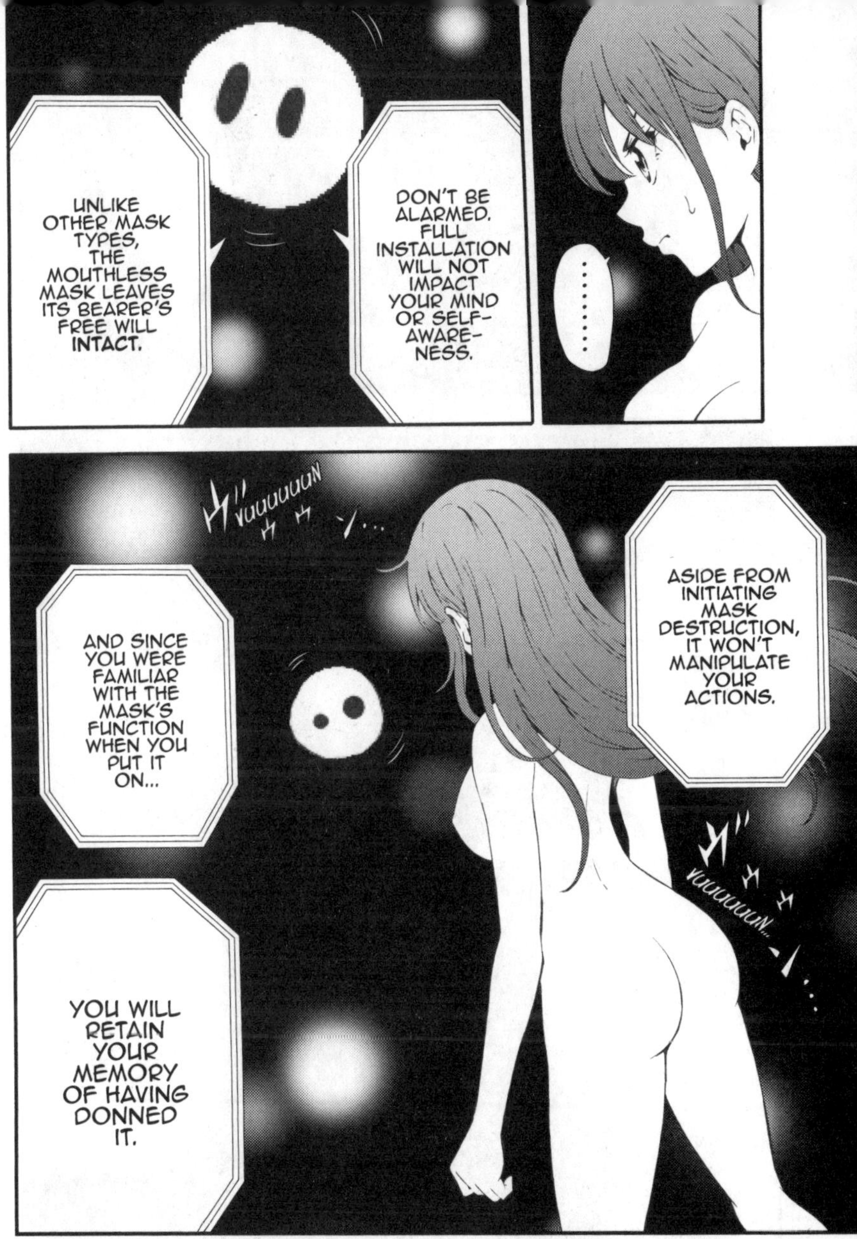

......
DON'T BE ALARMED. FULL INSTALLATION WILL NOT IMPACT YOUR MIND OR SELF-AWARENESS.
UNLIKE OTHER MASK TYPES, THE MOUTHLESS MASK LEAVES ITS BEARER'S FREE WILL **INTACT.**
ASIDE FROM INITIATING MASK DESTRUCTION, IT WON'T MANIPULATE YOUR ACTIONS.
VUUUUUUN...
AND SINCE YOU WERE FAMILIAR WITH THE MASK'S FUNCTION WHEN YOU PUT IT ON...
VUUUUUUN...
YOU WILL RETAIN YOUR MEMORY OF HAVING DONNED IT.

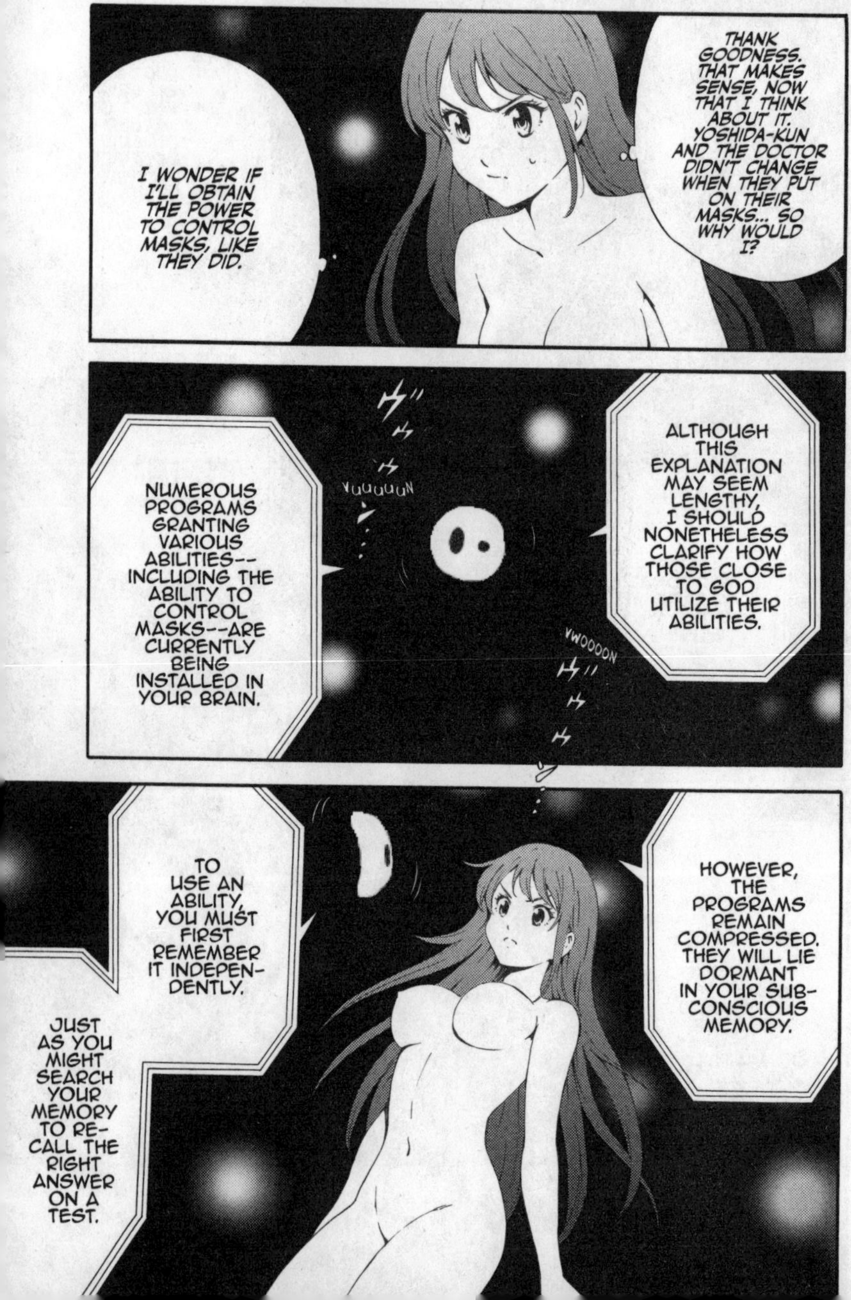
THANK GOODNESS. THAT MAKES SENSE, NOW THAT I THINK ABOUT IT. YOSHIDA-KUN AND THE DOCTOR DIDN'T CHANGE WHEN THEY PUT ON THEIR MASKS... SO WHY WOULD I?
I WONDER IF I'LL OBTAIN THE POWER TO CONTROL MASKS, LIKE THEY DID.
ALTHOUGH THIS EXPLANATION MAY SEEM LENGTHY, I SHOULD NONETHELESS CLARIFY HOW THOSE CLOSE TO GOD UTILIZE THEIR ABILITIES.
VWOOOON
VUUUUUN
NUMEROUS PROGRAMS GRANTING VARIOUS ABILITIES--INCLUDING THE ABILITY TO CONTROL MASKS--ARE CURRENTLY BEING INSTALLED IN YOUR BRAIN.
HOWEVER, THE PROGRAMS REMAIN COMPRESSED. THEY WILL LIE DORMANT IN YOUR SUB-CONSCIOUS MEMORY.
TO USE AN ABILITY, YOU MUST FIRST REMEMBER IT INDEPEN-DENTLY.
JUST AS YOU MIGHT SEARCH YOUR MEMORY TO RE-CALL THE RIGHT ANSWER ON A TEST.

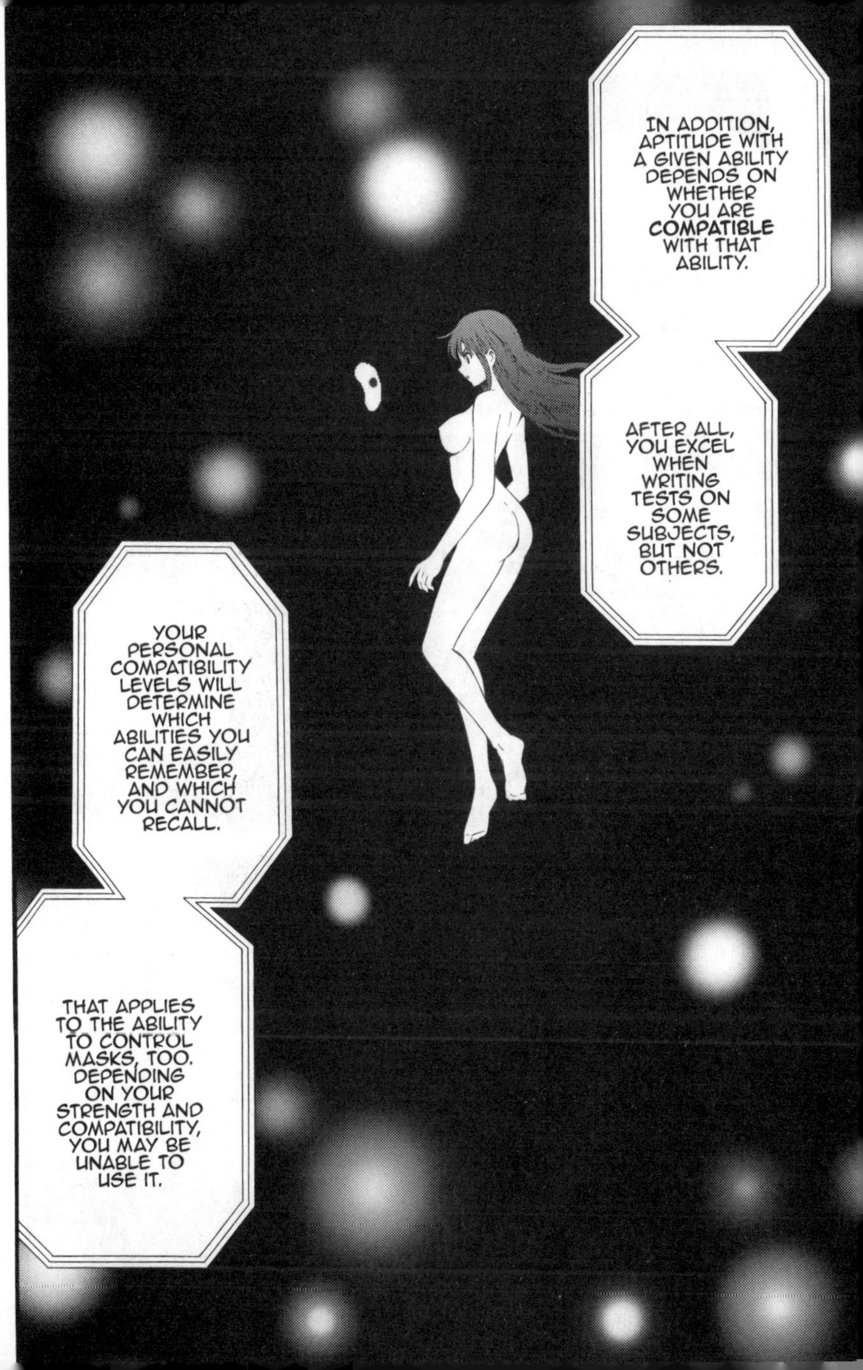
IN ADDITION, APTITUDE WITH A GIVEN ABILITY DEPENDS ON WHETHER YOU ARE **COMPATIBLE** WITH THAT ABILITY.
AFTER ALL, YOU EXCEL WHEN WRITING TESTS ON SOME SUBJECTS, BUT NOT OTHERS.
YOUR PERSONAL COMPATIBILITY LEVELS WILL DETERMINE WHICH ABILITIES YOU CAN EASILY REMEMBER, AND WHICH YOU CANNOT RECALL.
THAT APPLIES TO THE ABILITY TO CONTROL MASKS, TOO. DEPENDING ON YOUR STRENGTH AND COMPATIBILITY, YOU MAY BE UNABLE TO USE IT.

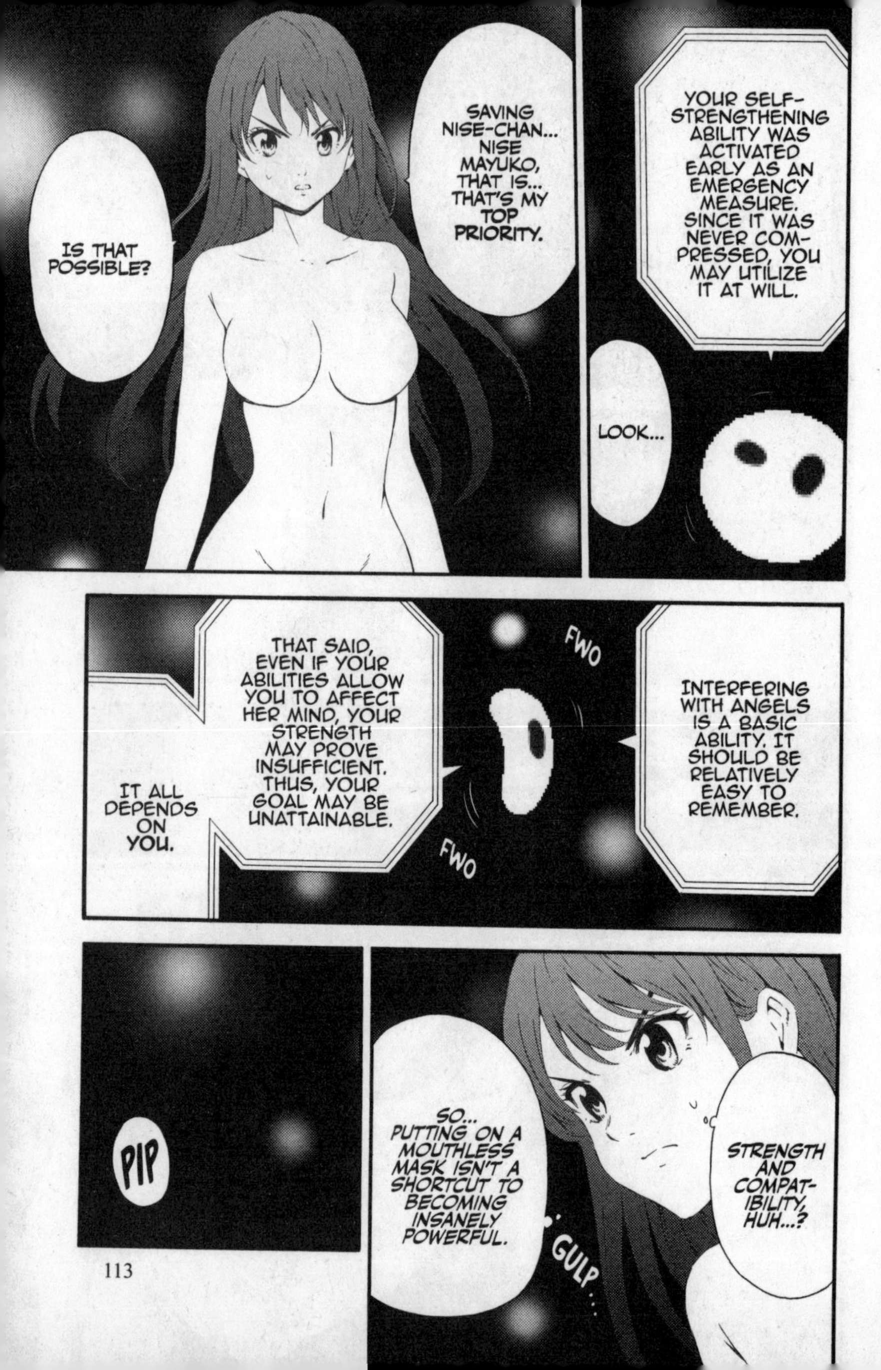

YOUR SELF-STRENGTHENING ABILITY WAS ACTIVATED EARLY AS AN EMERGENCY MEASURE. SINCE IT WAS NEVER COMPRESSED, YOU MAY UTILIZE IT AT WILL.
LOOK...
SAVING NISE-CHAN... NISE MAYUKO, THAT IS... THAT'S MY TOP PRIORITY.
IS THAT POSSIBLE?
INTERFERING WITH ANGELS IS A BASIC ABILITY. IT SHOULD BE RELATIVELY EASY TO REMEMBER.
FWO
FWO
THAT SAID, EVEN IF YOUR ABILITIES ALLOW YOU TO AFFECT HER MIND, YOUR STRENGTH MAY PROVE INSUFFICIENT. THUS, YOUR GOAL MAY BE UNATTAINABLE.
IT ALL DEPENDS ON YOU.
STRENGTH AND COMPATIBILITY, HUH...?
SO... PUTTING ON A MOUTHLESS MASK ISN'T A SHORTCUT TO BECOMING INSANELY POWERFUL.
GULP...
PIP

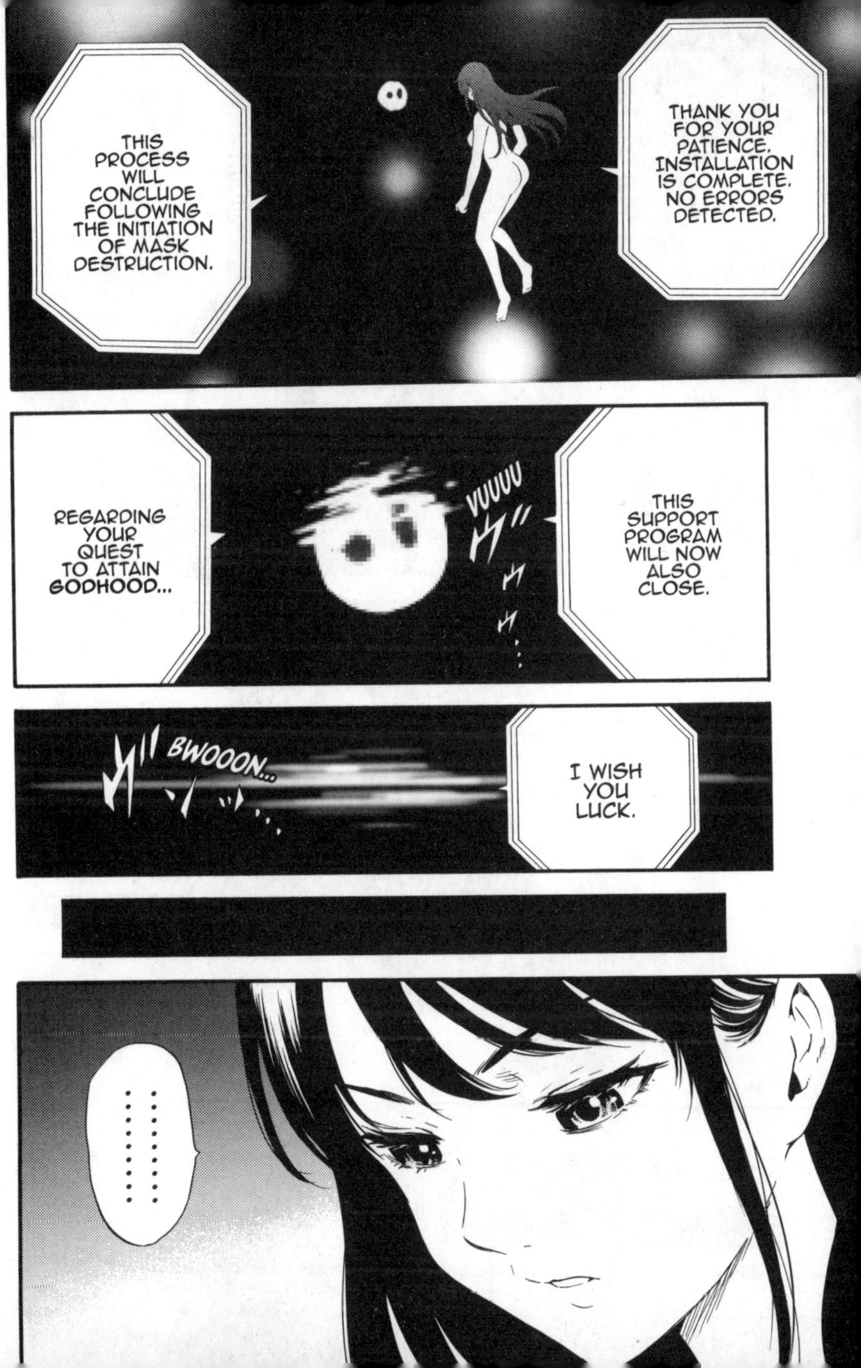
THANK YOU FOR YOUR PATIENCE. INSTALLATION IS COMPLETE. NO ERRORS DETECTED.
THIS PROCESS WILL CONCLUDE FOLLOWING THE INITIATION OF MASK DESTRUCTION.
THIS SUPPORT PROGRAM WILL NOW ALSO CLOSE.
VUUUU
REGARDING YOUR QUEST TO ATTAIN GODHOOD...
I WISH YOU LUCK.
BWOOON...
......

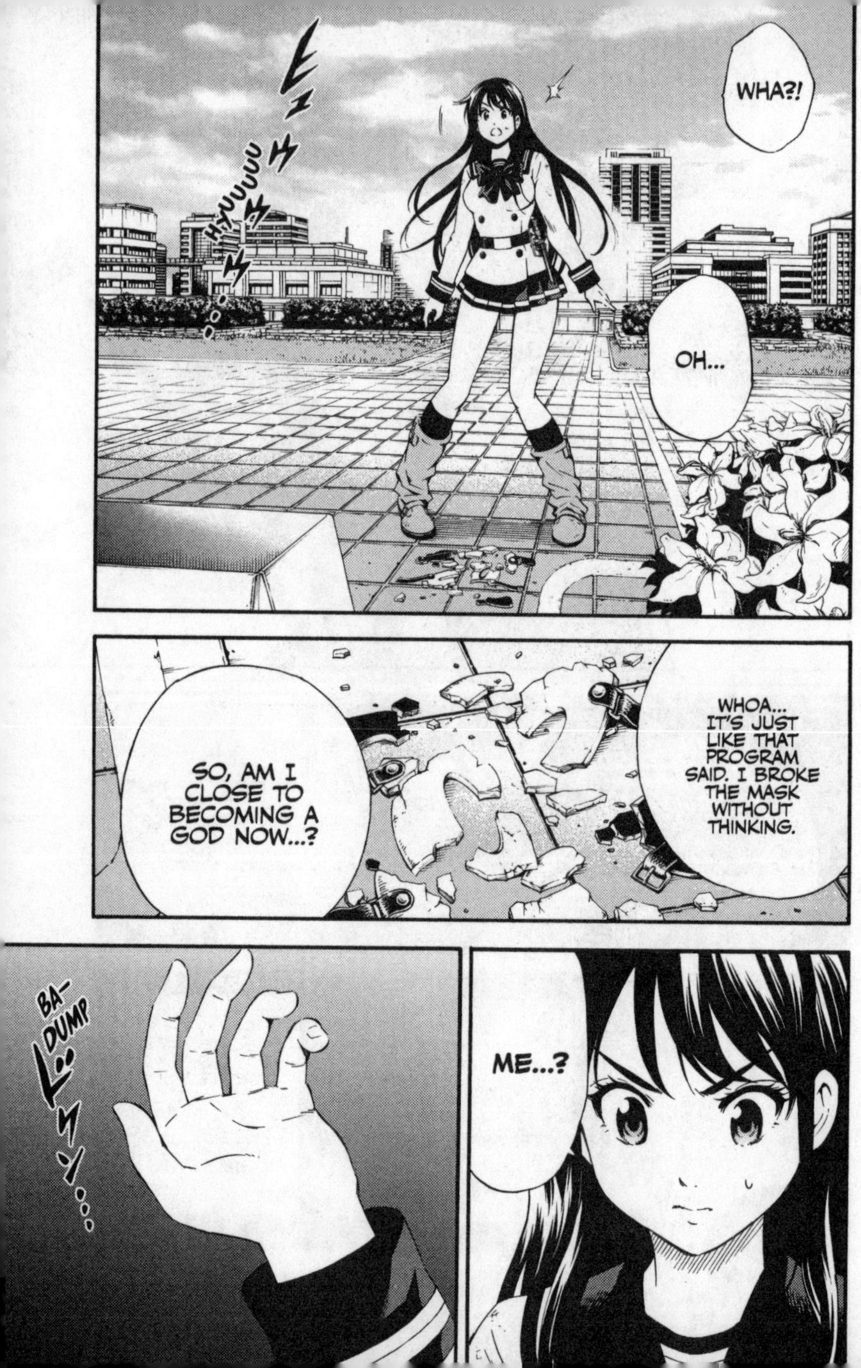
WHA?!
HYUUUUU...
OH...
WHOA... IT'S JUST LIKE THAT PROGRAM SAID. I BROKE THE MASK WITHOUT THINKING.
SO, AM I CLOSE TO BECOMING A GOD NOW...?
ME...?
BA-DUMP

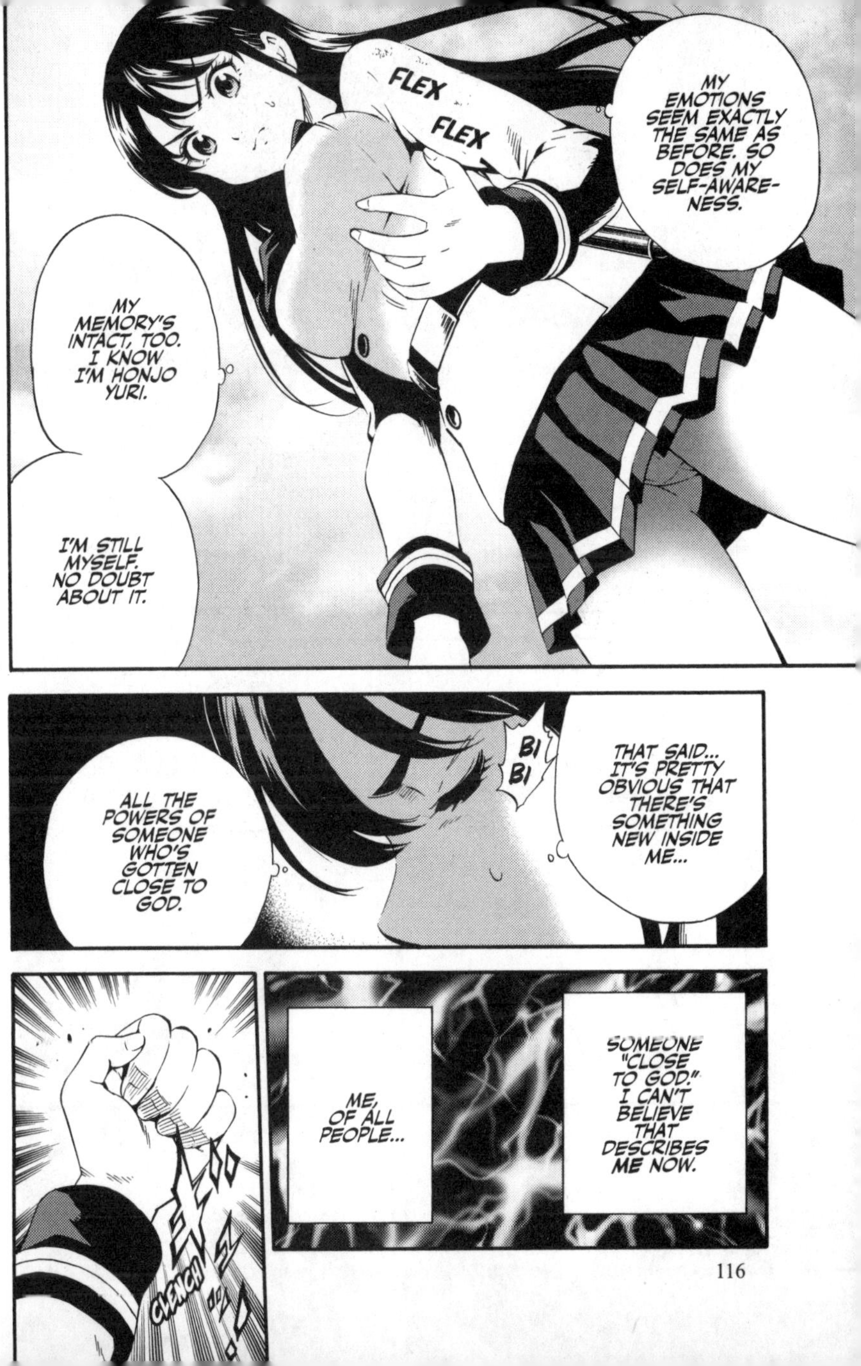
FLEX
FLEX
MY EMOTIONS SEEM EXACTLY THE SAME AS BEFORE. SO DOES MY SELF-AWARE-NESS.
MY MEMORY'S INTACT, TOO. I KNOW I'M HONJO YURI.
I'M STILL MYSELF. NO DOUBT ABOUT IT.
THAT SAID... IT'S PRETTY OBVIOUS THAT THERE'S SOMETHING NEW INSIDE ME...
BI
BI
ALL THE POWERS OF SOMEONE WHO'S GOTTEN CLOSE TO GOD.
SOMEONE "CLOSE TO GOD." I CAN'T BELIEVE THAT DESCRIBES ME NOW.
ME, OF ALL PEOPLE...
CLENCH

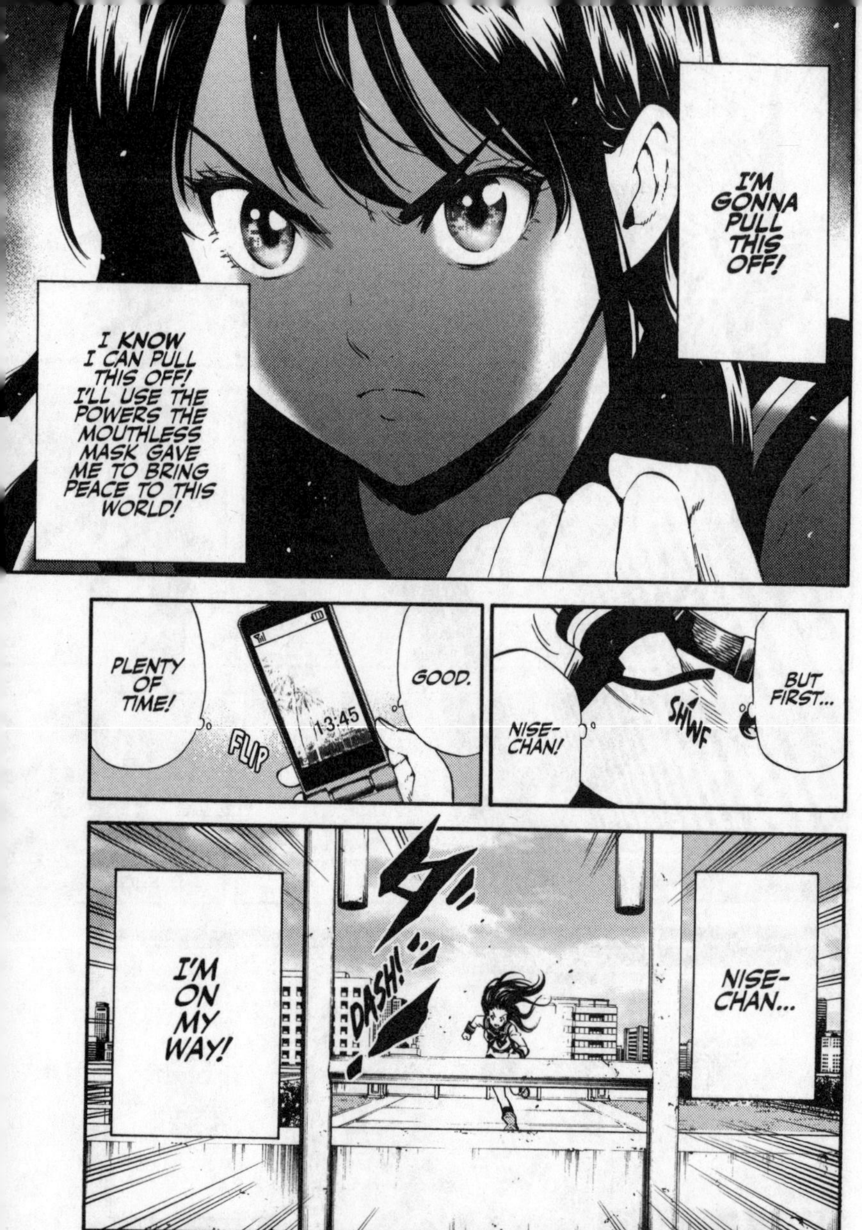
I'M GONNA PULL THIS OFF!
I KNOW I CAN PULL THIS OFF! I'LL USE THE POWERS THE MOUTHLESS MASK GAVE ME TO BRING PEACE TO THIS WORLD!
BUT FIRST...
SHWF
NISE-CHAN!
GOOD.
13:45
FLIP
PLENTY OF TIME!
NISE-CHAN...
DASH!
I'M ON MY WAY!

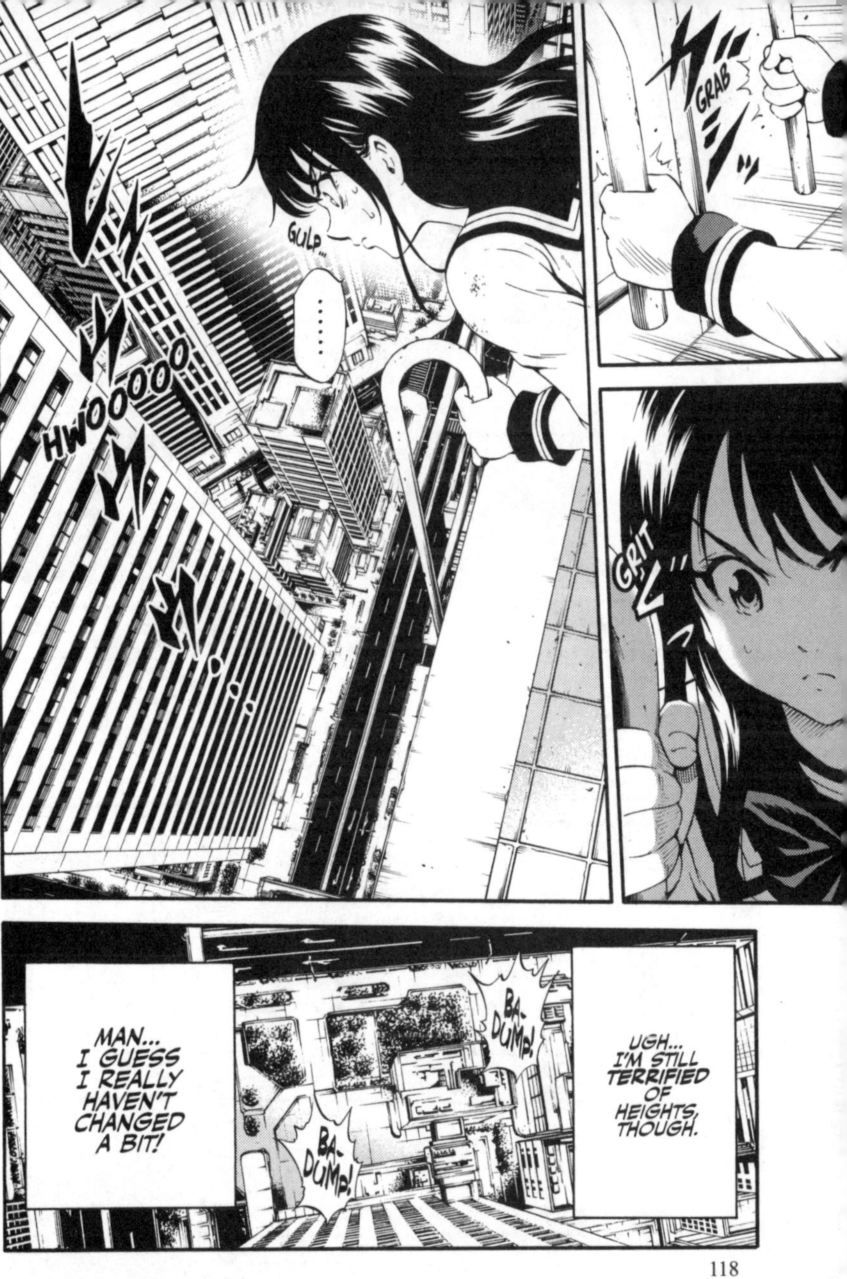

GRAB
GRIT
GULP...
......
HWOOOOO
UGH... I'M STILL TERRIFIED OF HEIGHTS, THOUGH.
BA-DUMP!
BA-DUMP!
MAN... I GUESS I REALLY HAVEN'T CHANGED A BIT!

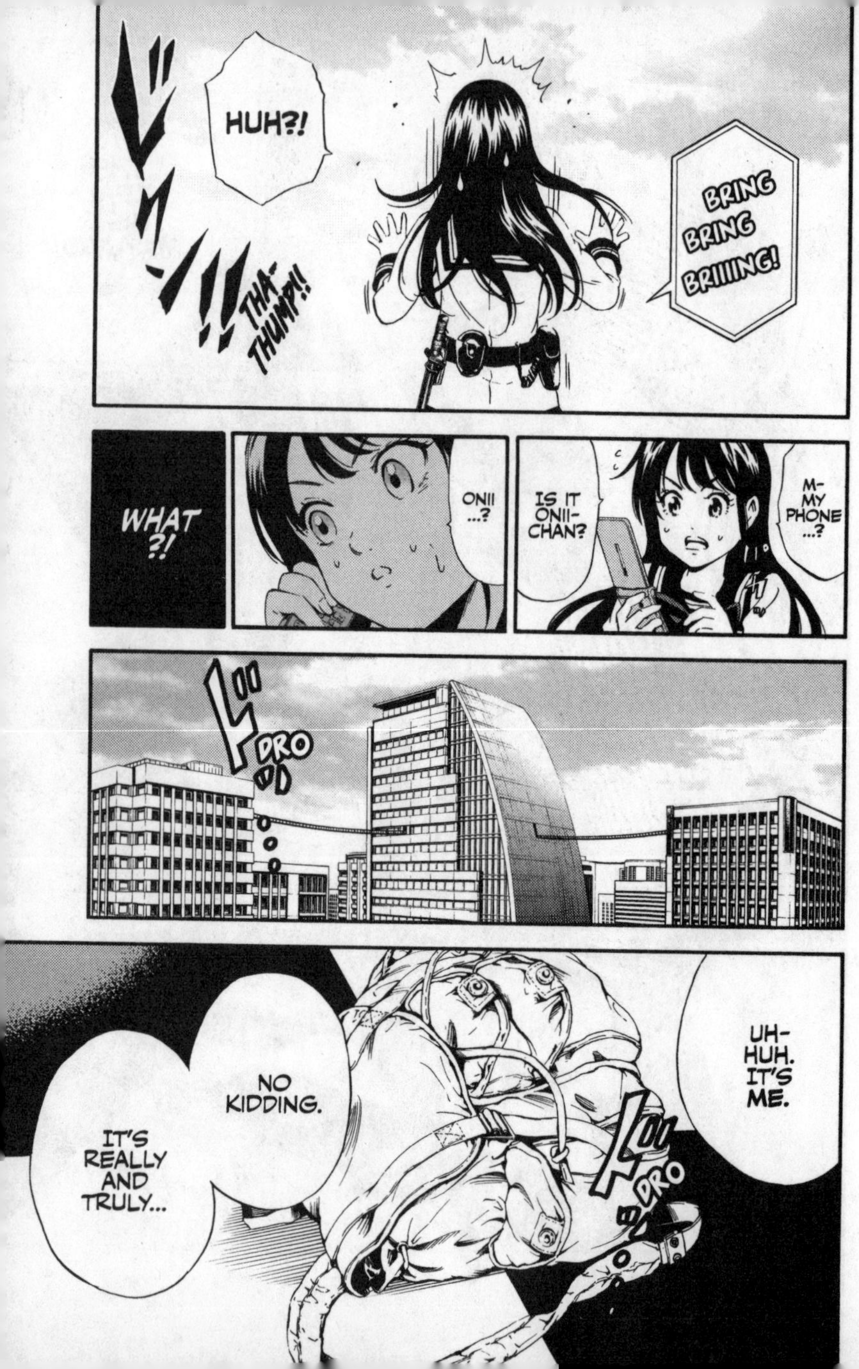
BRING BRING BRIIIING!
HUH?!
THA-THUMP!!
M-MY PHONE ...?
IS IT ONII-CHAN?
ONII ...?
WHAT ?!
DRO OO
UH-HUH. IT'S ME.
DRO OO
NO KIDDING.
IT'S REALLY AND TRULY...

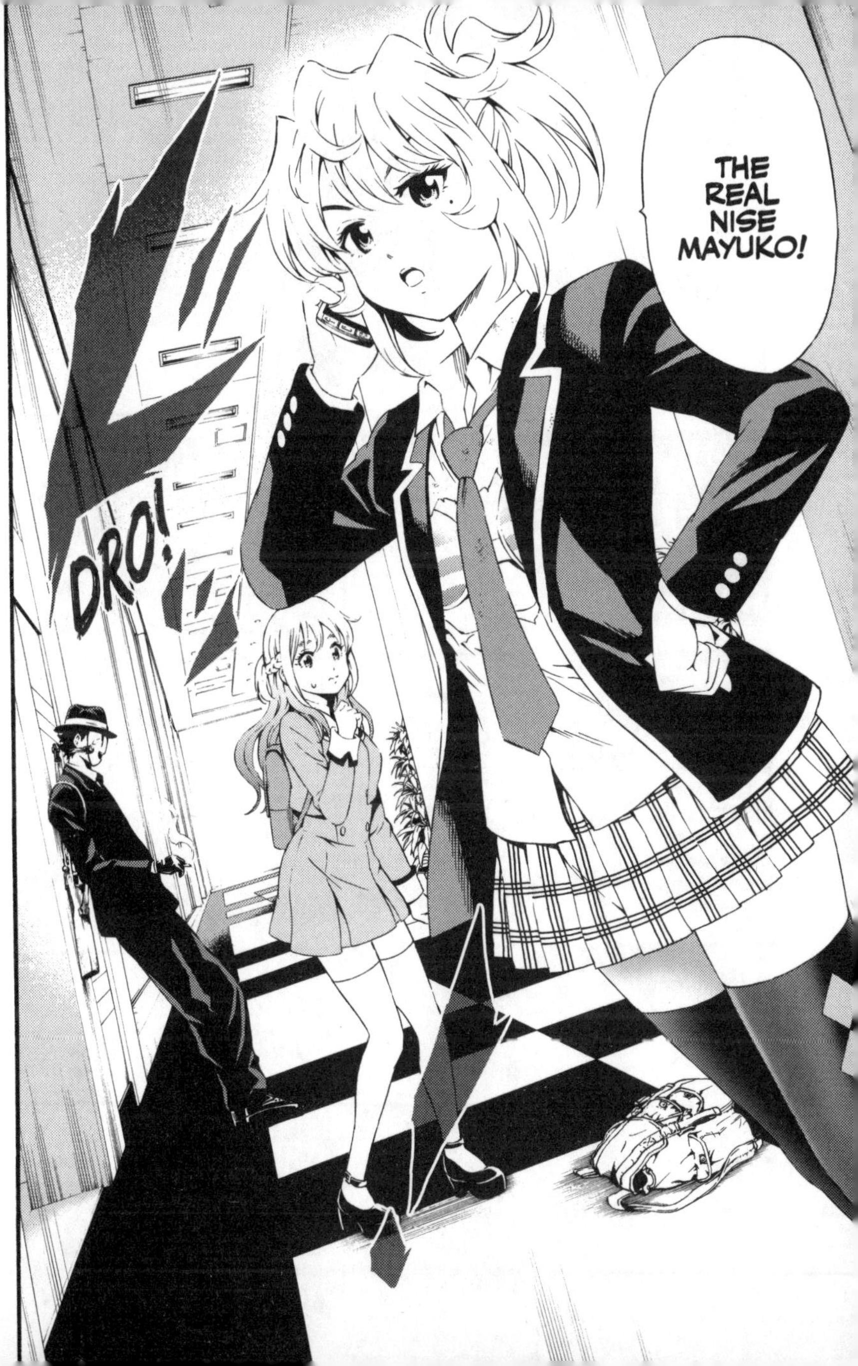
THE REAL NISE MAYUKO!
DRO!

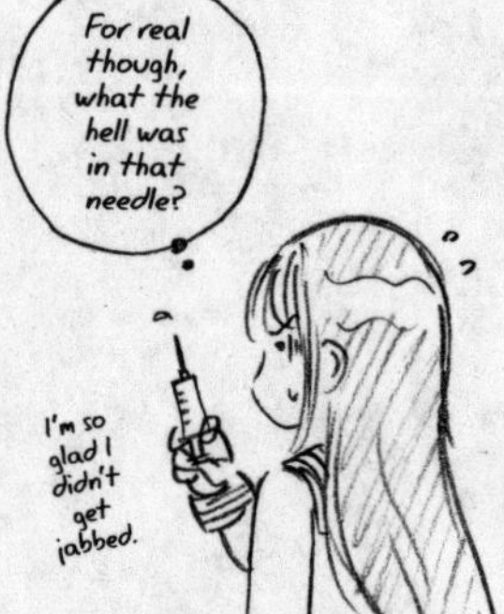
For real though, what the hell was in that needle?
I'm so glad I didn't get jabbed.

HIGH-RISE INVASION

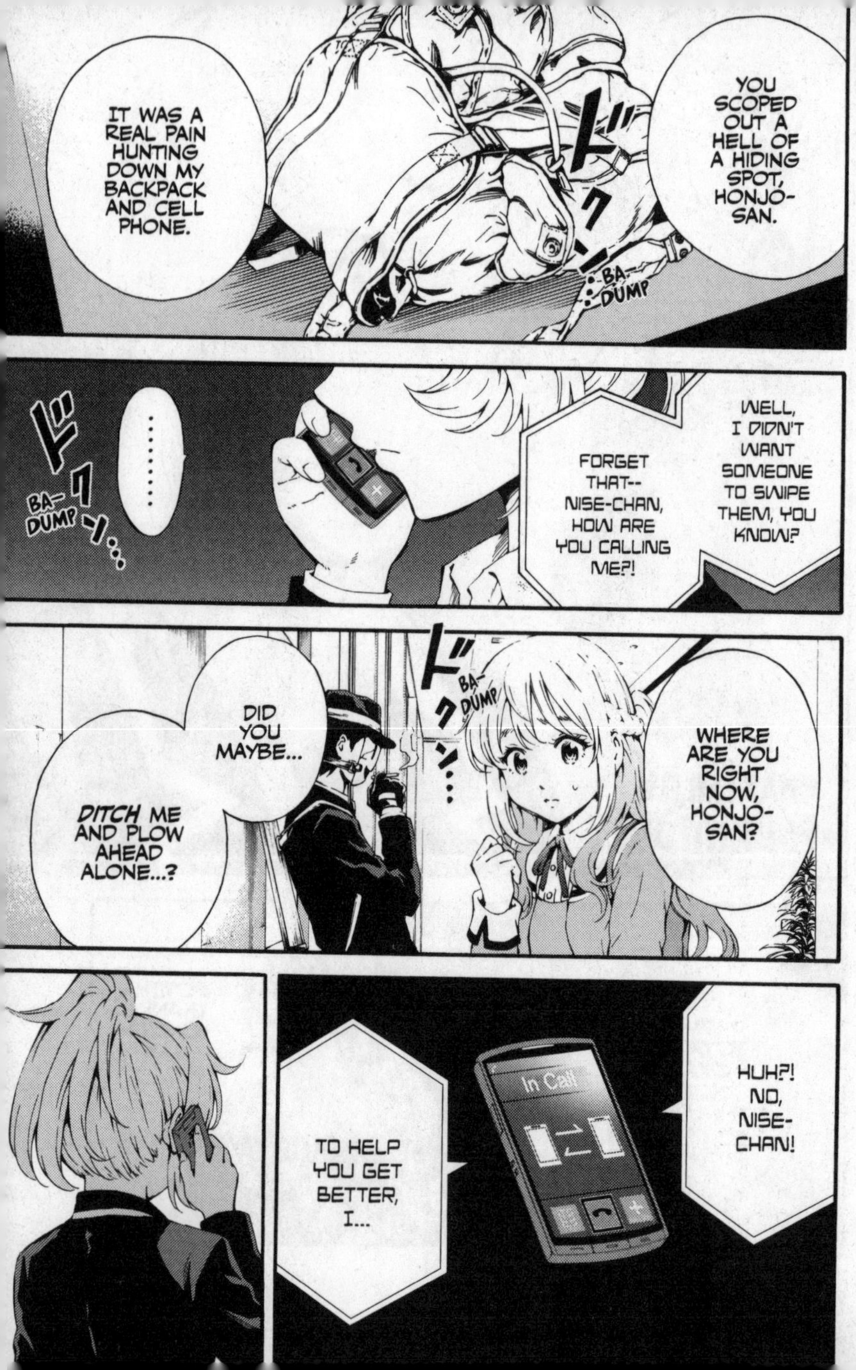
YOU SCOPED OUT A HELL OF A HIDING SPOT, HONJO-SAN.
ドクン
BA-DUMP
IT WAS A REAL PAIN HUNTING DOWN MY BACKPACK AND CELL PHONE.
WELL, I DIDN'T WANT SOMEONE TO SWIPE THEM, YOU KNOW?
FORGET THAT-- NISE-CHAN, HOW ARE YOU CALLING ME?!
......
ドクン...
BA-DUMP
WHERE ARE YOU RIGHT NOW, HONJO-SAN?
ドクン...
BA-DUMP
DID YOU MAYBE...
DITCH ME AND PLOW AHEAD ALONE...?
HUH?! NO, NISE-CHAN!
In Call
TO HELP YOU GET BETTER, I...

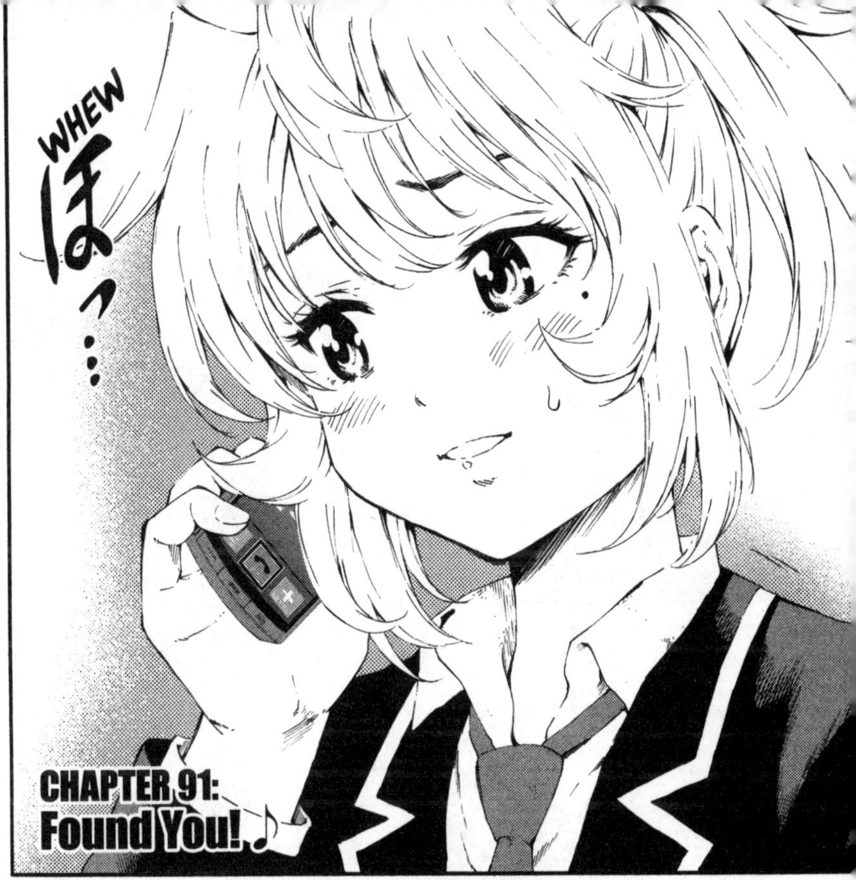
WHEW
ほっ…
CHAPTER 91:
Found You! ♪

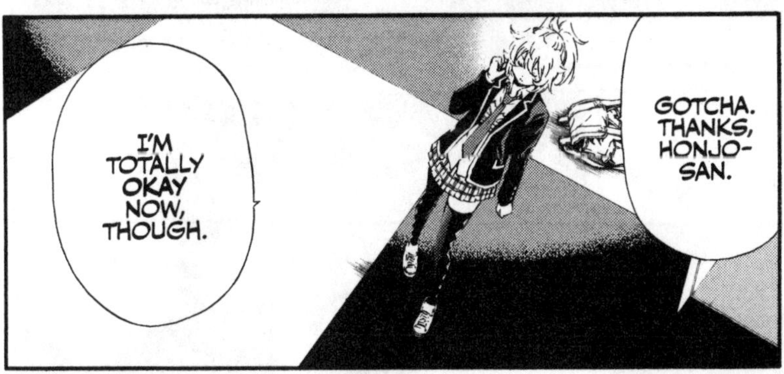
GOTCHA. THANKS, HONJO-SAN.
I'M TOTALLY OKAY NOW, THOUGH.

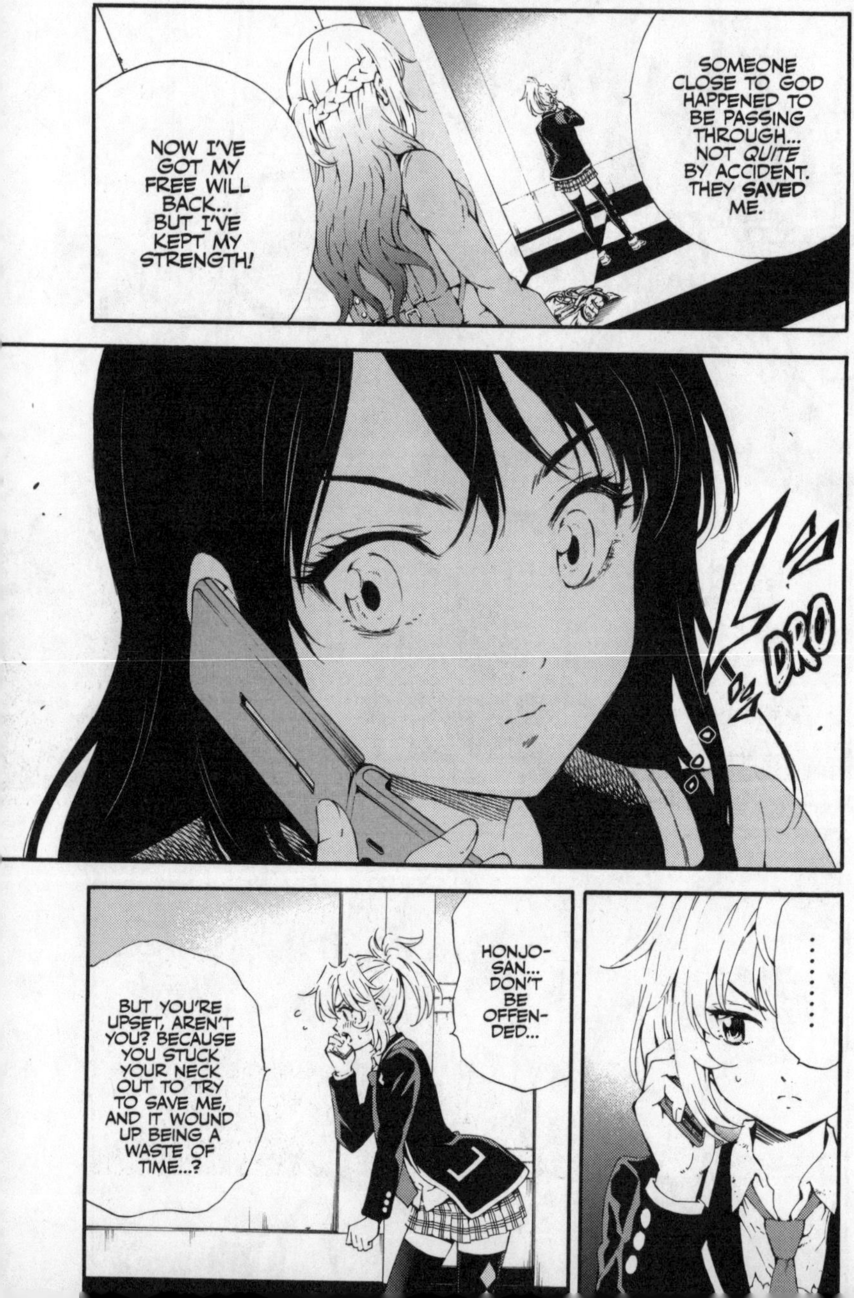
SOMEONE CLOSE TO GOD HAPPENED TO BE PASSING THROUGH... NOT *QUITE* BY ACCIDENT. THEY **SAVED** ME.
NOW I'VE GOT MY FREE WILL BACK... BUT I'VE KEPT MY STRENGTH!
DRO
....
HONJO-SAN... DON'T BE OFFEND-ED...
BUT YOU'RE UPSET, AREN'T YOU? BECAUSE YOU STUCK YOUR NECK OUT TO TRY TO SAVE ME, AND IT WOUND UP BEING A WASTE OF TIME...?

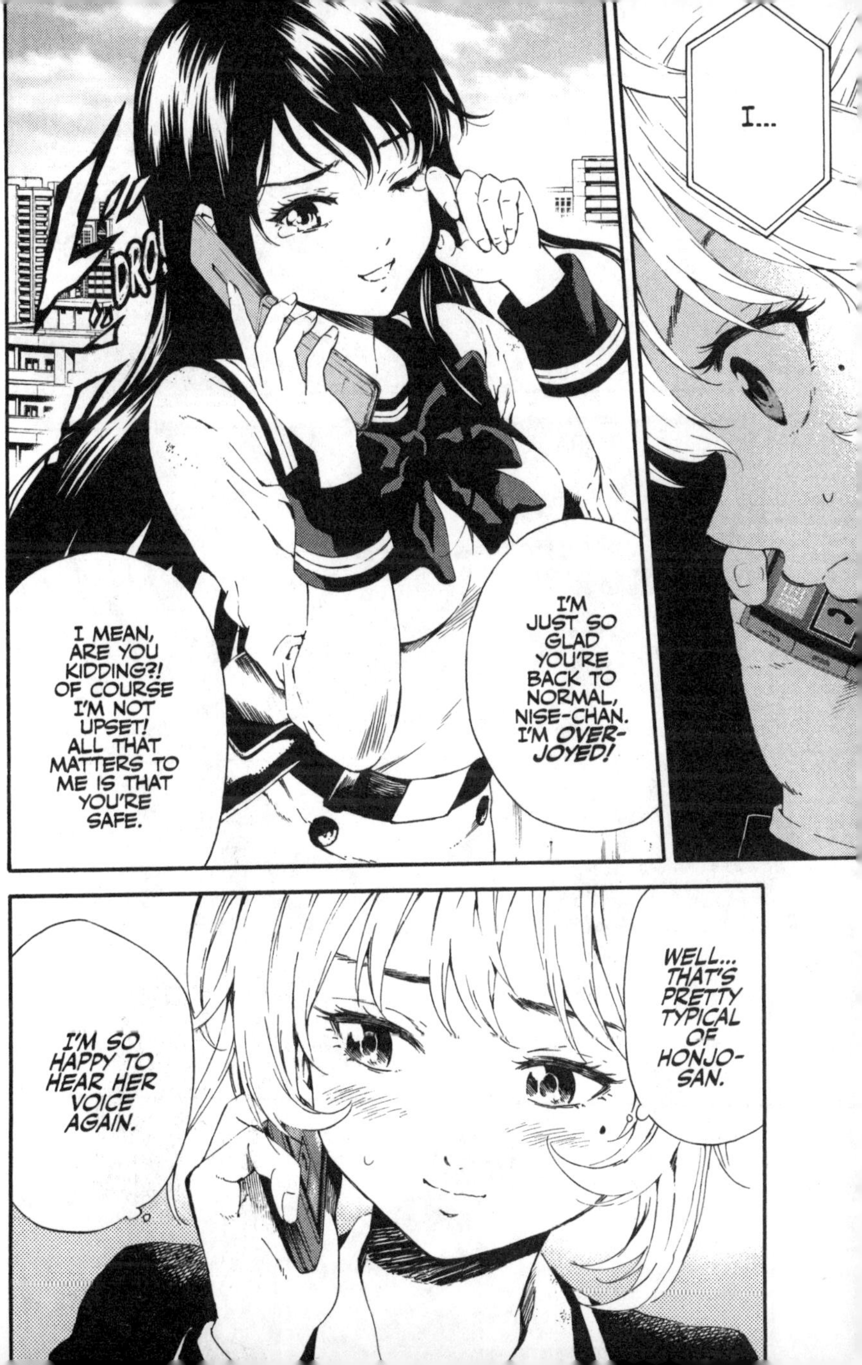
I...
I'M JUST SO GLAD YOU'RE BACK TO NORMAL, NISE-CHAN. I'M *OVER-JOYED!*
I MEAN, ARE YOU KIDDING?! OF COURSE I'M NOT UPSET! ALL THAT MATTERS TO ME IS THAT YOU'RE SAFE.
DRO!
WELL... THAT'S PRETTY TYPICAL OF HONJO-SAN.
I'M SO HAPPY TO HEAR HER VOICE AGAIN.

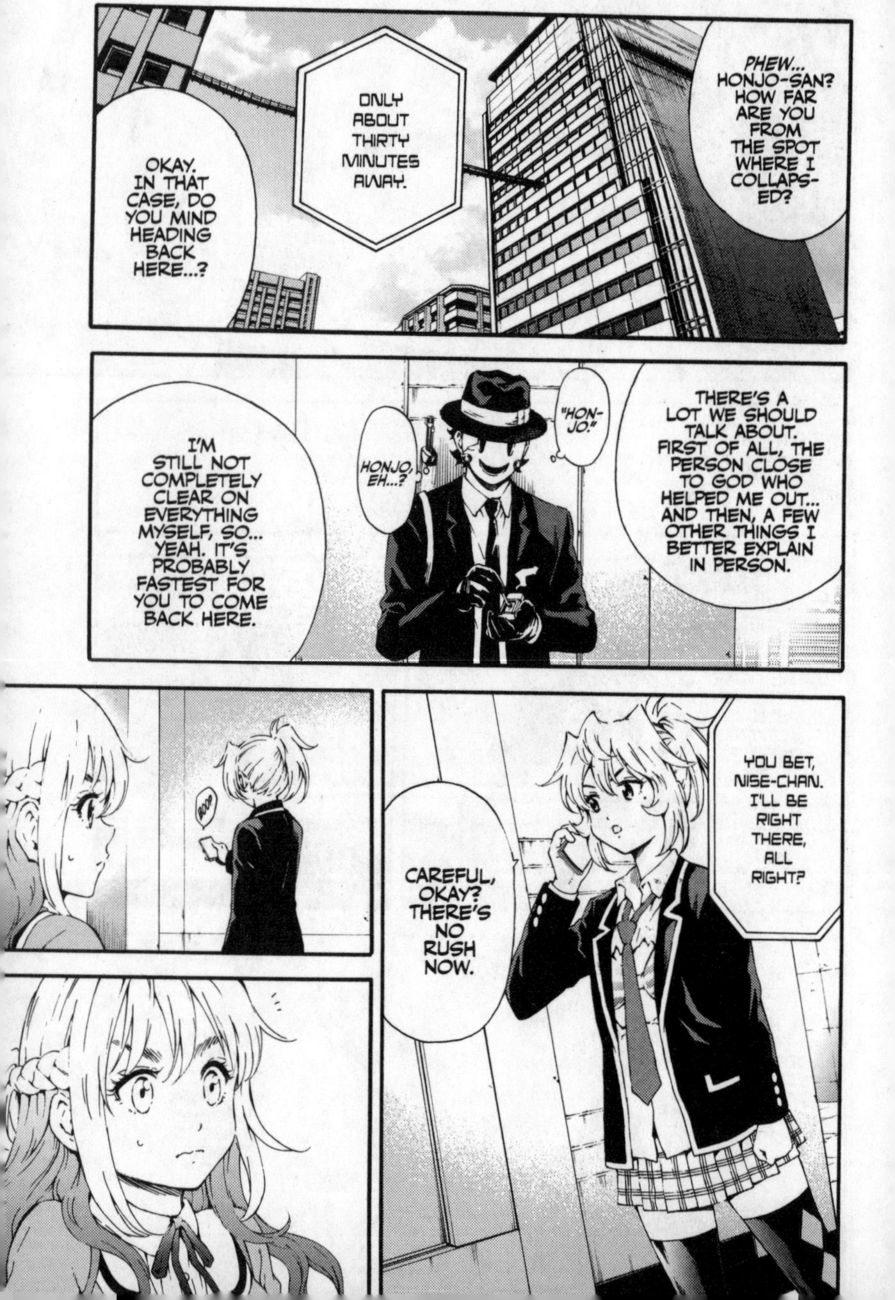
PHEW... HONJO-SAN? HOW FAR ARE YOU FROM THE SPOT WHERE I COLLAPSED?
ONLY ABOUT THIRTY MINUTES AWAY.
OKAY. IN THAT CASE, DO YOU MIND HEADING BACK HERE...?
THERE'S A LOT WE SHOULD TALK ABOUT. FIRST OF ALL, THE PERSON CLOSE TO GOD WHO HELPED ME OUT... AND THEN, A FEW OTHER THINGS I BETTER EXPLAIN IN PERSON.
"HONJO."
HONJO, EH...?
I'M STILL NOT COMPLETELY CLEAR ON EVERYTHING MYSELF, SO... YEAH. IT'S PROBABLY FASTEST FOR YOU TO COME BACK HERE.
YOU BET, NISE-CHAN. I'LL BE RIGHT THERE, ALL RIGHT?
CAREFUL, OKAY? THERE'S NO RUSH NOW.
BOOP

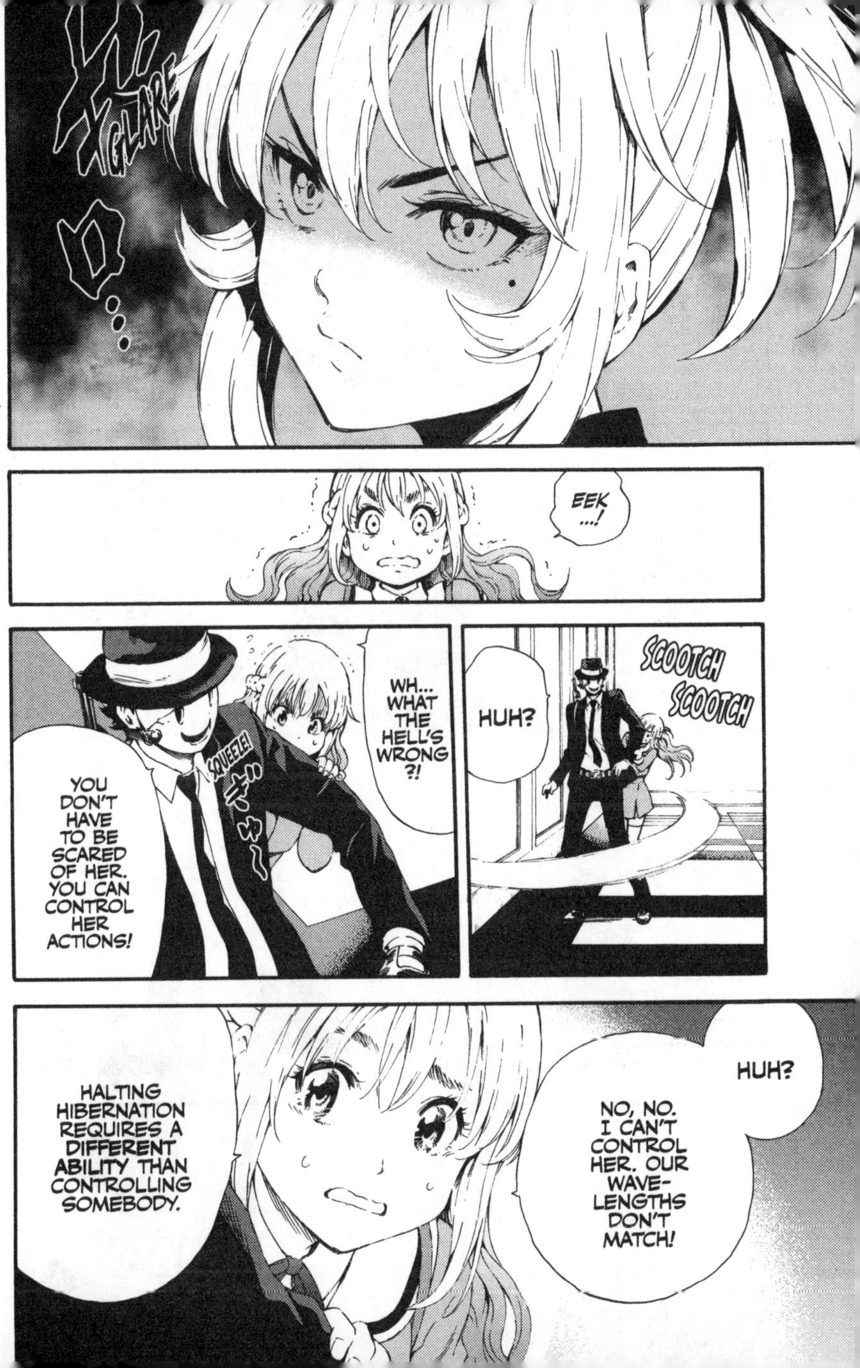
GLARE
EEK ...!
SCOOTCH
SCOOTCH
HUH?
WH... WHAT THE HELL'S WRONG?!
SQUEEZE!
YOU DON'T HAVE TO BE SCARED OF HER. YOU CAN CONTROL HER ACTIONS!
HUH?
NO, NO. I CAN'T CONTROL HER. OUR WAVE-LENGTHS DON'T MATCH!
HALTING HIBERNATION REQUIRES A DIFFERENT ABILITY THAN CONTROLLING SOMEBODY.

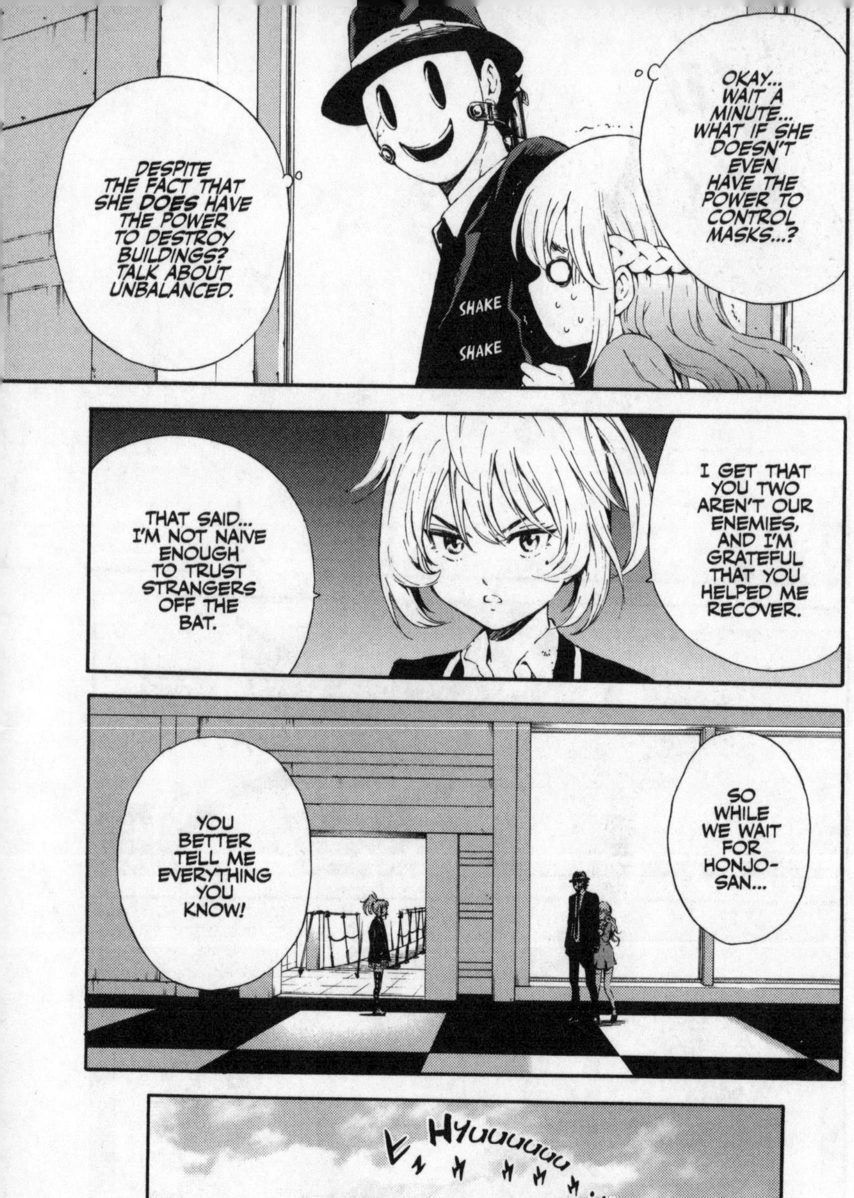
OKAY... WAIT A MINUTE... WHAT IF SHE DOESN'T EVEN HAVE THE POWER TO CONTROL MASKS...?
DESPITE THE FACT THAT SHE DOES HAVE THE POWER TO DESTROY BUILDINGS? TALK ABOUT UNBALANCED.
SHAKE
SHAKE
I GET THAT YOU TWO AREN'T OUR ENEMIES, AND I'M GRATEFUL THAT YOU HELPED ME RECOVER.
THAT SAID... I'M NOT NAIVE ENOUGH TO TRUST STRANGERS OFF THE BAT.
SO WHILE WE WAIT FOR HONJO-SAN...
YOU BETTER TELL ME EVERYTHING YOU KNOW!
HYUUUUUUU...

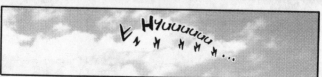

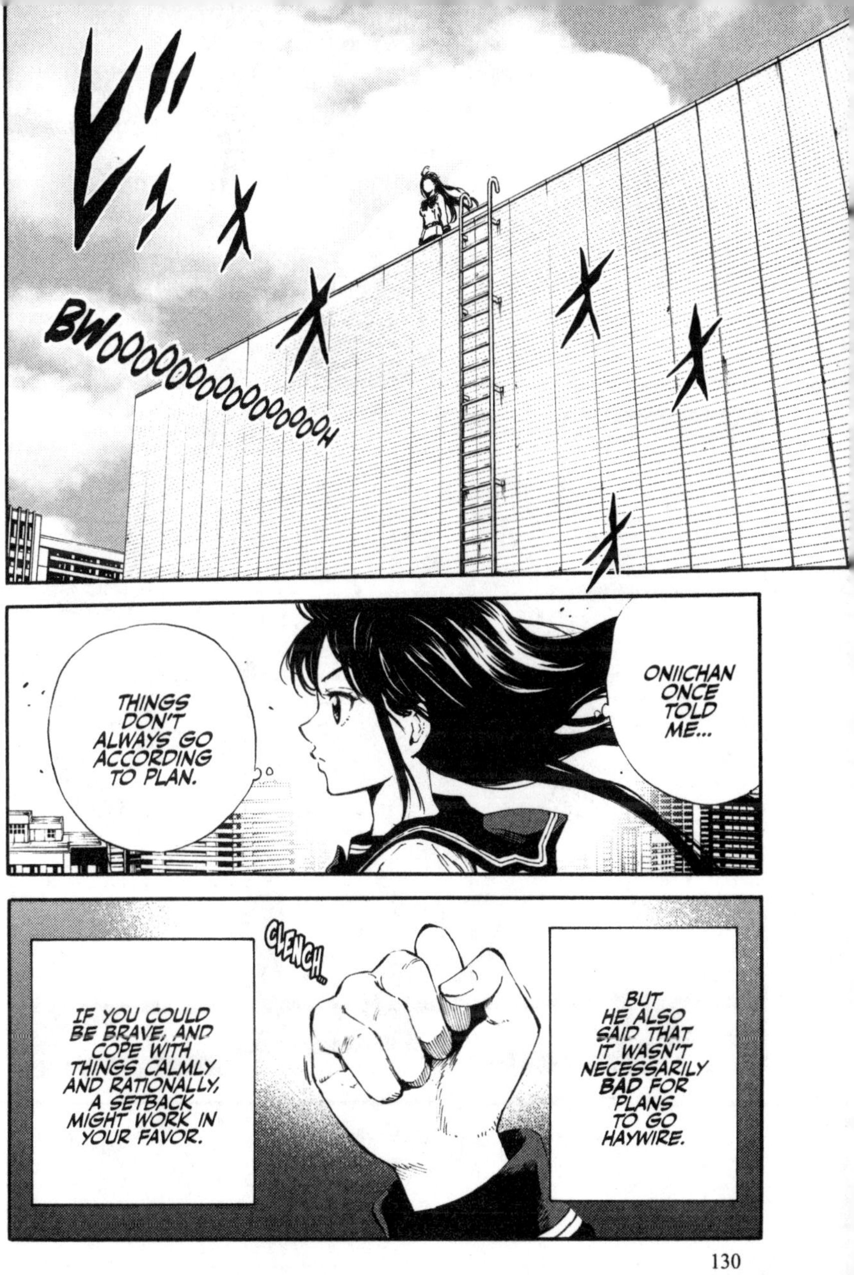

ビュォ
BWOOOOOOOOOOOOOOOH
ONIICHAN ONCE TOLD ME...
THINGS DON'T ALWAYS GO ACCORDING TO PLAN.
CLENCH...
BUT HE ALSO SAID THAT IT WASN'T NECESSARILY BAD FOR PLANS TO GO HAYWIRE.
IF YOU COULD BE BRAVE, AND COPE WITH THINGS CALMLY AND RATIONALLY, A SETBACK MIGHT WORK IN YOUR FAVOR.

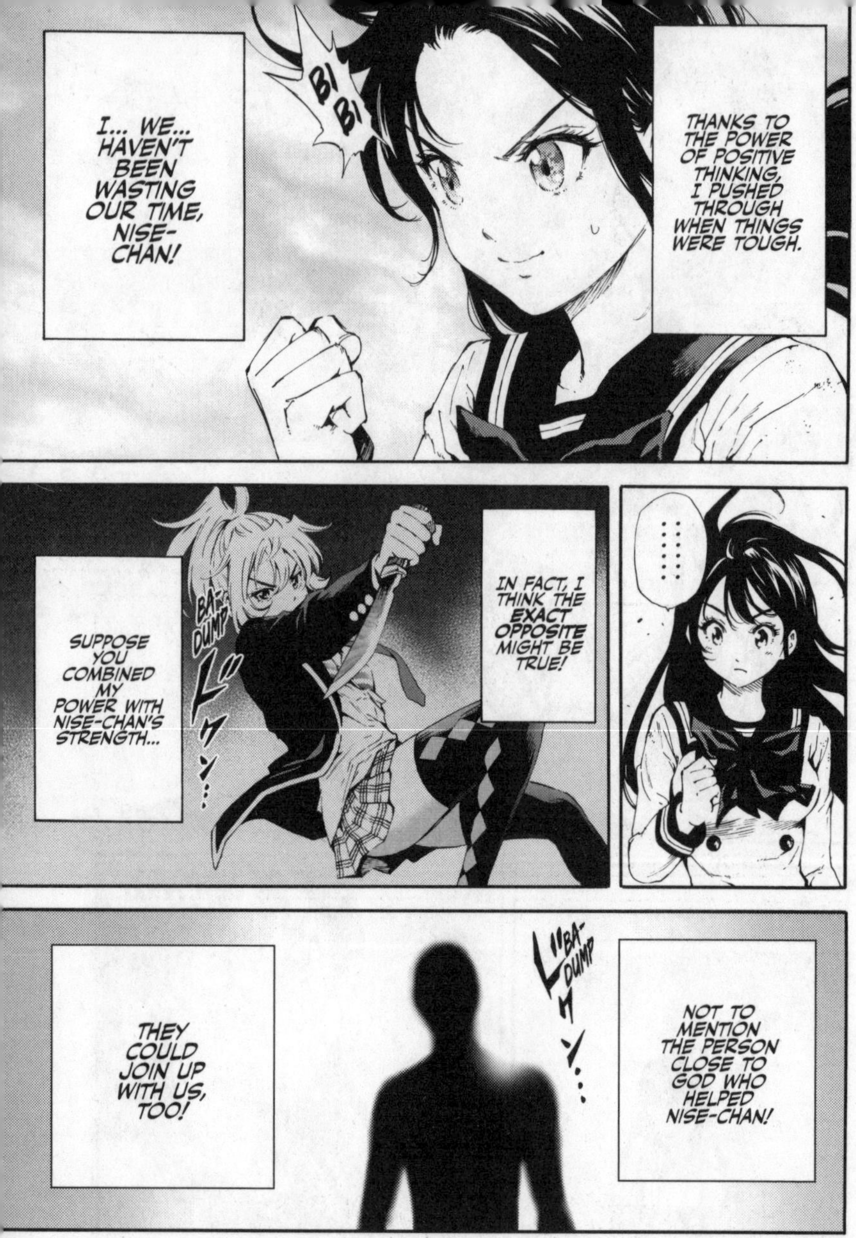
THANKS TO THE POWER OF POSITIVE THINKING, I PUSHED THROUGH WHEN THINGS WERE TOUGH.
BI BI
I... WE... HAVEN'T BEEN WASTING OUR TIME, NISE-CHAN!
......
IN FACT, I THINK THE EXACT OPPOSITE MIGHT BE TRUE!
BA-DUMP
SUPPOSE YOU COMBINED MY POWER WITH NISE-CHAN'S STRENGTH...
NOT TO MENTION THE PERSON CLOSE TO GOD WHO HELPED NISE-CHAN!
BA-DUMP
THEY COULD JOIN UP WITH US, TOO!

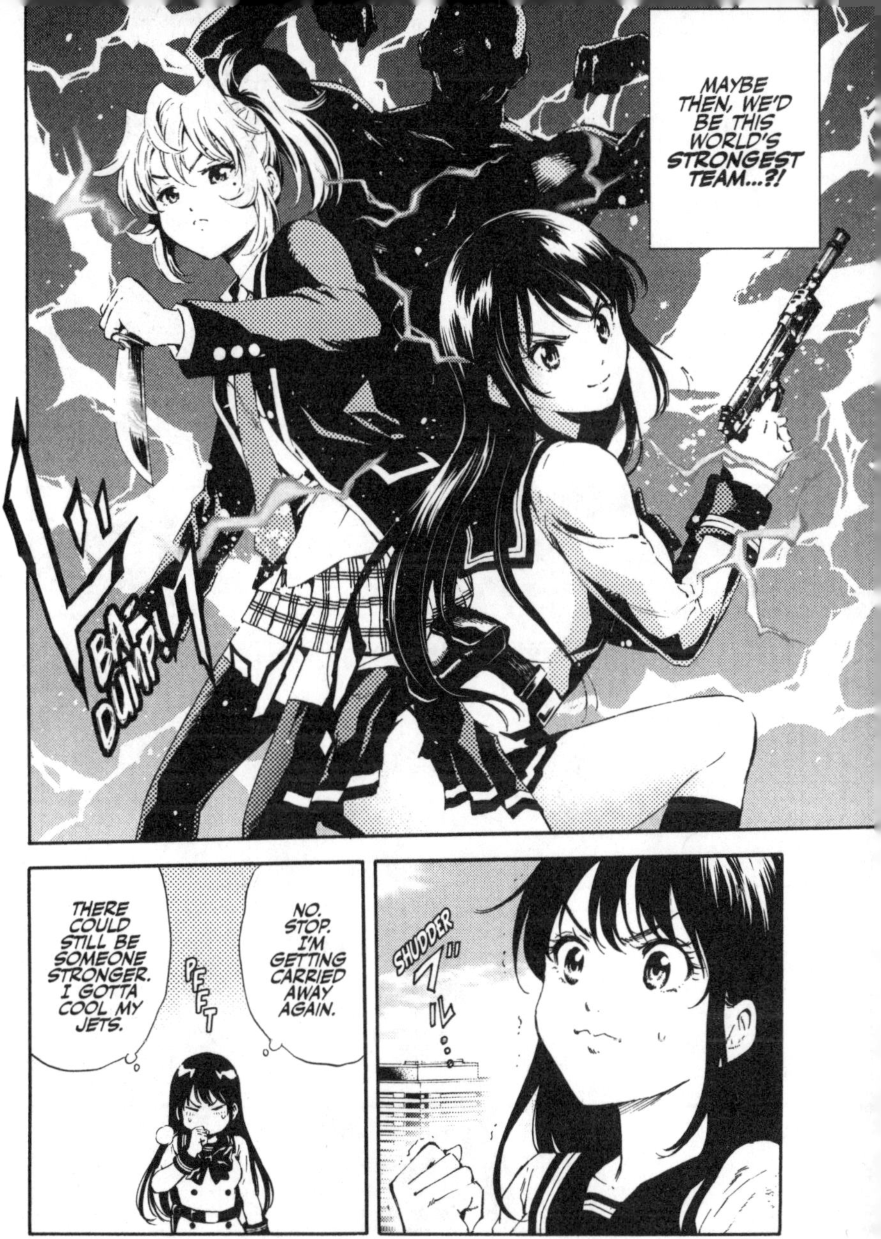
MAYBE THEN, WE'D BE THIS WORLD'S STRONGEST TEAM...?!
BA-DUMP!!
SHUDDER
NO. STOP. I'M GETTING CARRIED AWAY AGAIN.
THERE COULD STILL BE SOMEONE STRONGER. I GOTTA COOL MY JETS.
PFFT

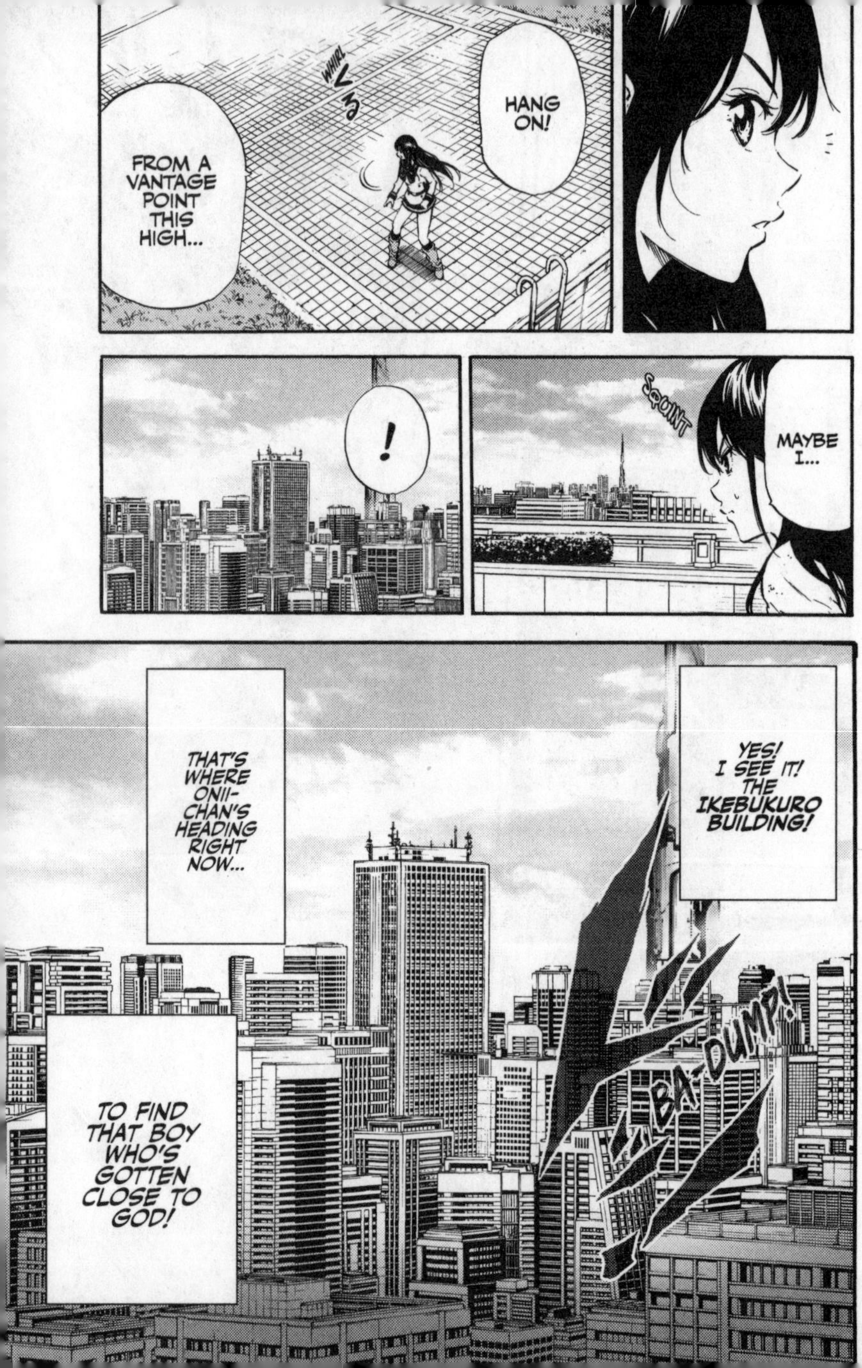
HANG ON!
WHIRL
くる
FROM A VANTAGE POINT THIS HIGH...
SQUINT
MAYBE I...
!
YES! I SEE IT! THE IKEBUKURO BUILDING!
BA-DUMP!
THAT'S WHERE ONII-CHAN'S HEADING RIGHT NOW...
TO FIND THAT BOY WHO'S GOTTEN CLOSE TO GOD!

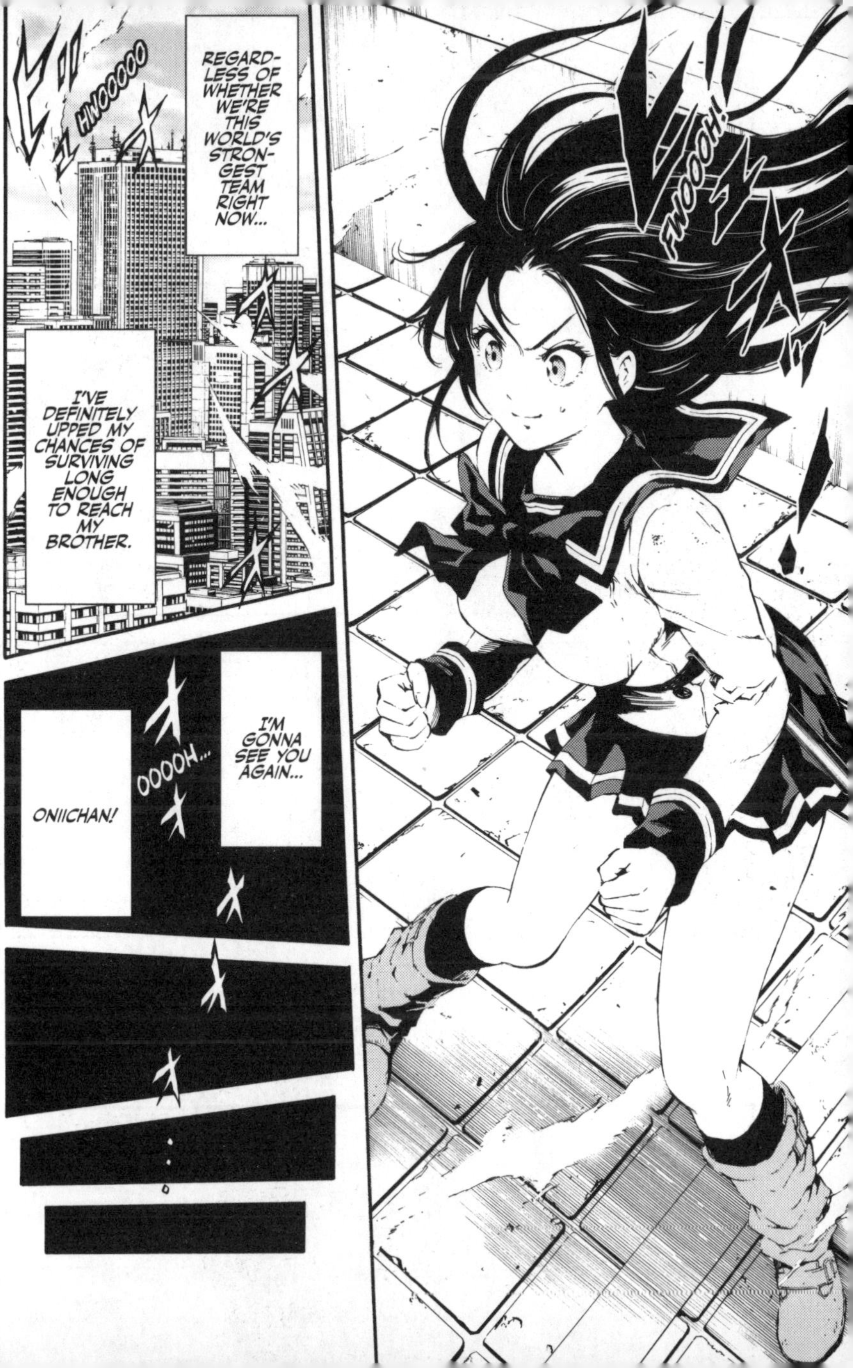
FWOOOOH!
REGARDLESS OF WHETHER WE'RE THIS WORLD'S STRONGEST TEAM RIGHT NOW...
HWOOOOO
I'VE DEFINITELY UPPED MY CHANCES OF SURVIVING LONG ENOUGH TO REACH MY BROTHER.
I'M GONNA SEE YOU AGAIN...
OOOOH...
ONIICHAN!

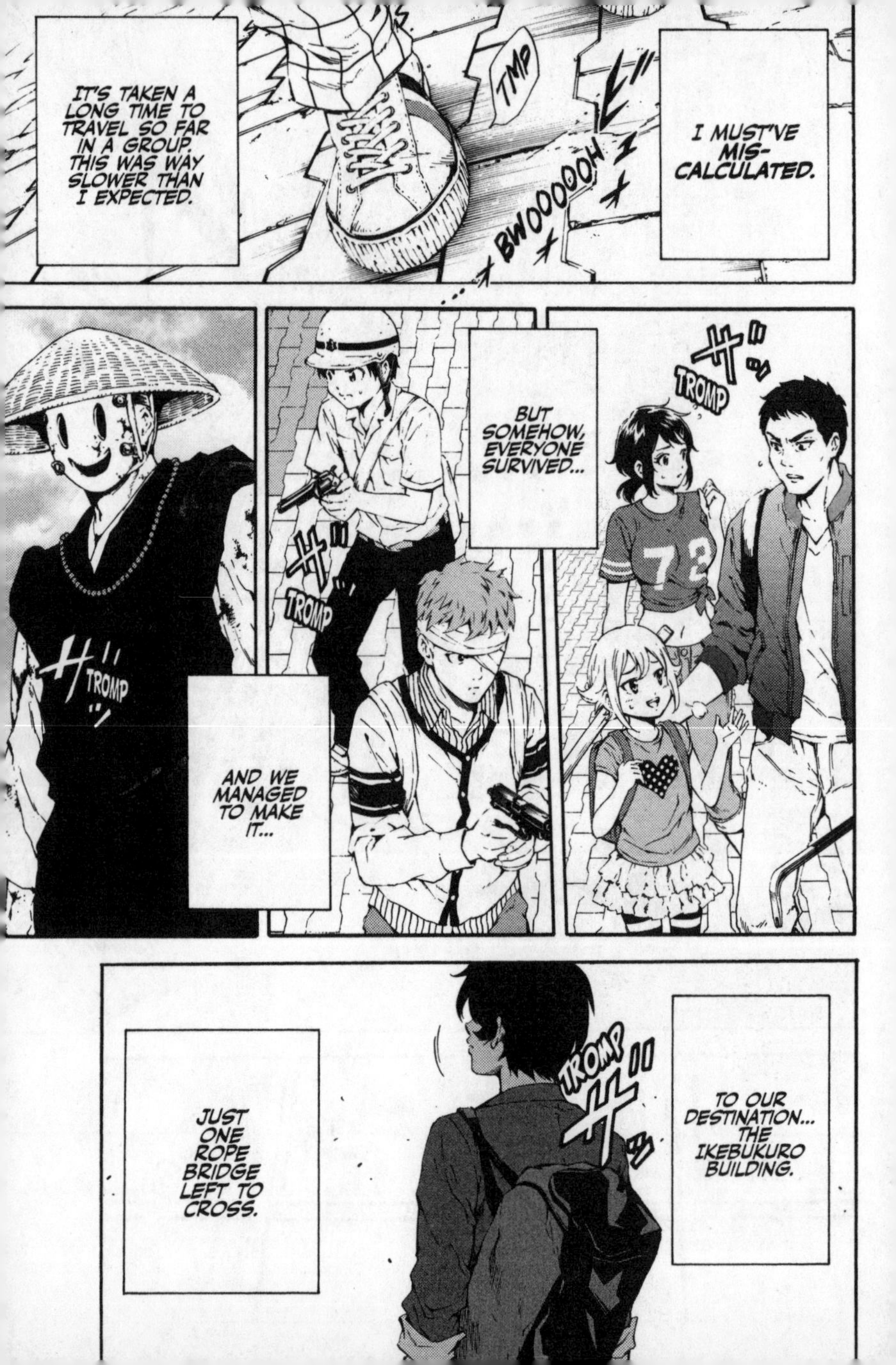

I MUST'VE MIS-CALCULATED.
TMP
BWOOOOOH
IT'S TAKEN A LONG TIME TO TRAVEL SO FAR IN A GROUP. THIS WAS WAY SLOWER THAN I EXPECTED.
TROMP
BUT SOMEHOW, EVERYONE SURVIVED...
TROMP
AND WE MANAGED TO MAKE IT...
TROMP
TO OUR DESTINATION... THE IKEBUKURO BUILDING.
TROMP
JUST ONE ROPE BRIDGE LEFT TO CROSS.

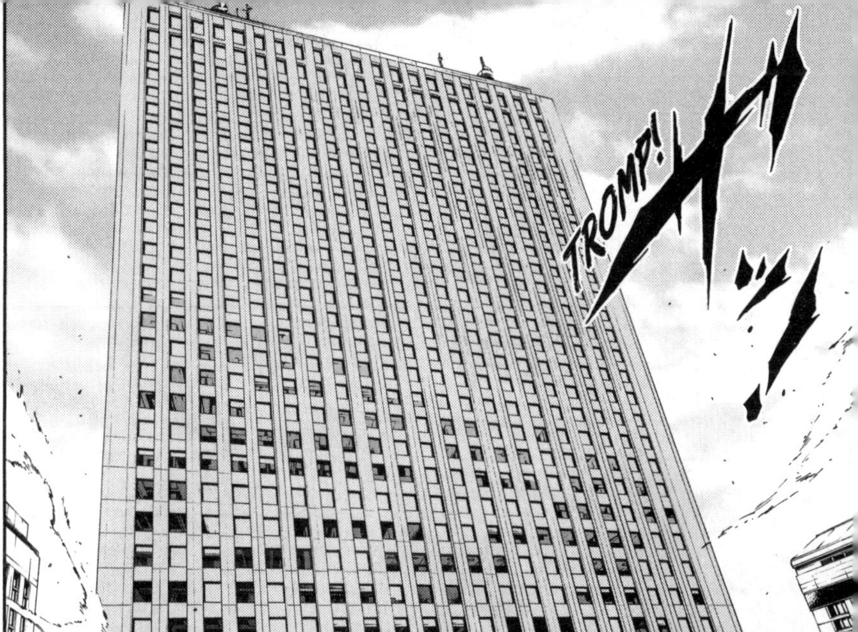
TROMP!

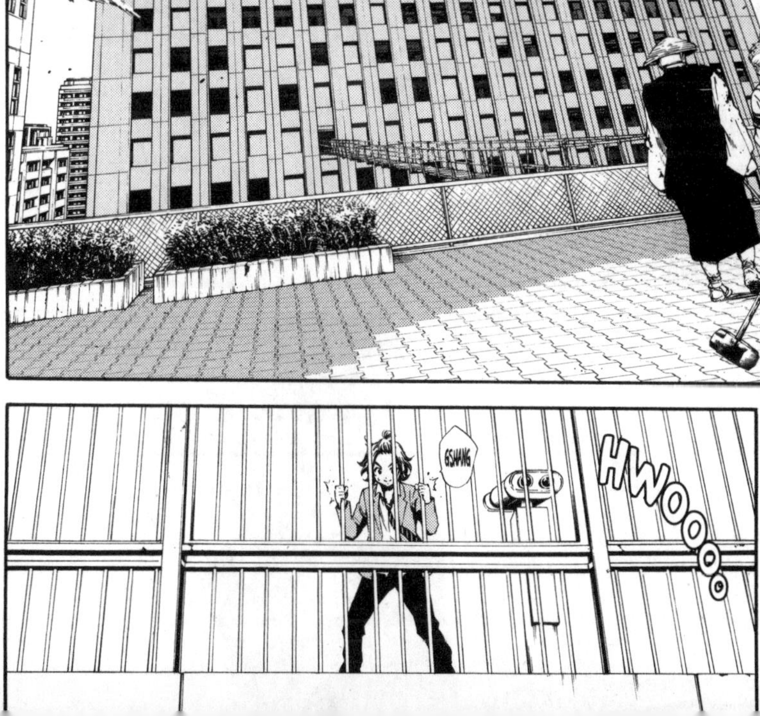
HWOOOOO
GSHANG

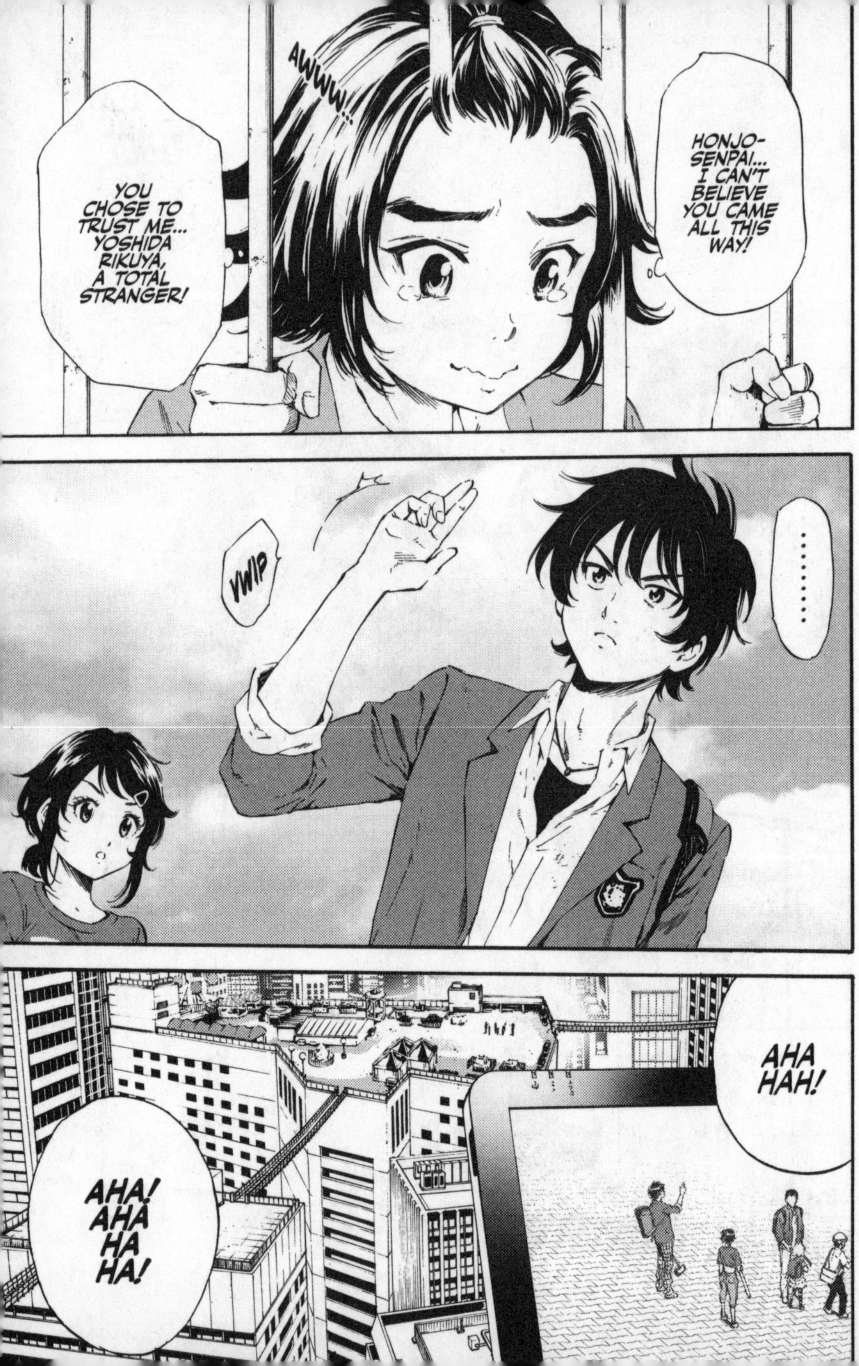
HONJO-SENPAI... I CAN'T BELIEVE YOU CAME ALL THIS WAY!
AWWW...!
YOU CHOSE TO TRUST ME... YOSHIDA RIKUYA, A TOTAL STRANGER!
....
VWIP
AHA HAH!
AHA! AHA HA HA!

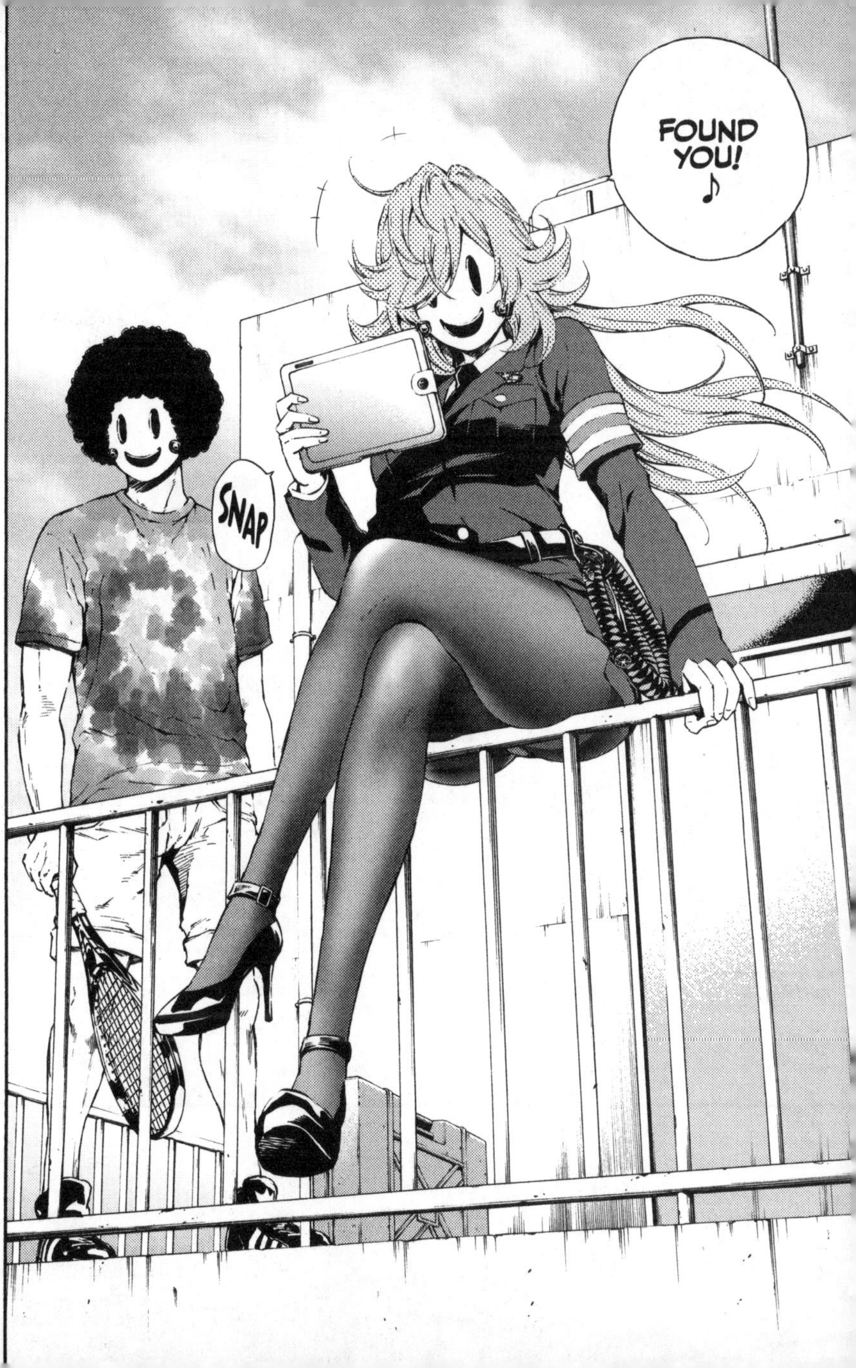
FOUND YOU! ♪
SNAP

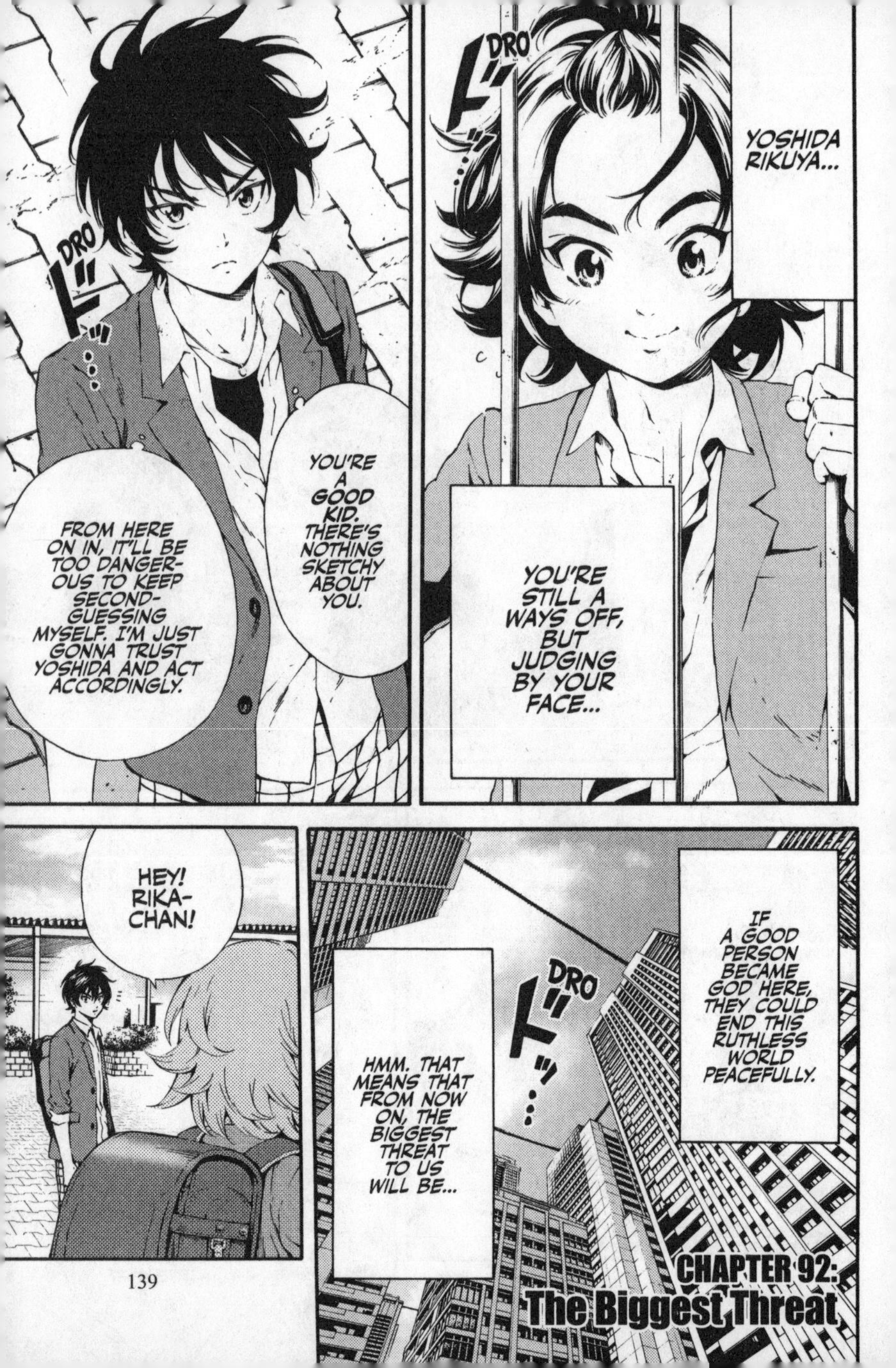
DRO
YOSHIDA RIKUYA...
YOU'RE STILL A WAYS OFF, BUT JUDGING BY YOUR FACE...
DRO
YOU'RE A GOOD KID. THERE'S NOTHING SKETCHY ABOUT YOU.
FROM HERE ON IN, IT'LL BE TOO DANGER-OUS TO KEEP SECOND-GUESSING MYSELF. I'M JUST GONNA TRUST YOSHIDA AND ACT ACCORDINGLY.
IF A GOOD PERSON BECAME GOD HERE, THEY COULD END THIS RUTHLESS WORLD PEACEFULLY.
DRO
HMM. THAT MEANS THAT FROM NOW ON, THE BIGGEST THREAT TO US WILL BE...
CHAPTER 92: The Biggest Threat
HEY! RIKA-CHAN!

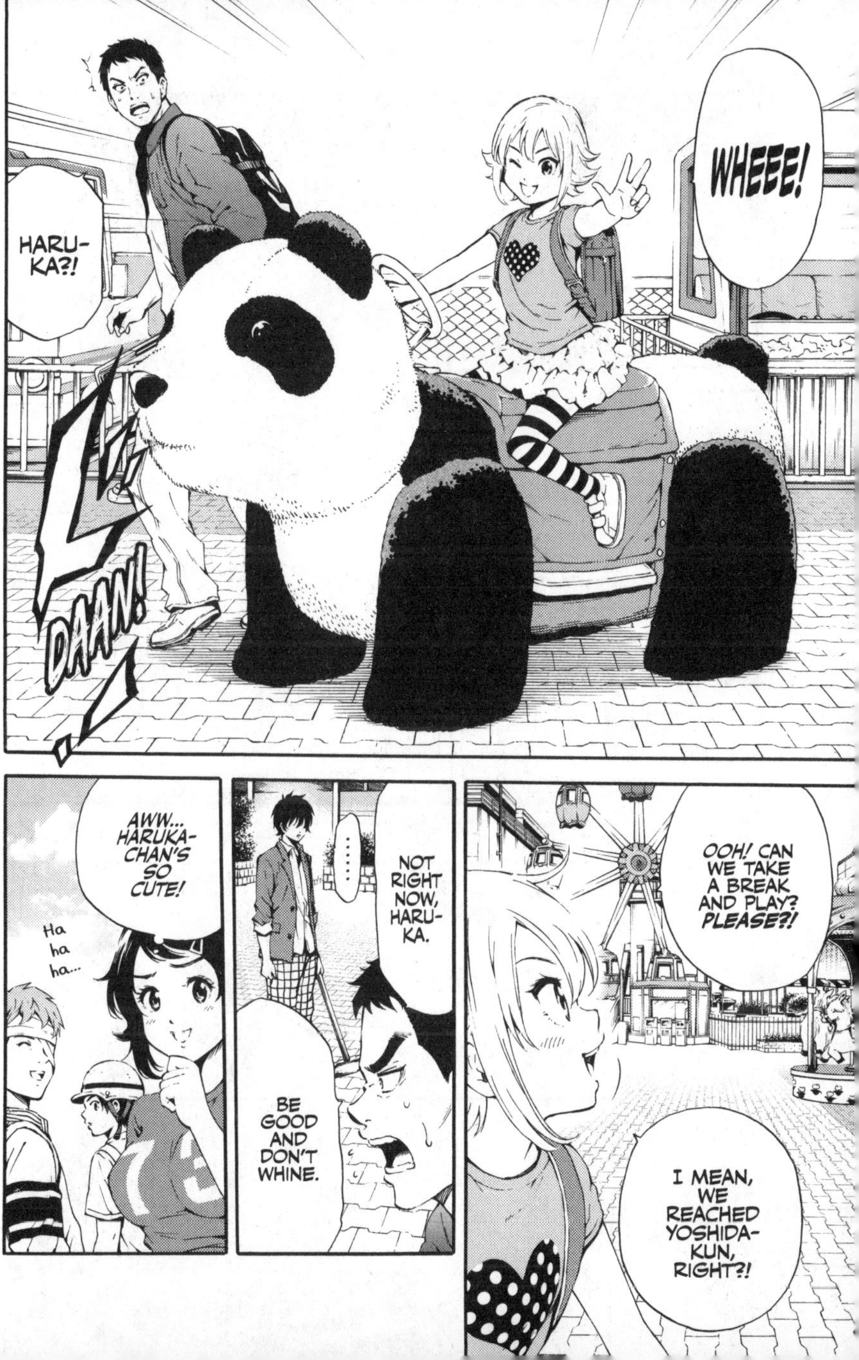
WHEEE!
HARU-KA?!
DAAN!
OOH! CAN WE TAKE A BREAK AND PLAY? PLEASE?!
I MEAN, WE REACHED YOSHIDA-KUN, RIGHT?!
NOT RIGHT NOW, HARU-KA.
......
BE GOOD AND DON'T WHINE.
AWW... HARUKA-CHAN'S SO CUTE!
Ha ha ha...

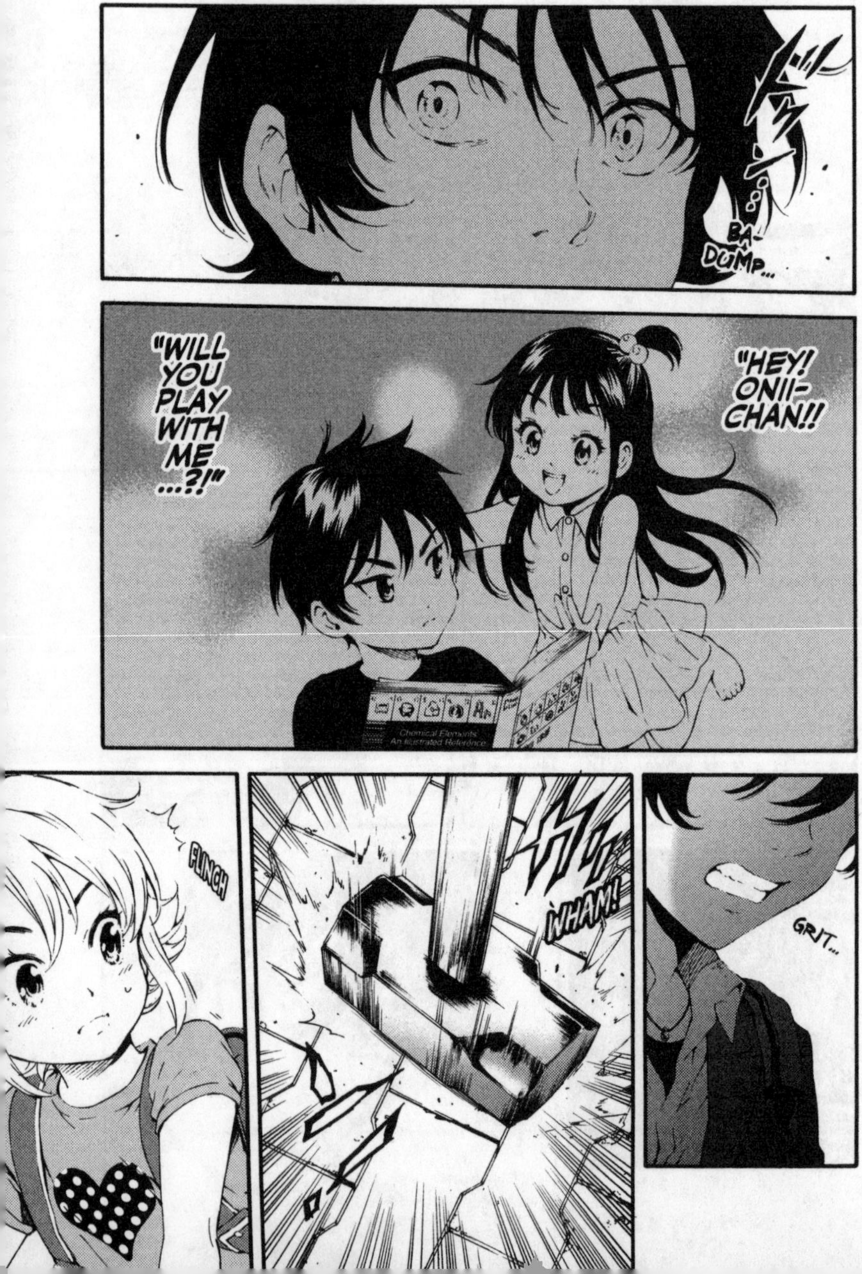
BA-DUMP...
"HEY! ONII-CHAN!!
"WILL YOU PLAY WITH ME ...?!"
Chemical Elements An Illustrated Reference
GRIT...
WHAM!
FLINCH

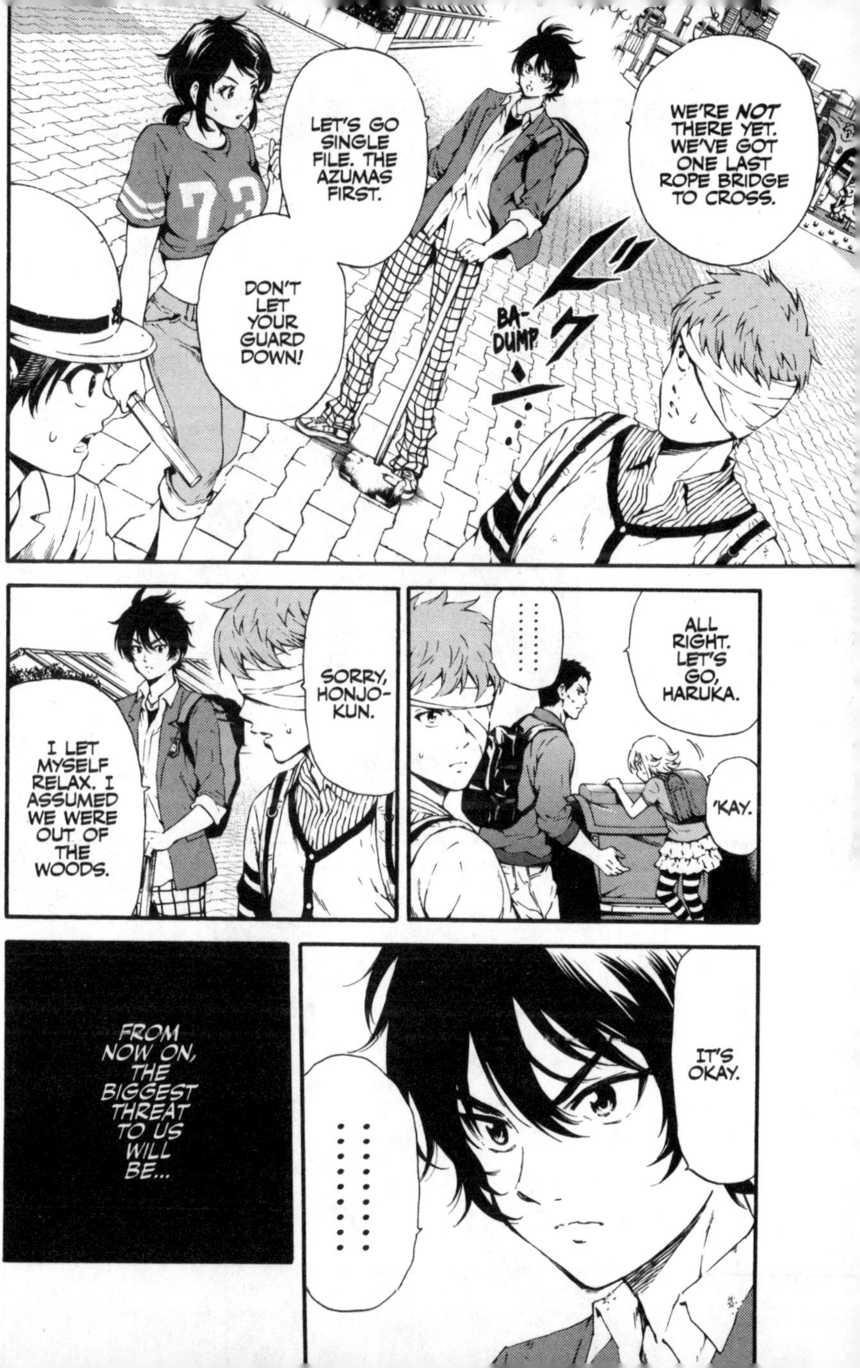
WE'RE NOT THERE YET. WE'VE GOT ONE LAST ROPE BRIDGE TO CROSS.
LET'S GO SINGLE FILE. THE AZUMAS FIRST.
DON'T LET YOUR GUARD DOWN!
BA-DUMP
ALL RIGHT. LET'S GO, HARUKA.
......
'KAY.
SORRY, HONJO-KUN.
I LET MYSELF RELAX. I ASSUMED WE WERE OUT OF THE WOODS.
IT'S OKAY.
......
FROM NOW ON, THE BIGGEST THREAT TO US WILL BE...

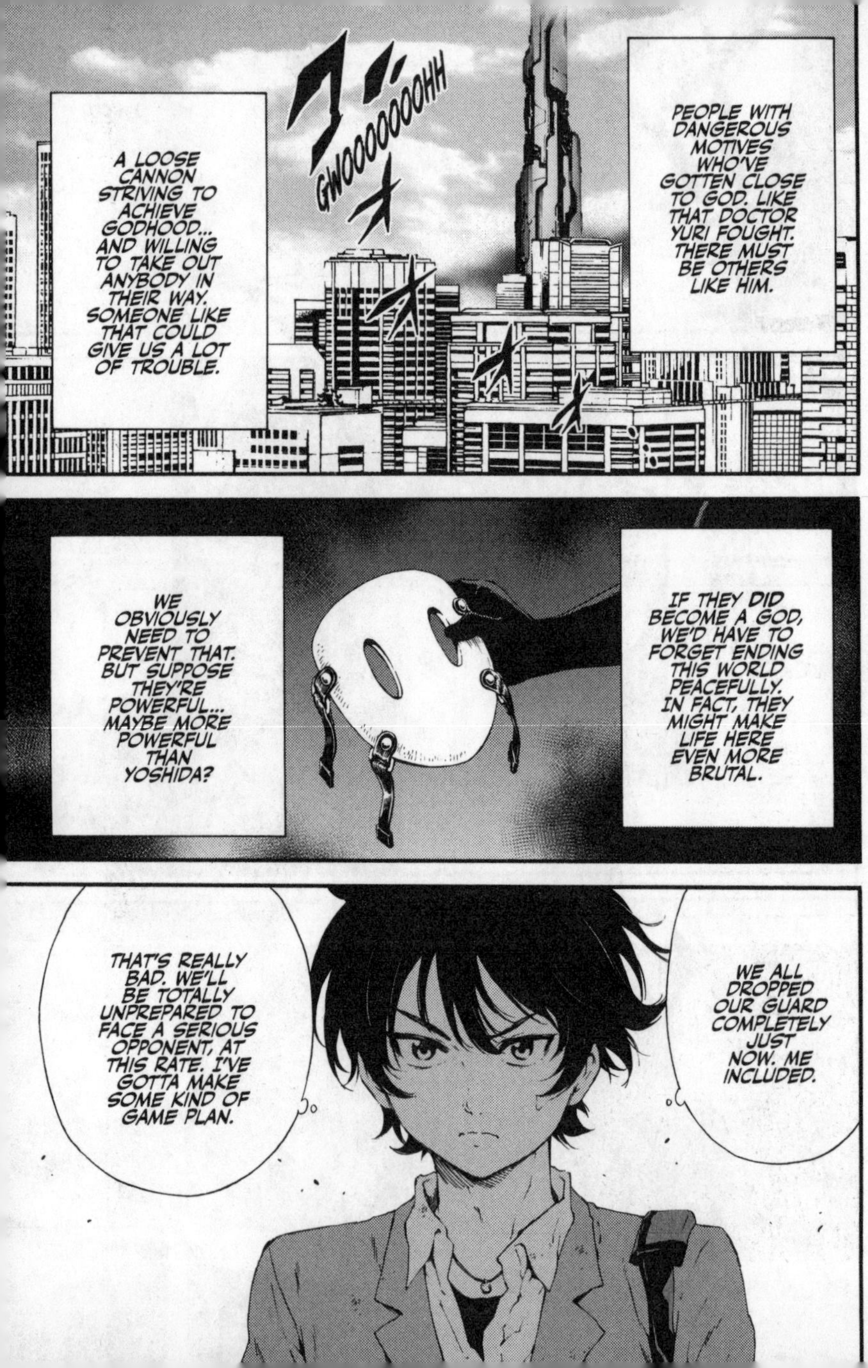
PEOPLE WITH DANGEROUS MOTIVES WHO'VE GOTTEN CLOSE TO GOD. LIKE THAT DOCTOR YURI FOUGHT. THERE MUST BE OTHERS LIKE HIM.
GWOOOOOOOHH
A LOOSE CANNON STRIVING TO ACHIEVE GODHOOD... AND WILLING TO TAKE OUT ANYBODY IN THEIR WAY. SOMEONE LIKE THAT COULD GIVE US A LOT OF TROUBLE.
IF THEY DID BECOME A GOD, WE'D HAVE TO FORGET ENDING THIS WORLD PEACEFULLY. IN FACT, THEY MIGHT MAKE LIFE HERE EVEN MORE BRUTAL.
WE OBVIOUSLY NEED TO PREVENT THAT. BUT SUPPOSE THEY'RE POWERFUL... MAYBE MORE POWERFUL THAN YOSHIDA?
WE ALL DROPPED OUR GUARD COMPLETELY JUST NOW. ME INCLUDED.
THAT'S REALLY BAD. WE'LL BE TOTALLY UNPREPARED TO FACE A SERIOUS OPPONENT, AT THIS RATE. I'VE GOTTA MAKE SOME KIND OF GAME PLAN.

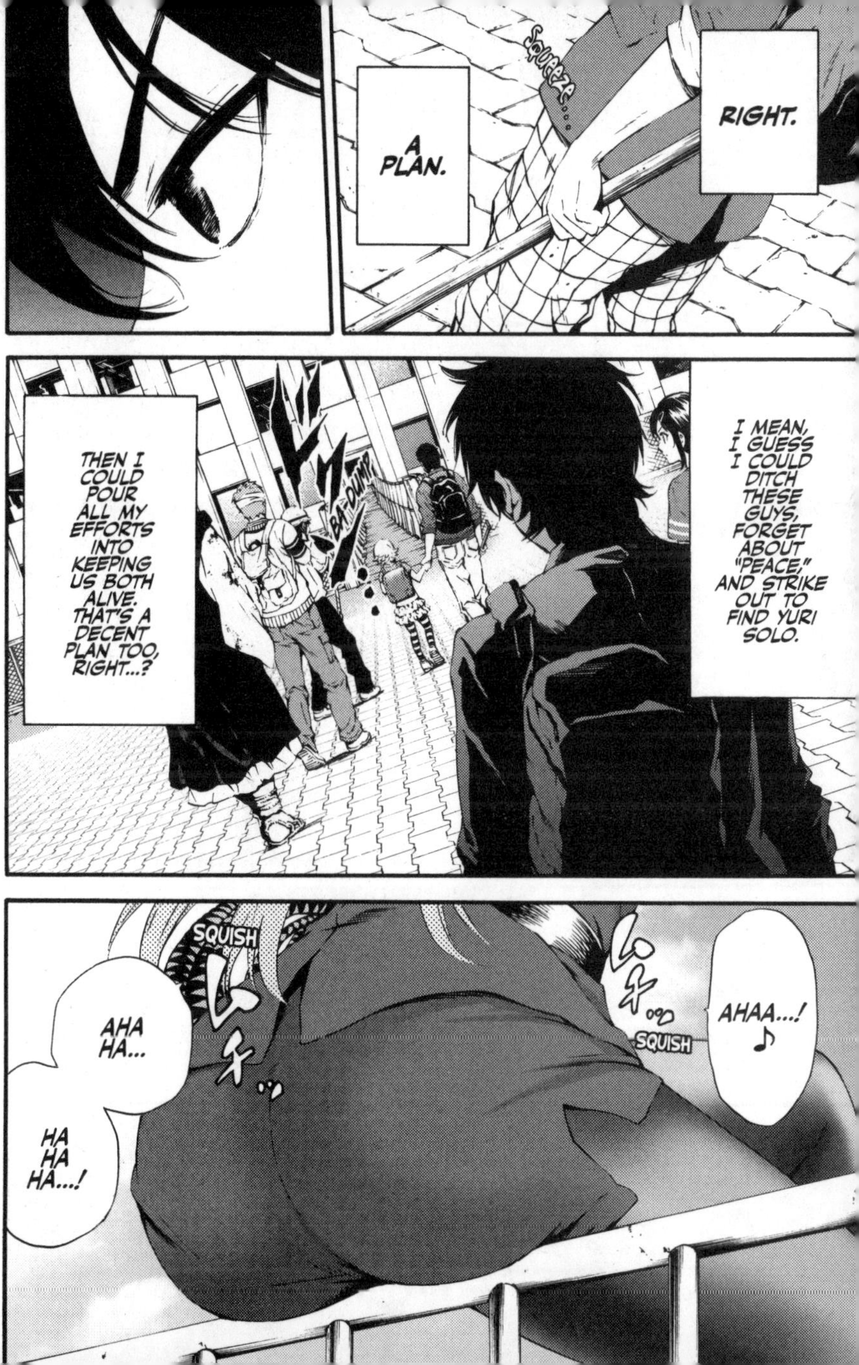
RIGHT.
Squeeze...
A PLAN.
I MEAN, I GUESS I COULD DITCH THESE GUYS, FORGET ABOUT "PEACE," AND STRIKE OUT TO FIND YURI SOLO.
BA-DUMP
THEN I COULD POUR ALL MY EFFORTS INTO KEEPING US BOTH ALIVE. THAT'S A DECENT PLAN TOO, RIGHT...?
AHAA...! ♪
SQUISH
SQUISH
AHA HA...
HA HA HA...!

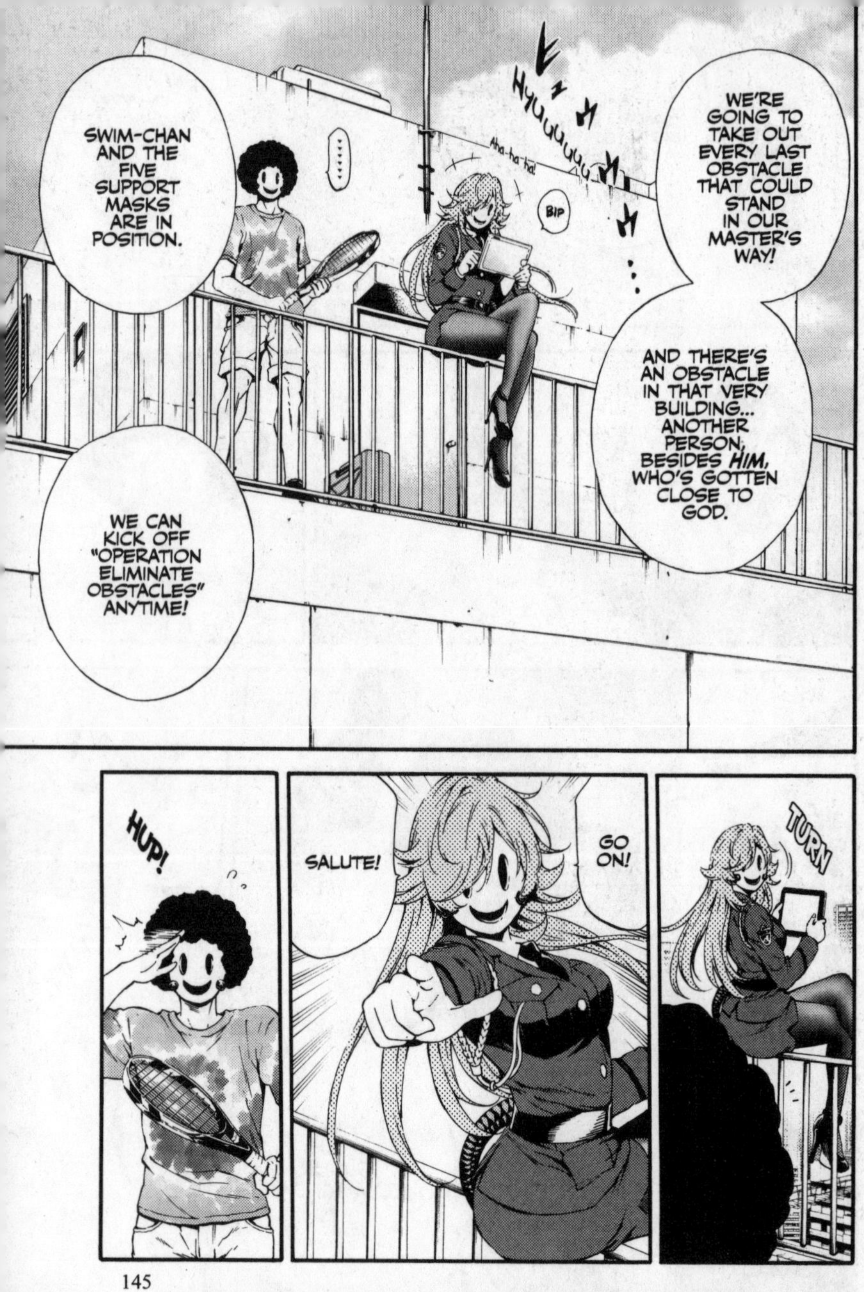

WE'RE GOING TO TAKE OUT EVERY LAST OBSTACLE THAT COULD STAND IN OUR MASTER'S WAY!
HYUUUUUU
AND THERE'S AN OBSTACLE IN THAT VERY BUILDING... ANOTHER PERSON, BESIDES *HIM*, WHO'S GOTTEN CLOSE TO GOD.
Aha-ha-ha!
BIP
......
SWIM-CHAN AND THE FIVE SUPPORT MASKS ARE IN POSITION.
WE CAN KICK OFF "OPERATION ELIMINATE OBSTACLES" ANYTIME!
TURN
GO ON!
SALUTE!
HUP!

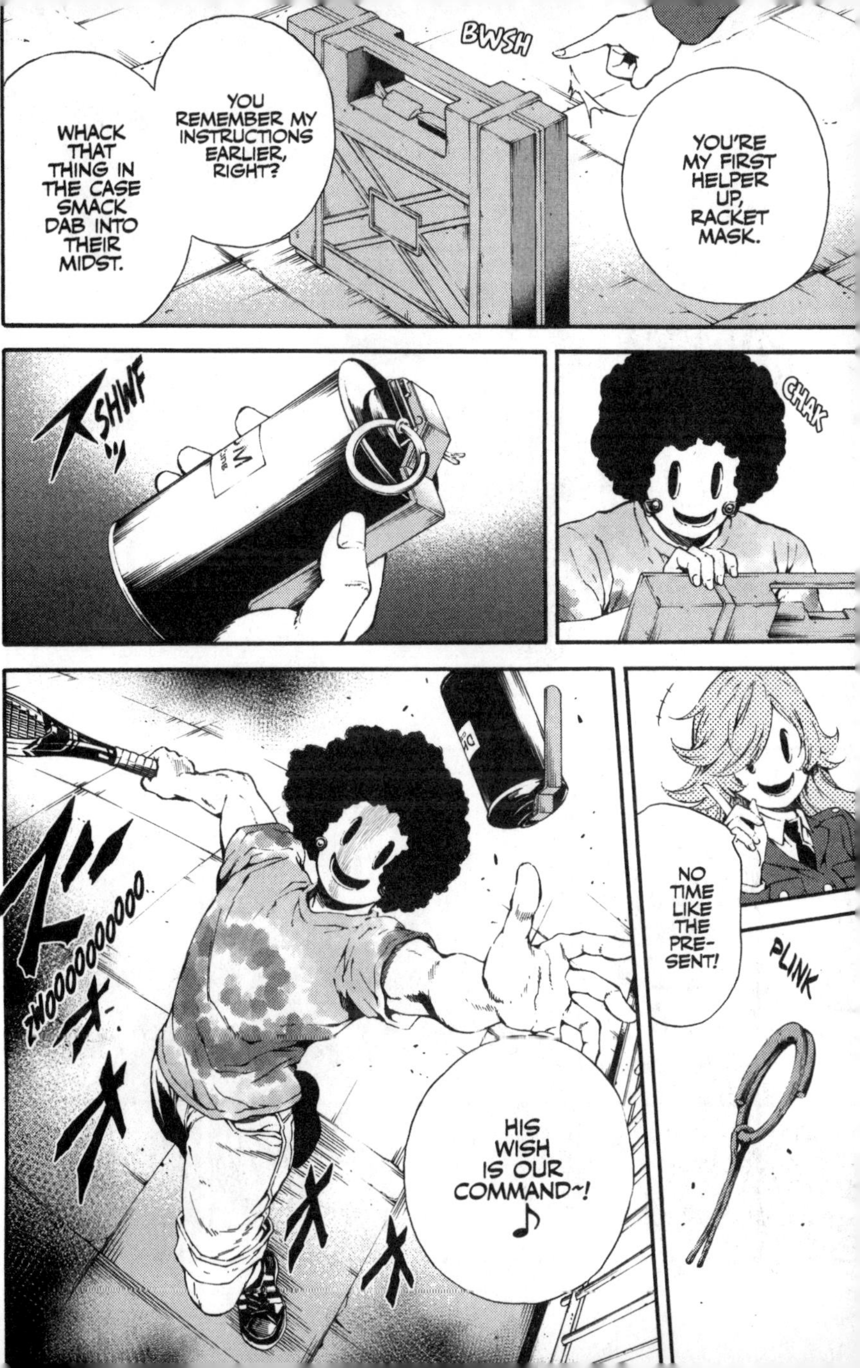
YOU'RE MY FIRST HELPER UP, RACKET MASK.
BWSH
YOU REMEMBER MY INSTRUCTIONS EARLIER, RIGHT?
WHACK THAT THING IN THE CASE SMACK DAB INTO THEIR MIDST.
CHAK
SHWF
NO TIME LIKE THE PRE-SENT!
PLINK
HIS WISH IS OUR COMMAND~! ♪
ZWOOOOOOOOOOO

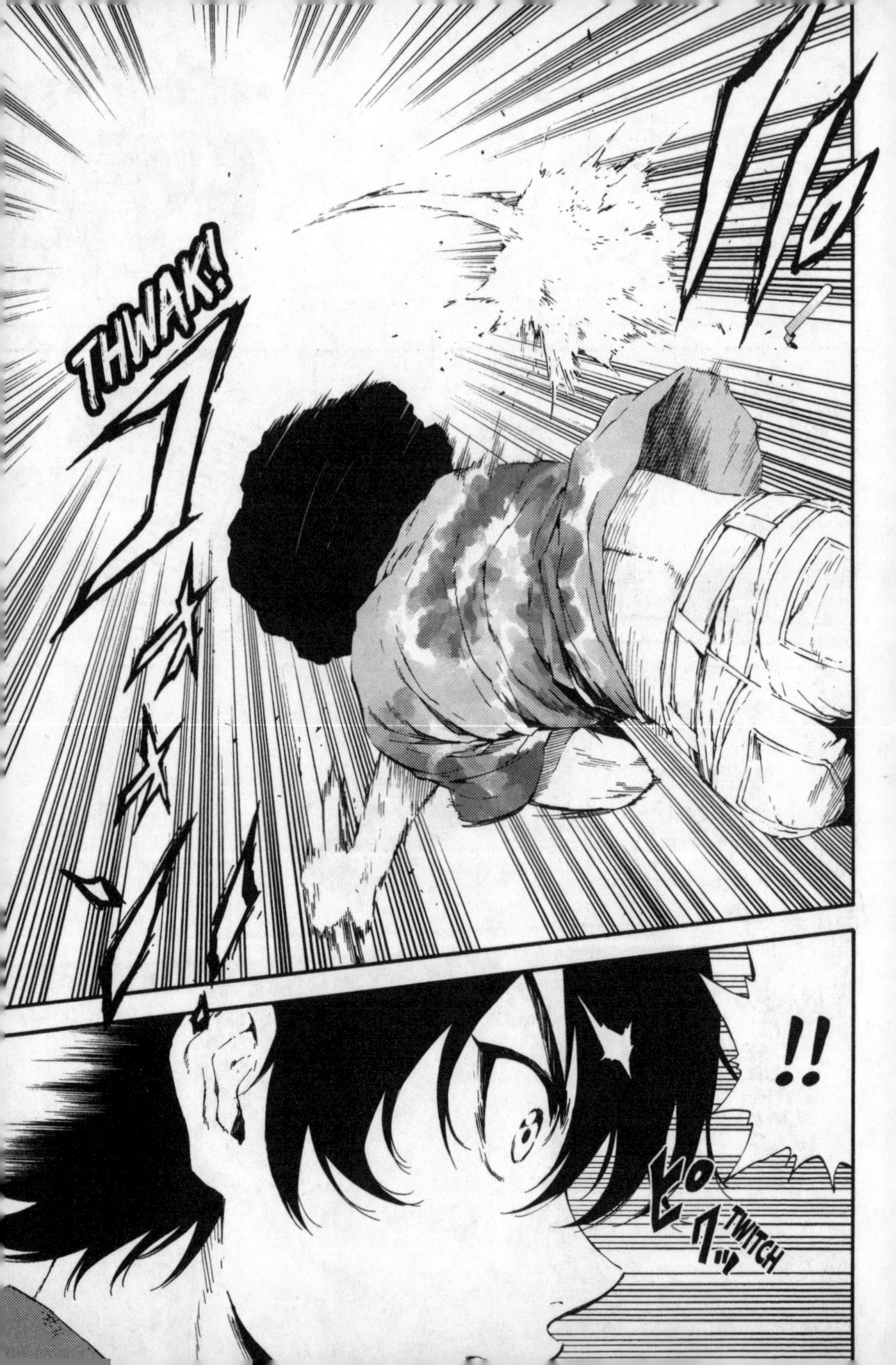
THWAK!
!!
TWITCH

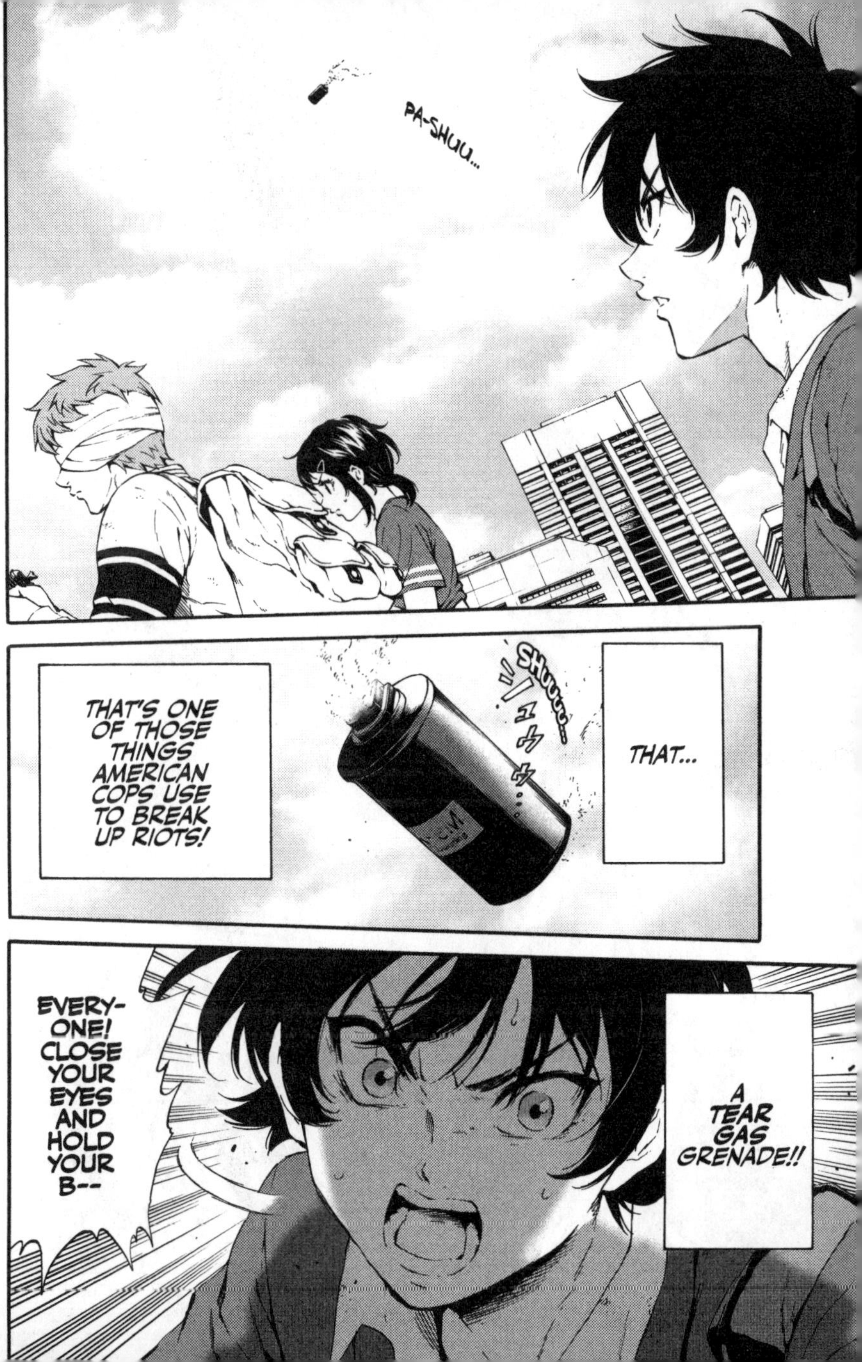
PA-SHUU...
THAT...
SHUUUU...
THAT'S ONE OF THOSE THINGS AMERICAN COPS USE TO BREAK UP RIOTS!
A TEAR GAS GRENADE!!
EVERY-ONE! CLOSE YOUR EYES AND HOLD YOUR B--

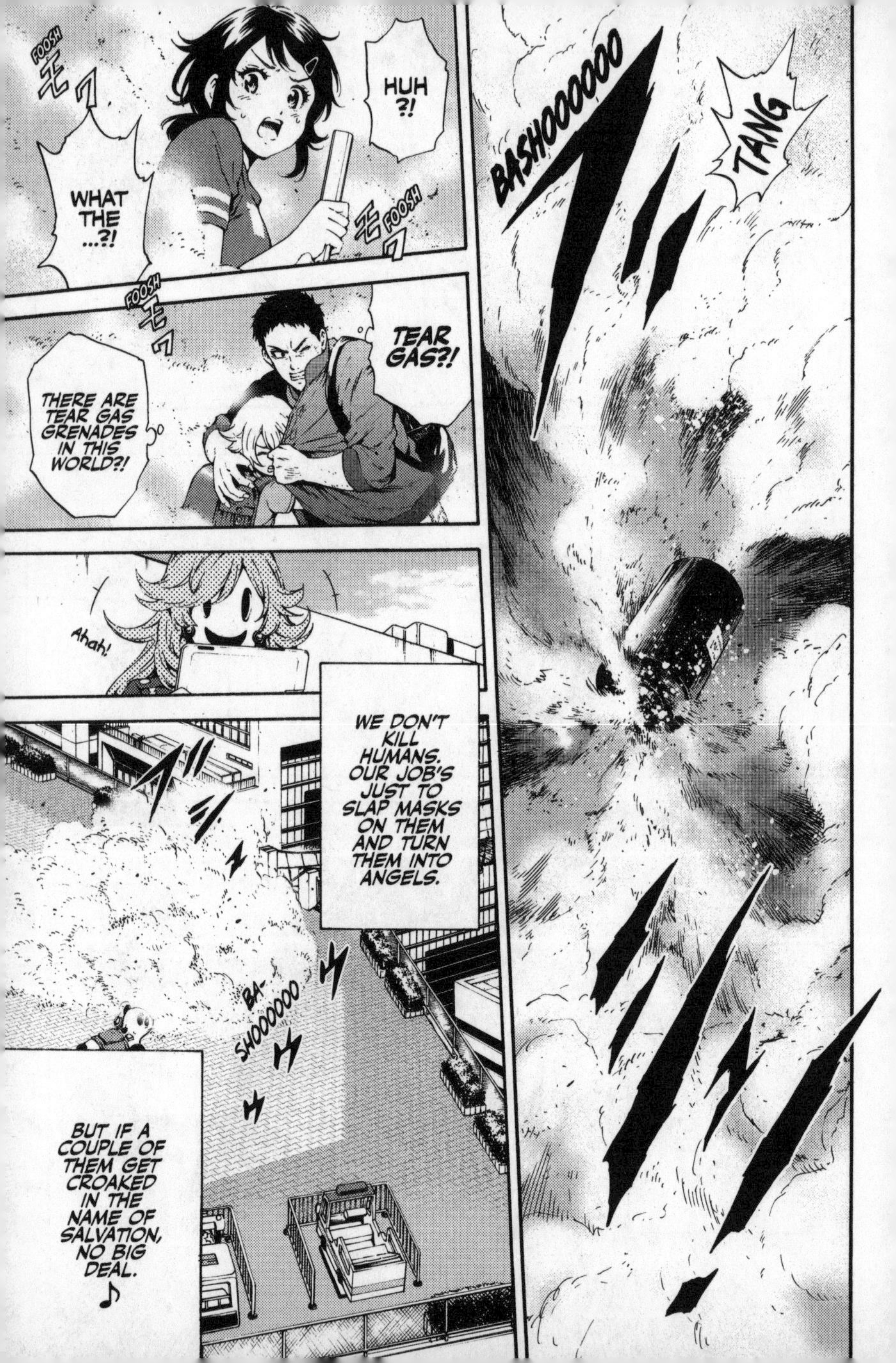
TANG
BASHOOOOOO
HUH ?!
FOOSH
WHAT THE ...?!
FOOSH
TEAR GAS?!
FOOSH
THERE ARE TEAR GAS GRENADES IN THIS WORLD?!
Ahah!
WE DON'T KILL HUMANS. OUR JOB'S JUST TO SLAP MASKS ON THEM AND TURN THEM INTO ANGELS.
BA-SHOOOOOO
BUT IF A COUPLE OF THEM GET CROAKED IN THE NAME OF SALVATION, NO BIG DEAL. ♪

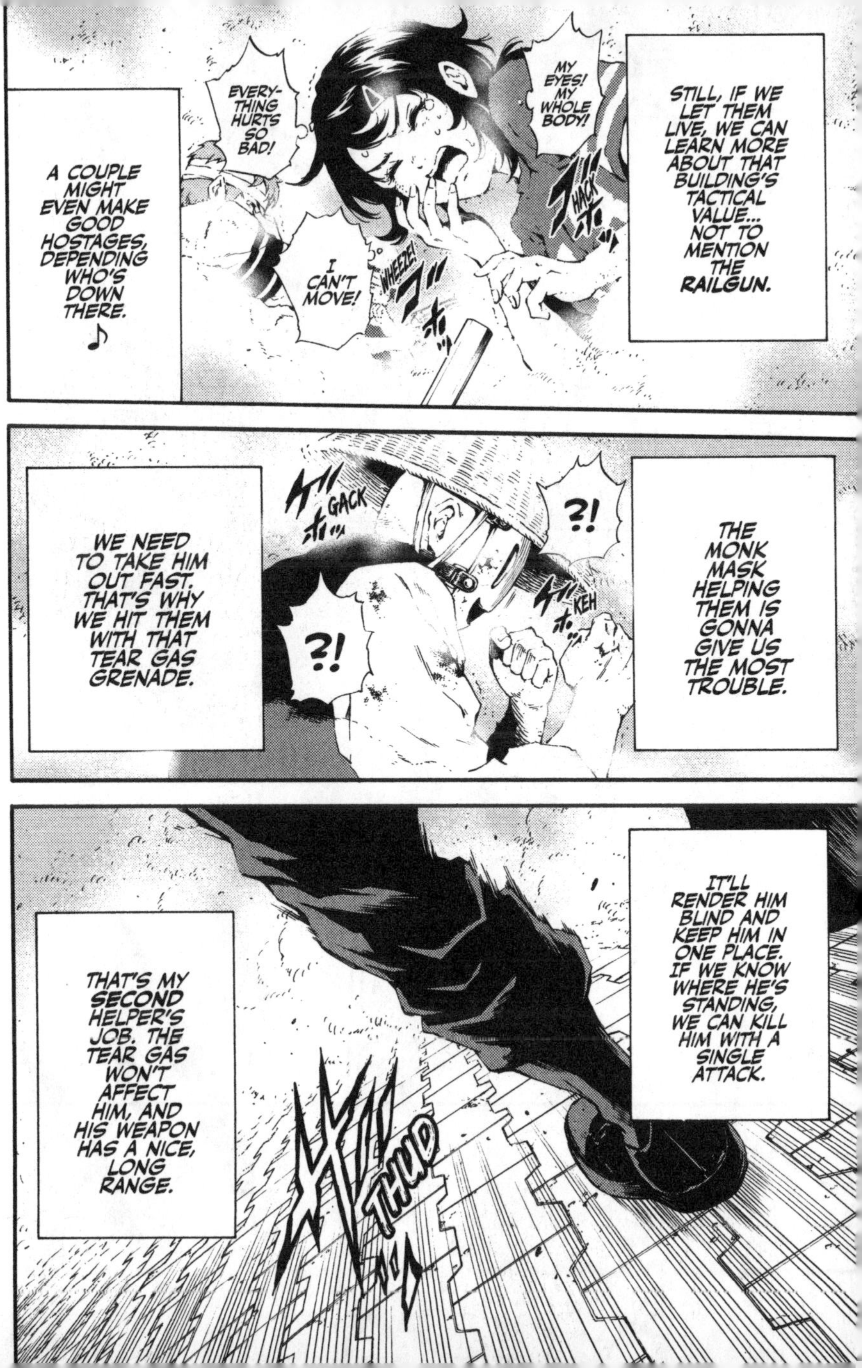
STILL, IF WE LET THEM LIVE, WE CAN LEARN MORE ABOUT THAT BUILDING'S TACTICAL VALUE... NOT TO MENTION THE RAILGUN.
MY EYES! MY WHOLE BODY!
HACK
EVERY-THING HURTS SO BAD!
I CAN'T MOVE!
WHEEZE!
A COUPLE MIGHT EVEN MAKE GOOD HOSTAGES, DEPENDING WHO'S DOWN THERE. ♪
THE MONK MASK HELPING THEM IS GONNA GIVE US THE MOST TROUBLE.
?!
KEH
GACK
?!
WE NEED TO TAKE HIM OUT FAST. THAT'S WHY WE HIT THEM WITH THAT TEAR GAS GRENADE.
IT'LL RENDER HIM BLIND AND KEEP HIM IN ONE PLACE. IF WE KNOW WHERE HE'S STANDING, WE CAN KILL HIM WITH A SINGLE ATTACK.
THUD
THAT'S MY SECOND HELPER'S JOB. THE TEAR GAS WON'T AFFECT HIM, AND HIS WEAPON HAS A NICE, LONG RANGE.

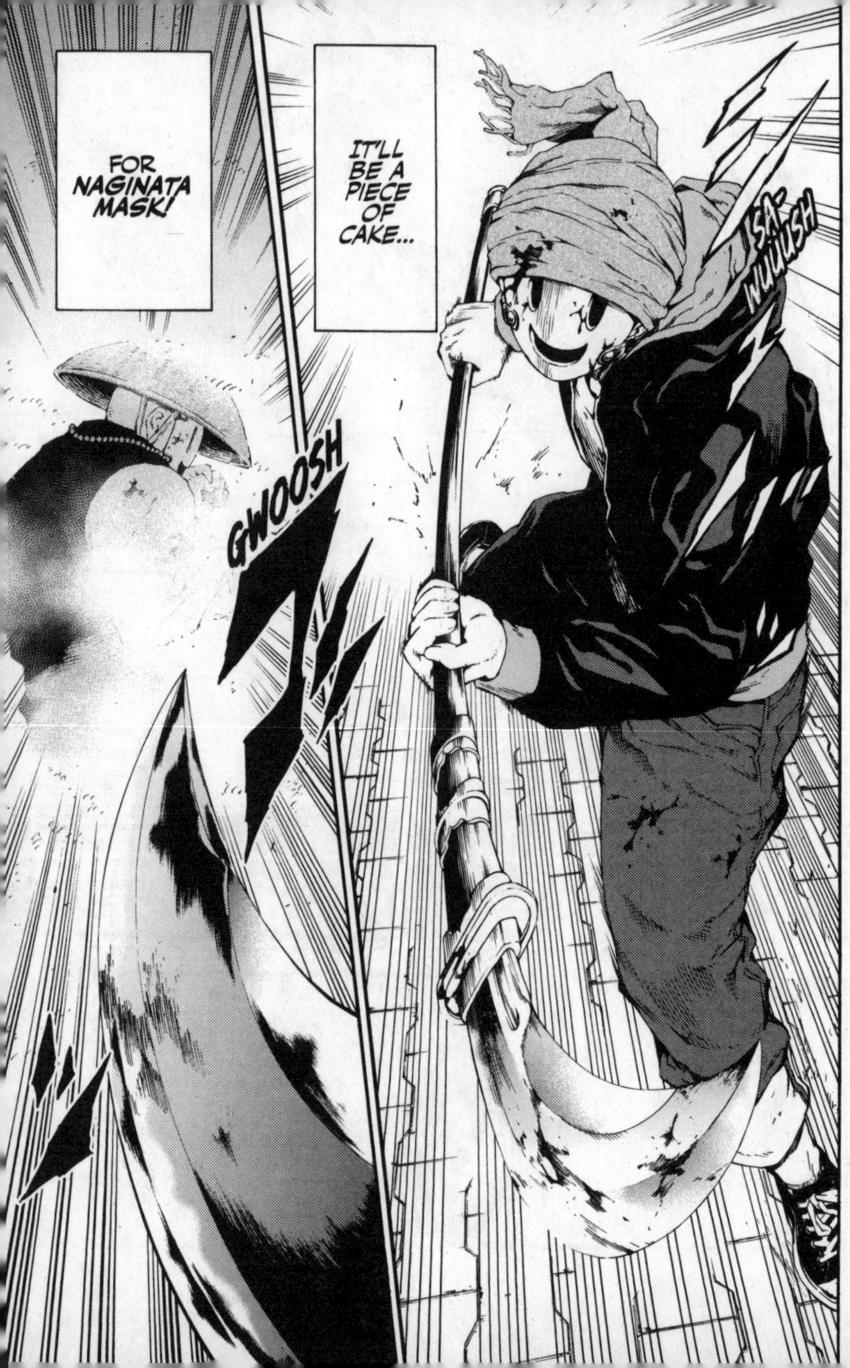

IT'LL BE A PIECE OF CAKE...
SA-WUUUSH
FOR NAGINATA MASK!
GWOOSH

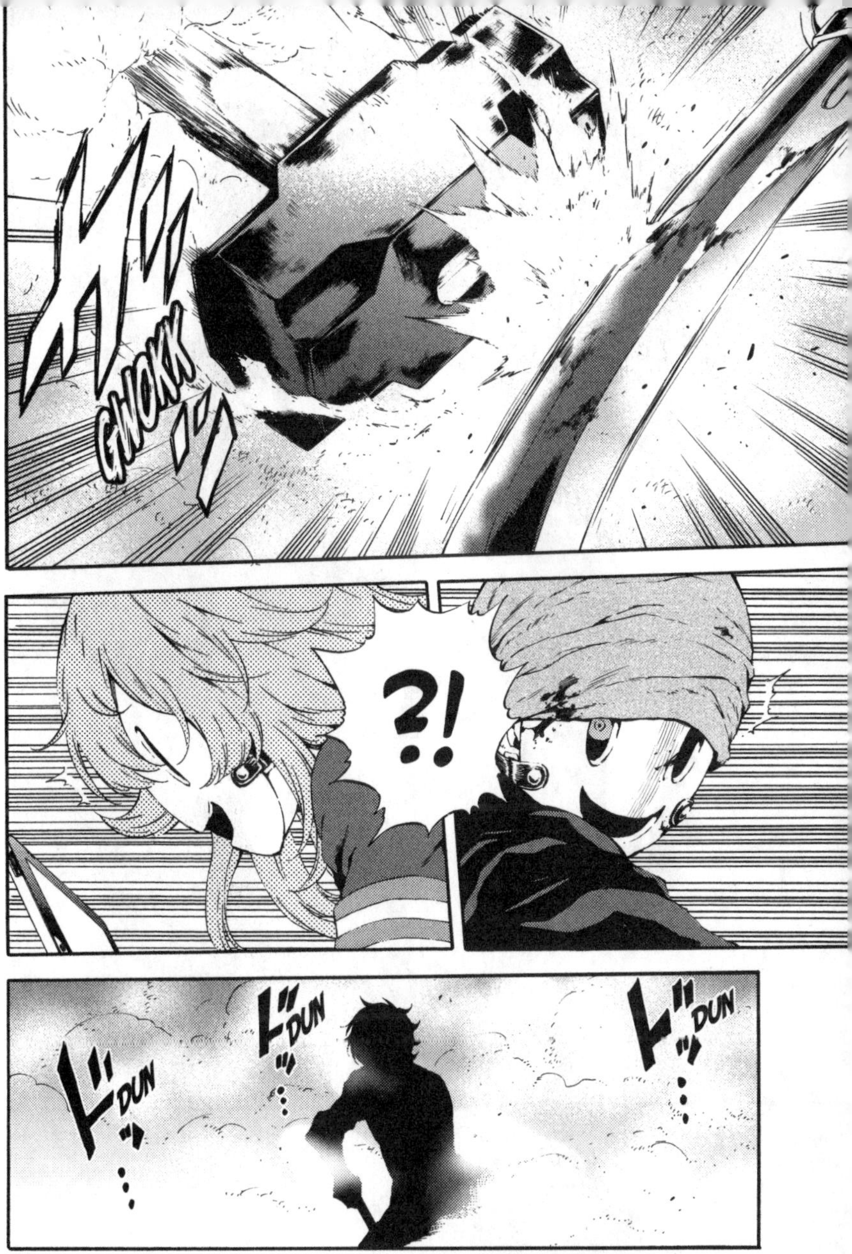
GWOKK
?!
DUN
DUN
DUN

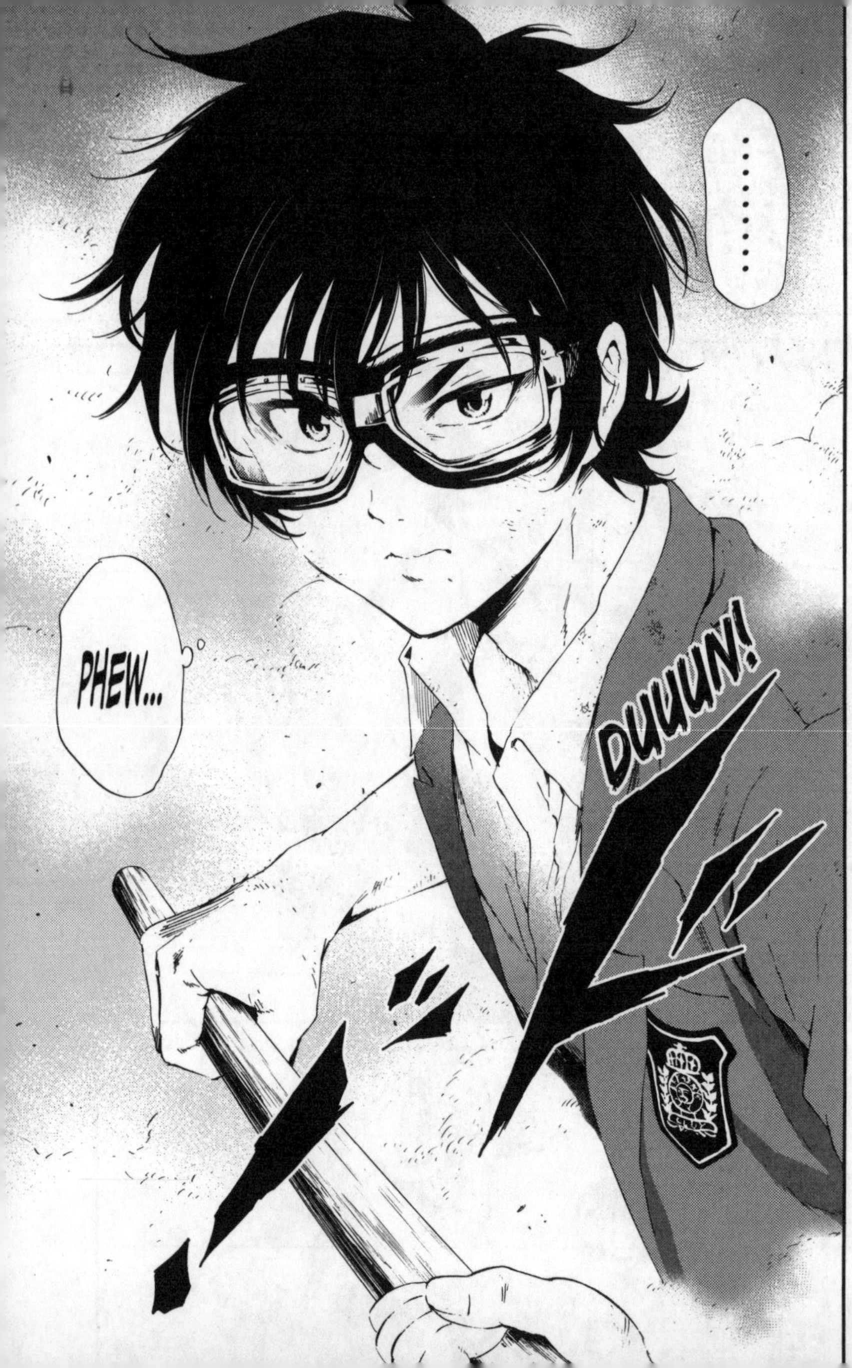

......
PHEW...
DUUUN!

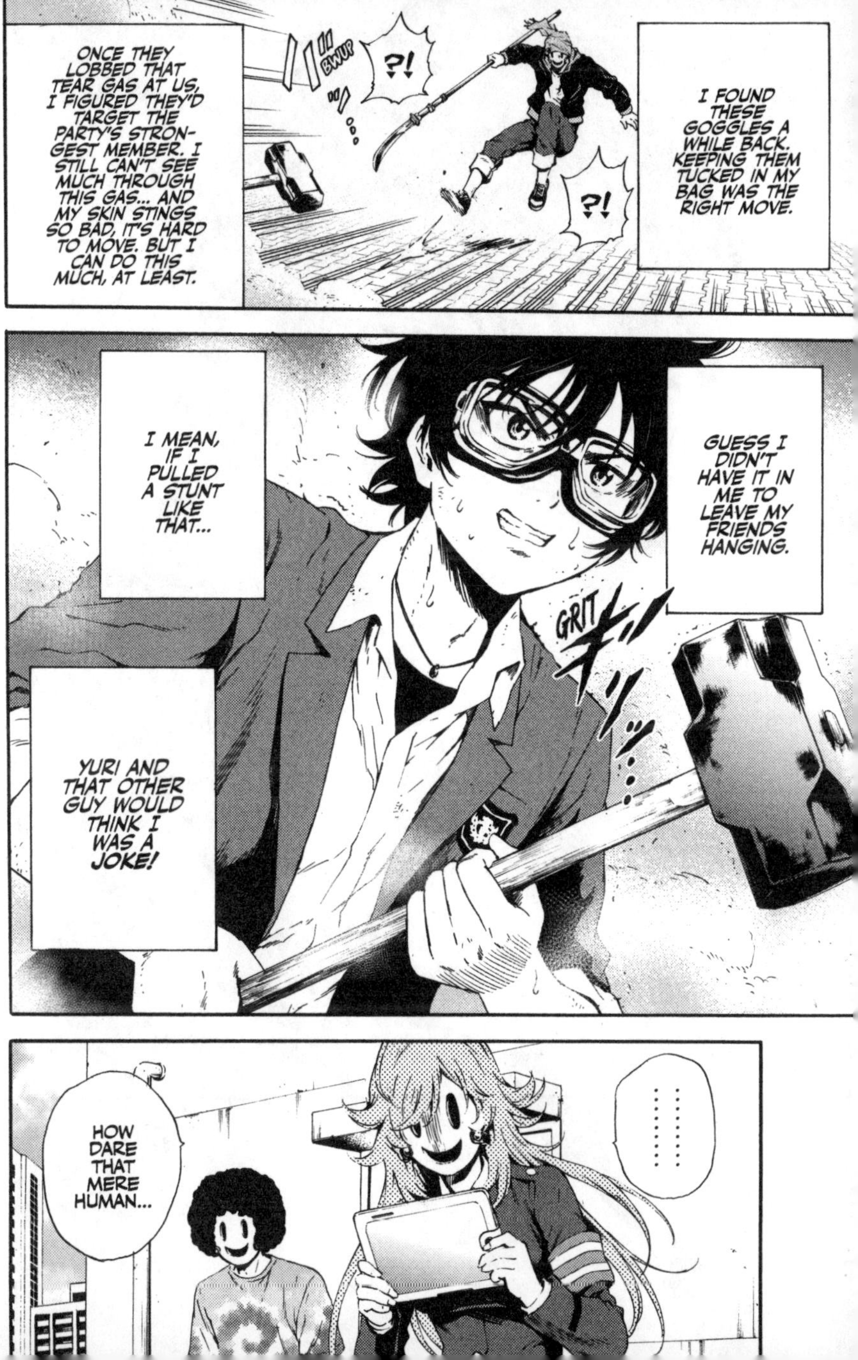
I FOUND THESE GOGGLES A WHILE BACK. KEEPING THEM TUCKED IN MY BAG WAS THE RIGHT MOVE.
?!
?!
BWUP
ONCE THEY LOBBED THAT TEAR GAS AT US, I FIGURED THEY'D TARGET THE PARTY'S STRONGEST MEMBER. I STILL CAN'T SEE MUCH THROUGH THIS GAS... AND MY SKIN STINGS SO BAD, IT'S HARD TO MOVE. BUT I CAN DO THIS MUCH, AT LEAST.
GUESS I DIDN'T HAVE IT IN ME TO LEAVE MY FRIENDS HANGING.
GRIT
I MEAN, IF I PULLED A STUNT LIKE THAT...
YURI AND THAT OTHER GUY WOULD THINK I WAS A JOKE!
......
HOW DARE THAT MERE HUMAN...

VOLUME 7 COVER ILLUSTRATION
ROUGH DRAFT

HIGH-RISE INVASION

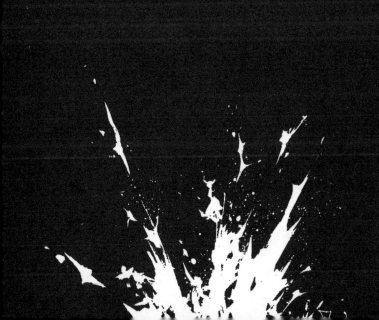

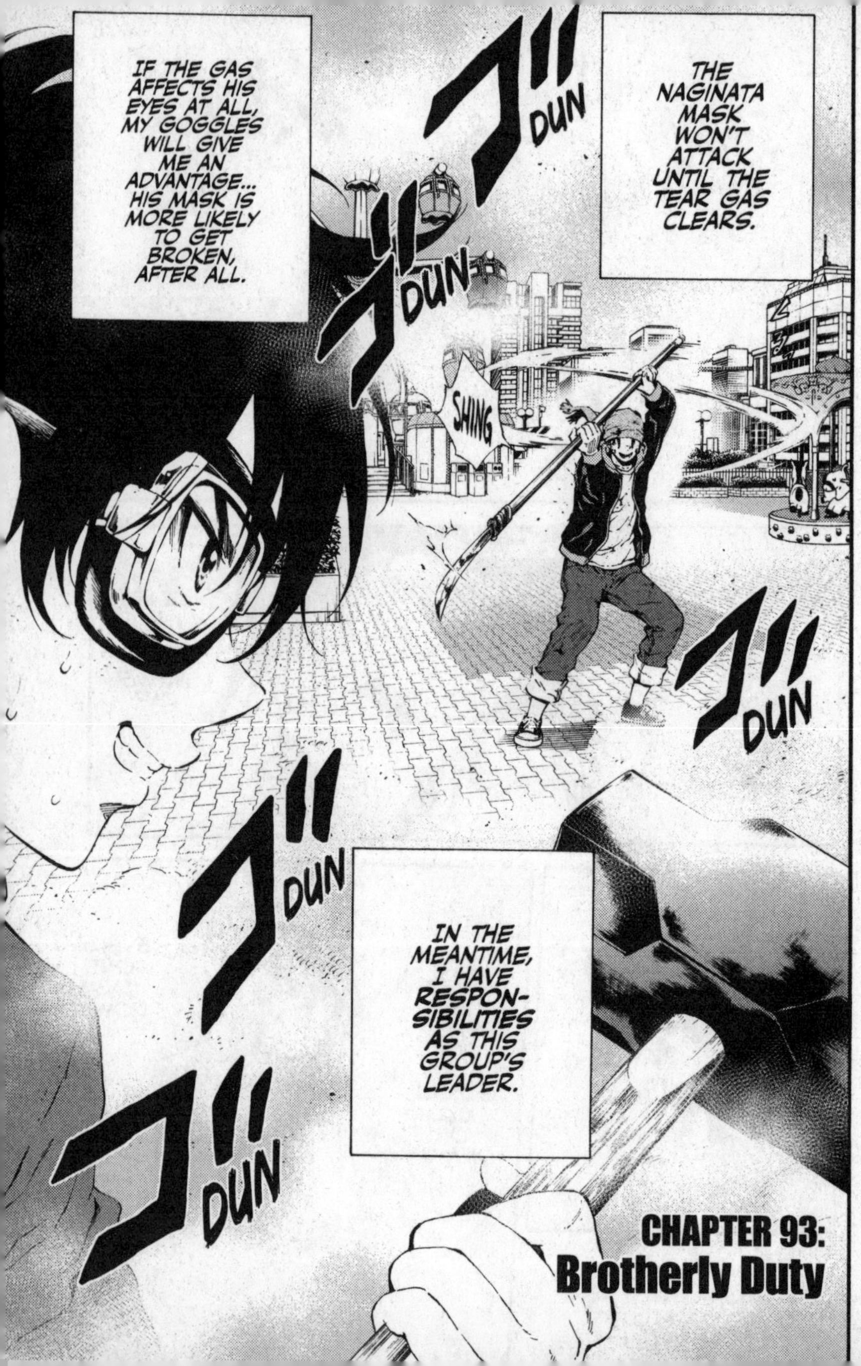
THE NAGINATA MASK WON'T ATTACK UNTIL THE TEAR GAS CLEARS.
DUN
DUN
IF THE GAS AFFECTS HIS EYES AT ALL, MY GOGGLES WILL GIVE ME AN ADVANTAGE... HIS MASK IS MORE LIKELY TO GET BROKEN, AFTER ALL.
DUN
SHING
DUN
IN THE MEANTIME, I HAVE RESPONSIBILITIES AS THIS GROUP'S LEADER.
DUN
DUN

CHAPTER 93: Brotherly Duty

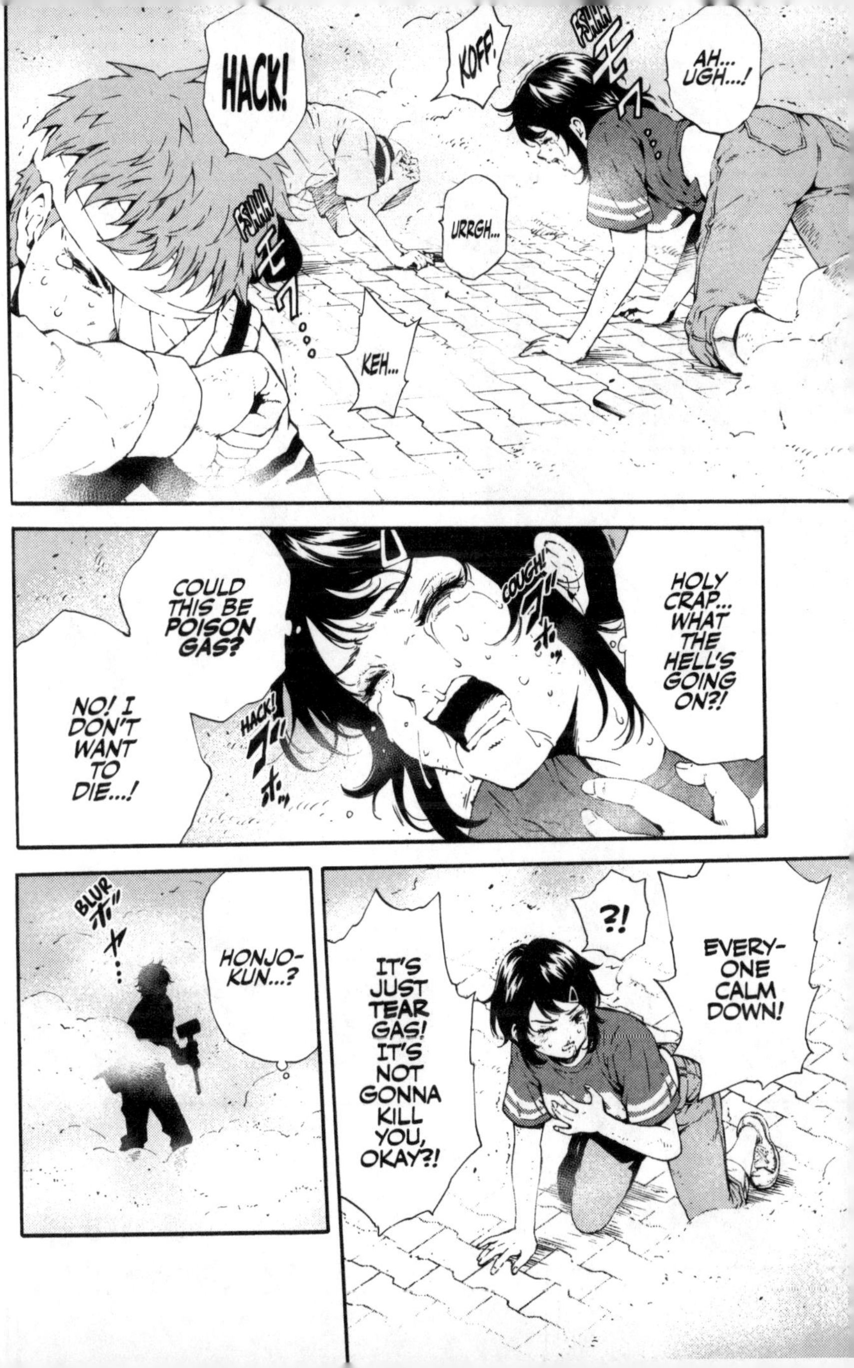
AH... UGH...!
FSHHH
KOFF!
HACK!
URRGH...
FSHHH
KEH...
HOLY CRAP... WHAT THE HELL'S GOING ON?!
COUGH!
COULD THIS BE POISON GAS?
HACK!
NO! I DON'T WANT TO DIE...!
EVERY-ONE CALM DOWN!
?!
IT'S JUST TEAR GAS! IT'S NOT GONNA KILL YOU, OKAY?!
HONJO-KUN...?
BLUR

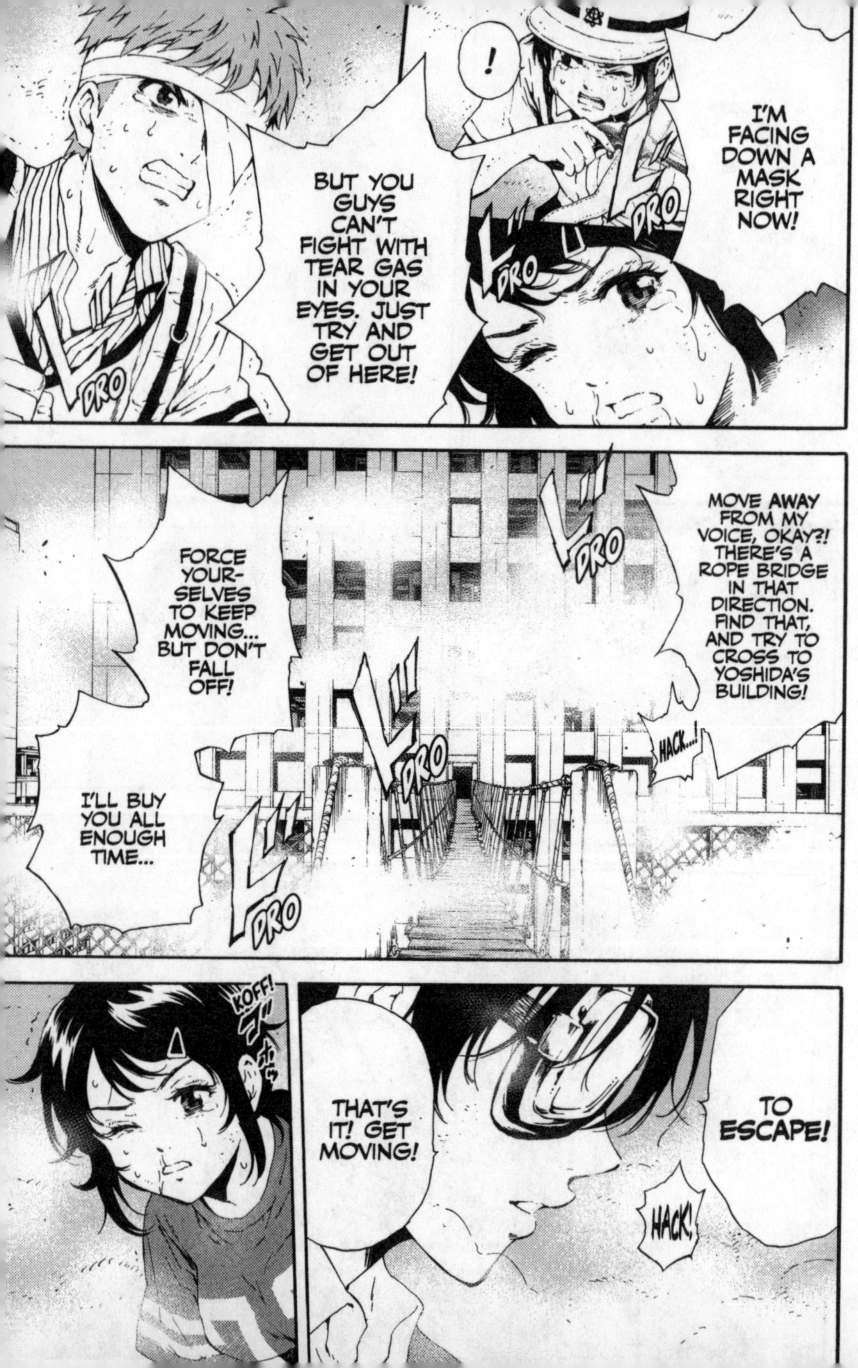
!
I'M FACING DOWN A MASK RIGHT NOW!
DRO
DRO
BUT YOU GUYS CAN'T FIGHT WITH TEAR GAS IN YOUR EYES. JUST TRY AND GET OUT OF HERE!
DRO
DRO
MOVE AWAY FROM MY VOICE, OKAY?! THERE'S A ROPE BRIDGE IN THAT DIRECTION. FIND THAT, AND TRY TO CROSS TO YOSHIDA'S BUILDING!
HACK...!
FORCE YOURSELVES TO KEEP MOVING... BUT DON'T FALL OFF!
DRO
I'LL BUY YOU ALL ENOUGH TIME...
DRO
TO ESCAPE!
HACK!
THAT'S IT! GET MOVING!
KOFF!

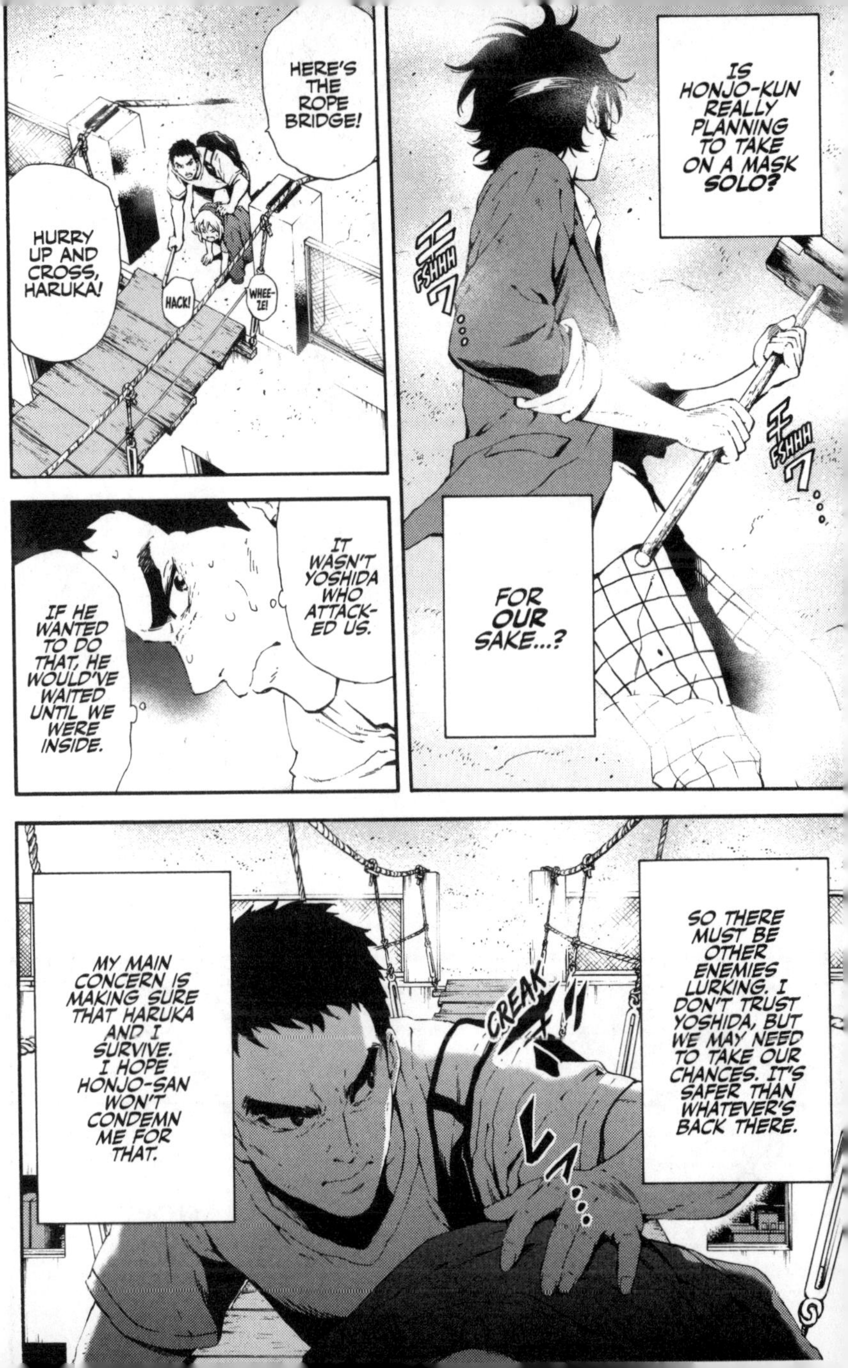

IS HONJO-KUN REALLY PLANNING TO TAKE ON A MASK SOLO?
FSHHH
FSHHH
FOR OUR SAKE...?
HERE'S THE ROPE BRIDGE!
HURRY UP AND CROSS, HARUKA!
WHEE-ZE!
HACK!
IT WASN'T YOSHIDA WHO ATTACKED US.
IF HE WANTED TO DO THAT, HE WOULD'VE WAITED UNTIL WE WERE INSIDE.
SO THERE MUST BE OTHER ENEMIES LURKING. I DON'T TRUST YOSHIDA, BUT WE MAY NEED TO TAKE OUR CHANCES. IT'S SAFER THAN WHATEVER'S BACK THERE.
CREAK
MY MAIN CONCERN IS MAKING SURE THAT HARUKA AND I SURVIVE. I HOPE HONJO-SAN WON'T CONDEMN ME FOR THAT.

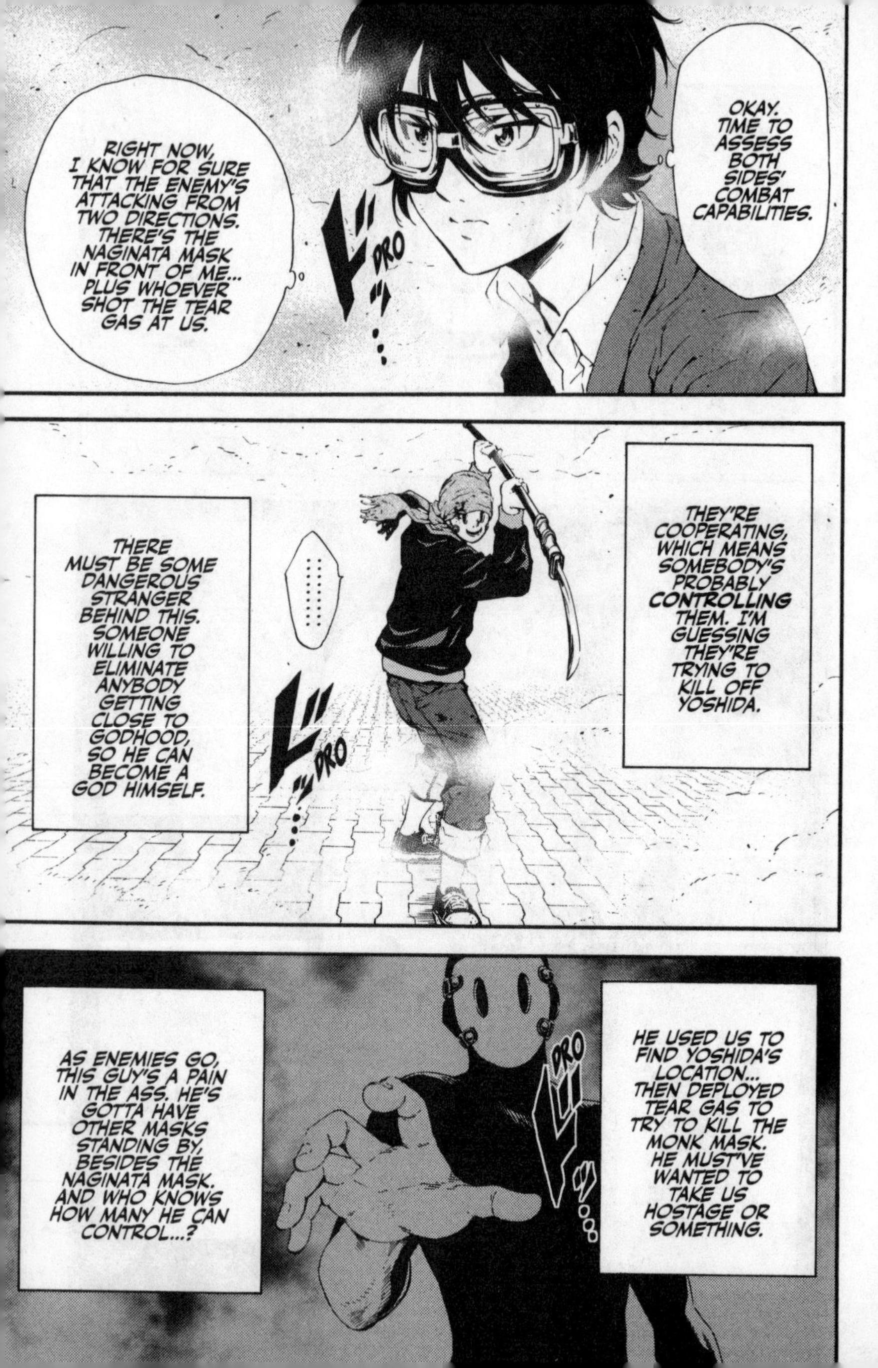
OKAY. TIME TO ASSESS BOTH SIDES' COMBAT CAPABILITIES.
RIGHT NOW, I KNOW FOR SURE THAT THE ENEMY'S ATTACKING FROM TWO DIRECTIONS. THERE'S THE NAGINATA MASK IN FRONT OF ME... PLUS WHOEVER SHOT THE TEAR GAS AT US.
DRO
THEY'RE COOPERATING, WHICH MEANS SOMEBODY'S PROBABLY **CONTROLLING** THEM. I'M GUESSING THEY'RE TRYING TO KILL OFF YOSHIDA.
....
THERE MUST BE SOME DANGEROUS STRANGER BEHIND THIS. SOMEONE WILLING TO ELIMINATE ANYBODY GETTING CLOSE TO GODHOOD, SO HE CAN BECOME A GOD HIMSELF.
DRO
HE USED US TO FIND YOSHIDA'S LOCATION... THEN DEPLOYED TEAR GAS TO TRY TO KILL THE MONK MASK. HE MUST'VE WANTED TO TAKE US HOSTAGE OR SOMETHING.
DRO
AS ENEMIES GO, THIS GUY'S A PAIN IN THE ASS. HE'S GOTTA HAVE OTHER MASKS STANDING BY, BESIDES THE NAGINATA MASK. AND WHO KNOWS HOW MANY HE CAN CONTROL...?

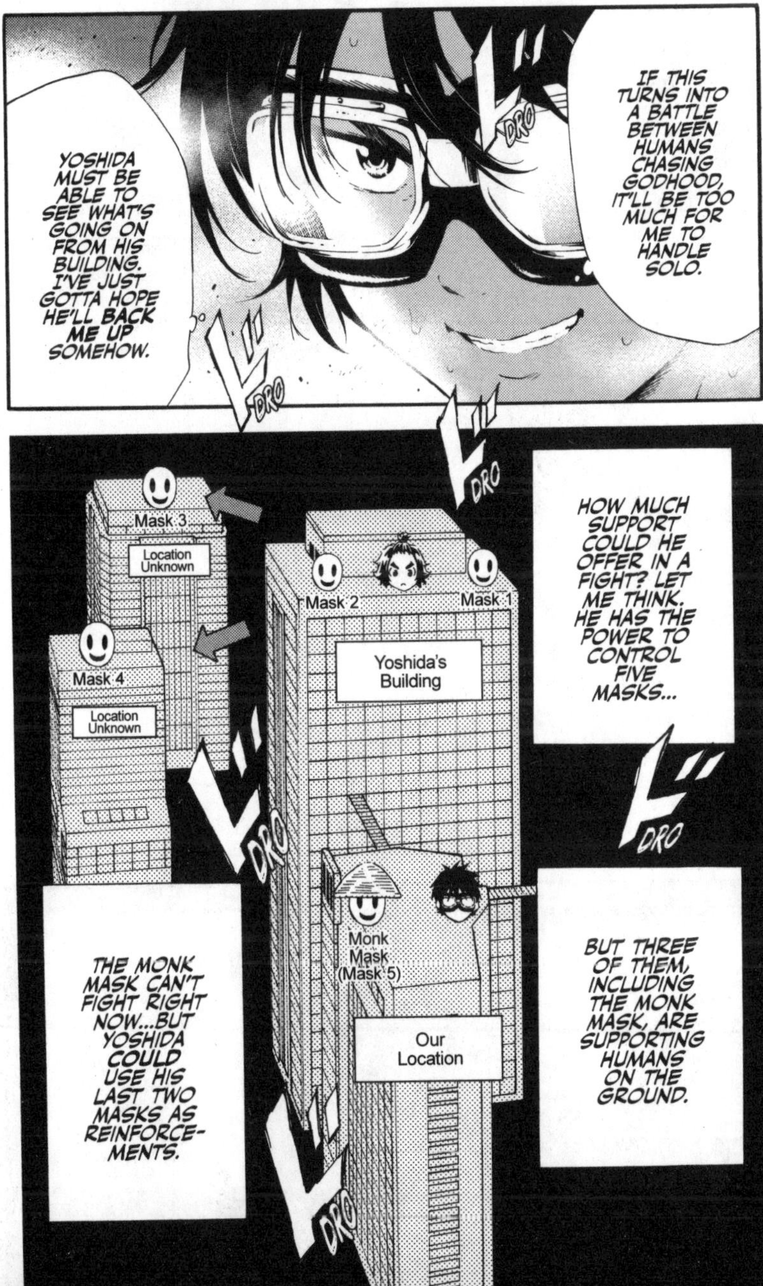
IF THIS TURNS INTO A BATTLE BETWEEN HUMANS CHASING GODHOOD, IT'LL BE TOO MUCH FOR ME TO HANDLE SOLO.
DRO
YOSHIDA MUST BE ABLE TO SEE WHAT'S GOING ON FROM HIS BUILDING. I'VE JUST GOTTA HOPE HE'LL BACK ME UP SOMEHOW.
DRO
DRO
HOW MUCH SUPPORT COULD HE OFFER IN A FIGHT? LET ME THINK. HE HAS THE POWER TO CONTROL FIVE MASKS...
Mask 3
Location Unknown
Mask 2
Mask 1
Yoshida's Building
Mask 4
Location Unknown
DRO
DRO
Monk Mask (Mask 5)
Our Location
BUT THREE OF THEM, INCLUDING THE MONK MASK, ARE SUPPORTING HUMANS ON THE GROUND.
THE MONK MASK CAN'T FIGHT RIGHT NOW...BUT YOSHIDA COULD USE HIS LAST TWO MASKS AS REINFORCE-MENTS.
DRO

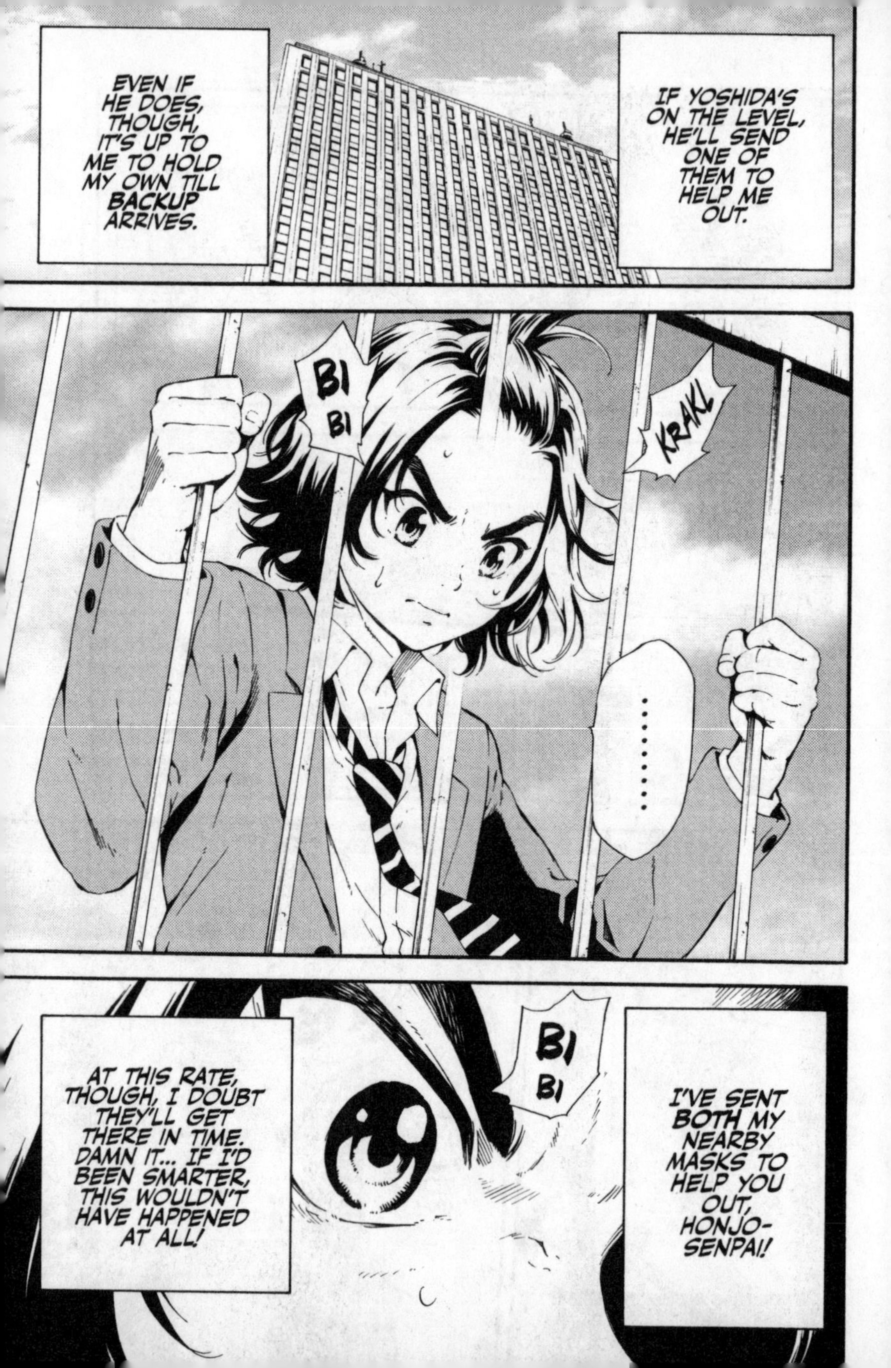
IF YOSHIDA'S ON THE LEVEL, HE'LL SEND ONE OF THEM TO HELP ME OUT.
EVEN IF HE DOES, THOUGH, IT'S UP TO ME TO HOLD MY OWN TILL BACKUP ARRIVES.
KRAK!
BI BI
......
I'VE SENT BOTH MY NEARBY MASKS TO HELP YOU OUT, HONJO-SENPAI!
BI BI
AT THIS RATE, THOUGH, I DOUBT THEY'LL GET THERE IN TIME. DAMN IT... IF I'D BEEN SMARTER, THIS WOULDN'T HAVE HAPPENED AT ALL!

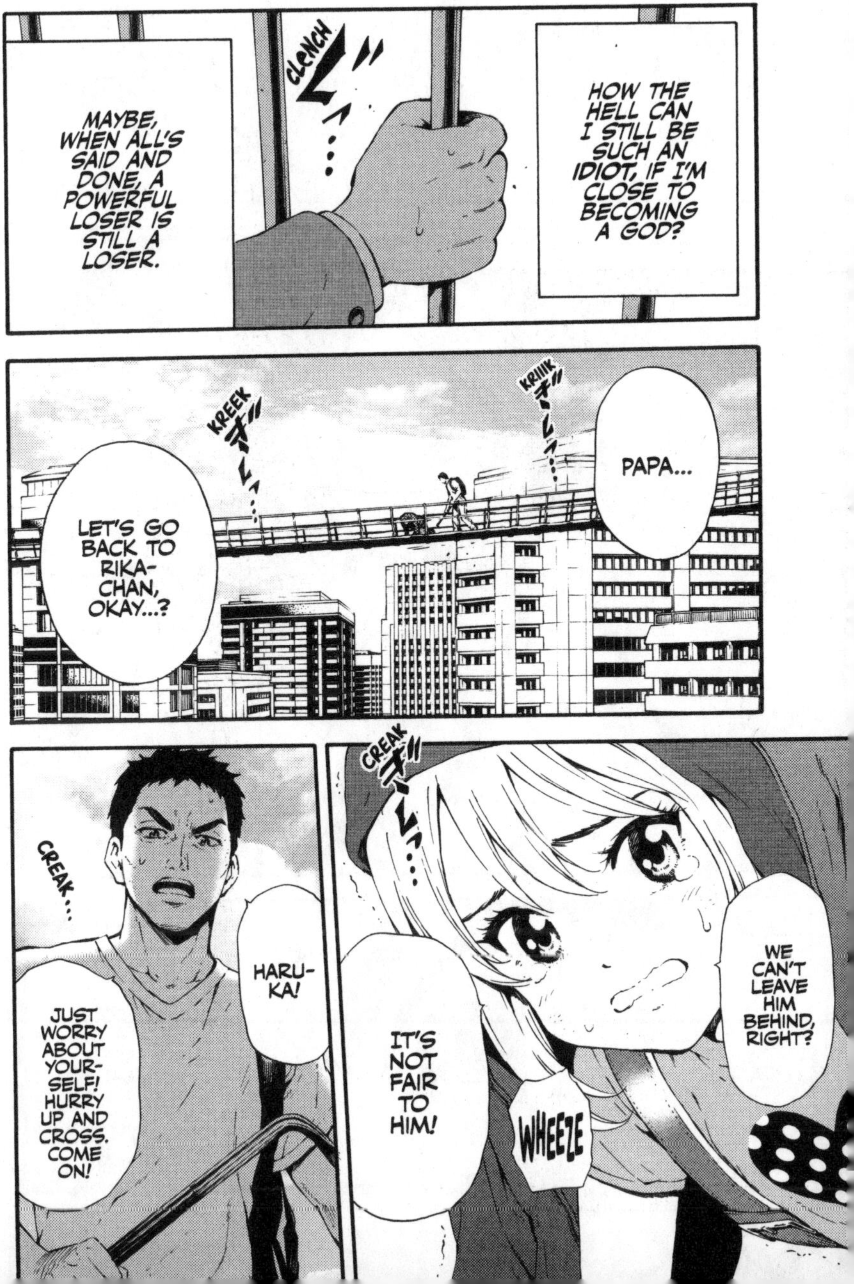
HOW THE HELL CAN I STILL BE SUCH AN IDIOT, IF I'M CLOSE TO BECOMING A GOD?
CLENCH
MAYBE, WHEN ALL'S SAID AND DONE, A POWERFUL LOSER IS STILL A LOSER.
PAPA...
KRIIIK
KREEK
LET'S GO BACK TO RIKA-CHAN, OKAY...?
WE CAN'T LEAVE HIM BEHIND, RIGHT?
CREAK
WHEEZE
IT'S NOT FAIR TO HIM!
HARU-KA!
CREAK...
JUST WORRY ABOUT YOUR-SELF! HURRY UP AND CROSS. COME ON!

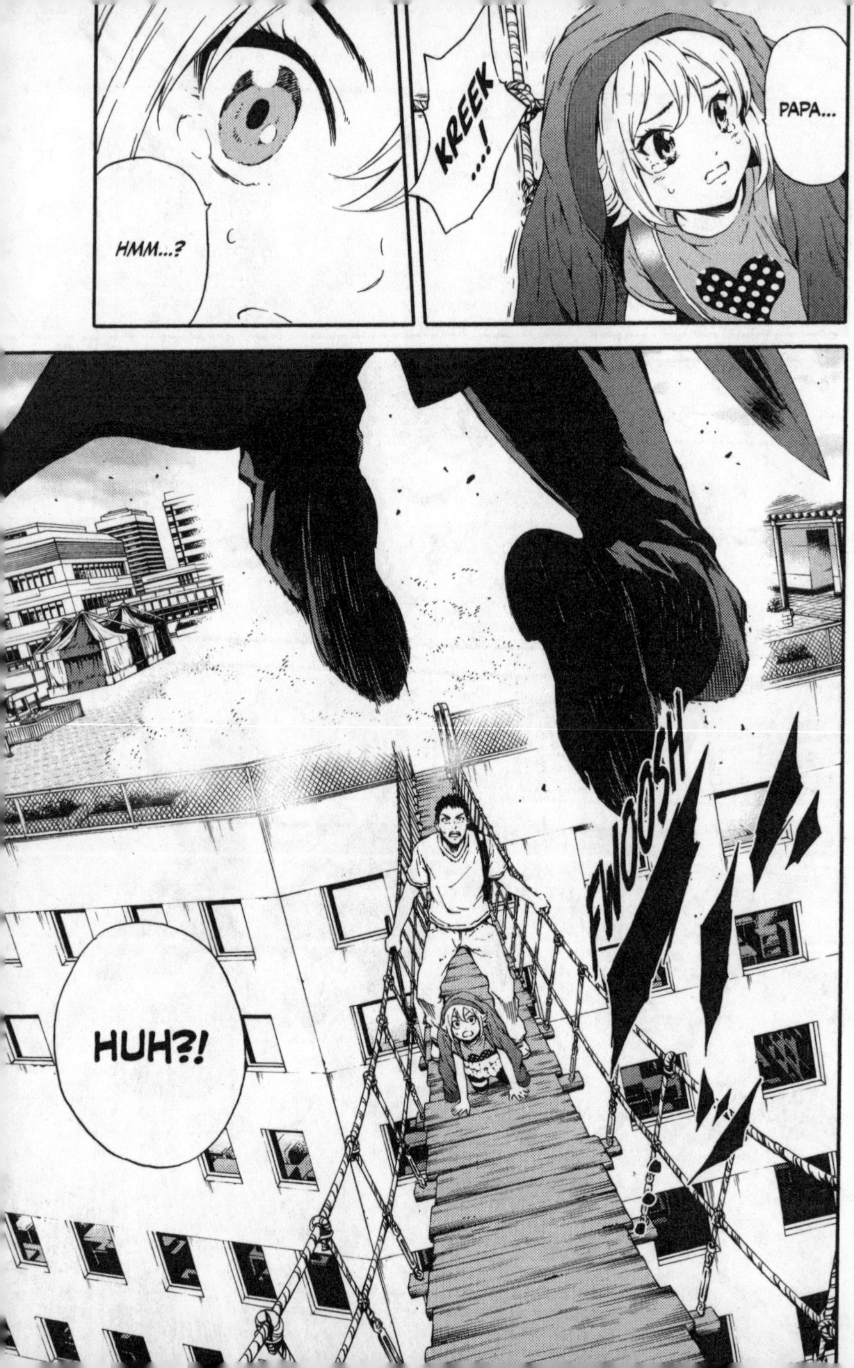
PAPA...
KREEK ...!
HMM...?
FWOOSH
HUH?!

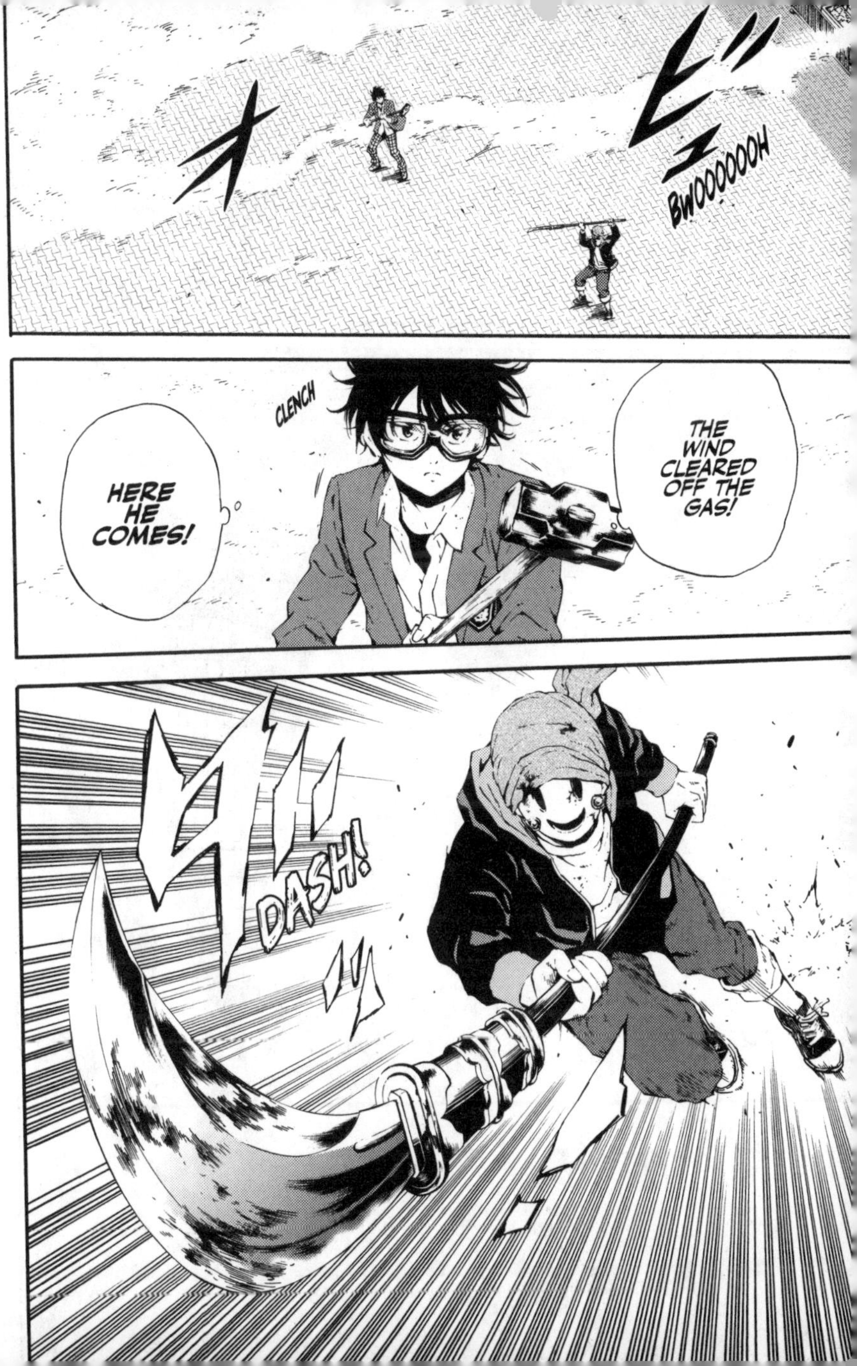
BWOOOOOOH
THE WIND CLEARED OFF THE GAS!
CLENCH
HERE HE COMES!
DASH!

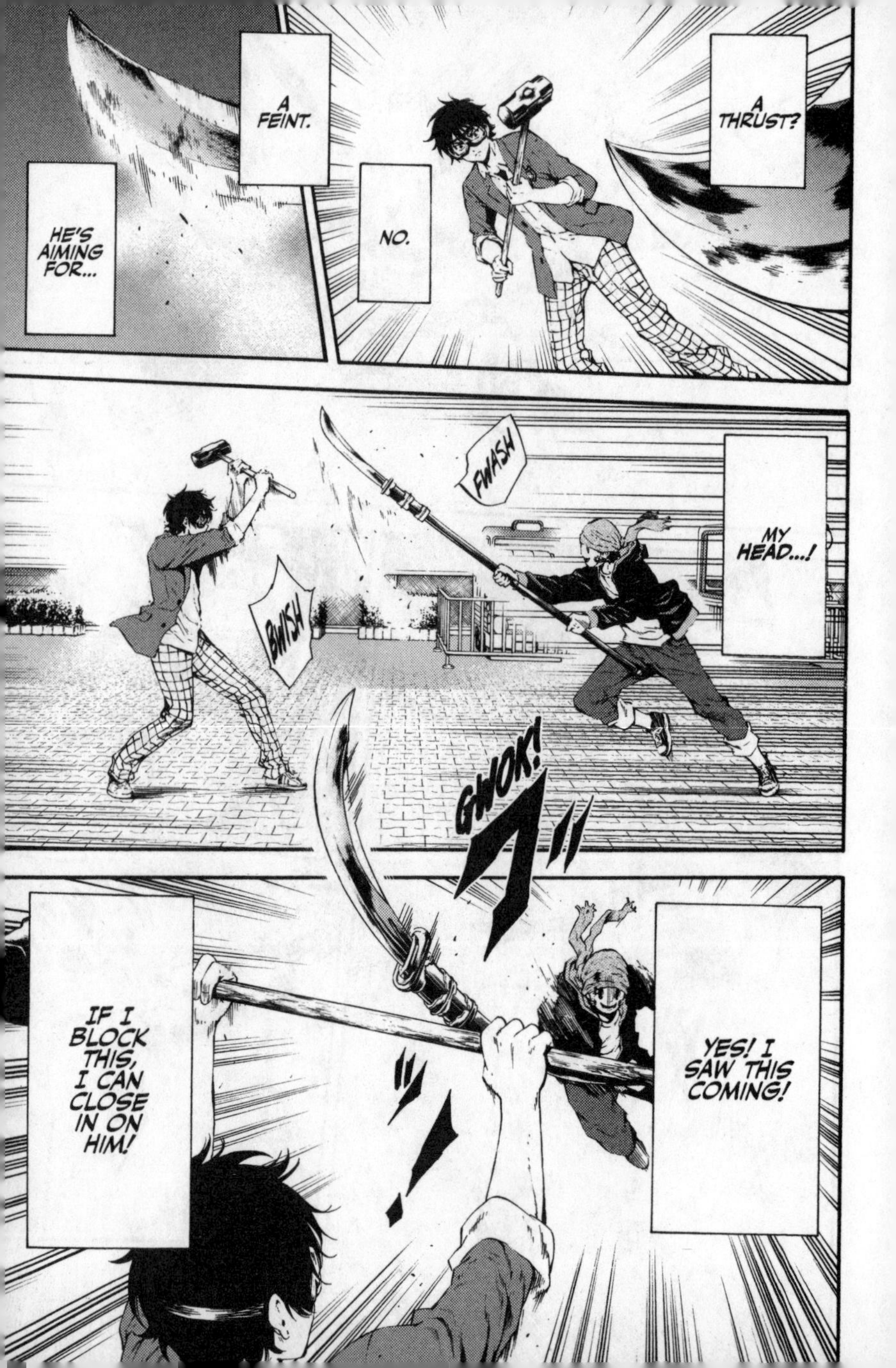
A THRUST?
A FEINT.
NO.
HE'S AIMING FOR...
MY HEAD...!
FWASH
BWISH
GWOK!
YES! I SAW THIS COMING!
IF I BLOCK THIS, I CAN CLOSE IN ON HIM!

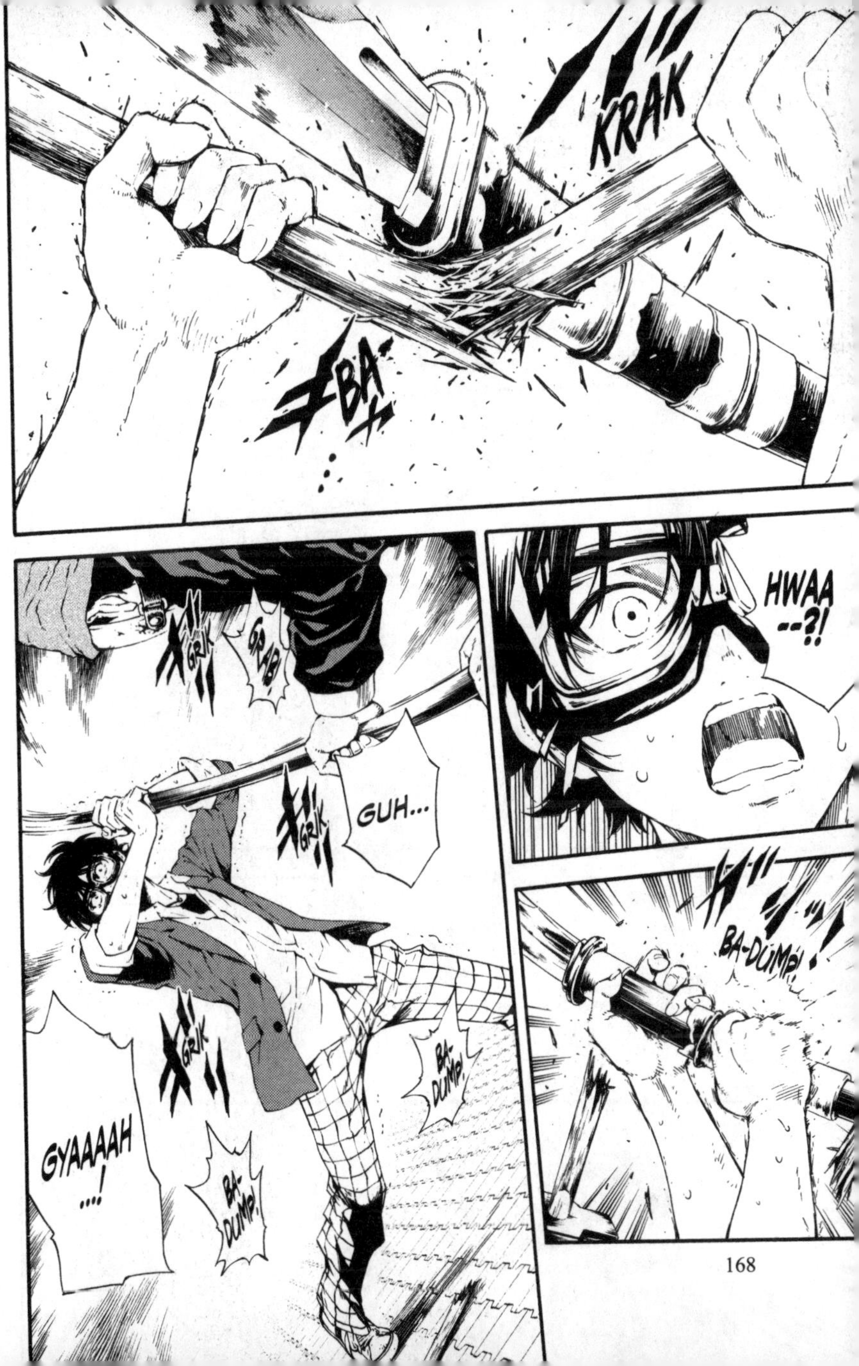
KRAK
BAK
HWAA --?!
BA-DUMP!
GRIK
GRAB!
GRIK
GUH...
GRIK
BA-DUMP!
GYAAAAH ...!
BA-DUMP!

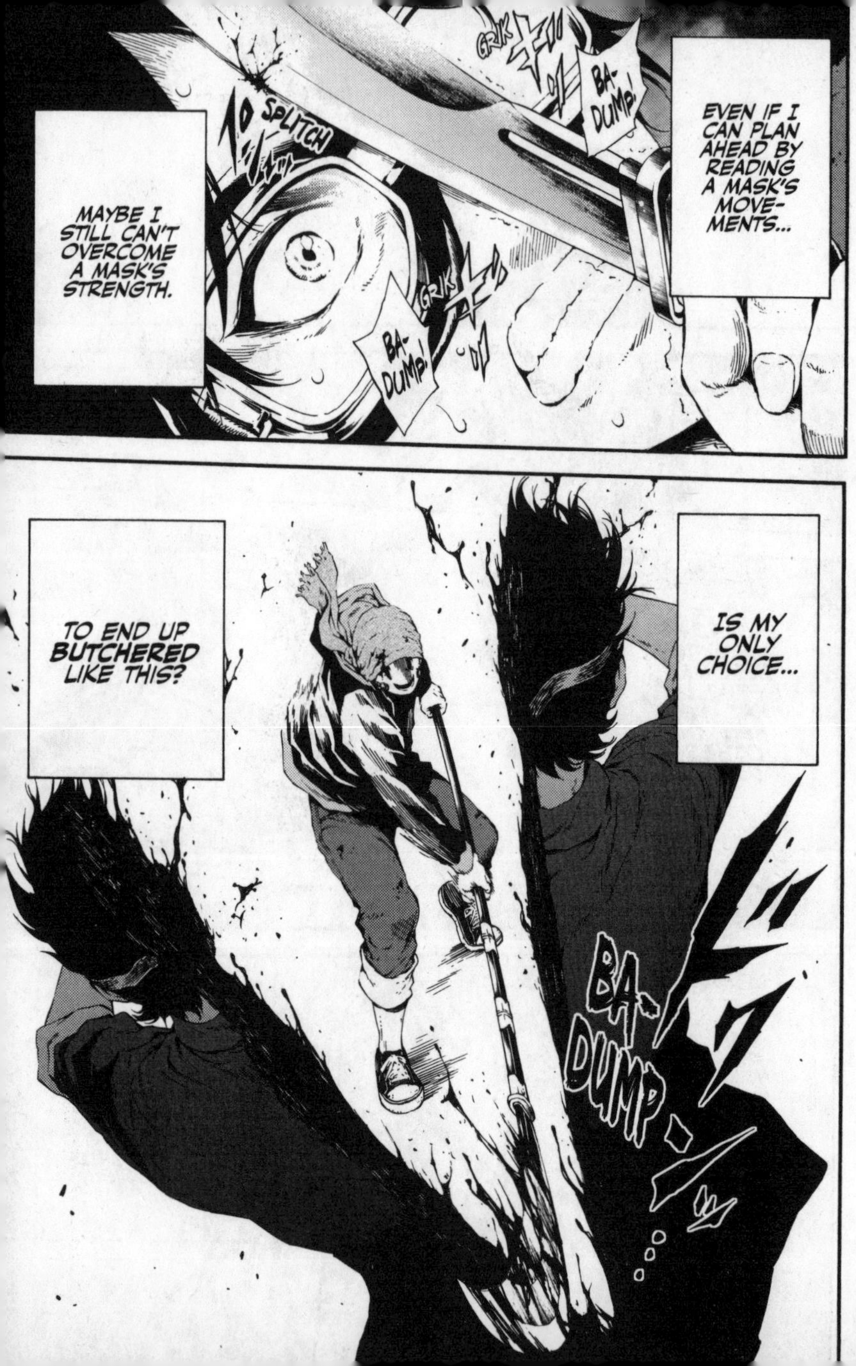

EVEN IF I CAN PLAN AHEAD BY READING A MASK'S MOVEMENTS...
GRIK
BA-DUMP!
SPLITCH
GRIK
BA-DUMP!
MAYBE I STILL CAN'T OVERCOME A MASK'S STRENGTH.
IS MY ONLY CHOICE...
BA-DUMP
TO END UP BUTCHERED LIKE THIS?

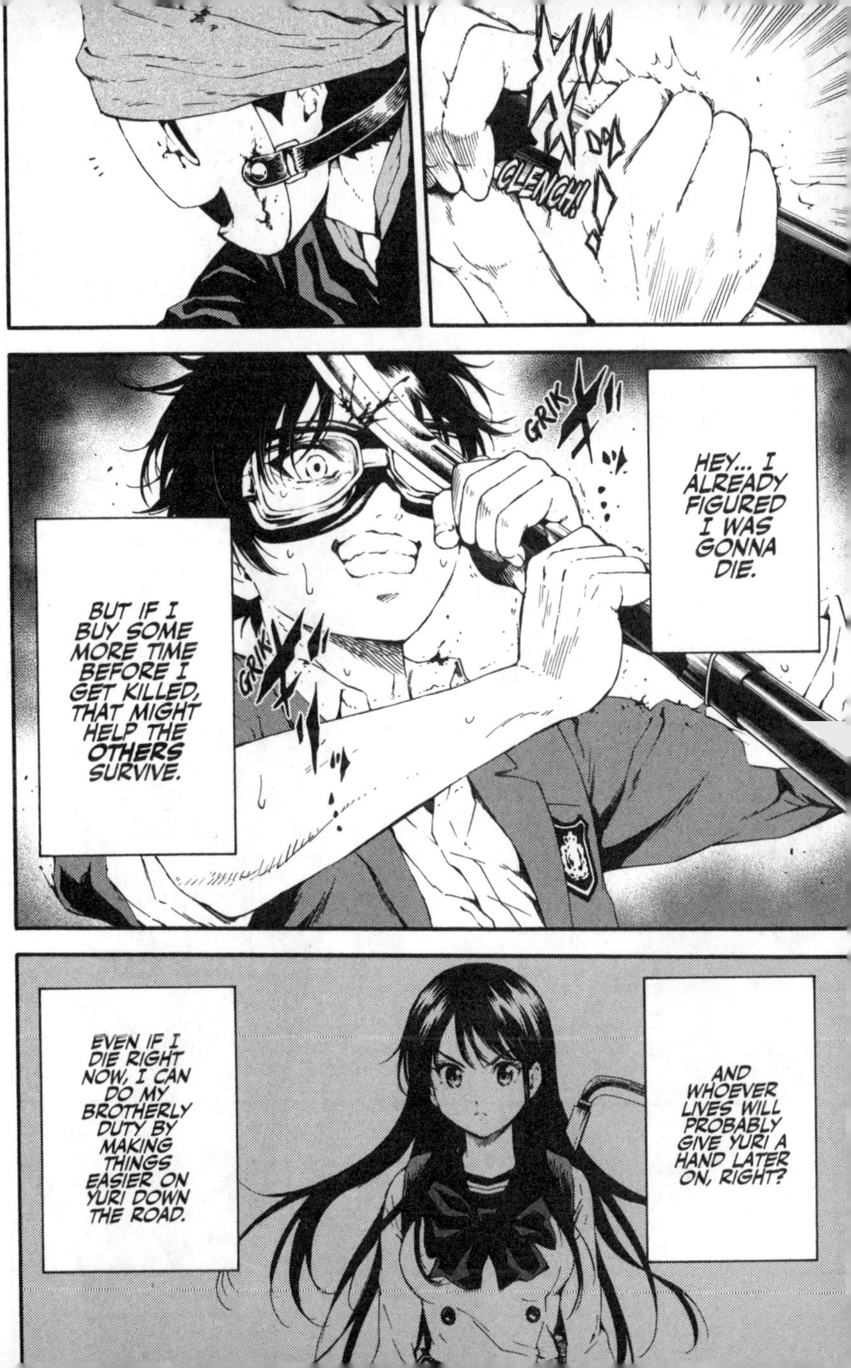
CLENCH!
HEY... I ALREADY FIGURED I WAS GONNA DIE.
GRIK
BUT IF I BUY SOME MORE TIME BEFORE I GET KILLED, THAT MIGHT HELP THE **OTHERS** SURVIVE.
GRIK
AND WHOEVER LIVES WILL PROBABLY GIVE YURI A HAND LATER ON, RIGHT?
EVEN IF I DIE RIGHT NOW, I CAN DO MY BROTHERLY DUTY BY MAKING THINGS EASIER ON YURI DOWN THE ROAD.

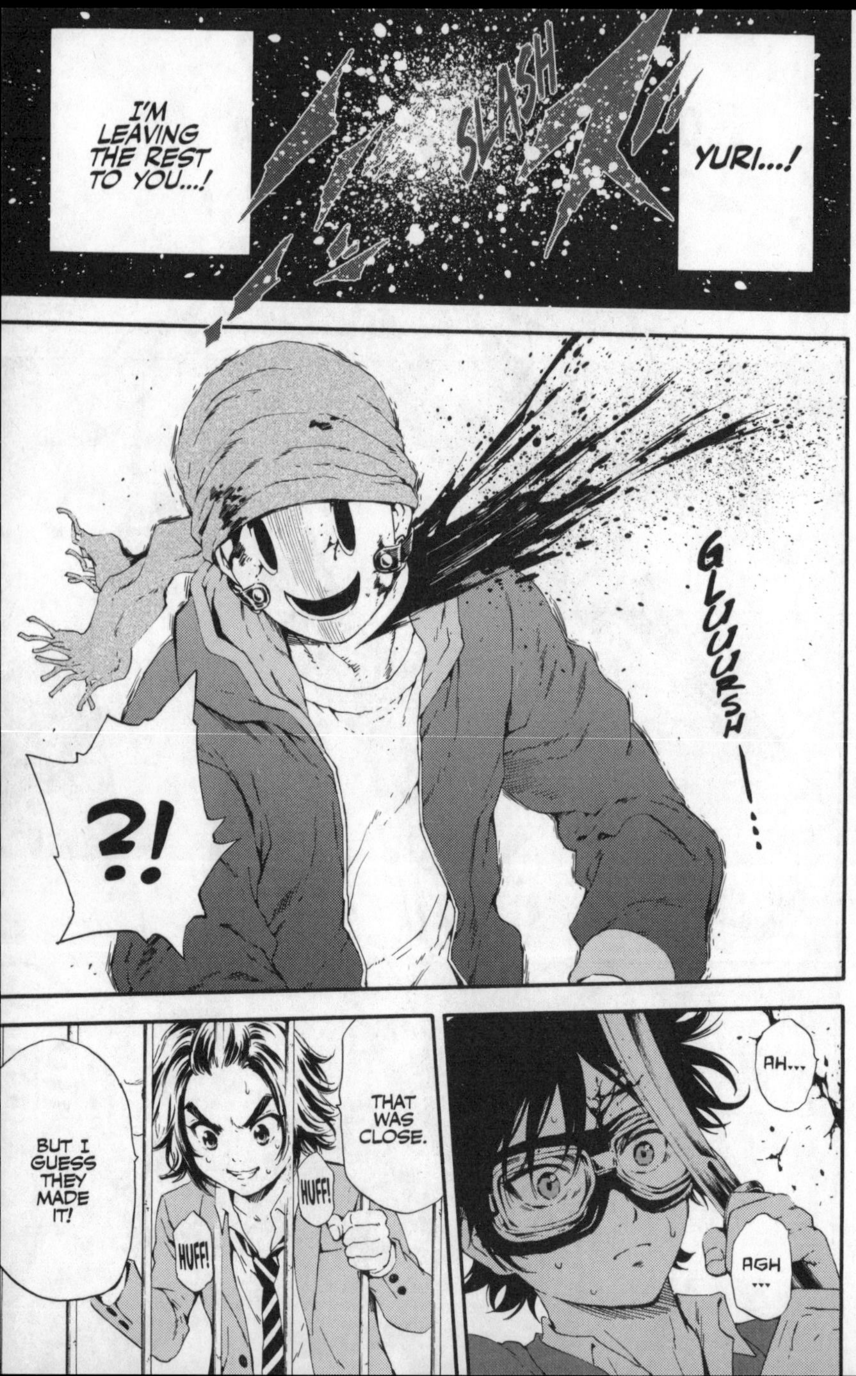
YURI...!
SLASH
I'M LEAVING THE REST TO YOU...!
GLUUURSH—...
?!
AH...
AGH...
THAT WAS CLOSE.
HUFF!
HUFF!
BUT I GUESS THEY MADE IT!

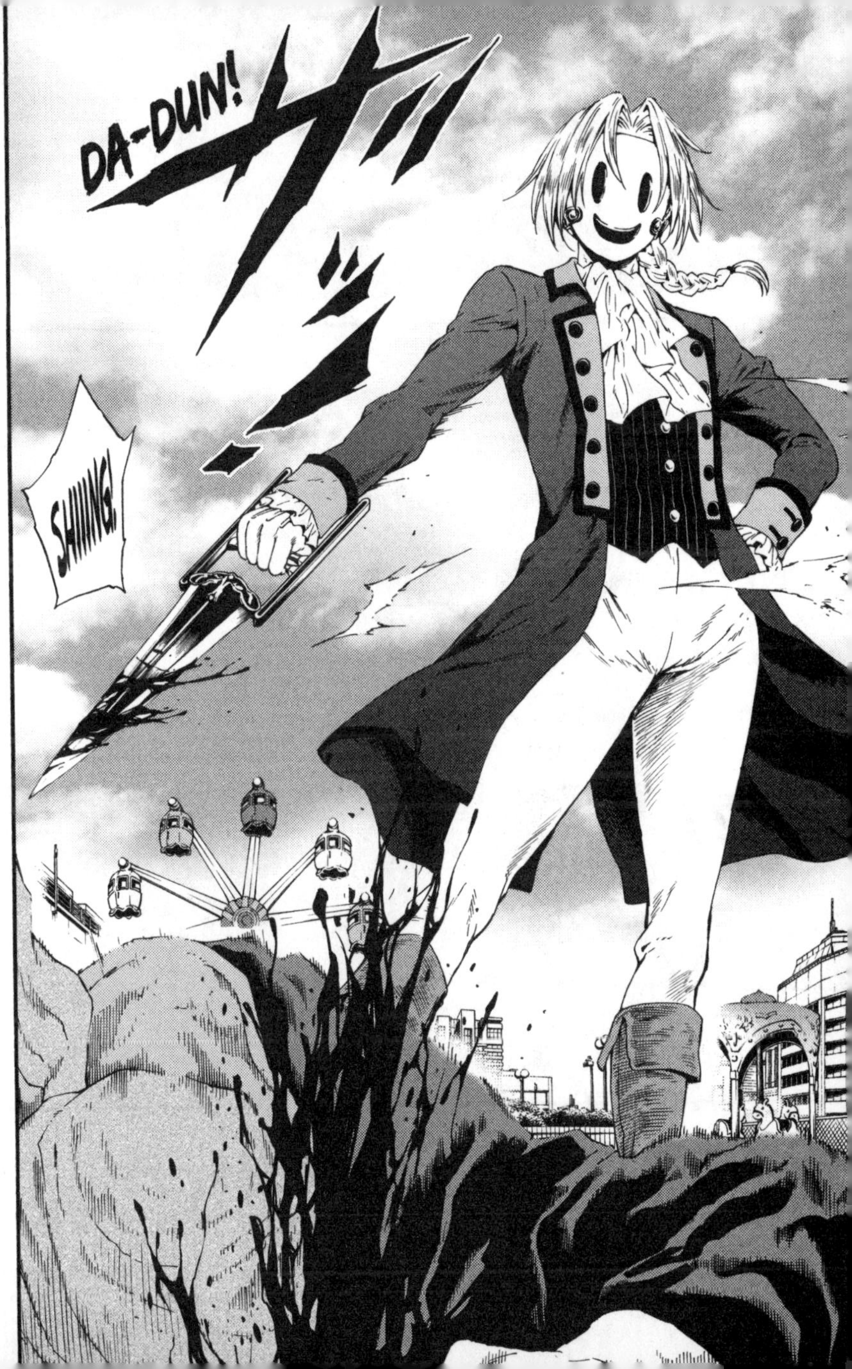
DA-DUN!
SHIIING!

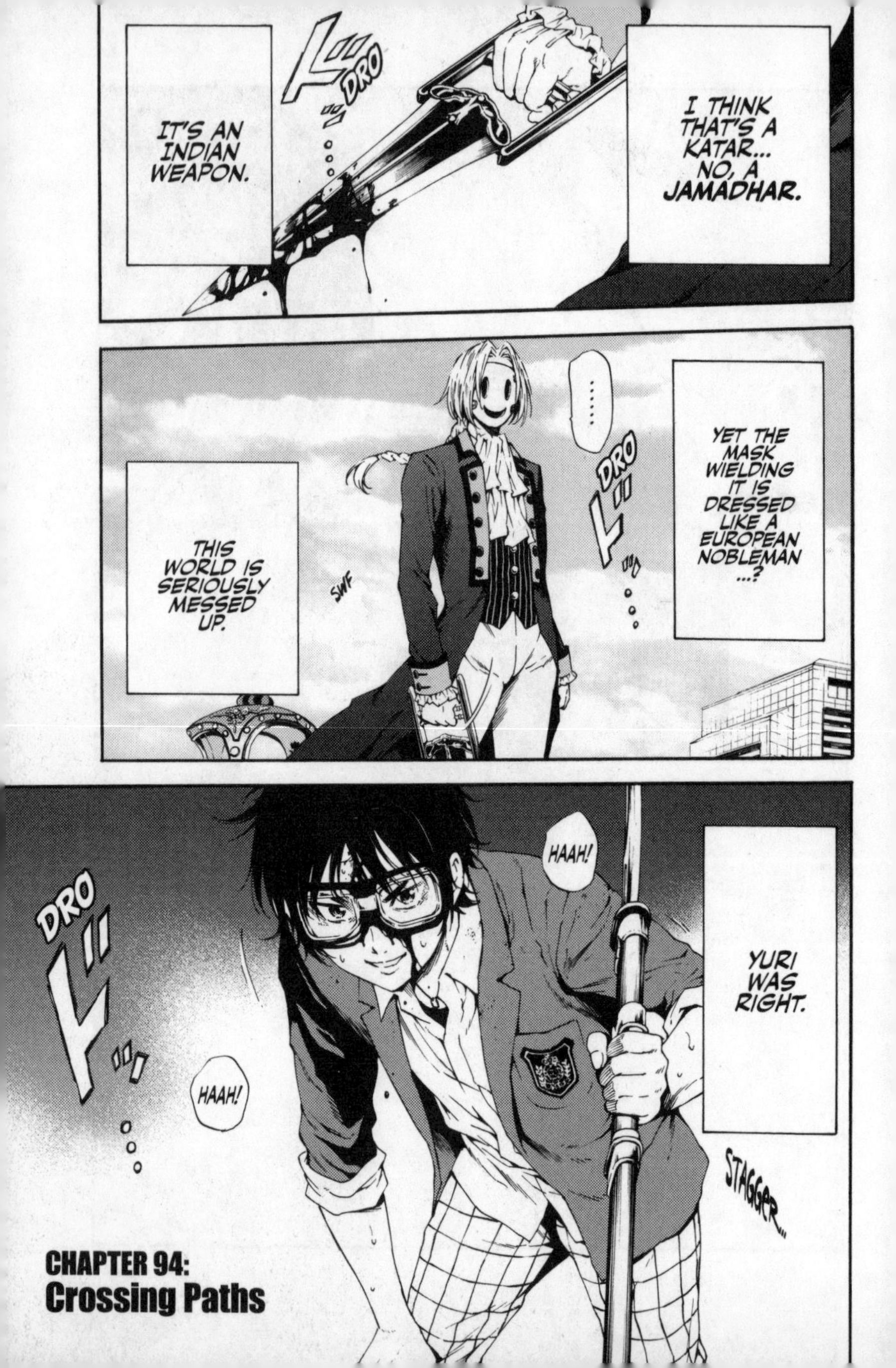
I THINK THAT'S A KATAR... NO, A JAMADHAR.
DRO
IT'S AN INDIAN WEAPON.
YET THE MASK WIELDING IT IS DRESSED LIKE A EUROPEAN NOBLEMAN ...?
DRO
......
SWF
THIS WORLD IS SERIOUSLY MESSED UP.
YURI WAS RIGHT.
HAAH!
STAGGER...
HAAH!
DRO

CHAPTER 94: Crossing Paths

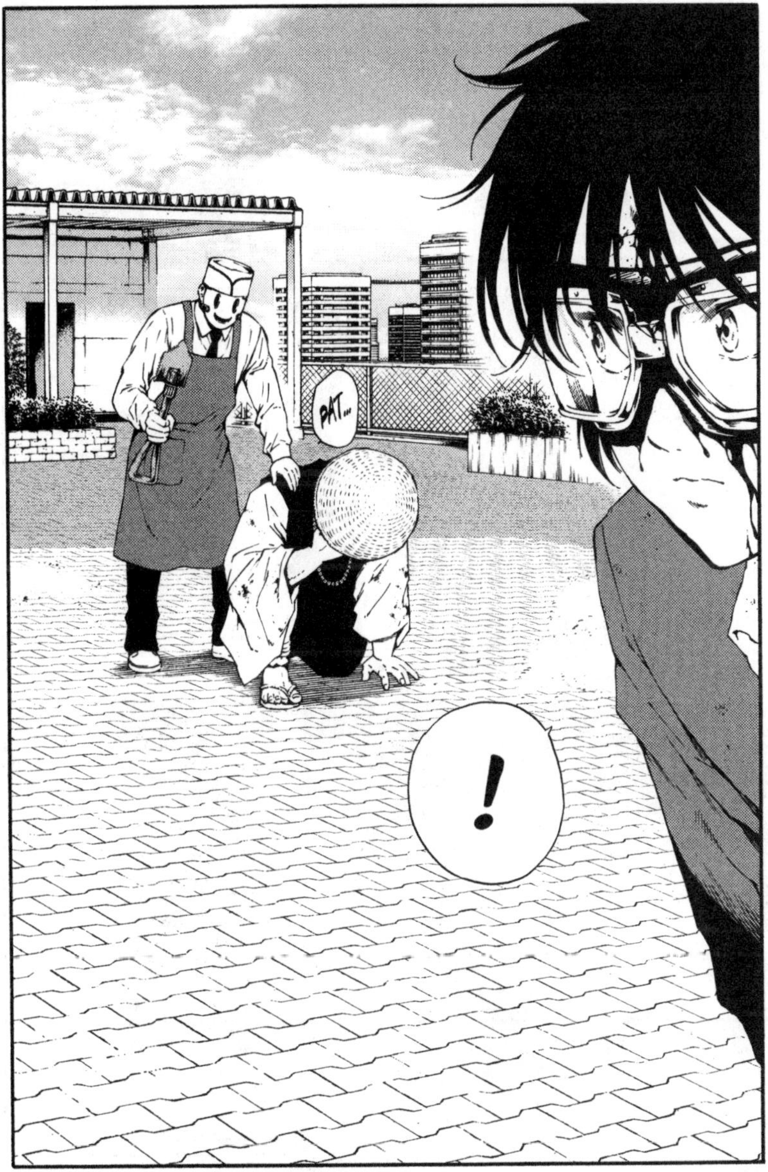
BAT...
!

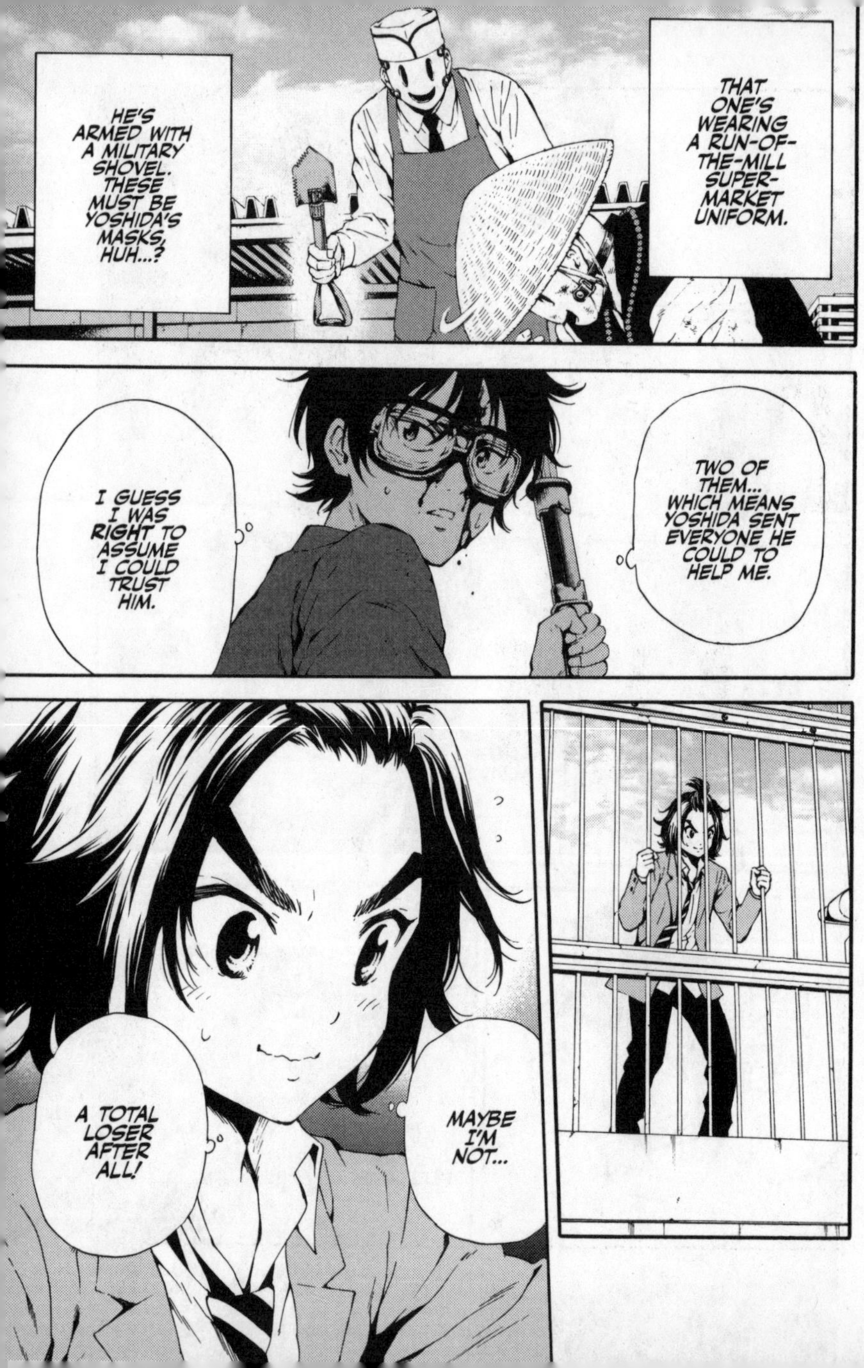
THAT ONE'S WEARING A RUN-OF-THE-MILL SUPER-MARKET UNIFORM.
HE'S ARMED WITH A MILITARY SHOVEL. THESE MUST BE YOSHIDA'S MASKS, HUH...?
TWO OF THEM... WHICH MEANS YOSHIDA SENT EVERYONE HE COULD TO HELP ME.
I GUESS I WAS RIGHT TO ASSUME I COULD TRUST HIM.
MAYBE I'M NOT...
A TOTAL LOSER AFTER ALL!

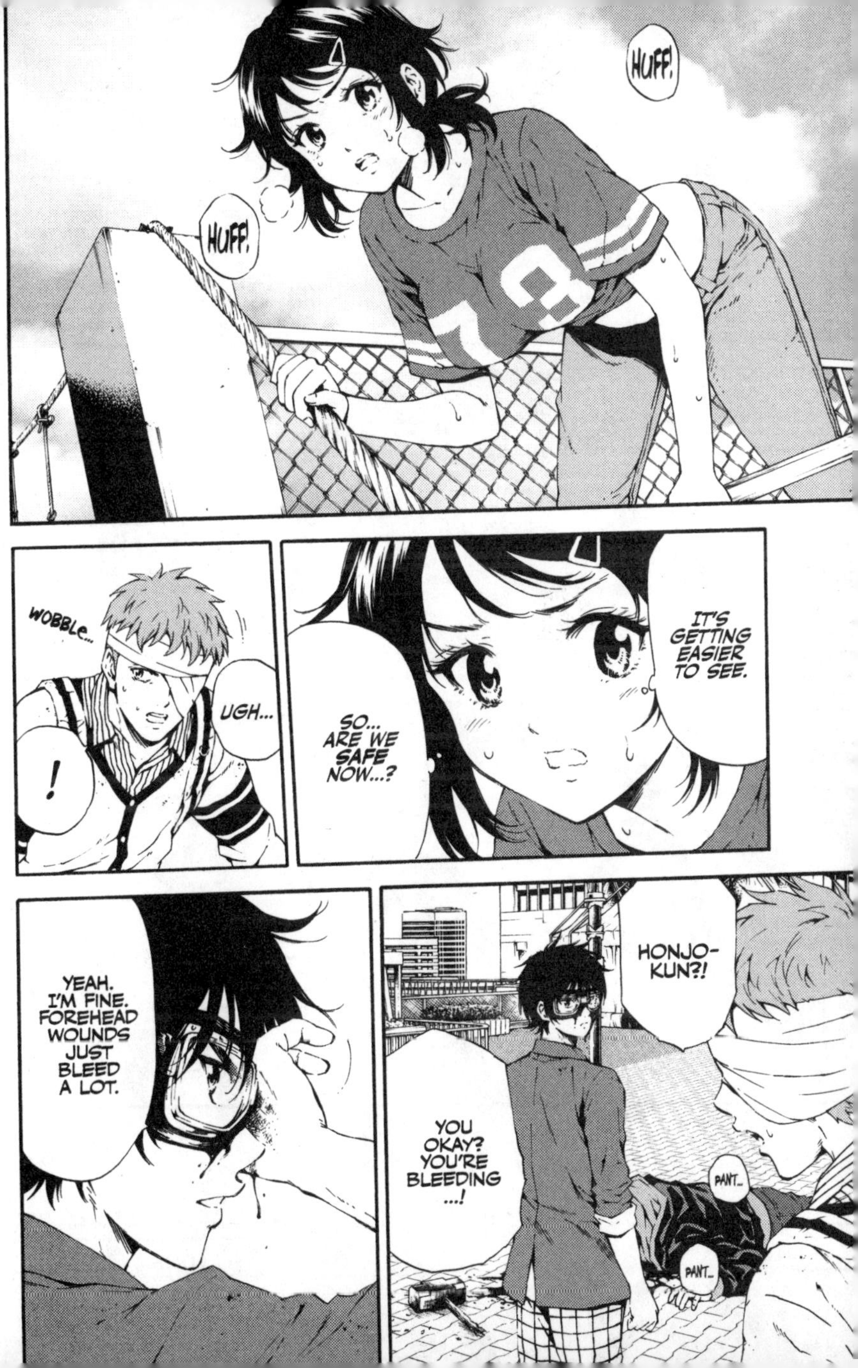
HUFF!
HUFF!
IT'S GETTING EASIER TO SEE.
SO... ARE WE SAFE NOW...?
WOBBLe...
UGH...
!
HONJO-KUN?!
YOU OKAY? YOU'RE BLEEDING ...!
PANT...
PANT...
YEAH. I'M FINE. FOREHEAD WOUNDS JUST BLEED A LOT.

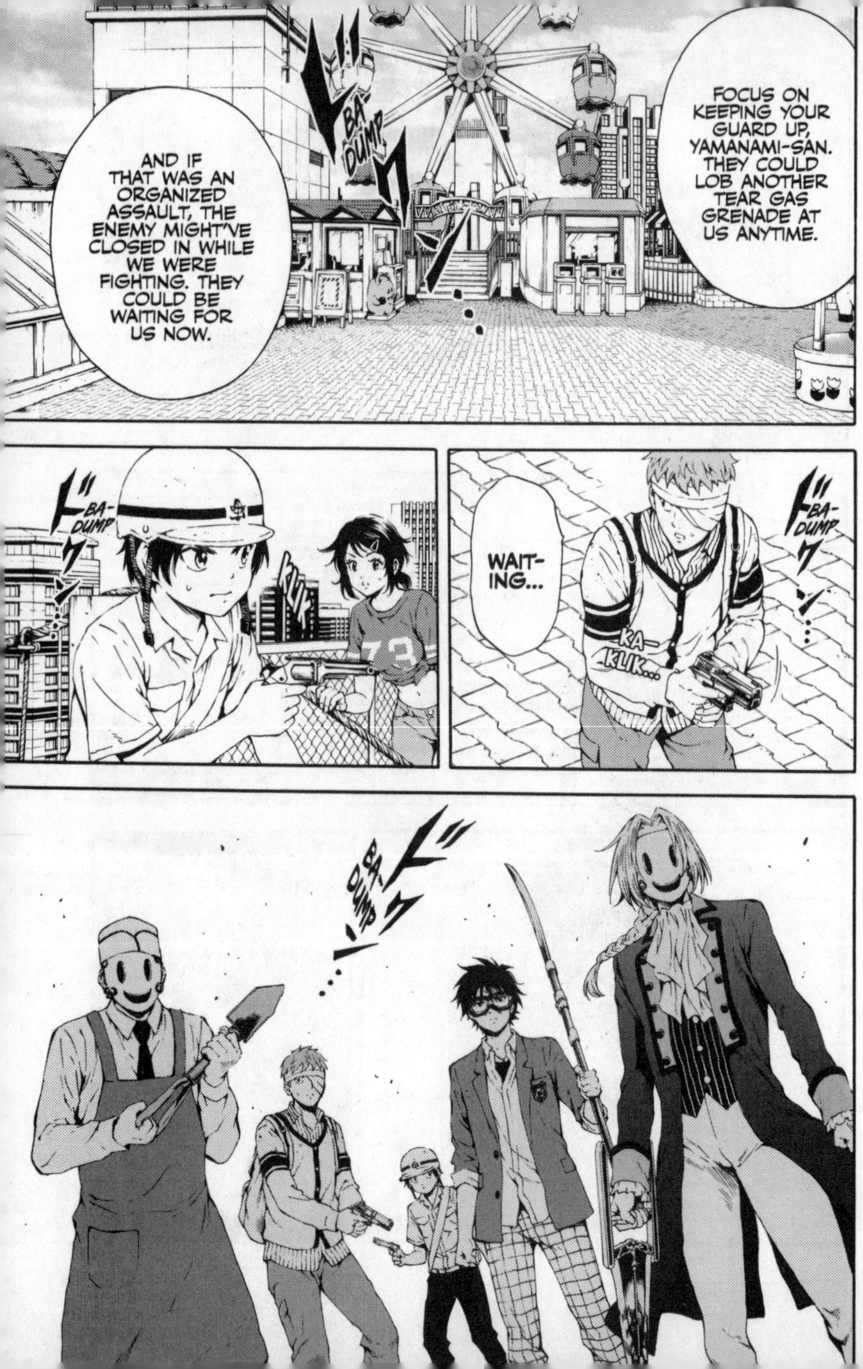
FOCUS ON KEEPING YOUR GUARD UP, YAMANAMI-SAN. THEY COULD LOB ANOTHER TEAR GAS GRENADE AT US ANYTIME.
BA-DUMP
AND IF THAT WAS AN ORGANIZED ASSAULT, THE ENEMY MIGHT'VE CLOSED IN WHILE WE WERE FIGHTING. THEY COULD BE WAITING FOR US NOW.
BA-DUMP
WAIT-ING...
KA-KLIK...
BA-DUMP
KLIK
BA-DUMP

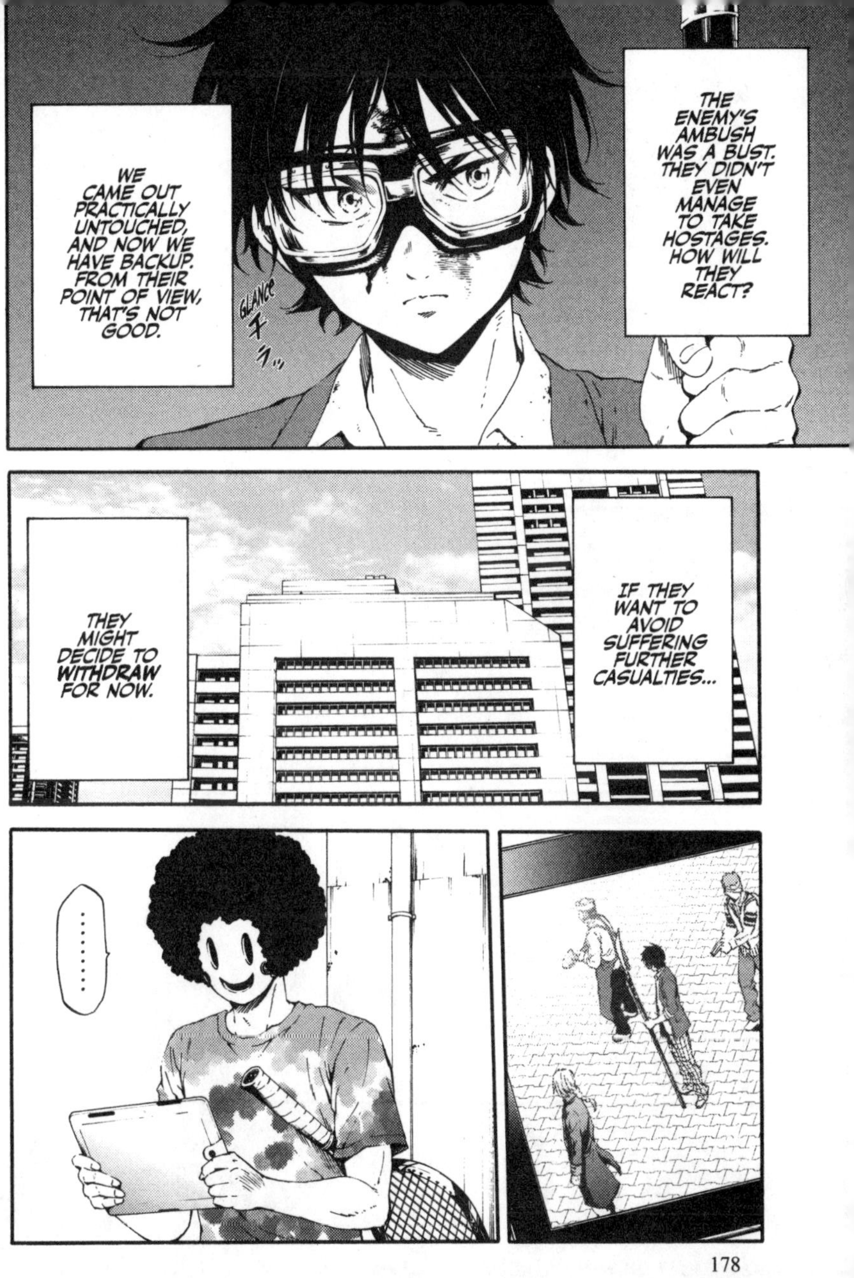
THE ENEMY'S AMBUSH WAS A BUST. THEY DIDN'T EVEN MANAGE TO TAKE HOSTAGES. HOW WILL THEY REACT?
WE CAME OUT PRACTICALLY UNTOUCHED, AND NOW WE HAVE BACKUP. FROM THEIR POINT OF VIEW, THAT'S NOT GOOD.
GLANCE
チラ
IF THEY WANT TO AVOID SUFFERING FURTHER CASUALTIES...
THEY MIGHT DECIDE TO WITHDRAW FOR NOW.
....

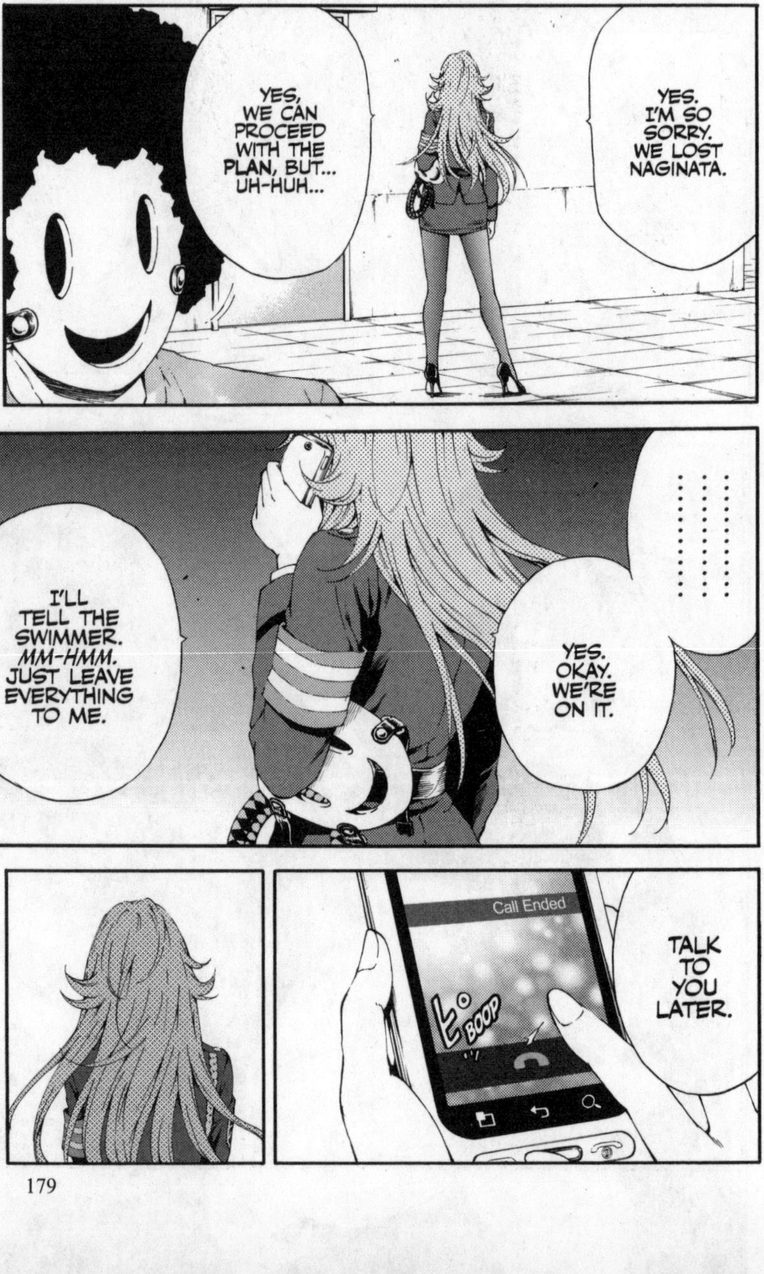
YES. I'M SO SORRY. WE LOST NAGINATA.
YES, WE CAN PROCEED WITH THE PLAN, BUT... UH-HUH...
......
YES. OKAY. WE'RE ON IT.
I'LL TELL THE SWIMMER. *MM-HMM.* JUST LEAVE EVERYTHING TO ME.
TALK TO YOU LATER.
Call Ended
BOOP

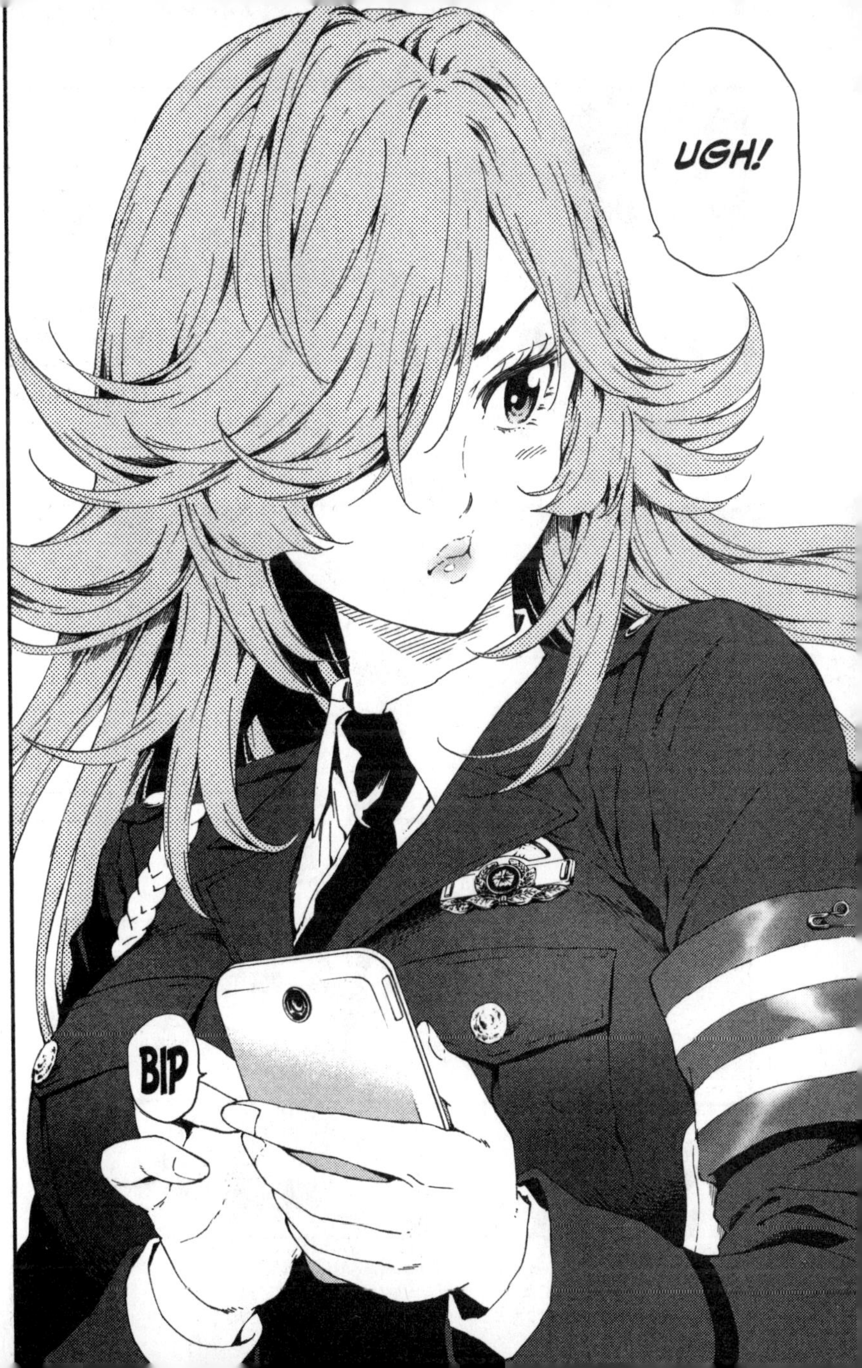
UGH!
BIP

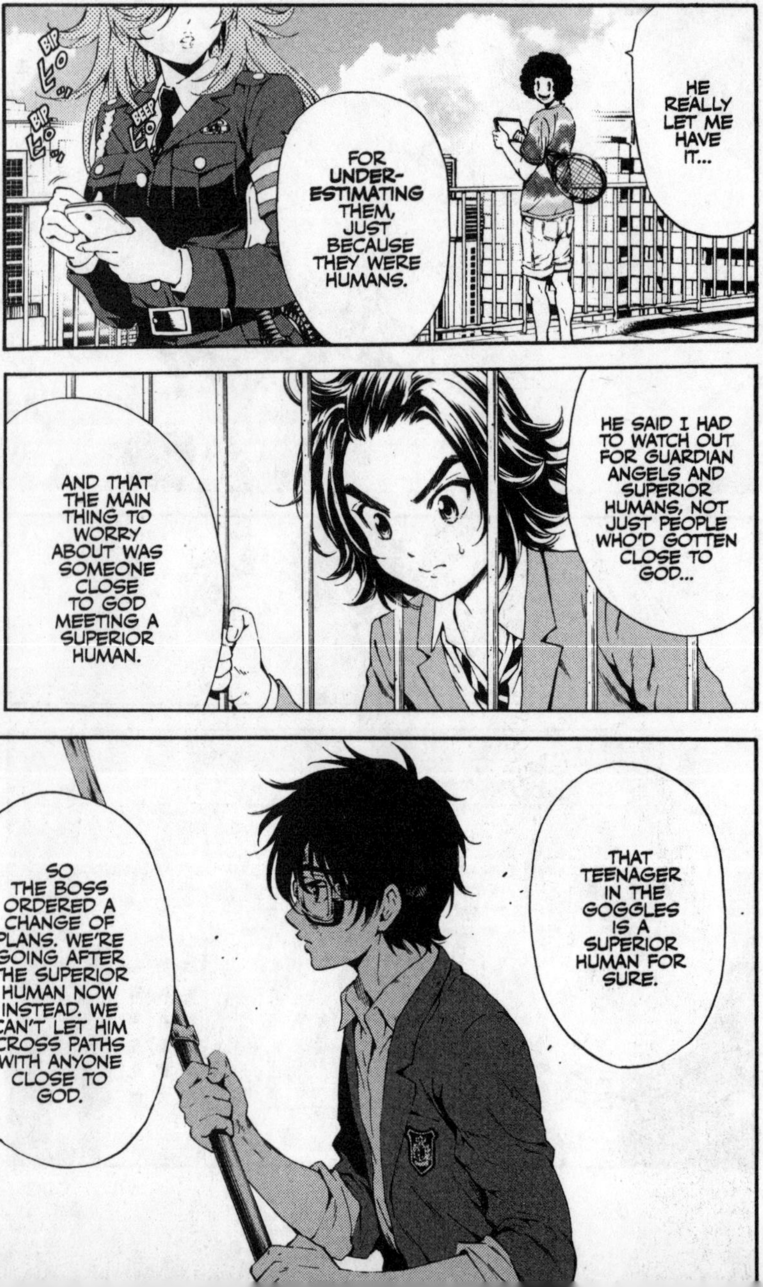
HE REALLY LET ME HAVE IT...
FOR UNDER-ESTIMATING THEM, JUST BECAUSE THEY WERE HUMANS.
BIP
BIP
BEEP
HE SAID I HAD TO WATCH OUT FOR GUARDIAN ANGELS AND SUPERIOR HUMANS, NOT JUST PEOPLE WHO'D GOTTEN CLOSE TO GOD...
AND THAT THE MAIN THING TO WORRY ABOUT WAS SOMEONE CLOSE TO GOD MEETING A SUPERIOR HUMAN.
THAT TEENAGER IN THE GOGGLES IS A SUPERIOR HUMAN FOR SURE.
SO THE BOSS ORDERED A CHANGE OF PLANS. WE'RE GOING AFTER THE SUPERIOR HUMAN NOW INSTEAD. WE CAN'T LET HIM CROSS PATHS WITH ANYONE CLOSE TO GOD.

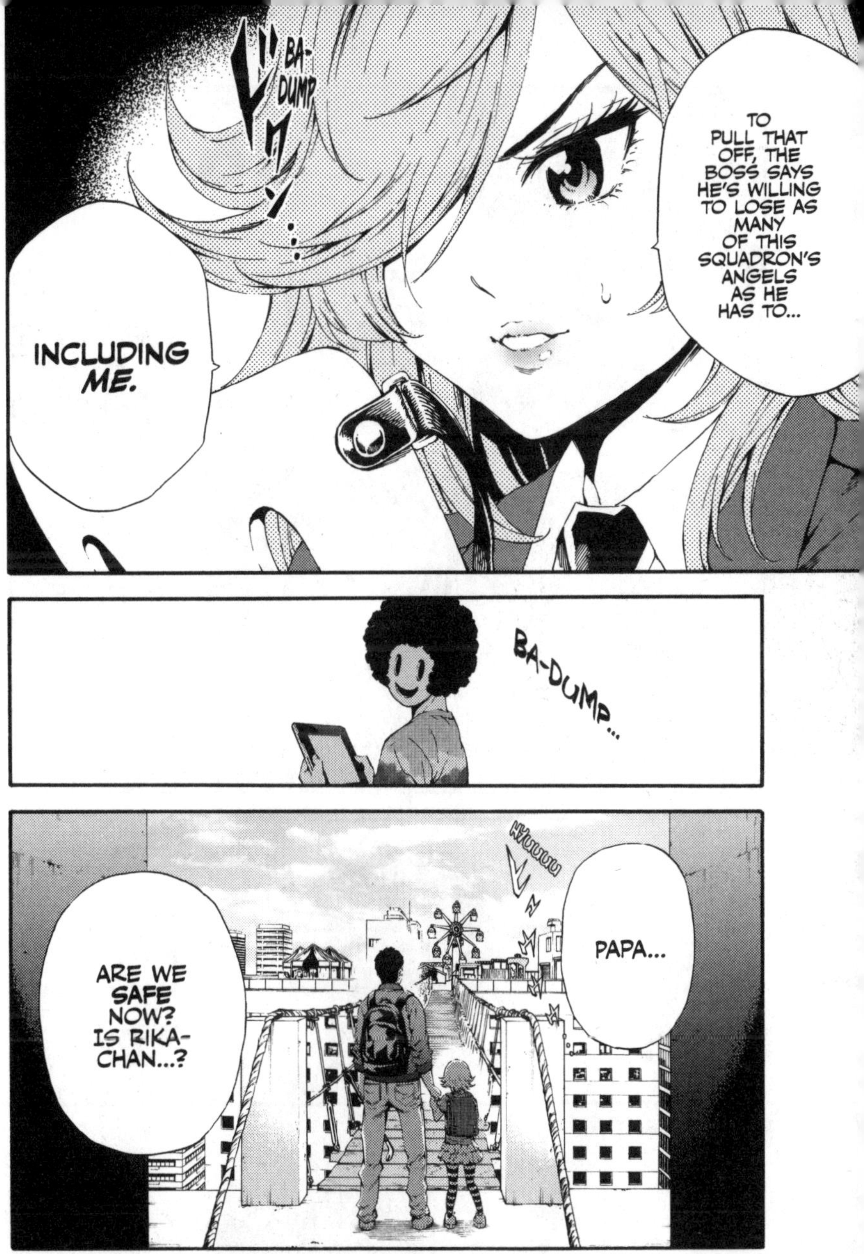
TO PULL THAT OFF, THE BOSS SAYS HE'S WILLING TO LOSE AS MANY OF THIS SQUADRON'S ANGELS AS HE HAS TO...
BA-DUMP
INCLUDING *ME.*
BA-DUMP...
PAPA...
ARE WE SAFE NOW? IS RIKA-CHAN...?

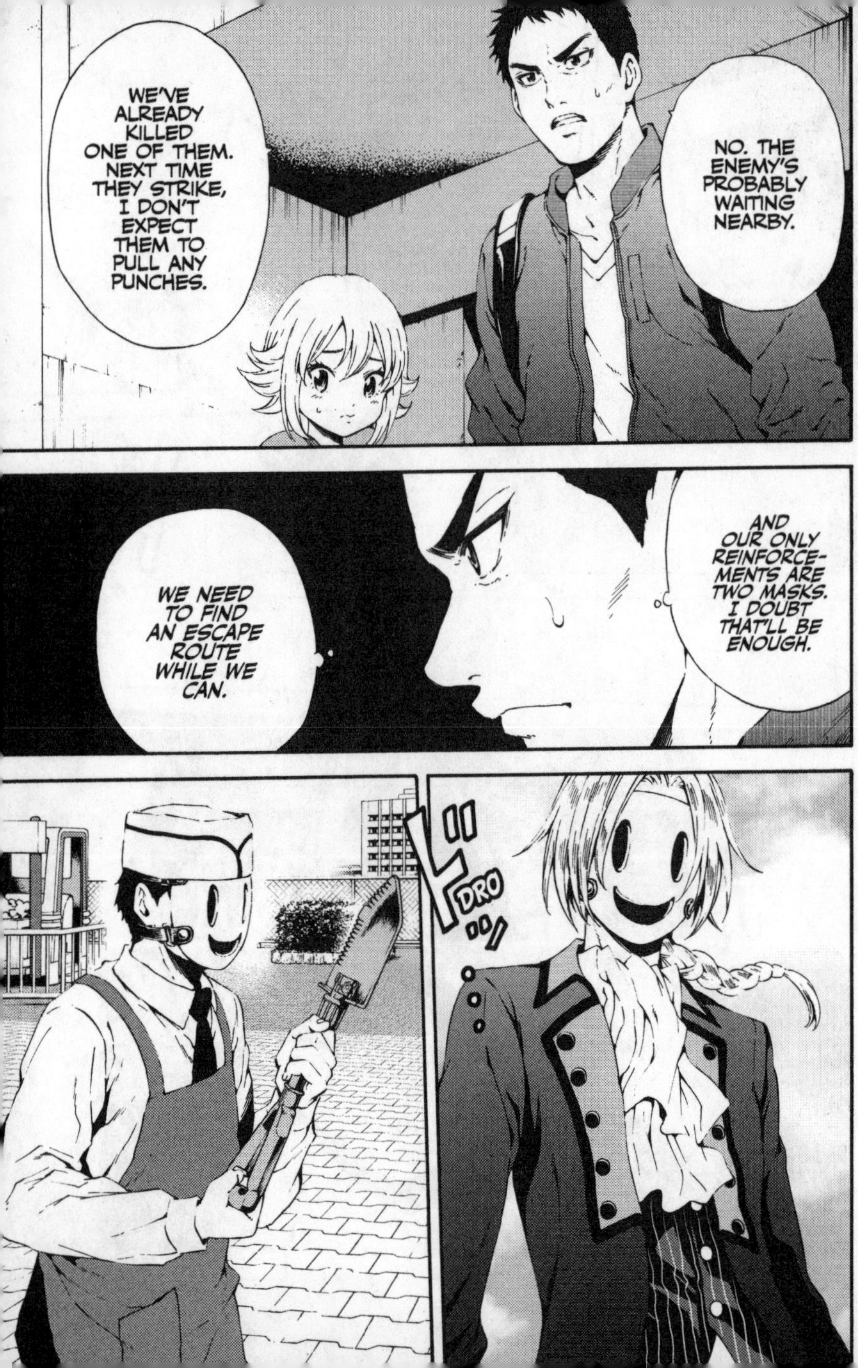
NO. THE ENEMY'S PROBABLY WAITING NEARBY.
WE'VE ALREADY KILLED ONE OF THEM. NEXT TIME THEY STRIKE, I DON'T EXPECT THEM TO PULL ANY PUNCHES.
AND OUR ONLY REINFORCE-MENTS ARE TWO MASKS. I DOUBT THAT'LL BE ENOUGH.
WE NEED TO FIND AN ESCAPE ROUTE WHILE WE CAN.
DRO

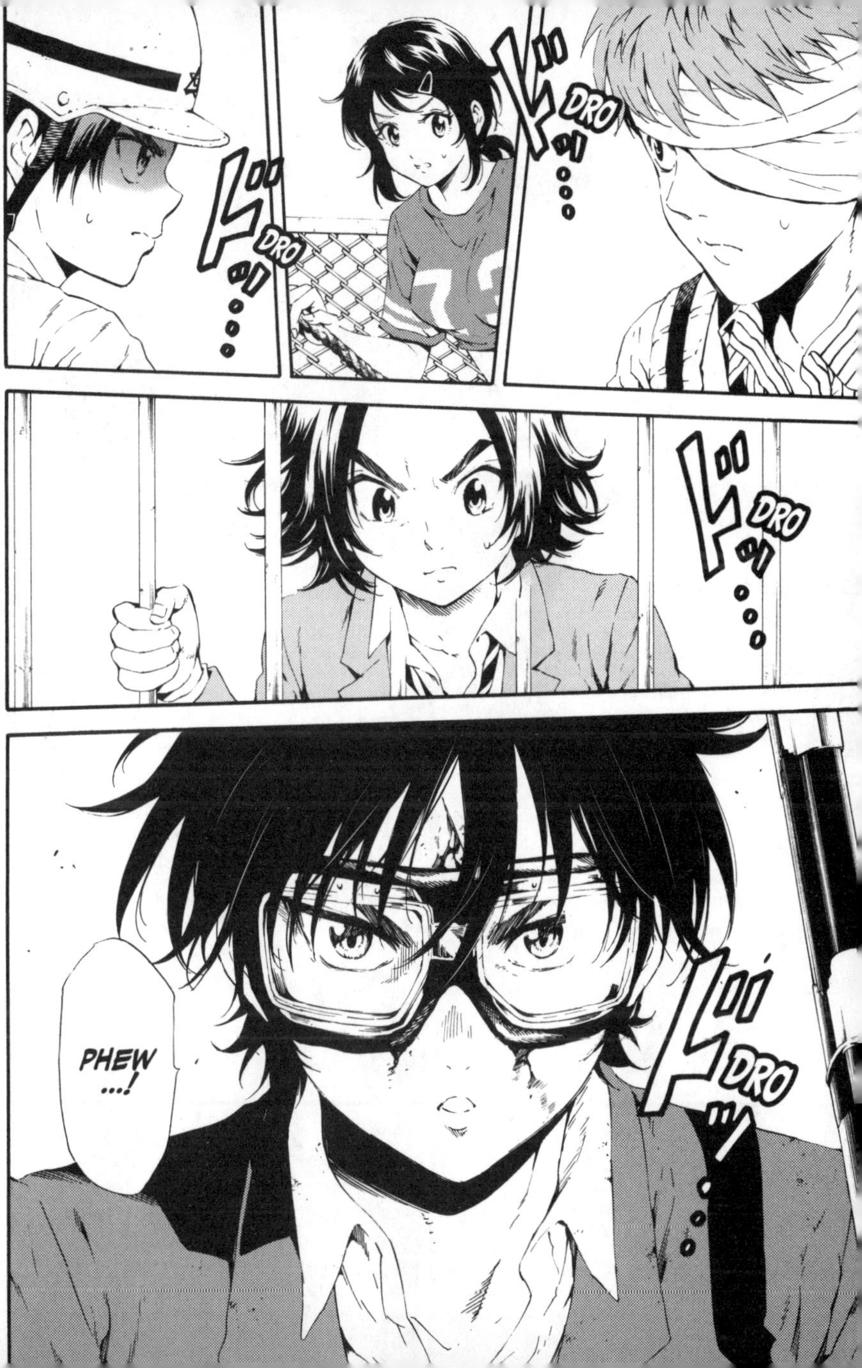
ド DRO ッ…
ド DRO ッ…
ド DRO ッ…
ド DRO ッ…
PHEW ...!

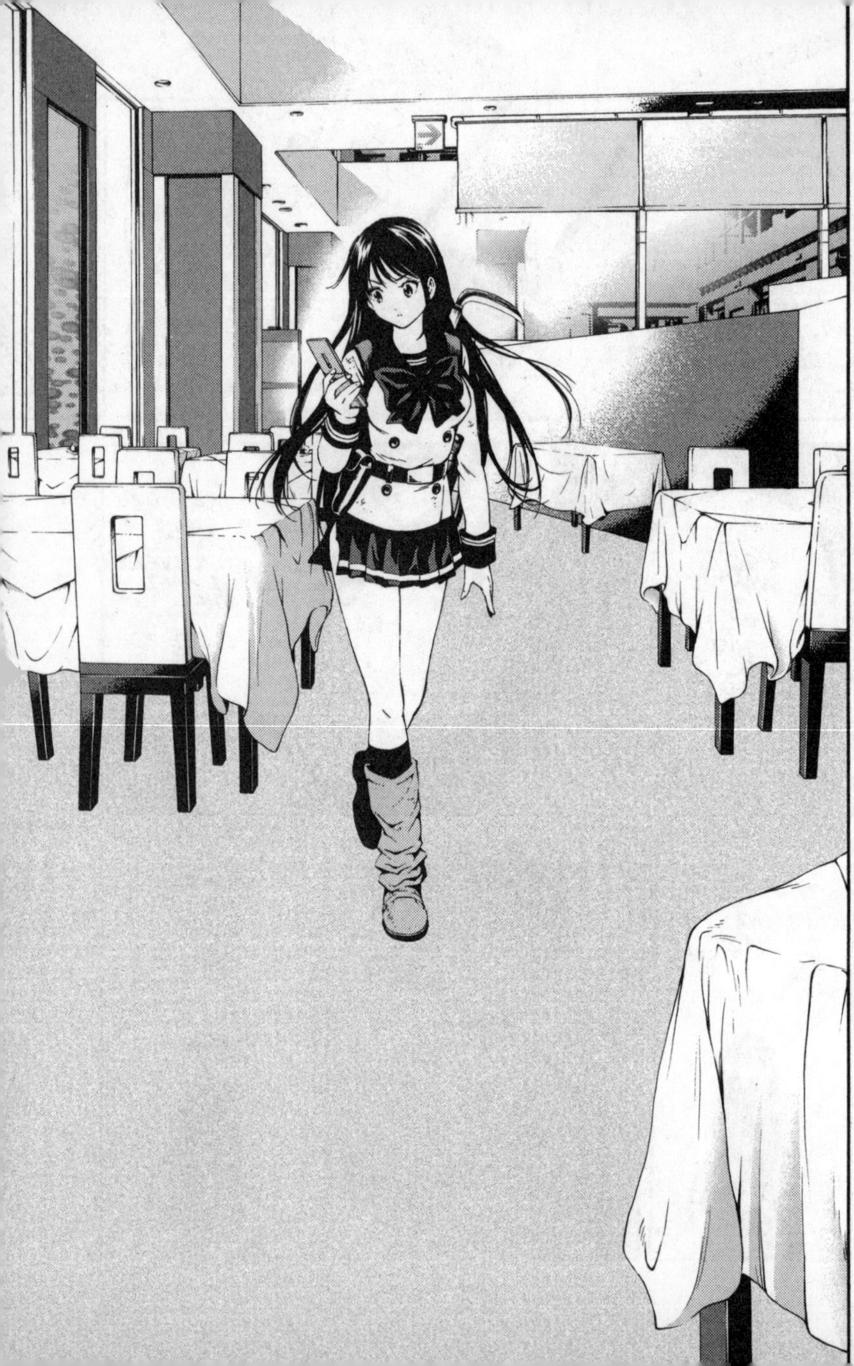

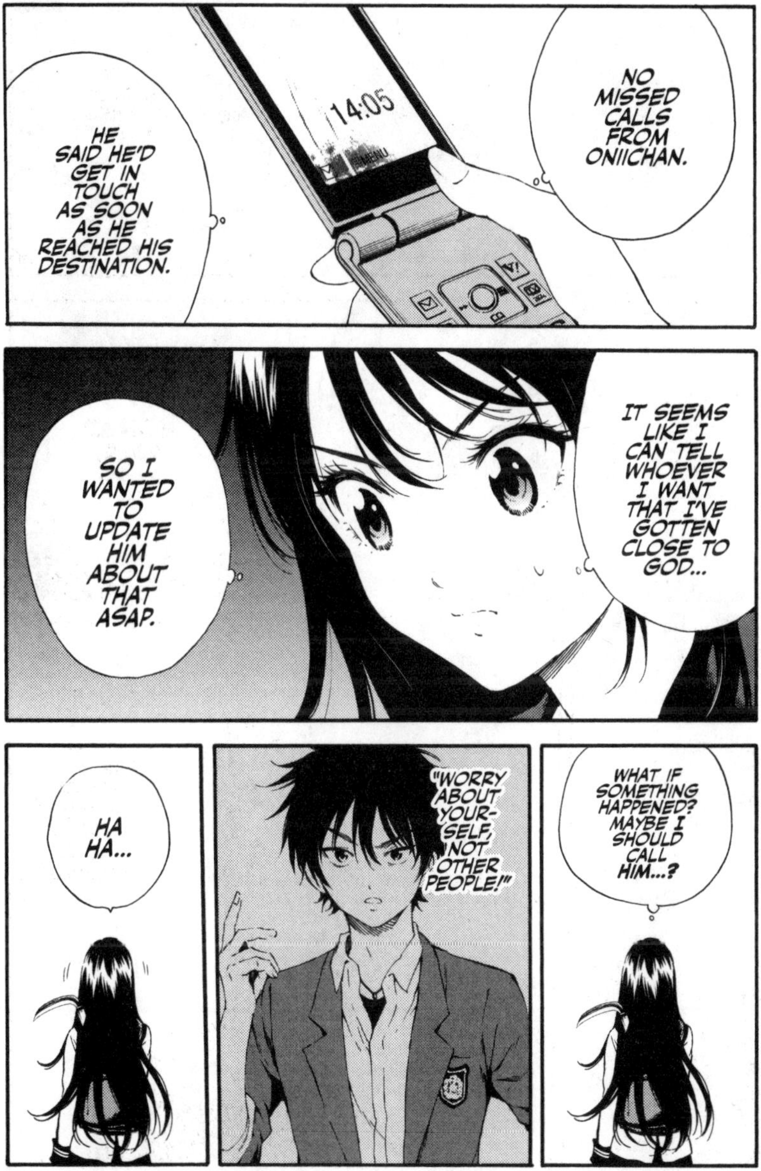
NO MISSED CALLS FROM ONIICHAN.
14:05
HE SAID HE'D GET IN TOUCH AS SOON AS HE REACHED HIS DESTINATION.
IT SEEMS LIKE I CAN TELL WHOEVER I WANT THAT I'VE GOTTEN CLOSE TO GOD...
SO I WANTED TO UPDATE HIM ABOUT THAT ASAP.
WHAT IF SOMETHING HAPPENED? MAYBE I SHOULD CALL HIM...?
"WORRY ABOUT YOUR-SELF, NOT OTHER PEOPLE!"
HA HA...

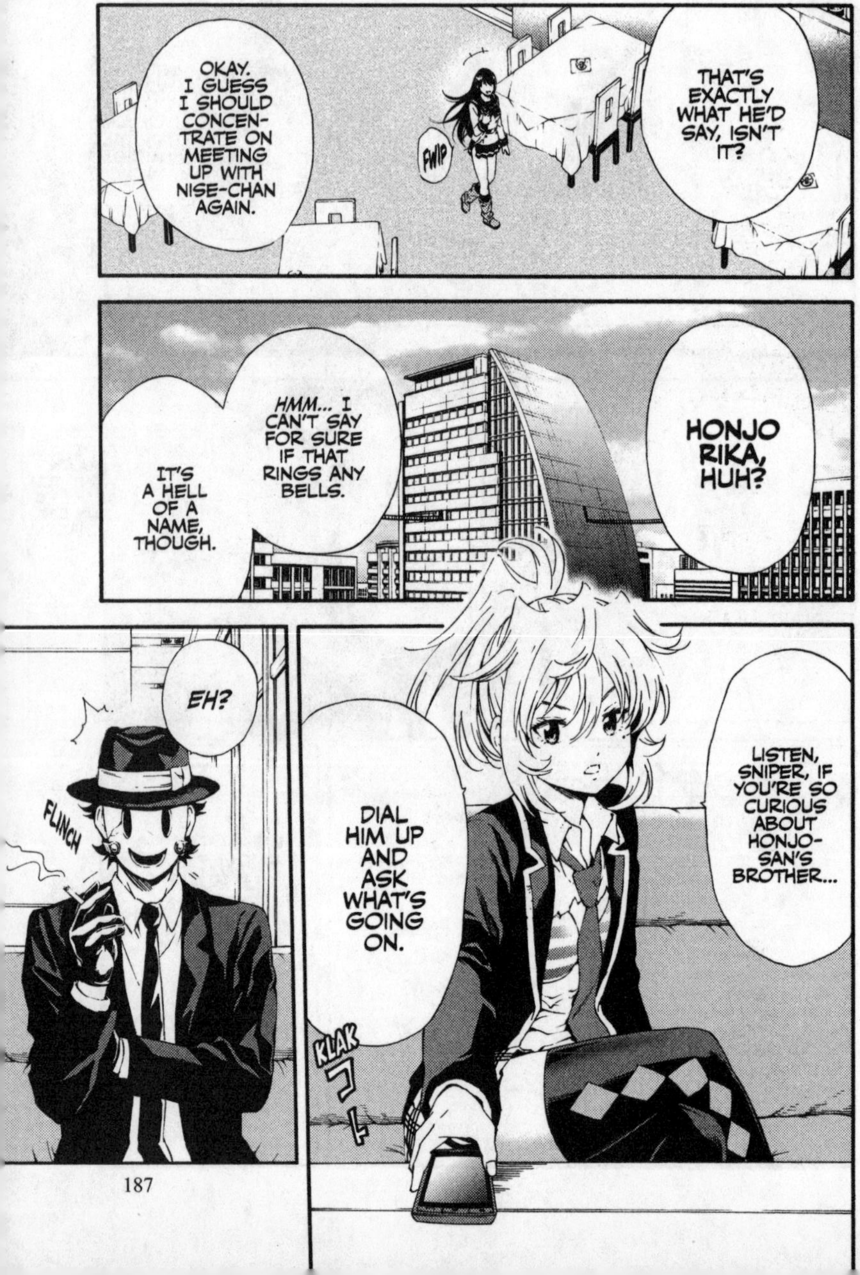
THAT'S EXACTLY WHAT HE'D SAY, ISN'T IT?
FWIP
OKAY. I GUESS I SHOULD CONCEN-TRATE ON MEETING UP WITH NISE-CHAN AGAIN.
HONJO RIKA, HUH?
HMM... I CAN'T SAY FOR SURE IF THAT RINGS ANY BELLS.
IT'S A HELL OF A NAME, THOUGH.
LISTEN, SNIPER, IF YOU'RE SO CURIOUS ABOUT HONJO-SAN'S BROTHER...
DIAL HIM UP AND ASK WHAT'S GOING ON.
KLAK
EH?
FLINCH

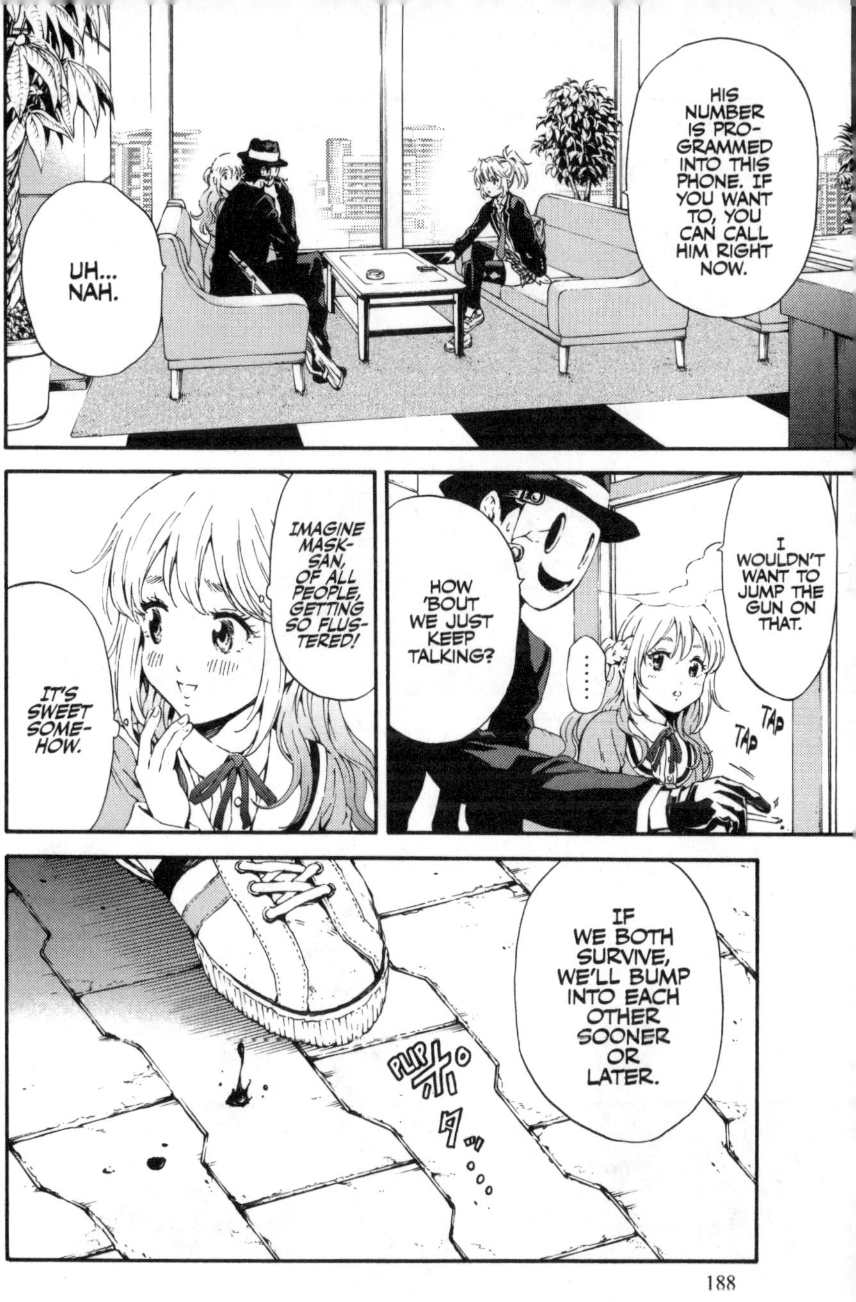
HIS NUMBER IS PRO-GRAMMED INTO THIS PHONE. IF YOU WANT TO, YOU CAN CALL HIM RIGHT NOW.
UH... NAH.
I WOULDN'T WANT TO JUMP THE GUN ON THAT.
HOW 'BOUT WE JUST KEEP TALKING?
TAP
TAP
......
IMAGINE MASK-SAN, OF ALL PEOPLE, GETTING SO FLUS-TERED!
IT'S SWEET SOME-HOW.
IF WE BOTH SURVIVE, WE'LL BUMP INTO EACH OTHER SOONER OR LATER.
PLIP

HIGH-RISE INVASION

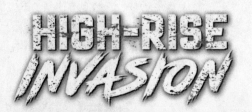

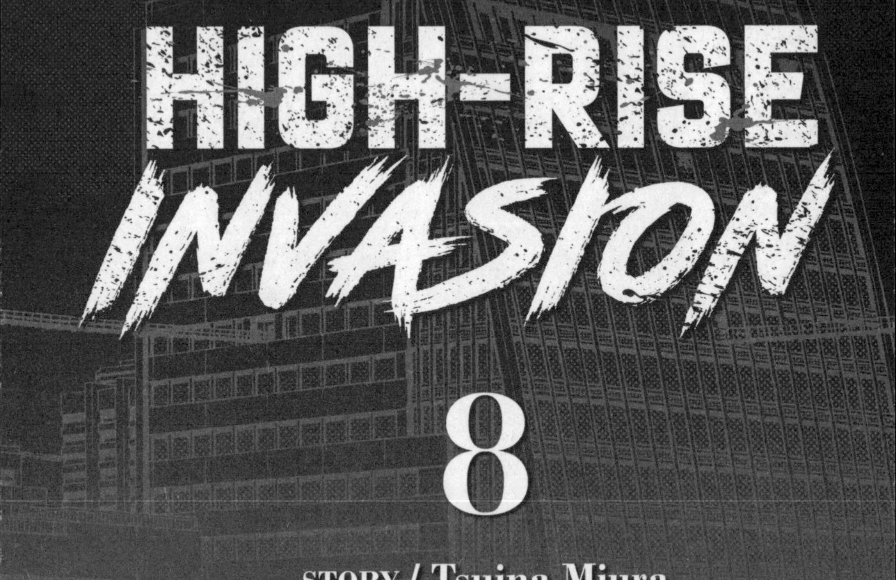

HIGH-RISE INVASION

8

STORY / Tsuina Miura
ART / Takahiro Oba

HIGH-RISE INVASION

8

CONTENTS

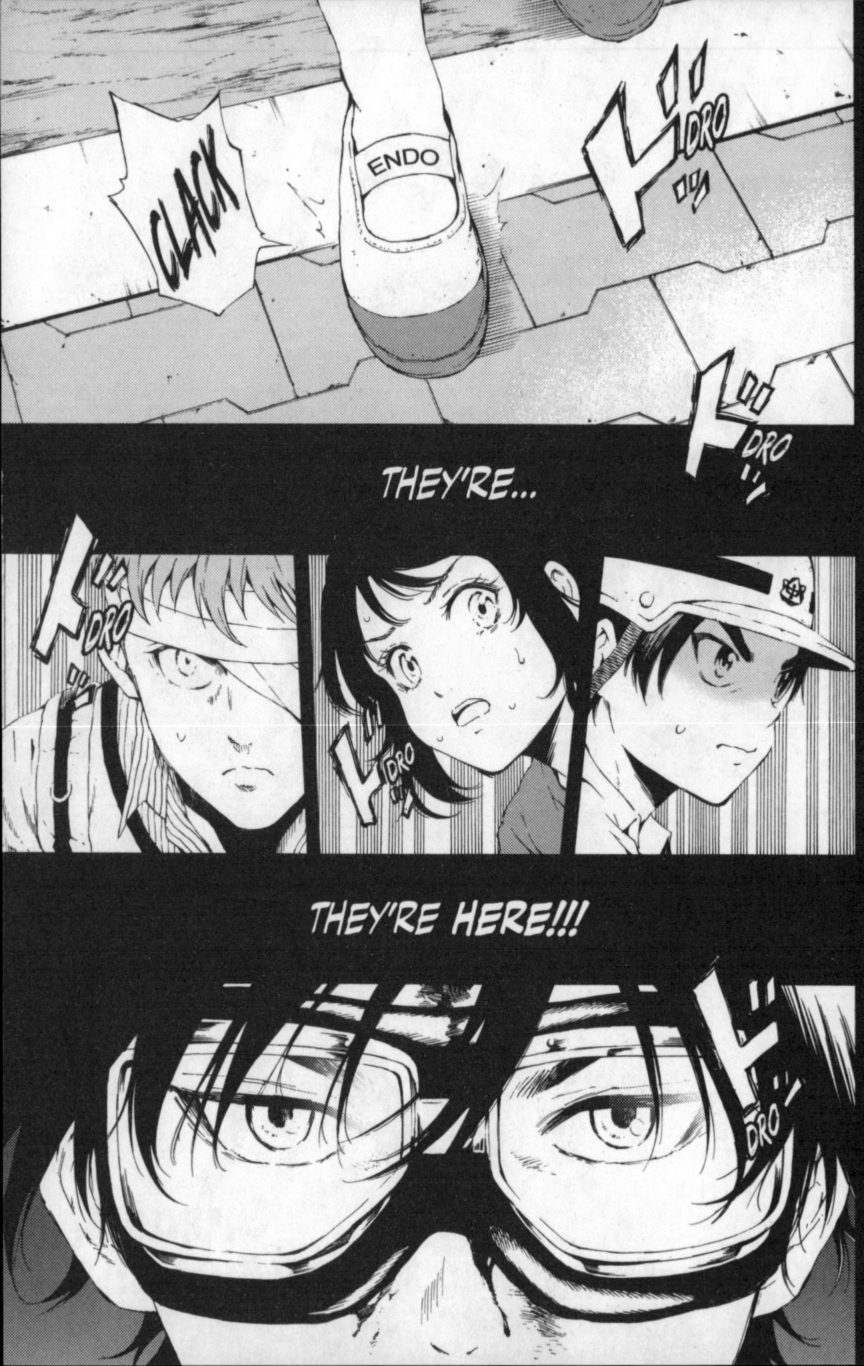
DRO
ENDO
CLACK
DRO
THEY'RE...
DRO
DRO
THEY'RE HERE!!!
DRO

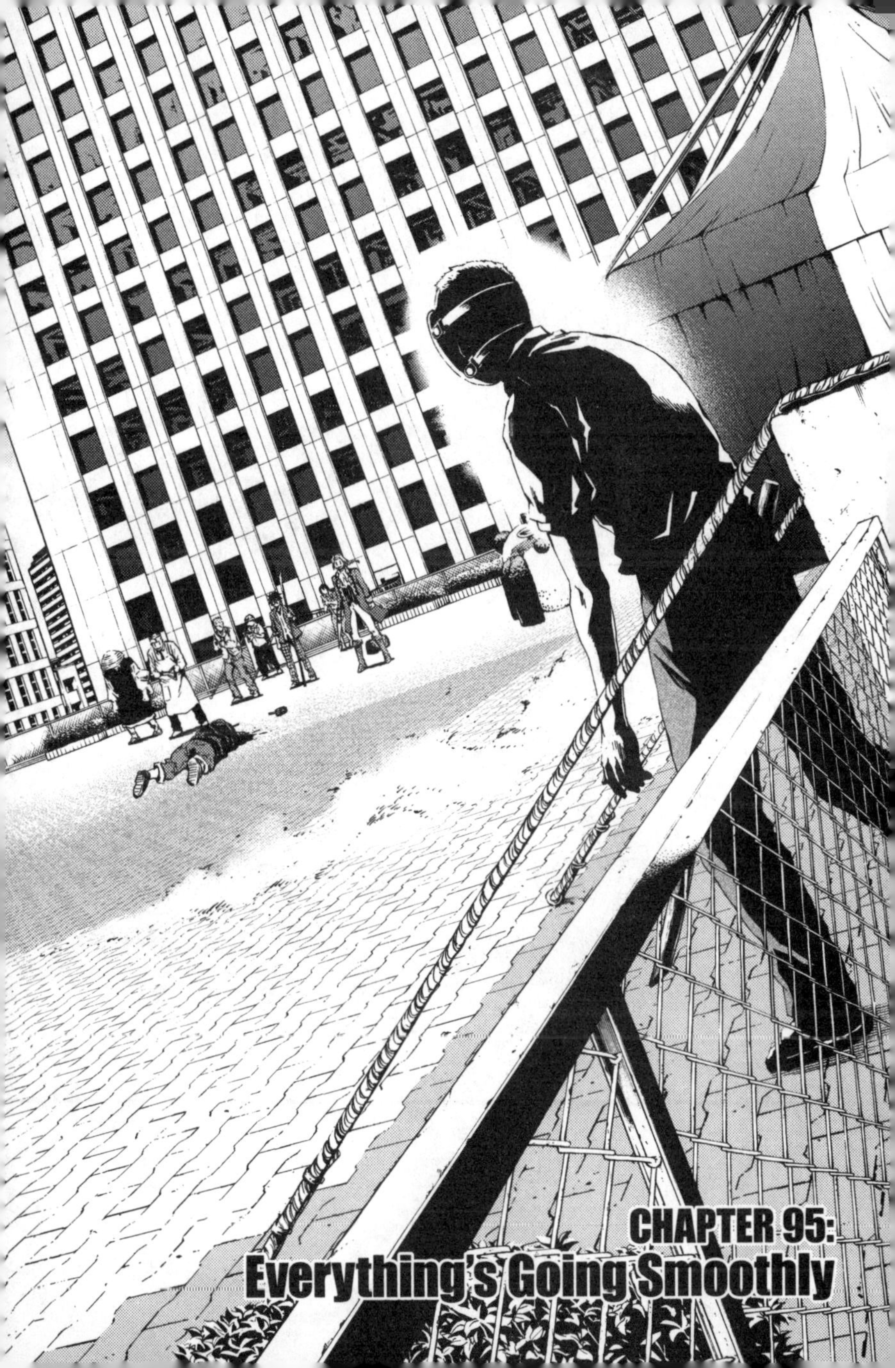

CHAPTER 95: Everything's Going Smoothly

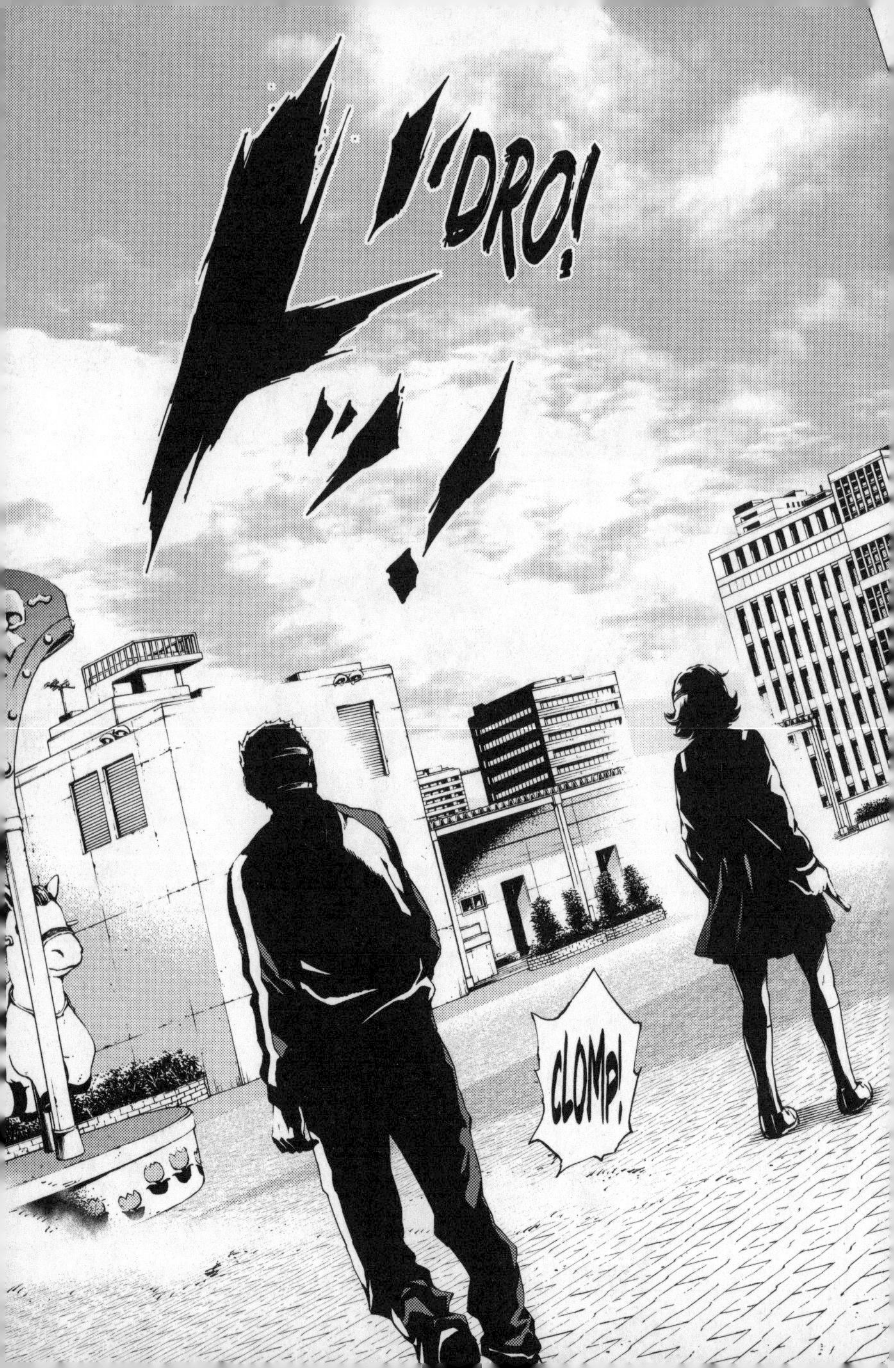
'DRO!
CLOMP!

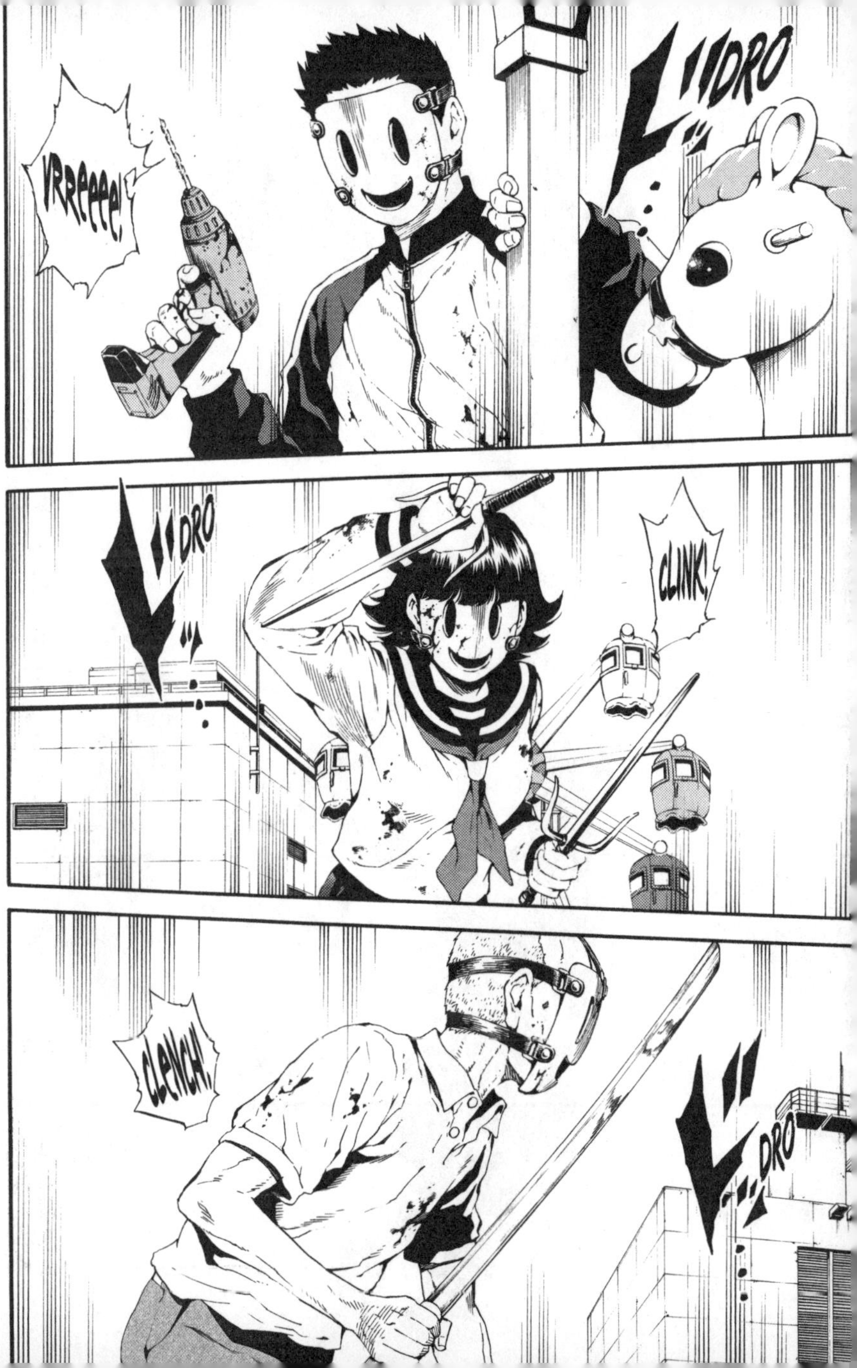
DRO
VRReeee!
CLINK!
DRO
DRO
CLENCH!

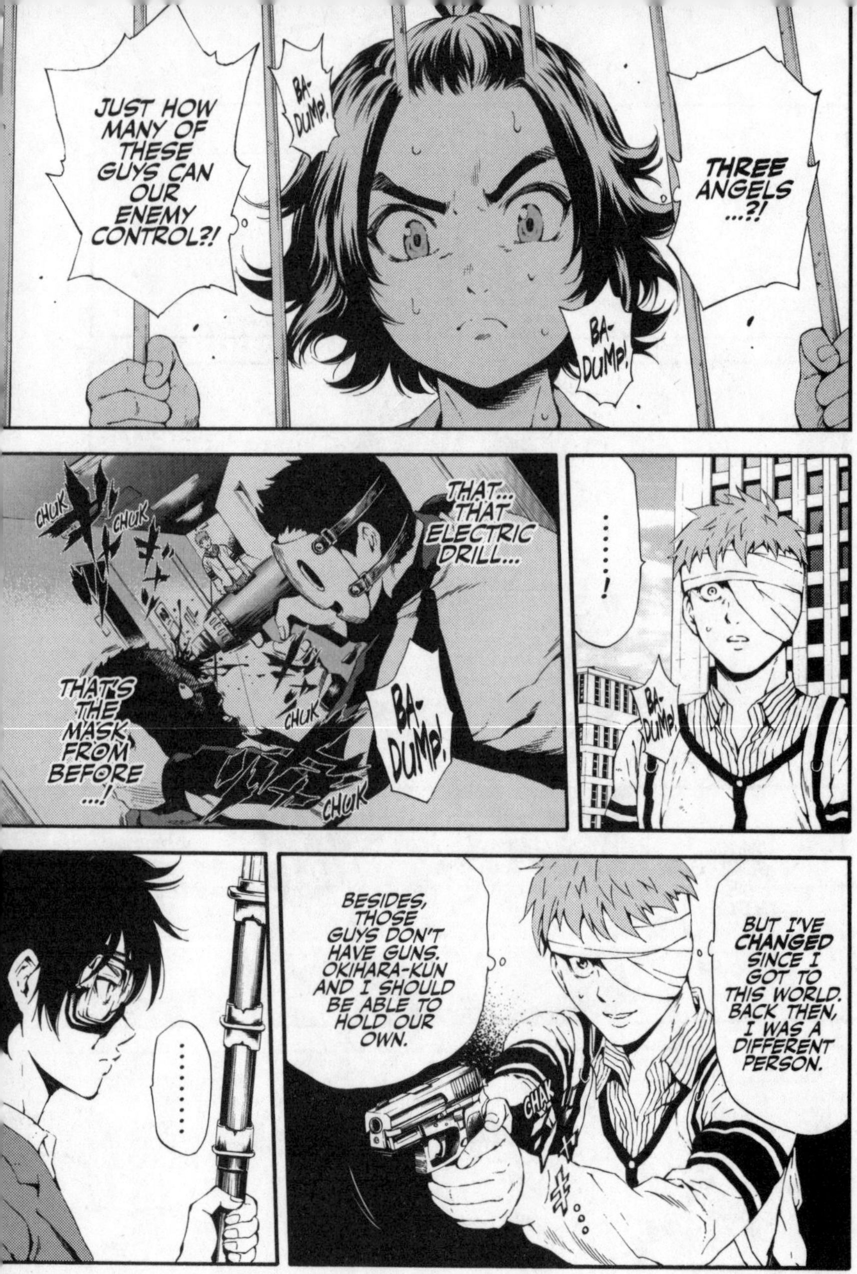

THREE ANGELS ...?!
BA-DUMP!
JUST HOW MANY OF THESE GUYS CAN OUR ENEMY CONTROL?!
BA-DUMP!
......!
BA-DUMP!
THAT... THAT ELECTRIC DRILL...
CHUK
CHUK
BA-DUMP!
THAT'S THE MASK FROM BEFORE ...!
CHUK
CHUK
BUT I'VE CHANGED SINCE I GOT TO THIS WORLD. BACK THEN, I WAS A DIFFERENT PERSON.
BESIDES, THOSE GUYS DON'T HAVE GUNS. OKIHARA-KUN AND I SHOULD BE ABLE TO HOLD OUR OWN.
CHAK
....

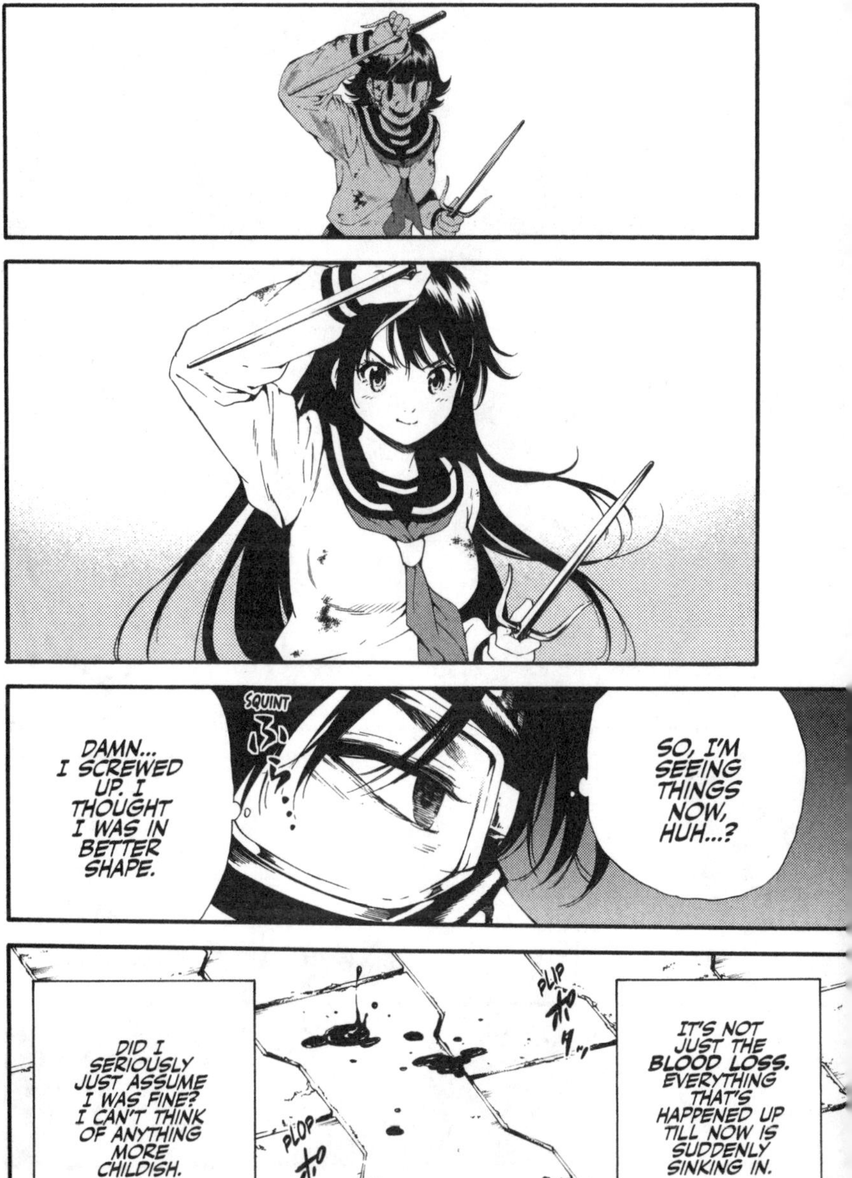
SO, I'M SEEING THINGS NOW, HUH...?
SQUINT
DAMN... I SCREWED UP. I THOUGHT I WAS IN BETTER SHAPE.
IT'S NOT JUST THE BLOOD LOSS. EVERYTHING THAT'S HAPPENED UP TILL NOW IS SUDDENLY SINKING IN.
PLIP
PLOP
DID I SERIOUSLY JUST ASSUME I WAS FINE? I CAN'T THINK OF ANYTHING MORE CHILDISH.

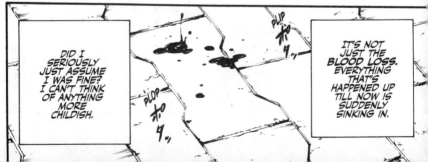

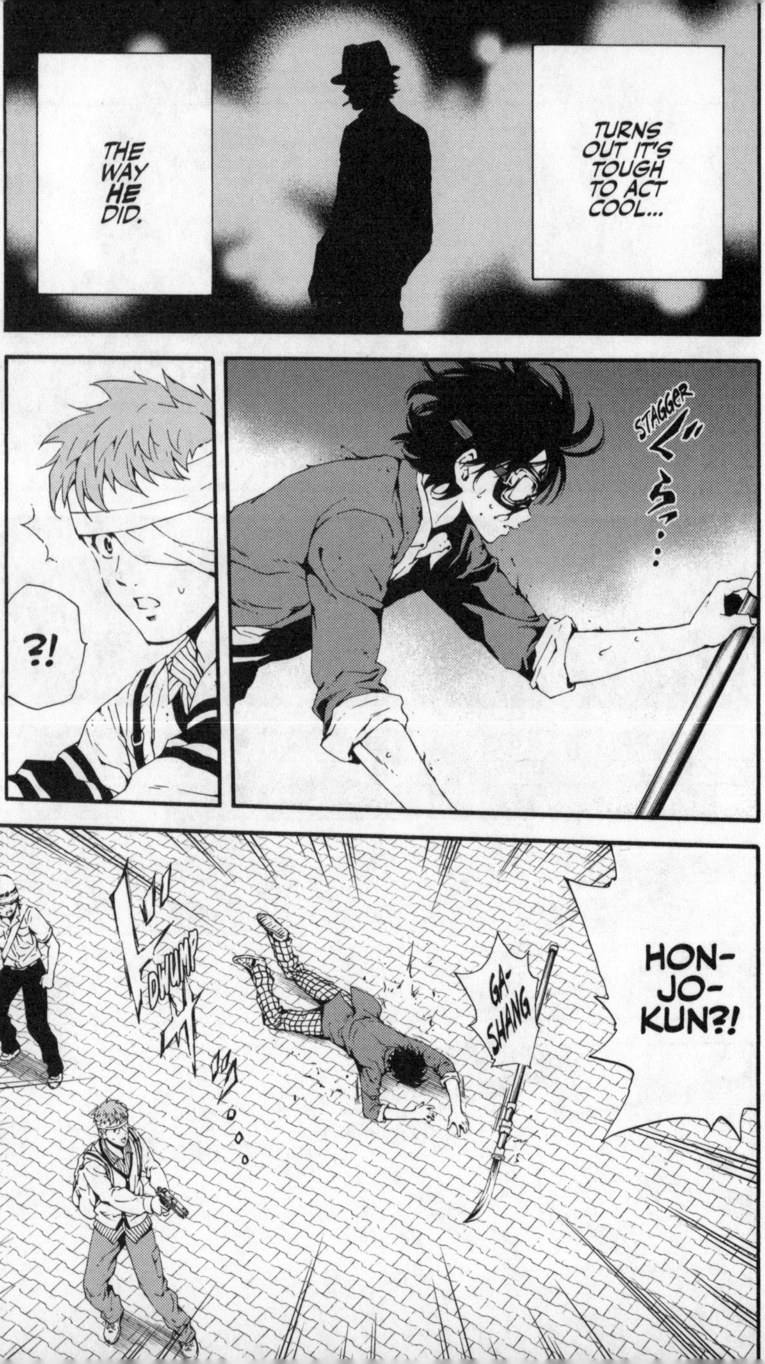
TURNS OUT IT'S TOUGH TO ACT COOL...
THE WAY HE DID.
STAGGER
?!
HON-JO-KUN?!
GA-SHANG
DWUMP

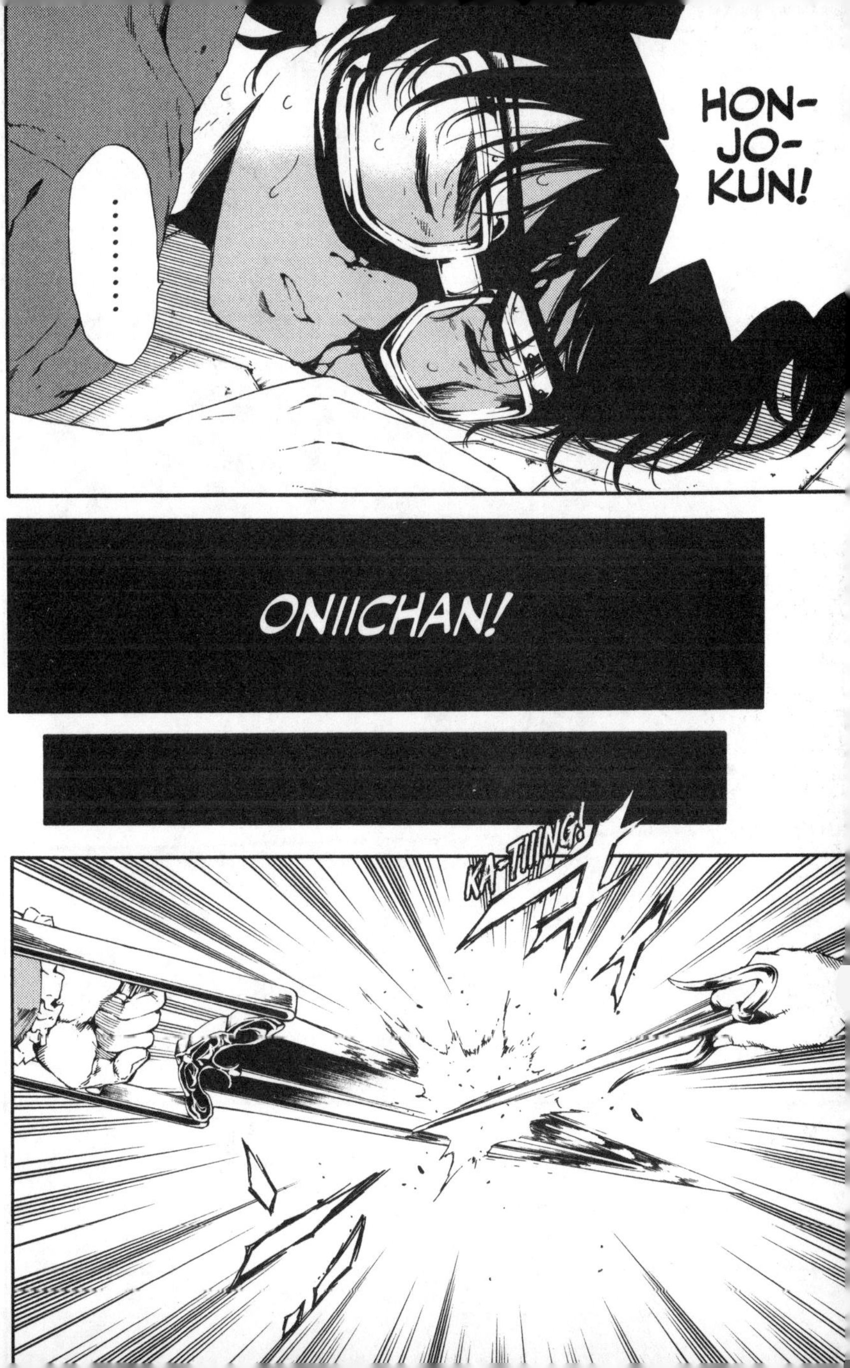
HON-JO-KUN!
....
ONIICHAN!
KA-TIIING!

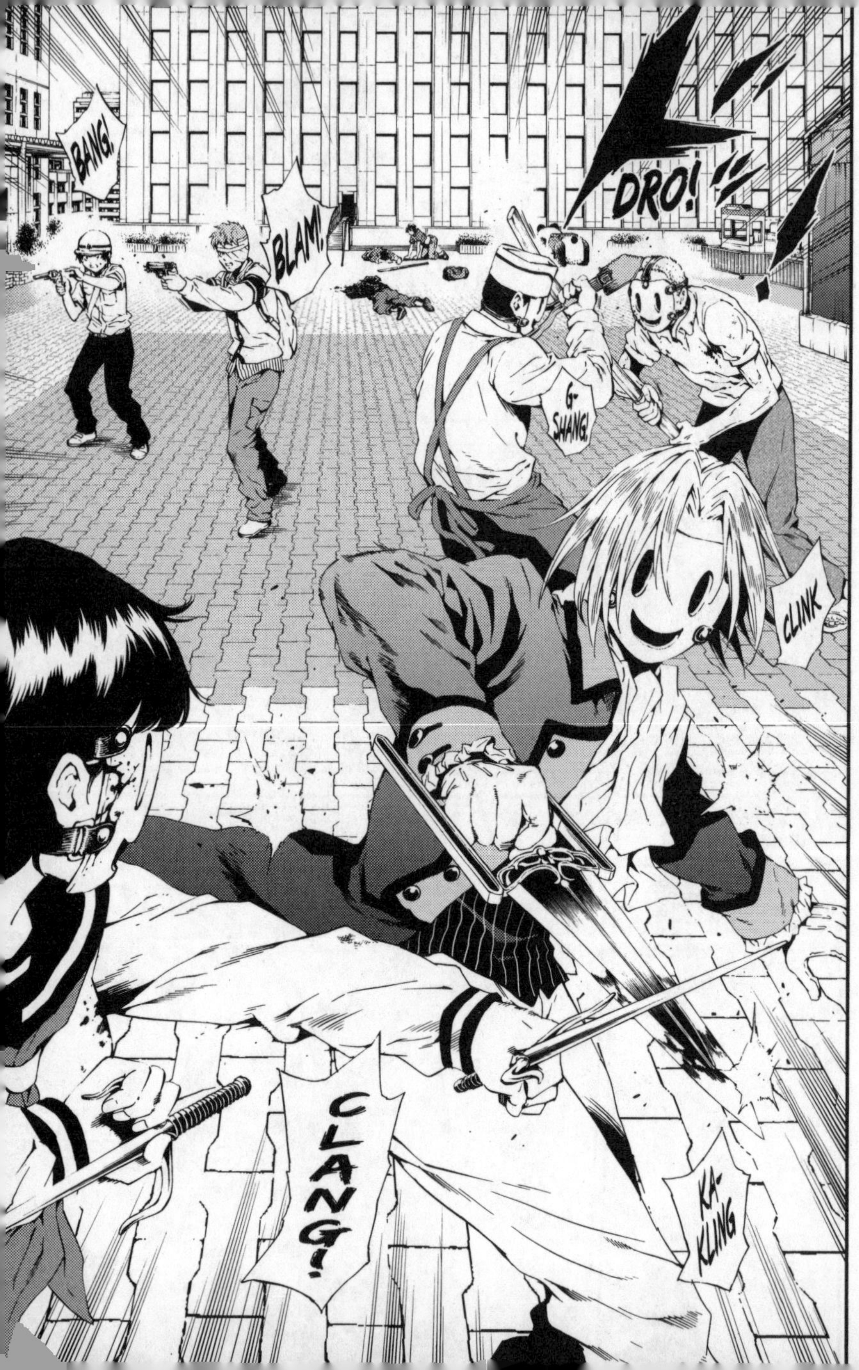
DRO!
BLAM!
BANG!
G-SHANG!
CLINK
KA-KLING
CLANG!

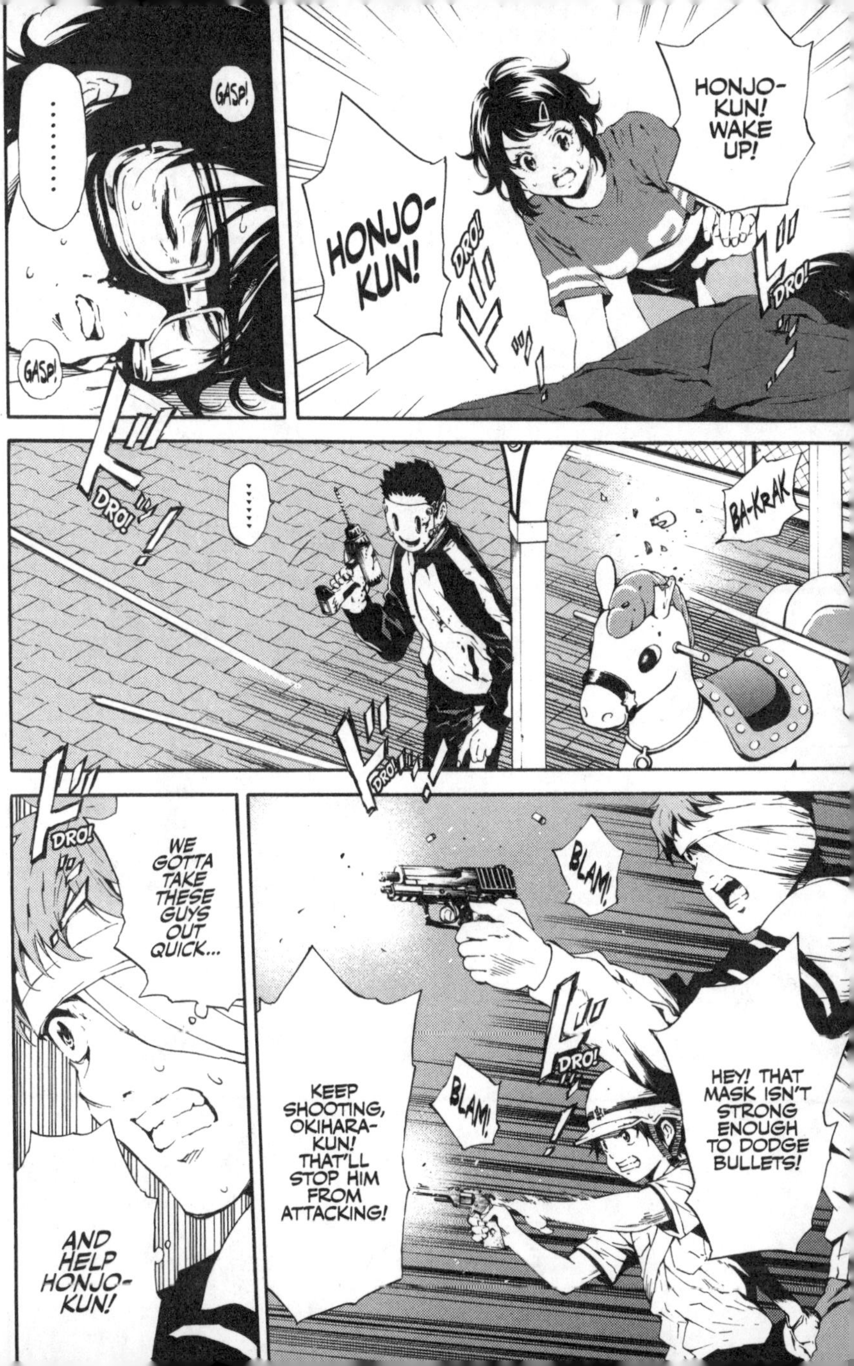
HONJO-KUN! WAKE UP!
HONJO-KUN!
DRO!
DRO!
GASP!
......
GASP!
BA-KRAK
......
DRO!
BLAM!
DRO!
BLAM!
HEY! THAT MASK ISN'T STRONG ENOUGH TO DODGE BULLETS!
KEEP SHOOTING, OKIHARA-KUN! THAT'LL STOP HIM FROM ATTACKING!
DRO!
WE GOTTA TAKE THESE GUYS OUT QUICK...
AND HELP HONJO-KUN!

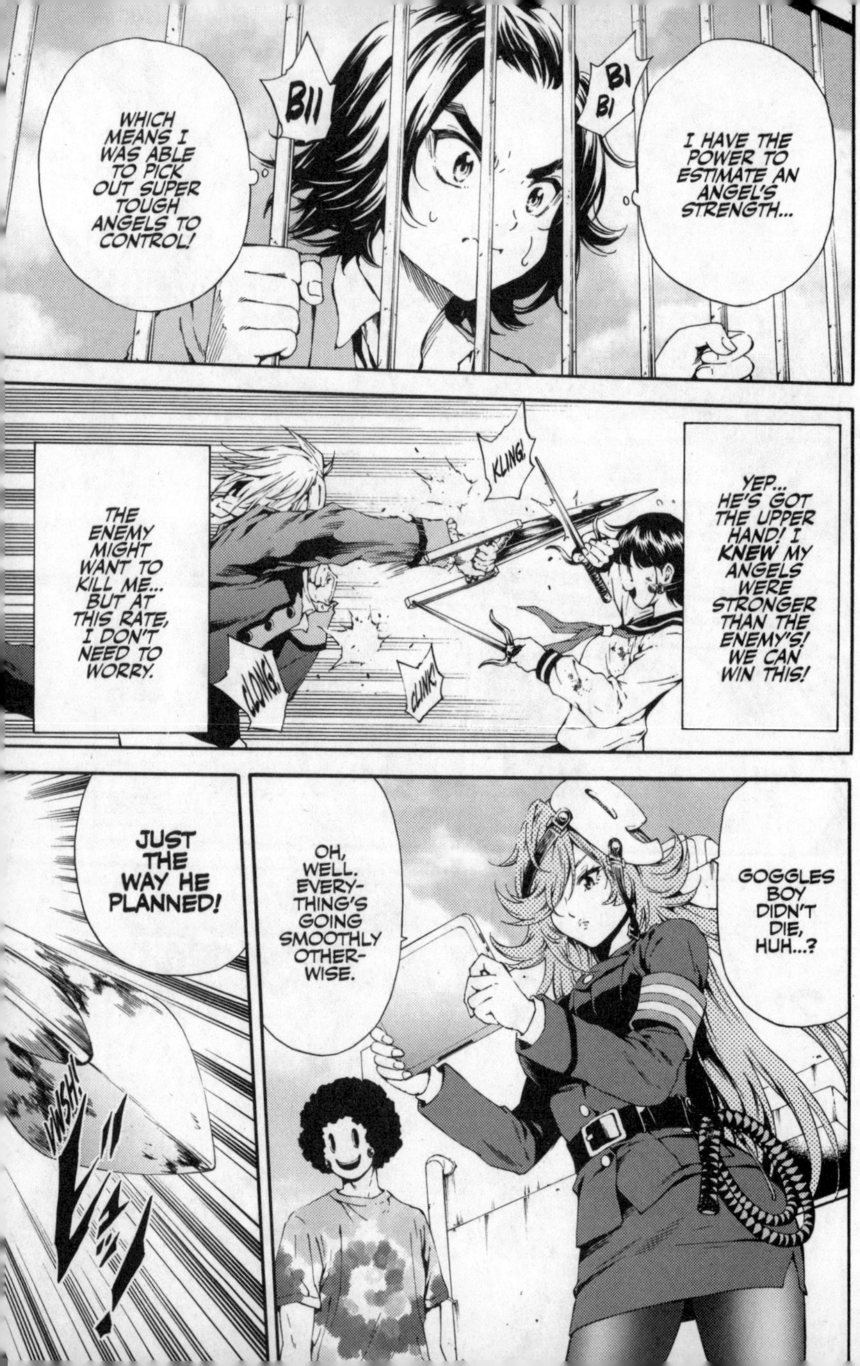
I HAVE THE POWER TO ESTIMATE AN ANGEL'S STRENGTH...
BI BI
BII
WHICH MEANS I WAS ABLE TO PICK OUT SUPER TOUGH ANGELS TO CONTROL!
YEP... HE'S GOT THE UPPER HAND! I KNEW MY ANGELS WERE STRONGER THAN THE ENEMY'S! WE CAN WIN THIS!
KLING!
THE ENEMY MIGHT WANT TO KILL ME... BUT AT THIS RATE, I DON'T NEED TO WORRY.
CLINK!
CLONG!
GOGGLES BOY DIDN'T DIE, HUH...?
OH, WELL. EVERYTHING'S GOING SMOOTHLY OTHERWISE.
JUST THE WAY HE PLANNED!
VWSH!

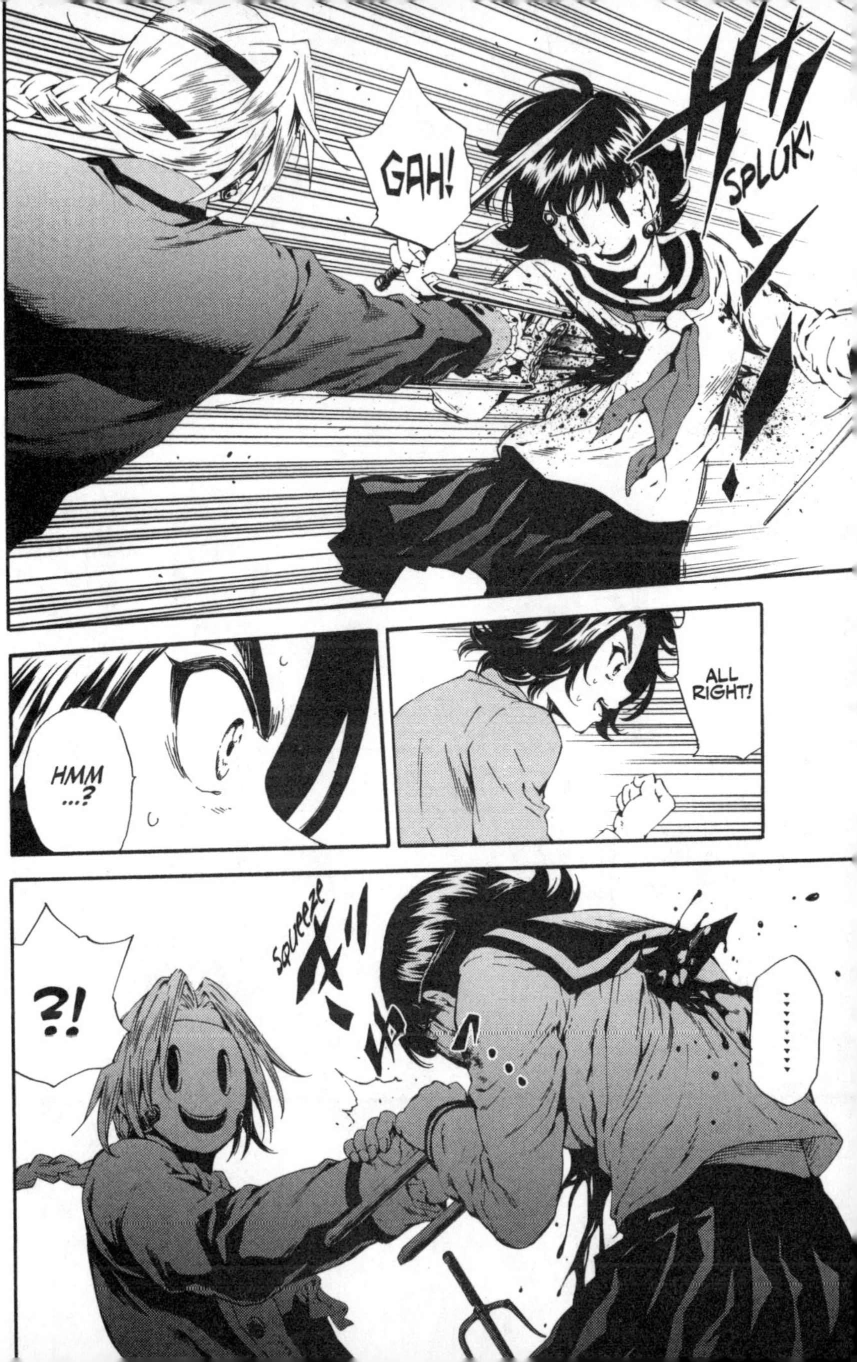
SPLUK!
GAH!
ALL RIGHT!
HMM ...?
......
Squeeze
?!

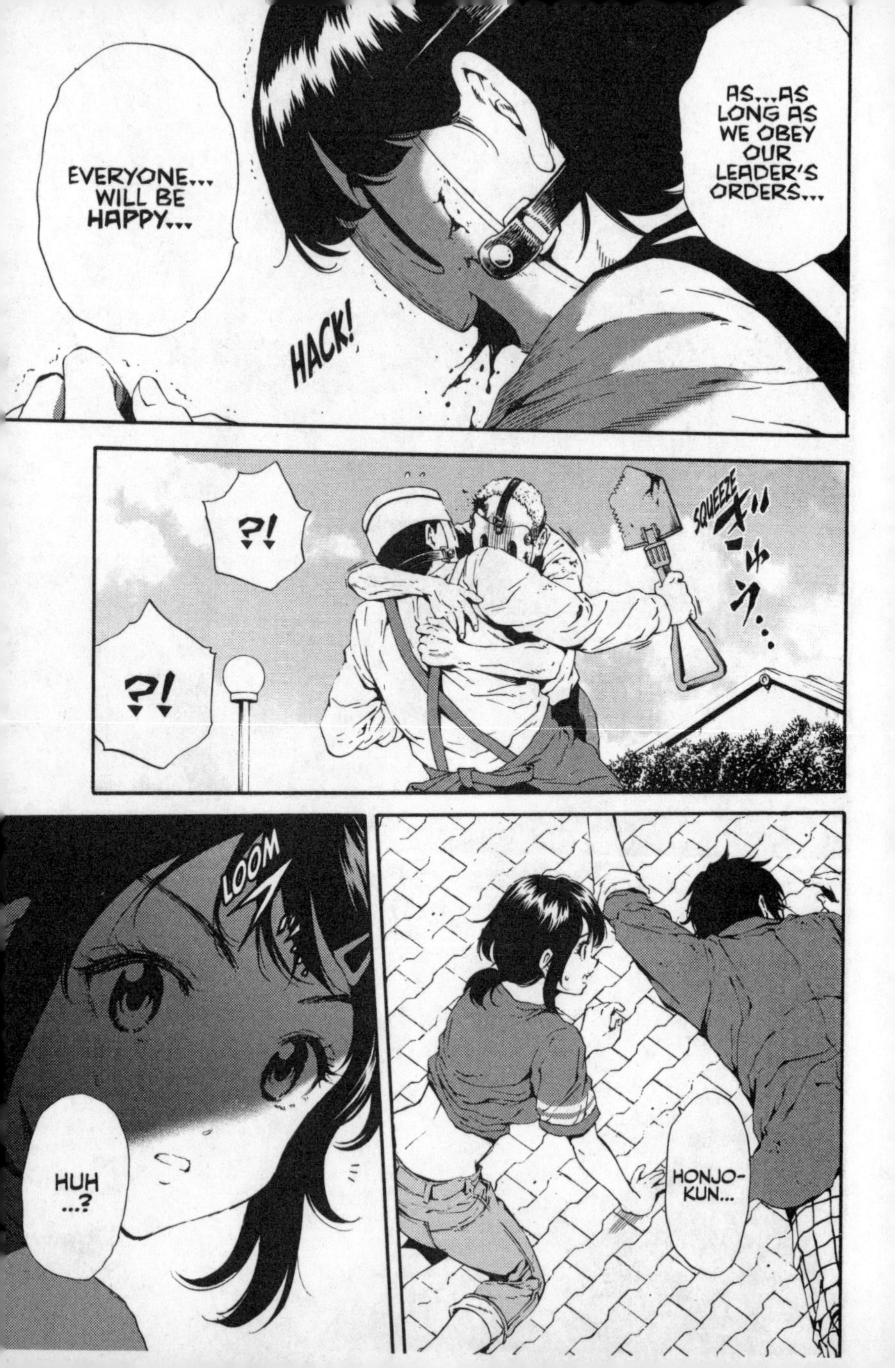
AS...AS LONG AS WE OBEY OUR LEADER'S ORDERS...
EVERYONE... WILL BE HAPPY...
HACK!
SQUEEZE
?!
?!
HONJO-KUN...
LOOM
HUH ...?

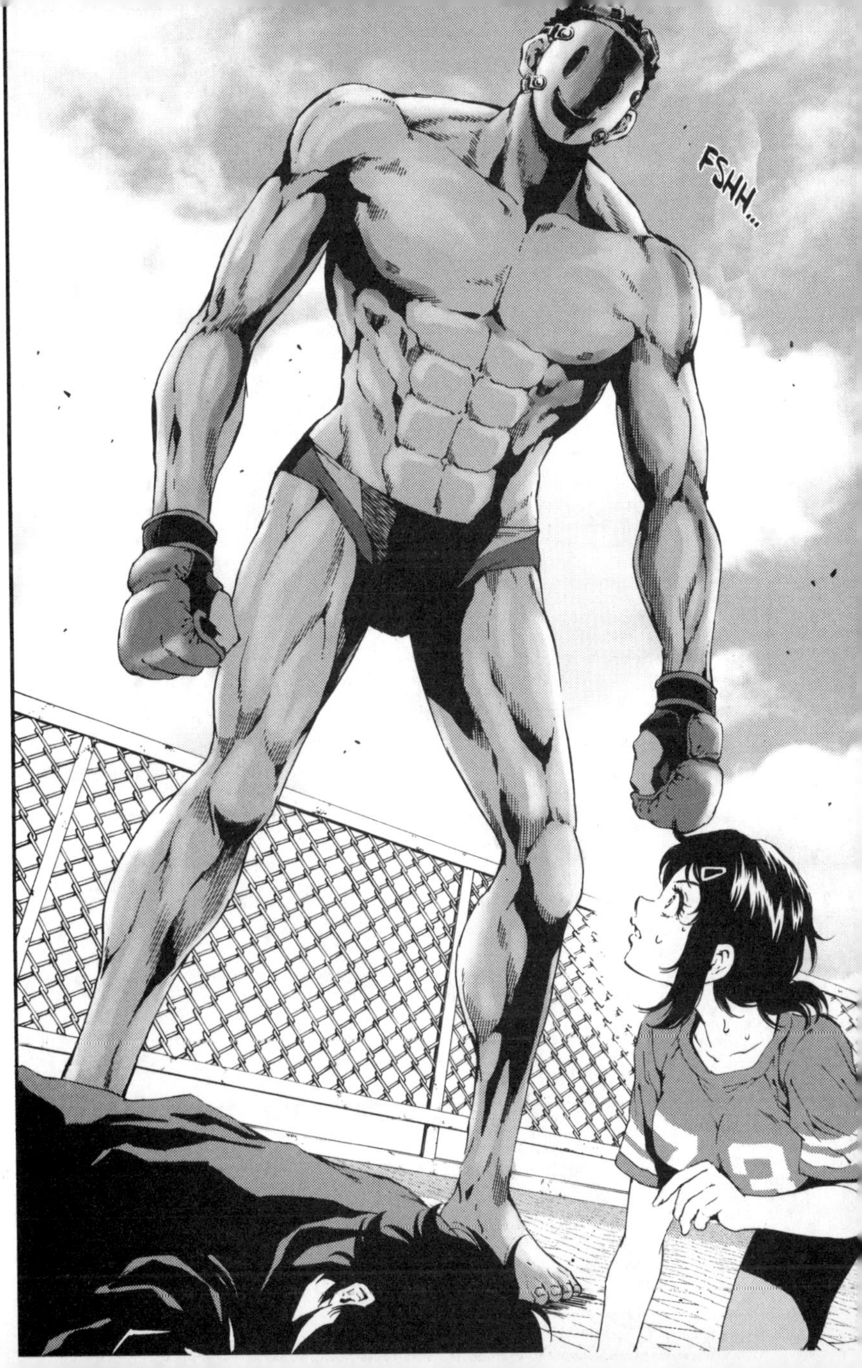
FSHH...

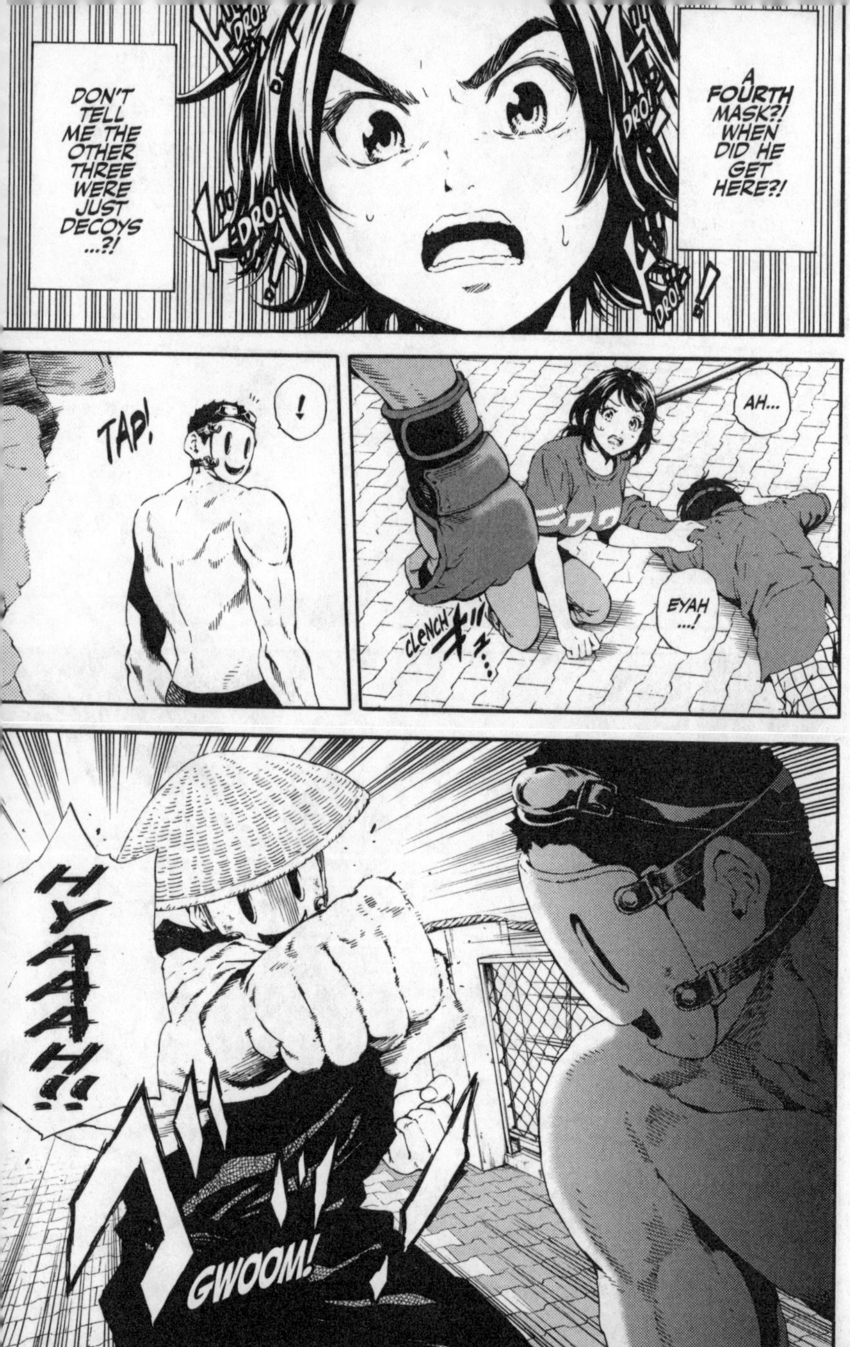
A FOURTH MASK?! WHEN DID HE GET HERE?!
DON'T TELL ME THE OTHER THREE WERE JUST DECOYS ...?!
AH...
EYAH ...!
CLENCH
!
TAP!
HYAAAH!!
GWOOM!

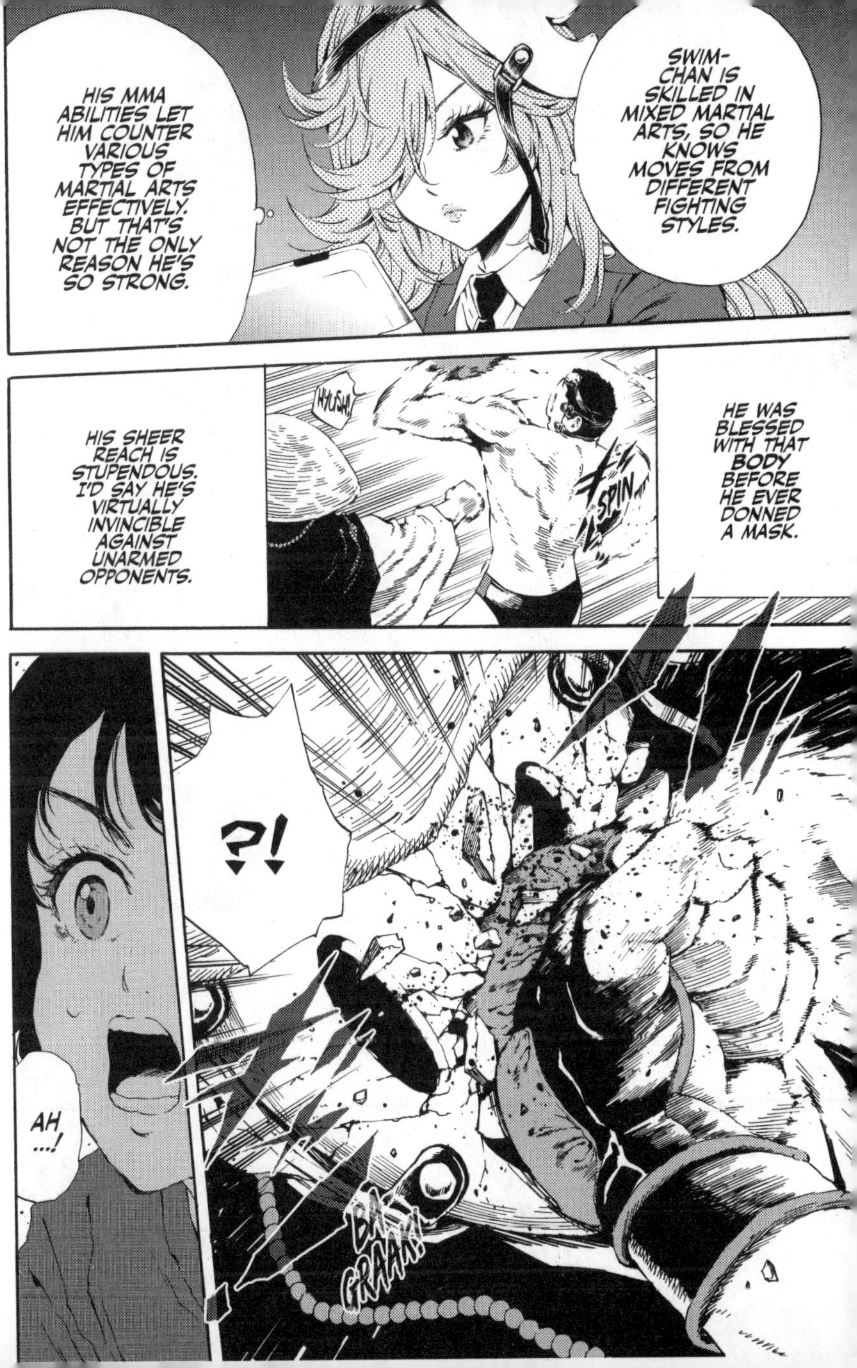
SWIM-CHAN IS SKILLED IN MIXED MARTIAL ARTS, SO HE KNOWS MOVES FROM DIFFERENT FIGHTING STYLES.
HIS MMA ABILITIES LET HIM COUNTER VARIOUS TYPES OF MARTIAL ARTS EFFECTIVELY. BUT THAT'S NOT THE ONLY REASON HE'S SO STRONG.
HE WAS BLESSED WITH THAT BODY BEFORE HE EVER DONNED A MASK.
HYUSH!
SPIN
HIS SHEER REACH IS STUPENDOUS. I'D SAY HE'S VIRTUALLY INVINCIBLE AGAINST UNARMED OPPONENTS.
?!
AH ...!
BA GRAAK!

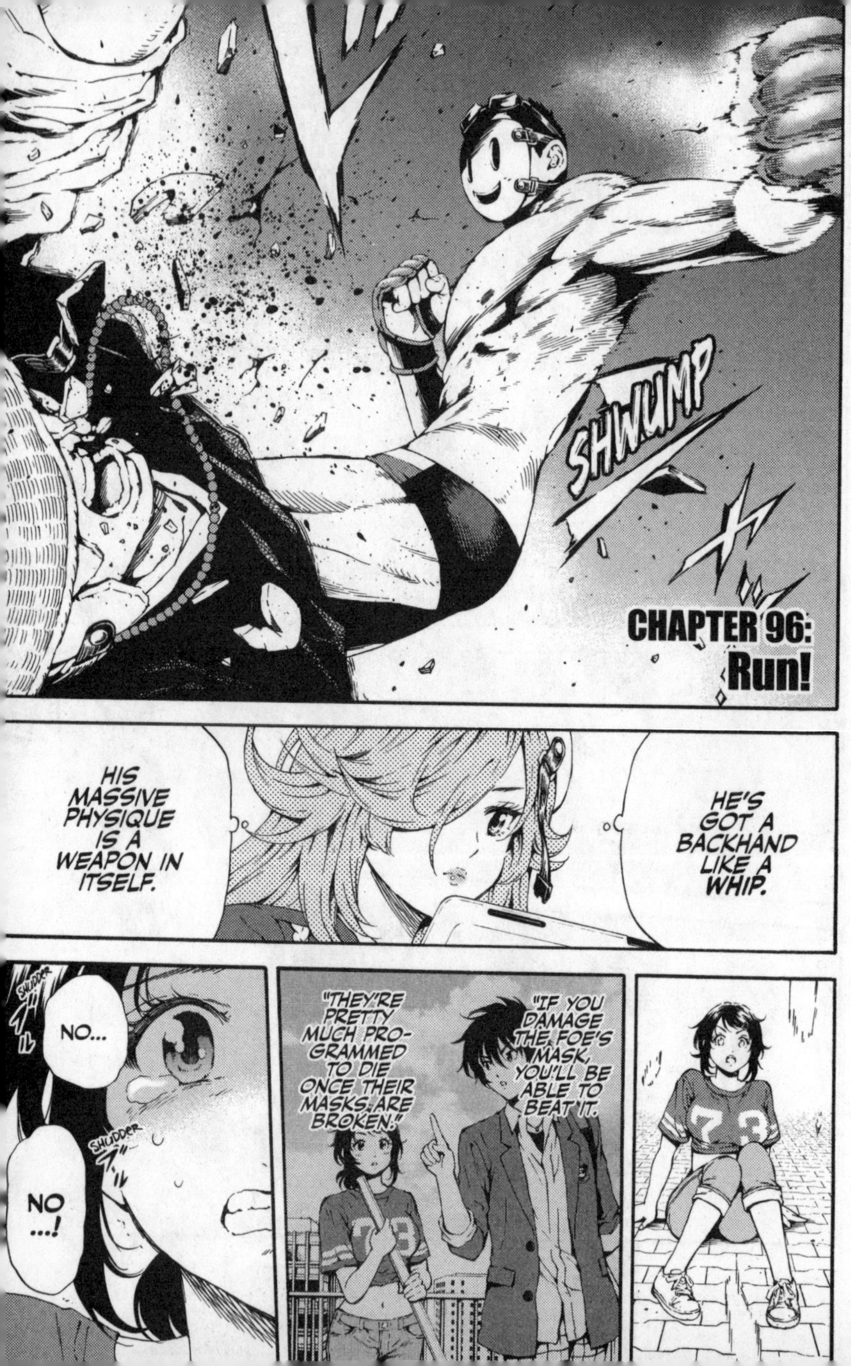
SHWUMP
CHAPTER 96:
Run!
HE'S GOT A BACKHAND LIKE A WHIP.
HIS MASSIVE PHYSIQUE IS A WEAPON IN ITSELF.
"IF YOU DAMAGE THE FOE'S MASK, YOU'LL BE ABLE TO BEAT IT.
"THEY'RE PRETTY MUCH PRO-GRAMMED TO DIE ONCE THEIR MASKS ARE BROKEN."
SHUDDER
NO...
SHUDDER
NO ...!

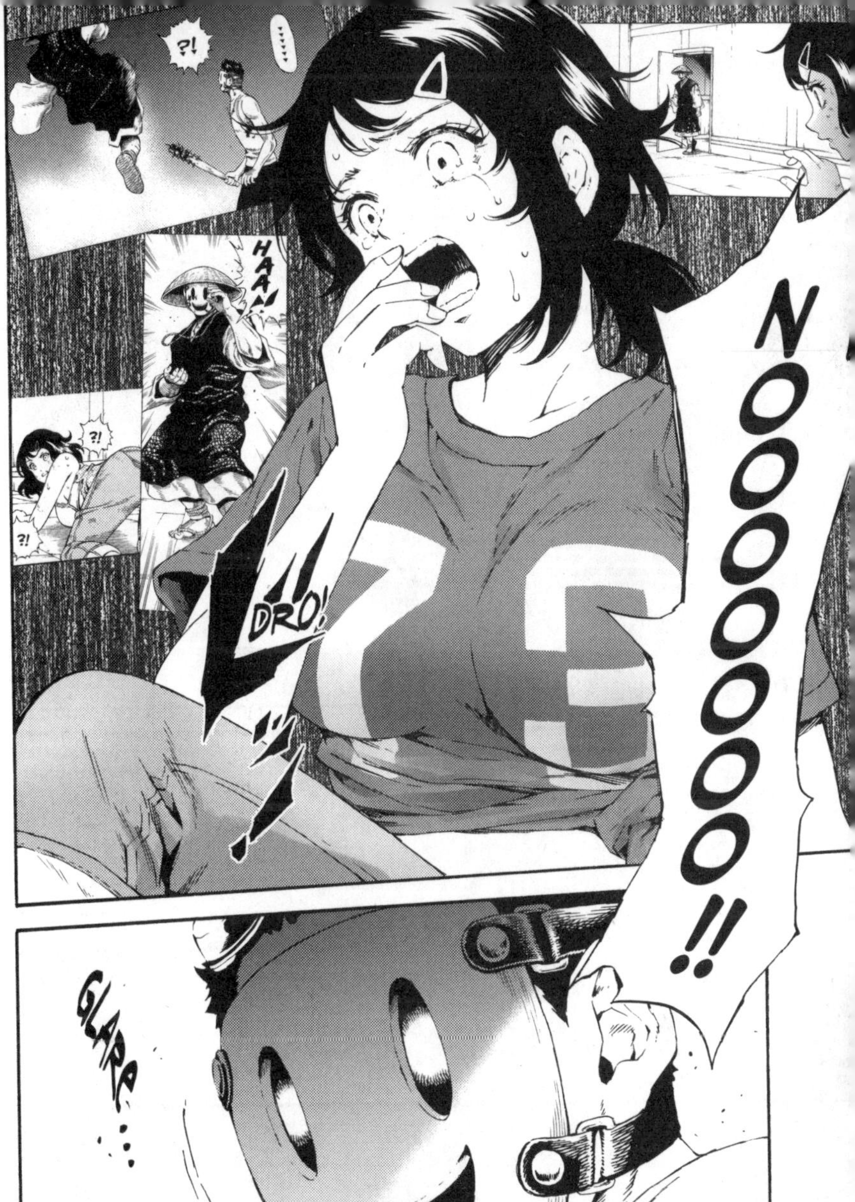

?!
......
HAAA!!
?!
?!
DRO!
NOOOOOOOO!!
GLARE...

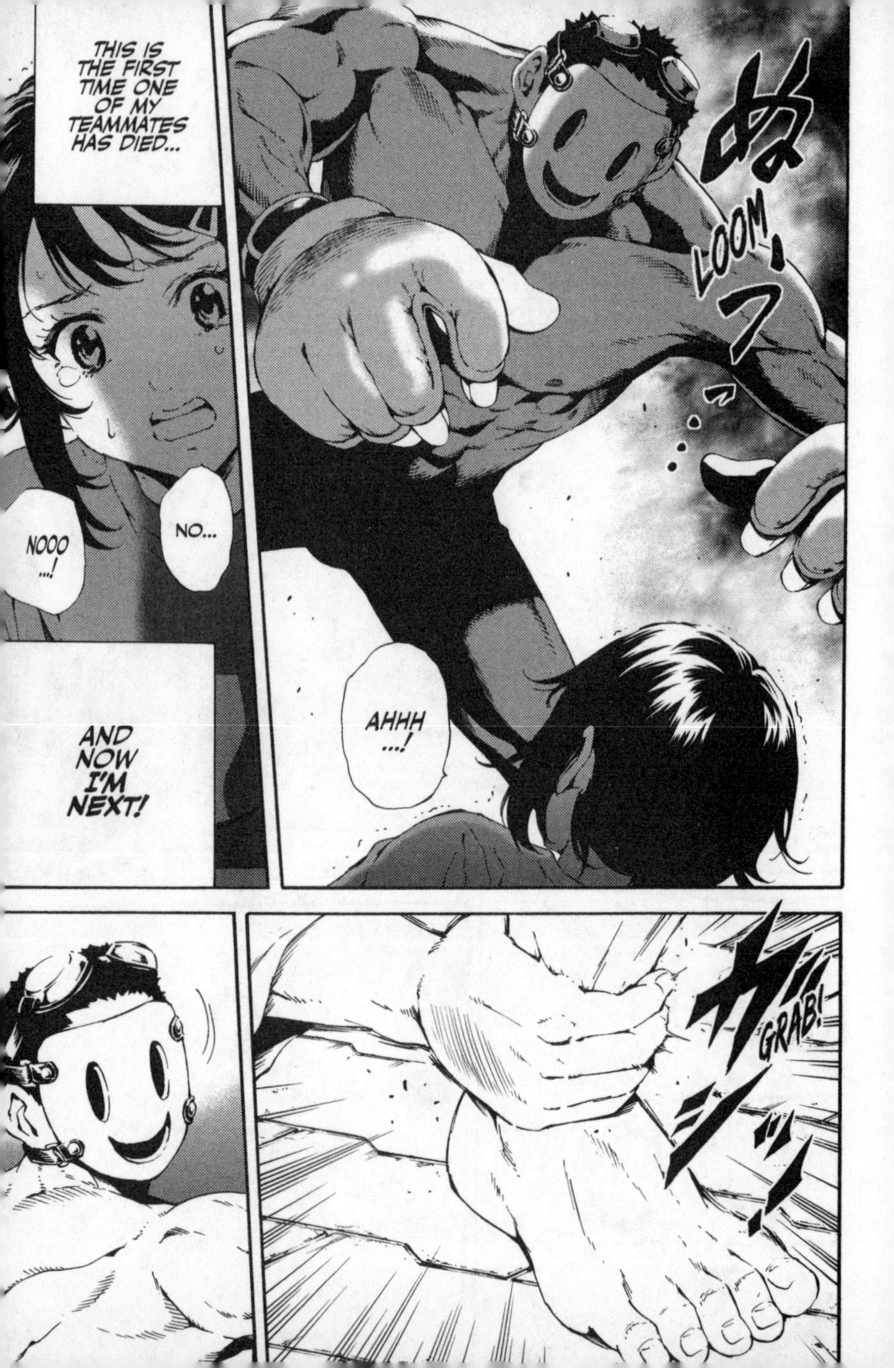
LOOM
AHHH ....!
THIS IS THE FIRST TIME ONE OF MY TEAMMATES HAS DIED...
NO...
NOOO ...!
AND NOW I'M NEXT!
GRAB!

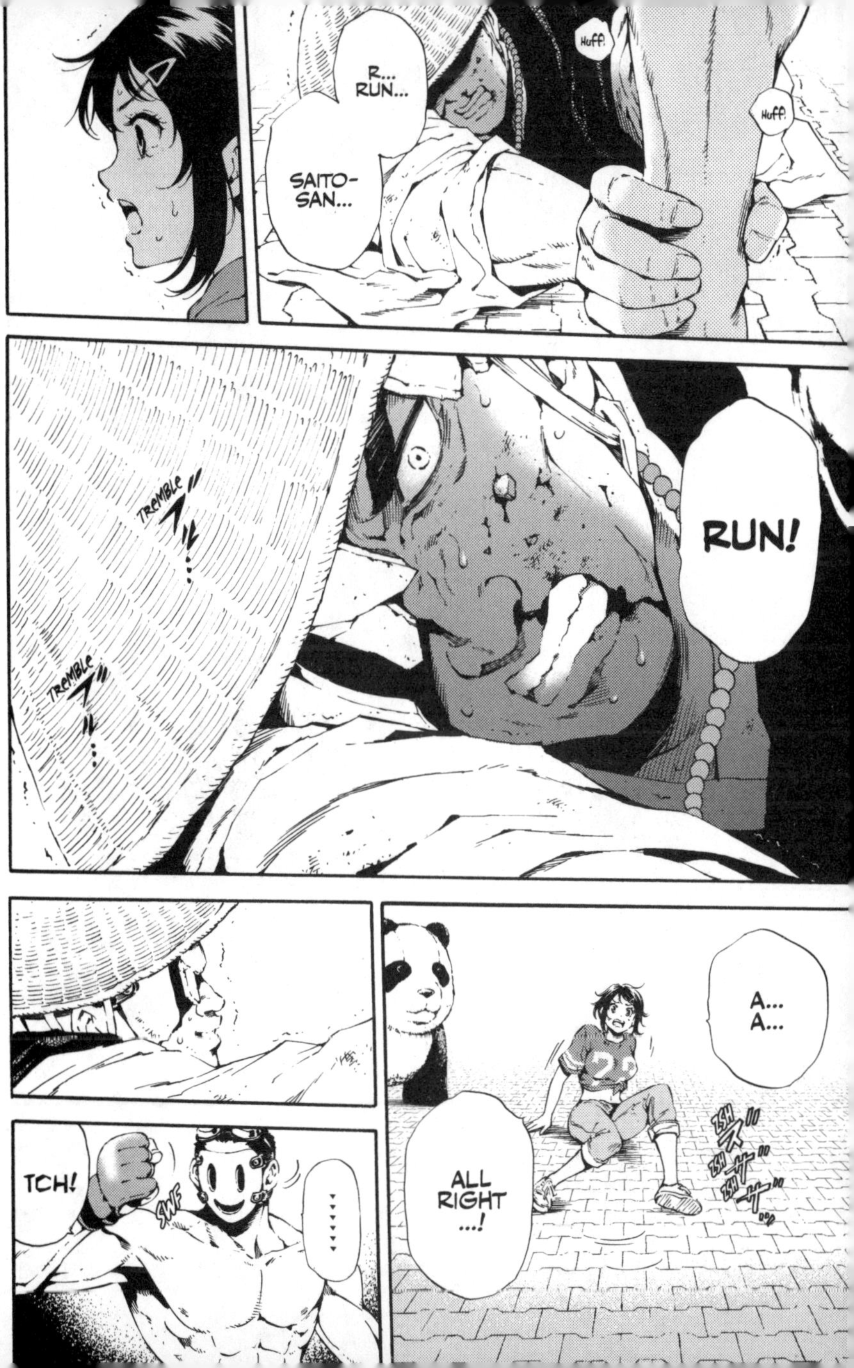

Huff!
Huff!
R... RUN...
SAITO-SAN...
RUN!
TREMBLE
TREMBLE
A... A...
ZSH
ZSH
ZSH
ALL RIGHT ...!
......
SWF
TCH!

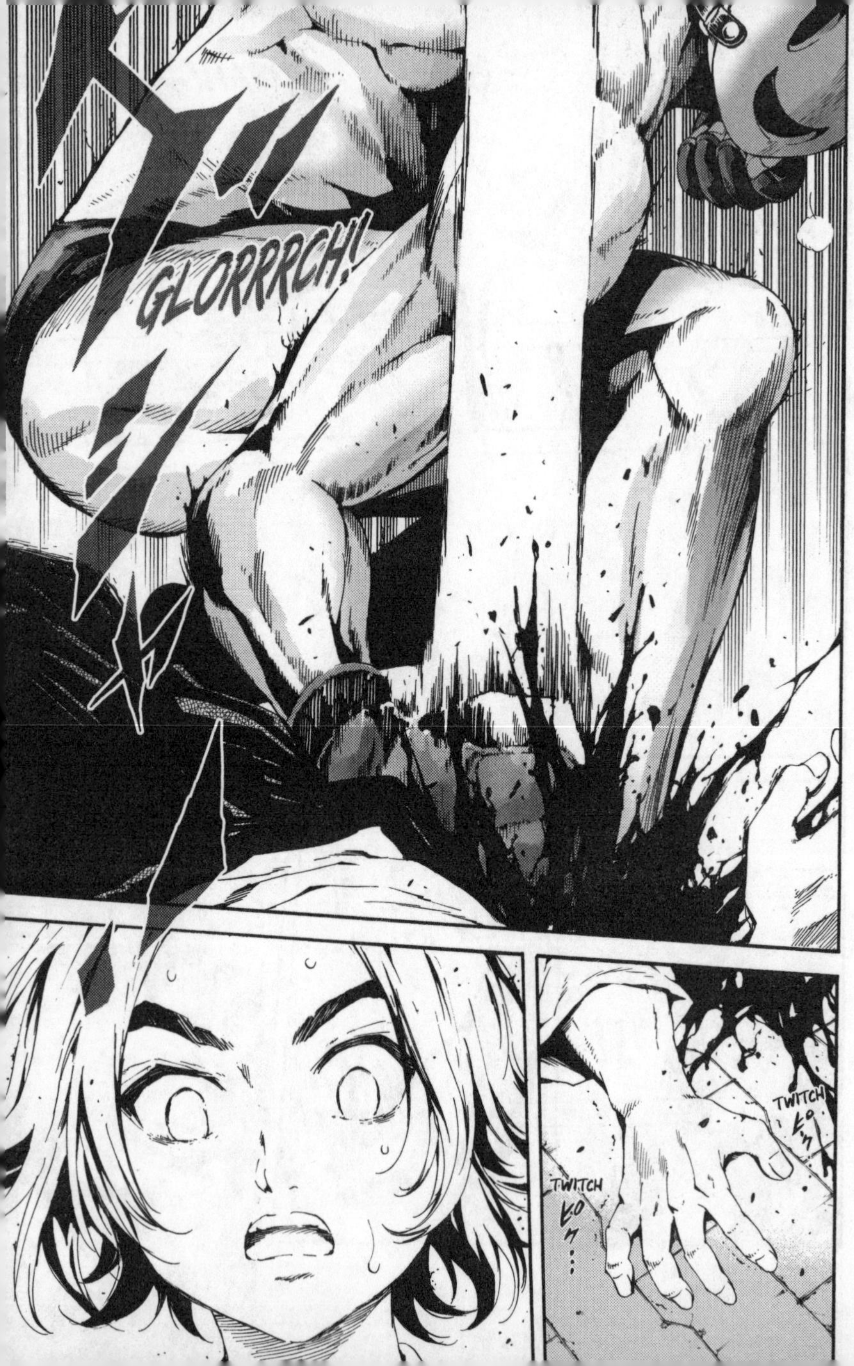
GLORRRCH!
TWITCH
TWITCH

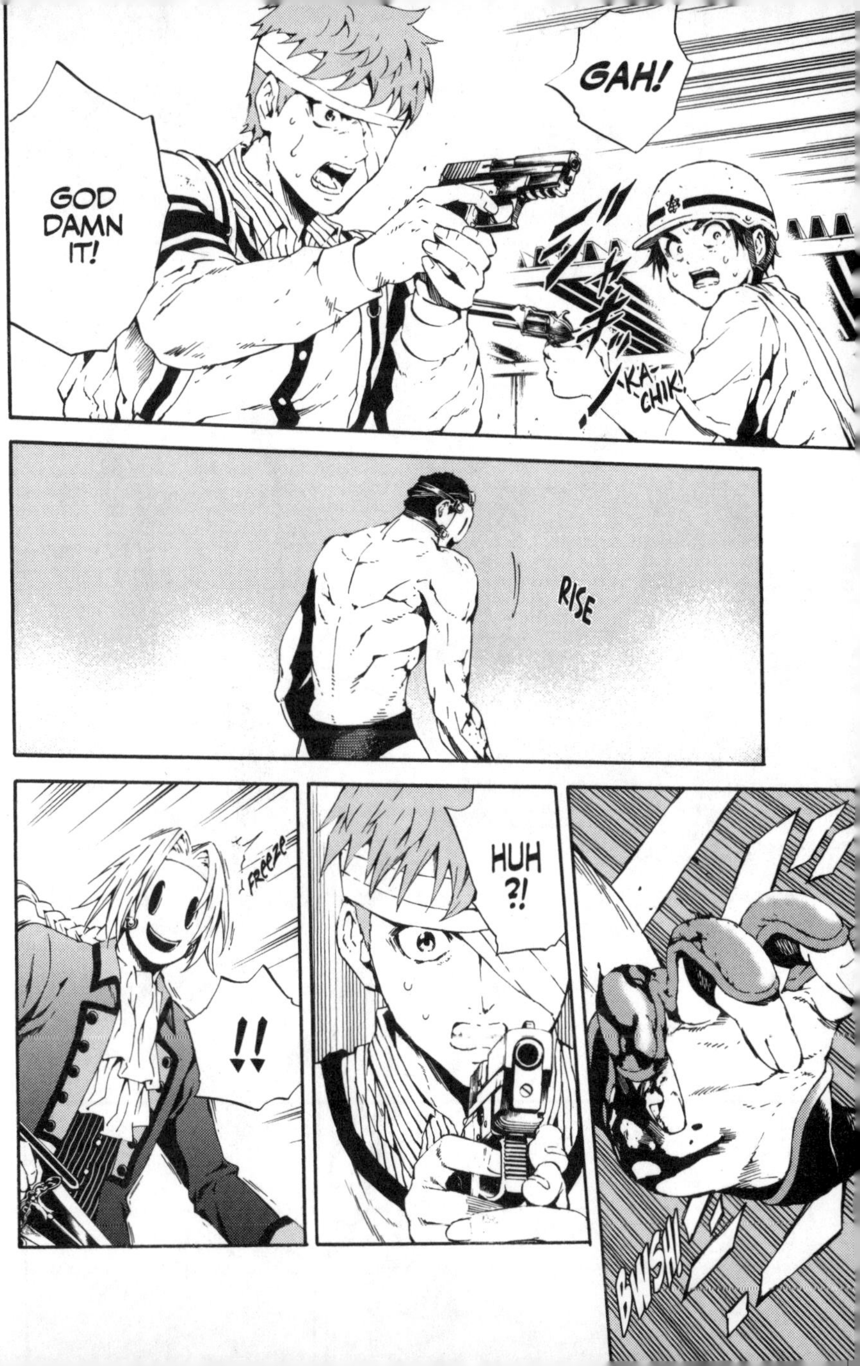
GAH!
GOD DAMN IT!
KA-CHIK!
RISE
BWSH!
HUH ?!
freeze
!!

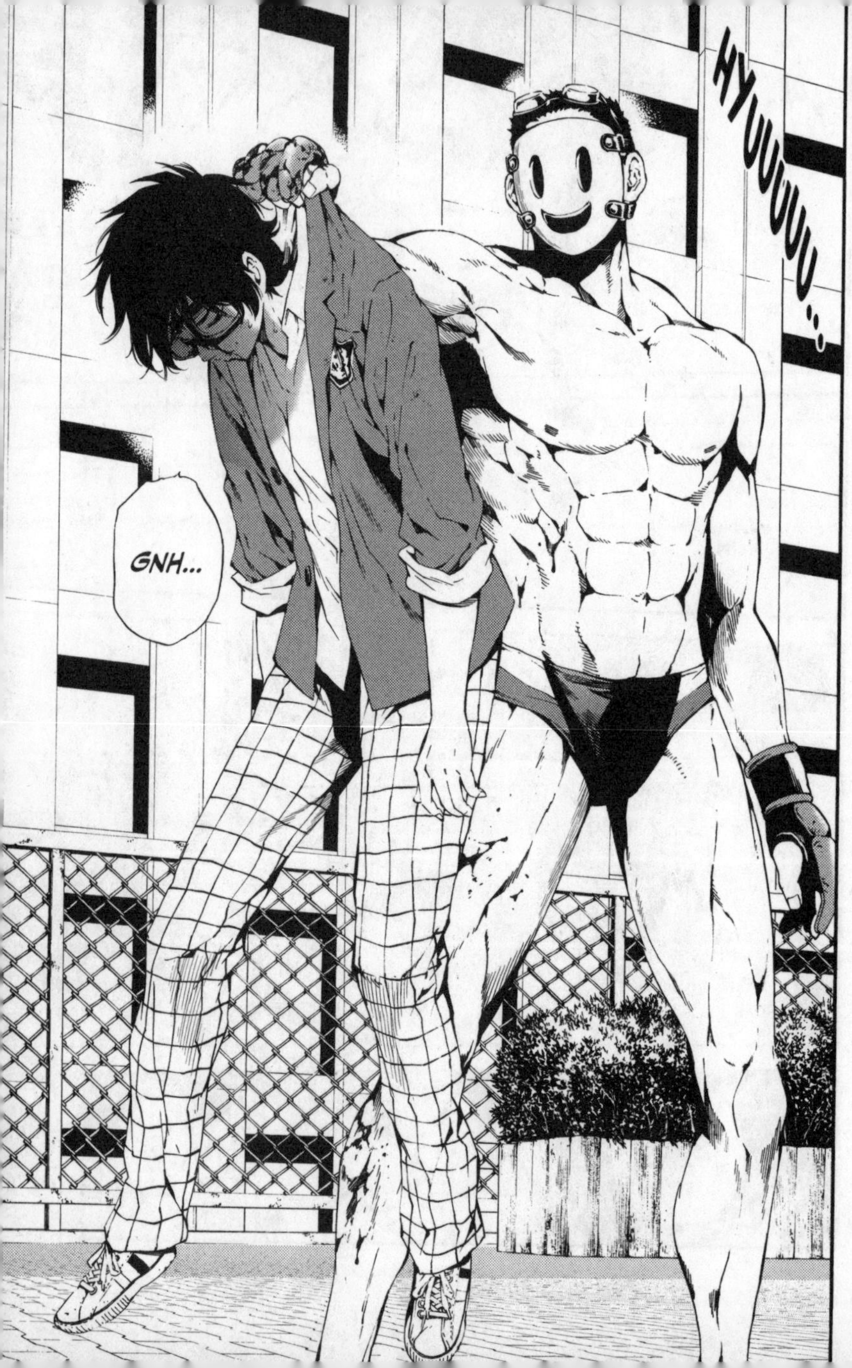
HYUUUUU...
GNH...

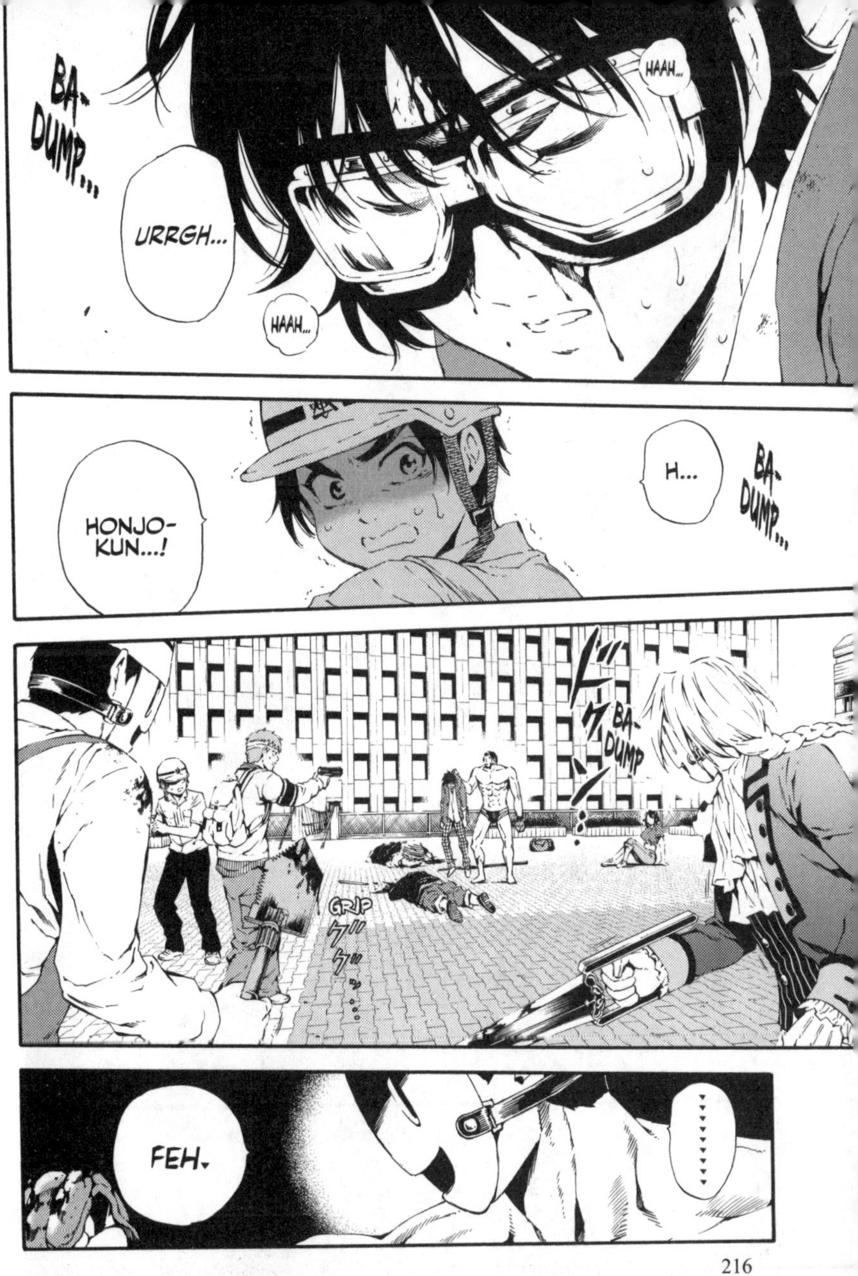
HAAH...
BA-DUMP...
URRGH...
HAAH...
BA-DUMP...
H...
HONJO-KUN...!
BA-DUMP
GRIP
....
FEH.

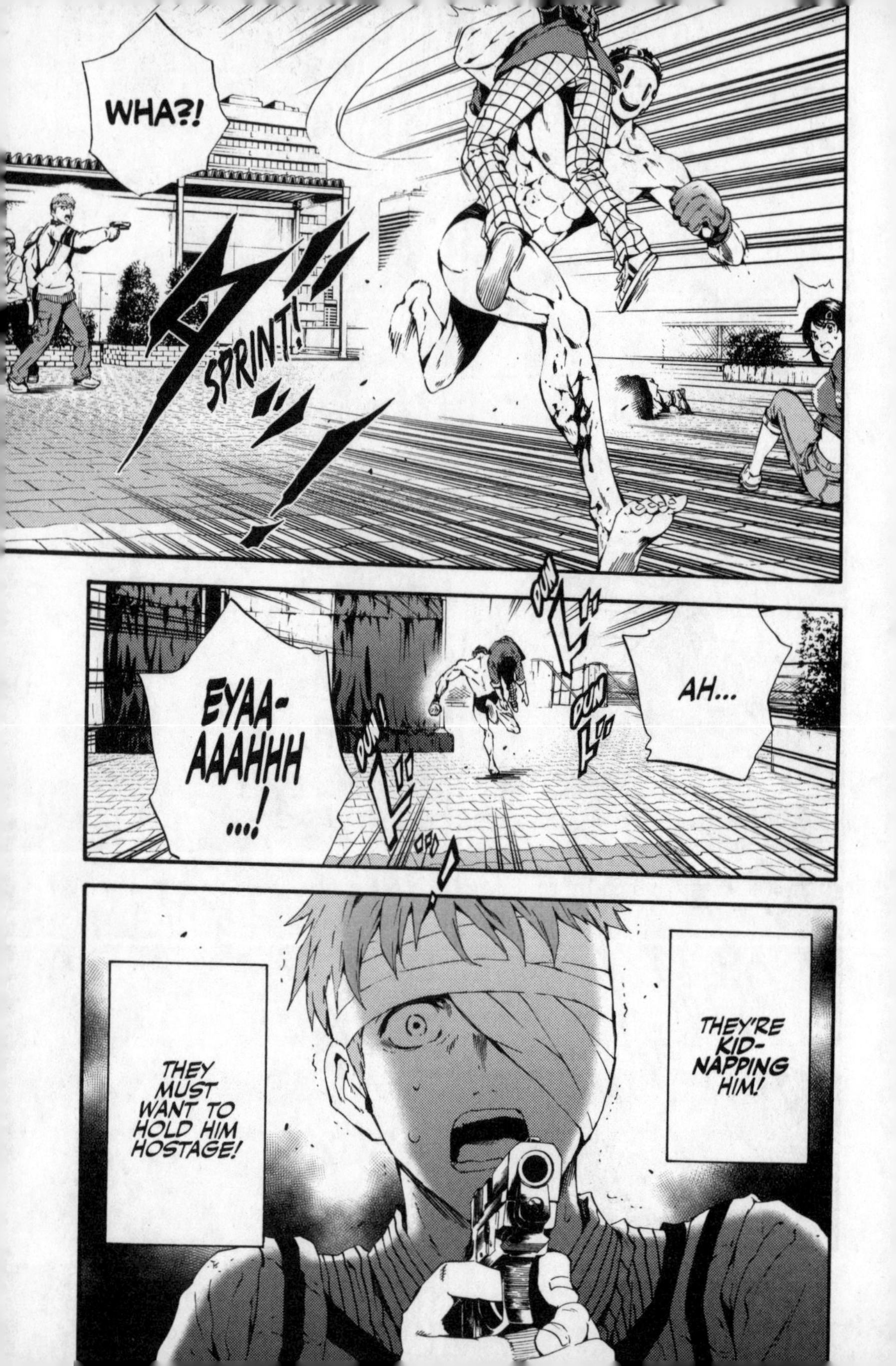
SPRINT!
WHA?!
AH...
DUN
DUN
DUN
EYAA-AAAHHH ...!
THEY'RE KID-NAPPING HIM!
THEY MUST WANT TO HOLD HIM HOSTAGE!

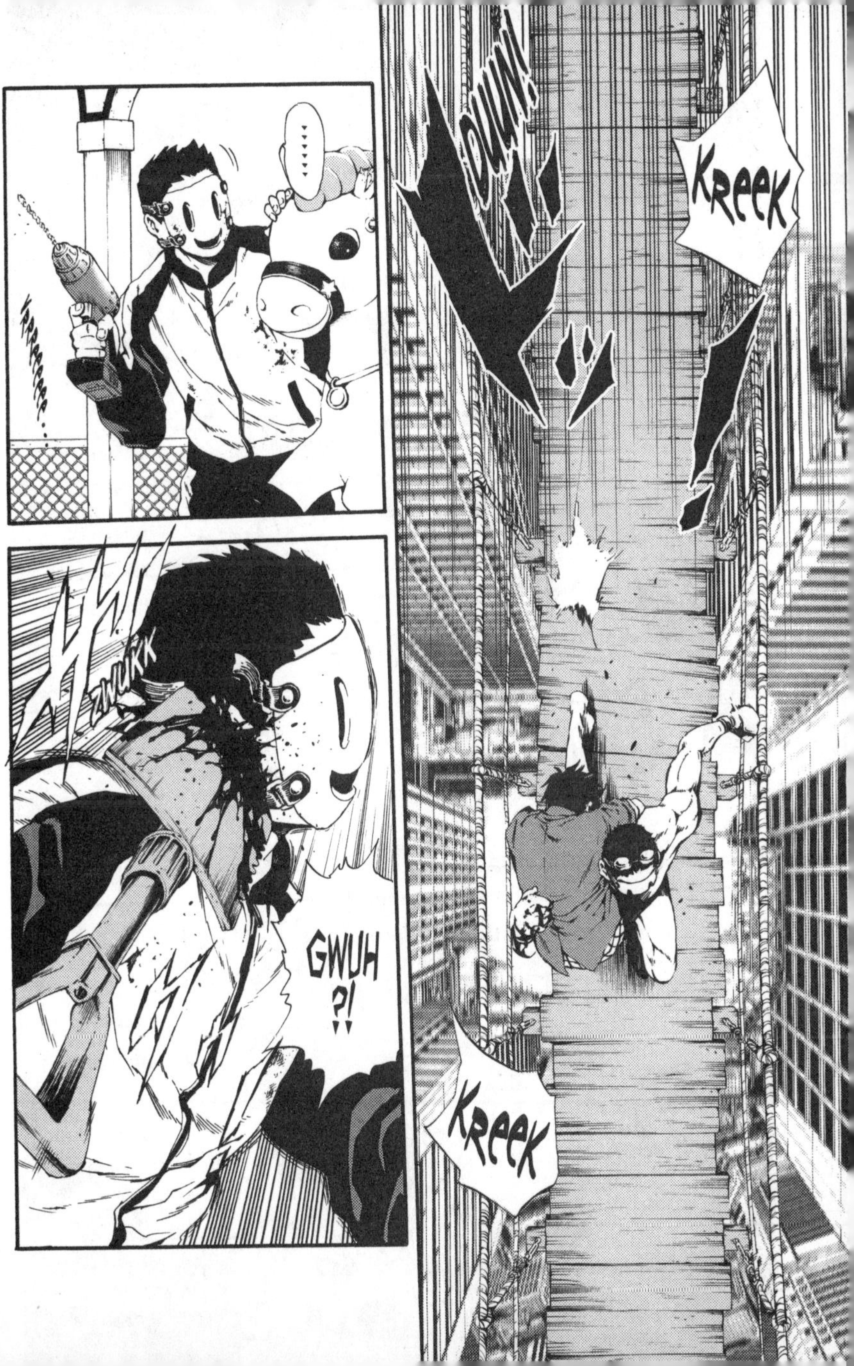

DWUN!
Kreek
Kreek
......
YRRRRRRRRR...
ZWUKK
GWUH ?!

THUD
HWOOOOO

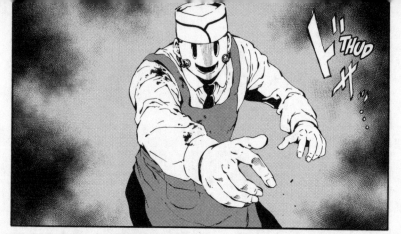

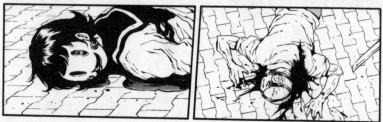

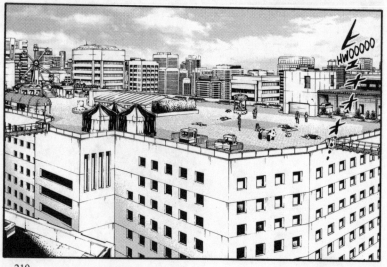

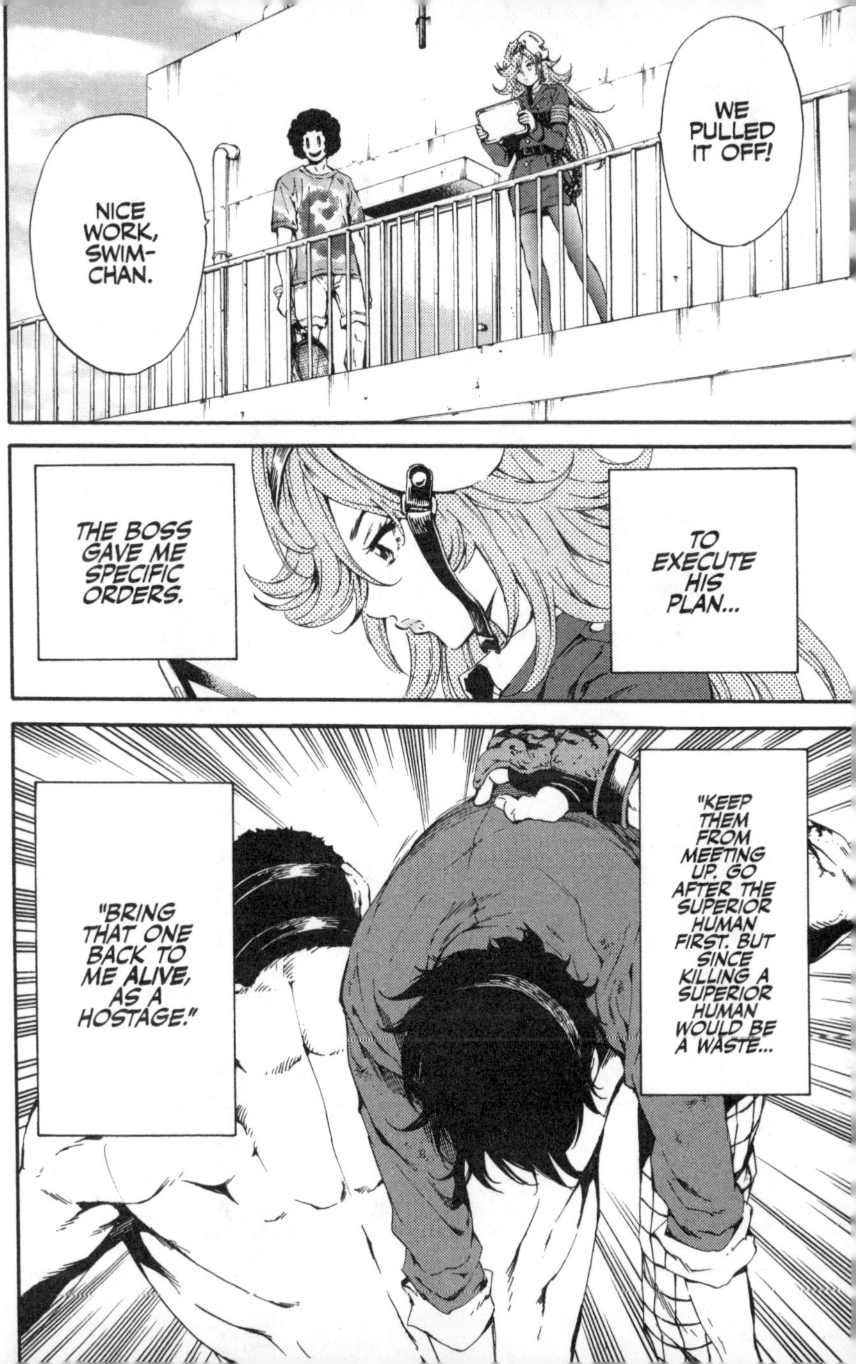
WE PULLED IT OFF!
NICE WORK, SWIM-CHAN.
TO EXECUTE HIS PLAN...
THE BOSS GAVE ME SPECIFIC ORDERS.
"KEEP THEM FROM MEETING UP. GO AFTER THE SUPERIOR HUMAN FIRST. BUT SINCE KILLING A SUPERIOR HUMAN WOULD BE A WASTE...
"BRING THAT ONE BACK TO ME ALIVE, AS A HOSTAGE."

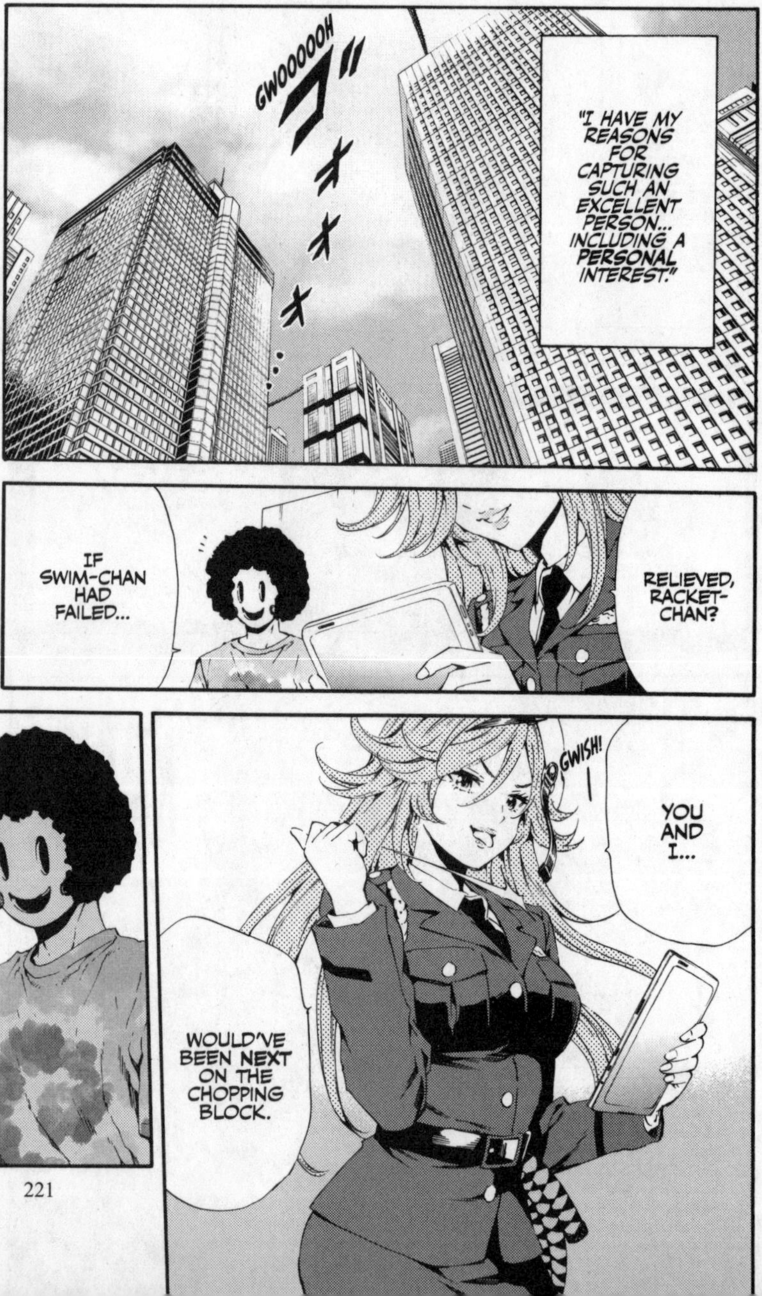
"I HAVE MY REASONS FOR CAPTURING SUCH AN EXCELLENT PERSON... INCLUDING A PERSONAL INTEREST."
GWOOOOOH
RELIEVED, RACKET-CHAN?
IF SWIM-CHAN HAD FAILED...
GWISH!
YOU AND I...
WOULD'VE BEEN NEXT ON THE CHOPPING BLOCK.
......

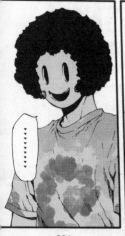

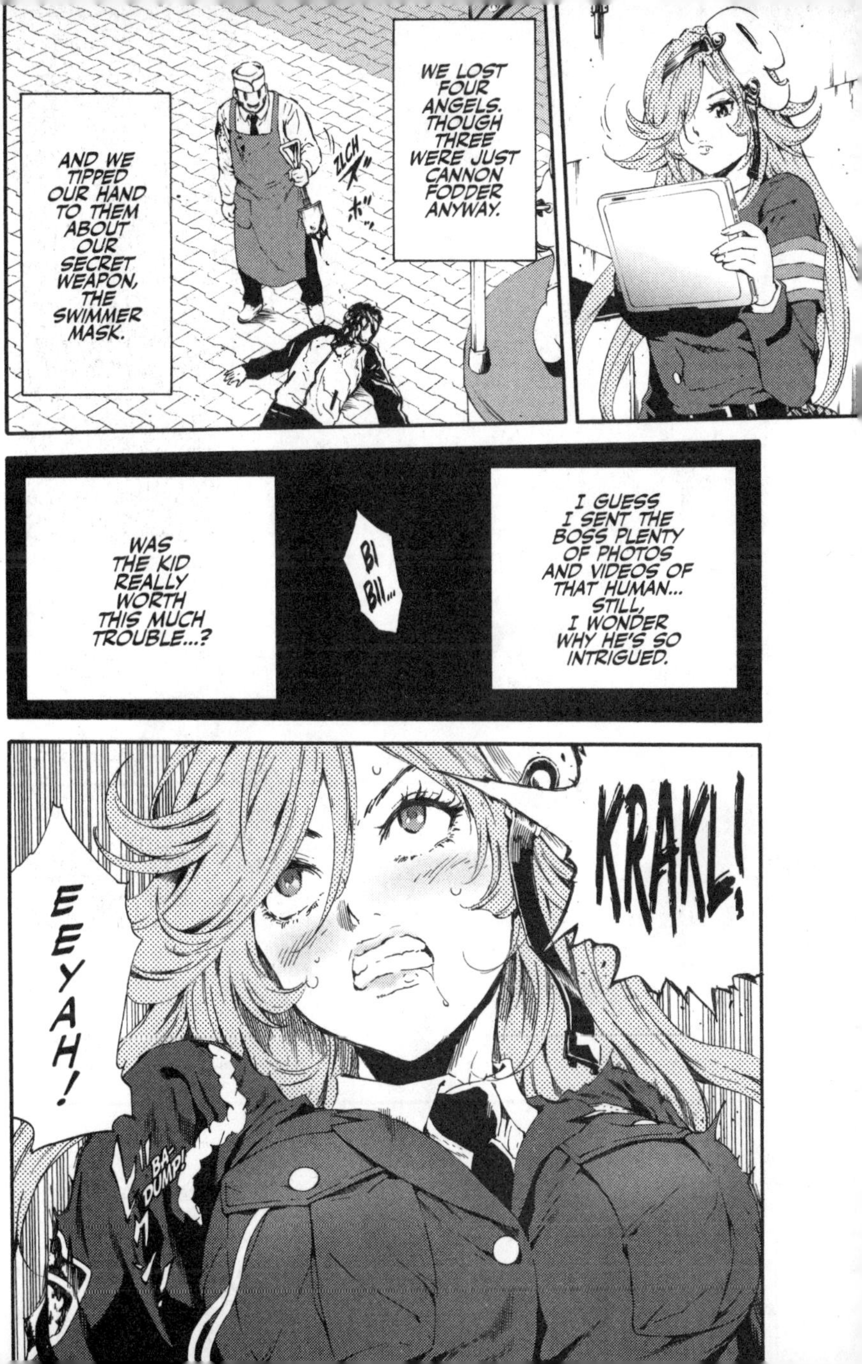
WE LOST FOUR ANGELS. THOUGH THREE WERE JUST CANNON FODDER ANYWAY.
AND WE TIPPED OUR HAND TO THEM ABOUT OUR SECRET WEAPON, THE SWIMMER MASK.
ZLCH
I GUESS I SENT THE BOSS PLENTY OF PHOTOS AND VIDEOS OF THAT HUMAN... STILL, I WONDER WHY HE'S SO INTRIGUED.
BI BII...
WAS THE KID REALLY WORTH THIS MUCH TROUBLE...?
KRAKL!
EEYAH!
BA-DUMP!

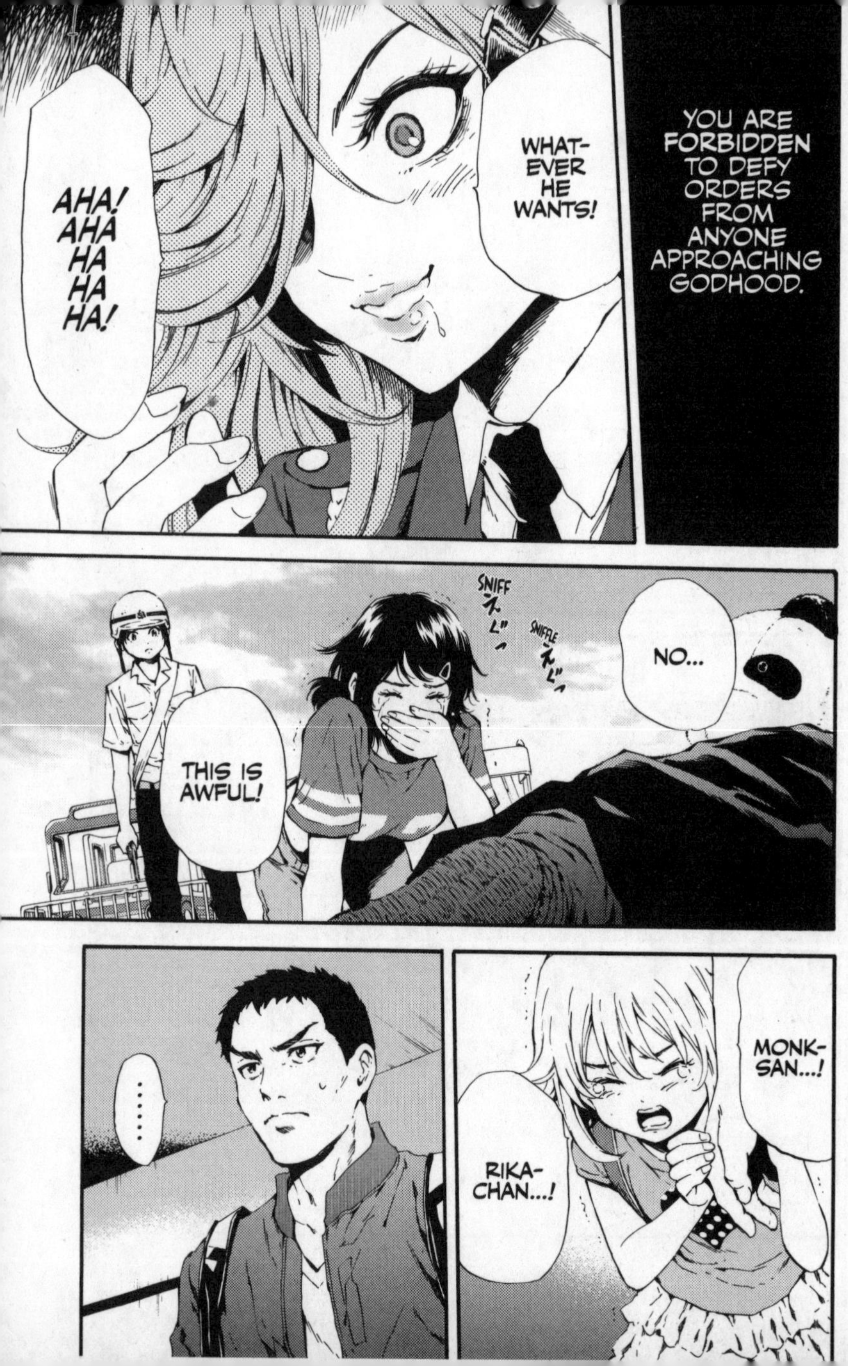

YOU ARE FORBIDDEN TO DEFY ORDERS FROM ANYONE APPROACHING GODHOOD.
WHAT-EVER HE WANTS!
AHA! AHA HA HA HA!
NO...
SNIFFLE
SNIFF
THIS IS AWFUL!
MONK-SAN...!
RIKA-CHAN...!
......

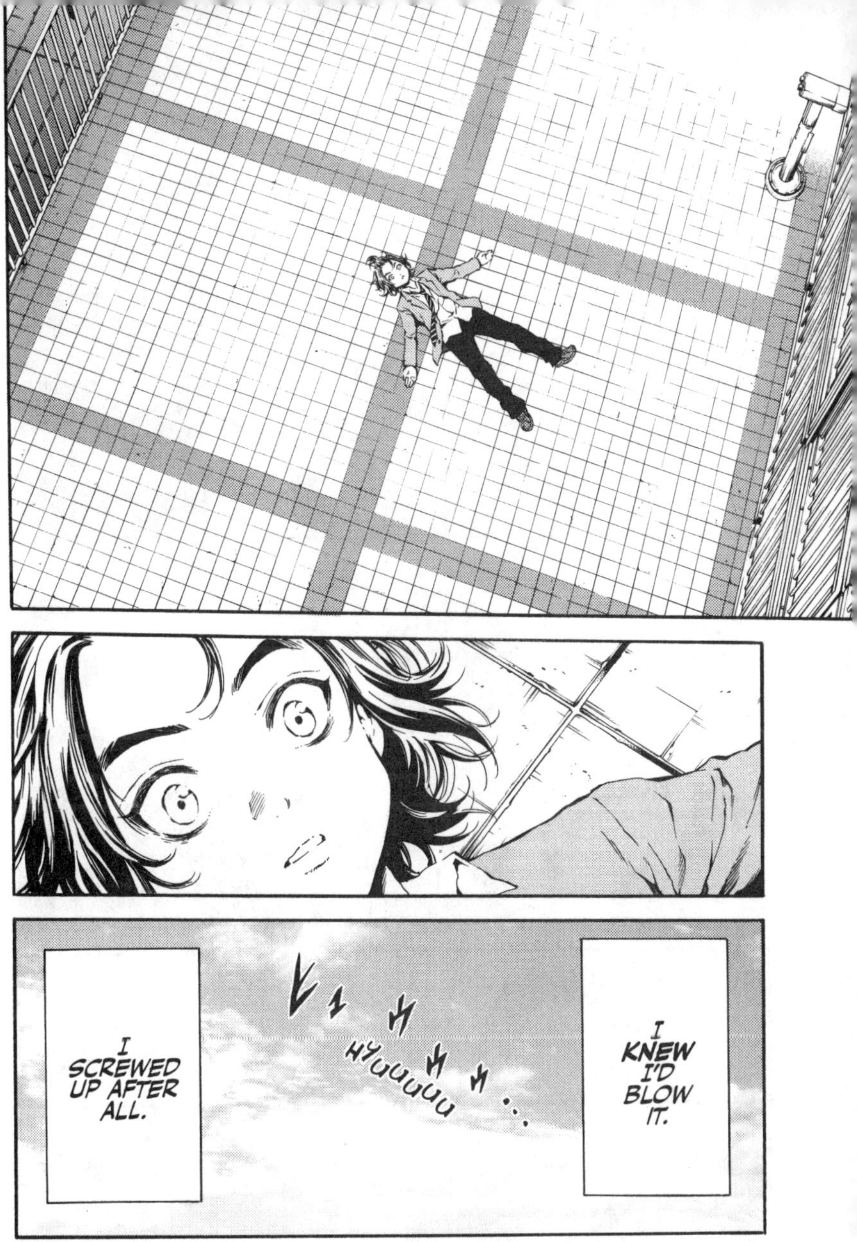
I KNEW I'D BLOW IT.
HYUUUUU
I SCREWED UP AFTER ALL.

HIGH-RISE INVASION

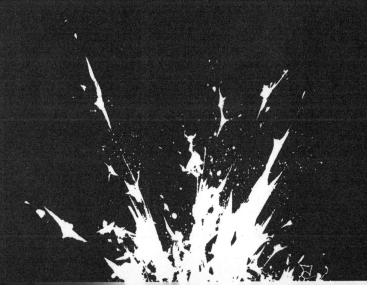

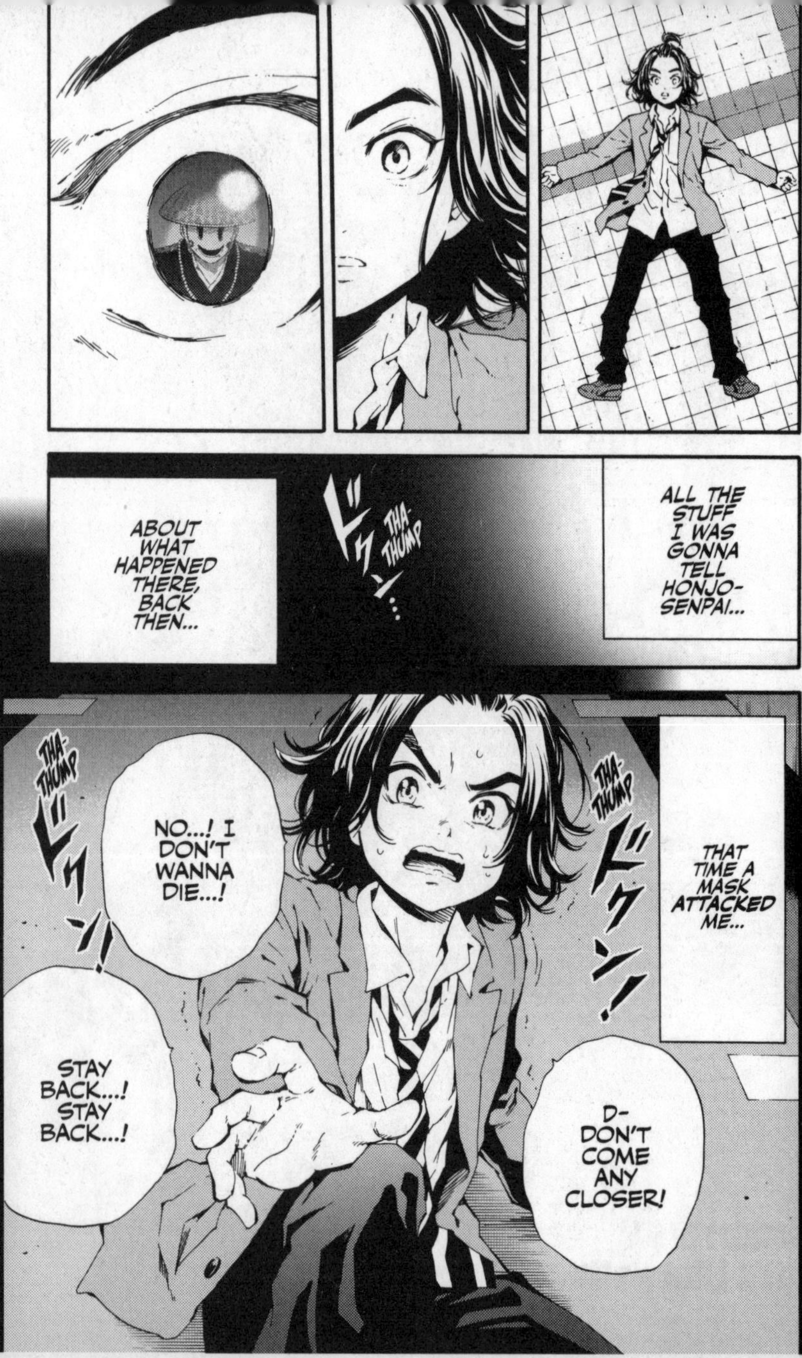

ALL THE STUFF I WAS GONNA TELL HONJO-SENPAI...
THA-THUMP
ABOUT WHAT HAPPENED THERE, BACK THEN...
THAT TIME A MASK ATTACKED ME...
THA-THUMP
NO...! I DON'T WANNA DIE...!
THA-THUMP
D-DON'T COME ANY CLOSER!
STAY BACK...! STAY BACK...!

CHAPTER 97:
It's Like Nothing's Changed

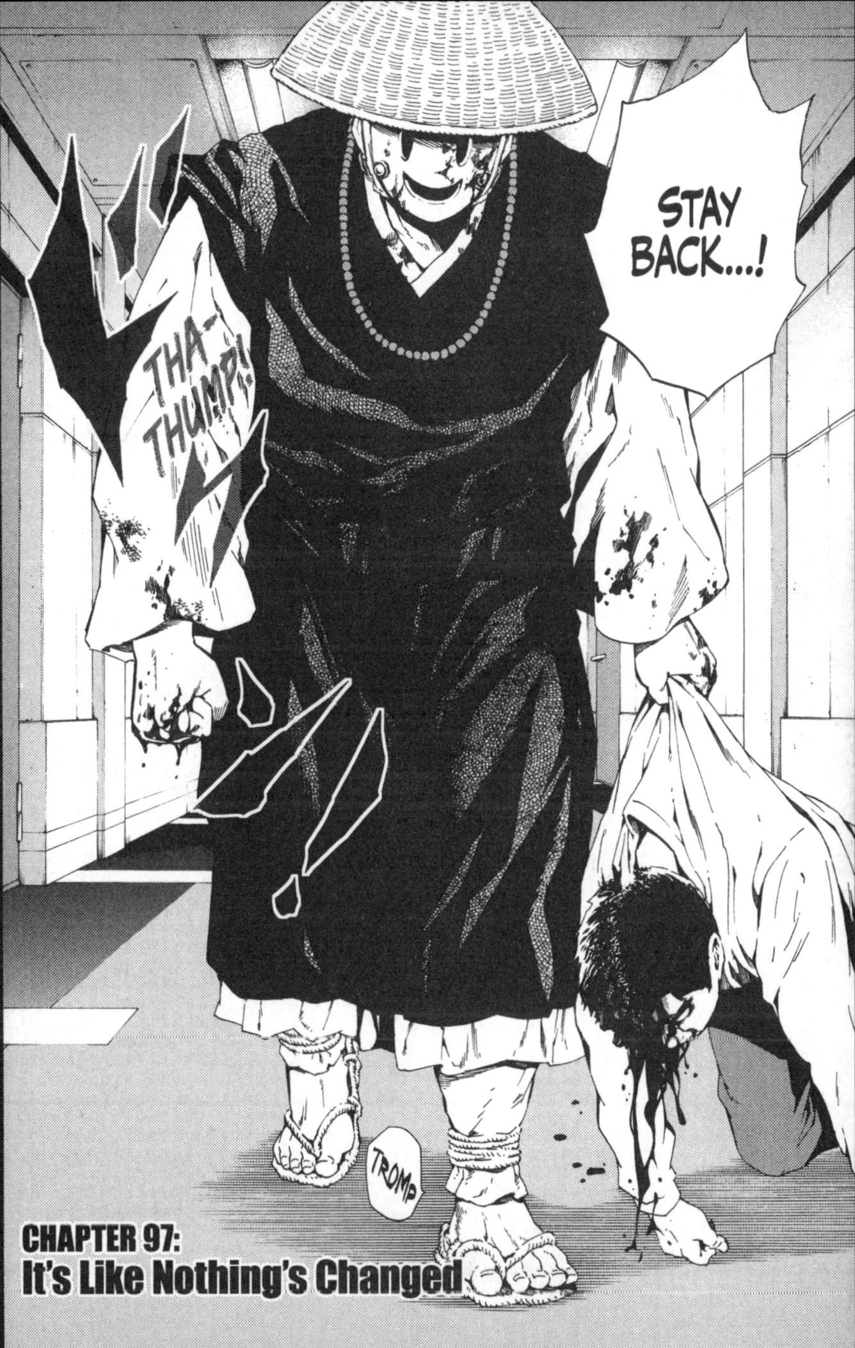
STAY BACK...!
THA-THUMP!!
TROMP

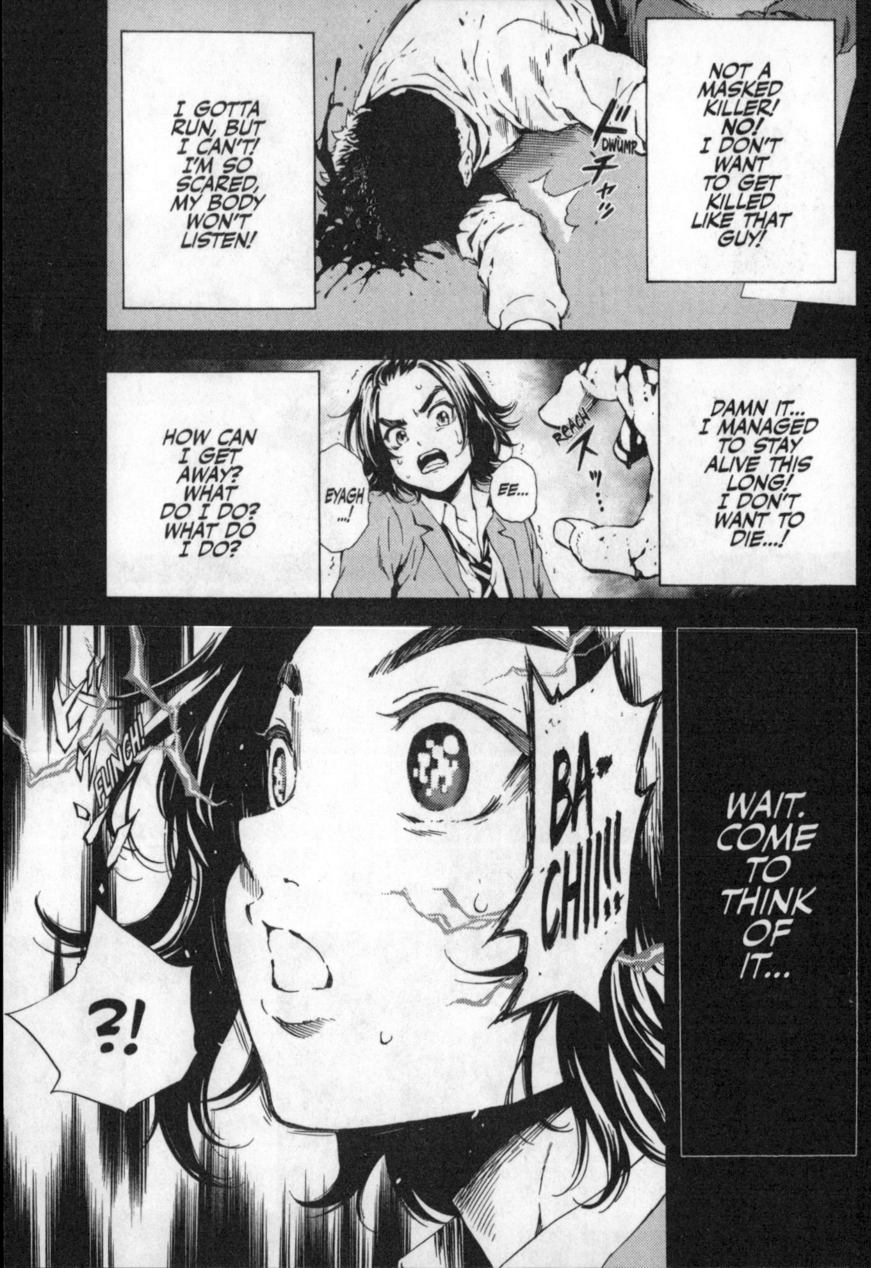
NOT A MASKED KILLER! NO! I DON'T WANT TO GET KILLED LIKE THAT GUY!
DWUMP
I GOTTA RUN, BUT I CAN'T! I'M SO SCARED, MY BODY WON'T LISTEN!
DAMN IT... I MANAGED TO STAY ALIVE THIS LONG! I DON'T WANT TO DIE...!
REACH
EE...
EYAGH ...!
HOW CAN I GET AWAY? WHAT DO I DO? WHAT DO I DO?
WAIT. COME TO THINK OF IT...
BA-CHI!!!
FLINCH!
?!

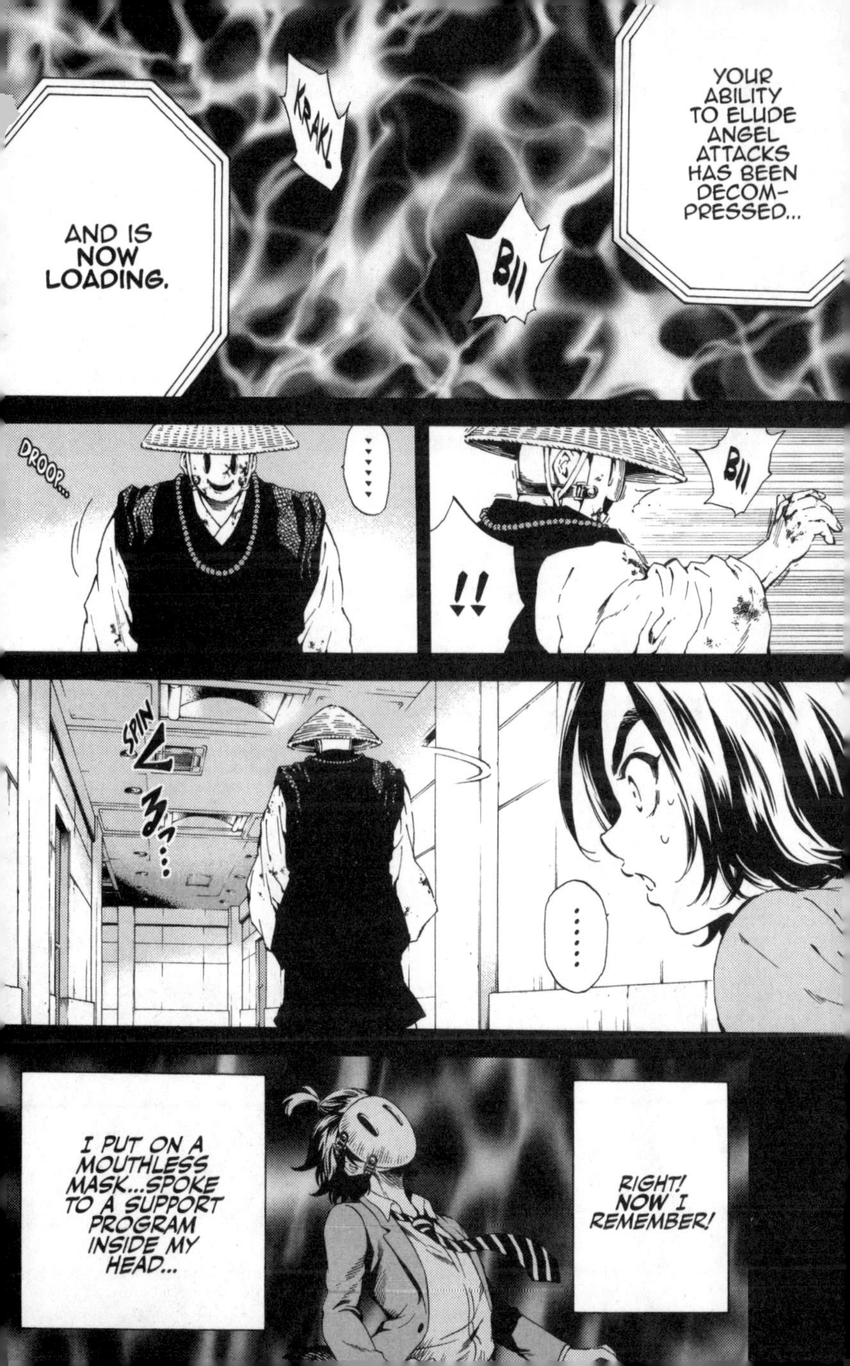
YOUR ABILITY TO ELUDE ANGEL ATTACKS HAS BEEN DECOM-PRESSED...
KRAK!
BII
AND IS NOW LOADING.
BII
!!
......
DROOP...
......
SPIN
RIGHT! NOW I REMEMBER!
I PUT ON A MOUTHLESS MASK...SPOKE TO A SUPPORT PROGRAM INSIDE MY HEAD...

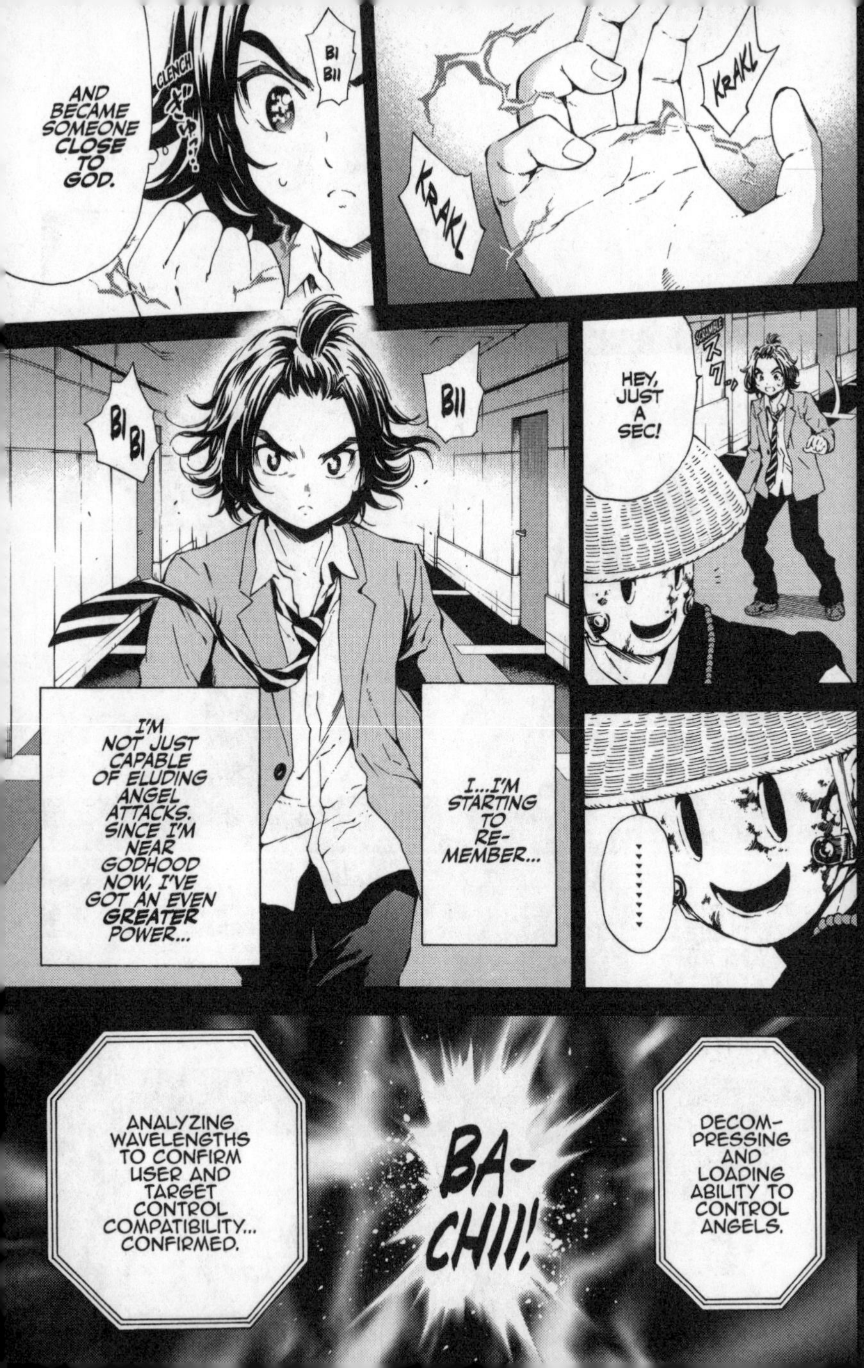
KRAKL
KRAKL
BI BII
CLENCH
AND BECAME SOMEONE CLOSE TO GOD.
SCRAMBLE
HEY, JUST A SEC!
......
BII
BI BI
I...I'M STARTING TO RE-MEMBER...
I'M NOT JUST CAPABLE OF ELUDING ANGEL ATTACKS. SINCE I'M NEAR GODHOOD NOW, I'VE GOT AN EVEN GREATER POWER...
DECOM-PRESSING AND LOADING ABILITY TO CONTROL ANGELS.
BA-CHII!
ANALYZING WAVELENGTHS TO CONFIRM USER AND TARGET CONTROL COMPATIBILITY... CONFIRMED.

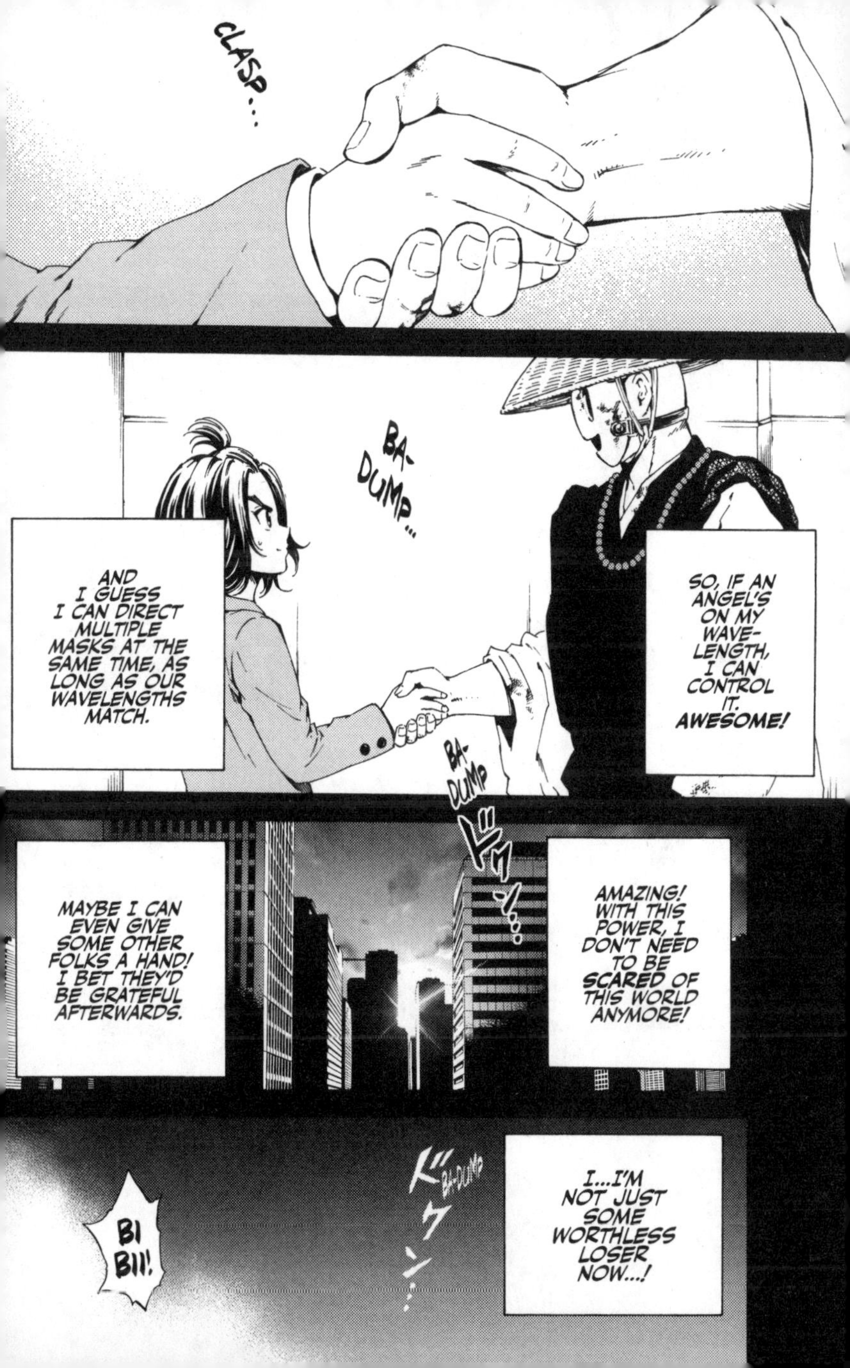
CLASP...
SO, IF AN ANGEL'S ON MY WAVE-LENGTH, I CAN CONTROL IT. AWESOME!
BA-DUMP...
AND I GUESS I CAN DIRECT MULTIPLE MASKS AT THE SAME TIME, AS LONG AS OUR WAVELENGTHS MATCH.
BA-DUMP
ドクン...
AMAZING! WITH THIS POWER, I DON'T NEED TO BE SCARED OF THIS WORLD ANYMORE!
MAYBE I CAN EVEN GIVE SOME OTHER FOLKS A HAND! I BET THEY'D BE GRATEFUL AFTERWARDS.
ドクン...
BA-DUMP
I...I'M NOT JUST SOME WORTHLESS LOSER NOW...!
BI BII!

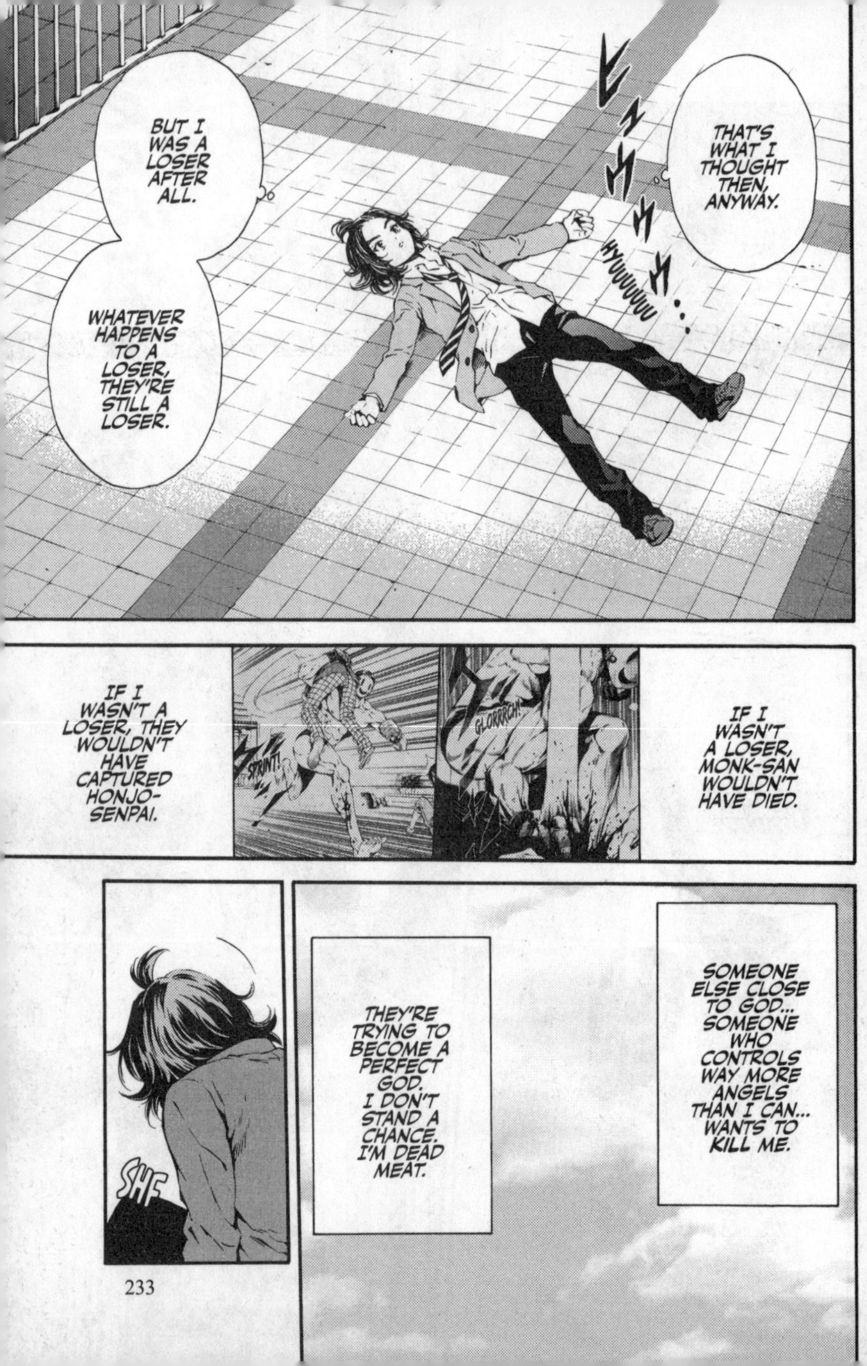
THAT'S WHAT I THOUGHT THEN, ANYWAY.
HYUUUUUUU
BUT I WAS A LOSER AFTER ALL.
WHATEVER HAPPENS TO A LOSER, THEY'RE STILL A LOSER.
IF I WASN'T A LOSER, MONK-SAN WOULDN'T HAVE DIED.
GLORRRCH!
SPRINT!
IF I WASN'T A LOSER, THEY WOULDN'T HAVE CAPTURED HONJO-SENPAI.
SOMEONE ELSE CLOSE TO GOD... SOMEONE WHO CONTROLS WAY MORE ANGELS THAN I CAN... WANTS TO KILL ME.
THEY'RE TRYING TO BECOME A PERFECT GOD. I DON'T STAND A CHANCE. I'M DEAD MEAT.
SHF

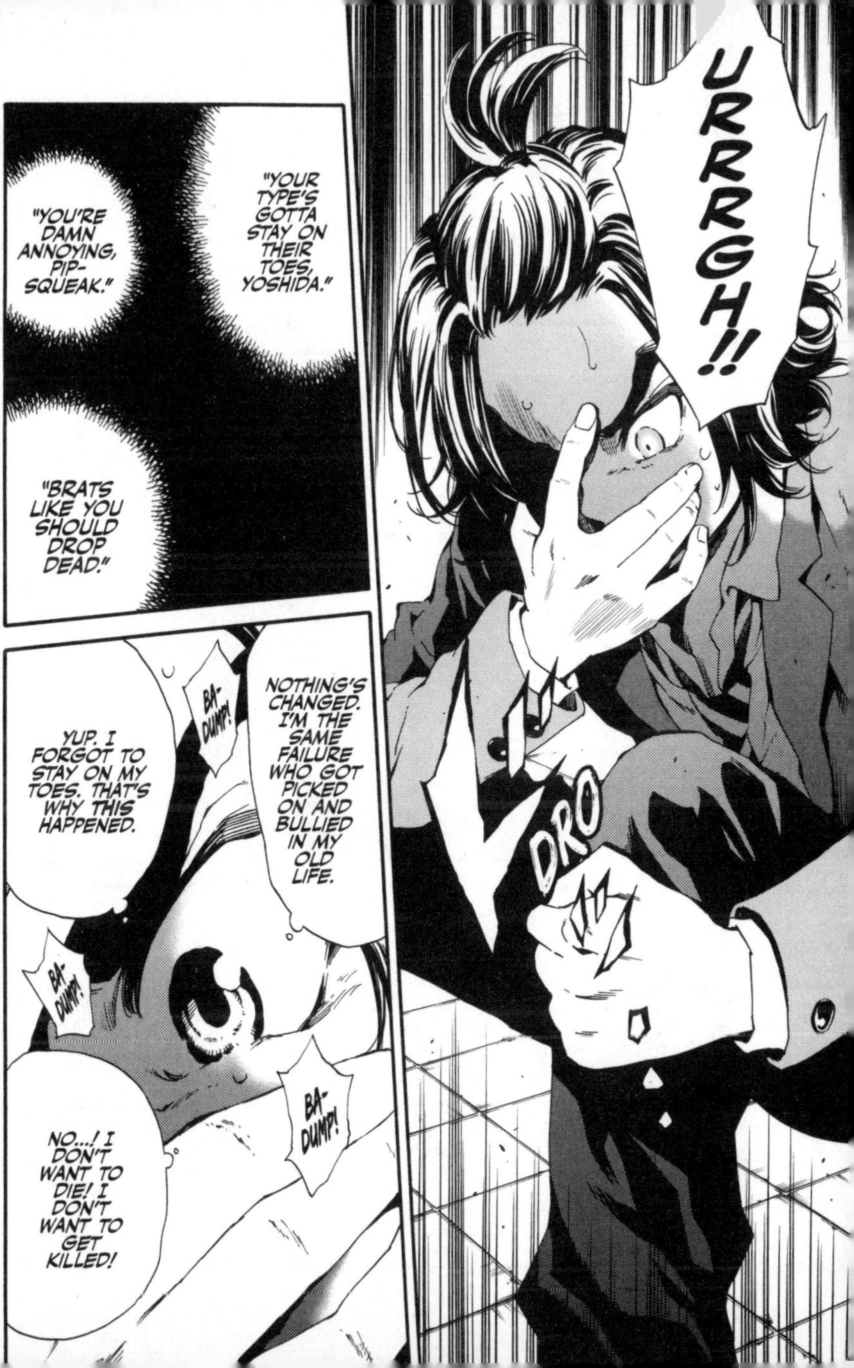
URRRGH!!
DRO
"YOUR TYPE'S GOTTA STAY ON THEIR TOES, YOSHIDA."
"YOU'RE DAMN ANNOYING, PIP-SQUEAK."
"BRATS LIKE YOU SHOULD DROP DEAD."
NOTHING'S CHANGED. I'M THE SAME FAILURE WHO GOT PICKED ON AND BULLIED IN MY OLD LIFE.
BA-DUMP!
YUP. I FORGOT TO STAY ON MY TOES. THAT'S WHY THIS HAPPENED.
BA-DUMP!
BA-DUMP!
NO...! I DON'T WANT TO DIE! I DON'T WANT TO GET KILLED!

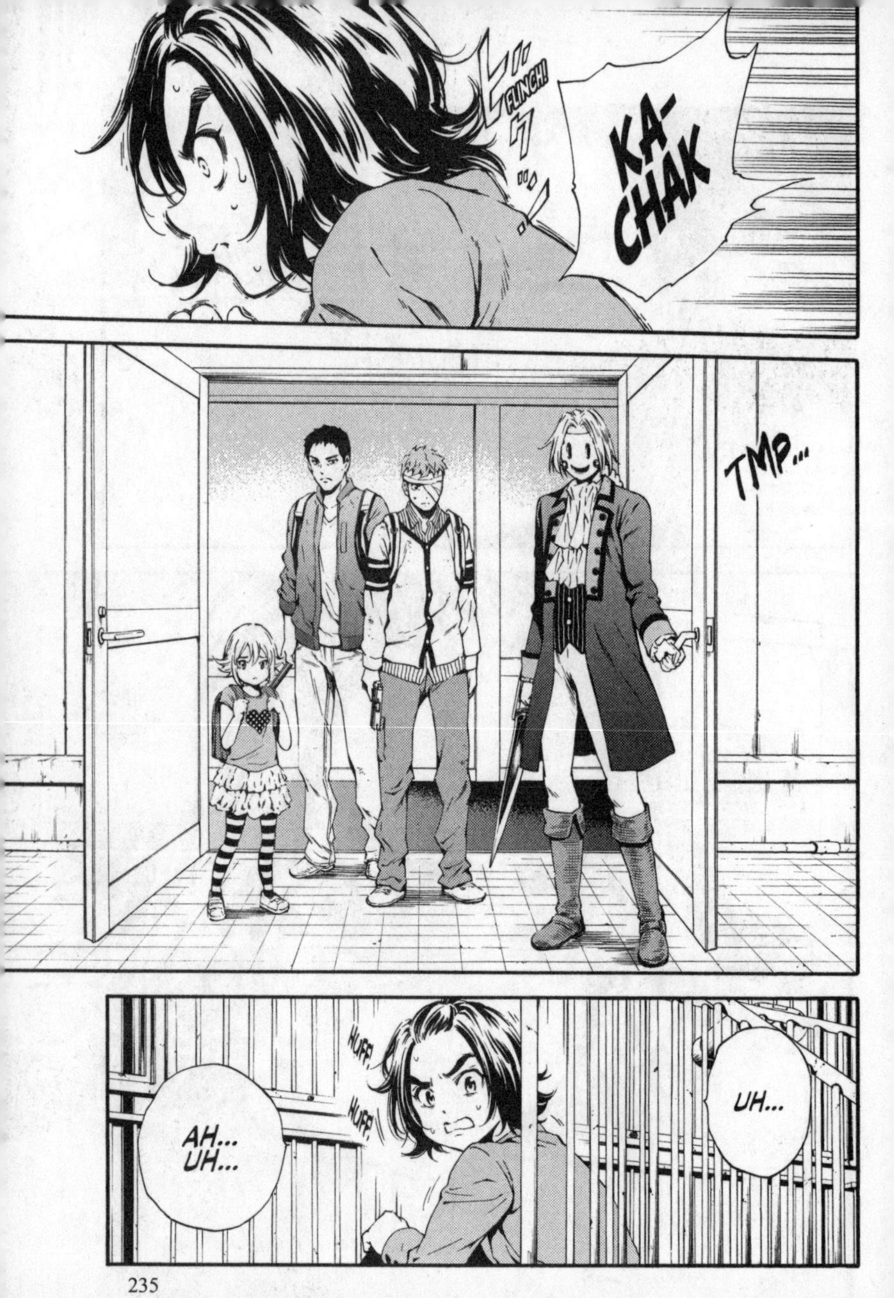
KA-
CHAK
FLINCH!
TMP...
UH...
HUFF!
HUFF!
AH...
UH...

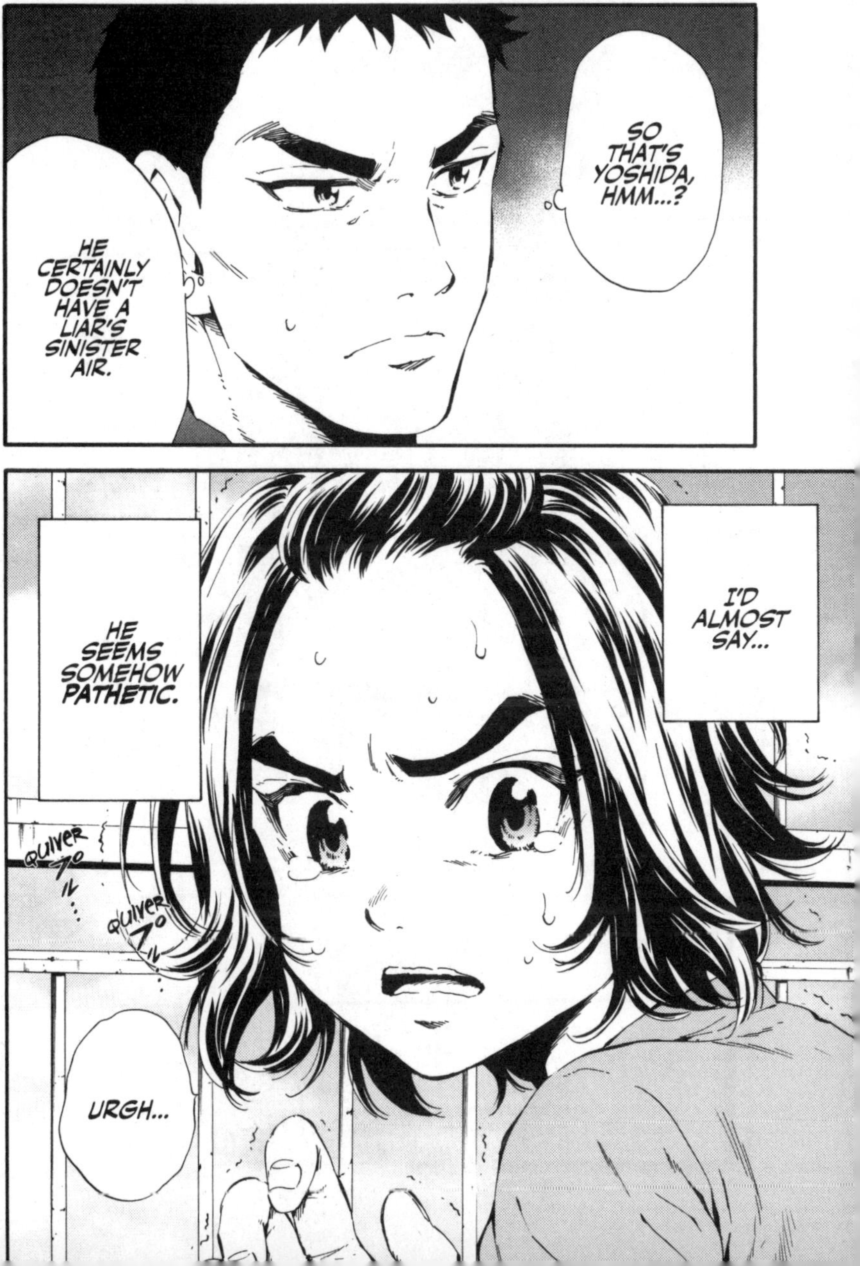
SO THAT'S YOSHIDA, HMM...?
HE CERTAINLY DOESN'T HAVE A LIAR'S SINISTER AIR.
I'D ALMOST SAY...
HE SEEMS SOMEHOW PATHETIC.
QUIVER
QUIVER
URGH...

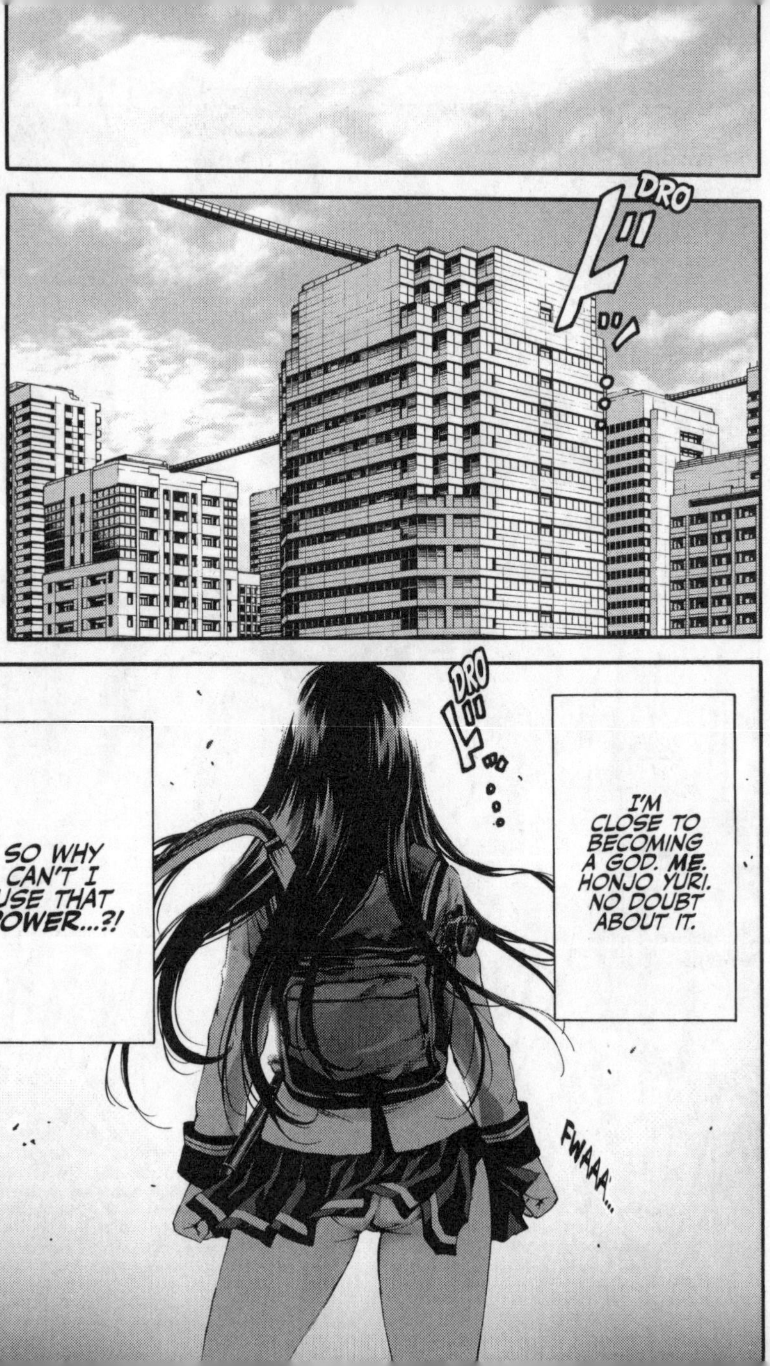
DRO
DRO
I'M CLOSE TO BECOMING A GOD. ME. HONJO YURI. NO DOUBT ABOUT IT.
SO WHY CAN'T I USE THAT POWER...?!
FWAAA...

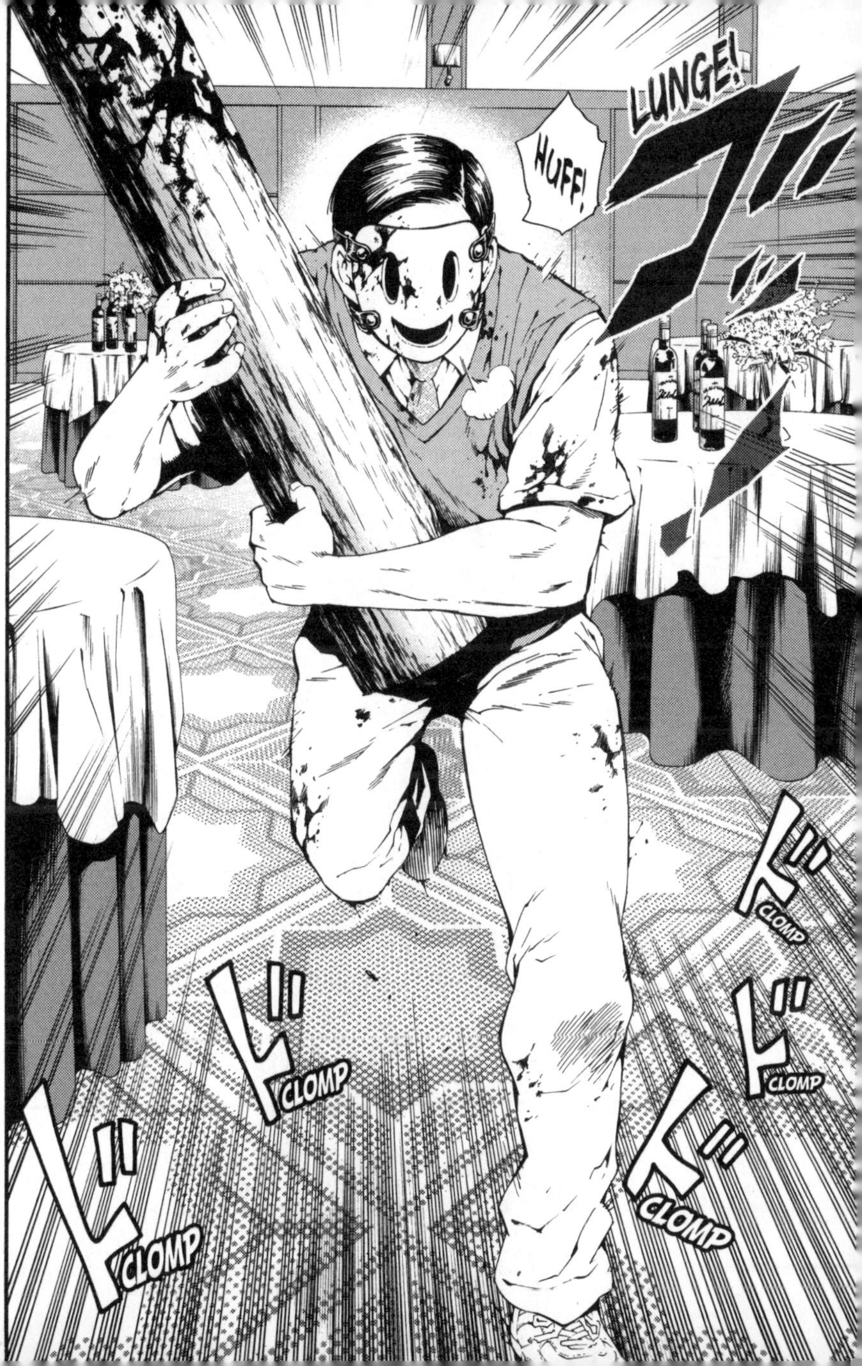

LUNGE!
HUFF!
CLOMP
CLOMP
CLOMP
CLOMP
CLOMP

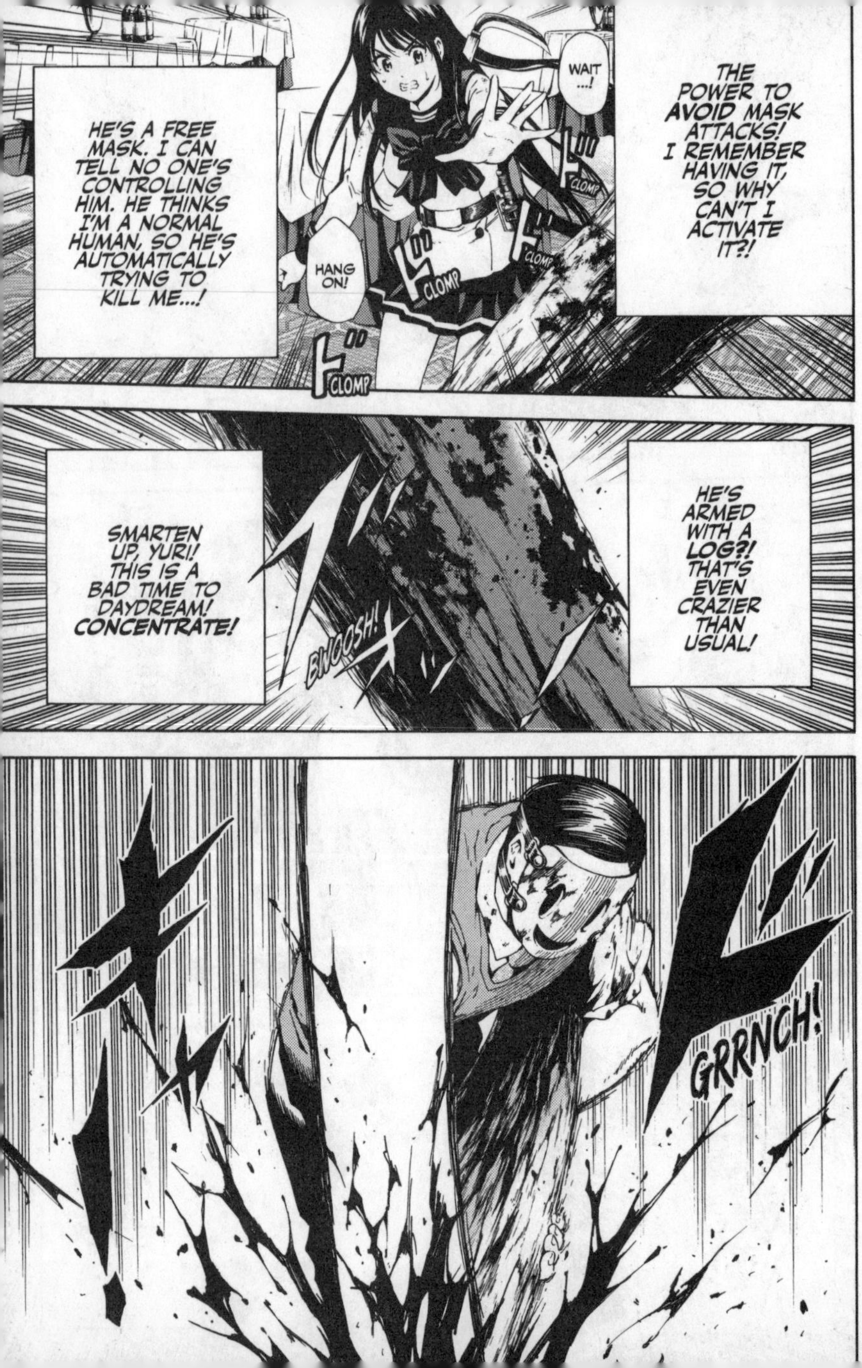
THE POWER TO AVOID MASK ATTACKS! I REMEMBER HAVING IT, SO WHY CAN'T I ACTIVATE IT?!
WAIT ...!
CLOMP
CLOMP
CLOMP
HANG ON!
HE'S A FREE MASK. I CAN TELL NO ONE'S CONTROLLING HIM. HE THINKS I'M A NORMAL HUMAN, SO HE'S AUTOMATICALLY TRYING TO KILL ME...!
CLOMP
HE'S ARMED WITH A LOG?! THAT'S EVEN CRAZIER THAN USUAL!
BWOOSH!
SMARTEN UP, YURI! THIS IS A BAD TIME TO DAYDREAM! CONCENTRATE!
GRRNCH!

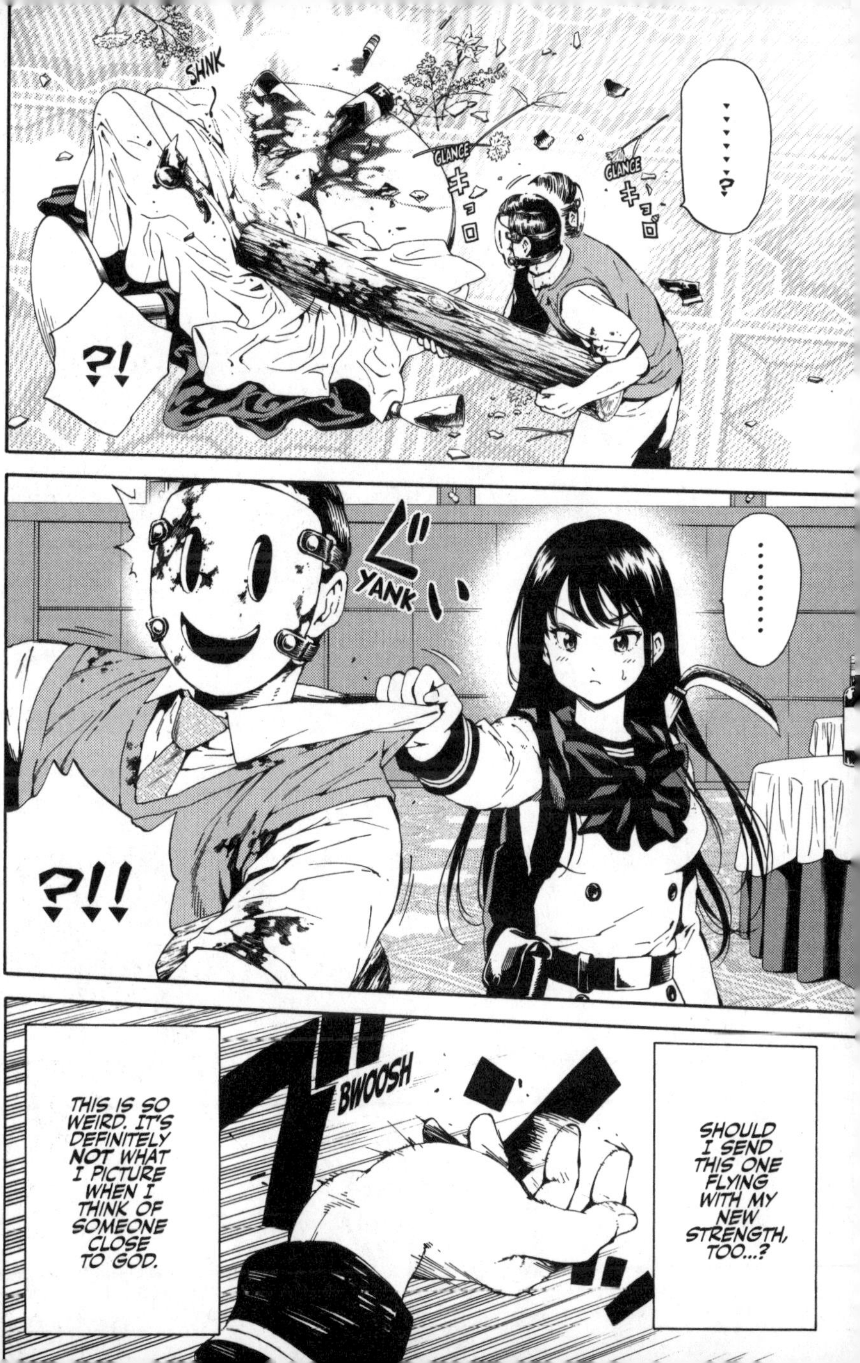

........?
GLANCE
キョロ
GLANCE
キョロ
SHNK
?!
....
YANK
ぐい
?!!
SHOULD I SEND THIS ONE FLYING WITH MY NEW STRENGTH, TOO...?
BWOOSH
THIS IS SO WEIRD. IT'S DEFINITELY NOT WHAT I PICTURE WHEN I THINK OF SOMEONE CLOSE TO GOD.

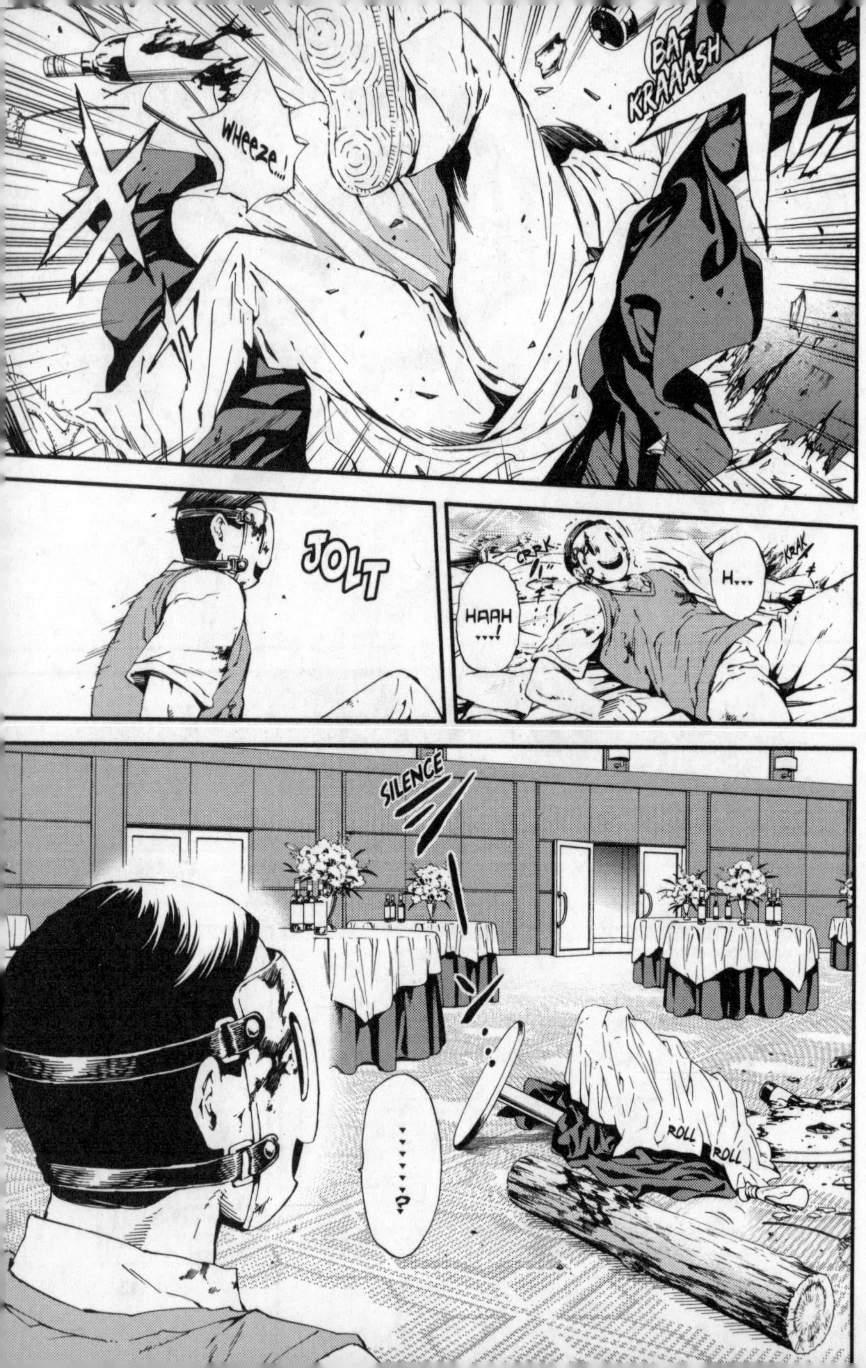
BA-KRAAASH
wheeze...!
KRAK
H...
CRRK
HAAH...!
JOLT
SILENCE
......?
ROLL
ROLL

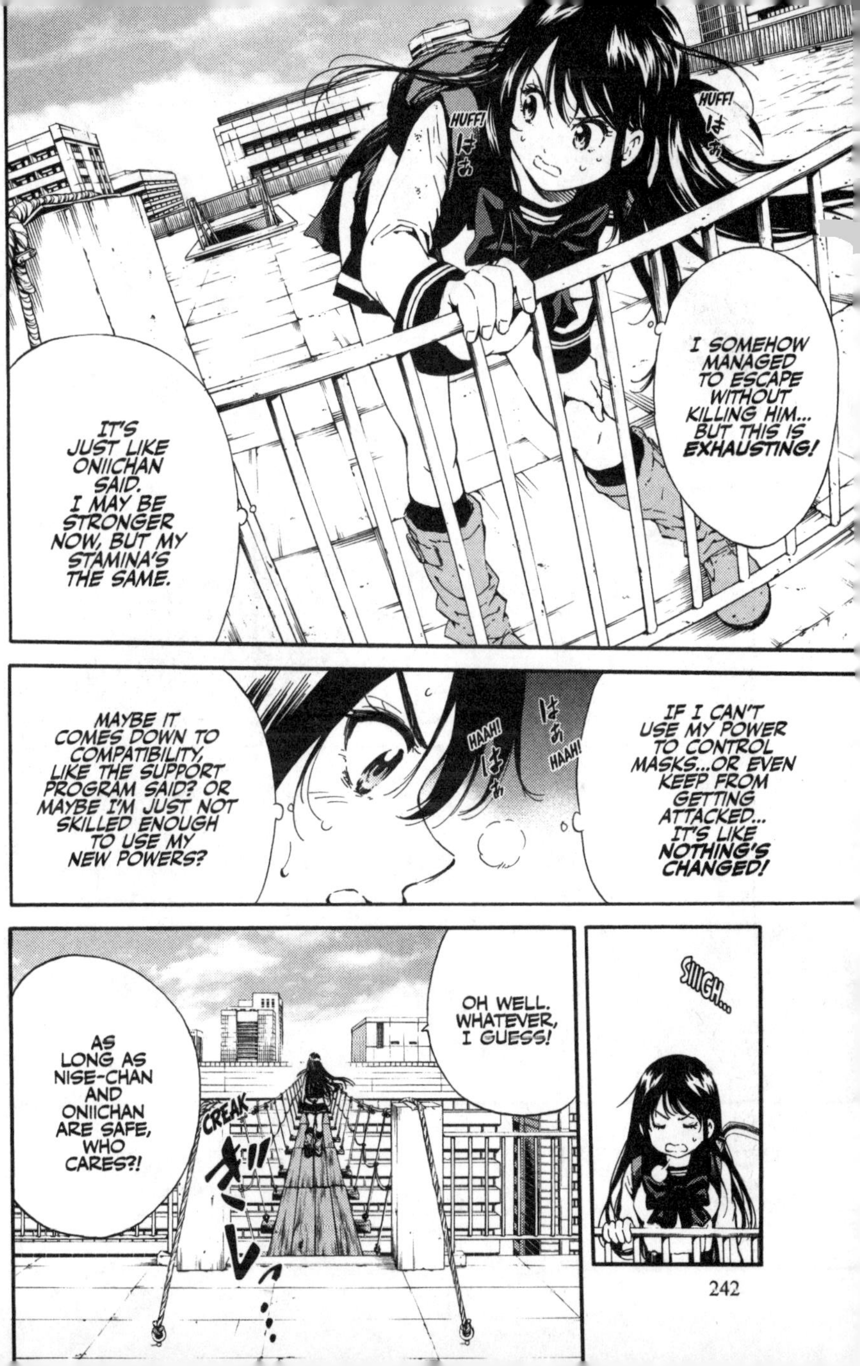
HUFF! はぁ
HUFF! はぁ
I SOMEHOW MANAGED TO ESCAPE WITHOUT KILLING HIM... BUT THIS IS EXHAUSTING!
IT'S JUST LIKE ONIICHAN SAID. I MAY BE STRONGER NOW, BUT MY STAMINA'S THE SAME.
IF I CAN'T USE MY POWER TO CONTROL MASKS...OR EVEN KEEP FROM GETTING ATTACKED... IT'S LIKE NOTHING'S CHANGED!
HAAH! はぁ
HAAH! はぁ
MAYBE IT COMES DOWN TO COMPATIBILITY, LIKE THE SUPPORT PROGRAM SAID? OR MAYBE I'M JUST NOT SKILLED ENOUGH TO USE MY NEW POWERS?
SIIIGH...
OH WELL. WHATEVER, I GUESS!
AS LONG AS NISE-CHAN AND ONIICHAN ARE SAFE, WHO CARES?!
CREAK

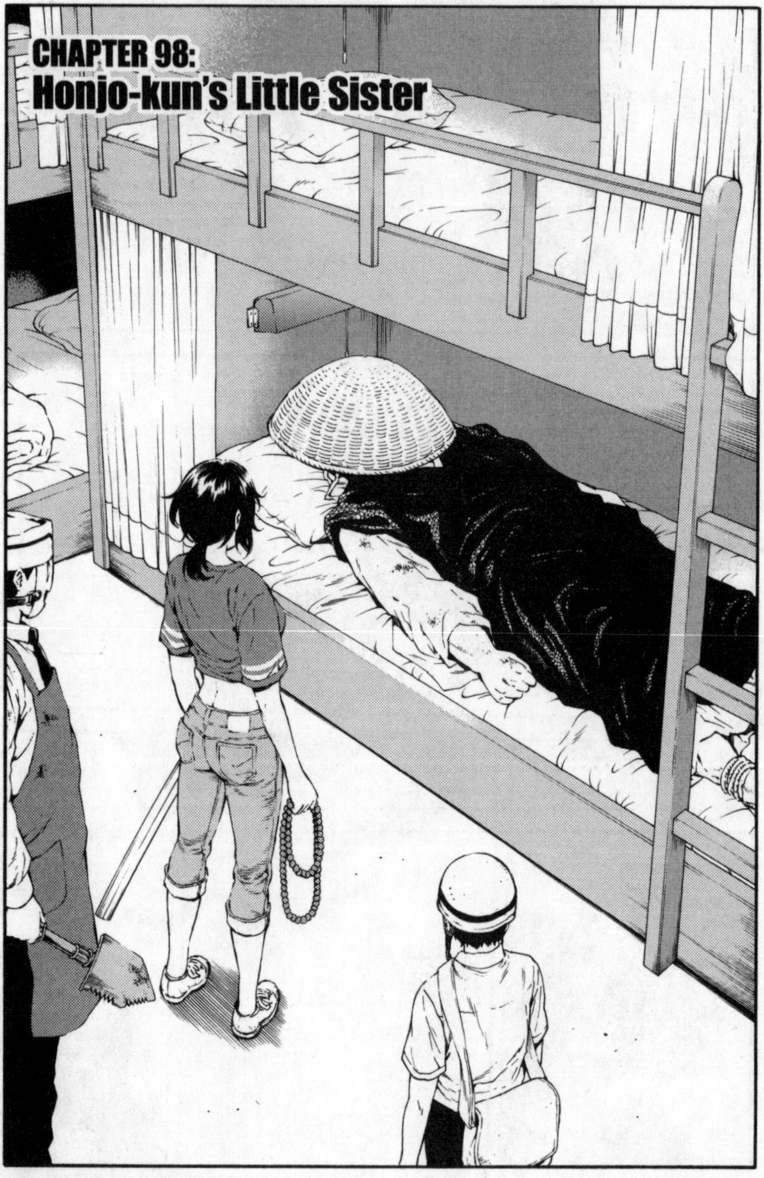
CHAPTER 98:
Honjo-kun's Little Sister

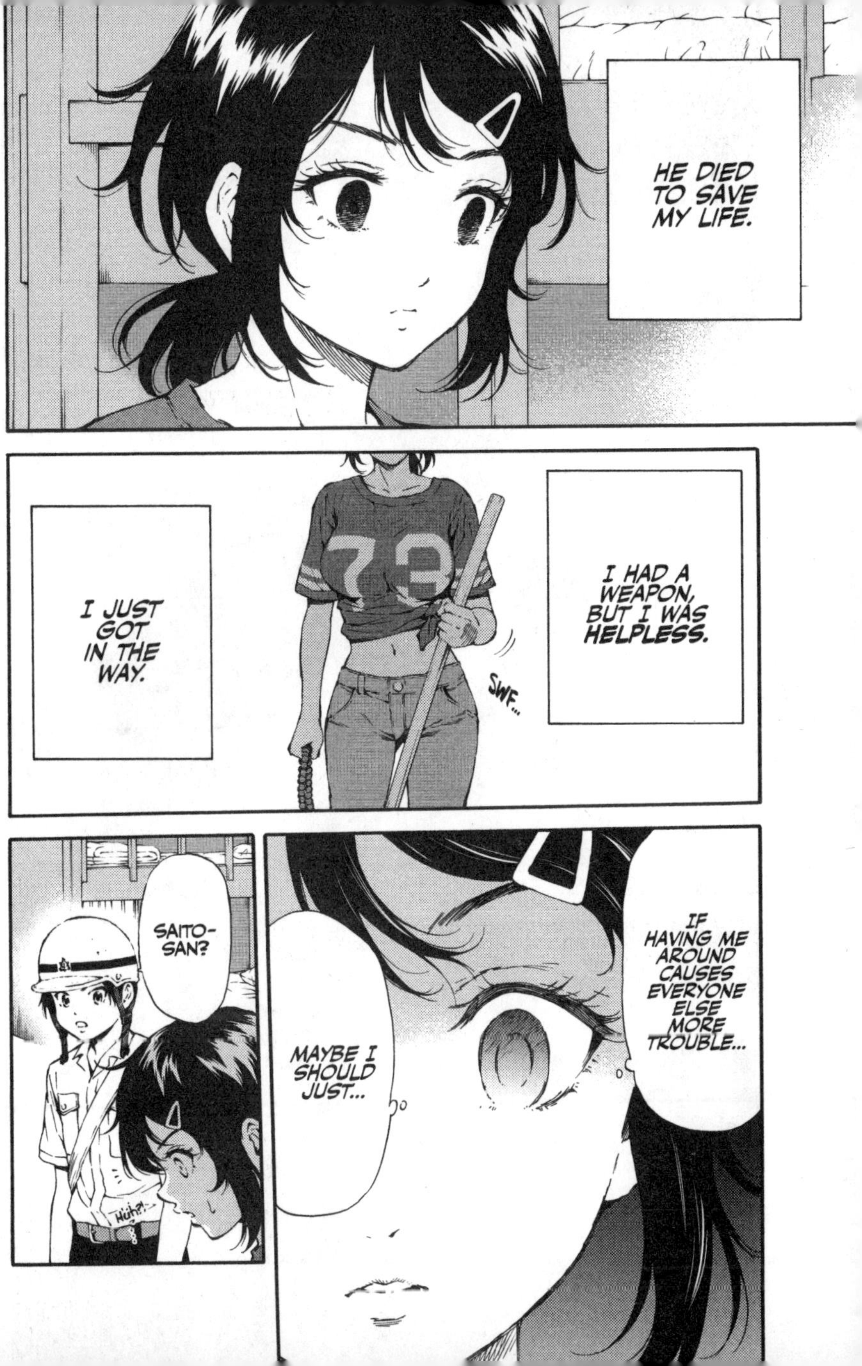
HE DIED TO SAVE MY LIFE.
I HAD A WEAPON, BUT I WAS HELPLESS.
SWF...
I JUST GOT IN THE WAY.
IF HAVING ME AROUND CAUSES EVERYONE ELSE MORE TROUBLE...
MAYBE I SHOULD JUST...
SAITO-SAN?
Huh?!

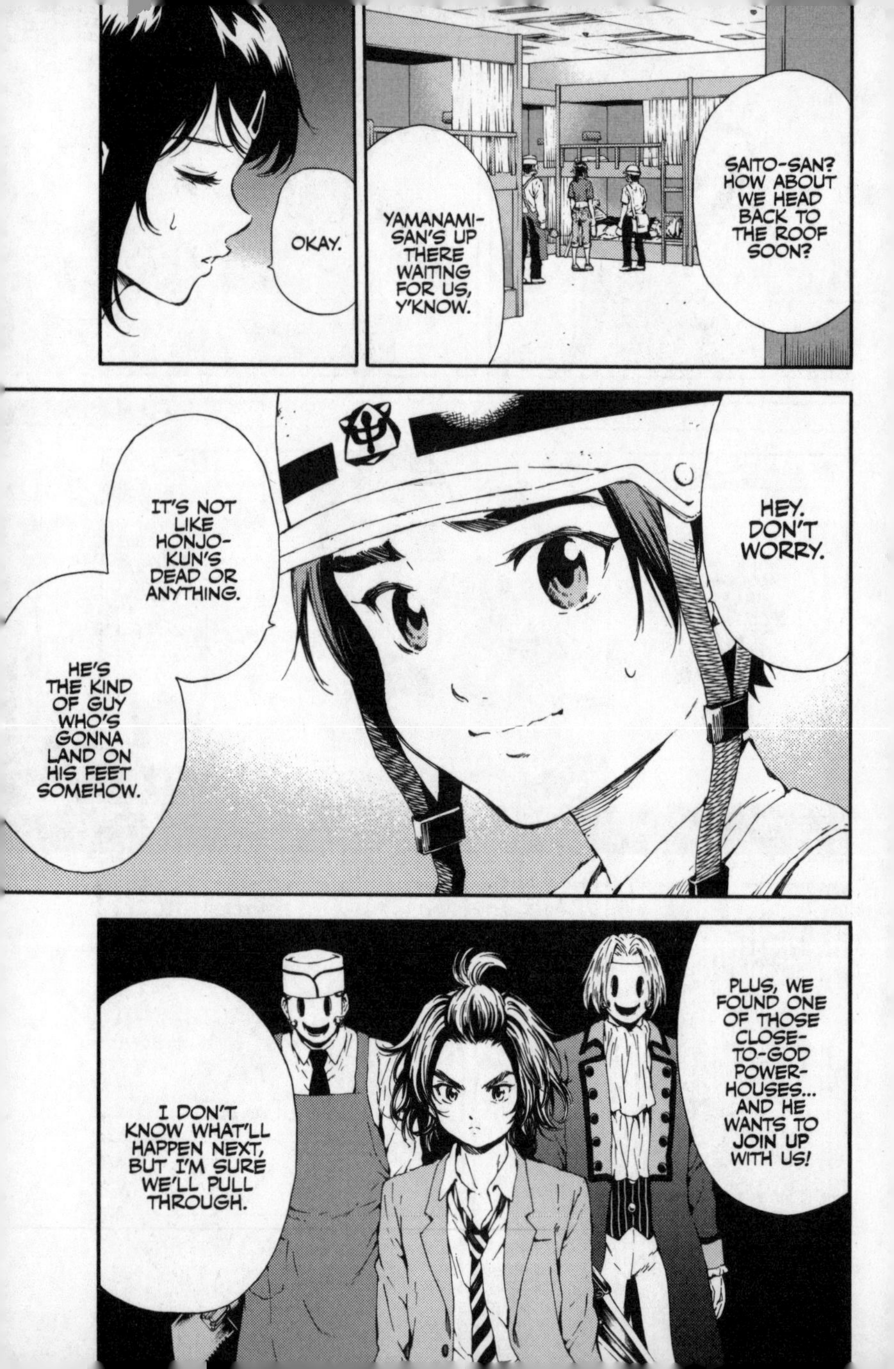
SAITO-SAN? HOW ABOUT WE HEAD BACK TO THE ROOF SOON?
YAMANAMI-SAN'S UP THERE WAITING FOR US, Y'KNOW.
OKAY.
HEY. DON'T WORRY.
IT'S NOT LIKE HONJO-KUN'S DEAD OR ANYTHING.
HE'S THE KIND OF GUY WHO'S GONNA LAND ON HIS FEET SOMEHOW.
PLUS, WE FOUND ONE OF THOSE CLOSE-TO-GOD POWER-HOUSES... AND HE WANTS TO JOIN UP WITH US!
I DON'T KNOW WHAT'LL HAPPEN NEXT, BUT I'M SURE WE'LL PULL THROUGH.

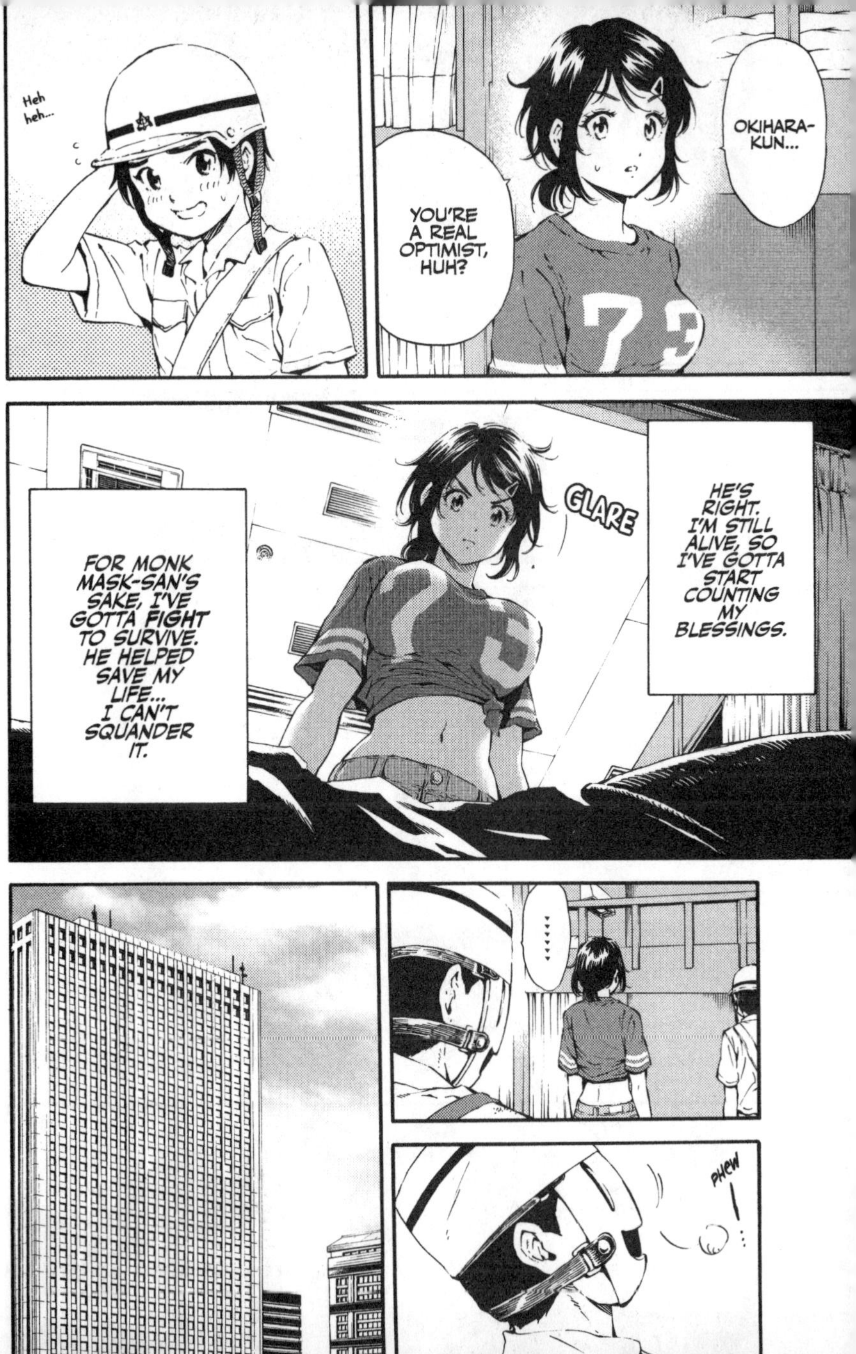
OKIHARA-KUN...
YOU'RE A REAL OPTIMIST, HUH?
Heh heh...
HE'S RIGHT. I'M STILL ALIVE, SO I'VE GOTTA START COUNTING MY BLESSINGS.
GLARE
FOR MONK MASK-SAN'S SAKE, I'VE GOTTA FIGHT TO SURVIVE. HE HELPED SAVE MY LIFE... I CAN'T SQUANDER IT.
......
PHEW

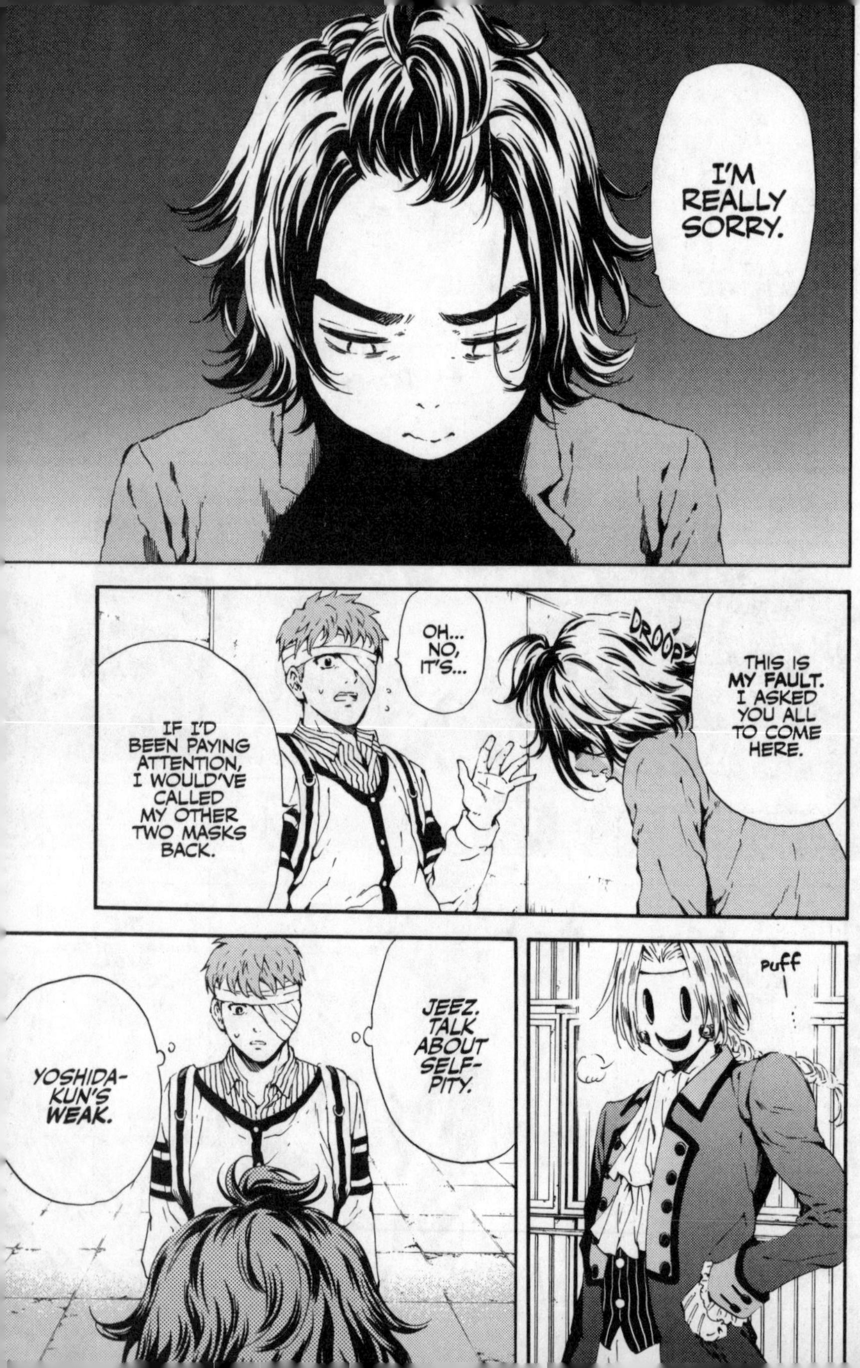
I'M REALLY SORRY.
DROOP
THIS IS MY FAULT. I ASKED YOU ALL TO COME HERE.
OH... NO, IT'S...
IF I'D BEEN PAYING ATTENTION, I WOULD'VE CALLED MY OTHER TWO MASKS BACK.
puff
JEEZ. TALK ABOUT SELF-PITY.
YOSHIDA-KUN'S WEAK.

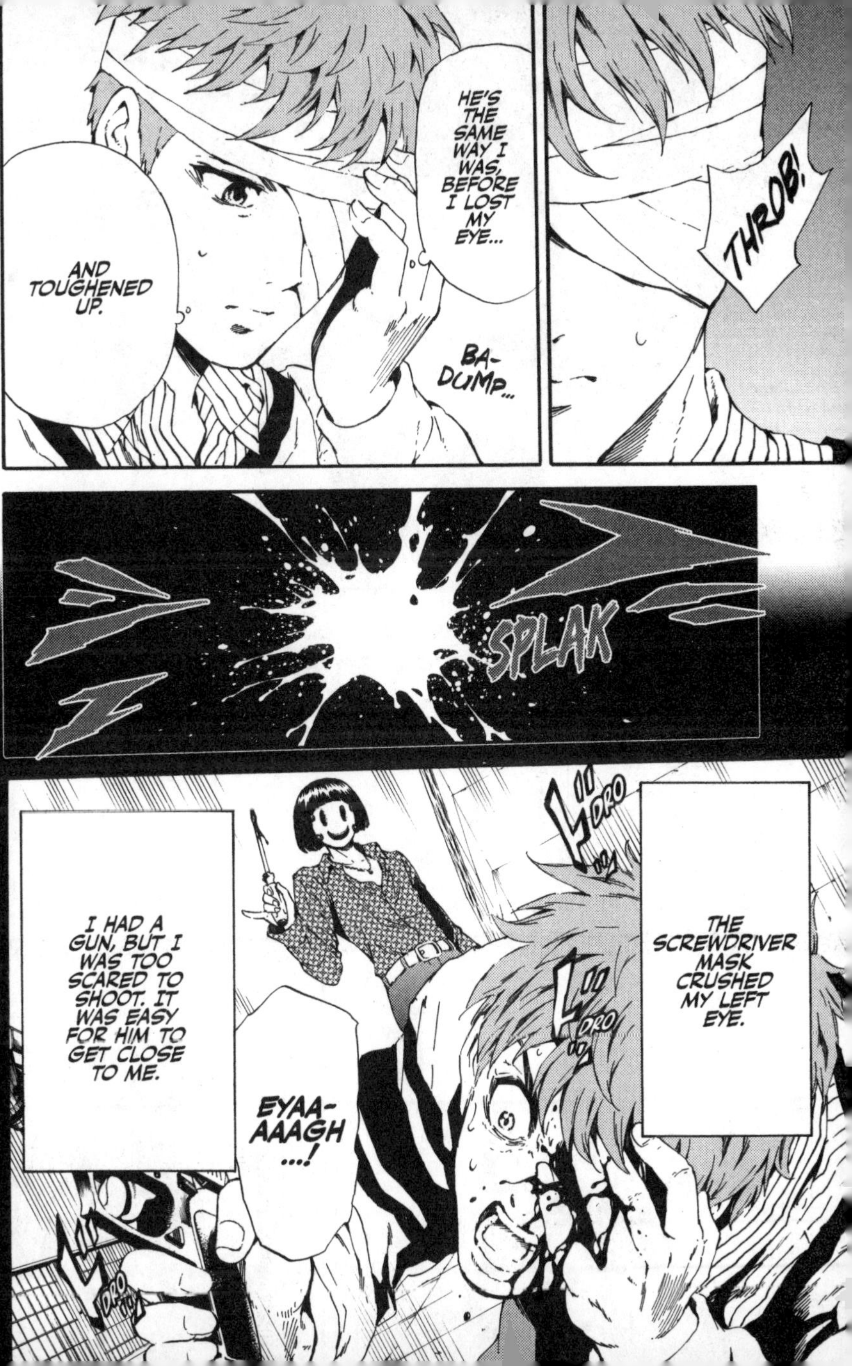
THROB!
HE'S THE SAME WAY I WAS, BEFORE I LOST MY EYE...
AND TOUGHENED UP.
BA-DUMP...
SPLAK
DRO
THE SCREWDRIVER MASK CRUSHED MY LEFT EYE.
DRO
I HAD A GUN, BUT I WAS TOO SCARED TO SHOOT. IT WAS EASY FOR HIM TO GET CLOSE TO ME.
EYAA-AAAGH ...!
DRO

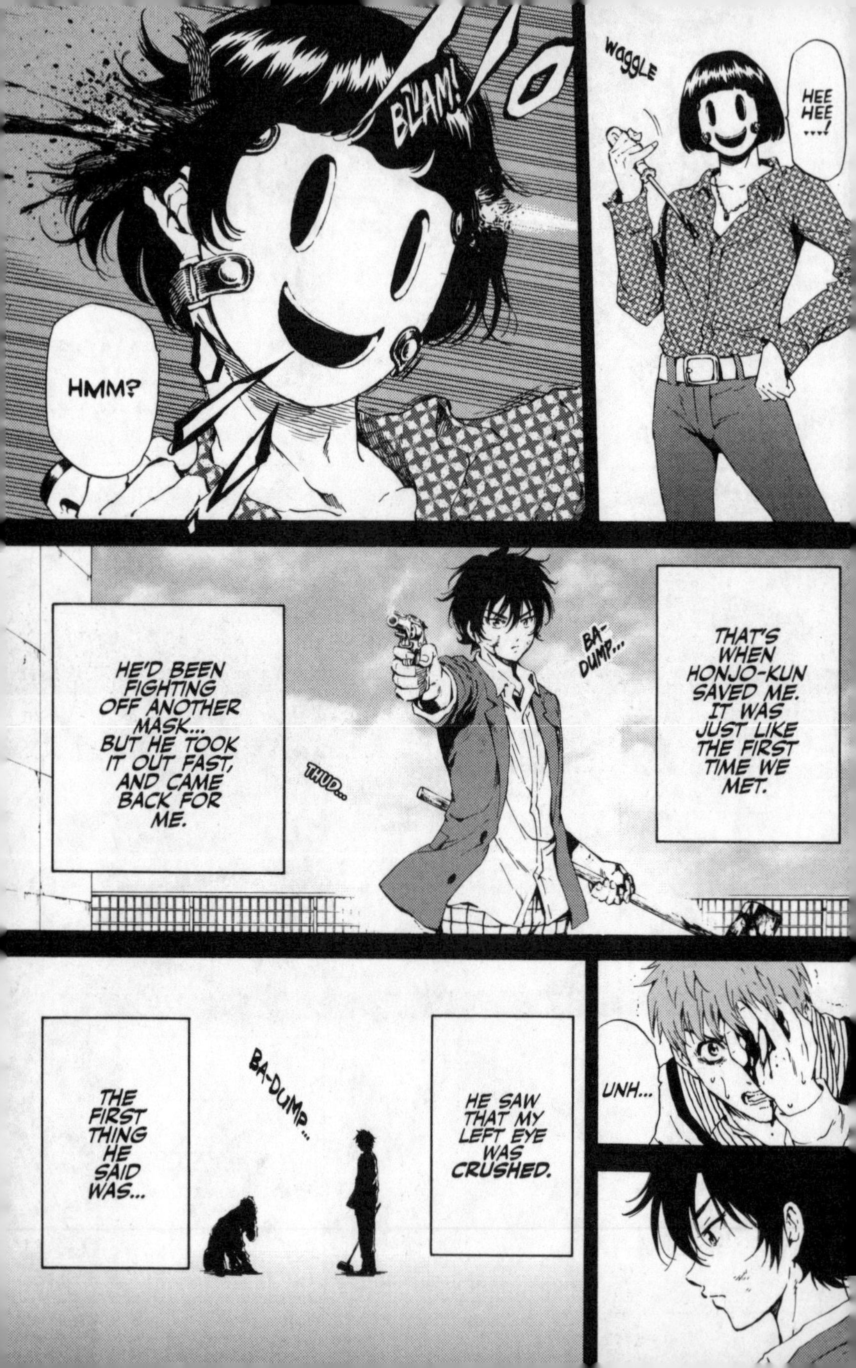
WAGGLE
HEE HEE...!
BLAM!
HMM?
THAT'S WHEN HONJO-KUN SAVED ME. IT WAS JUST LIKE THE FIRST TIME WE MET.
BA-DUMP...
THUD...
HE'D BEEN FIGHTING OFF ANOTHER MASK... BUT HE TOOK IT OUT FAST, AND CAME BACK FOR ME.
UNH...
HE SAW THAT MY LEFT EYE WAS CRUSHED.
BA-DUMP...
THE FIRST THING HE SAID WAS...

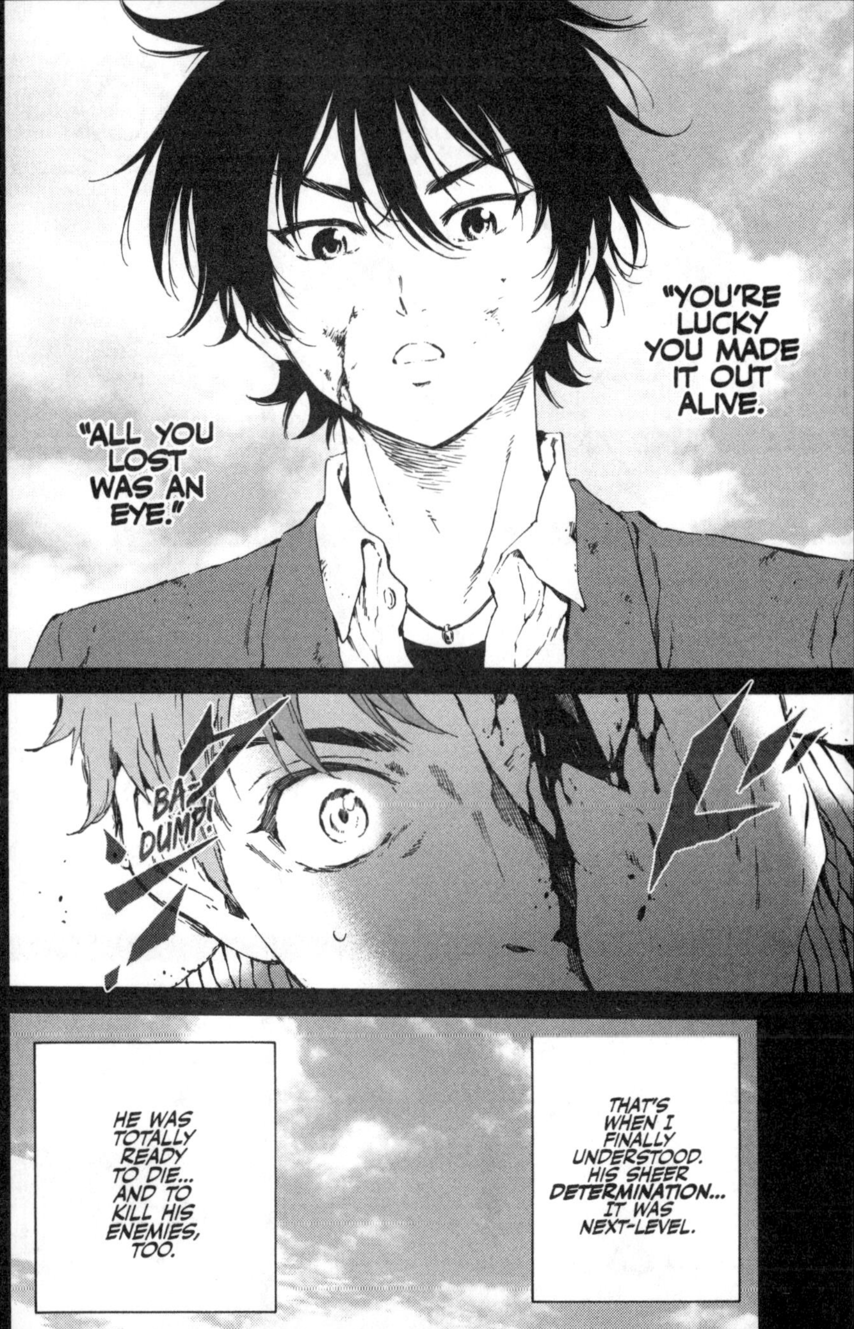
"YOU'RE LUCKY YOU MADE IT OUT ALIVE.
"ALL YOU LOST WAS AN EYE."
BA-DUMP!
THAT'S WHEN I FINALLY UNDERSTOOD. HIS SHEER DETERMINATION... IT WAS NEXT-LEVEL.
HE WAS TOTALLY READY TO DIE... AND TO KILL HIS ENEMIES, TOO.

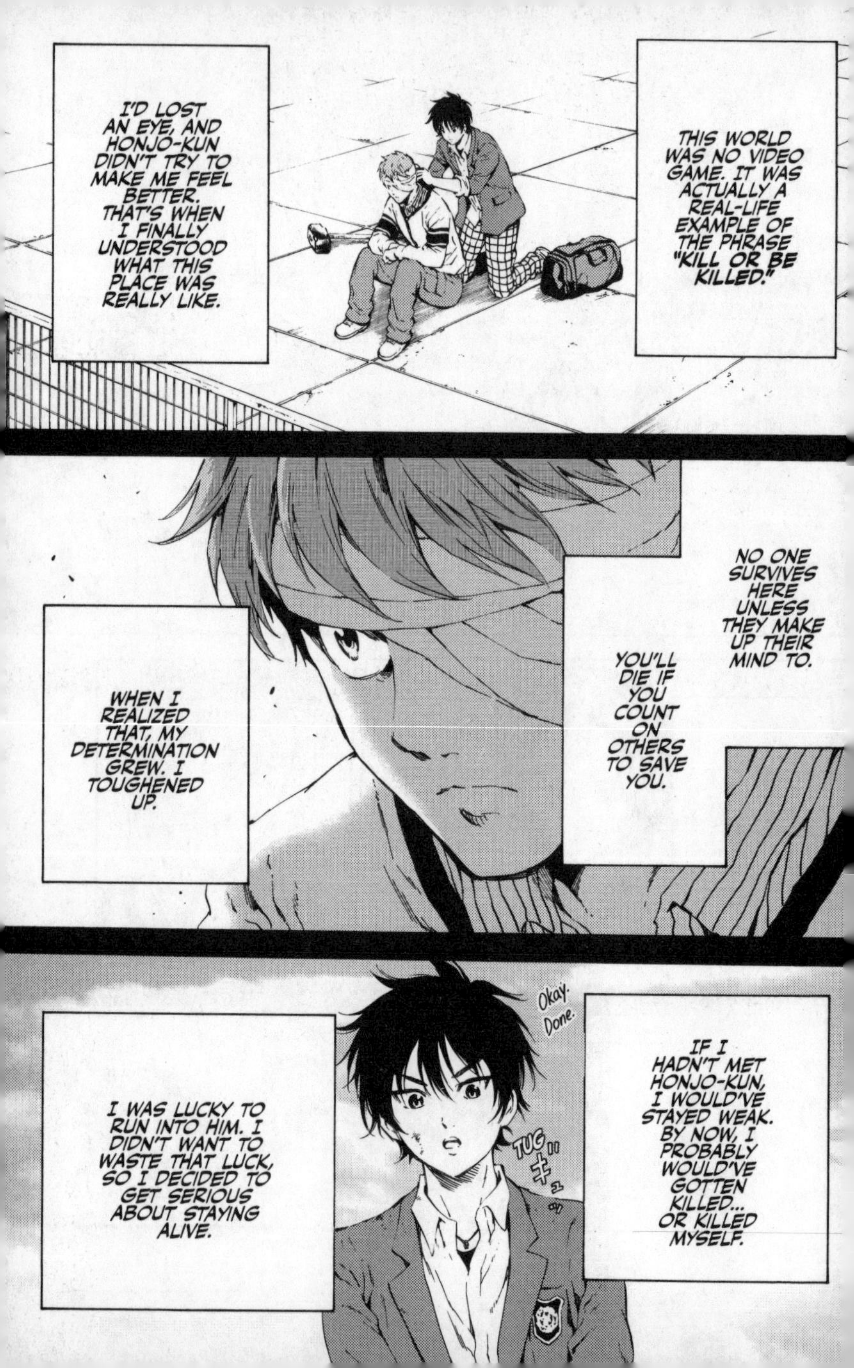
THIS WORLD WAS NO VIDEO GAME. IT WAS ACTUALLY A REAL-LIFE EXAMPLE OF THE PHRASE "KILL OR BE KILLED."
I'D LOST AN EYE, AND HONJO-KUN DIDN'T TRY TO MAKE ME FEEL BETTER. THAT'S WHEN I FINALLY UNDERSTOOD WHAT THIS PLACE WAS REALLY LIKE.
NO ONE SURVIVES HERE UNLESS THEY MAKE UP THEIR MIND TO.
YOU'LL DIE IF YOU COUNT ON OTHERS TO SAVE YOU.
WHEN I REALIZED THAT, MY DETERMINATION GREW. I TOUGHENED UP.
IF I HADN'T MET HONJO-KUN, I WOULD'VE STAYED WEAK. BY NOW, I PROBABLY WOULD'VE GOTTEN KILLED... OR KILLED MYSELF.
Okay. Done.
TUG
I WAS LUCKY TO RUN INTO HIM. I DIDN'T WANT TO WASTE THAT LUCK, SO I DECIDED TO GET SERIOUS ABOUT STAYING ALIVE.

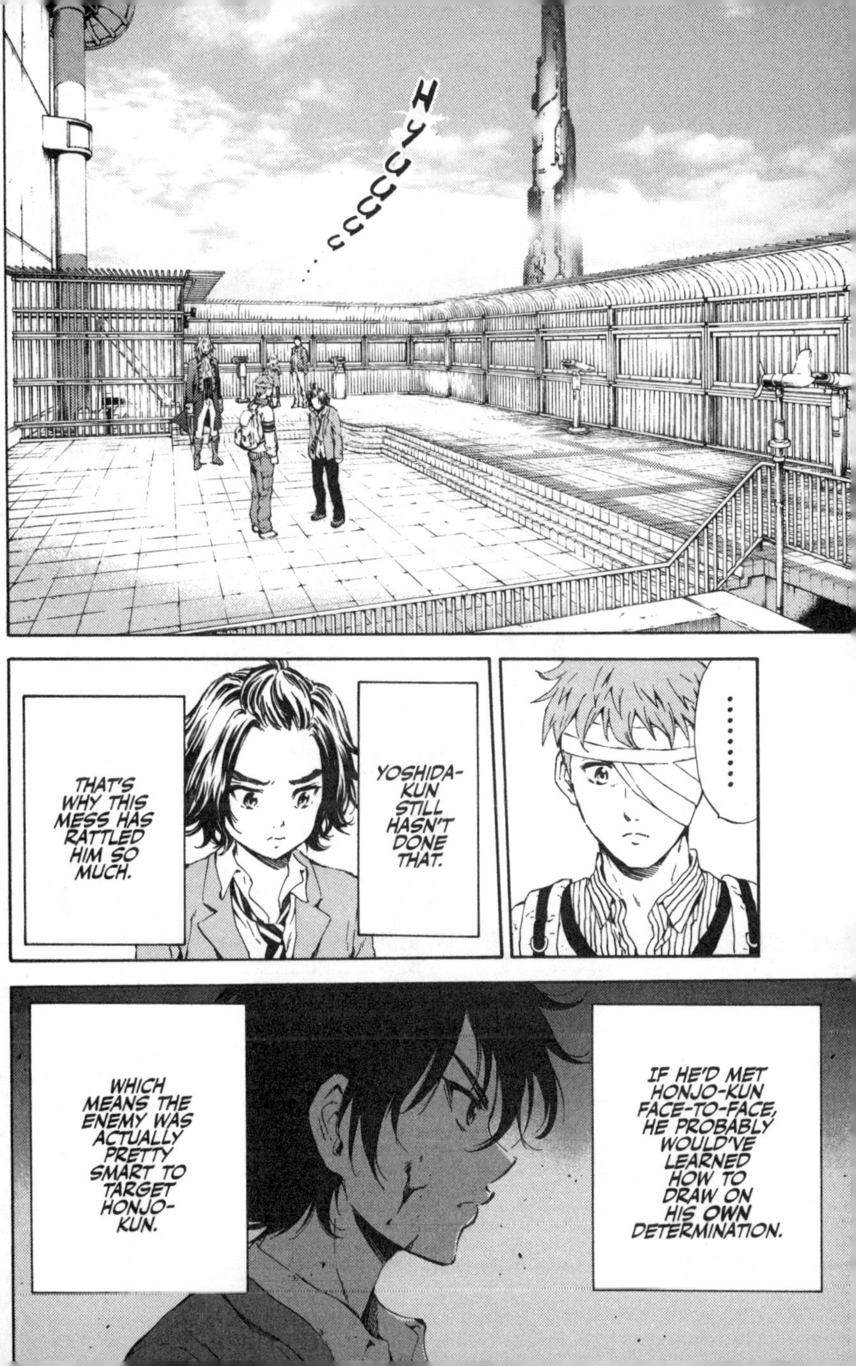
HYUUUUU...
......
YOSHIDA-KUN STILL HASN'T DONE THAT.
THAT'S WHY THIS MESS HAS RATTLED HIM SO MUCH.
IF HE'D MET HONJO-KUN FACE-TO-FACE, HE PROBABLY WOULD'VE LEARNED HOW TO DRAW ON HIS OWN DETERMINATION.
WHICH MEANS THE ENEMY WAS ACTUALLY PRETTY SMART TO TARGET HONJO-KUN.

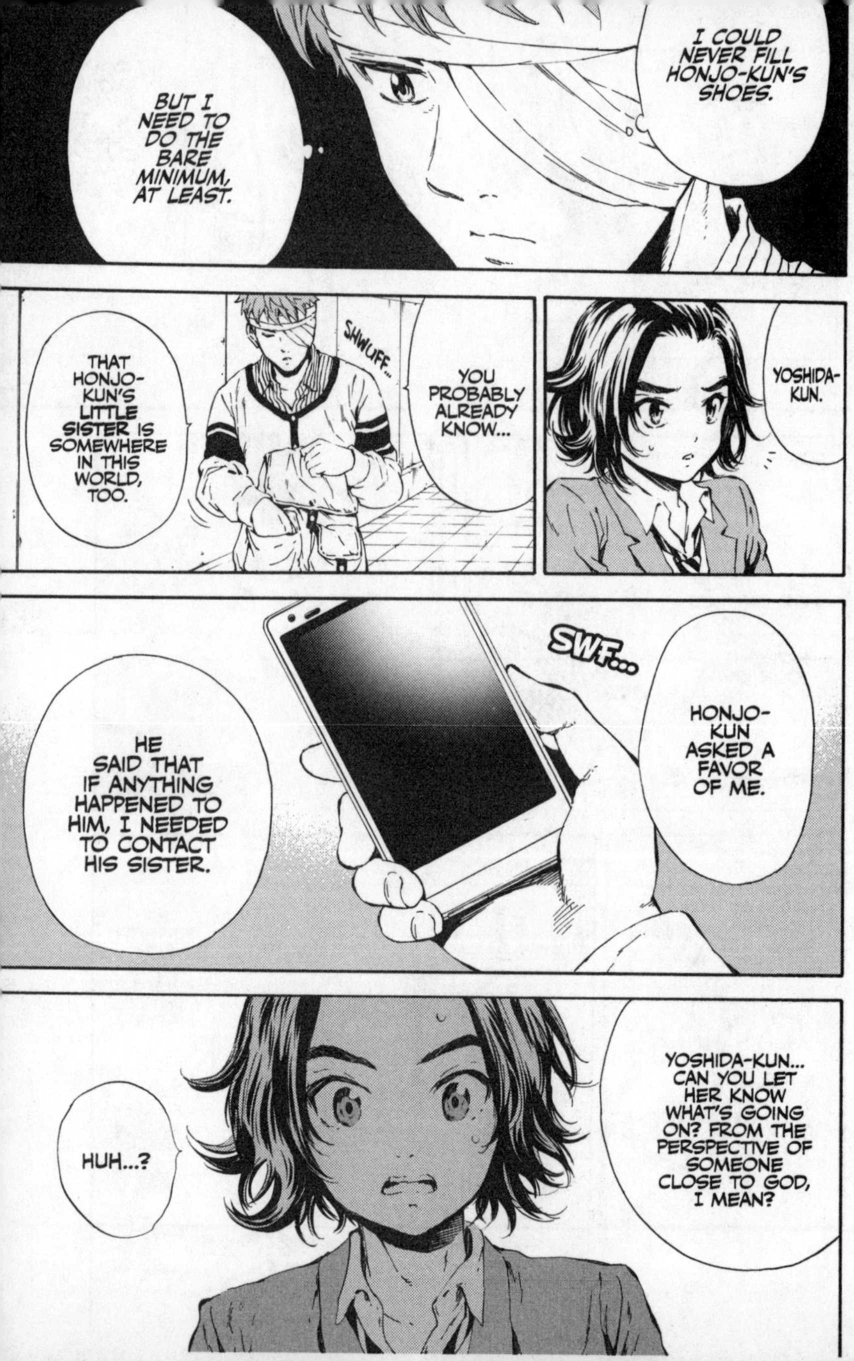
I COULD NEVER FILL HONJO-KUN'S SHOES.
BUT I NEED TO DO THE BARE MINIMUM, AT LEAST.
YOSHIDA-KUN.
SHWUFF...
YOU PROBABLY ALREADY KNOW...
THAT HONJO-KUN'S LITTLE SISTER IS SOMEWHERE IN THIS WORLD, TOO.
SWF...
HONJO-KUN ASKED A FAVOR OF ME.
HE SAID THAT IF ANYTHING HAPPENED TO HIM, I NEEDED TO CONTACT HIS SISTER.
YOSHIDA-KUN... CAN YOU LET HER KNOW WHAT'S GOING ON? FROM THE PERSPECTIVE OF SOMEONE CLOSE TO GOD, I MEAN?
HUH...?

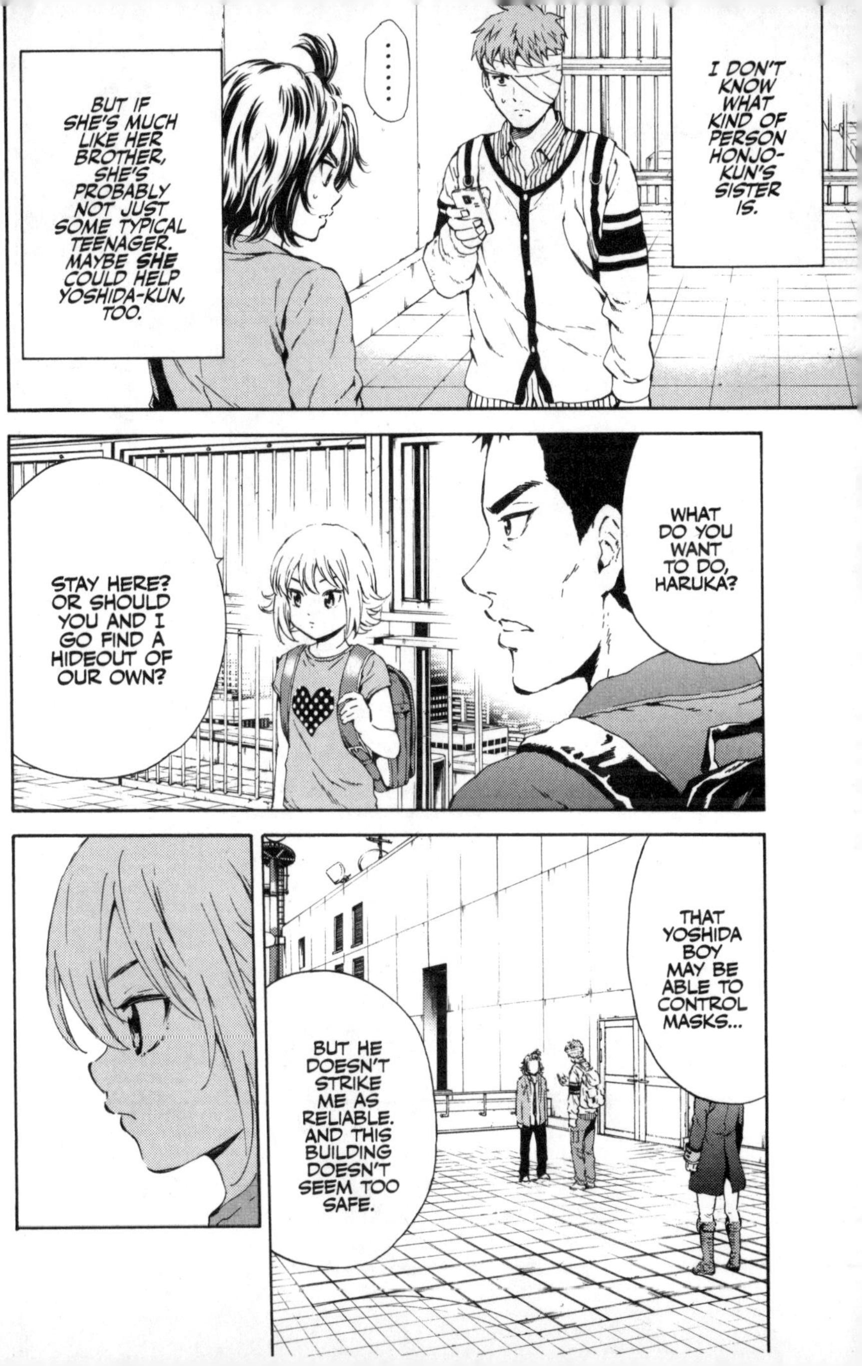
I DON'T KNOW WHAT KIND OF PERSON HONJO-KUN'S SISTER IS.
......
BUT IF SHE'S MUCH LIKE HER BROTHER, SHE'S PROBABLY NOT JUST SOME TYPICAL TEENAGER. MAYBE SHE COULD HELP YOSHIDA-KUN, TOO.
WHAT DO YOU WANT TO DO, HARUKA?
STAY HERE? OR SHOULD YOU AND I GO FIND A HIDEOUT OF OUR OWN?
THAT YOSHIDA BOY MAY BE ABLE TO CONTROL MASKS...
BUT HE DOESN'T STRIKE ME AS RELIABLE. AND THIS BUILDING DOESN'T SEEM TOO SAFE.

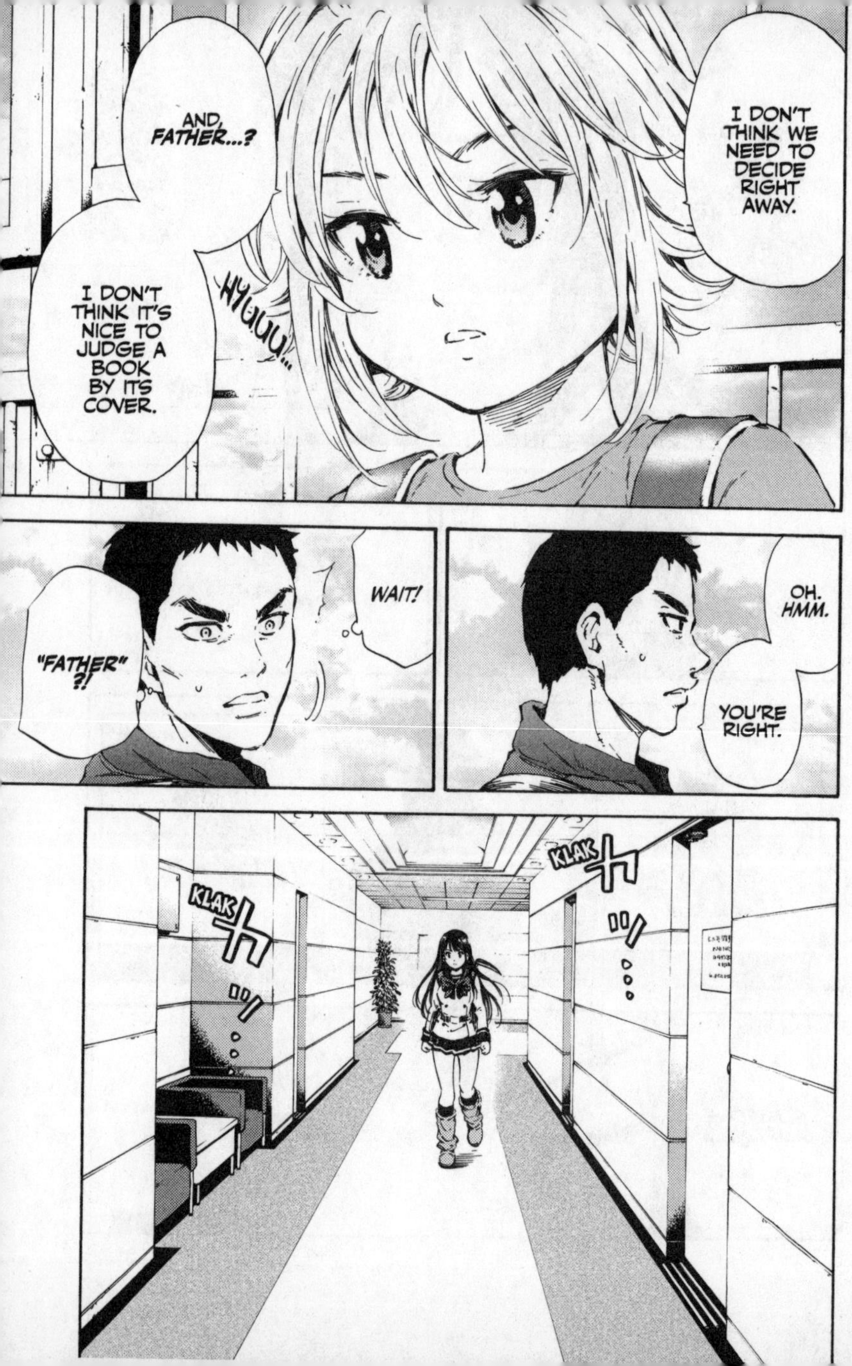
I DON'T THINK WE NEED TO DECIDE RIGHT AWAY.
AND, FATHER...?
HYUUU...
I DON'T THINK IT'S NICE TO JUDGE A BOOK BY ITS COVER.
OH. HMM.
YOU'RE RIGHT.
WAIT!
"FATHER" ?!
KLAK
KLAK

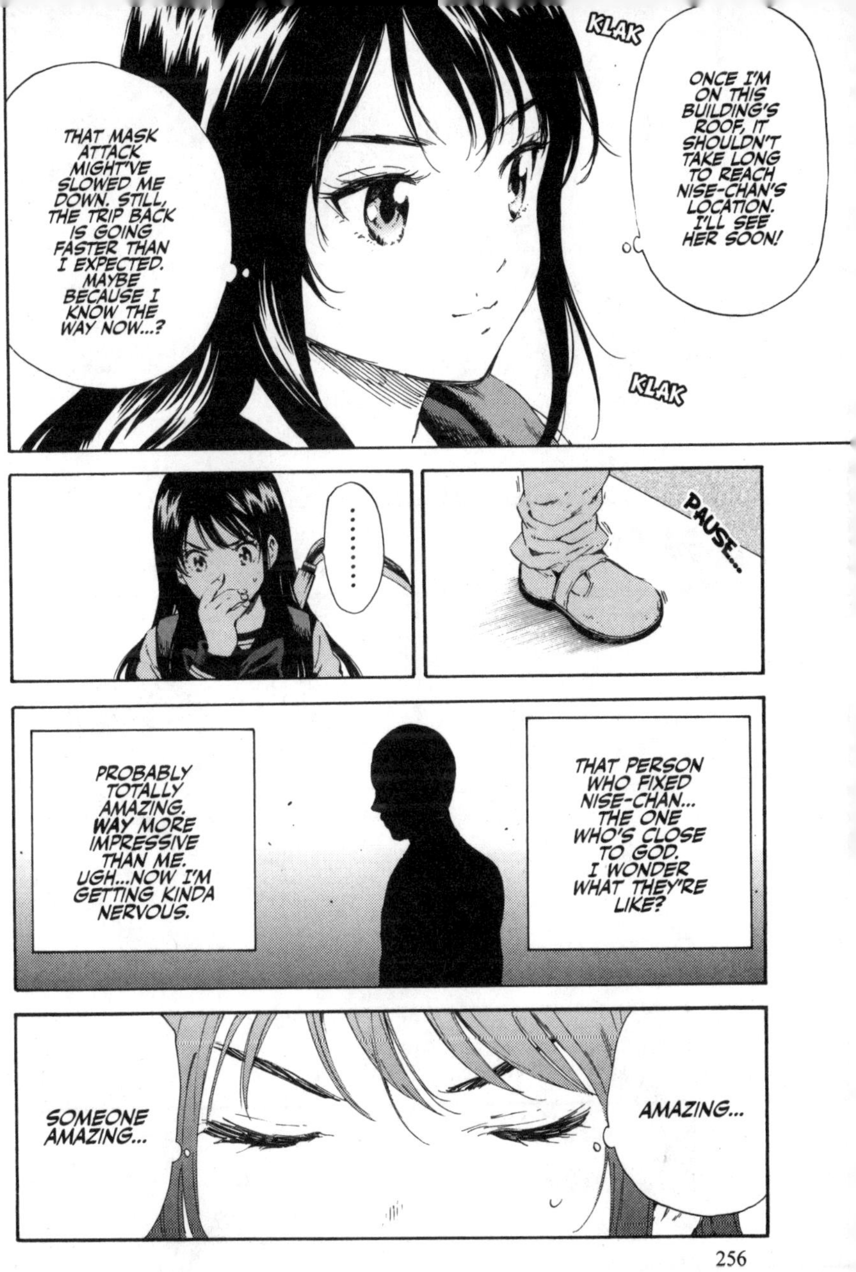
KLAK
ONCE I'M ON THIS BUILDING'S ROOF, IT SHOULDN'T TAKE LONG TO REACH NISE-CHAN'S LOCATION. I'LL SEE HER SOON!
THAT MASK ATTACK MIGHT'VE SLOWED ME DOWN. STILL, THE TRIP BACK IS GOING FASTER THAN I EXPECTED. MAYBE BECAUSE I KNOW THE WAY NOW...?
KLAK
PAUSE...
....
THAT PERSON WHO FIXED NISE-CHAN... THE ONE WHO'S CLOSE TO GOD. I WONDER WHAT THEY'RE LIKE?
PROBABLY TOTALLY AMAZING. WAY MORE IMPRESSIVE THAN ME. UGH...NOW I'M GETTING KINDA NERVOUS.
AMAZING...
SOMEONE AMAZING...

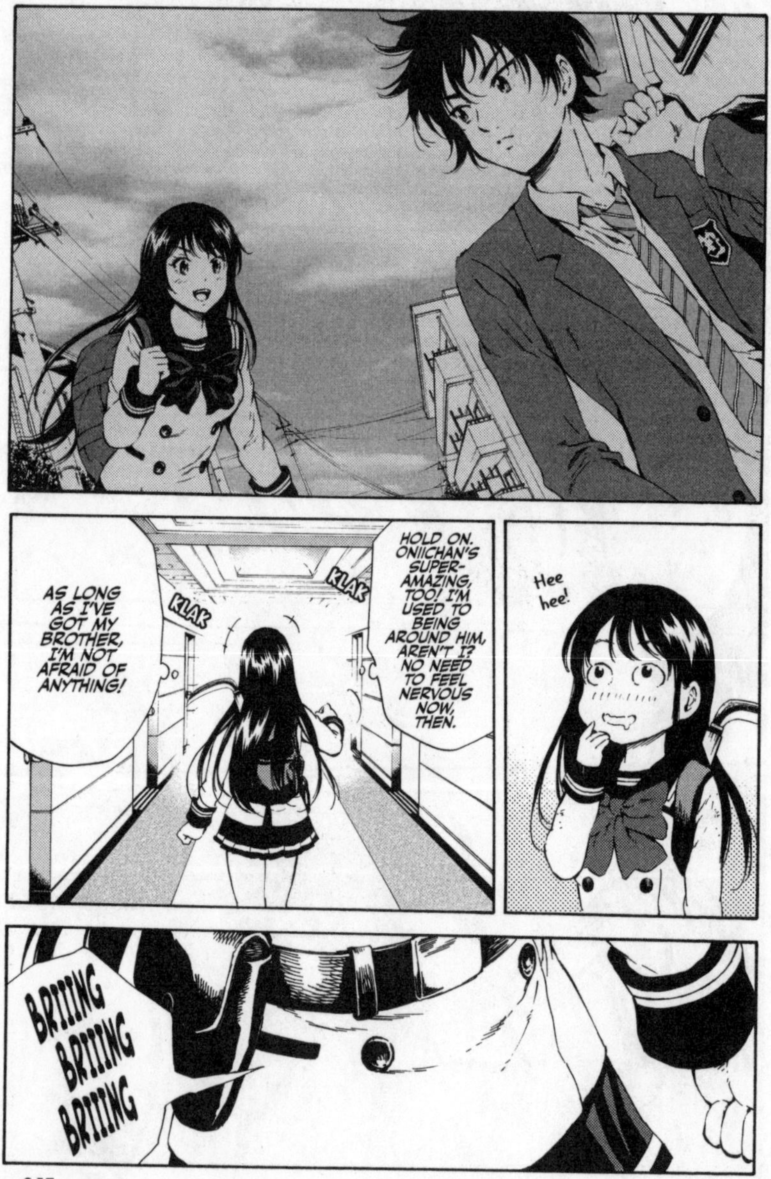
Hee hee!
HOLD ON. ONIICHAN'S SUPER-AMAZING, TOO! I'M USED TO BEING AROUND HIM, AREN'T I? NO NEED TO FEEL NERVOUS NOW, THEN.
KLAK
KLAK
AS LONG AS I'VE GOT MY BROTHER, I'M NOT AFRAID OF ANYTHING!
BRIIING BRIIING BRIIING

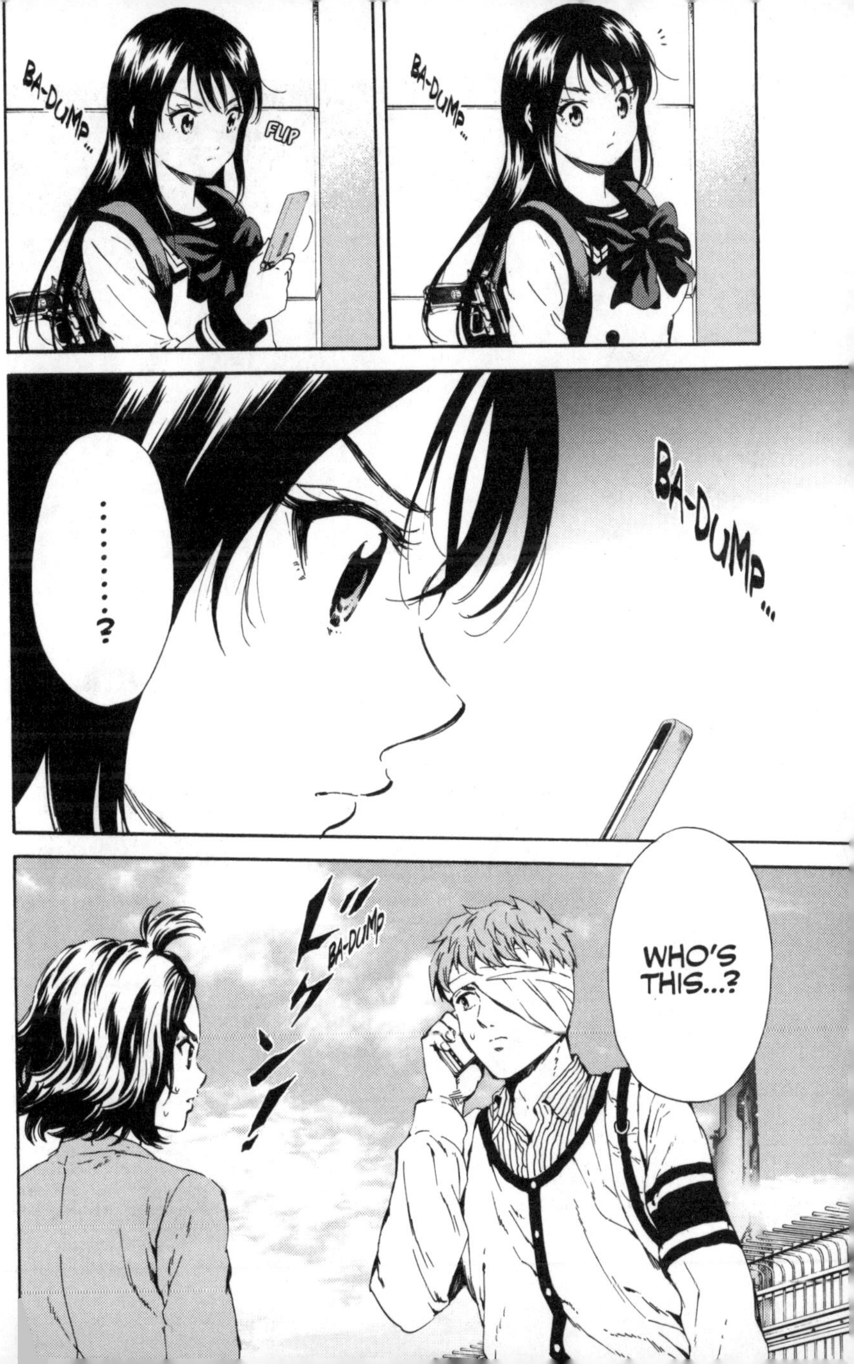

BA-DUMP...
BA-DUMP...
FLIP
BA-DUMP...
.........?
WHO'S THIS...?
BA-DUMP

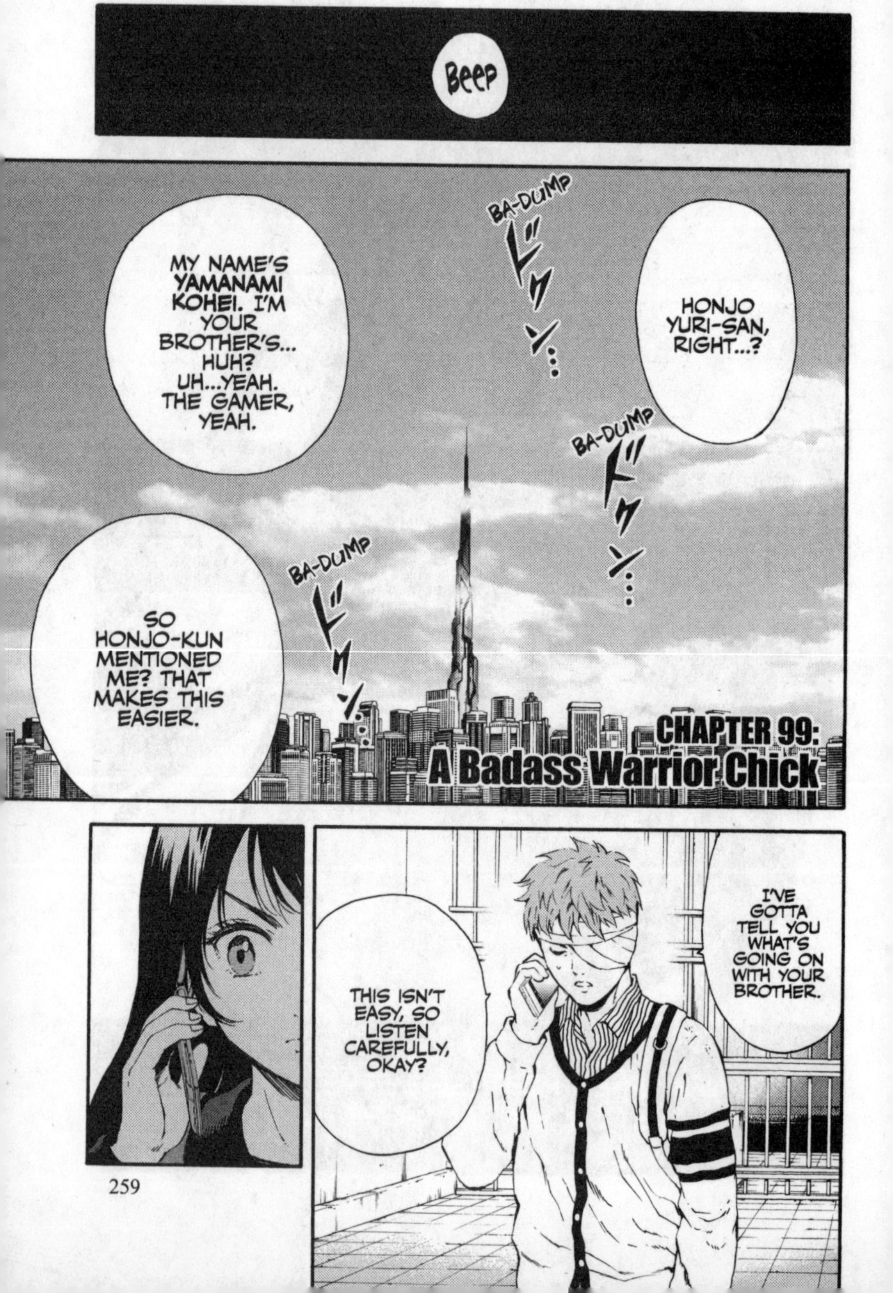
Beep
HONJO YURI-SAN, RIGHT...?
BA-DUMP
ドクン…
MY NAME'S YAMANAMI KOHEI. I'M YOUR BROTHER'S... HUH? UH...YEAH. THE GAMER, YEAH.
BA-DUMP
ドクン…
BA-DUMP
ドクン…
SO HONJO-KUN MENTIONED ME? THAT MAKES THIS EASIER.
CHAPTER 99: A Badass Warrior Chick
I'VE GOTTA TELL YOU WHAT'S GOING ON WITH YOUR BROTHER.
THIS ISN'T EASY, SO LISTEN CAREFULLY, OKAY?

A FEW MINUTES AGO, OUR TEAM
CLASHED WITH AN ENEMY GANG.

YOUR BROTHER, HONJO RIKA...

WAS TAKEN HOSTAGE BY THE ENEMY.
WE DON'T KNOW WHERE HE IS.

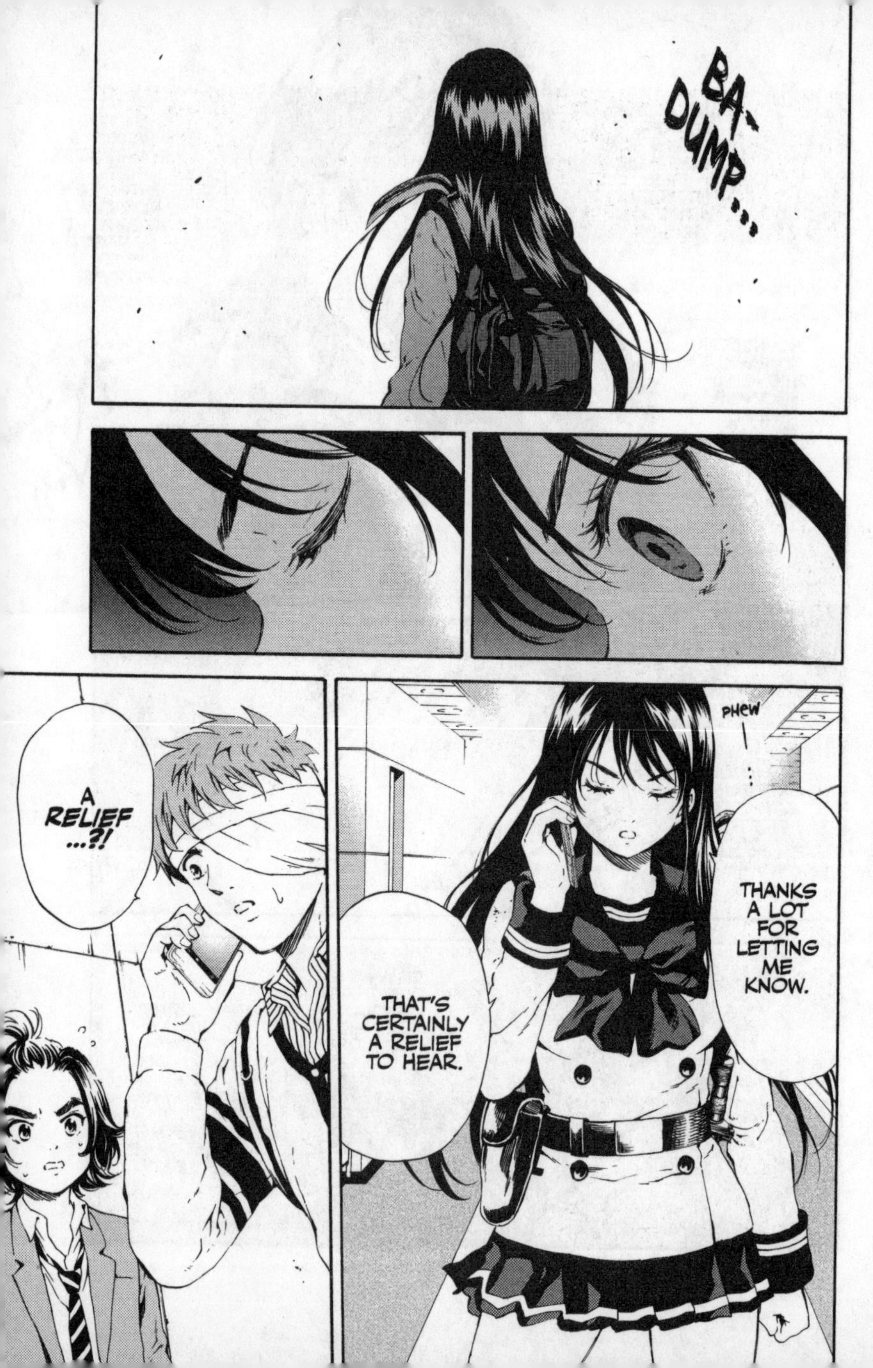
BA-DUMP...
PHEW
...
THANKS A LOT FOR LETTING ME KNOW.
THAT'S CERTAINLY A RELIEF TO HEAR.
A RELIEF ...?!

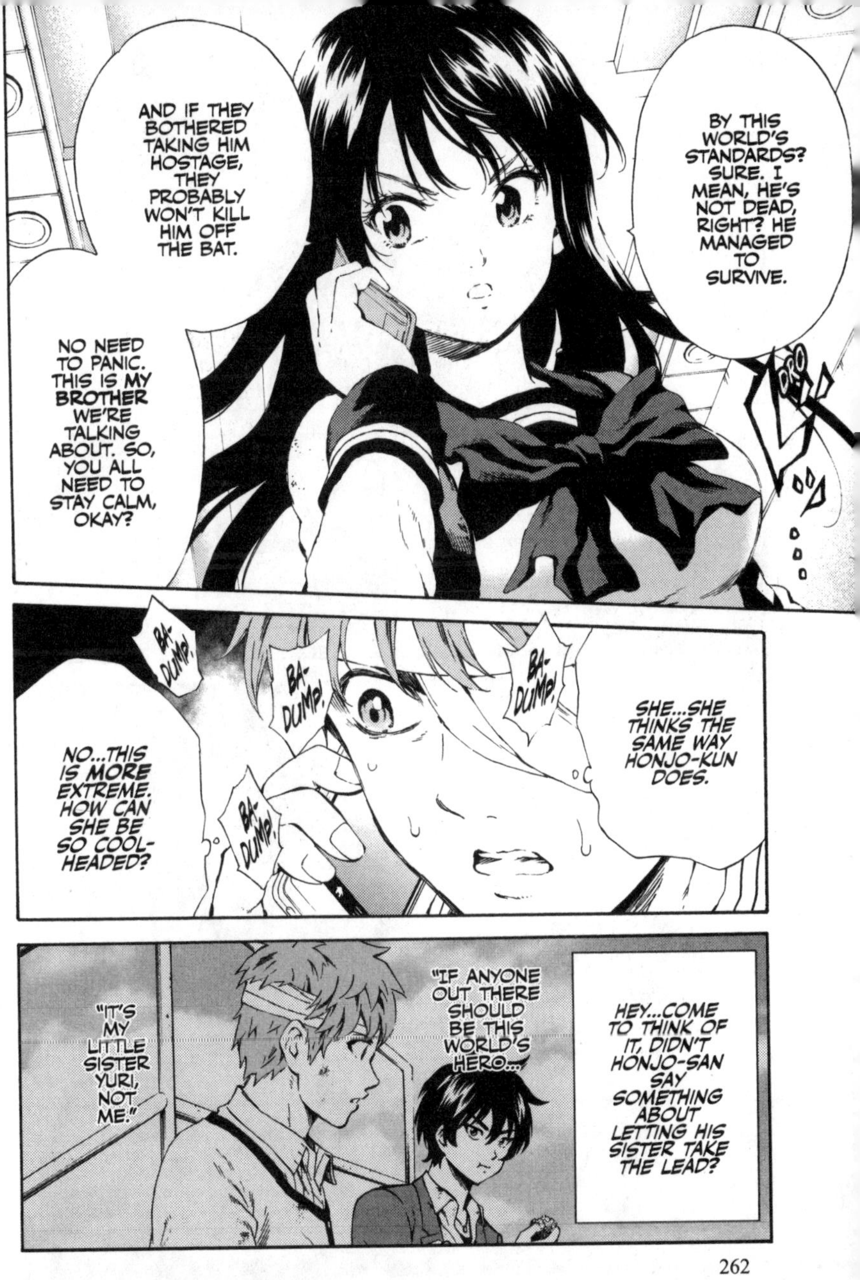
BY THIS WORLD'S STANDARDS? SURE. I MEAN, HE'S NOT DEAD, RIGHT? HE MANAGED TO SURVIVE.
AND IF THEY BOTHERED TAKING HIM HOSTAGE, THEY PROBABLY WON'T KILL HIM OFF THE BAT.
NO NEED TO PANIC. THIS IS MY BROTHER WE'RE TALKING ABOUT. SO, YOU ALL NEED TO STAY CALM, OKAY?
SHE...SHE THINKS THE SAME WAY HONJO-KUN DOES.
BA-DUMP!
BA-DUMP!
BA-DUMP!
BA-DUMP!
NO...THIS IS MORE EXTREME. HOW CAN SHE BE SO COOL-HEADED?
HEY...COME TO THINK OF IT, DIDN'T HONJO-SAN SAY SOMETHING ABOUT LETTING HIS SISTER TAKE THE LEAD?
"IF ANYONE OUT THERE SHOULD BE THIS WORLD'S HERO...
"IT'S MY LITTLE SISTER YURI, NOT ME."

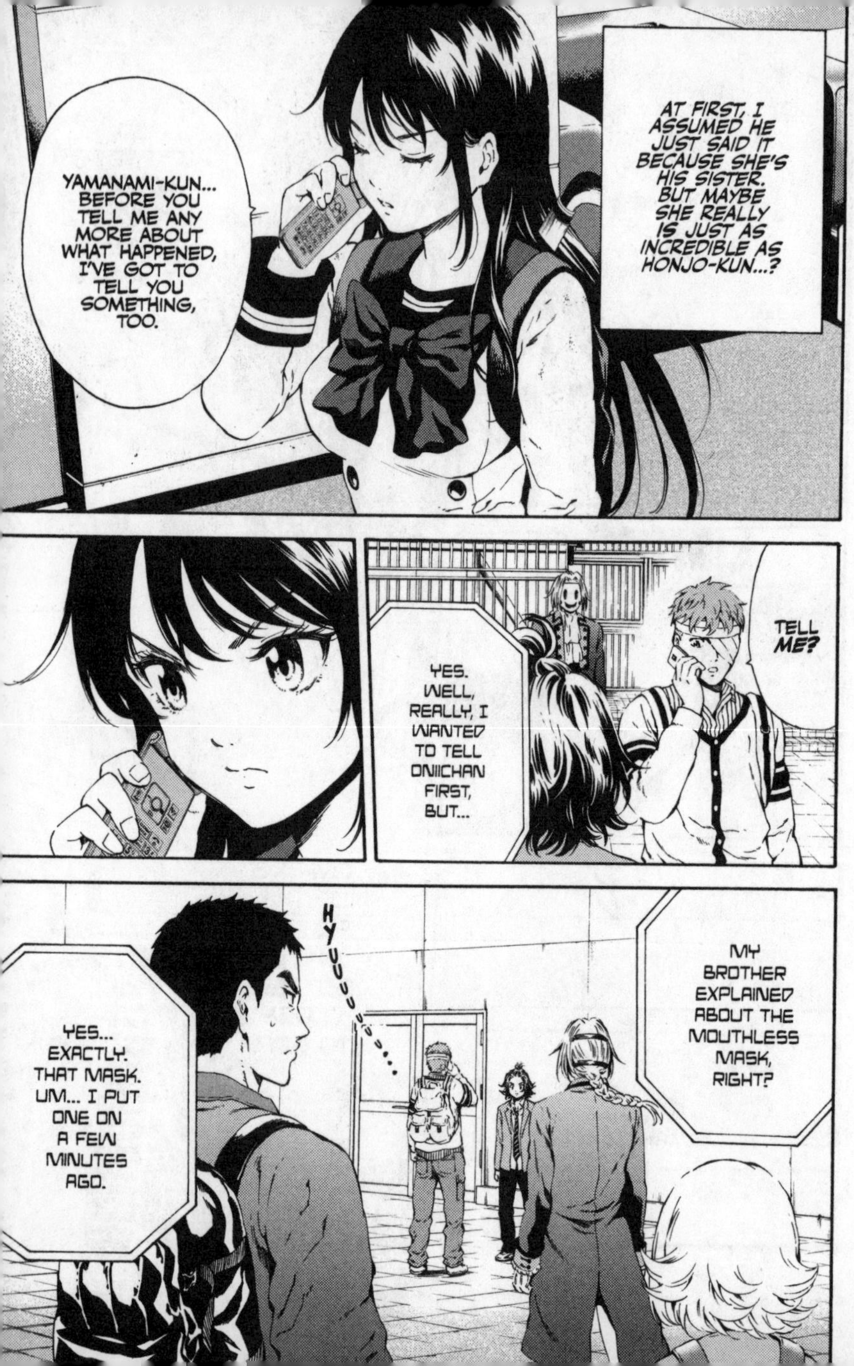
AT FIRST, I ASSUMED HE JUST SAID IT BECAUSE SHE'S HIS SISTER. BUT MAYBE SHE REALLY IS JUST AS INCREDIBLE AS HONJO-KUN...?
YAMANAMI-KUN... BEFORE YOU TELL ME ANY MORE ABOUT WHAT HAPPENED, I'VE GOT TO TELL YOU SOMETHING, TOO.
TELL *ME*?
YES. WELL, REALLY, I WANTED TO TELL ONIICHAN FIRST, BUT...
MY BROTHER EXPLAINED ABOUT THE MOUTHLESS MASK, RIGHT?
HYUUUUUU...
YES... EXACTLY. THAT MASK. UM... I PUT ONE ON A FEW MINUTES AGO.

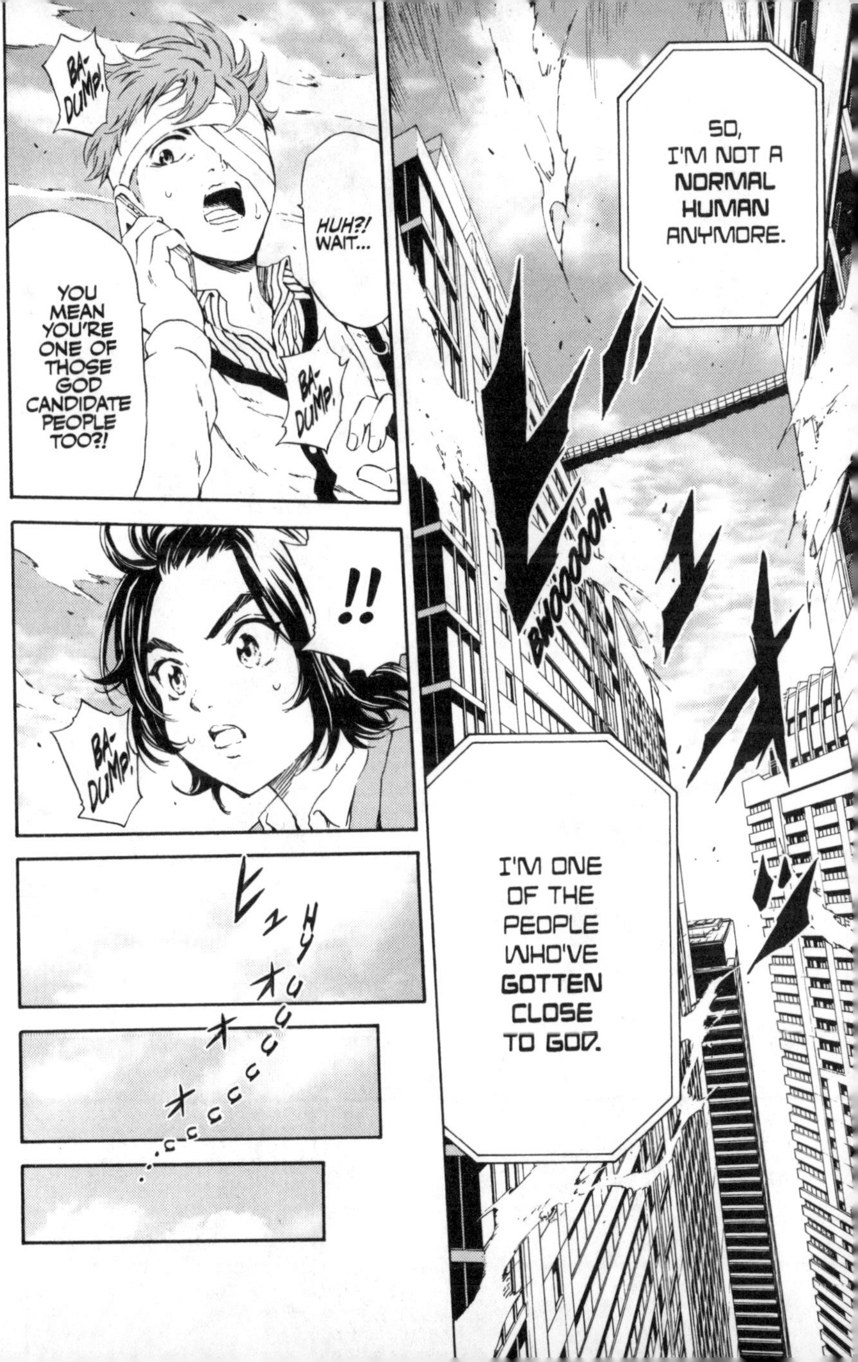
SO, I'M NOT A NORMAL HUMAN ANYMORE.
BWOOOOOOH
I'M ONE OF THE PEOPLE WHO'VE GOTTEN CLOSE TO GOD.
BA-DUMP!
HUH?! WAIT...
YOU MEAN YOU'RE ONE OF THOSE GOD CANDIDATE PEOPLE TOO?!
BA-DUMP!
!!
BA-DUMP!
HYUUUCCCCCC...

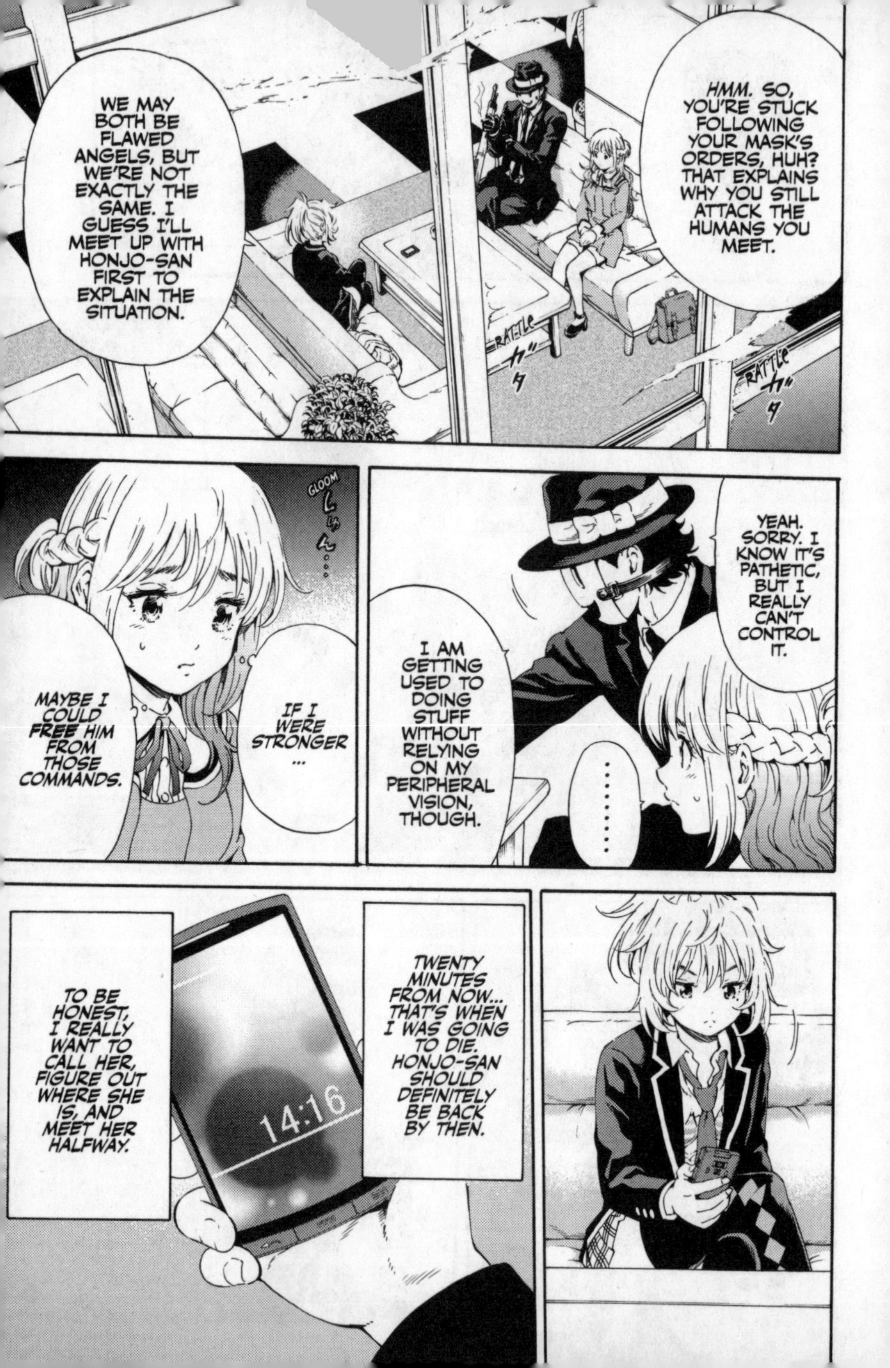
HMM. SO, YOU'RE STUCK FOLLOWING YOUR MASK'S ORDERS, HUH? THAT EXPLAINS WHY YOU STILL ATTACK THE HUMANS YOU MEET.
RATTLE
ガタ
RATTLE
ガタ
WE MAY BOTH BE FLAWED ANGELS, BUT WE'RE NOT EXACTLY THE SAME. I GUESS I'LL MEET UP WITH HONJO-SAN FIRST TO EXPLAIN THE SITUATION.
YEAH. SORRY. I KNOW IT'S PATHETIC, BUT I REALLY CAN'T CONTROL IT.
I AM GETTING USED TO DOING STUFF WITHOUT RELYING ON MY PERIPHERAL VISION, THOUGH.
......
GLOOM
しゅん...
IF I WERE STRONGER ...
MAYBE I COULD FREE HIM FROM THOSE COMMANDS.
TWENTY MINUTES FROM NOW... THAT'S WHEN I WAS GOING TO DIE. HONJO-SAN SHOULD DEFINITELY BE BACK BY THEN.
14:16
TO BE HONEST, I REALLY WANT TO CALL HER, FIGURE OUT WHERE SHE IS, AND MEET HER HALFWAY.

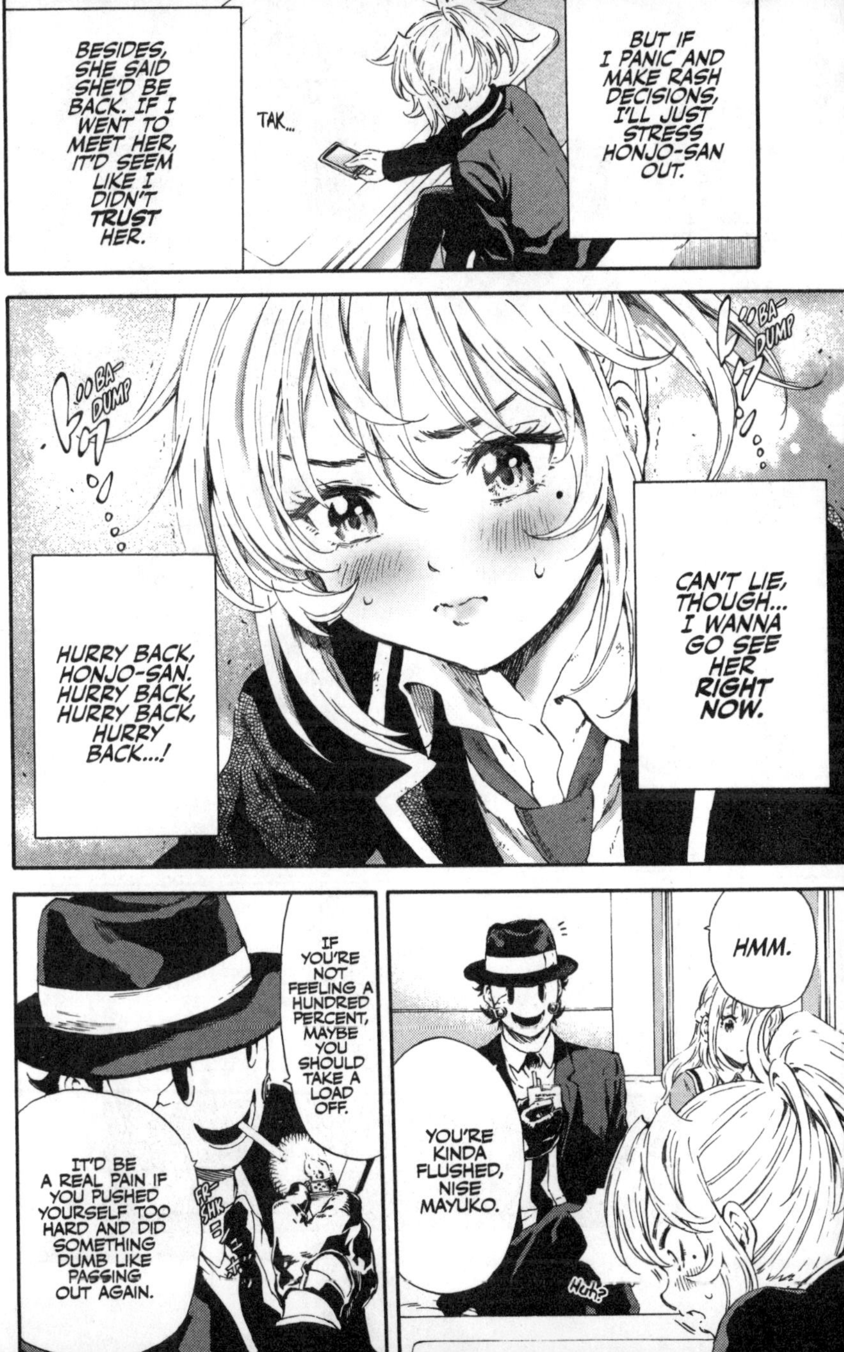

BUT IF I PANIC AND MAKE RASH DECISIONS, I'LL JUST STRESS HONJO-SAN OUT.
TAK...
BESIDES, SHE SAID SHE'D BE BACK. IF I WENT TO MEET HER, IT'D SEEM LIKE I DIDN'T TRUST HER.
BA-DUMP
CAN'T LIE, THOUGH... I WANNA GO SEE HER RIGHT NOW.
BA-DUMP
HURRY BACK, HONJO-SAN. HURRY BACK, HURRY BACK, HURRY BACK...!
HMM.
YOU'RE KINDA FLUSHED, NISE MAYUKO.
Huh?
IF YOU'RE NOT FEELING A HUNDRED PERCENT, MAYBE YOU SHOULD TAKE A LOAD OFF.
FRSHK
IT'D BE A REAL PAIN IF YOU PUSHED YOURSELF TOO HARD AND DID SOMETHING DUMB LIKE PASSING OUT AGAIN.

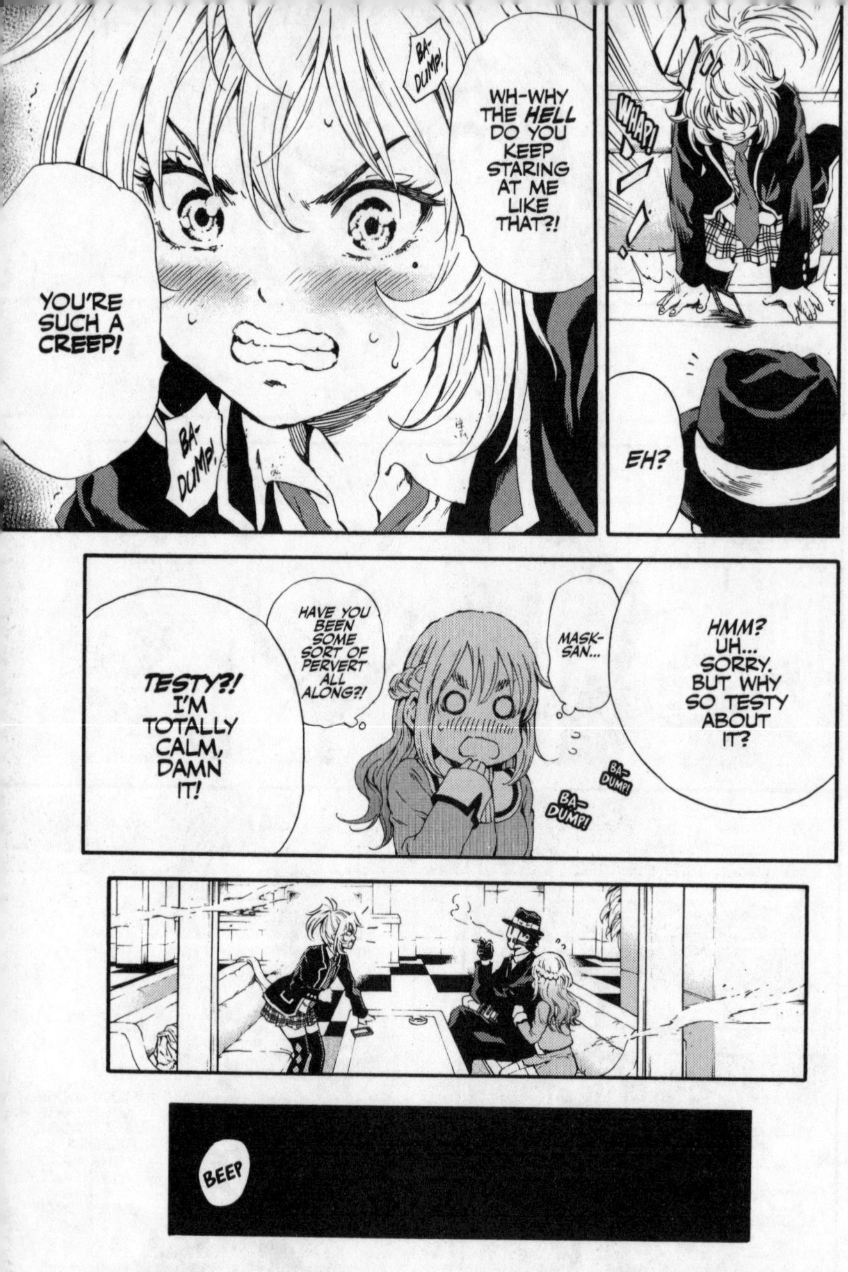
WHAP!
EH?
BA-DUMP!
WH-WHY THE HELL DO YOU KEEP STARING AT ME LIKE THAT?!
YOU'RE SUCH A CREEP!
BA-DUMP!
HMM? UH... SORRY. BUT WHY SO TESTY ABOUT IT?
BA-DUMP!
BA-DUMP!
MASK-SAN...
HAVE YOU BEEN SOME SORT OF PERVERT ALL ALONG?!
TESTY?! I'M TOTALLY CALM, DAMN IT!
BEEP

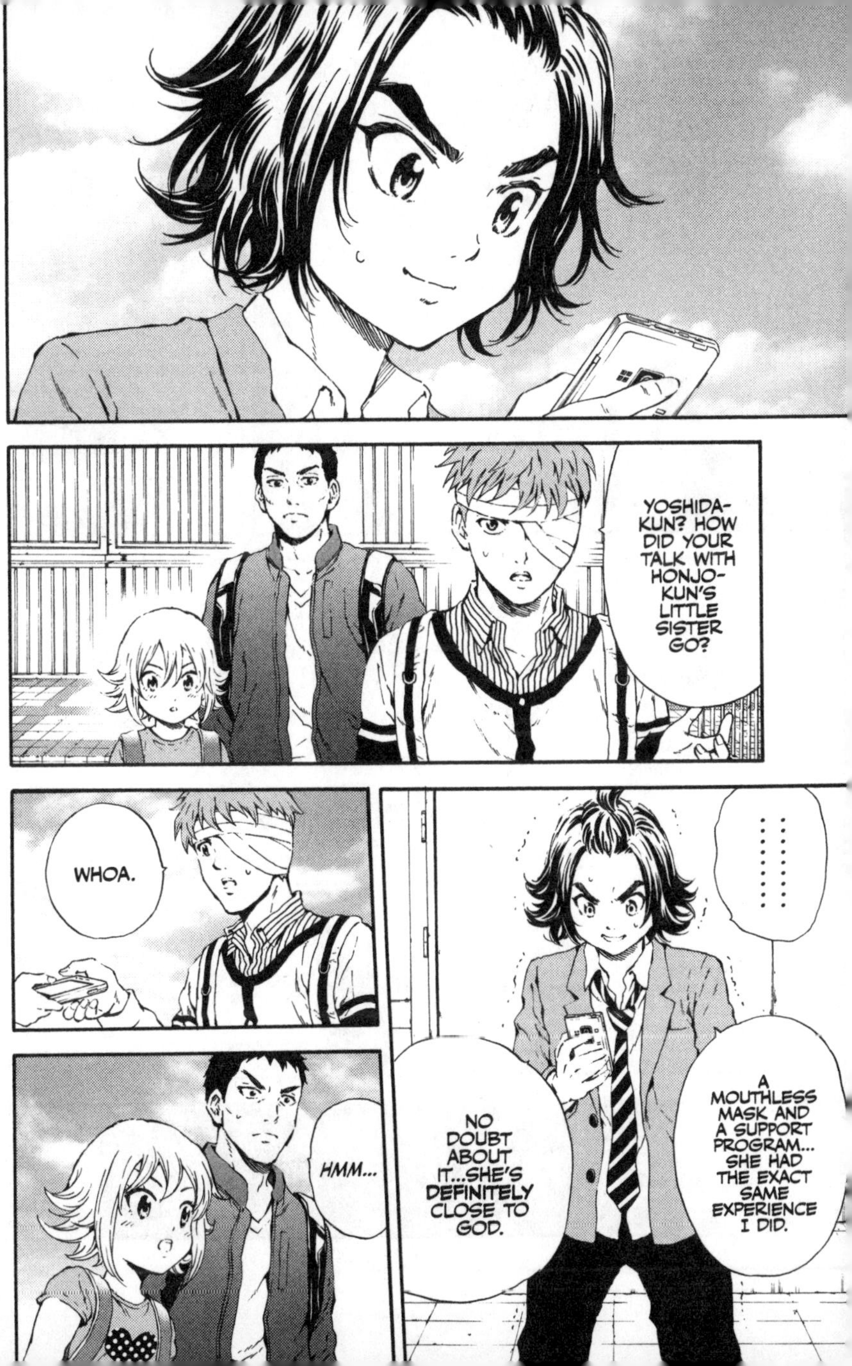
YOSHIDA-KUN? HOW DID YOUR TALK WITH HONJO-KUN'S LITTLE SISTER GO?
......
A MOUTHLESS MASK AND A SUPPORT PROGRAM... SHE HAD THE EXACT SAME EXPERIENCE I DID.
NO DOUBT ABOUT IT...SHE'S DEFINITELY CLOSE TO GOD.
WHOA.
HMM...

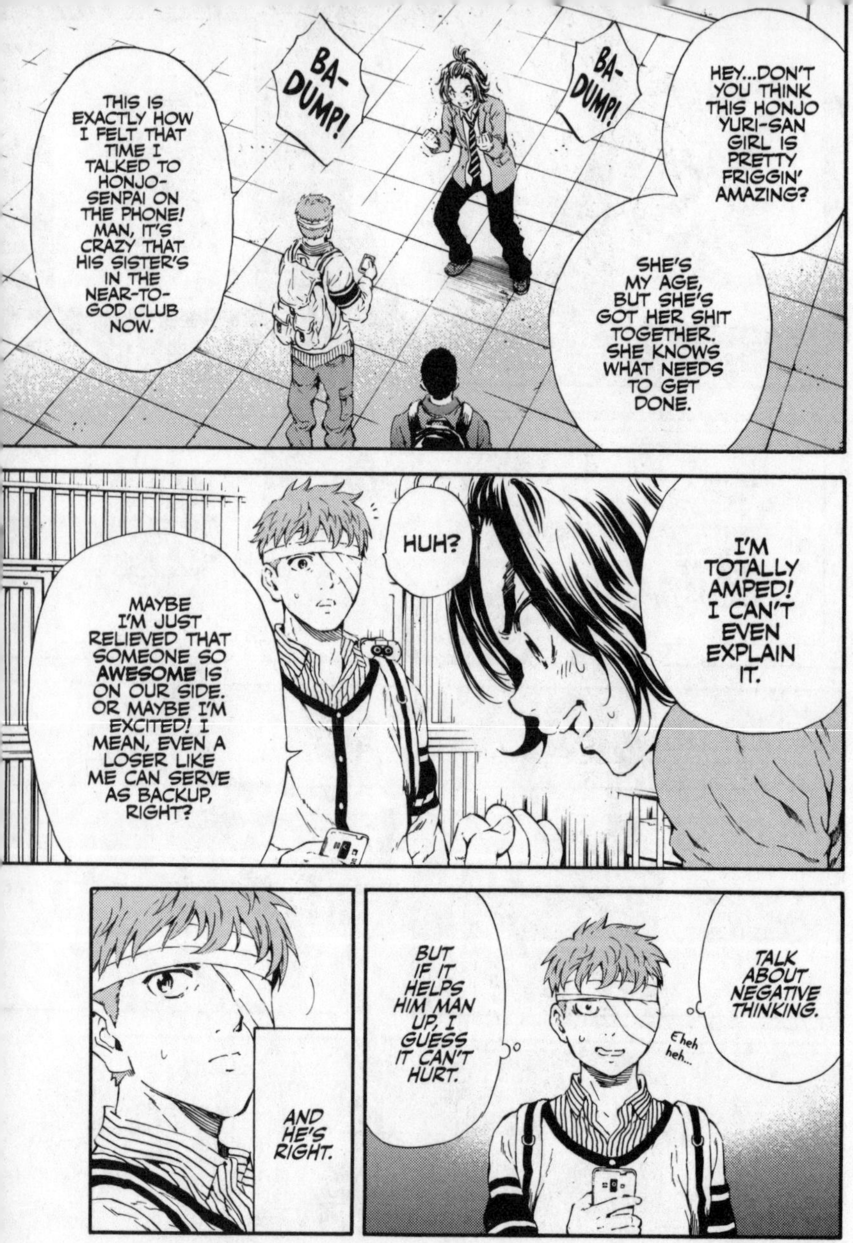
HEY...DON'T YOU THINK THIS HONJO YURI-SAN GIRL IS PRETTY FRIGGIN' AMAZING?
SHE'S MY AGE, BUT SHE'S GOT HER SHIT TOGETHER. SHE KNOWS WHAT NEEDS TO GET DONE.
BA-DUMP!
BA-DUMP!
THIS IS EXACTLY HOW I FELT THAT TIME I TALKED TO HONJO-SENPAI ON THE PHONE! MAN, IT'S CRAZY THAT HIS SISTER'S IN THE NEAR-TO-GOD CLUB NOW.
I'M TOTALLY AMPED! I CAN'T EVEN EXPLAIN IT.
HUH?
MAYBE I'M JUST RELIEVED THAT SOMEONE SO **AWESOME** IS ON OUR SIDE. OR MAYBE I'M EXCITED! I MEAN, EVEN A LOSER LIKE ME CAN SERVE AS BACKUP, RIGHT?
TALK ABOUT NEGATIVE THINKING.
Eheh heh...
BUT IF IT HELPS HIM MAN UP, I GUESS IT CAN'T HURT.
AND HE'S RIGHT.

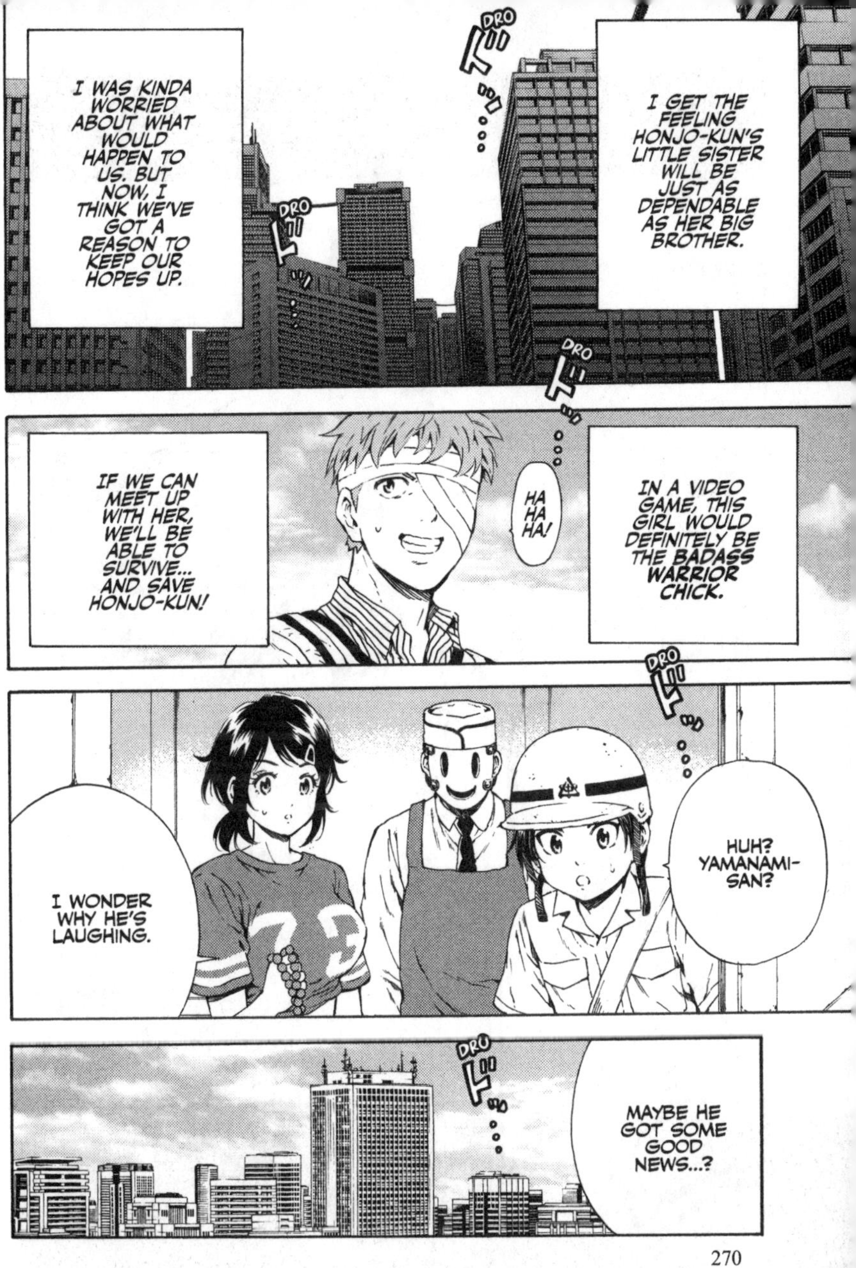
DRO
I GET THE FEELING HONJO-KUN'S LITTLE SISTER WILL BE JUST AS DEPENDABLE AS HER BIG BROTHER.
I WAS KINDA WORRIED ABOUT WHAT WOULD HAPPEN TO US. BUT NOW, I THINK WE'VE GOT A REASON TO KEEP OUR HOPES UP.
DRO
DRO
IN A VIDEO GAME, THIS GIRL WOULD DEFINITELY BE THE BADASS WARRIOR CHICK.
HA HA HA!
IF WE CAN MEET UP WITH HER, WE'LL BE ABLE TO SURVIVE... AND SAVE HONJO-KUN!
DRO
HUH? YAMANAMI-SAN?
I WONDER WHY HE'S LAUGHING.
MAYBE HE GOT SOME GOOD NEWS...?
DRO

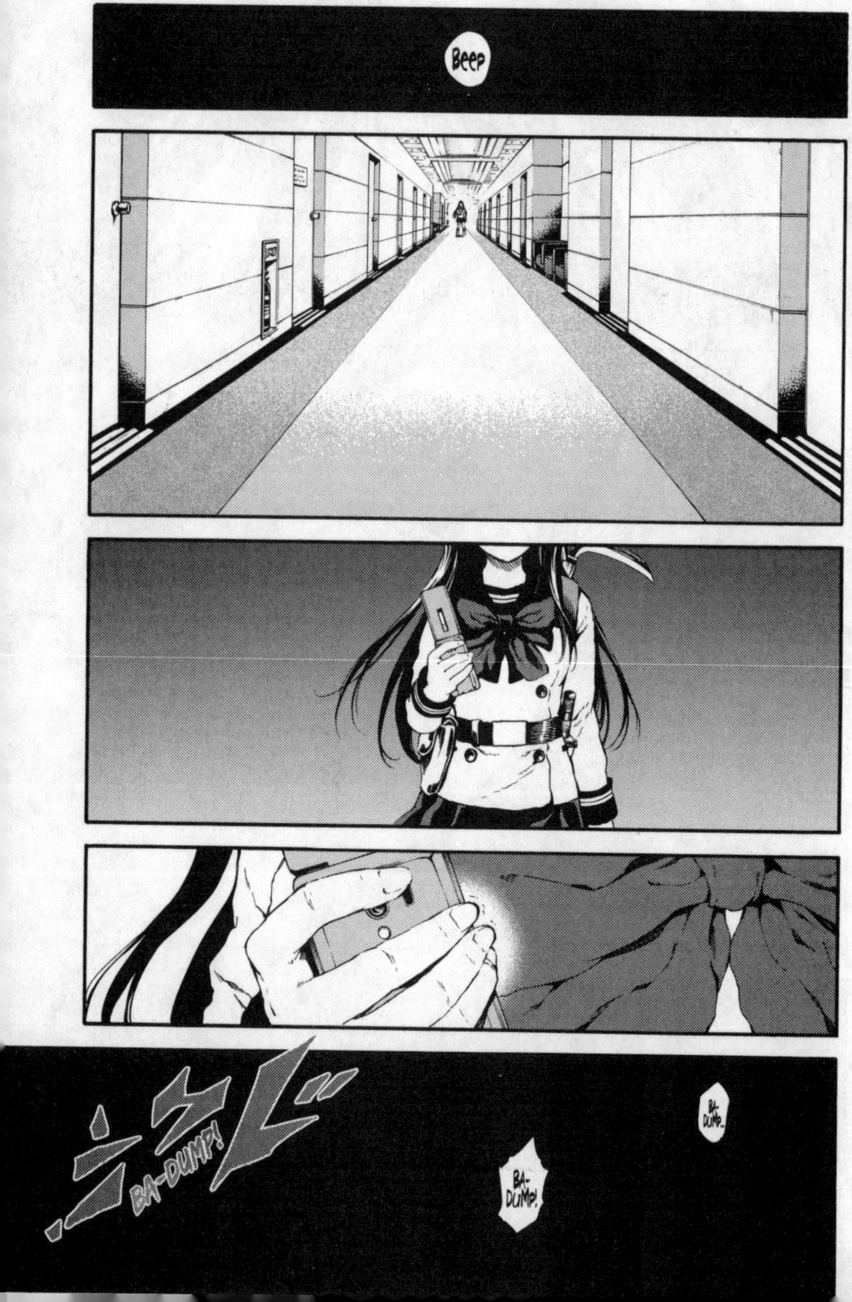
Beep
BA-DUMP...
BA-DUMP!
BA-DUMP!

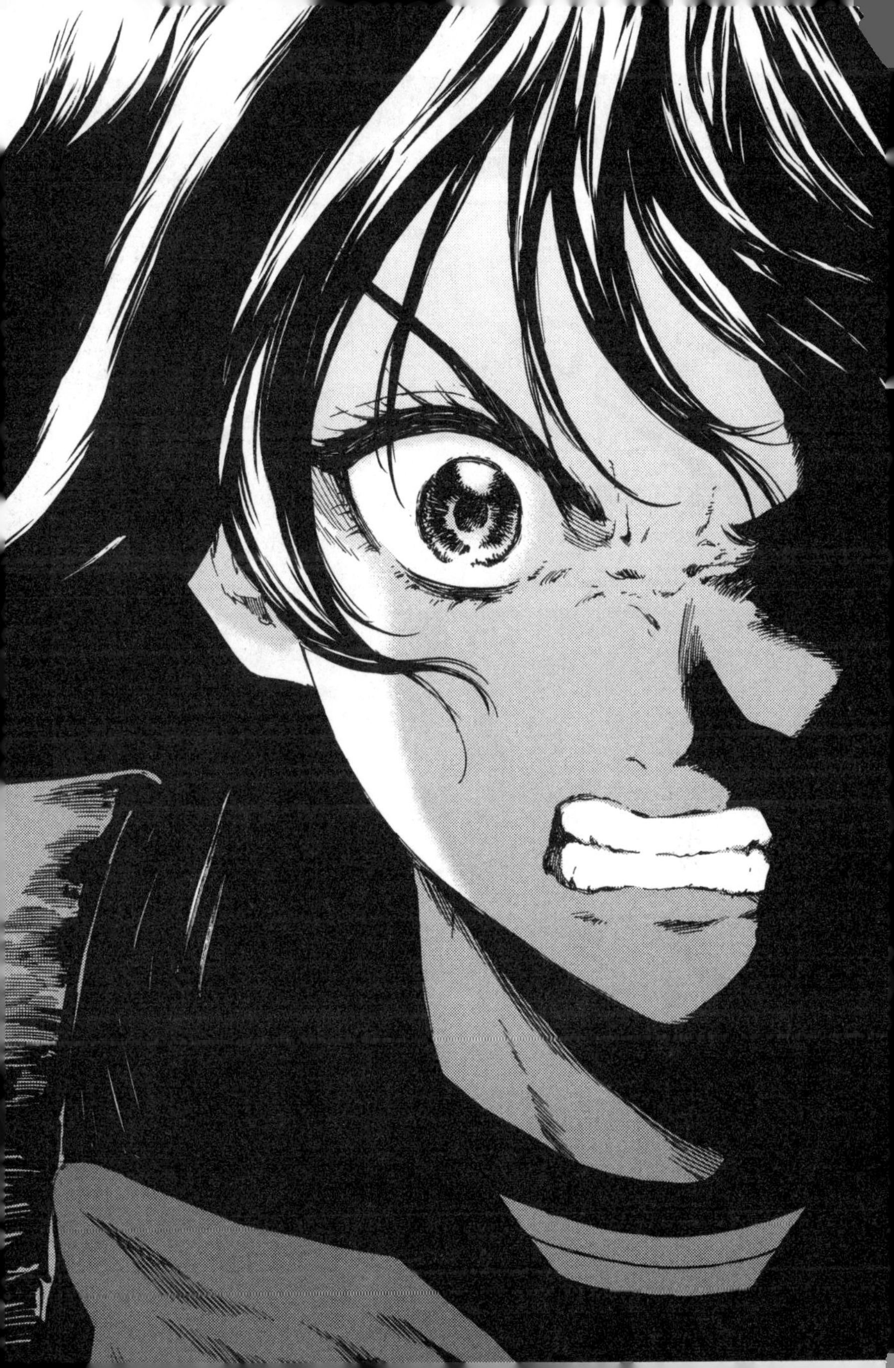

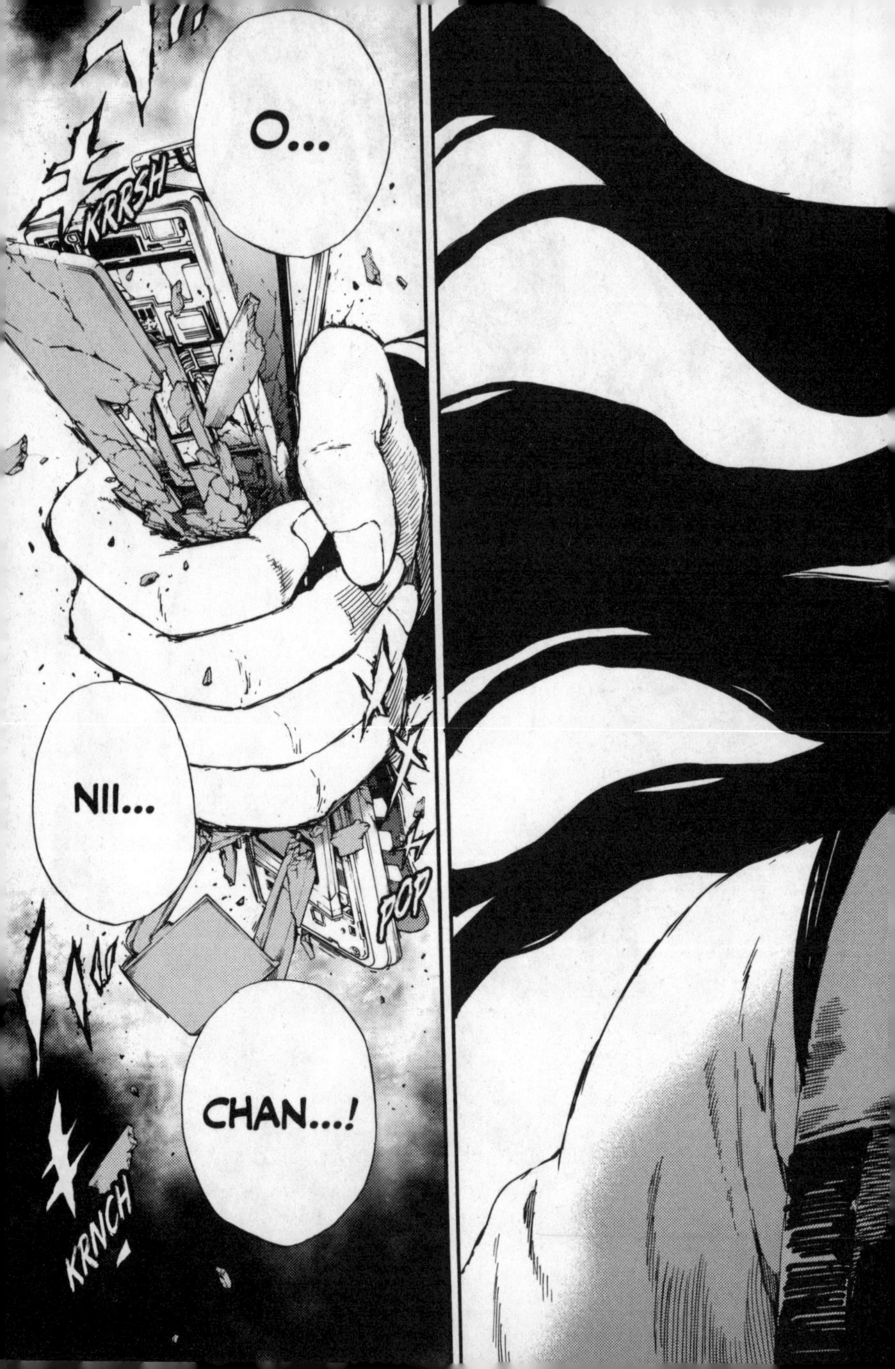
O...
KRRSH
POP
NII...
CHAN...!
KRNCH

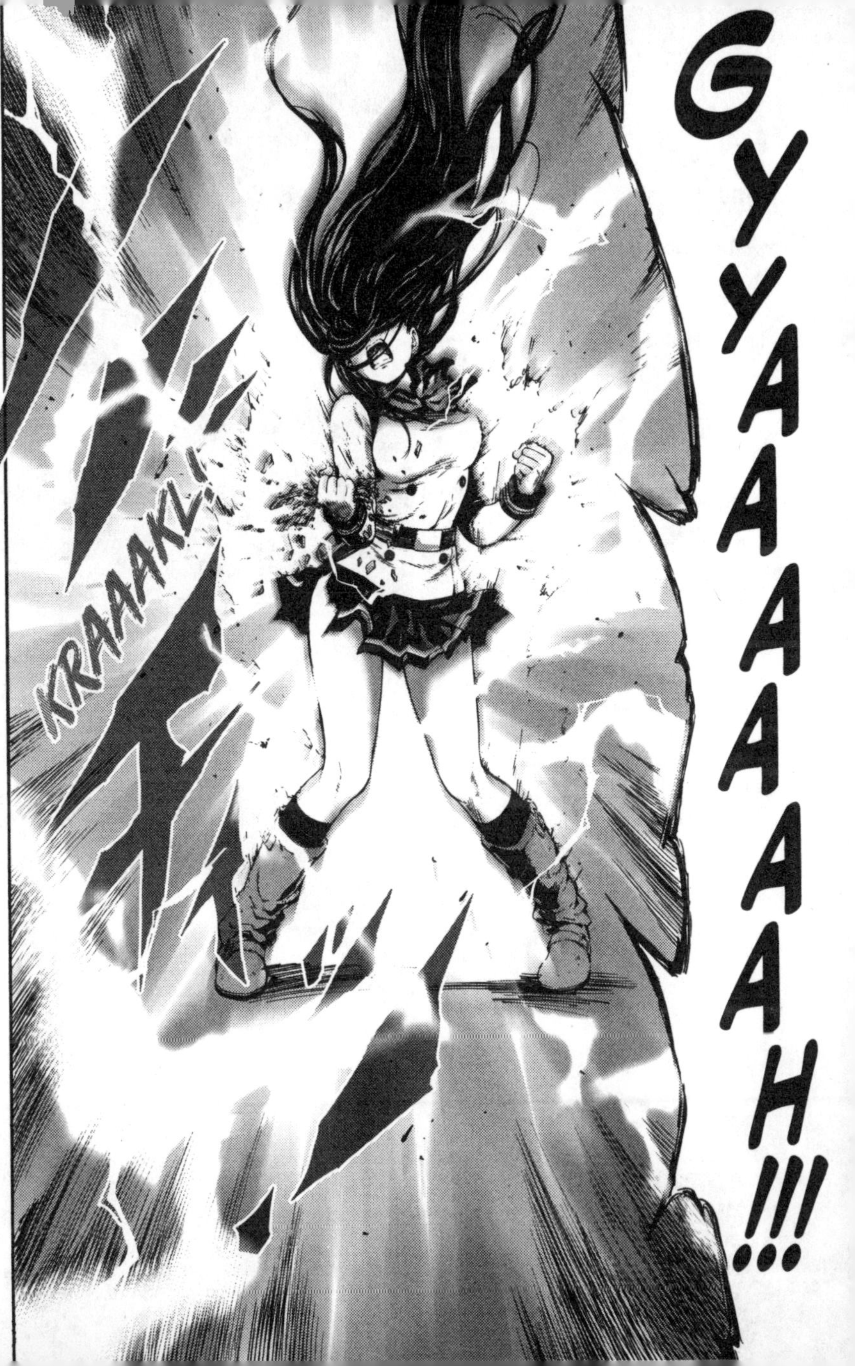
GYAAAAAAAH!!!
KRAAAKL!!

HIGH-RISE INVASION

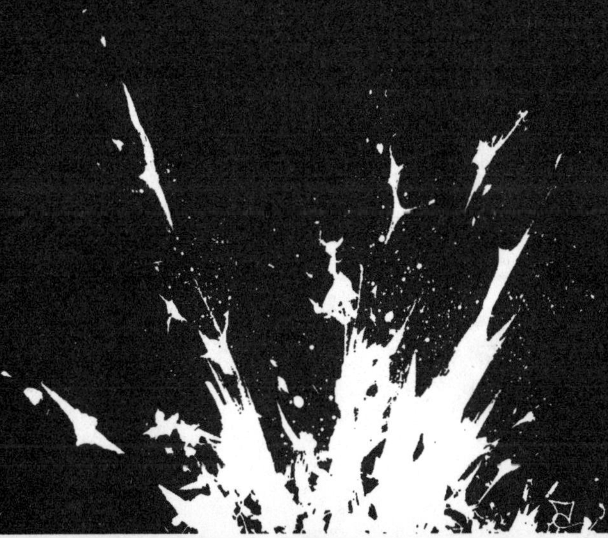

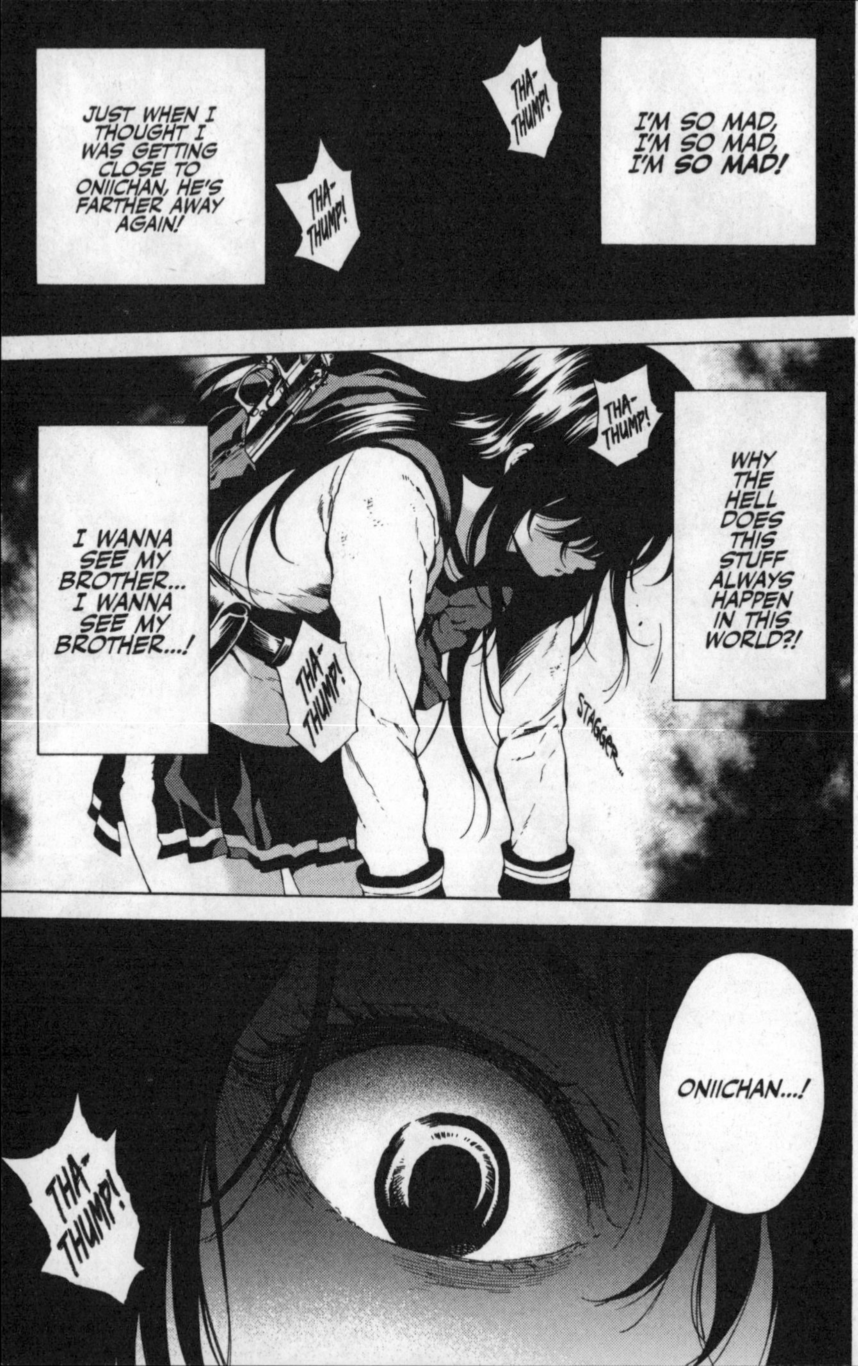

I'M SO MAD, I'M SO MAD, I'M SO MAD!
THA-THUMP!
JUST WHEN I THOUGHT I WAS GETTING CLOSE TO ONIICHAN, HE'S FARTHER AWAY AGAIN!
THA-THUMP!
THA-THUMP!
WHY THE HELL DOES THIS STUFF ALWAYS HAPPEN IN THIS WORLD?!
I WANNA SEE MY BROTHER... I WANNA SEE MY BROTHER...!
THA-THUMP!
STAGGER...
ONIICHAN...!
THA-THUMP!

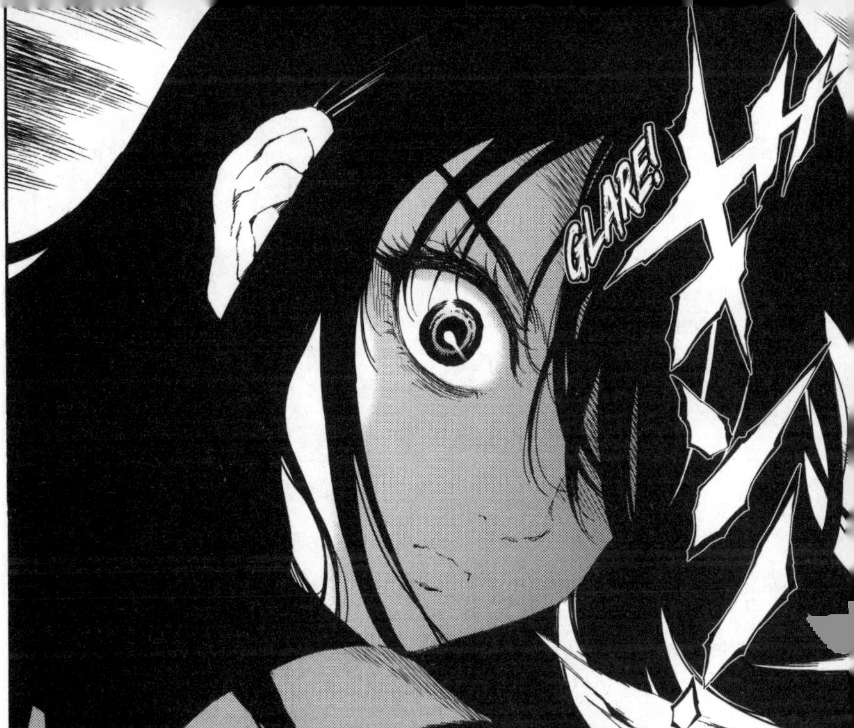
GLARE!

CHAPTER 100: Howling

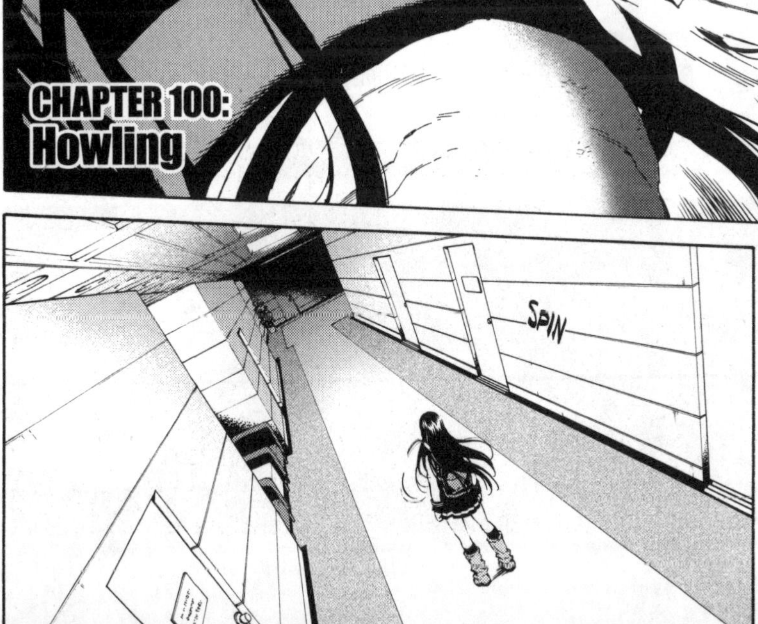
SPIN

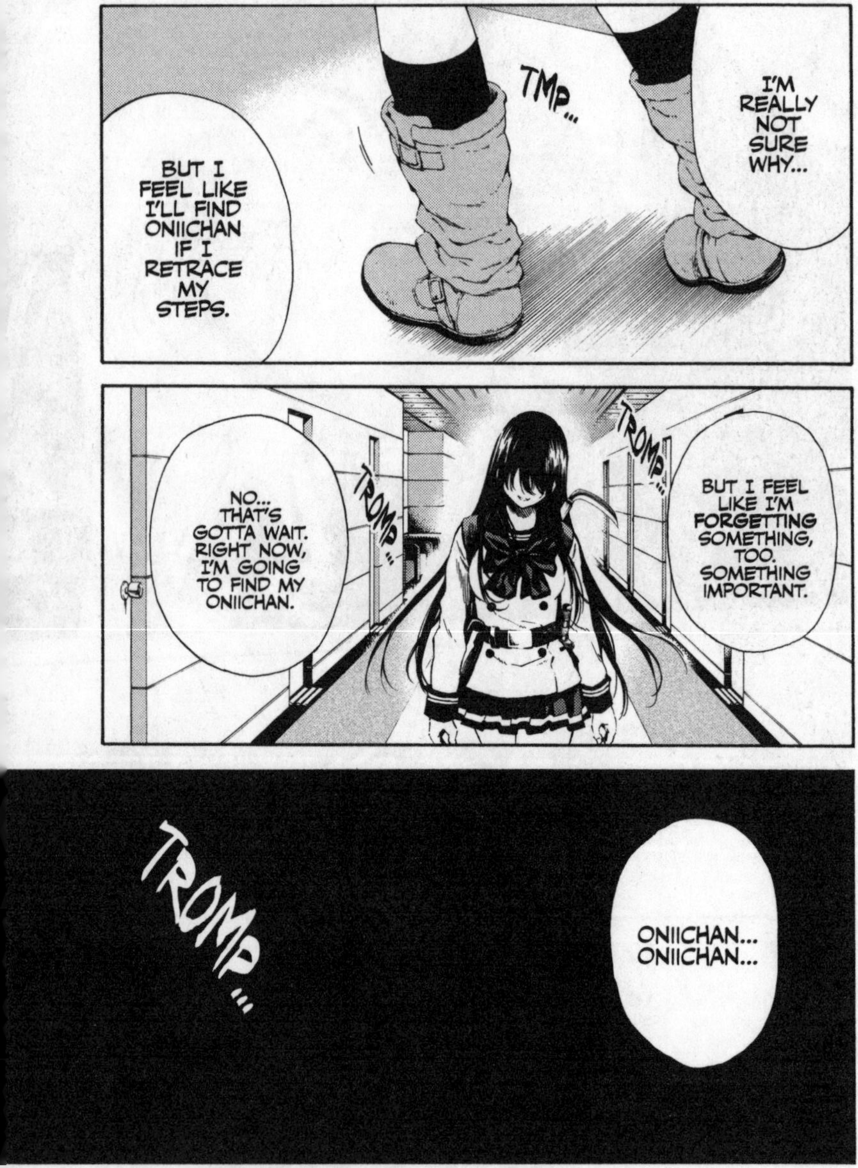
I'M REALLY NOT SURE WHY...
TMP...
BUT I FEEL LIKE I'LL FIND ONIICHAN IF I RETRACE MY STEPS.
BUT I FEEL LIKE I'M FORGETTING SOMETHING, TOO. SOMETHING IMPORTANT.
TROMP...
TROMP...
NO... THAT'S GOTTA WAIT. RIGHT NOW, I'M GOING TO FIND MY ONIICHAN.
ONIICHAN... ONIICHAN...
TROMP...

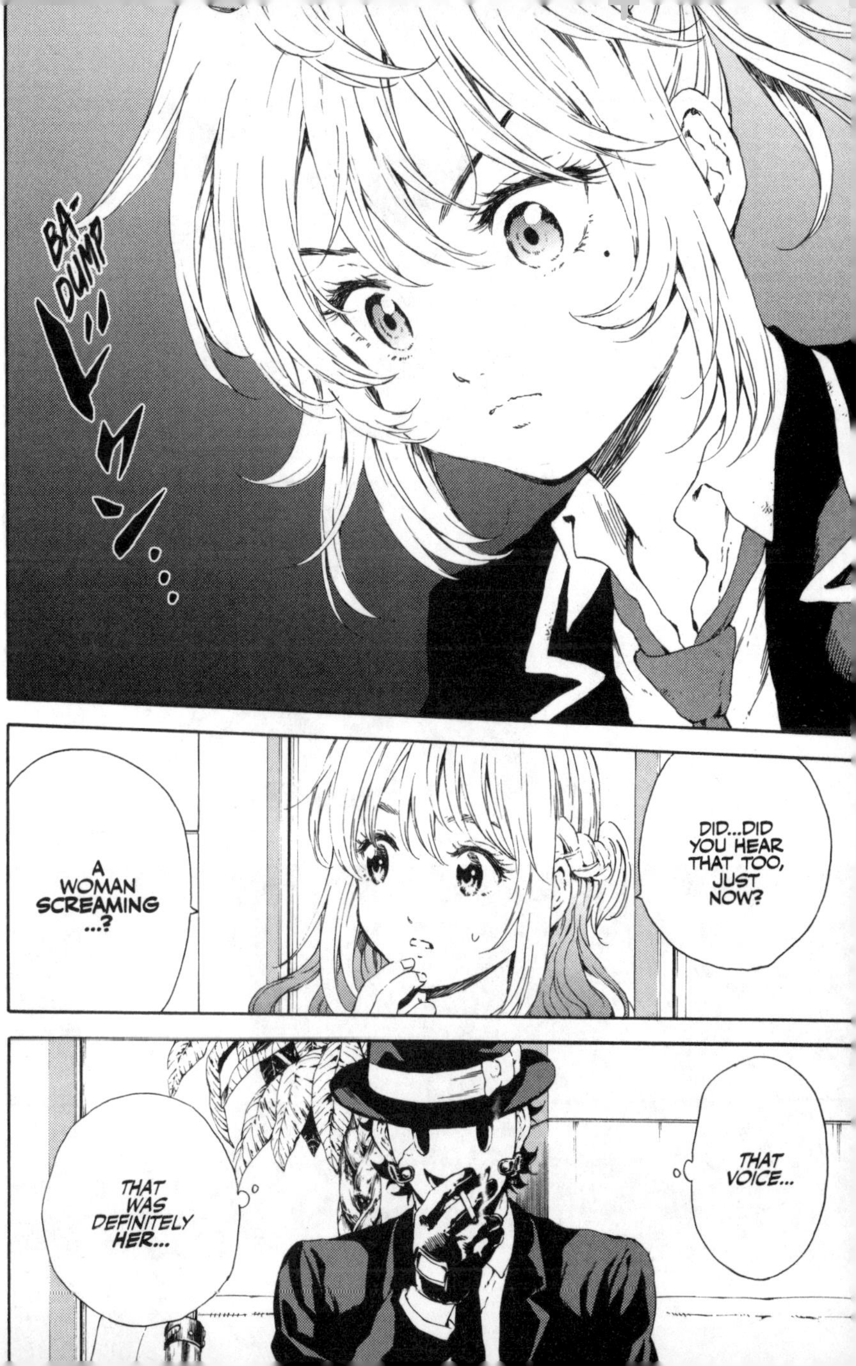
BA-DUMP
DID...DID YOU HEAR THAT TOO, JUST NOW?
A WOMAN SCREAMING ...?
THAT VOICE...
THAT WAS DEFINITELY HER...

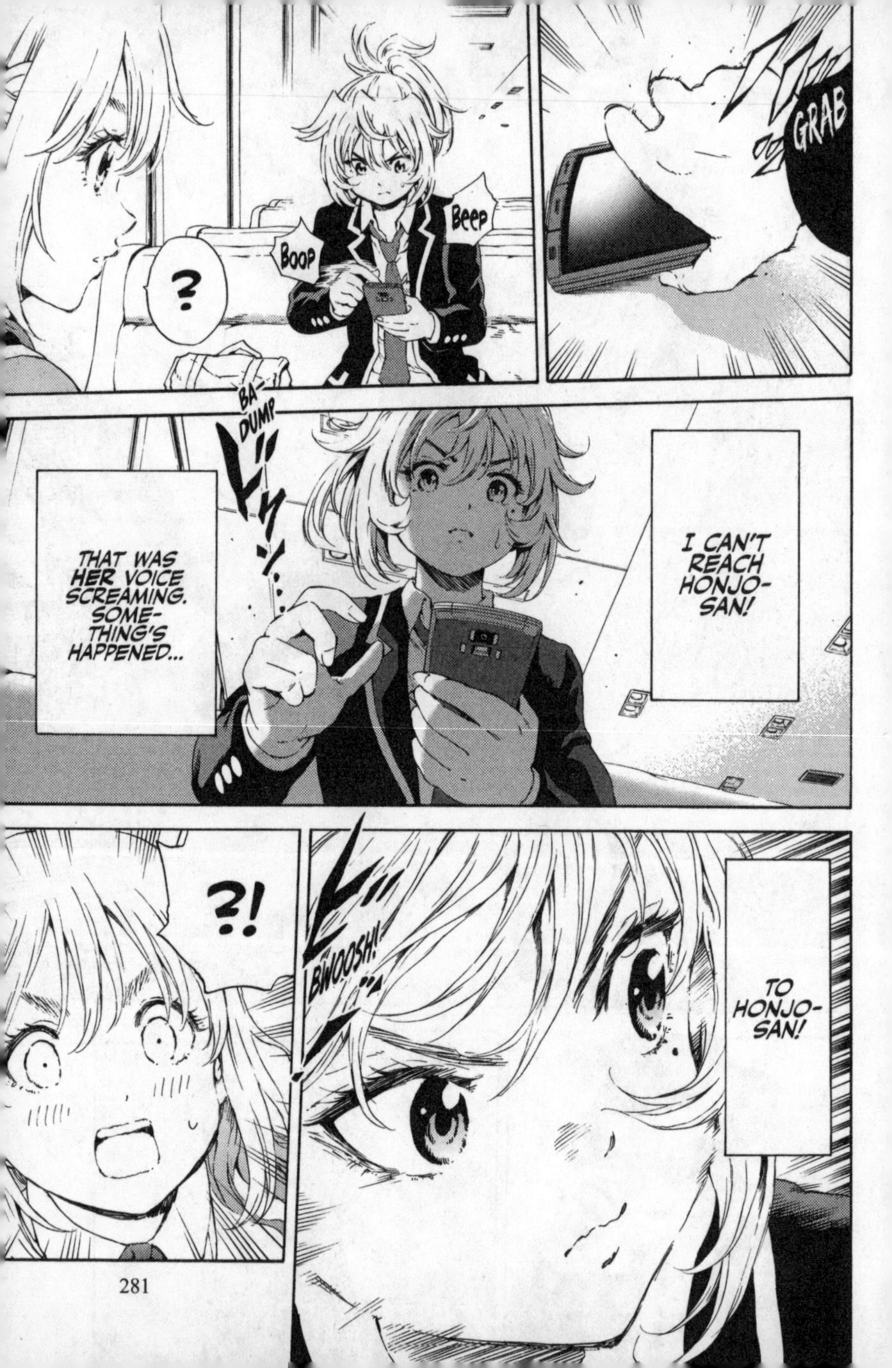
GRAB
Beep
Boop
?
I CAN'T REACH HONJO-SAN!
BA-DUMP
THAT WAS HER VOICE SCREAMING. SOME-THING'S HAPPENED...
TO HONJO-SAN!
BWOOSH!
?!

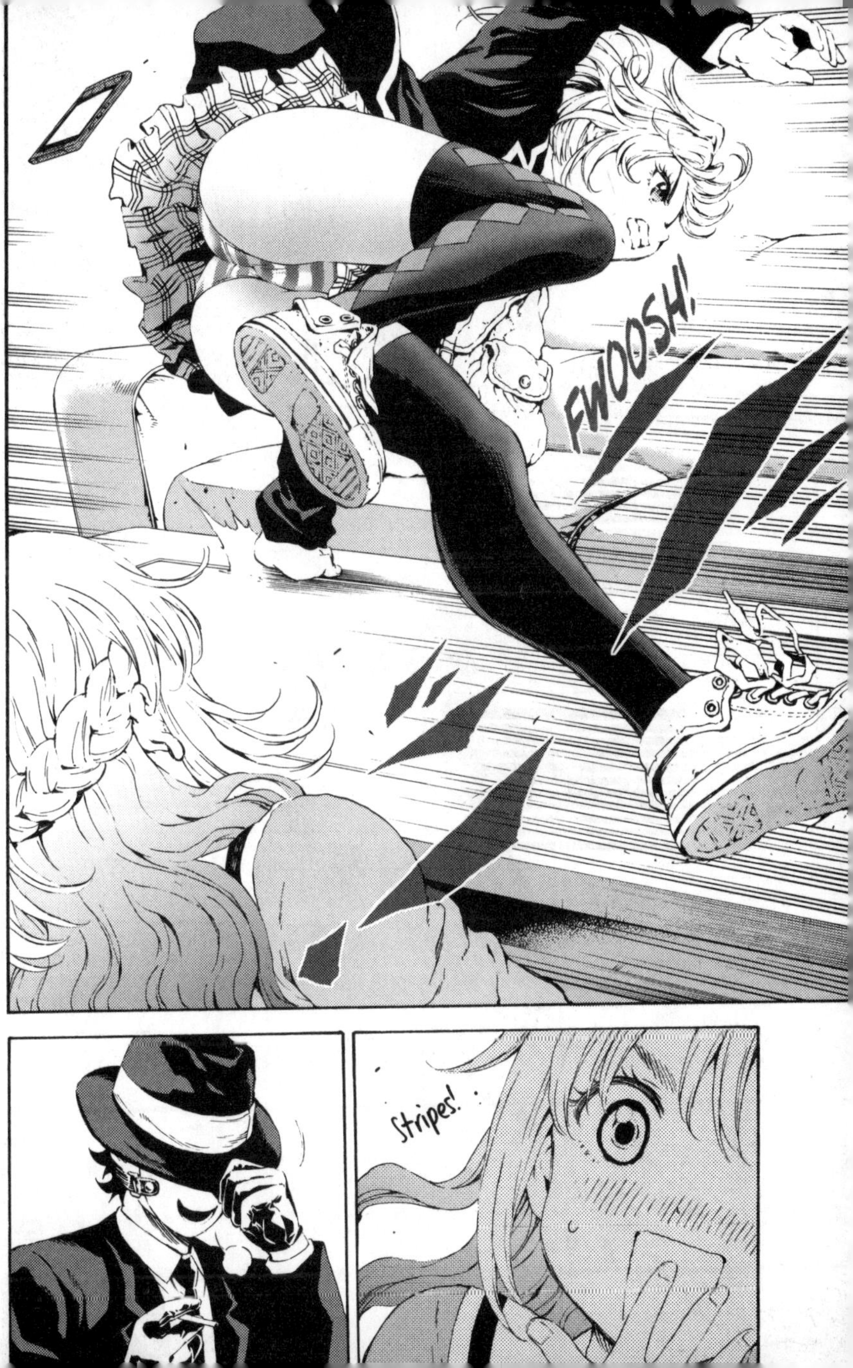
FWOOSH!
Stripes!

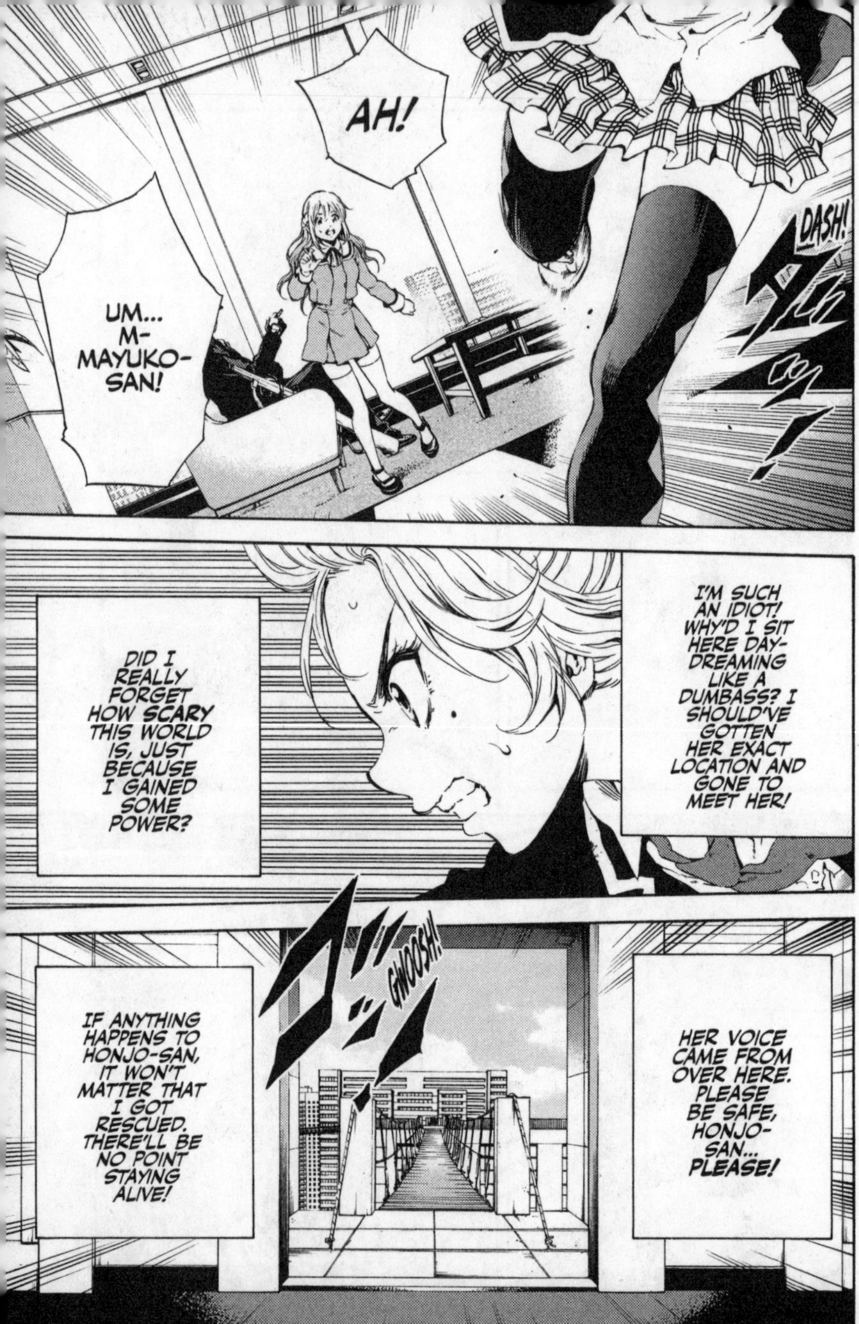
AH!
DASH!
UM... M-MAYUKO-SAN!
I'M SUCH AN IDIOT! WHY'D I SIT HERE DAY-DREAMING LIKE A DUMBASS? I SHOULD'VE GOTTEN HER EXACT LOCATION AND GONE TO MEET HER!
DID I REALLY FORGET HOW SCARY THIS WORLD IS, JUST BECAUSE I GAINED SOME POWER?
HER VOICE CAME FROM OVER HERE. PLEASE BE SAFE, HONJO-SAN... PLEASE!
GWOOSH!
IF ANYTHING HAPPENS TO HONJO-SAN, IT WON'T MATTER THAT I GOT RESCUED. THERE'LL BE NO POINT STAYING ALIVE!

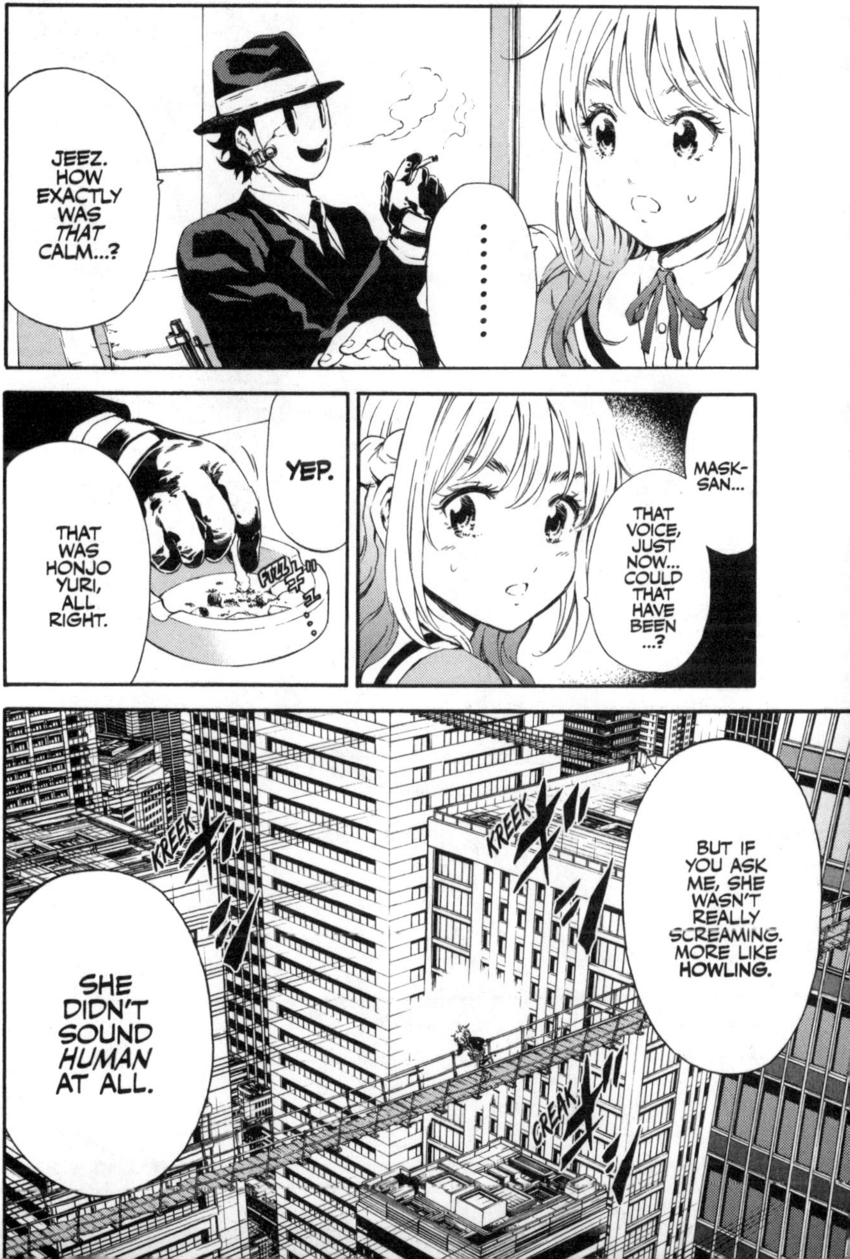
......
JEEZ. HOW EXACTLY WAS *THAT* CALM...?
MASK-SAN...
THAT VOICE, JUST NOW... COULD THAT HAVE BEEN ...?
YEP.
THAT WAS HONJO YURI, ALL RIGHT.
FIZZ
BUT IF YOU ASK ME, SHE WASN'T REALLY SCREAMING. MORE LIKE **HOWLING.**
KREEK
KREEK
CREAK
SHE DIDN'T SOUND *HUMAN* AT ALL.

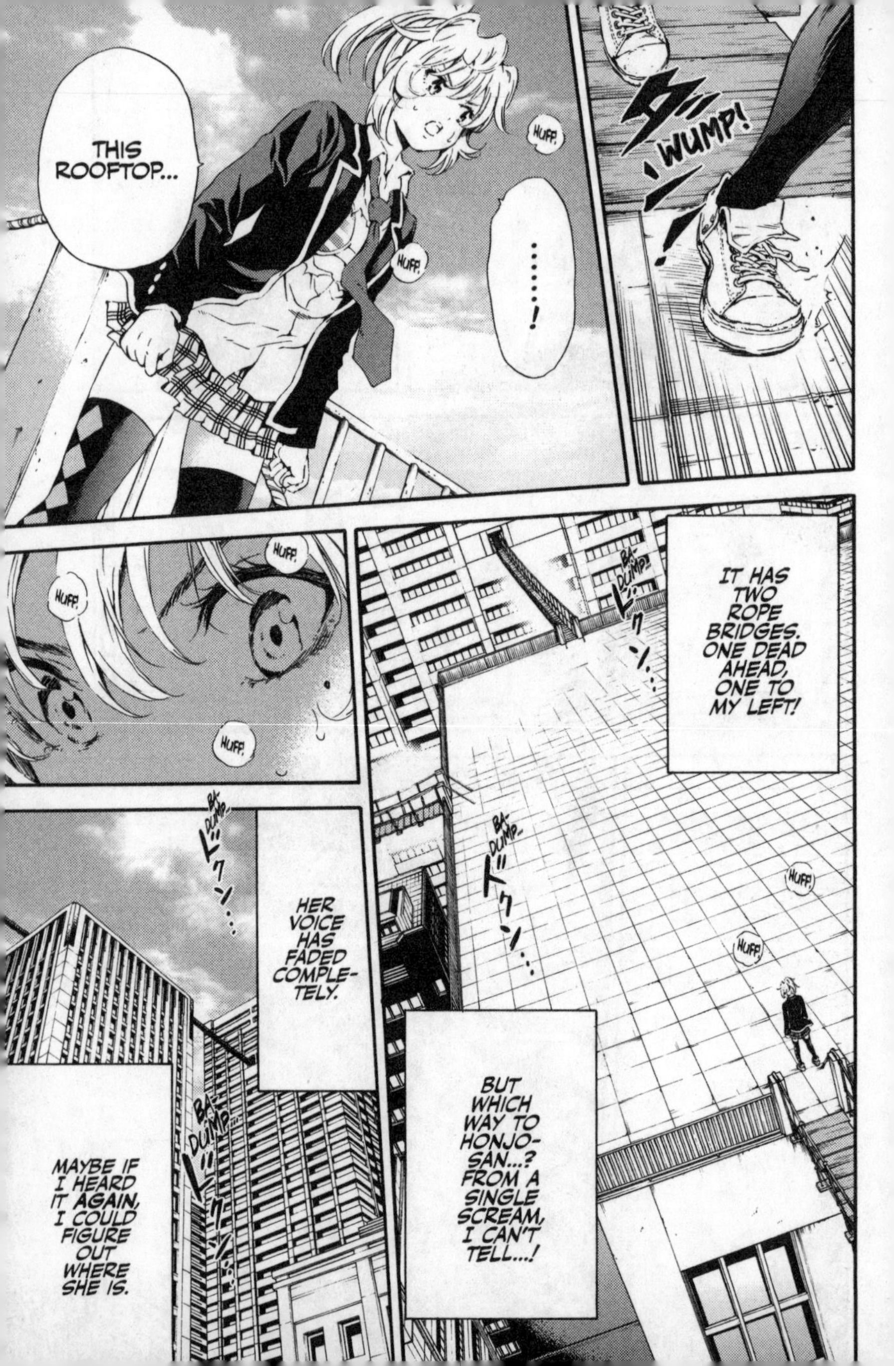
WUMP!
HUFF!
THIS ROOFTOP...
......!
HUFF!
IT HAS TWO ROPE BRIDGES. ONE DEAD AHEAD, ONE TO MY LEFT!
BA-DUMP...
BA-DUMP...
HUFF!
HUFF!
BUT WHICH WAY TO HONJO-SAN...? FROM A SINGLE SCREAM, I CAN'T TELL...!
HUFF!
HUFF!
HUFF!
BA-DUMP...
HER VOICE HAS FADED COMPLETE-TELY.
BA-DUMP...
MAYBE IF I HEARD IT AGAIN, I COULD FIGURE OUT WHERE SHE IS.

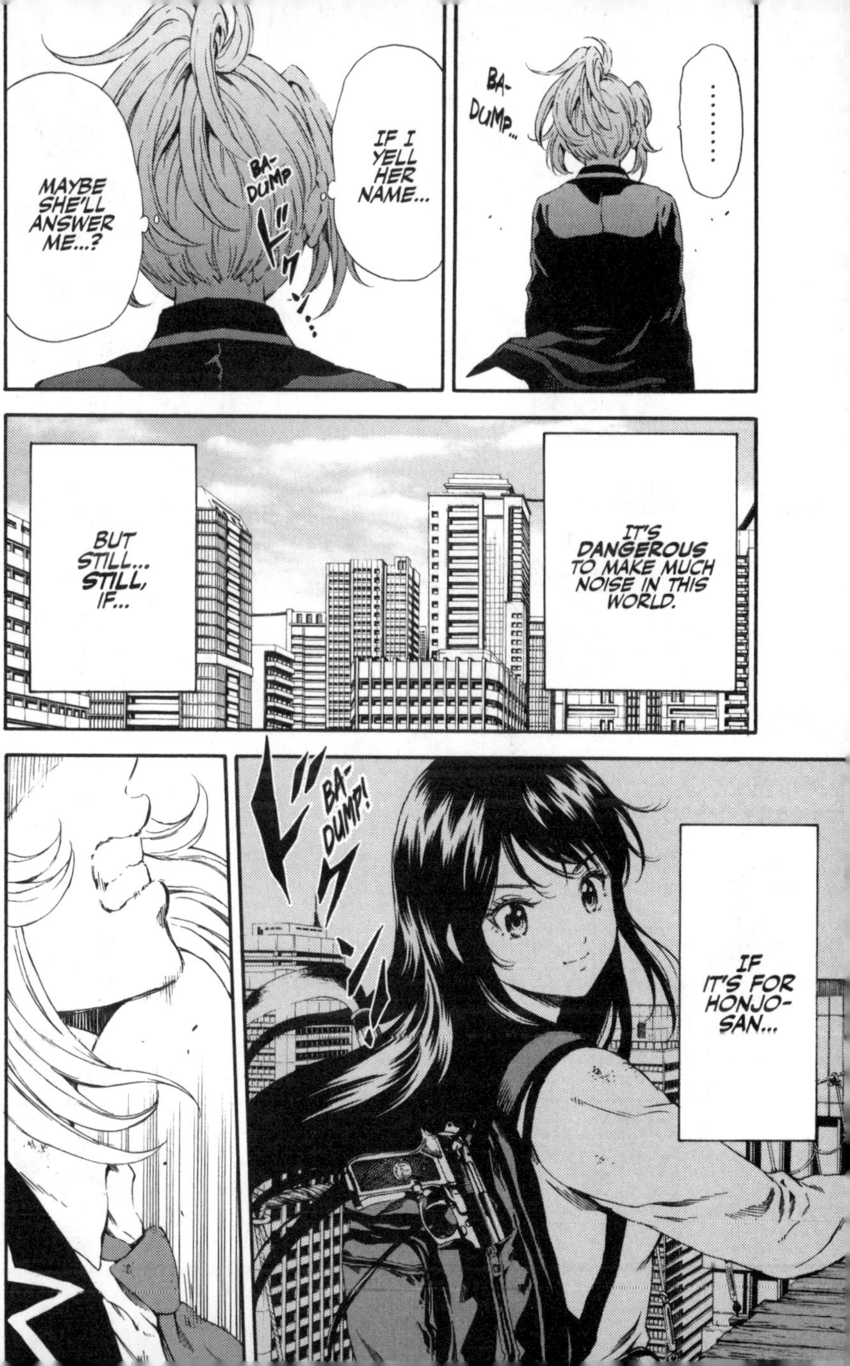
......
BA-DUMP...
IF I YELL HER NAME...
BA-DUMP
MAYBE SHE'LL ANSWER ME...?
IT'S **DANGEROUS** TO MAKE MUCH NOISE IN THIS WORLD.
BUT STILL... **STILL,** IF...
IF IT'S FOR HONJO-SAN...
BA-DUMP!

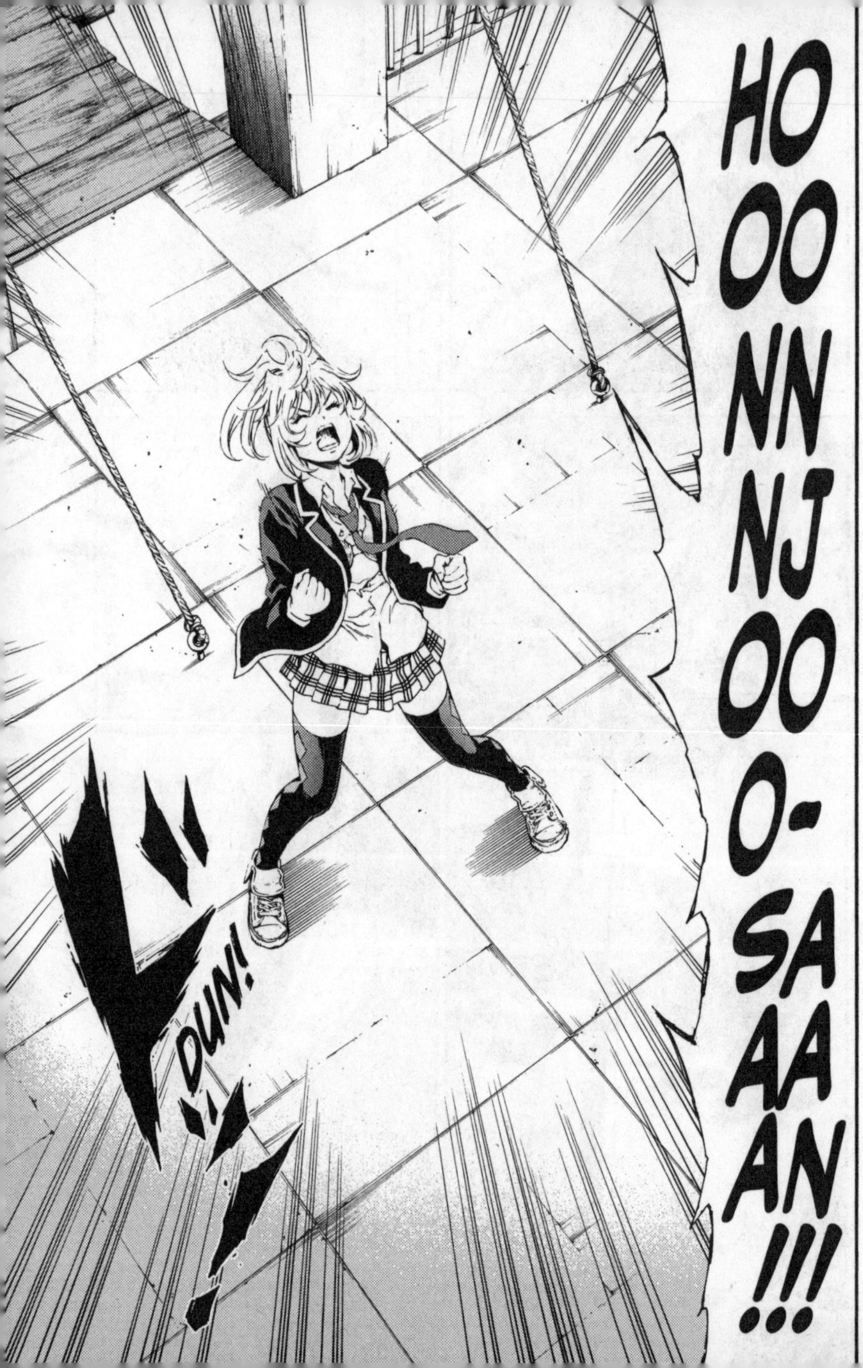
HOOONNNJOOO-SAAAAN!!!
DUN!

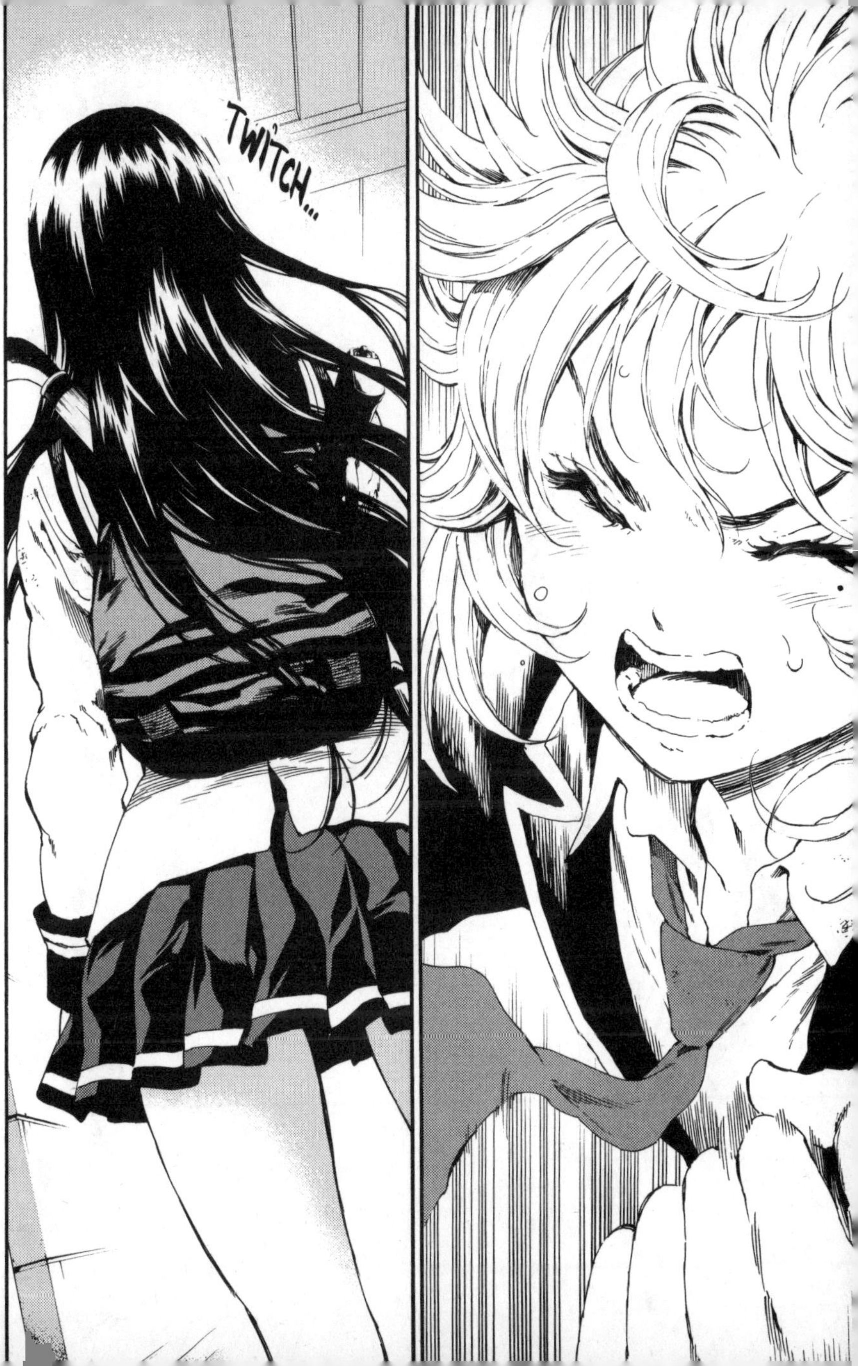
TWITCH...

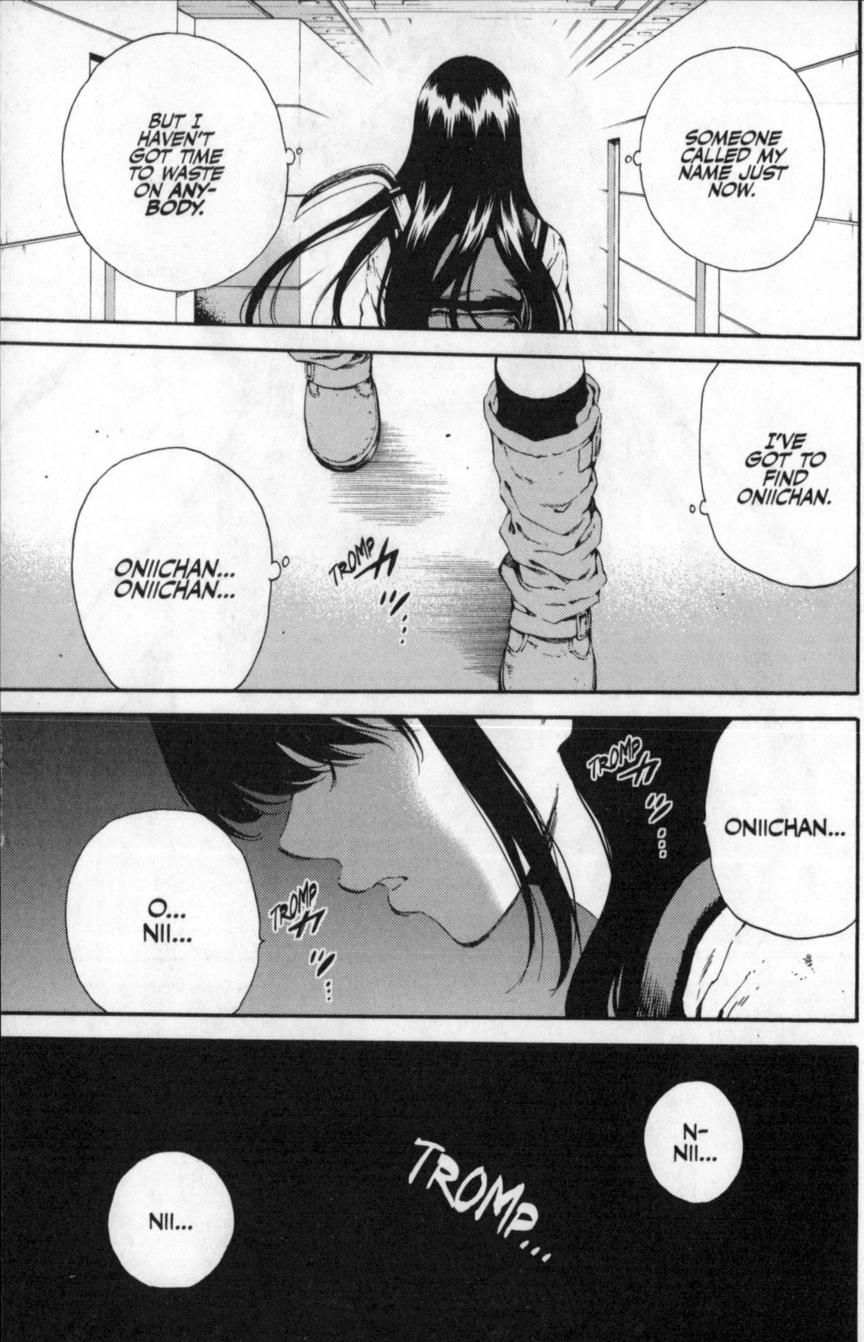
SOMEONE CALLED MY NAME JUST NOW.
BUT I HAVEN'T GOT TIME TO WASTE ON ANY-BODY.
I'VE GOT TO FIND ONIICHAN.
TROMP
ONIICHAN... ONIICHAN...
TROMP
ONIICHAN...
TROMP
O... NII...
N- NII...
TROMP...
NII...

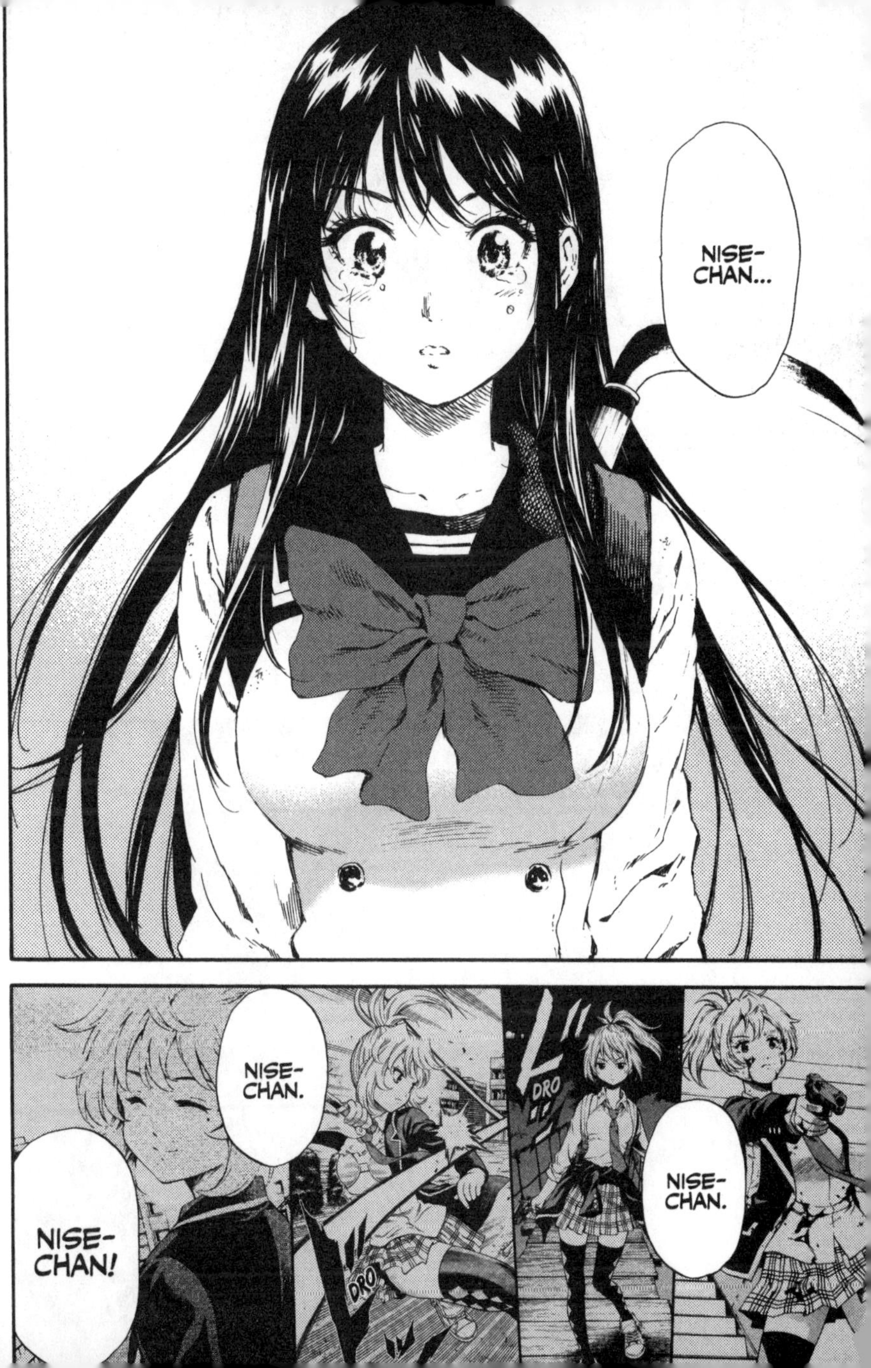
NISE-CHAN...
NISE-CHAN.
DRO
NISE-CHAN.
DRO
NISE-CHAN!

NIIISEEE-
CHAAAN!!!

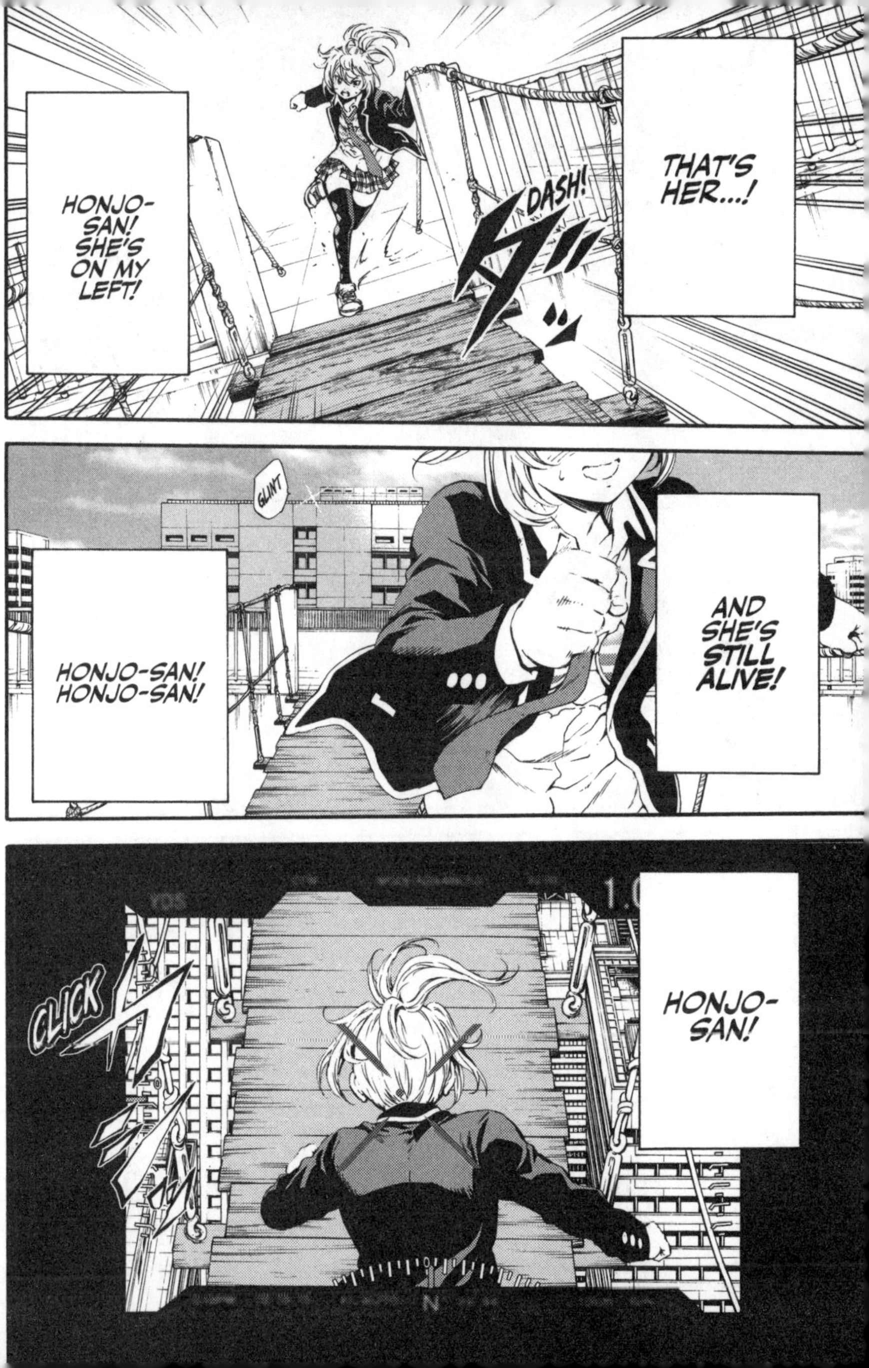
THAT'S HER...!
DASH!
HONJO-SAN! SHE'S ON MY LEFT!
AND SHE'S STILL ALIVE!
GLINT
HONJO-SAN! HONJO-SAN!
HONJO-SAN!
CLICK

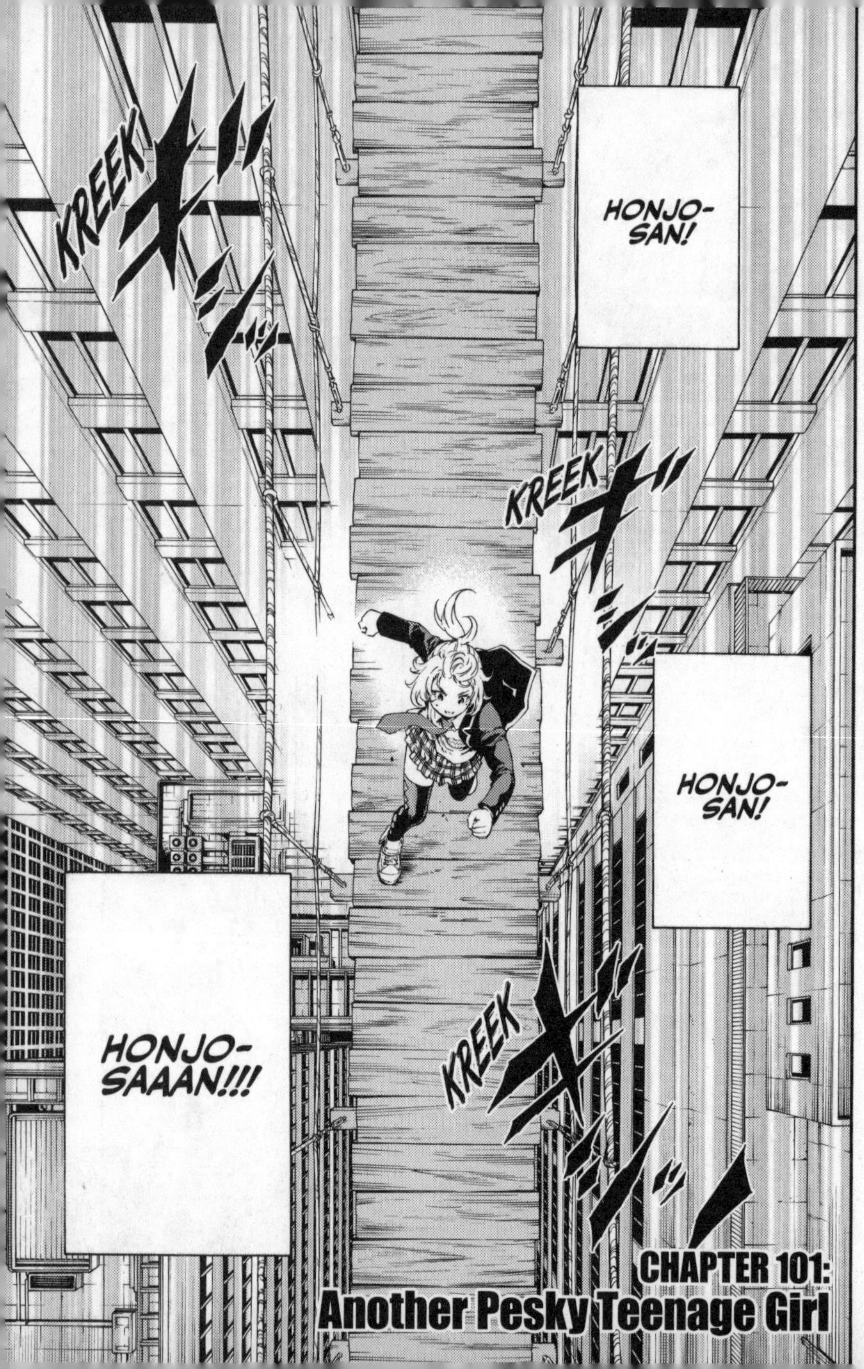
HONJO-SAN!
KREEK
KREEK
HONJO-SAN!
HONJO-SAAAN!!!
KREEK
CHAPTER 101:
Another Pesky Teenage Girl

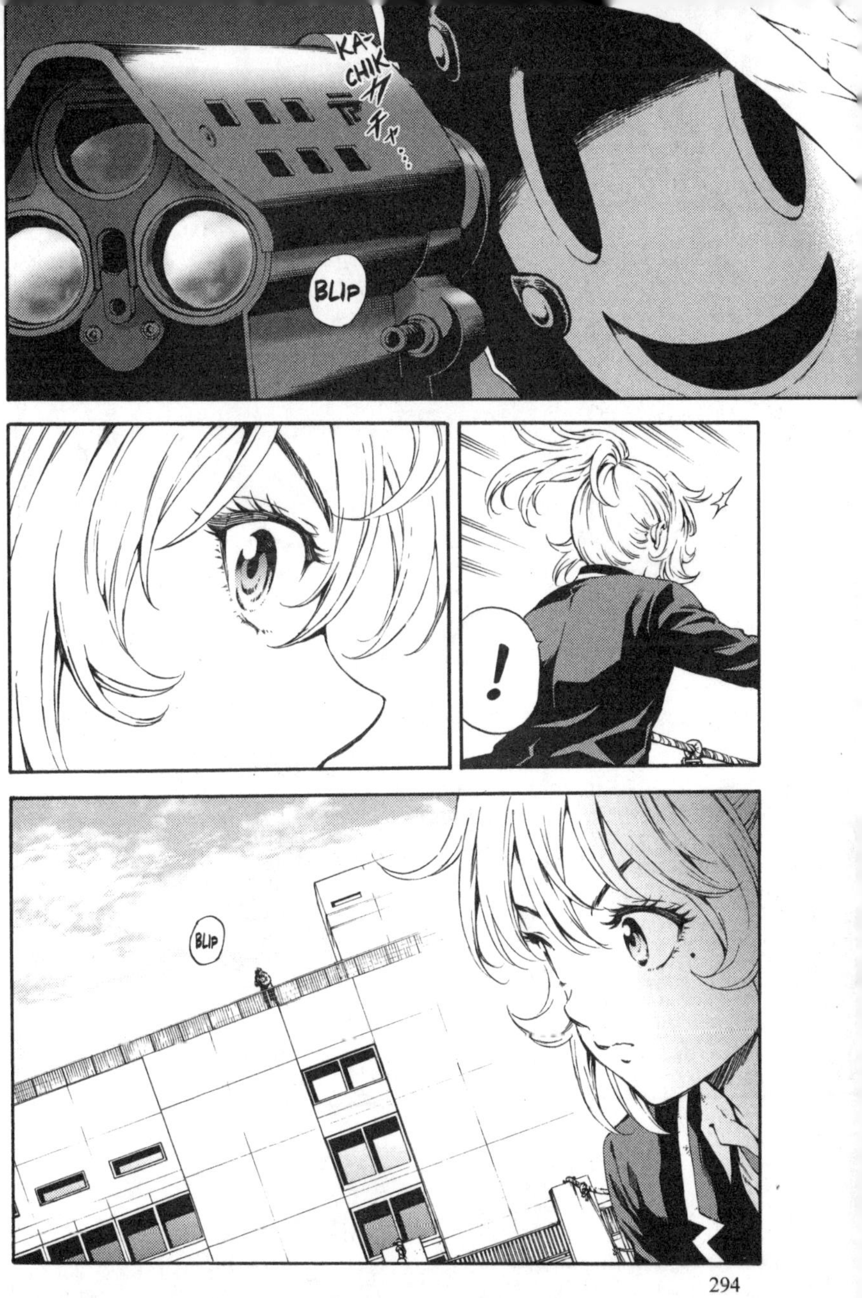
KA-CHIK
カチャ...
BLIP
!
BLIP

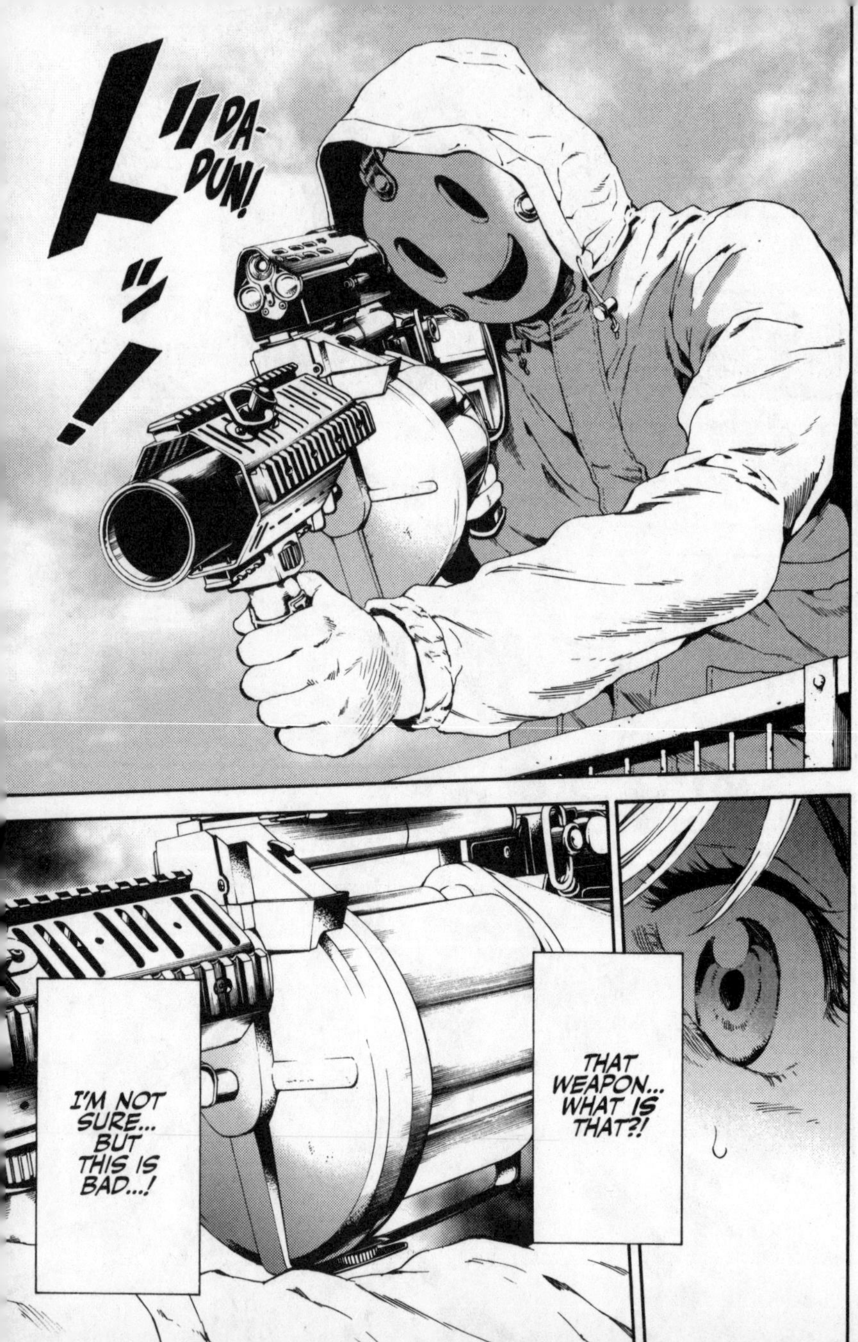
DA-DUN!
THAT WEAPON... WHAT IS THAT?!
I'M NOT SURE... BUT THIS IS BAD...!

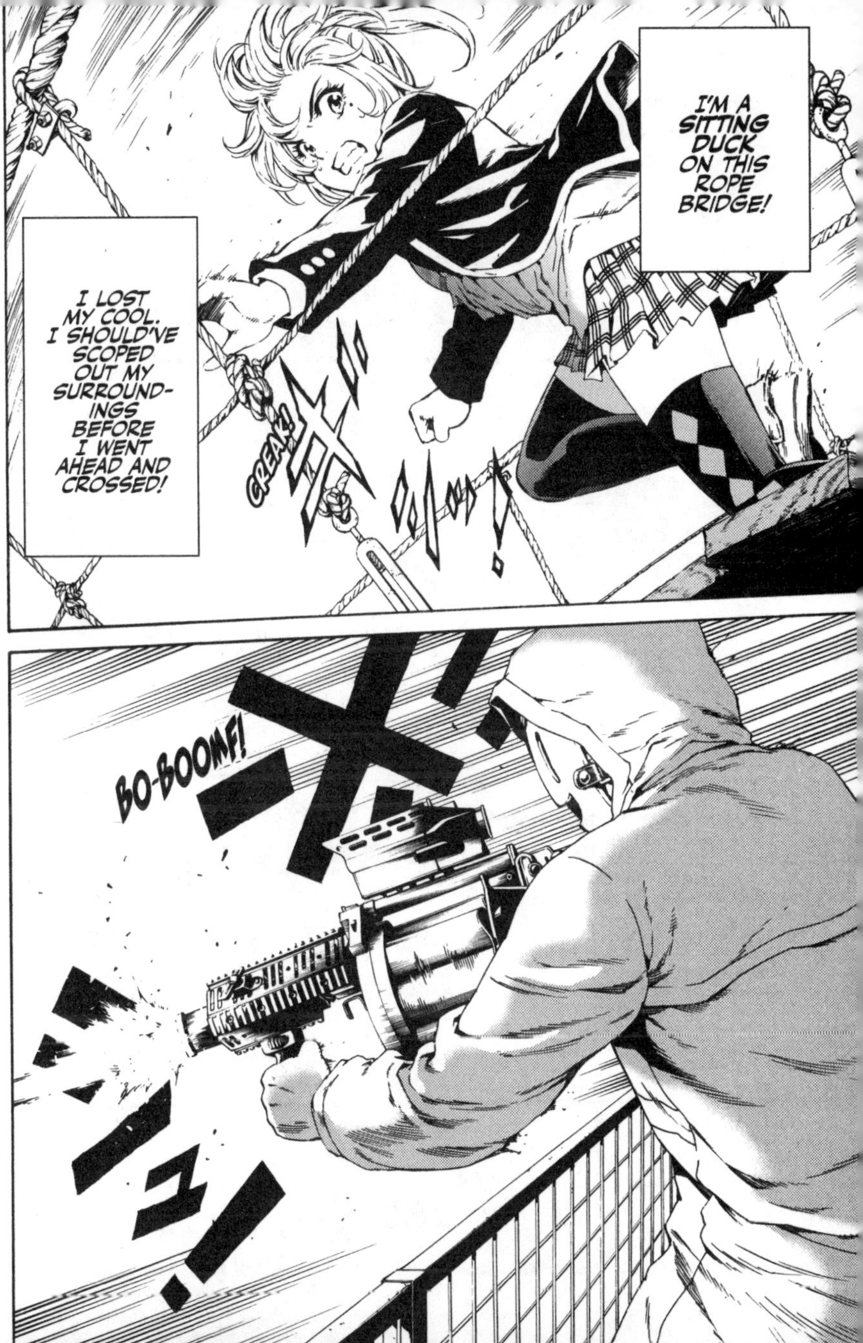
I'M A SITTING DUCK ON THIS ROPE BRIDGE!
I LOST MY COOL. I SHOULD'VE SCOPED OUT MY SURROUND-INGS BEFORE I WENT AHEAD AND CROSSED!
CREAK!
BO-BOOMF!

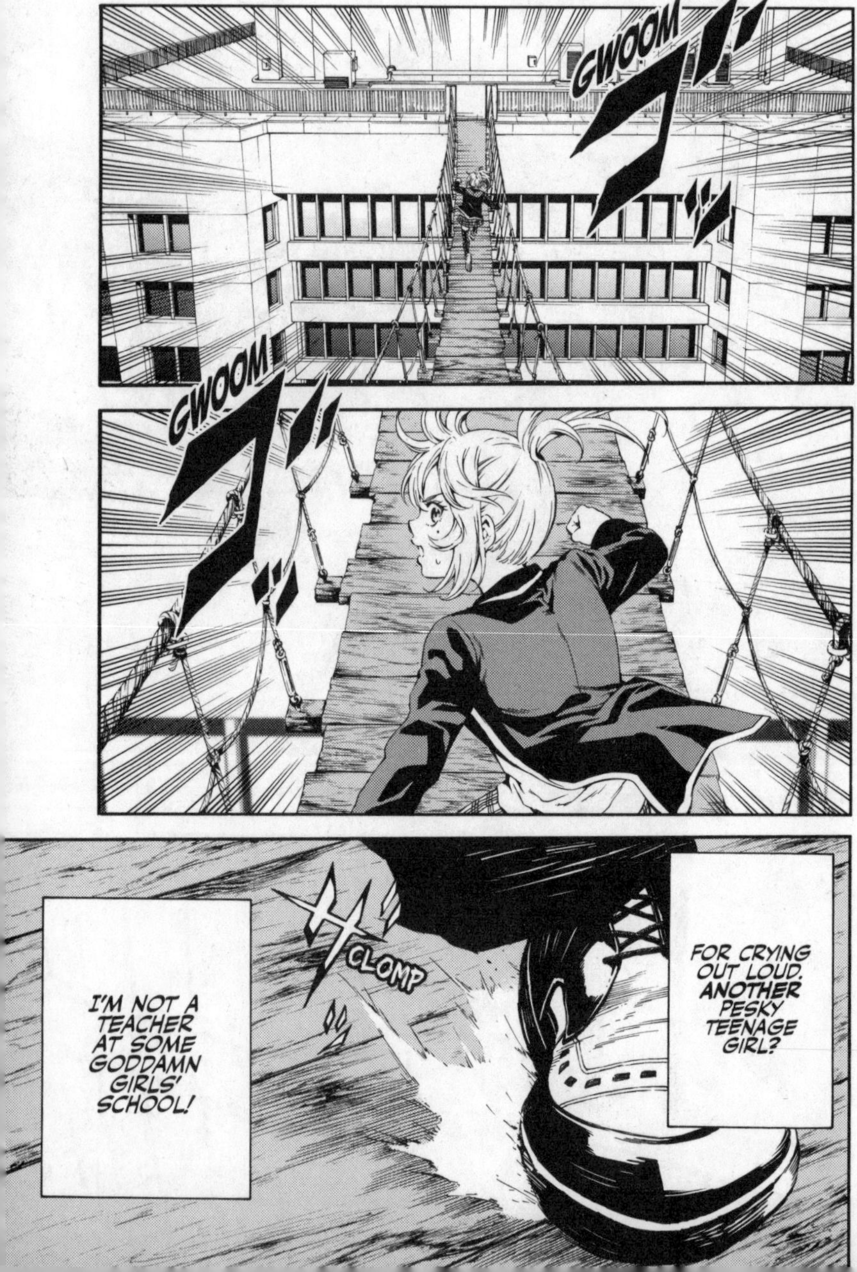
GWOOM
GWOOM
FOR CRYING OUT LOUD. ANOTHER PESKY TEENAGE GIRL?
CLOMP
I'M NOT A TEACHER AT SOME GODDAMN GIRLS' SCHOOL!

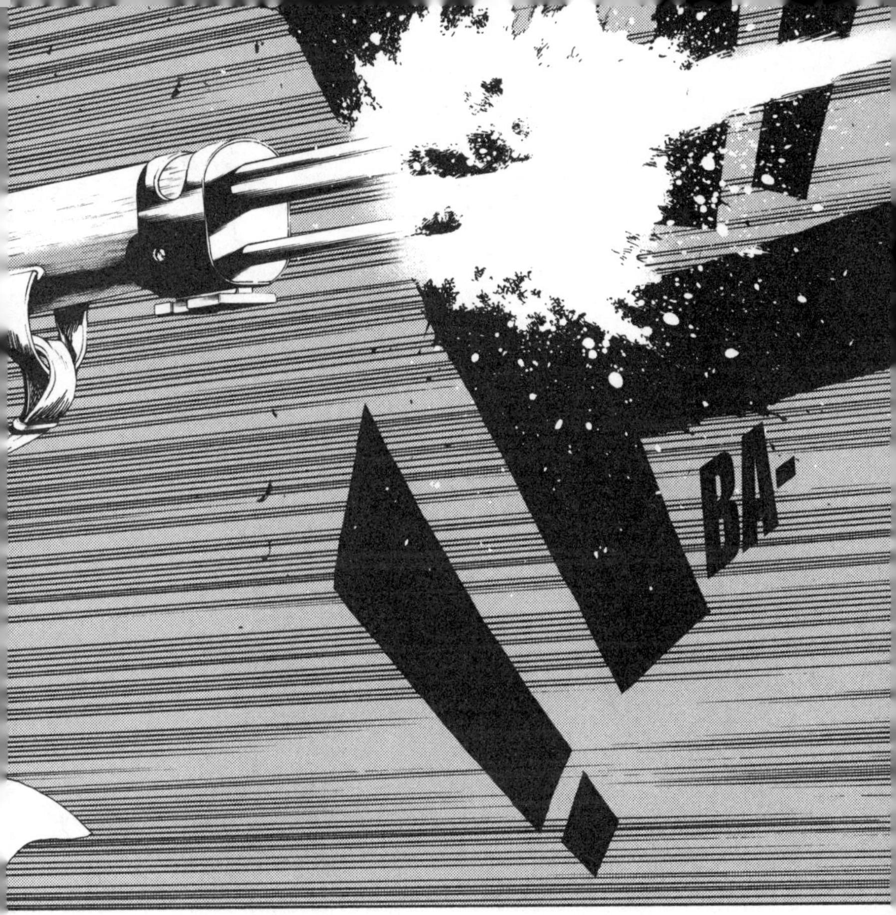
BA-
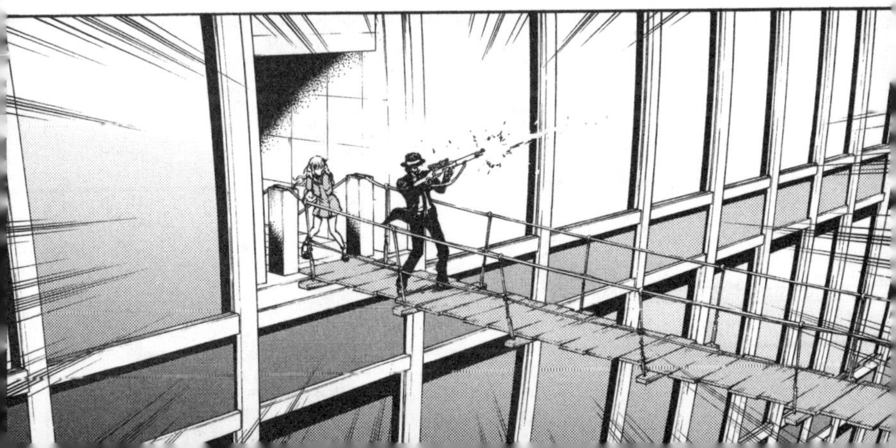

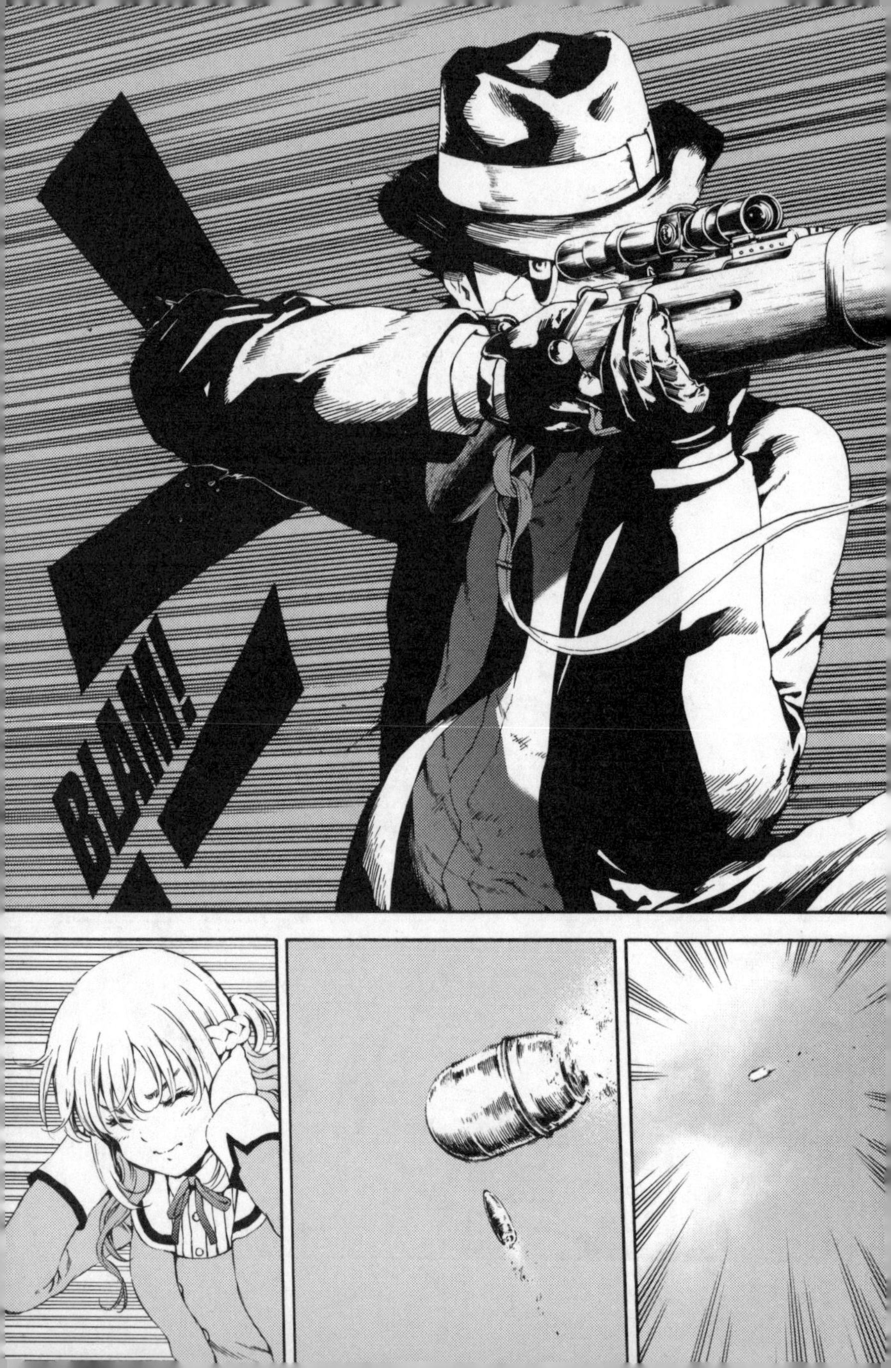
BLAM!

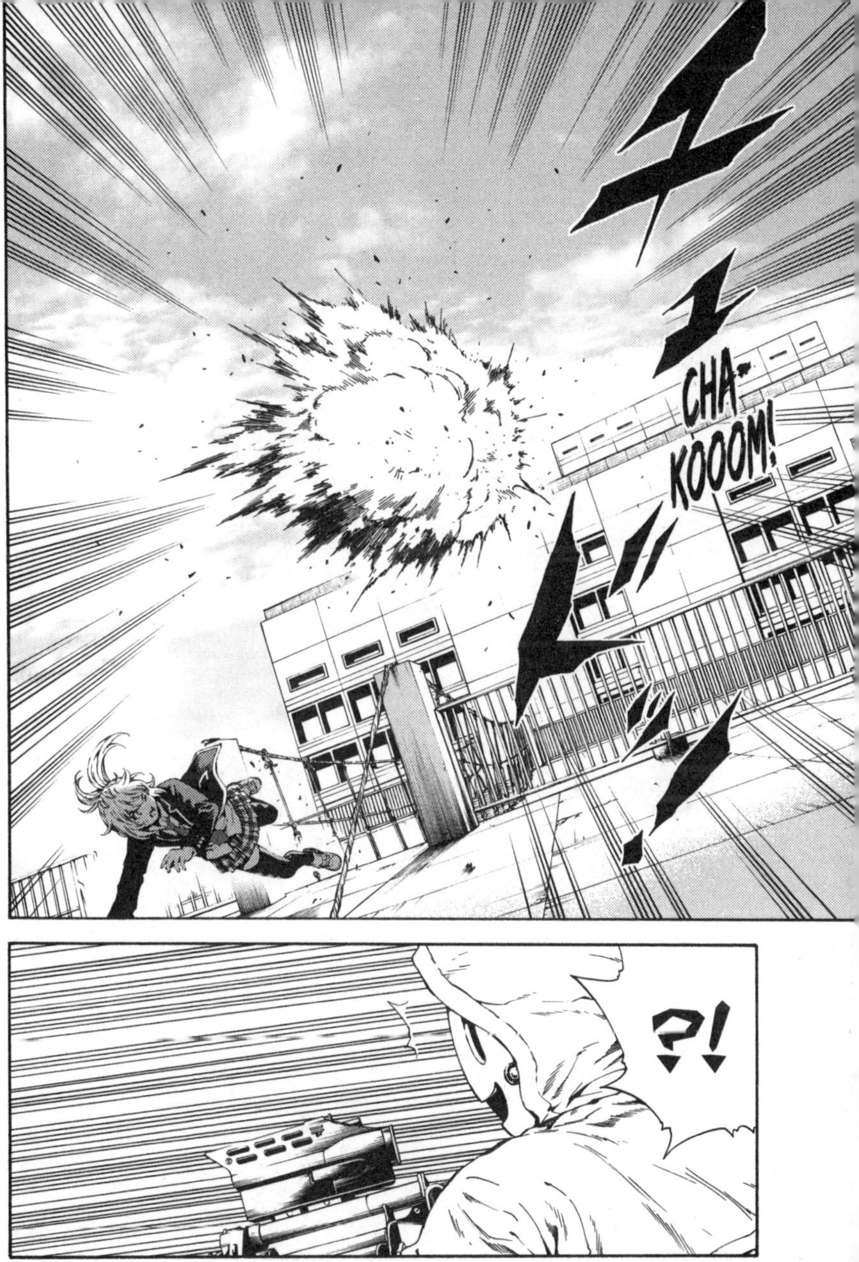
CHA-KOOOM!
?!

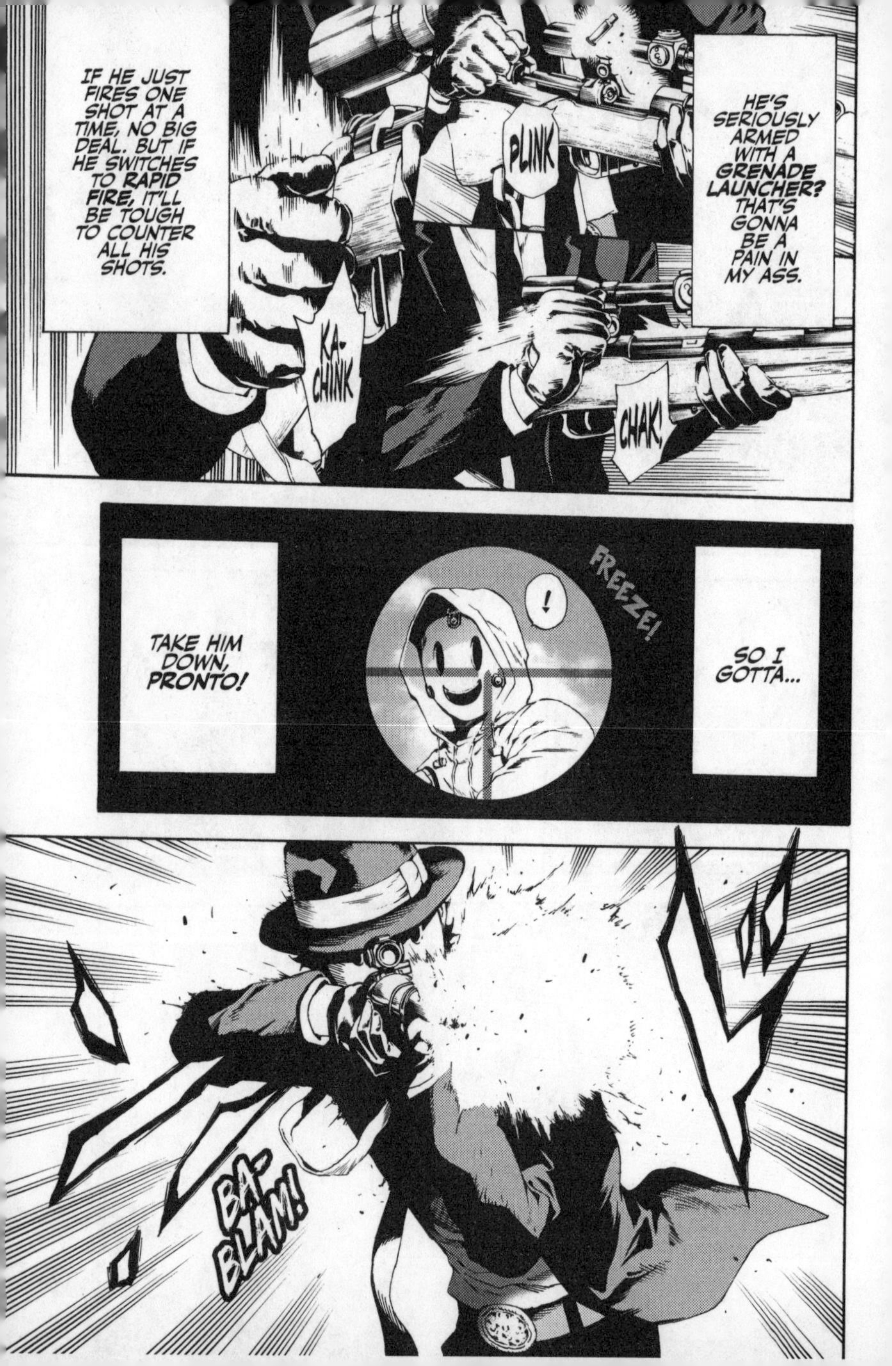
HE'S SERIOUSLY ARMED WITH A GRENADE LAUNCHER? THAT'S GONNA BE A PAIN IN MY ASS.
PLINK
IF HE JUST FIRES ONE SHOT AT A TIME, NO BIG DEAL. BUT IF HE SWITCHES TO RAPID FIRE, IT'LL BE TOUGH TO COUNTER ALL HIS SHOTS.
CHAK!
KA-CHINK
SO I GOTTA...
FREEZE!
!
TAKE HIM DOWN, PRONTO!
BA-BLAM!

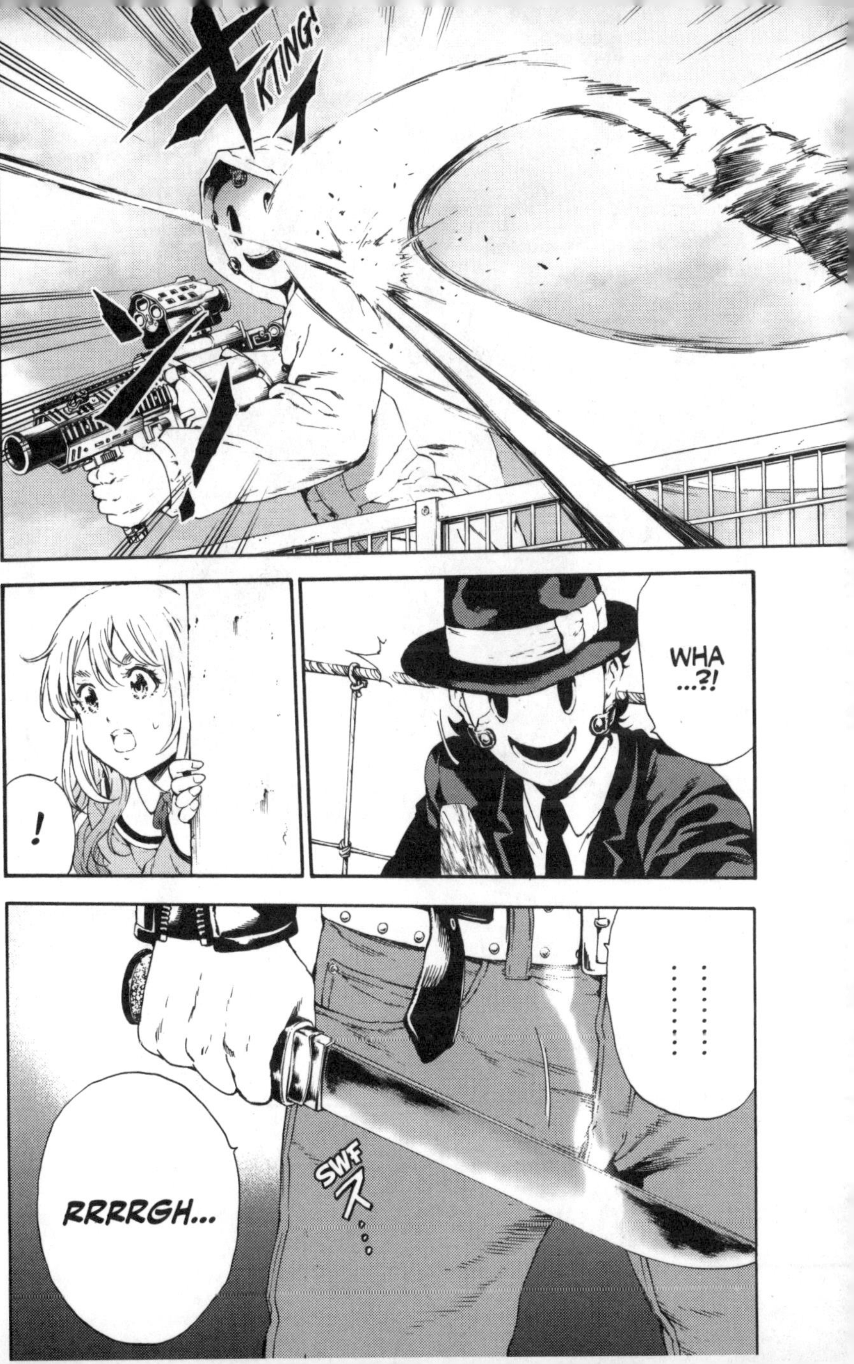
KTING!
WHA ...?!
!
......
SWF
RRRRGH...

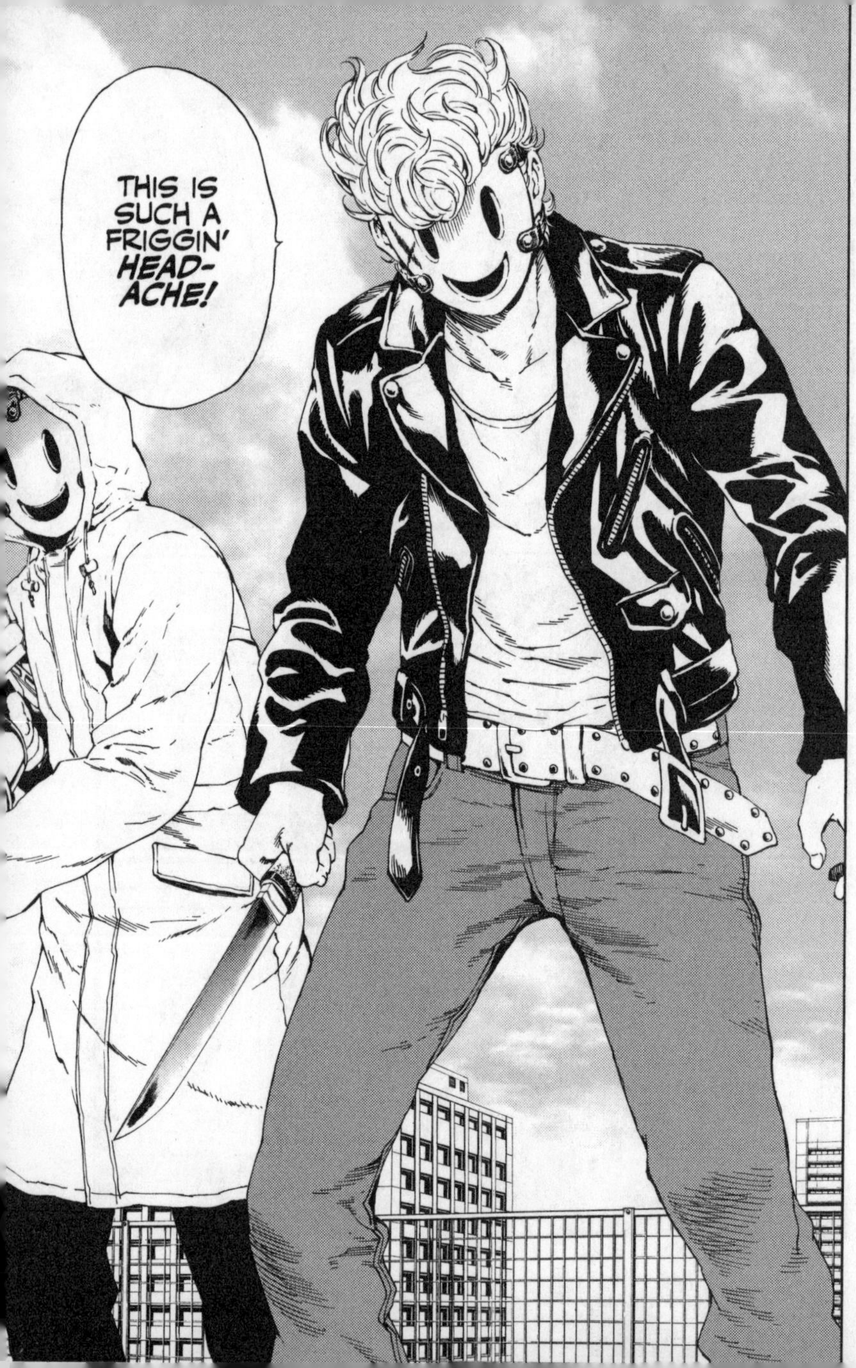
THIS IS SUCH A FRIGGIN' HEAD-ACHE!

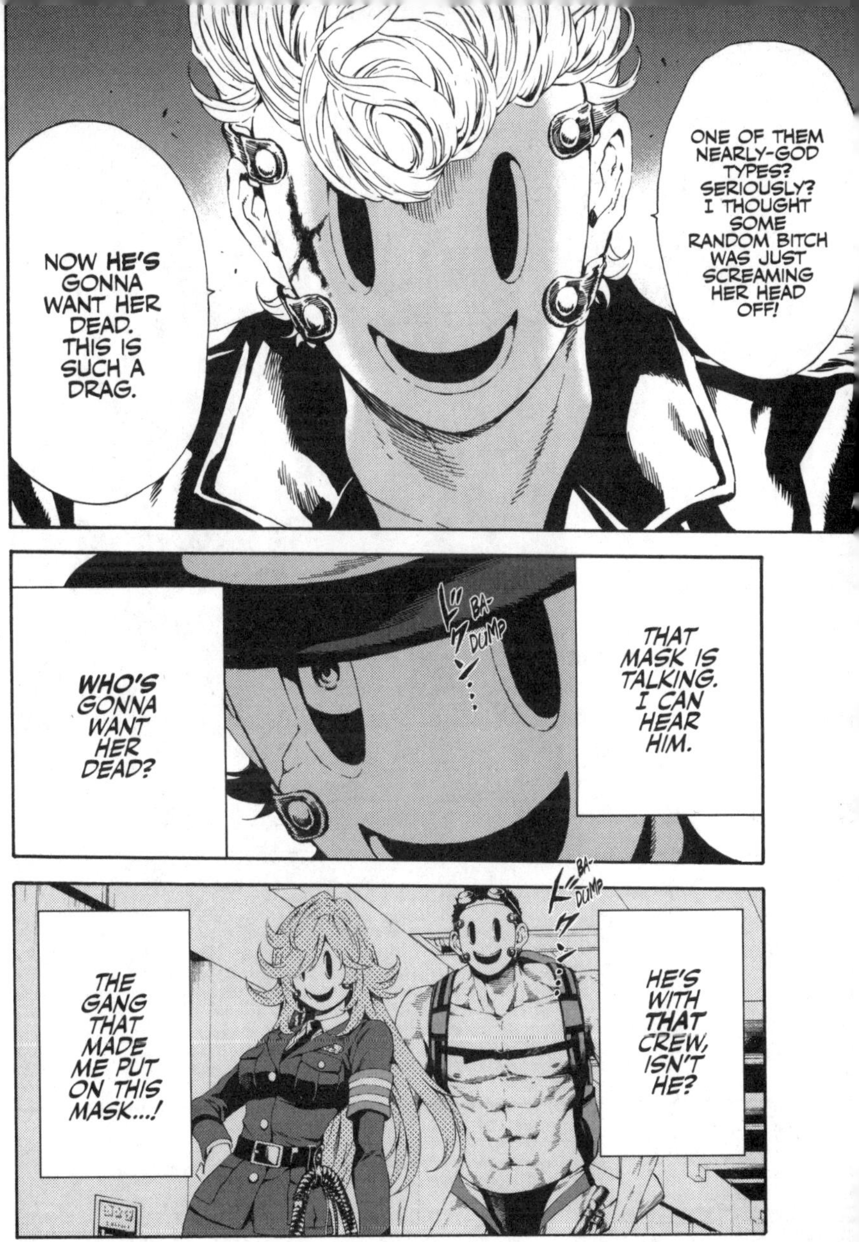
ONE OF THEM NEARLY-GOD TYPES? SERIOUSLY? I THOUGHT SOME RANDOM BITCH WAS JUST SCREAMING HER HEAD OFF!
NOW HE'S GONNA WANT HER DEAD. THIS IS SUCH A DRAG.
THAT MASK IS TALKING. I CAN HEAR HIM.
BA-DUMP
WHO'S GONNA WANT HER DEAD?
HE'S WITH THAT CREW, ISN'T HE?
BA-DUMP
THE GANG THAT MADE ME PUT ON THIS MASK...!

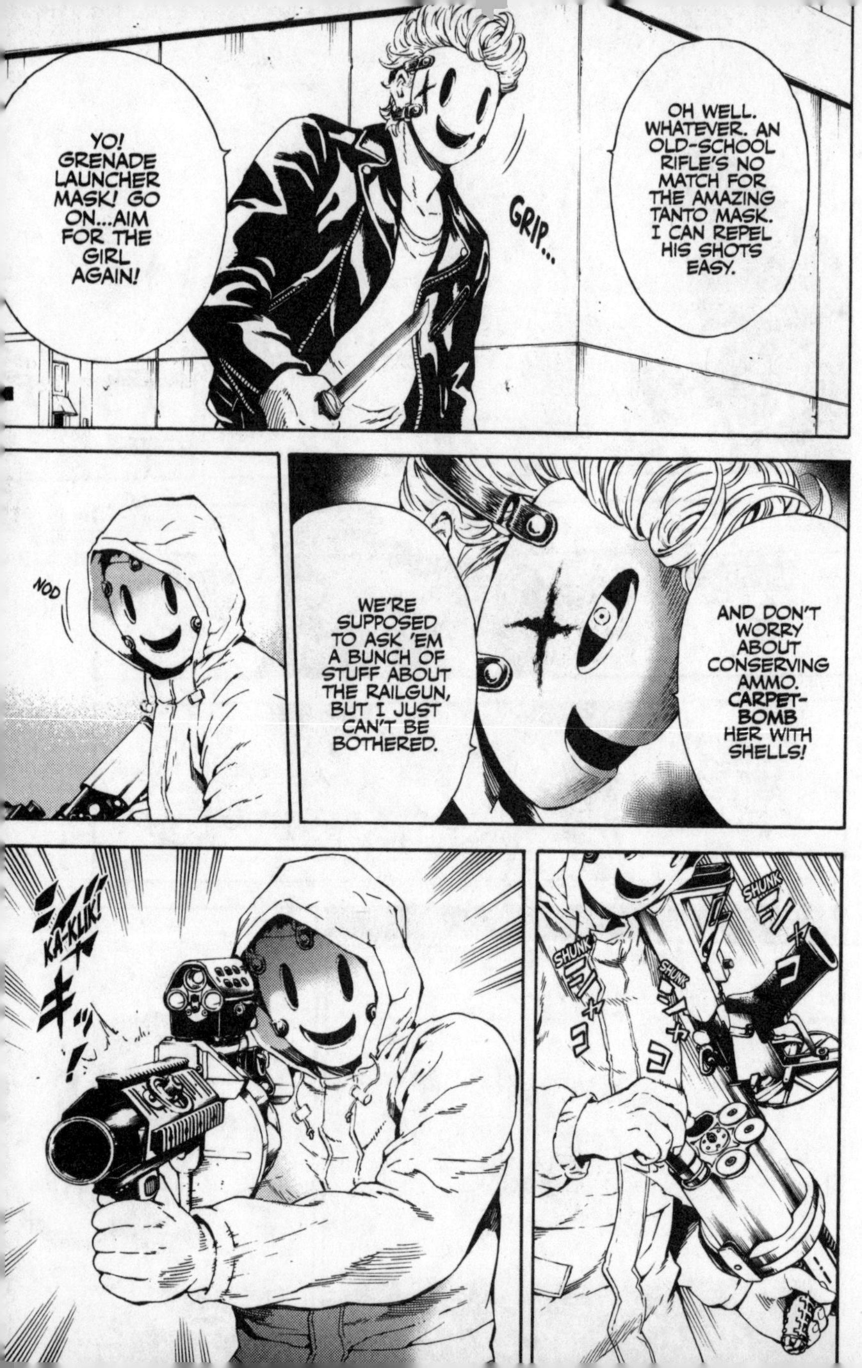
OH WELL. WHATEVER. AN OLD-SCHOOL RIFLE'S NO MATCH FOR THE AMAZING TANTO MASK. I CAN REPEL HIS SHOTS EASY.
GRIP...
YO! GRENADE LAUNCHER MASK! GO ON...AIM FOR THE GIRL AGAIN!
AND DON'T WORRY ABOUT CONSERVING AMMO. CARPET-BOMB HER WITH SHELLS!
WE'RE SUPPOSED TO ASK 'EM A BUNCH OF STUFF ABOUT THE RAILGUN, BUT I JUST CAN'T BE BOTHERED.
NOD
SHUNK
SHUNK
SHUNK
KA-KLIK!

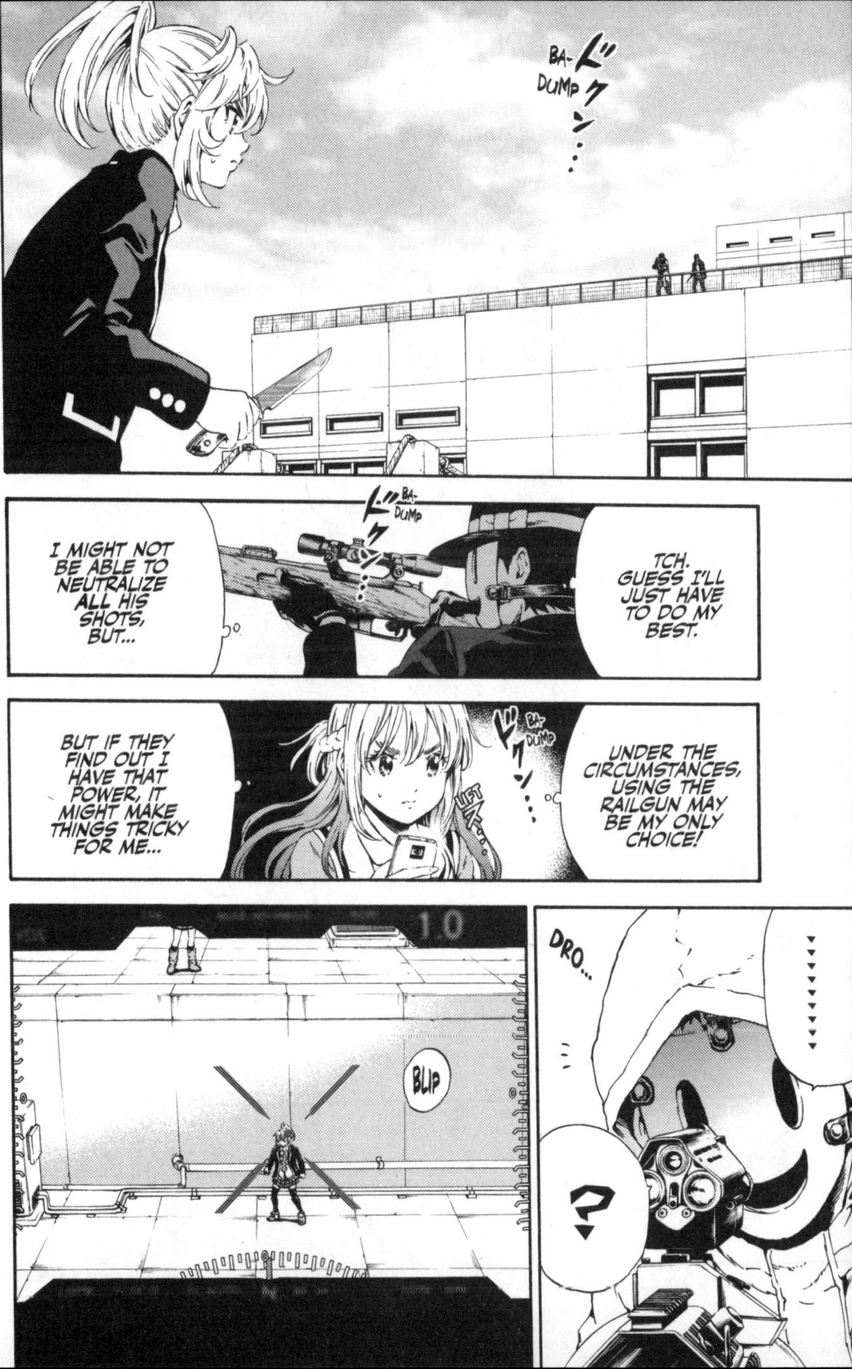
BA-DUMP
ドクン…
TCH. GUESS I'LL JUST HAVE TO DO MY BEST.
BA-DUMP
I MIGHT NOT BE ABLE TO NEUTRALIZE ALL HIS SHOTS, BUT...
UNDER THE CIRCUMSTANCES, USING THE RAILGUN MAY BE MY ONLY CHOICE!
BA-DUMP
LIFT
BUT IF THEY FIND OUT I HAVE THAT POWER, IT MIGHT MAKE THINGS TRICKY FOR ME...
DRO...
?
1.0
BLIP

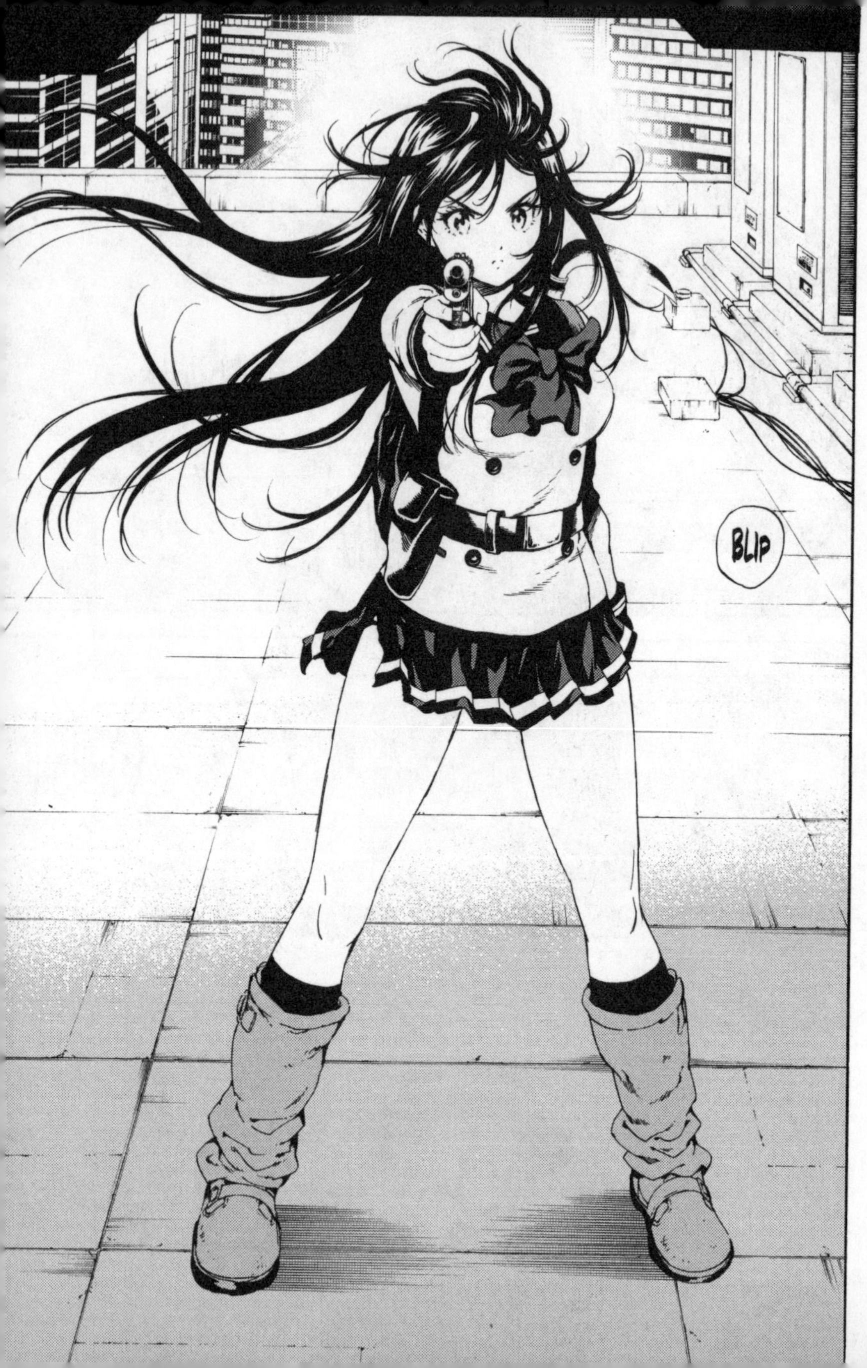
BLIP

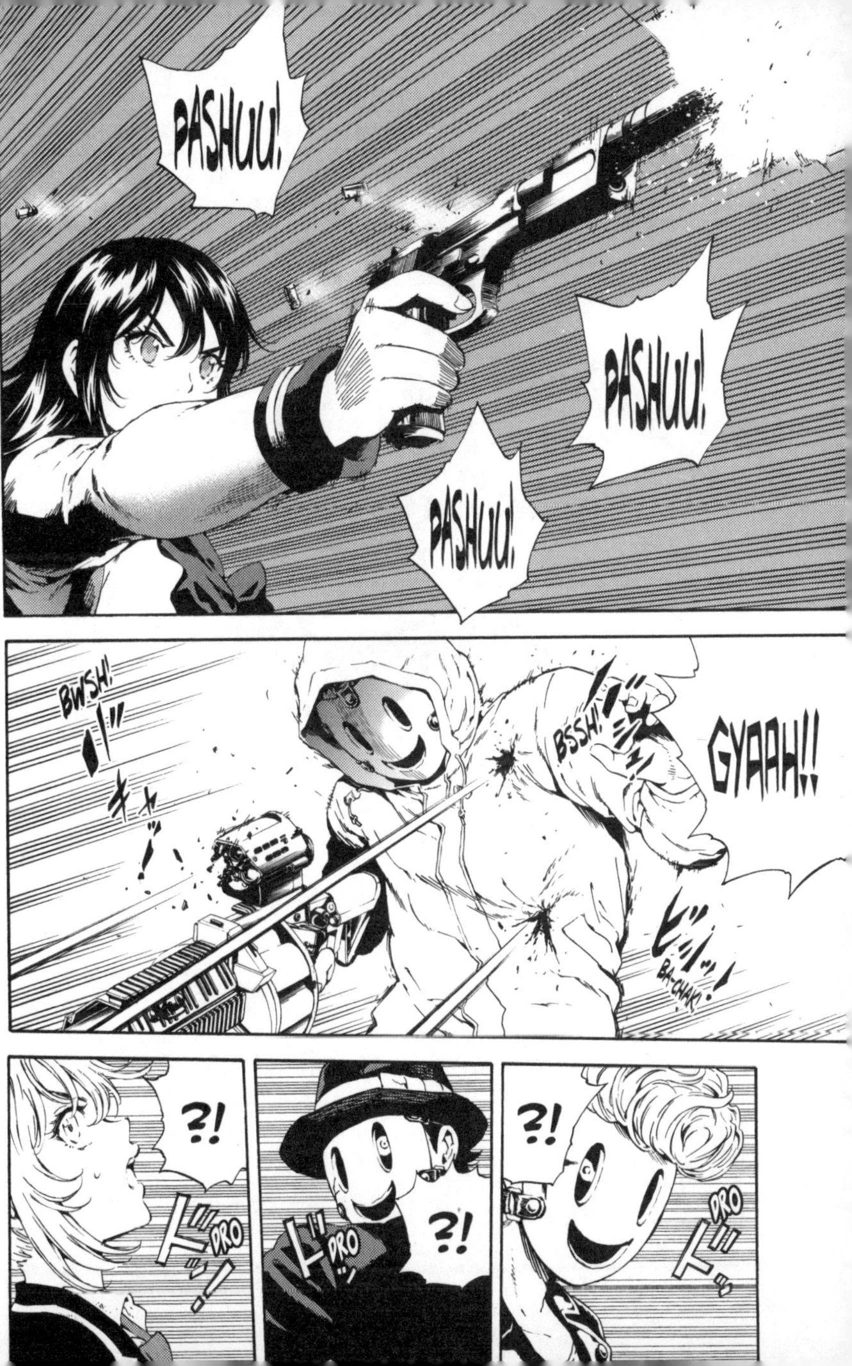
PASHUU!
PASHUU!
PASHUU!
GYAAH!!!
BSSH!
BWSH!
BA-CHAK!
?!
DRO
?!
DRO
?!
DRO

HIGH-RISE INVASION

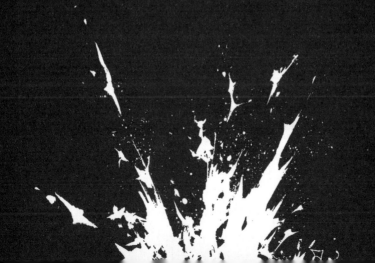

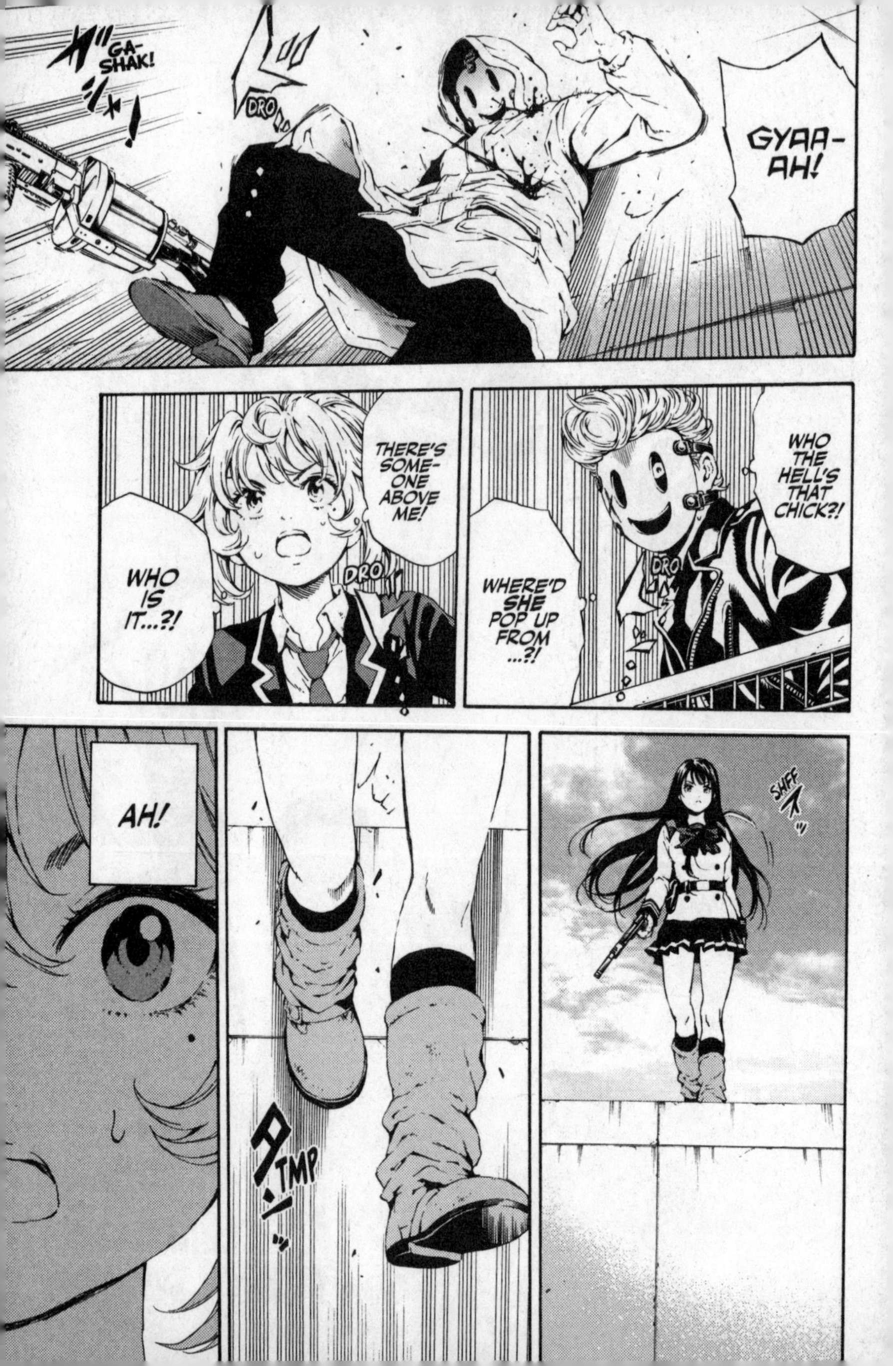
GYAA-AH!
DRO
GA-SHAK!
WHO THE HELL'S THAT CHICK?!
DRO
WHERE'D SHE POP UP FROM ...?!
THERE'S SOME-ONE ABOVE ME!
DRO
WHO IS IT...?!
SHFF
TMP
AH!

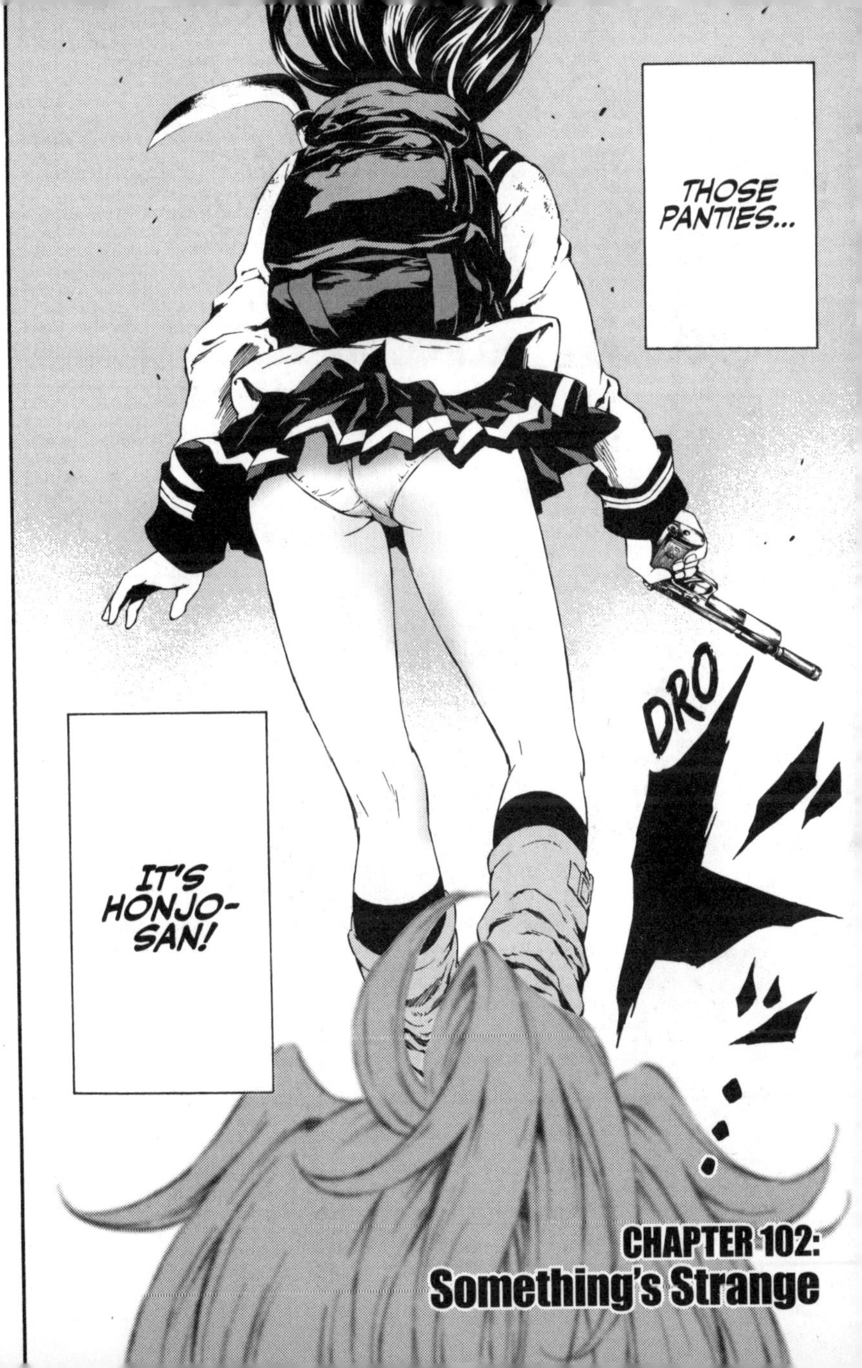
THOSE PANTIES...
DRO
IT'S HONJO-SAN!
CHAPTER 102:
Something's Strange

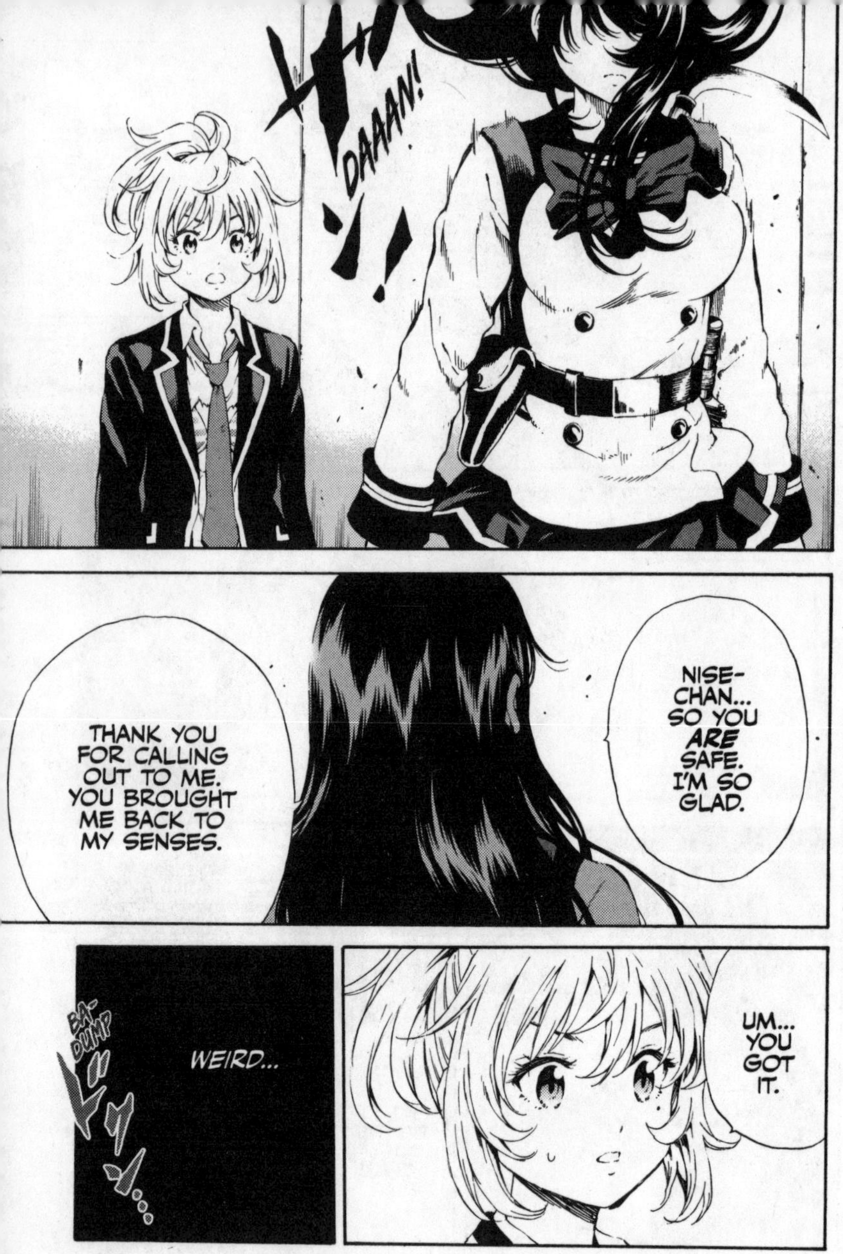
DAAAN!
NISE-CHAN... SO YOU *ARE* SAFE. I'M SO GLAD.
THANK YOU FOR CALLING OUT TO ME. YOU BROUGHT ME BACK TO MY SENSES.
UM... YOU GOT IT.
WEIRD...
BA-DUMP

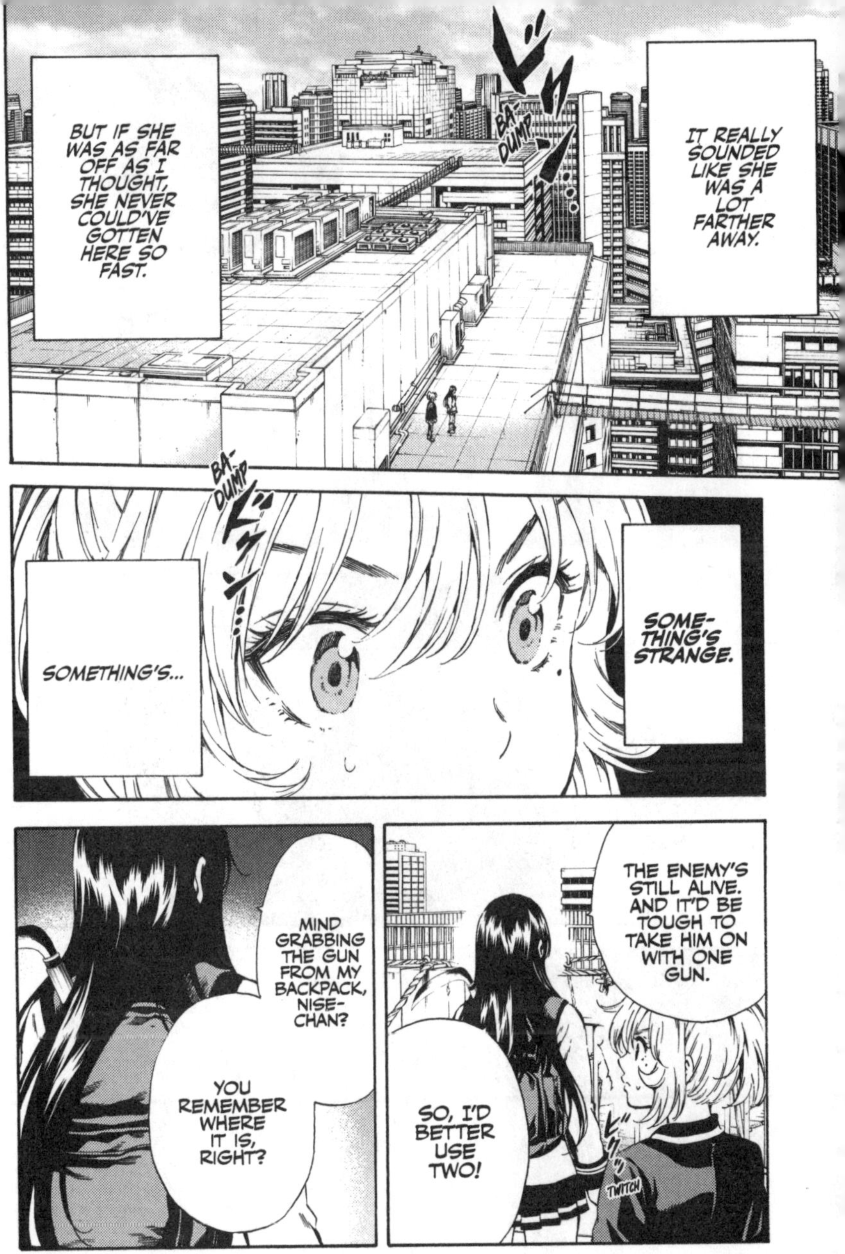
IT REALLY SOUNDED LIKE SHE WAS A LOT FARTHER AWAY.
BA-DUMP
BUT IF SHE WAS AS FAR OFF AS I THOUGHT, SHE NEVER COULD'VE GOTTEN HERE SO FAST.
SOME-THING'S STRANGE.
BA-DUMP
SOMETHING'S...
THE ENEMY'S STILL ALIVE. AND IT'D BE TOUGH TO TAKE HIM ON WITH ONE GUN.
SO, I'D BETTER USE TWO!
TWITCH
MIND GRABBING THE GUN FROM MY BACKPACK, NISE-CHAN?
YOU REMEMBER WHERE IT IS, RIGHT?

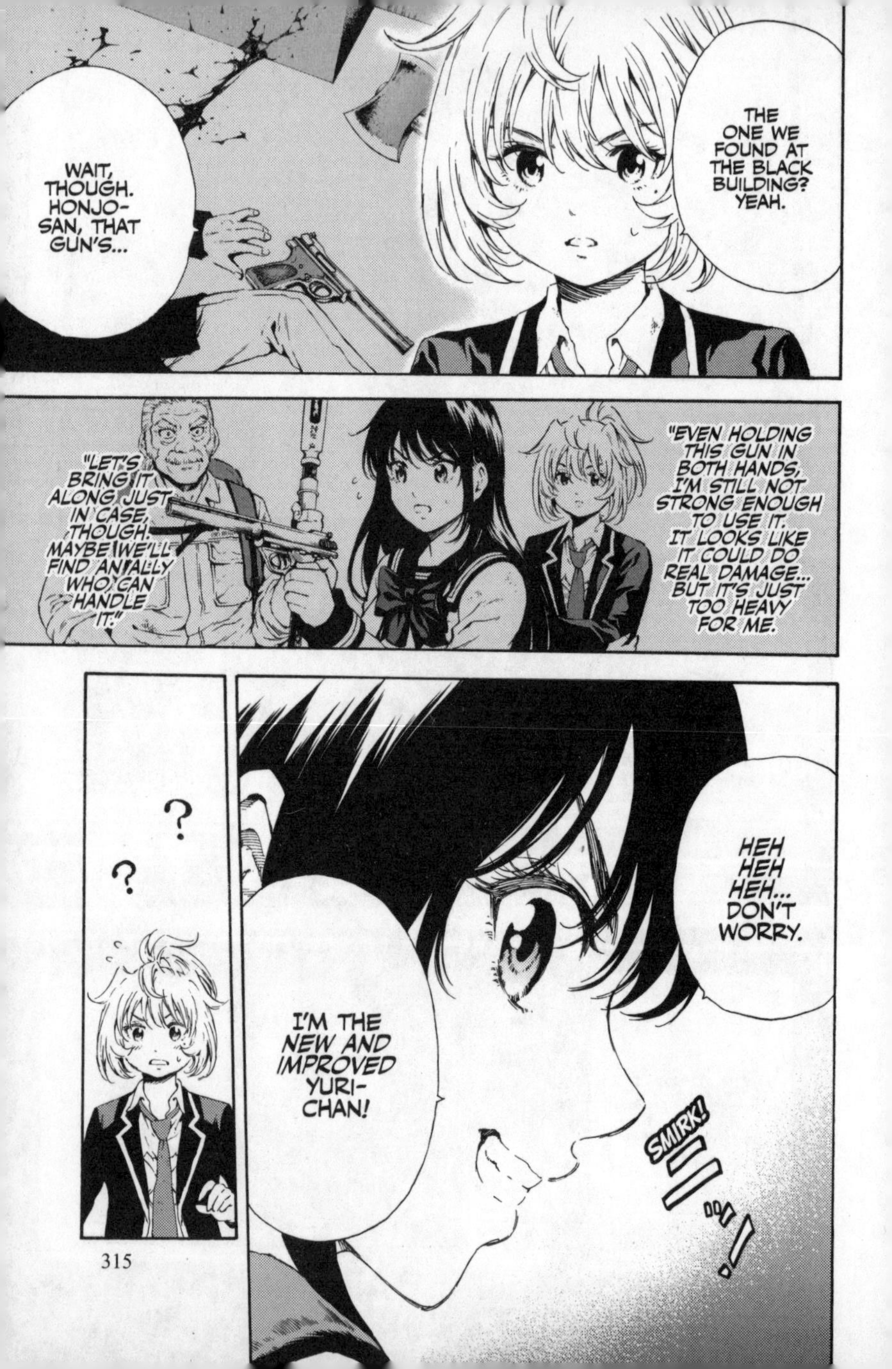

WAIT, THOUGH. HONJO-SAN, THAT GUN'S...
THE ONE WE FOUND AT THE BLACK BUILDING? YEAH.
"EVEN HOLDING THIS GUN IN BOTH HANDS, I'M STILL NOT STRONG ENOUGH TO USE IT. IT LOOKS LIKE IT COULD DO REAL DAMAGE... BUT IT'S JUST TOO HEAVY FOR ME.
"LET'S BRING IT ALONG JUST IN CASE, THOUGH. MAYBE WE'LL FIND AN ALLY WHO CAN HANDLE IT."
HEH HEH HEH... DON'T WORRY.
I'M THE NEW AND IMPROVED YURI-CHAN!
SMIRK!
? ?

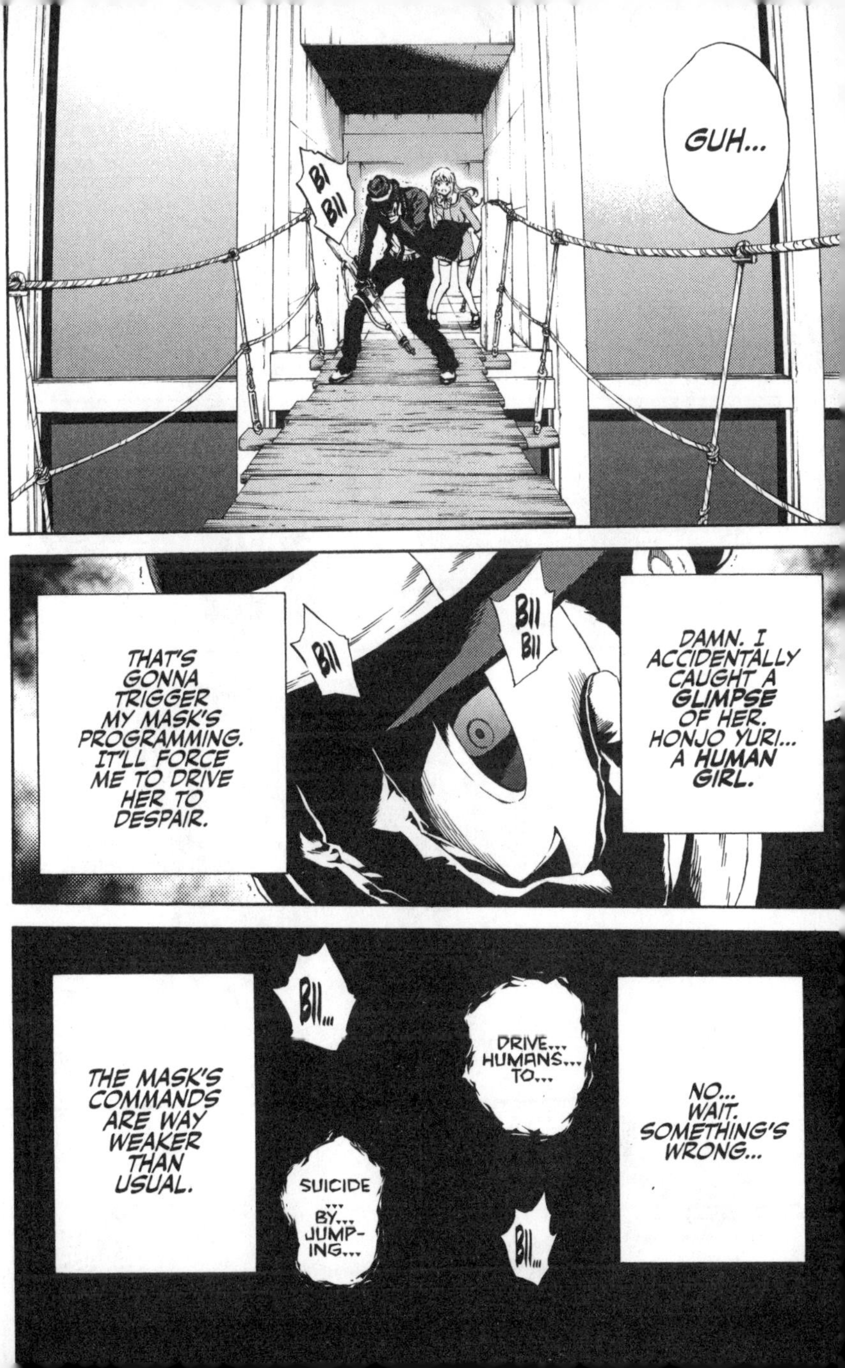
GUH...
BI BII
DAMN. I ACCIDENTALLY CAUGHT A GLIMPSE OF HER. HONJO YURI... A HUMAN GIRL.
BII BII
BII
THAT'S GONNA TRIGGER MY MASK'S PROGRAMMING. IT'LL FORCE ME TO DRIVE HER TO DESPAIR.
NO... WAIT. SOMETHING'S WRONG...
DRIVE... HUMANS... TO...
BII...
BII...
SUICIDE ... BY... JUMP-ING...
THE MASK'S COMMANDS ARE WAY WEAKER THAN USUAL.

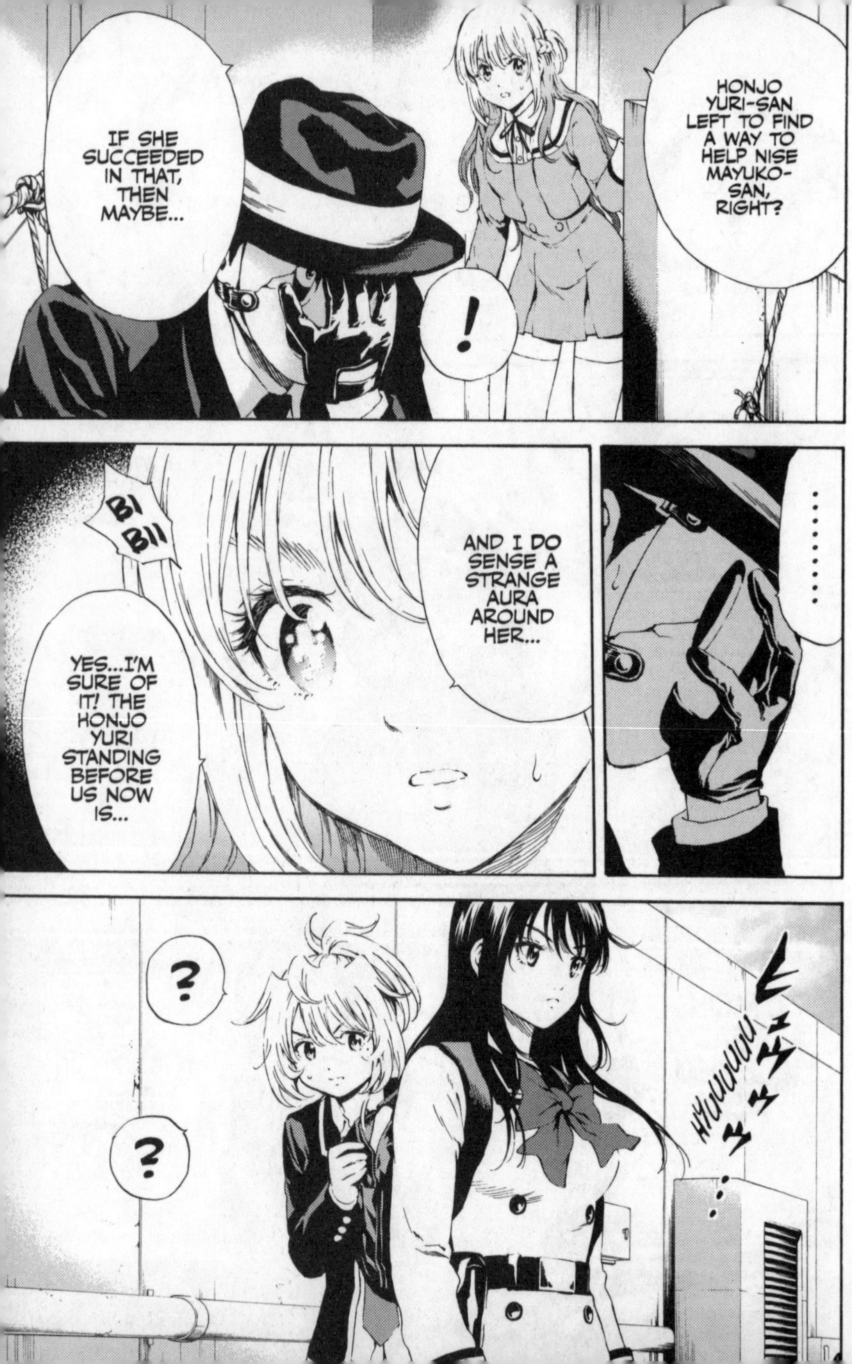
HONJO YURI-SAN LEFT TO FIND A WAY TO HELP NISE MAYUKO-SAN, RIGHT?
IF SHE SUCCEEDED IN THAT, THEN MAYBE...
!
......
AND I DO SENSE A STRANGE AURA AROUND HER...
BI BII
YES...I'M SURE OF IT! THE HONJO YURI STANDING BEFORE US NOW IS...
HYUUUUUU
?
?

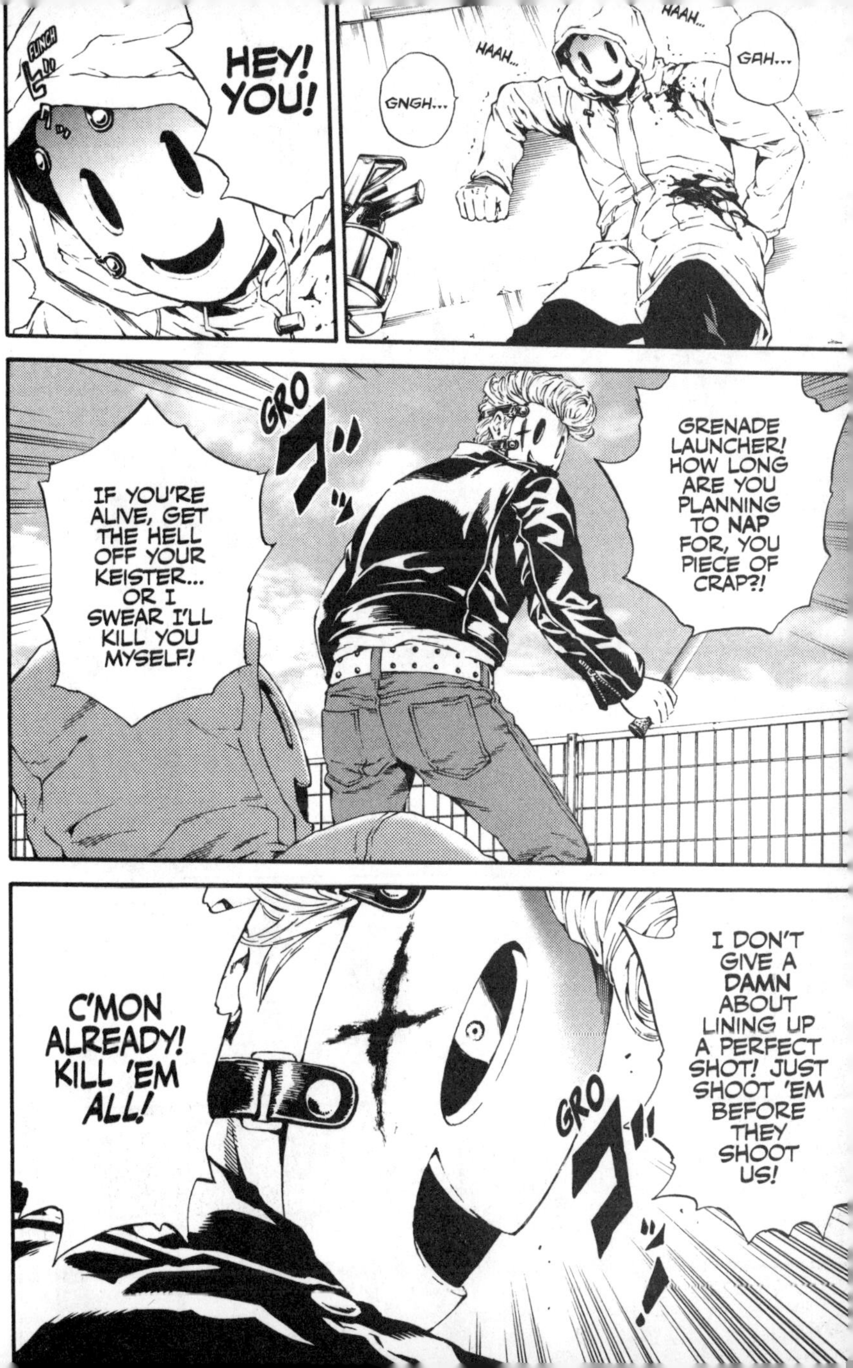
HAAH...
GAH...
HAAH...
GNGH...
FLINCH
HEY! YOU!
GRENADE LAUNCHER! HOW LONG ARE YOU PLANNING TO NAP FOR, YOU PIECE OF CRAP?!
GRO
IF YOU'RE ALIVE, GET THE HELL OFF YOUR KEISTER... OR I SWEAR I'LL KILL YOU MYSELF!
I DON'T GIVE A DAMN ABOUT LINING UP A PERFECT SHOT! JUST SHOOT 'EM BEFORE THEY SHOOT US!
GRO
C'MON ALREADY! KILL 'EM ALL!

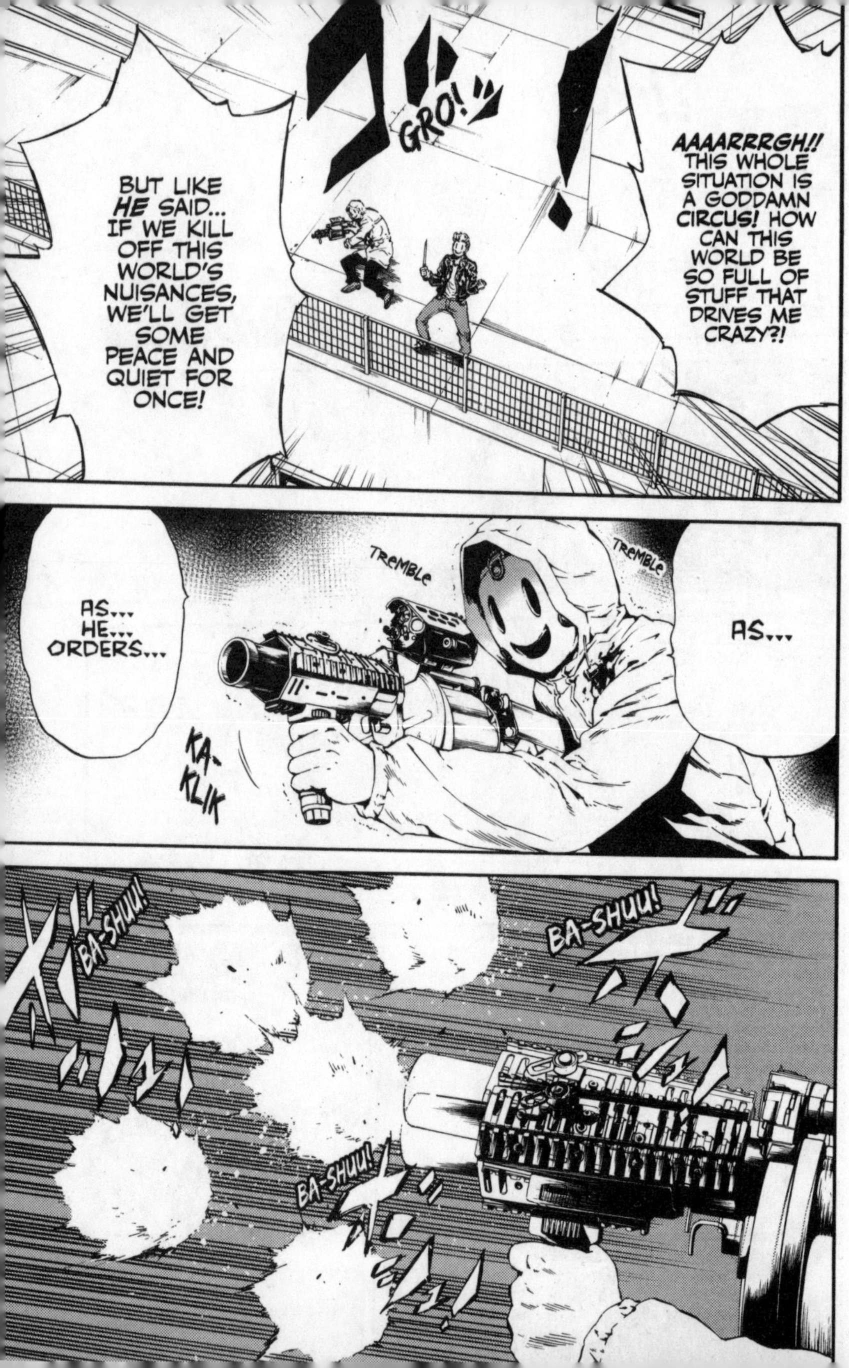
AAAARRRGH!! THIS WHOLE SITUATION IS A GODDAMN CIRCUS! HOW CAN THIS WORLD BE SO FULL OF STUFF THAT DRIVES ME CRAZY?!
GRO!
BUT LIKE HE SAID... IF WE KILL OFF THIS WORLD'S NUISANCES, WE'LL GET SOME PEACE AND QUIET FOR ONCE!
AS...
TREMBLE
TREMBLE
AS... HE... ORDERS...
KA-KLIK
BA-SHUU!
BA-SHUU!
BA-SHUU!

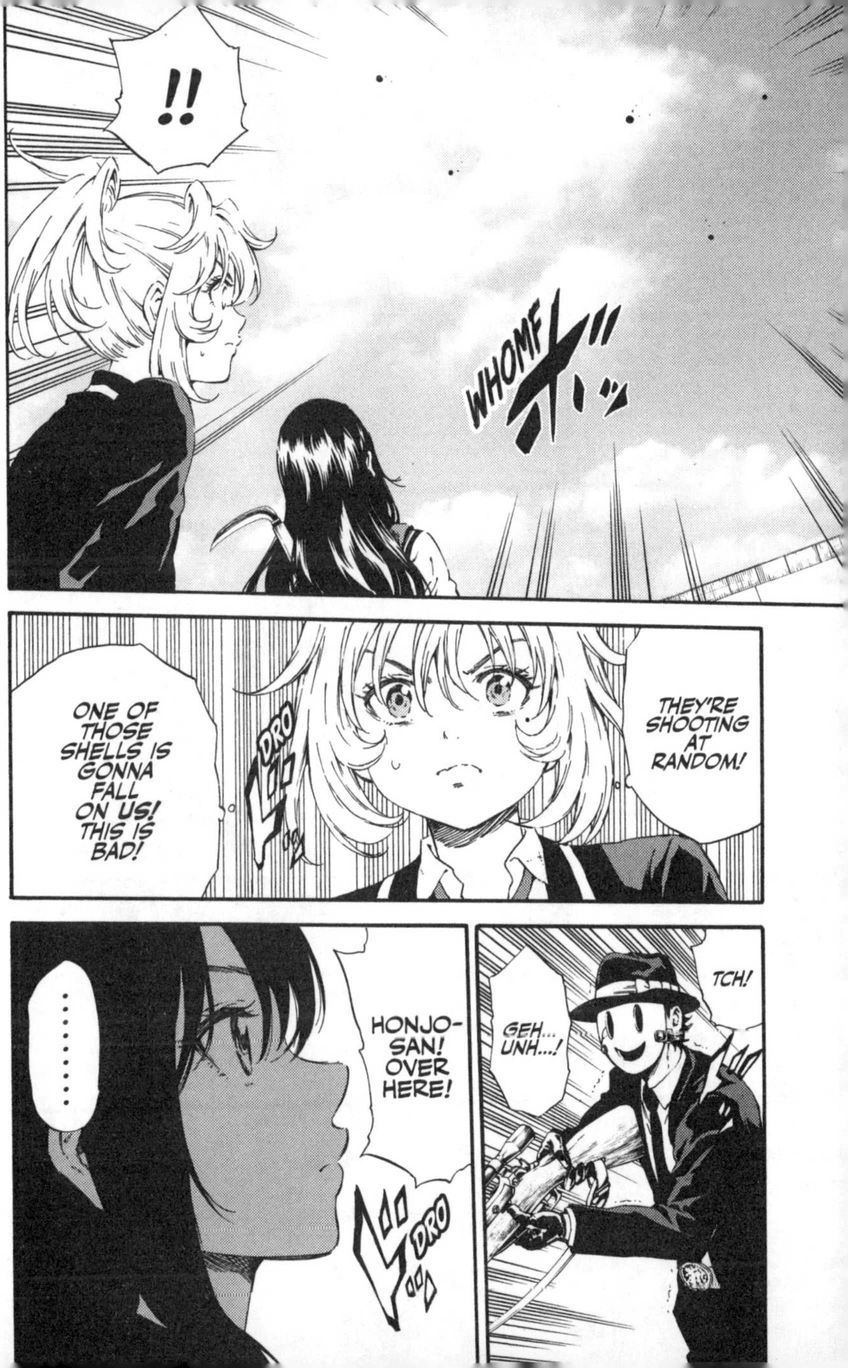
!!
WHOMF
THEY'RE SHOOTING AT RANDOM!
DRO
ONE OF THOSE SHELLS IS GONNA FALL ON US! THIS IS BAD!
TCH!
GEH... UNH...!
HONJO-SAN! OVER HERE!
DRO
....

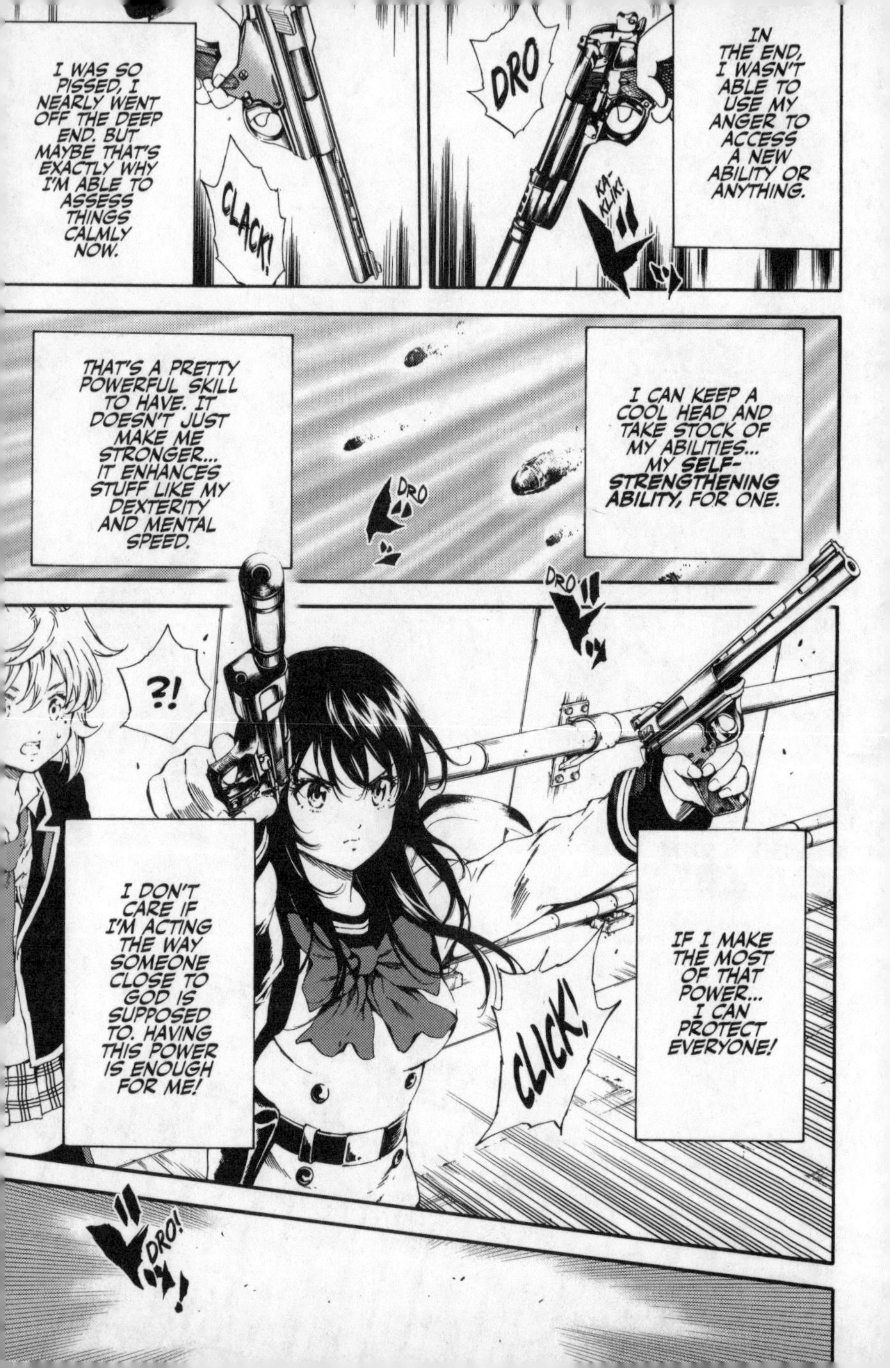
DRO
IN THE END, I WASN'T ABLE TO USE MY ANGER TO ACCESS A NEW ABILITY OR ANYTHING.
KA-KLIK!!
I WAS SO PISSED, I NEARLY WENT OFF THE DEEP END. BUT MAYBE THAT'S EXACTLY WHY I'M ABLE TO ASSESS THINGS CALMLY NOW.
CLACK!
I CAN KEEP A COOL HEAD AND TAKE STOCK OF MY ABILITIES... MY SELF-STRENGTHENING ABILITY, FOR ONE.
THAT'S A PRETTY POWERFUL SKILL TO HAVE. IT DOESN'T JUST MAKE ME STRONGER... IT ENHANCES STUFF LIKE MY DEXTERITY AND MENTAL SPEED.
DRO
DRO!!
IF I MAKE THE MOST OF THAT POWER... I CAN PROTECT EVERYONE!
CLICK!
?!
I DON'T CARE IF I'M ACTING THE WAY SOMEONE CLOSE TO GOD IS SUPPOSED TO. HAVING THIS POWER IS ENOUGH FOR ME!
DRO!!

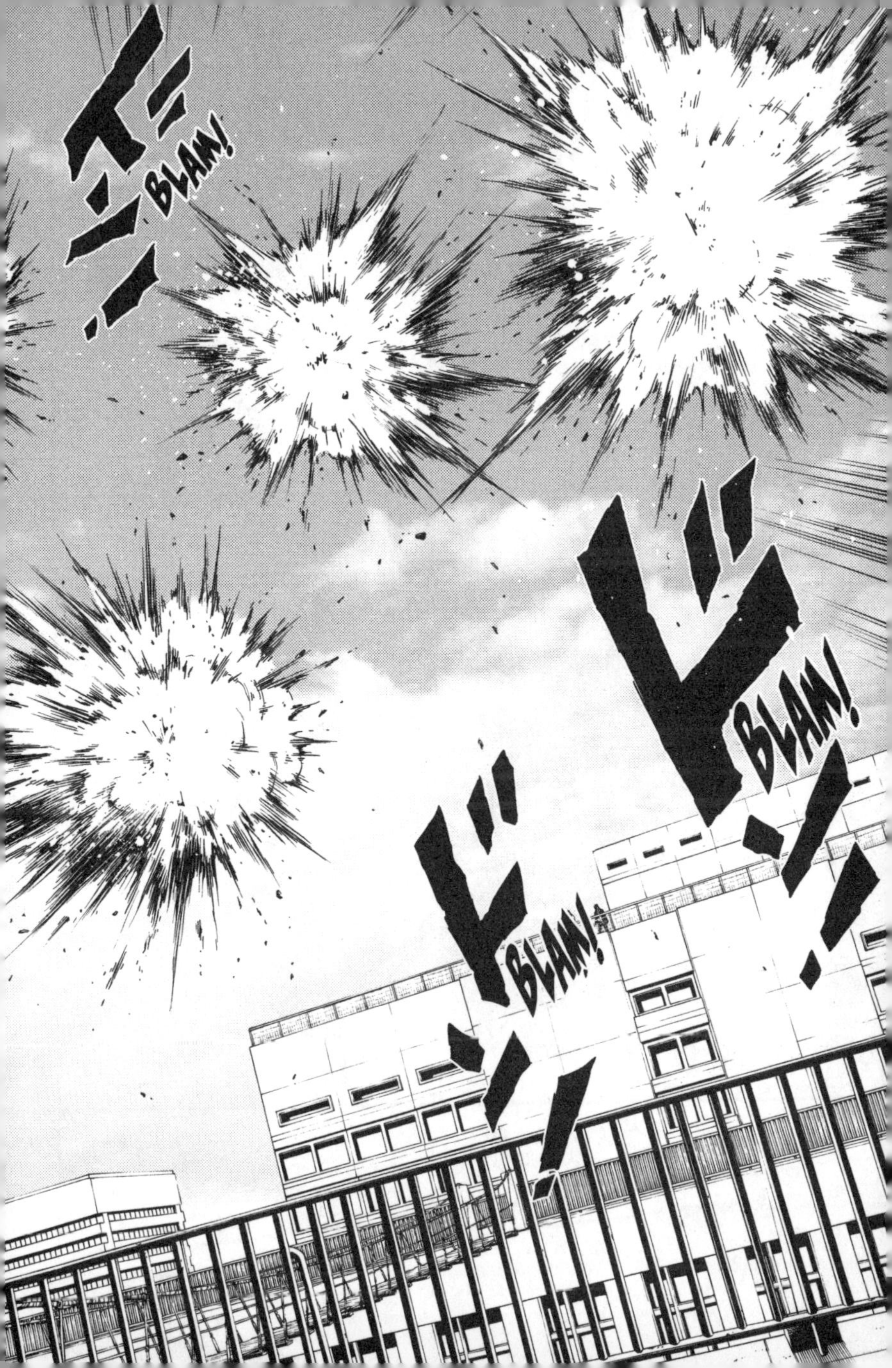
BLAM!
BLAM!
BLAM!

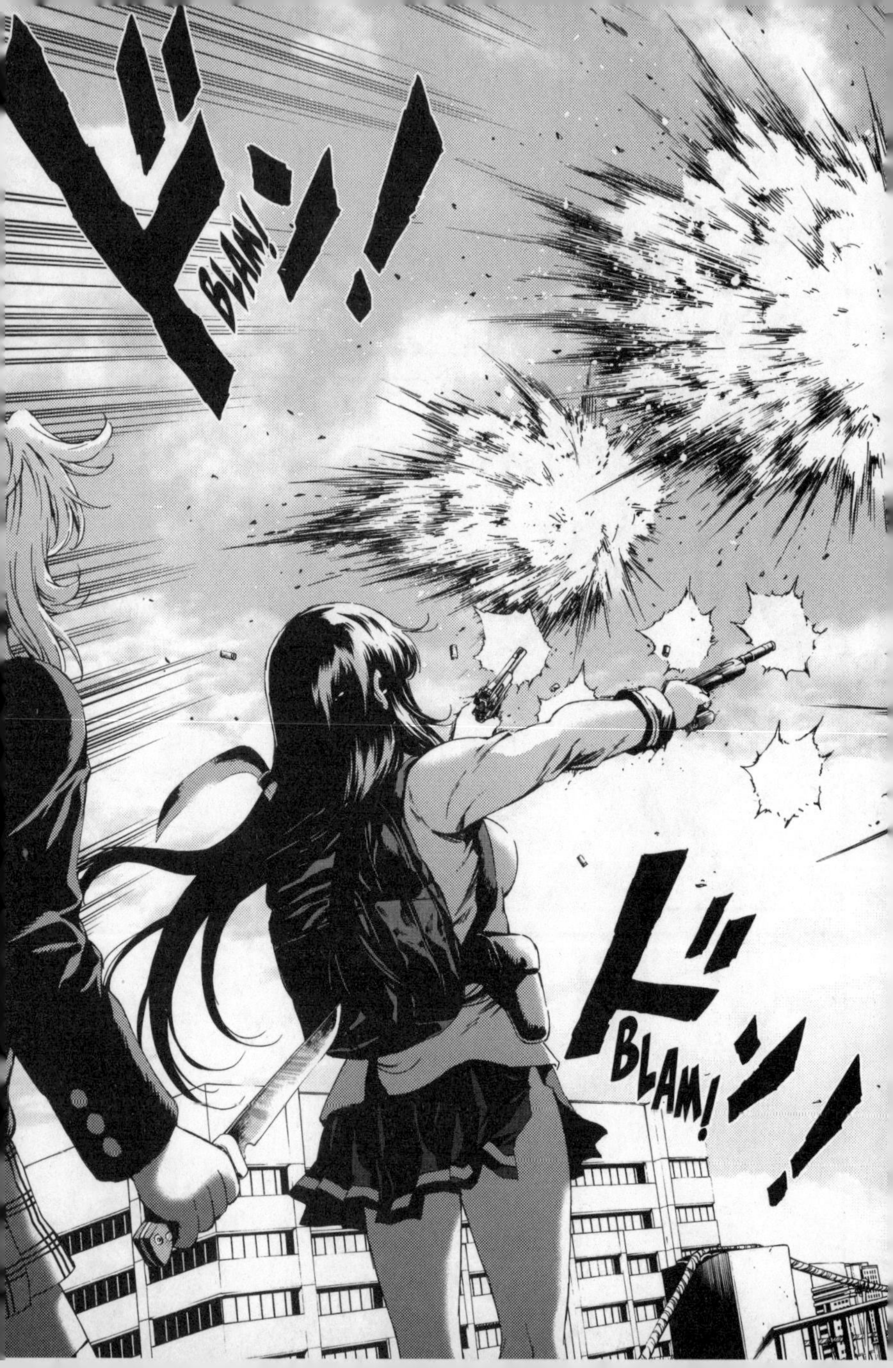
ドン!!
BLAM!
ドン!!
BLAM!

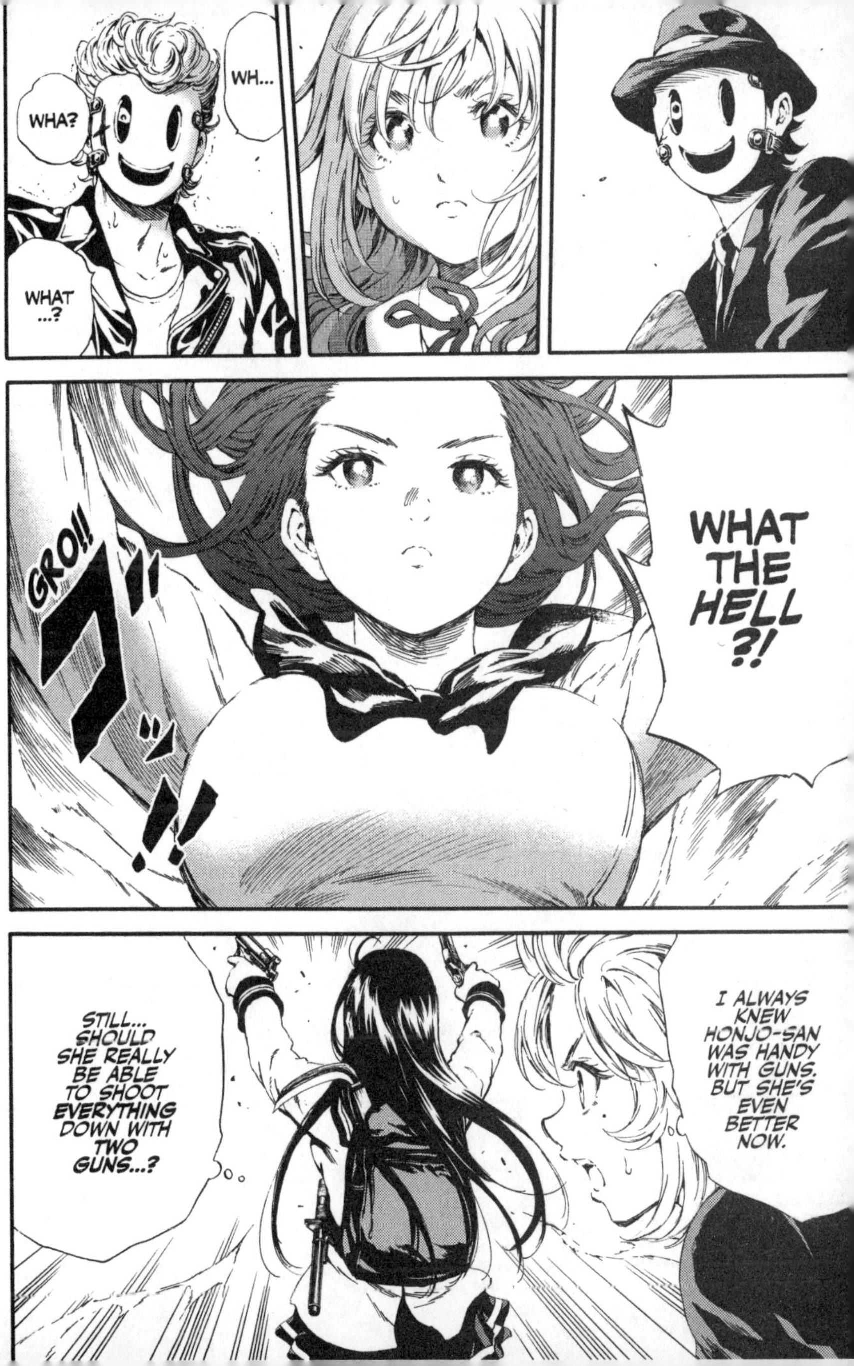
WH...
WHA?
WHAT ...?
WHAT THE HELL ?!
GRO!!
I ALWAYS KNEW HONJO-SAN WAS HANDY WITH GUNS. BUT SHE'S EVEN BETTER NOW.
STILL... SHOULD SHE REALLY BE ABLE TO SHOOT EVERYTHING DOWN WITH TWO GUNS...?

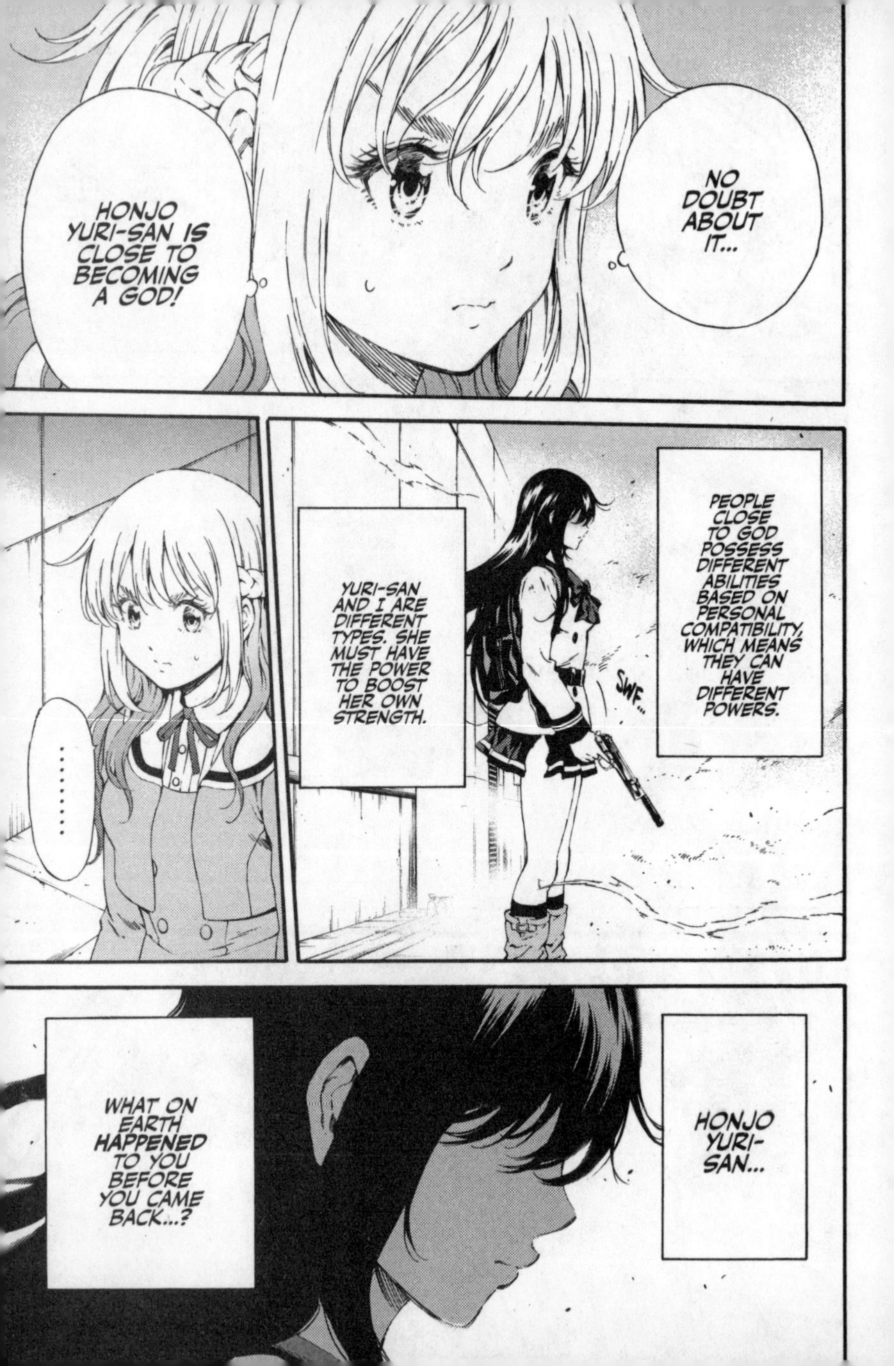
NO DOUBT ABOUT IT...
HONJO YURI-SAN IS CLOSE TO BECOMING A GOD!
PEOPLE CLOSE TO GOD POSSESS DIFFERENT ABILITIES BASED ON PERSONAL COMPATIBILITY, WHICH MEANS THEY CAN HAVE DIFFERENT POWERS.
SWF...
YURI-SAN AND I ARE DIFFERENT TYPES. SHE MUST HAVE THE POWER TO BOOST HER OWN STRENGTH.
......
HONJO YURI-SAN...
WHAT ON EARTH HAPPENED TO YOU BEFORE YOU CAME BACK...?

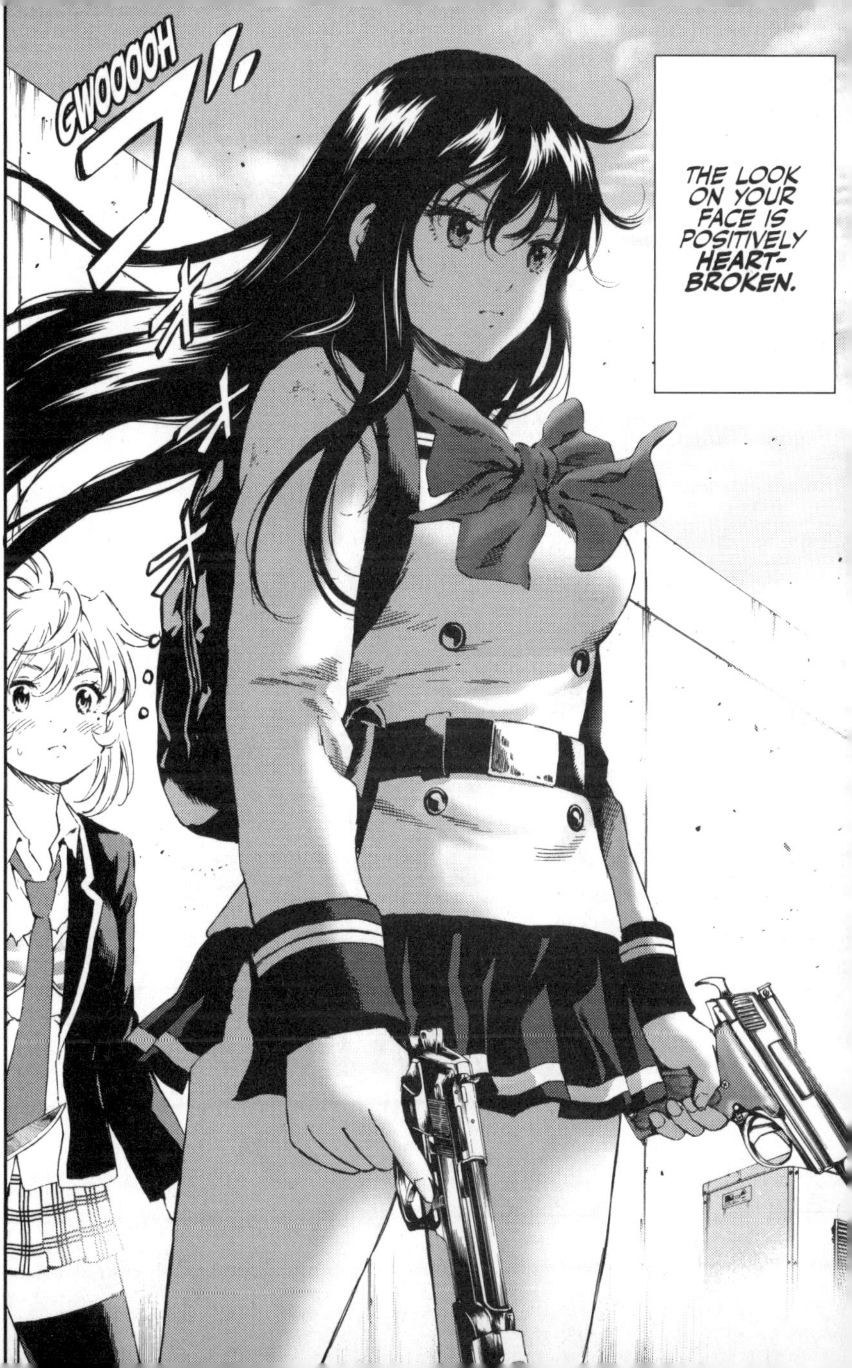
THE LOOK ON YOUR FACE IS POSITIVELY HEART-BROKEN.
GWOOOOH

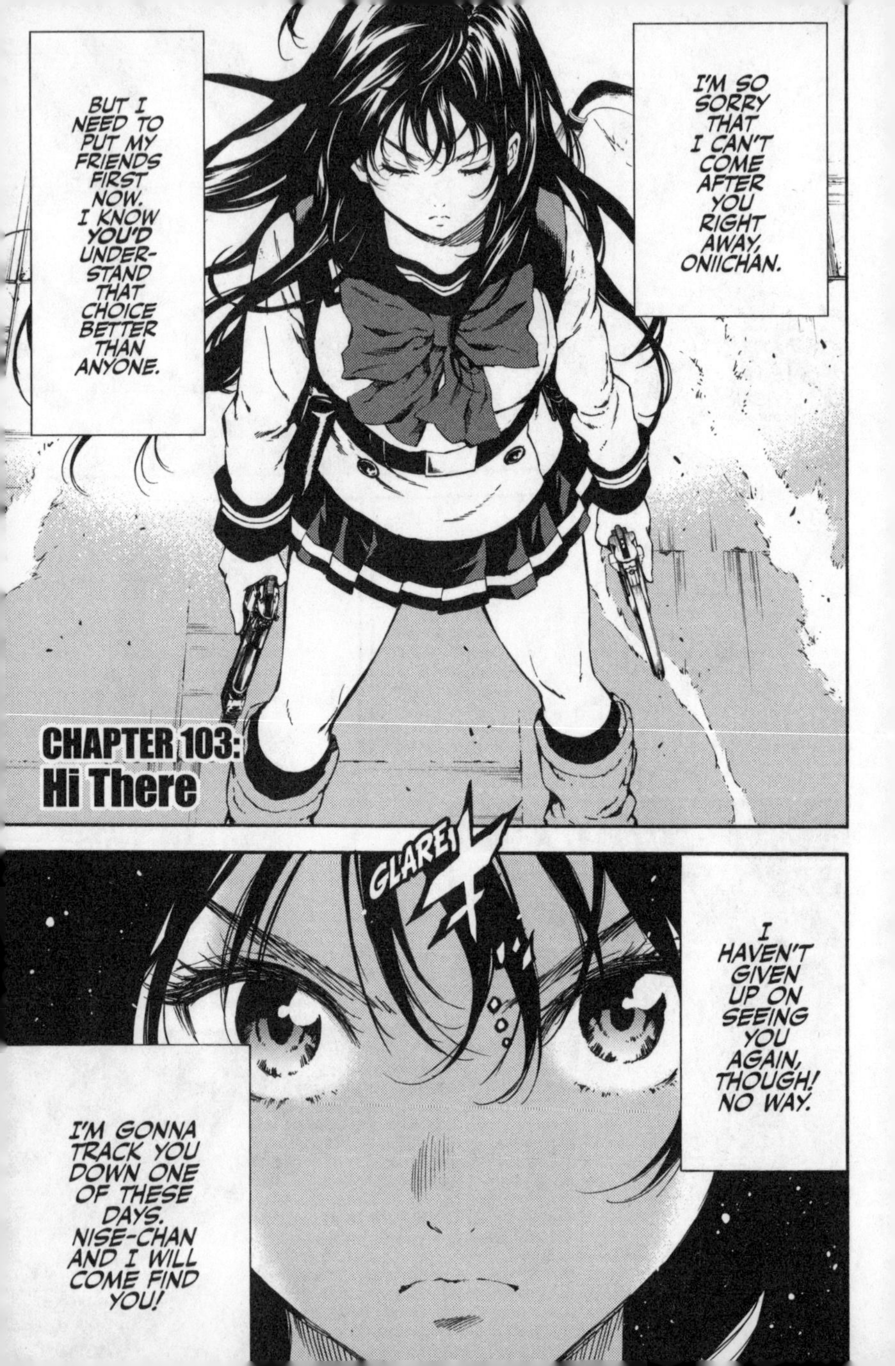
I'M SO SORRY THAT I CAN'T COME AFTER YOU RIGHT AWAY, ONIICHAN.
BUT I NEED TO PUT MY FRIENDS FIRST NOW. I KNOW YOU'D UNDER-STAND THAT CHOICE BETTER THAN ANYONE.
CHAPTER 103:
Hi There
I HAVEN'T GIVEN UP ON SEEING YOU AGAIN, THOUGH! NO WAY.
GLARE
I'M GONNA TRACK YOU DOWN ONE OF THESE DAYS. NISE-CHAN AND I WILL COME FIND YOU!

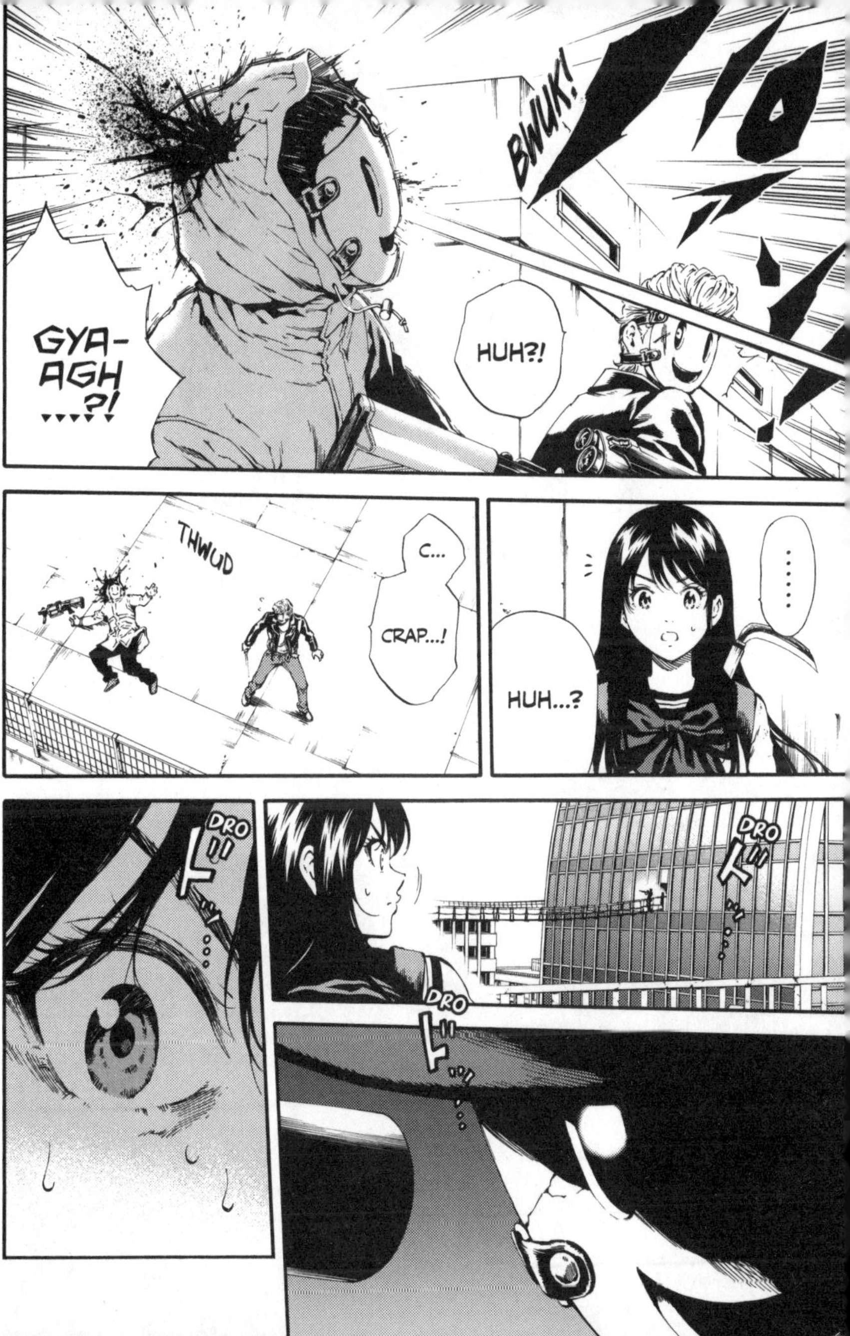
BWUK!
HUH?!
GYA-AGH.....?!
......
HUH...?
C... CRAP...!
THWUD
DRO
DRO
DRO

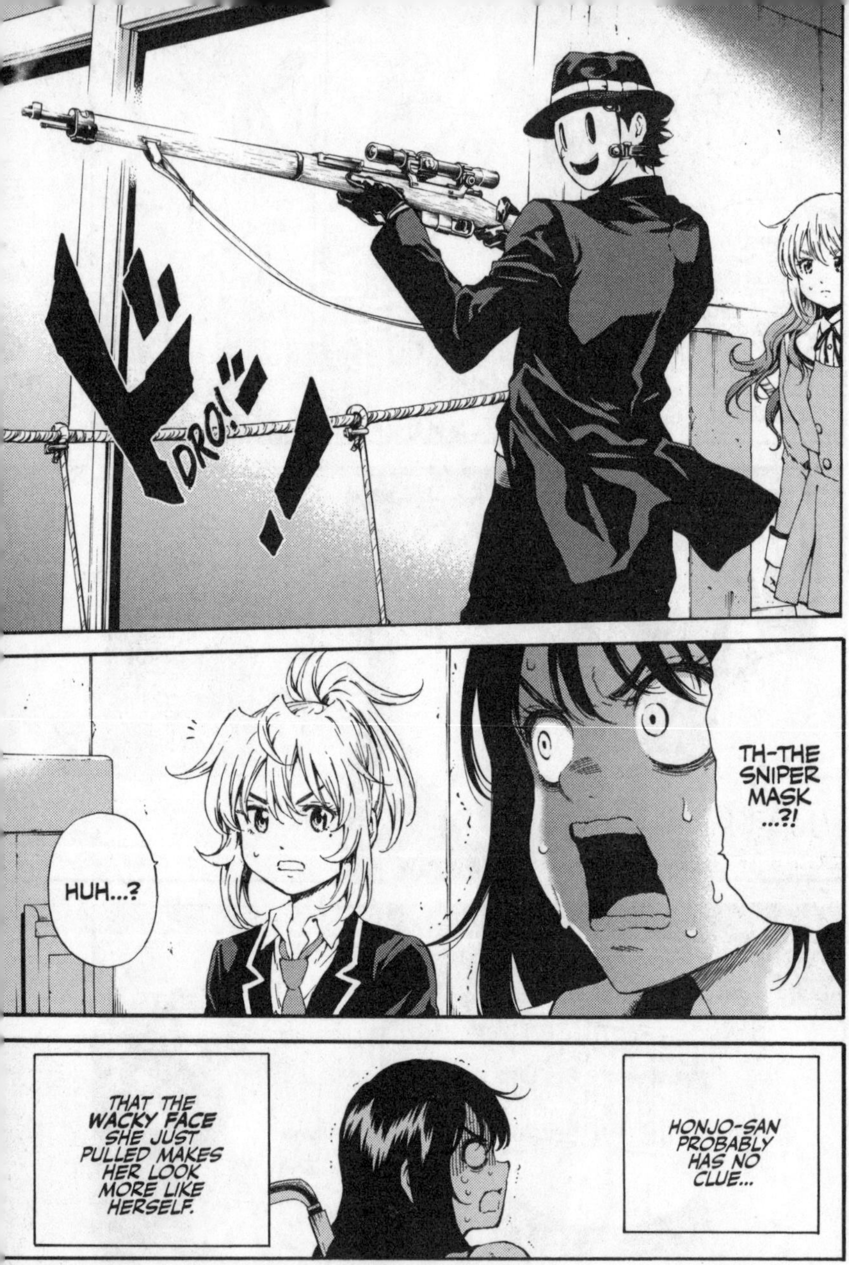
DRO!
TH-THE SNIPER MASK ...?!
HUH...?
HONJO-SAN PROBABLY HAS NO CLUE...
THAT THE WACKY FACE SHE JUST PULLED MAKES HER LOOK MORE LIKE HERSELF.

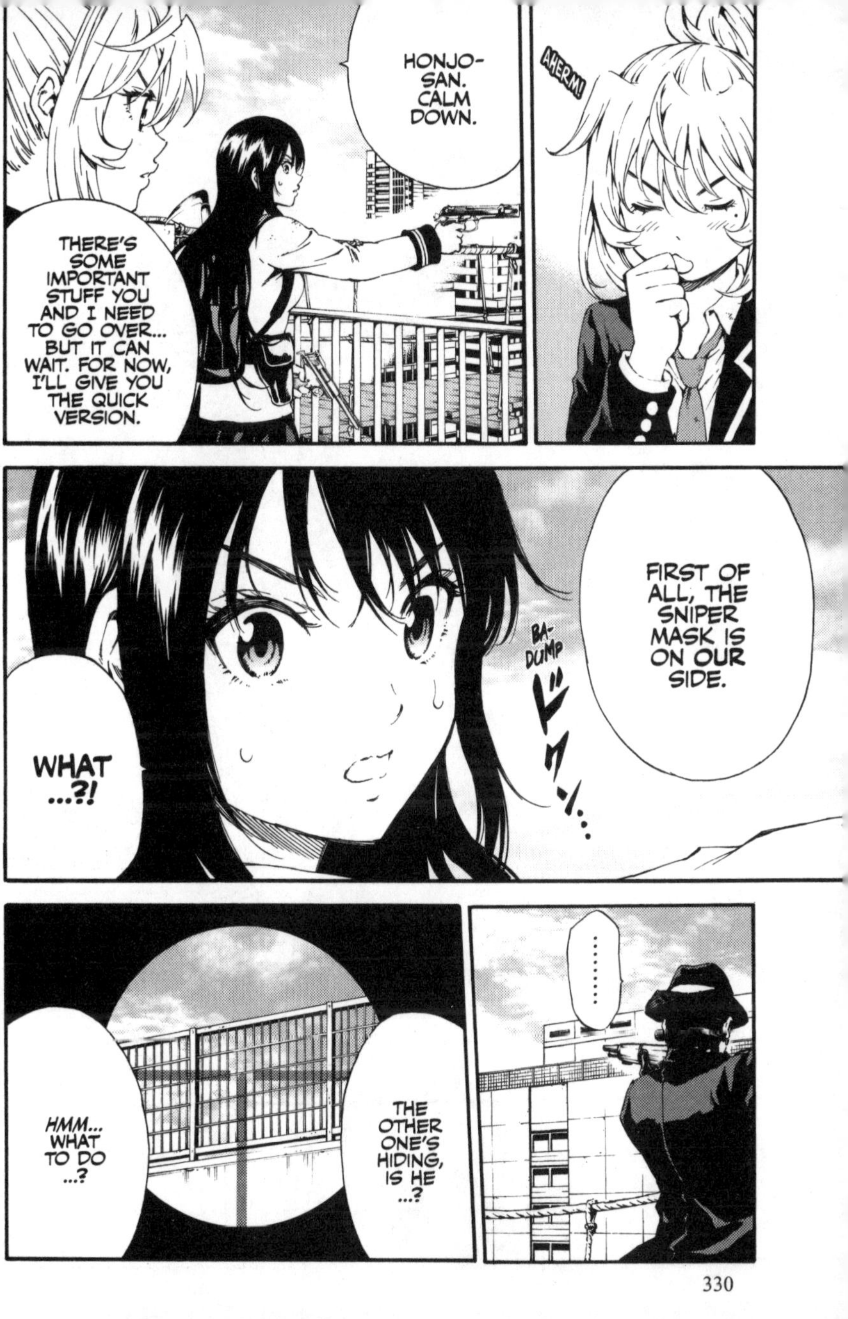
AHERM!
HONJO-SAN. CALM DOWN.
THERE'S SOME IMPORTANT STUFF YOU AND I NEED TO GO OVER... BUT IT CAN WAIT. FOR NOW, I'LL GIVE YOU THE QUICK VERSION.
FIRST OF ALL, THE SNIPER MASK IS ON OUR SIDE.
BA-DUMP
WHAT ...?!
....
THE OTHER ONE'S HIDING, IS HE ...?
HMM... WHAT TO DO ...?

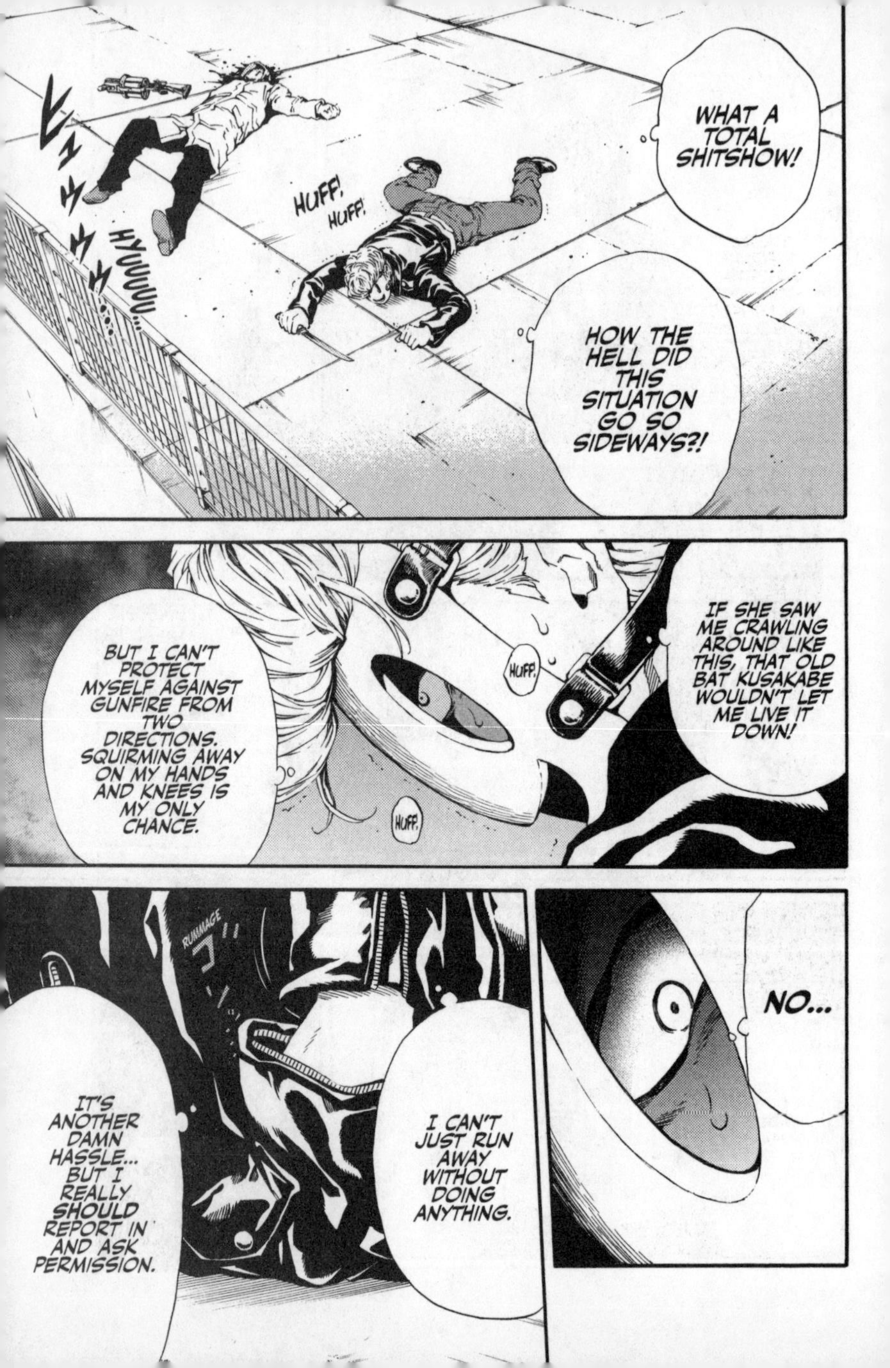
WHAT A TOTAL SHITSHOW!
HOW THE HELL DID THIS SITUATION GO SO SIDEWAYS?!
HUFF! HUFF!
HYUUUUU...
IF SHE SAW ME CRAWLING AROUND LIKE THIS, THAT OLD BAT KUSAKABE WOULDN'T LET ME LIVE IT DOWN!
HUFF!
BUT I CAN'T PROTECT MYSELF AGAINST GUNFIRE FROM TWO DIRECTIONS. SQUIRMING AWAY ON MY HANDS AND KNEES IS MY ONLY CHANCE.
HUFF!
NO...
I CAN'T JUST RUN AWAY WITHOUT DOING ANYTHING.
RUMMAGE
IT'S ANOTHER DAMN HASSLE... BUT I REALLY SHOULD REPORT IN AND ASK PERMISSION.

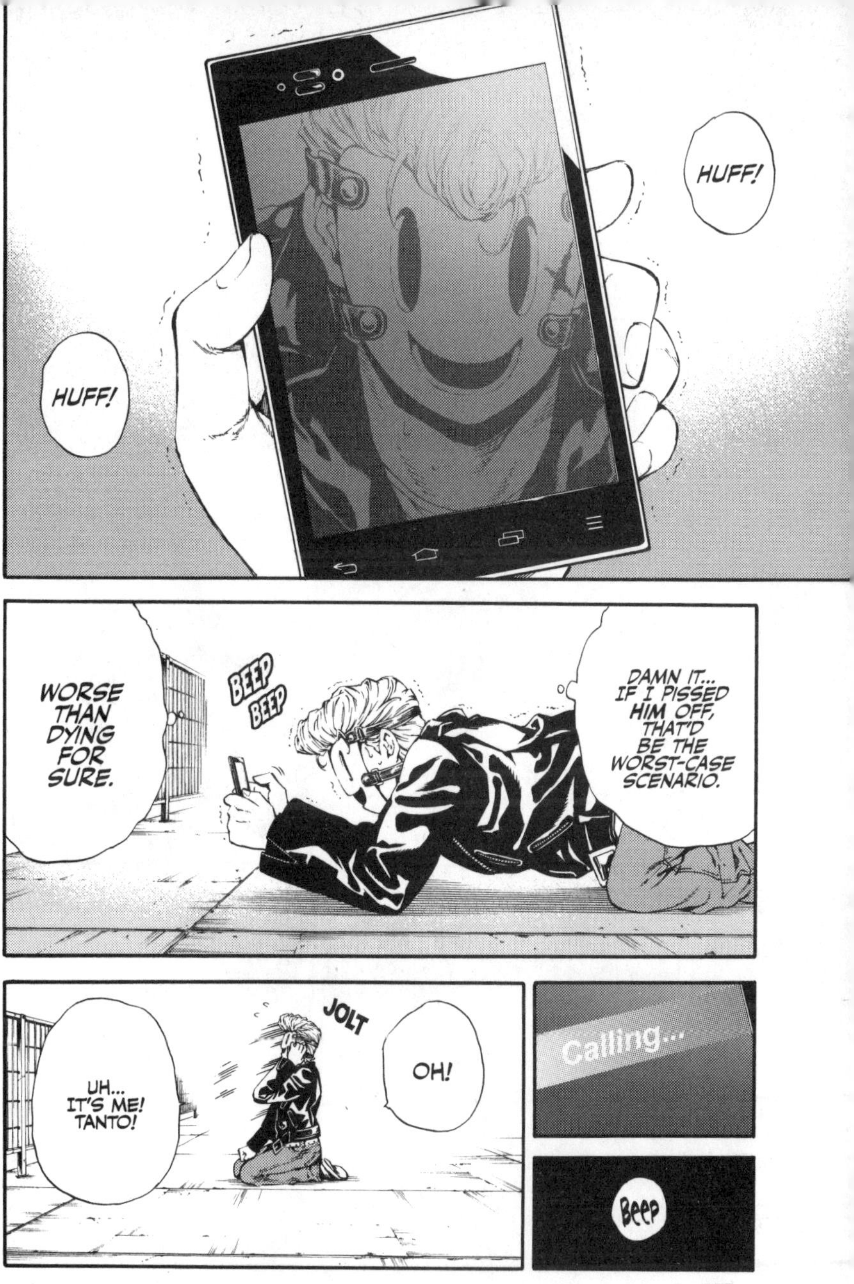
HUFF!
HUFF!
DAMN IT... IF I PISSED HIM OFF, THAT'D BE THE WORST-CASE SCENARIO.
BEEP BEEP
WORSE THAN DYING FOR SURE.
Calling...
Beep
OH!
JOLT
UH... IT'S ME! TANTO!

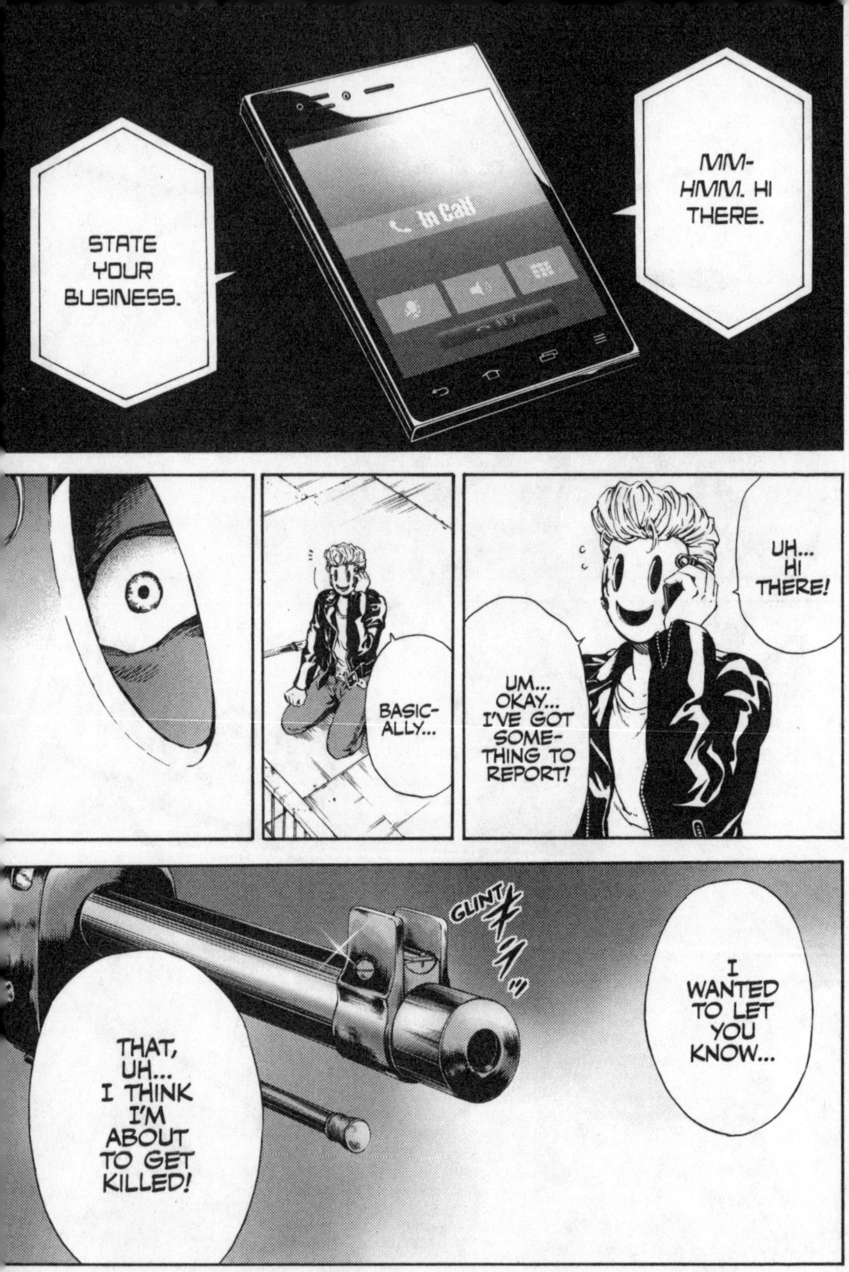
MM-HMM. HI THERE.
In Call
STATE YOUR BUSINESS.
UH... HI THERE!
UM... OKAY... I'VE GOT SOMETHING TO REPORT!
BASIC-ALLY...
I WANTED TO LET YOU KNOW...
GLINT
THAT, UH... I THINK I'M ABOUT TO GET KILLED!

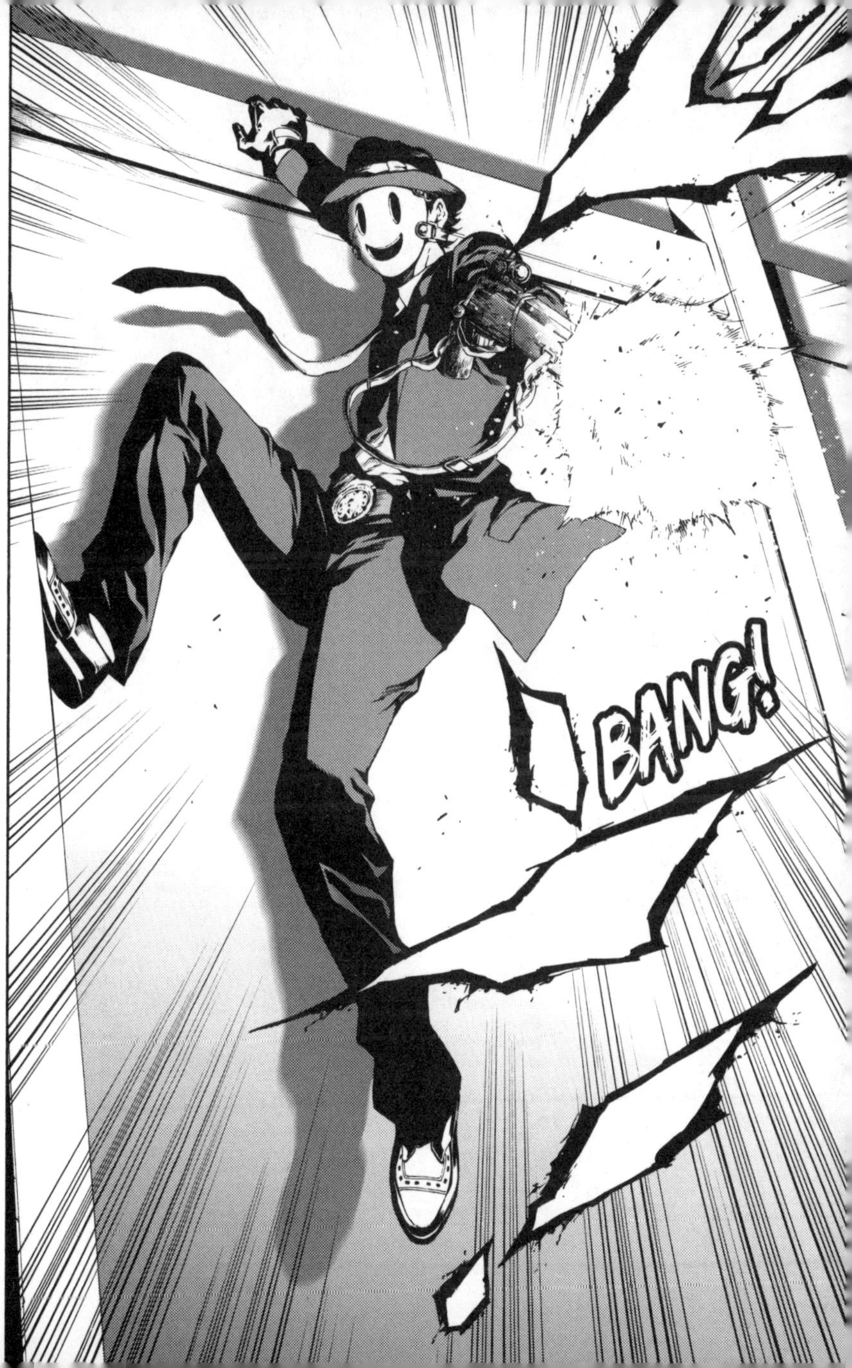
BANG!

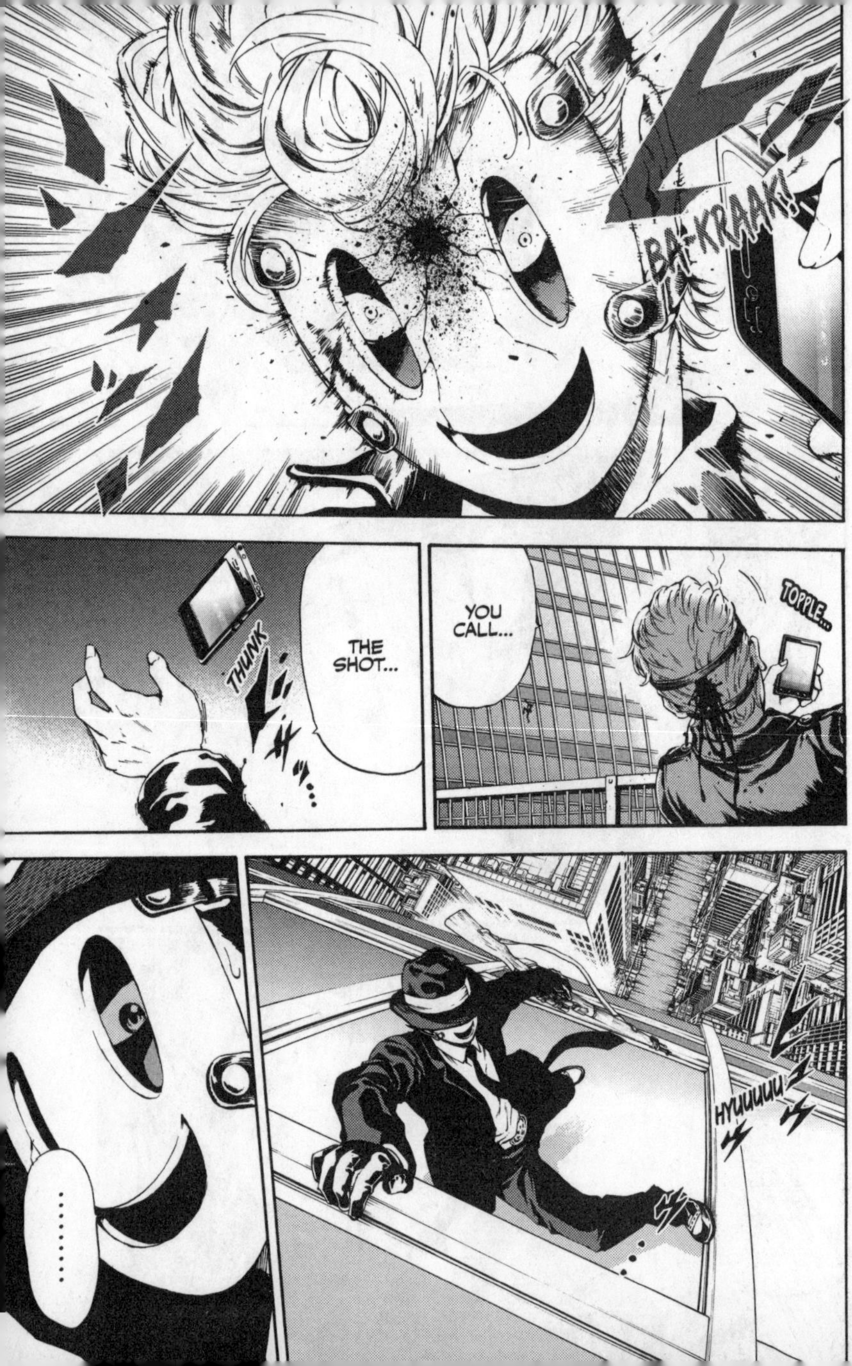
BA-KRAAK!
TOPPLE...
YOU CALL...
THE SHOT...
THUNK
HYUUUUU
......

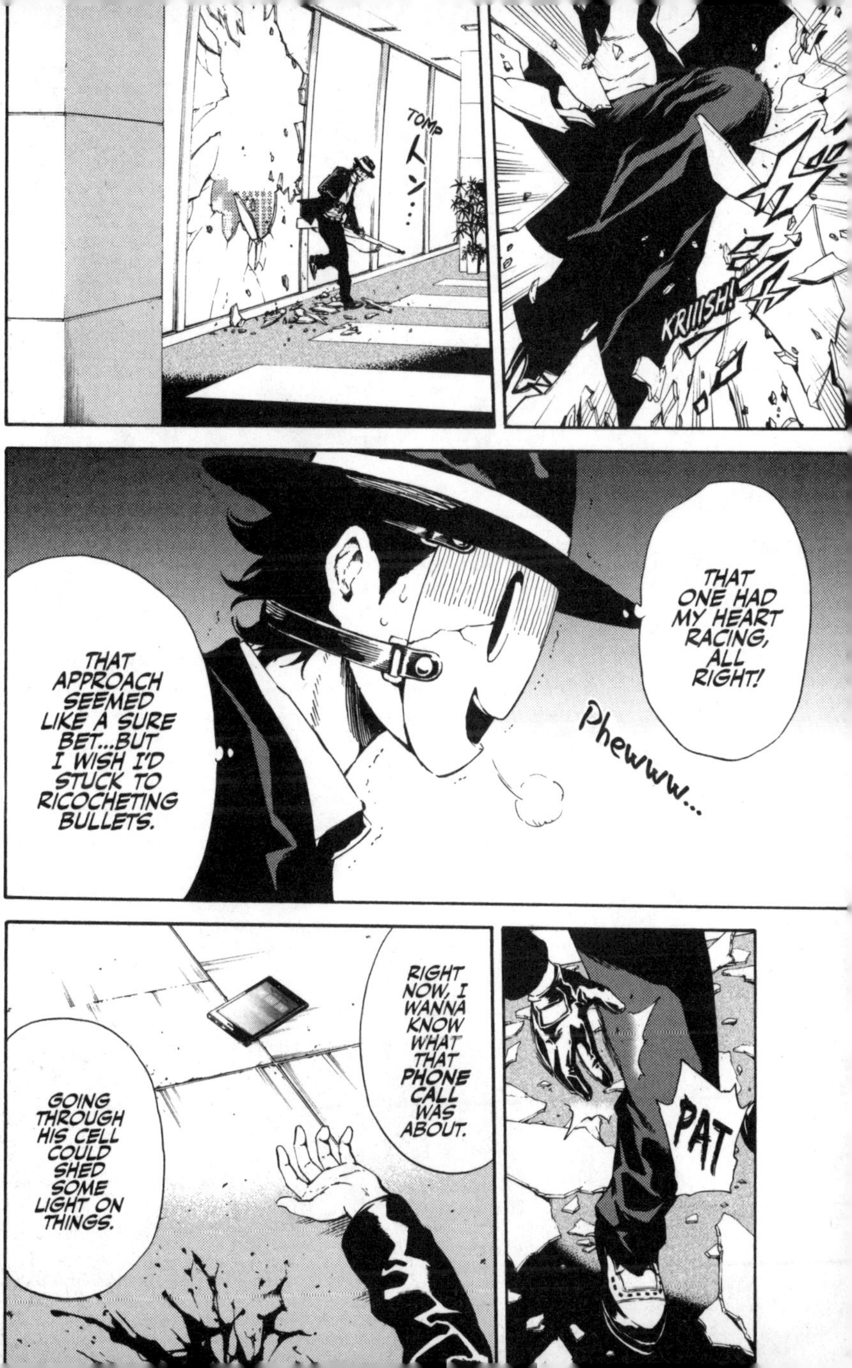
KRUISH!
TOMP
トン…
THAT ONE HAD MY HEART RACING, ALL RIGHT!
Phewww...
THAT APPROACH SEEMED LIKE A SURE BET...BUT I WISH I'D STUCK TO RICOCHETING BULLETS.
PAT
RIGHT NOW, I WANNA KNOW WHAT THAT PHONE CALL WAS ABOUT.
GOING THROUGH HIS CELL COULD SHED SOME LIGHT ON THINGS.

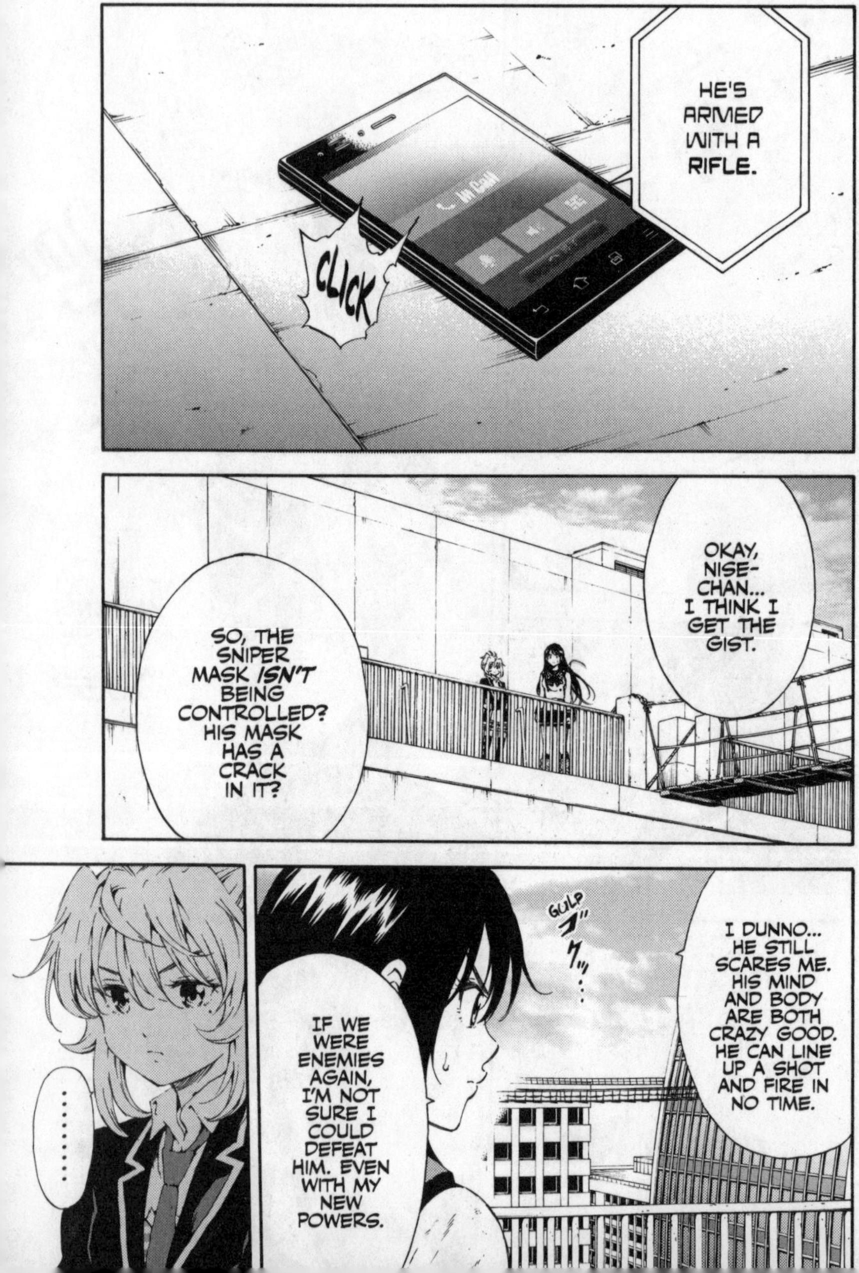

HE'S ARMED WITH A RIFLE.
CLICK
OKAY, NISE-CHAN... I THINK I GET THE GIST.
SO, THE SNIPER MASK *ISN'T* BEING CONTROLLED? HIS MASK HAS A CRACK IN IT?
I DUNNO... HE STILL SCARES ME. HIS MIND AND BODY ARE BOTH CRAZY GOOD. HE CAN LINE UP A SHOT AND FIRE IN NO TIME.
GULP
IF WE WERE ENEMIES AGAIN, I'M NOT SURE I COULD DEFEAT HIM. EVEN WITH MY NEW POWERS.
....

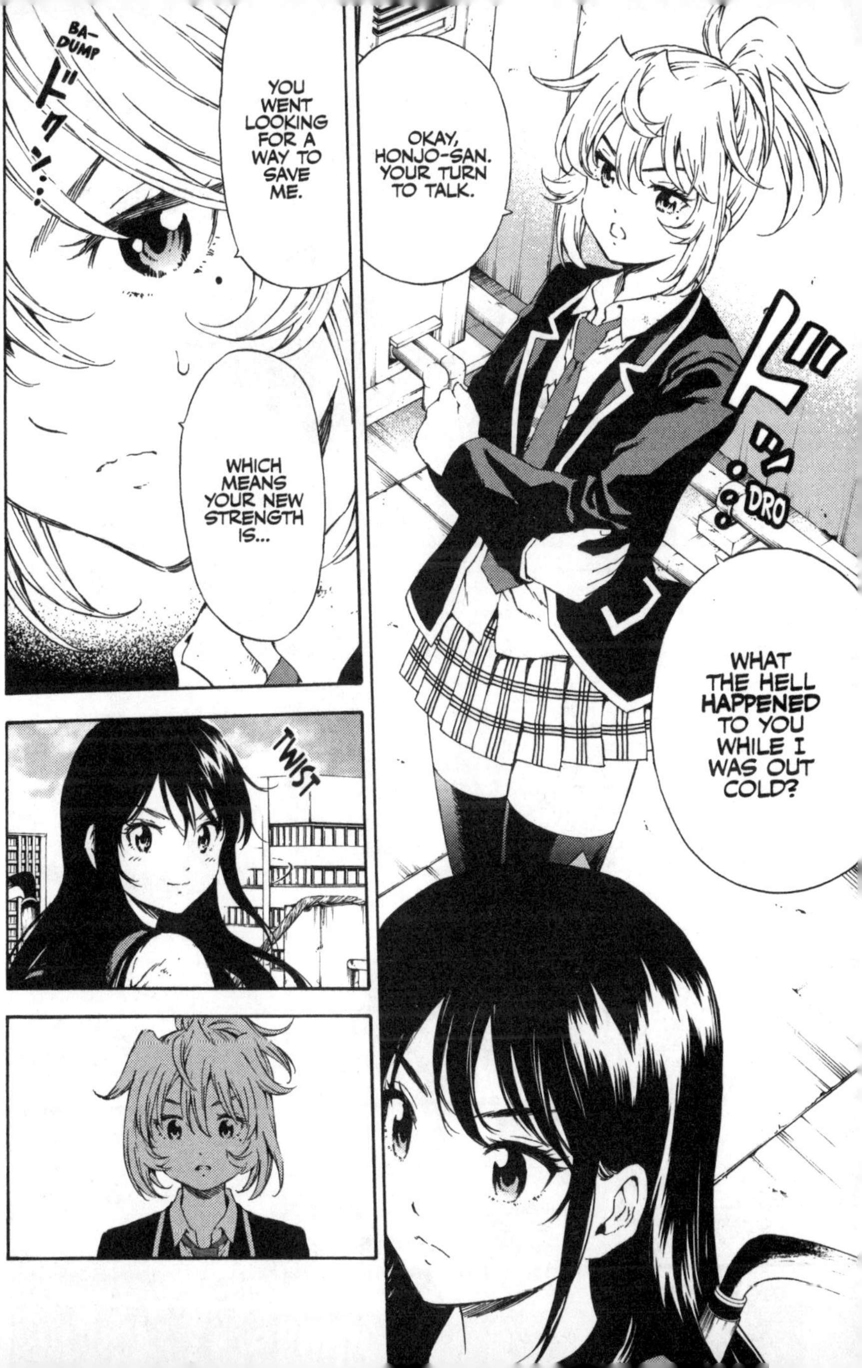
OKAY, HONJO-SAN. YOUR TURN TO TALK.
DRO
WHAT THE HELL HAPPENED TO YOU WHILE I WAS OUT COLD?
BA-DUMP
YOU WENT LOOKING FOR A WAY TO SAVE ME.
WHICH MEANS YOUR NEW STRENGTH IS...
TWIST

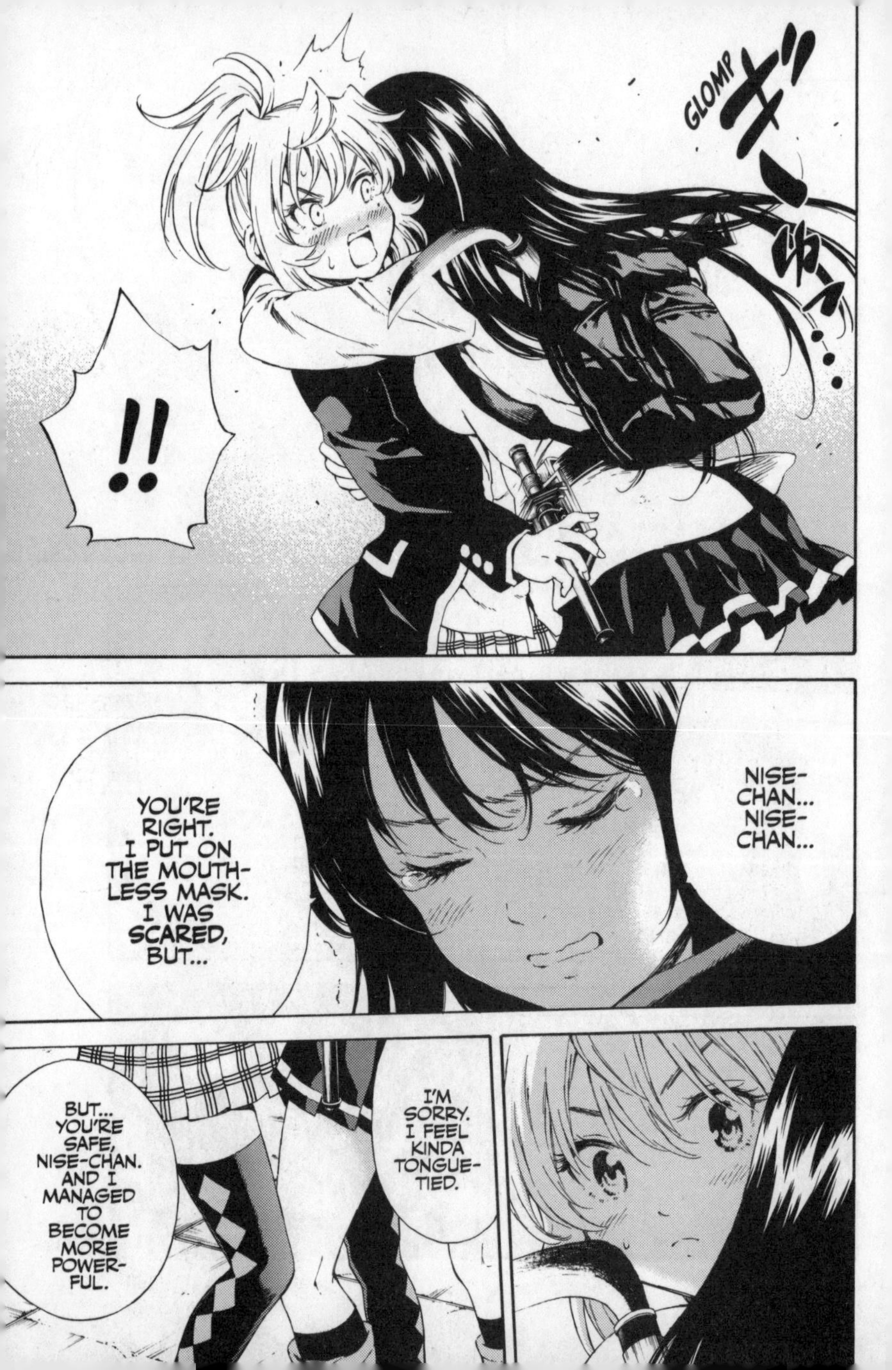
GLOMP
ぎゅーっ…
!!
NISE-CHAN... NISE-CHAN...
YOU'RE RIGHT. I PUT ON THE MOUTH-LESS MASK. I WAS SCARED, BUT...
I'M SORRY. I FEEL KINDA TONGUE-TIED.
BUT... YOU'RE SAFE, NISE-CHAN. AND I MANAGED TO BECOME MORE POWER-FUL.

NOW WE CAN BE TOGETHER AGAIN...

FOREVER AND EVER...!

H... HONJO-SAN...

CAN'T BREATHE, HERE...!

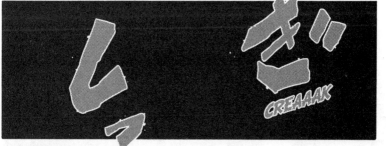

CREAAAK

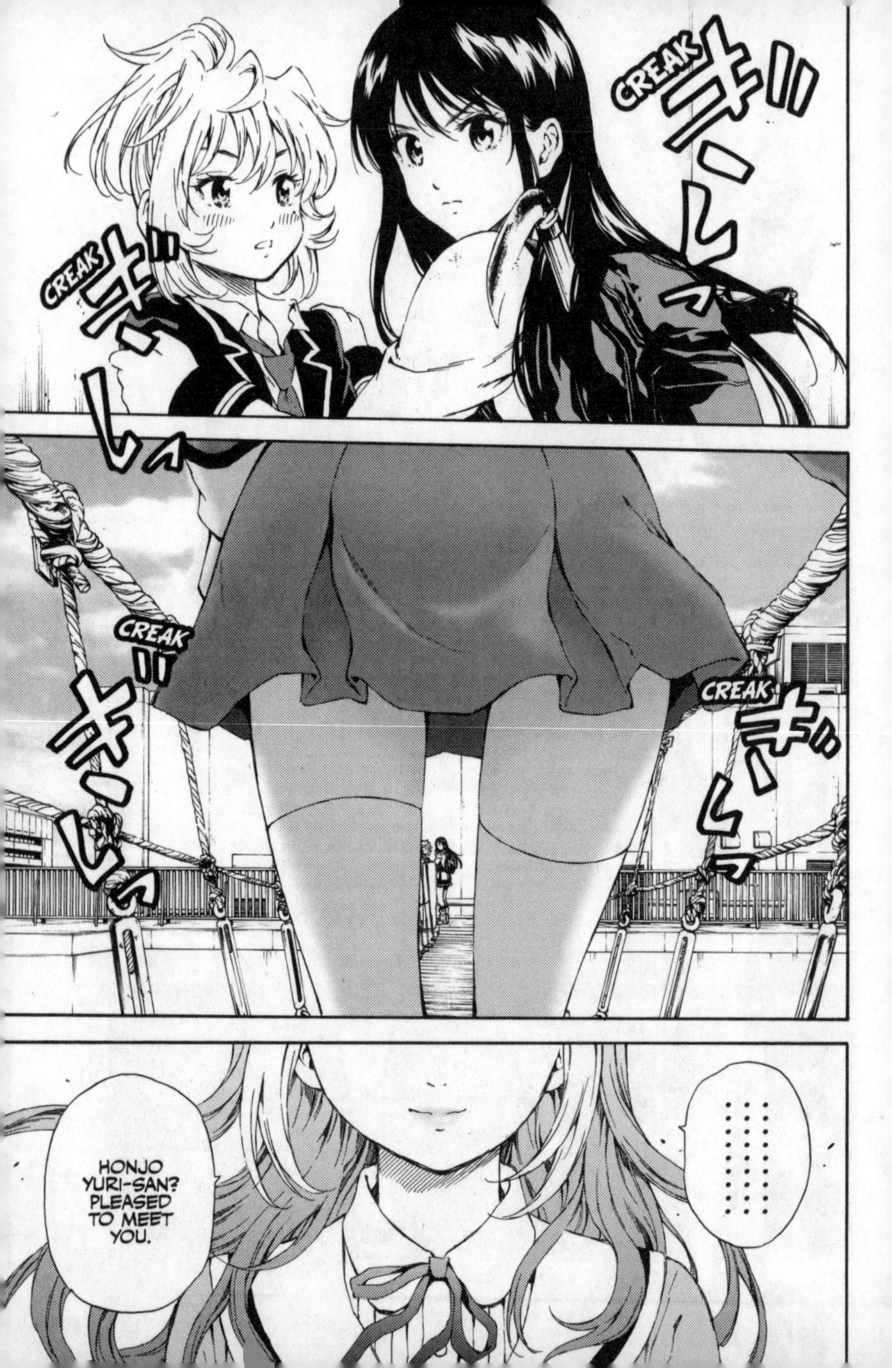
CREAK
CREAK
CREAK
CREAK
......
HONJO YURI-SAN? PLEASED TO MEET YOU.

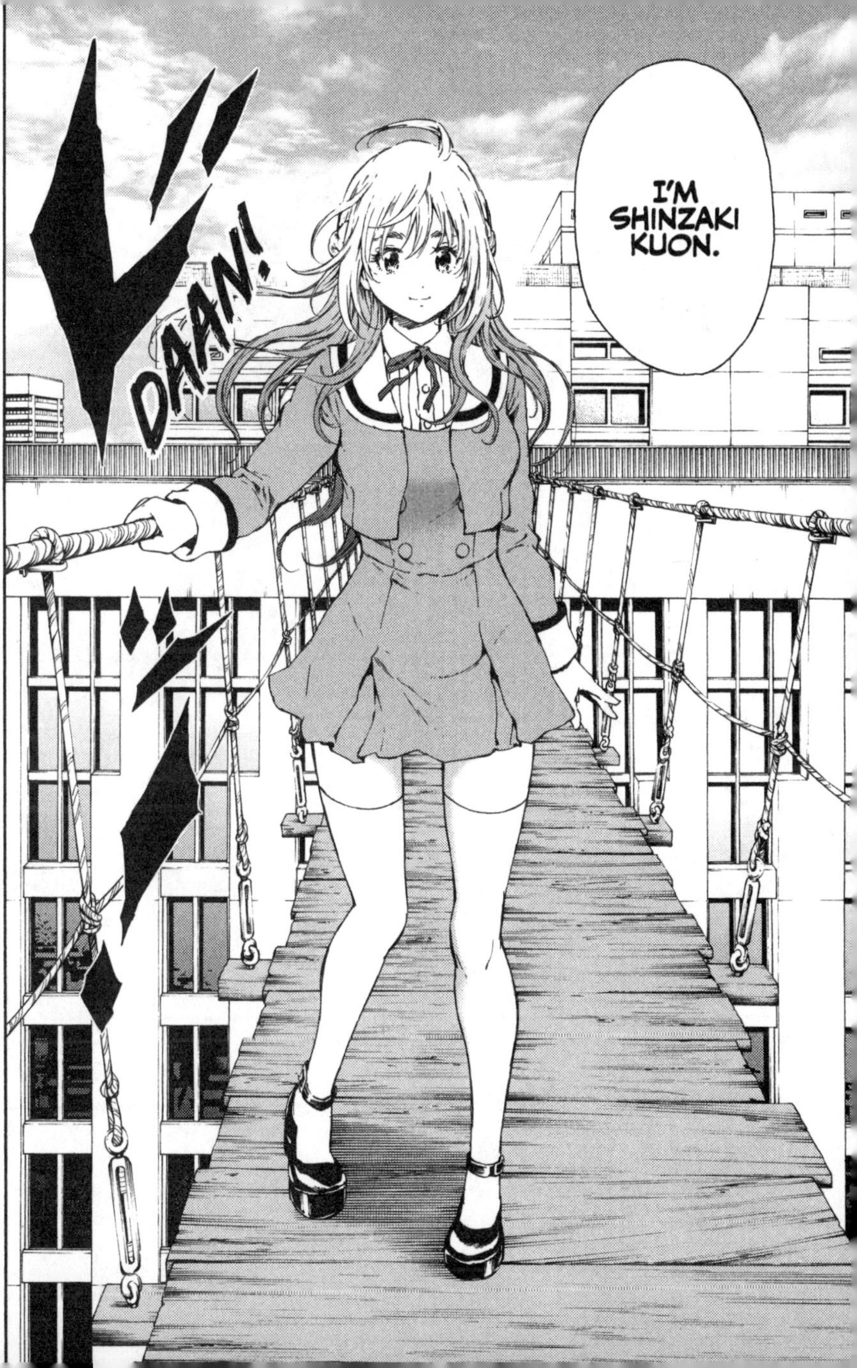
I'M SHINZAKI KUON.
DAAN!

HIGH-RISE INVASION

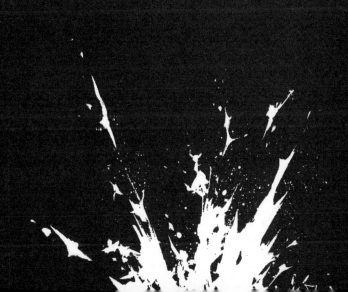

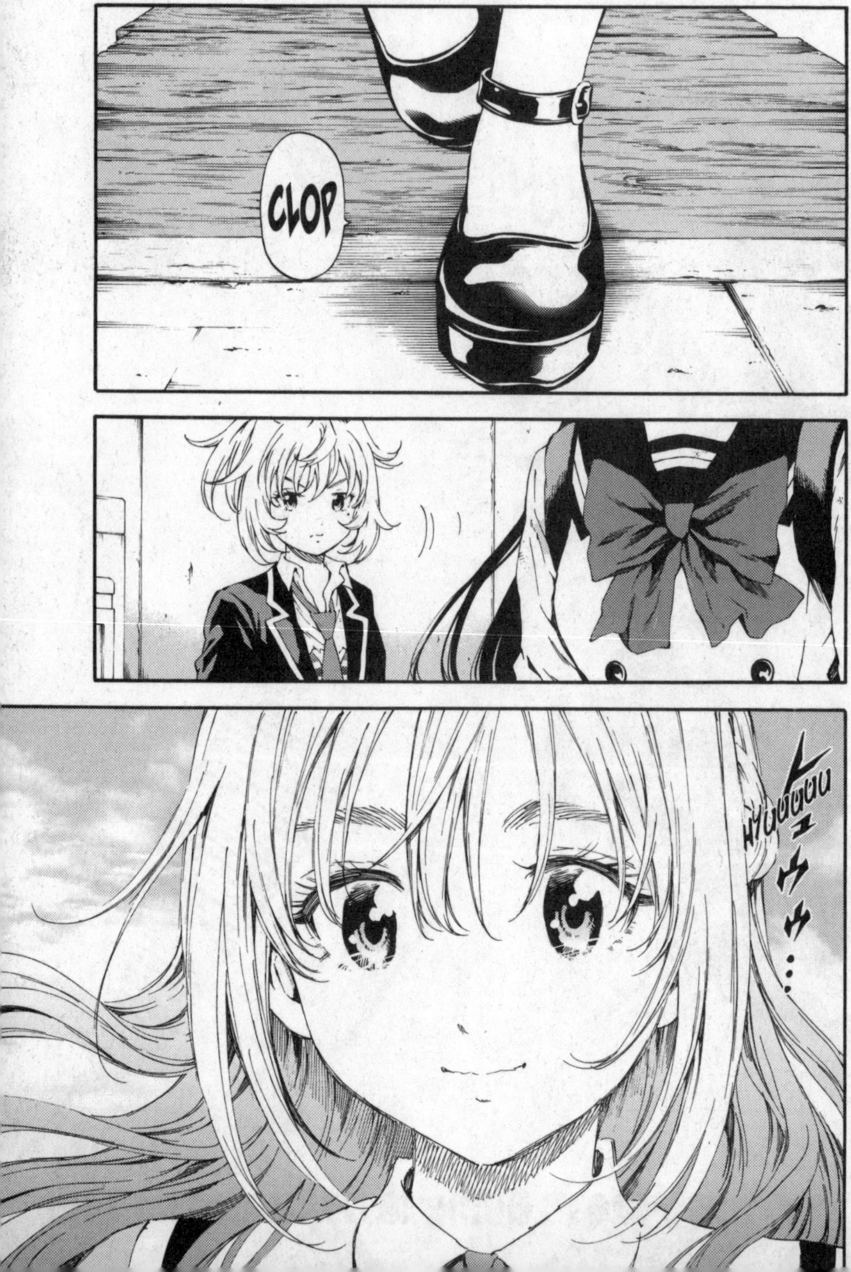
CLOP
HYUUUUUU

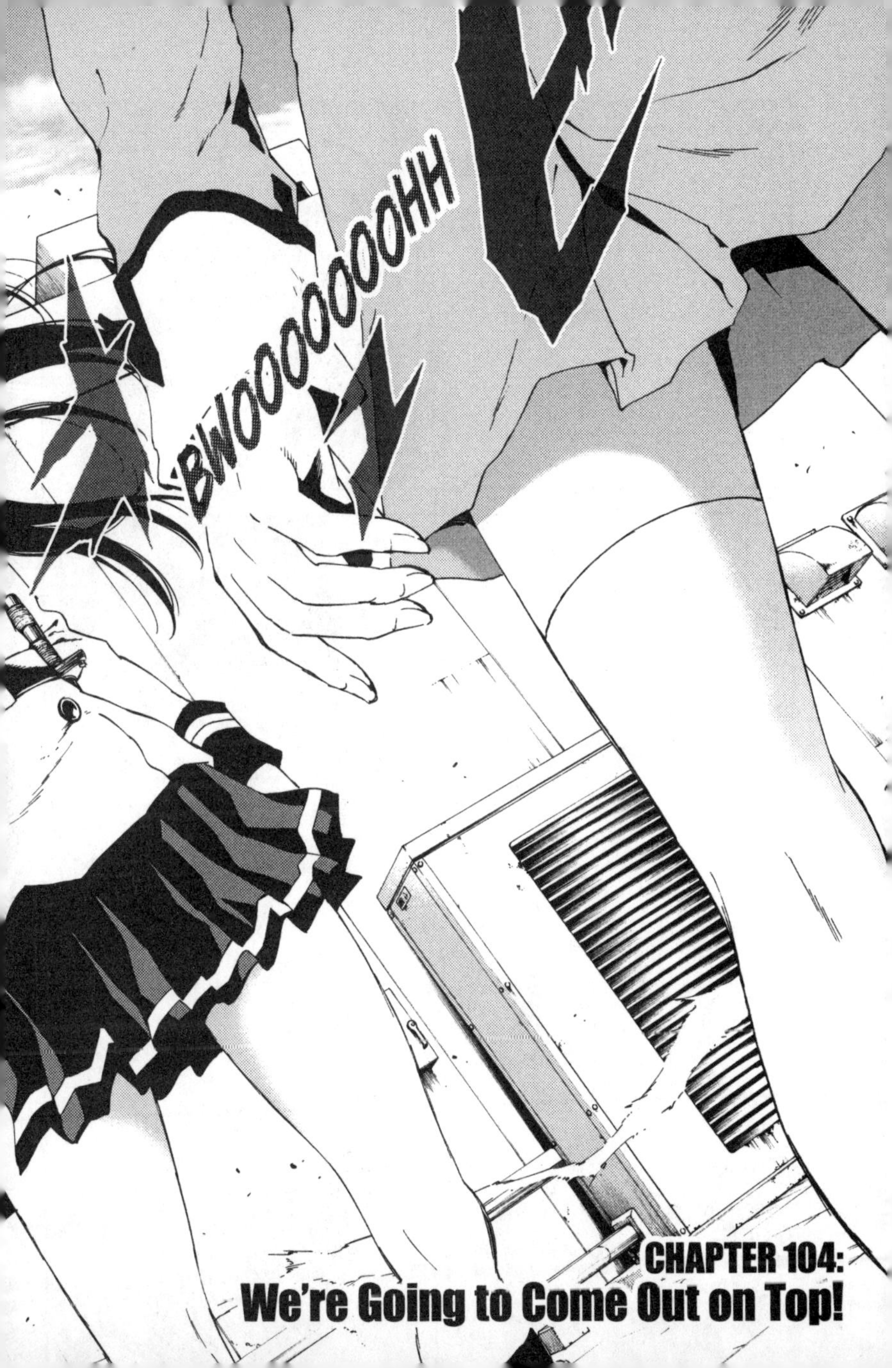
BWOOOOOOOHH

CHAPTER 104:
We're Going to Come Out on Top!

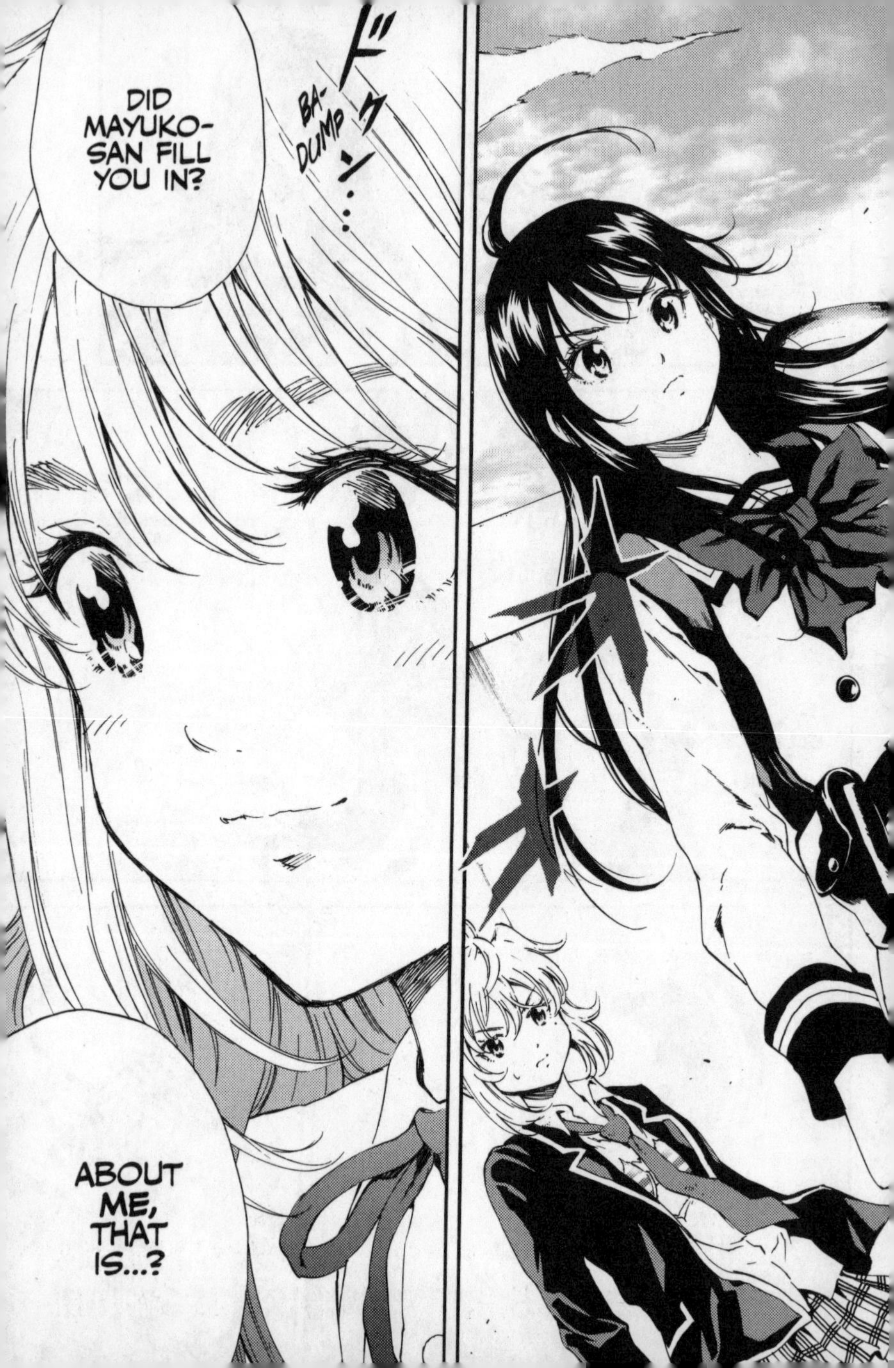
ドクン…
BA-DUMP
DID MAYUKO-SAN FILL YOU IN?
ABOUT ME, THAT IS...?

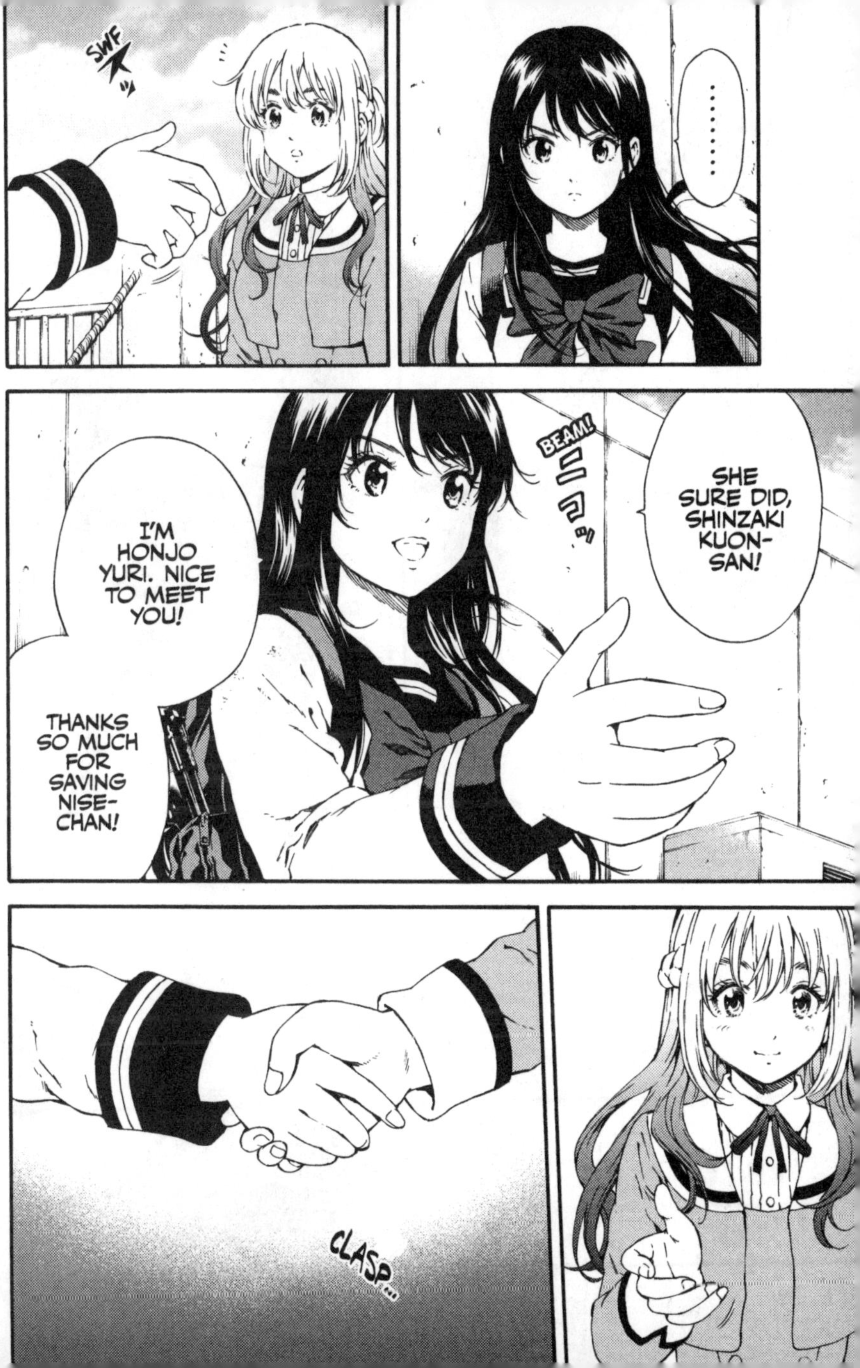
....
SWF
SHE SURE DID, SHINZAKI KUON-SAN!
BEAM!
I'M HONJO YURI. NICE TO MEET YOU!
THANKS SO MUCH FOR SAVING NISE-CHAN!
CLASP...

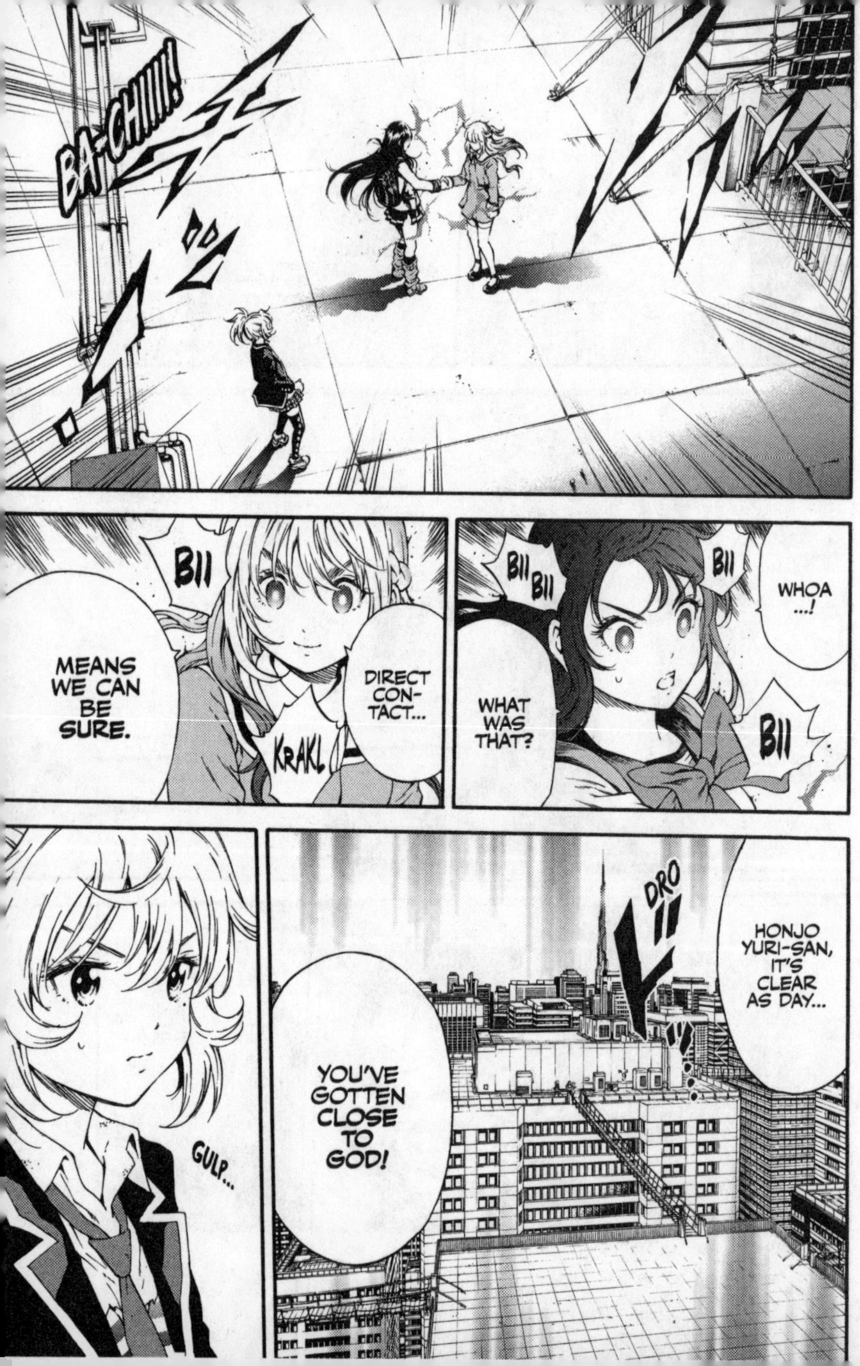
BA-CHIII!
BII
WHOA ...!
BII
BII BII
WHAT WAS THAT?
BII
BII
DIRECT CON-TACT...
KRAKL
MEANS WE CAN BE SURE.
HONJO YURI-SAN, IT'S CLEAR AS DAY...
DRO!!
YOU'VE GOTTEN CLOSE TO GOD!
GULP...

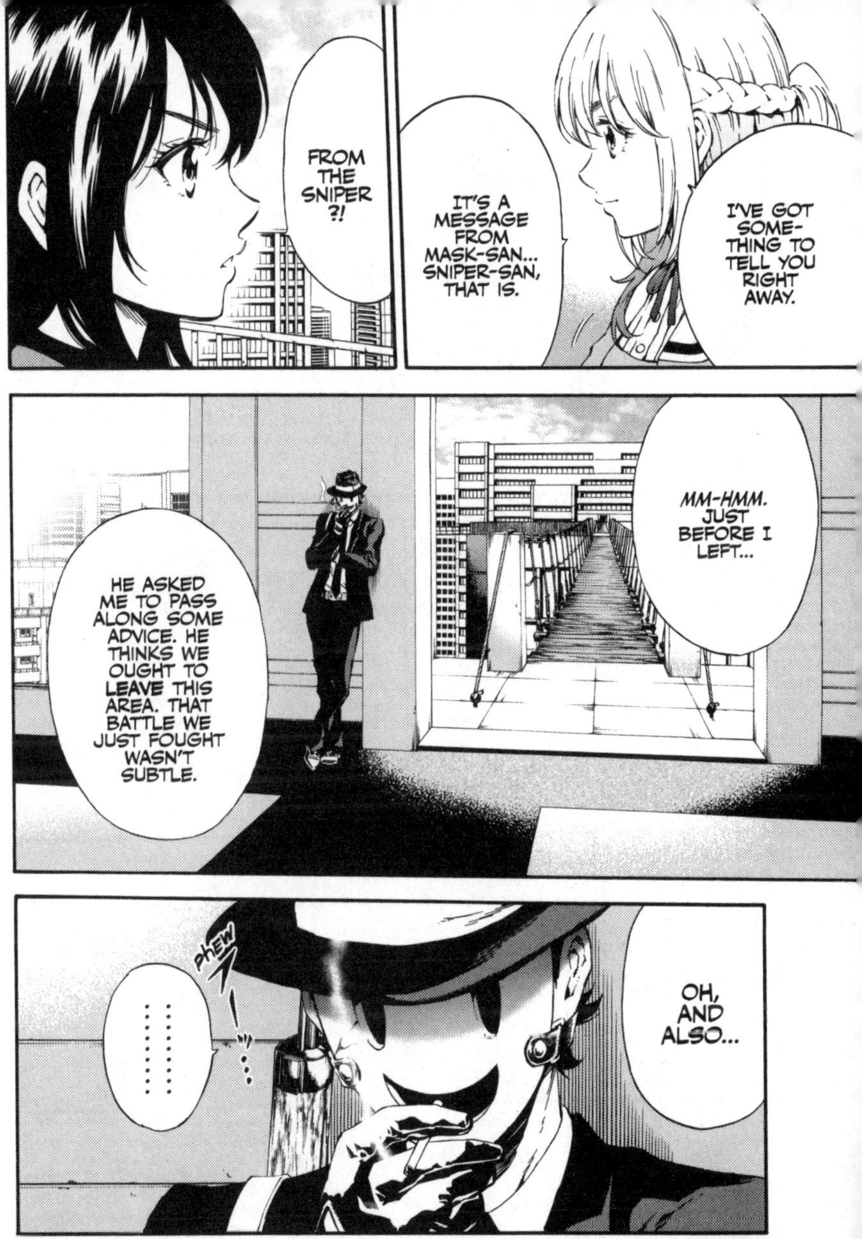
I'VE GOT SOME-THING TO TELL YOU RIGHT AWAY.
IT'S A MESSAGE FROM MASK-SAN... SNIPER-SAN, THAT IS.
FROM THE SNIPER ?!
MM-HMM. JUST BEFORE I LEFT...
HE ASKED ME TO PASS ALONG SOME ADVICE. HE THINKS WE OUGHT TO **LEAVE** THIS AREA. THAT BATTLE WE JUST FOUGHT WASN'T SUBTLE.
OH, AND ALSO...
PHEW
......

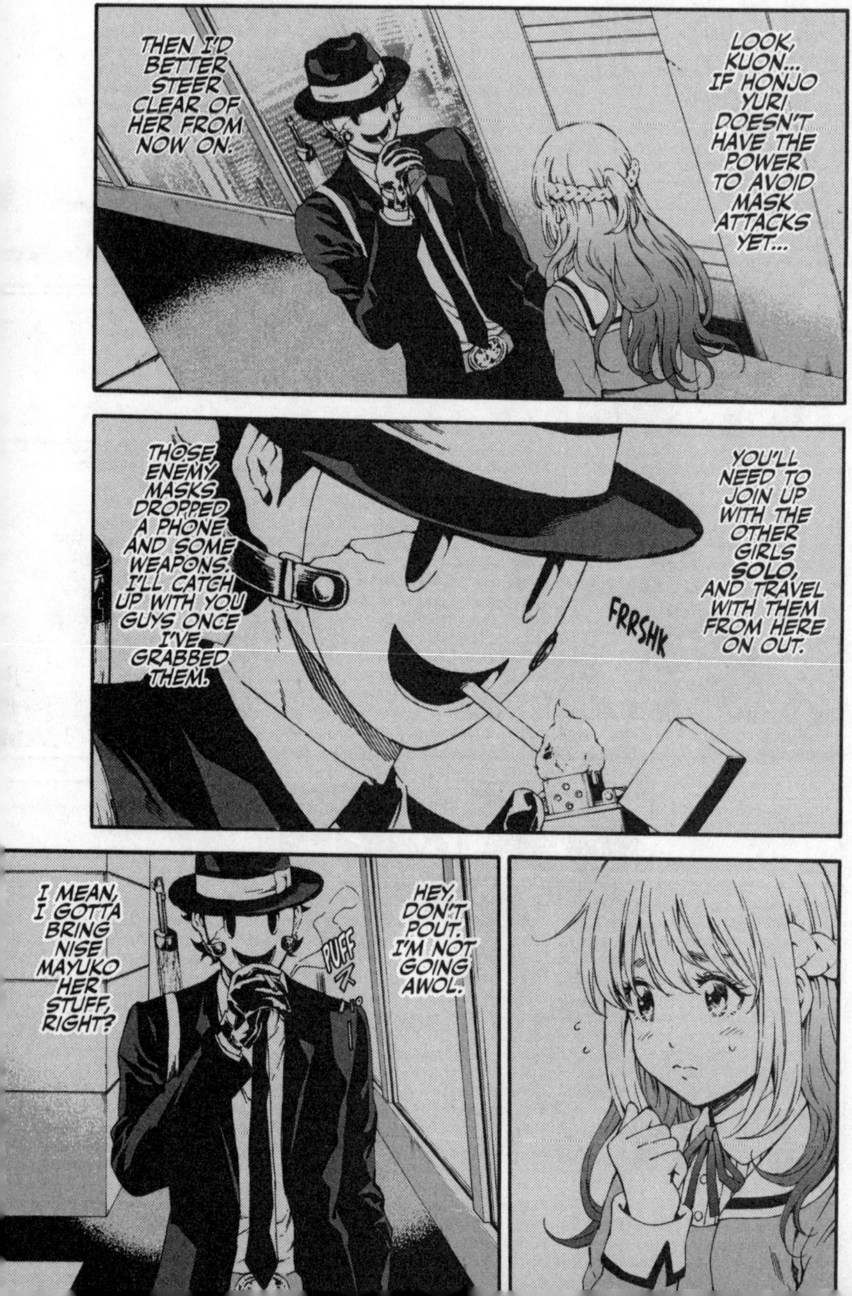
LOOK, KUON... IF HONJO YURI DOESN'T HAVE THE POWER TO AVOID MASK ATTACKS YET...
THEN I'D BETTER STEER CLEAR OF HER FROM NOW ON.
YOU'LL NEED TO JOIN UP WITH THE OTHER GIRLS SOLO, AND TRAVEL WITH THEM FROM HERE ON OUT.
FRRSHK
THOSE ENEMY MASKS DROPPED A PHONE AND SOME WEAPONS. I'LL CATCH UP WITH YOU GUYS ONCE I'VE GRABBED THEM.
HEY, DON'T POUT. I'M NOT GOING AWOL.
PUFF
I MEAN, I GOTTA BRING NISE MAYUKO HER STUFF, RIGHT?

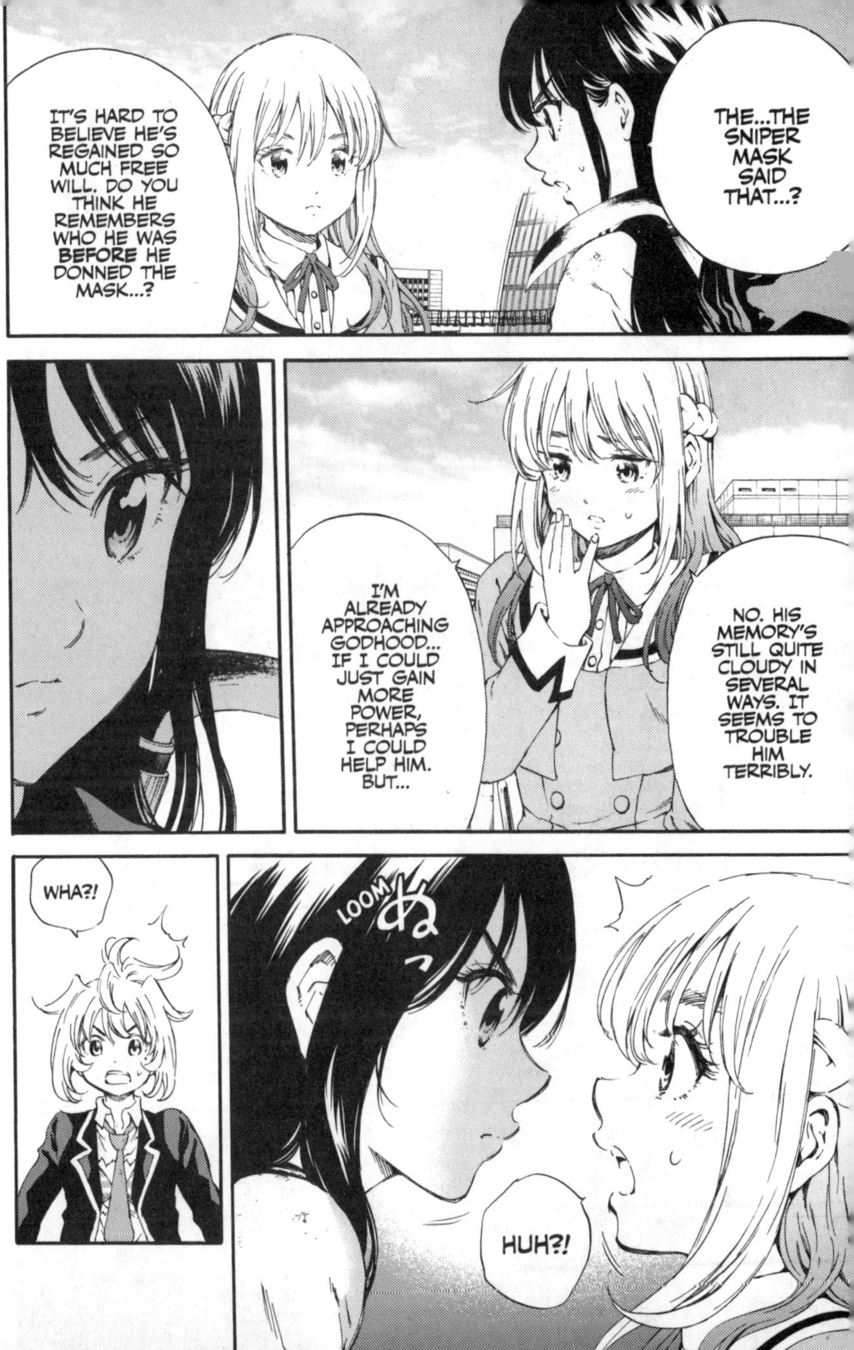
THE...THE SNIPER MASK SAID THAT...?
IT'S HARD TO BELIEVE HE'S REGAINED SO MUCH FREE WILL. DO YOU THINK HE REMEMBERS WHO HE WAS BEFORE HE DONNED THE MASK...?
NO. HIS MEMORY'S STILL QUITE CLOUDY IN SEVERAL WAYS. IT SEEMS TO TROUBLE HIM TERRIBLY.
I'M ALREADY APPROACHING GODHOOD... IF I COULD JUST GAIN MORE POWER, PERHAPS I COULD HELP HIM. BUT...
LOOM
ぬっ
HUH?!
WHA?!

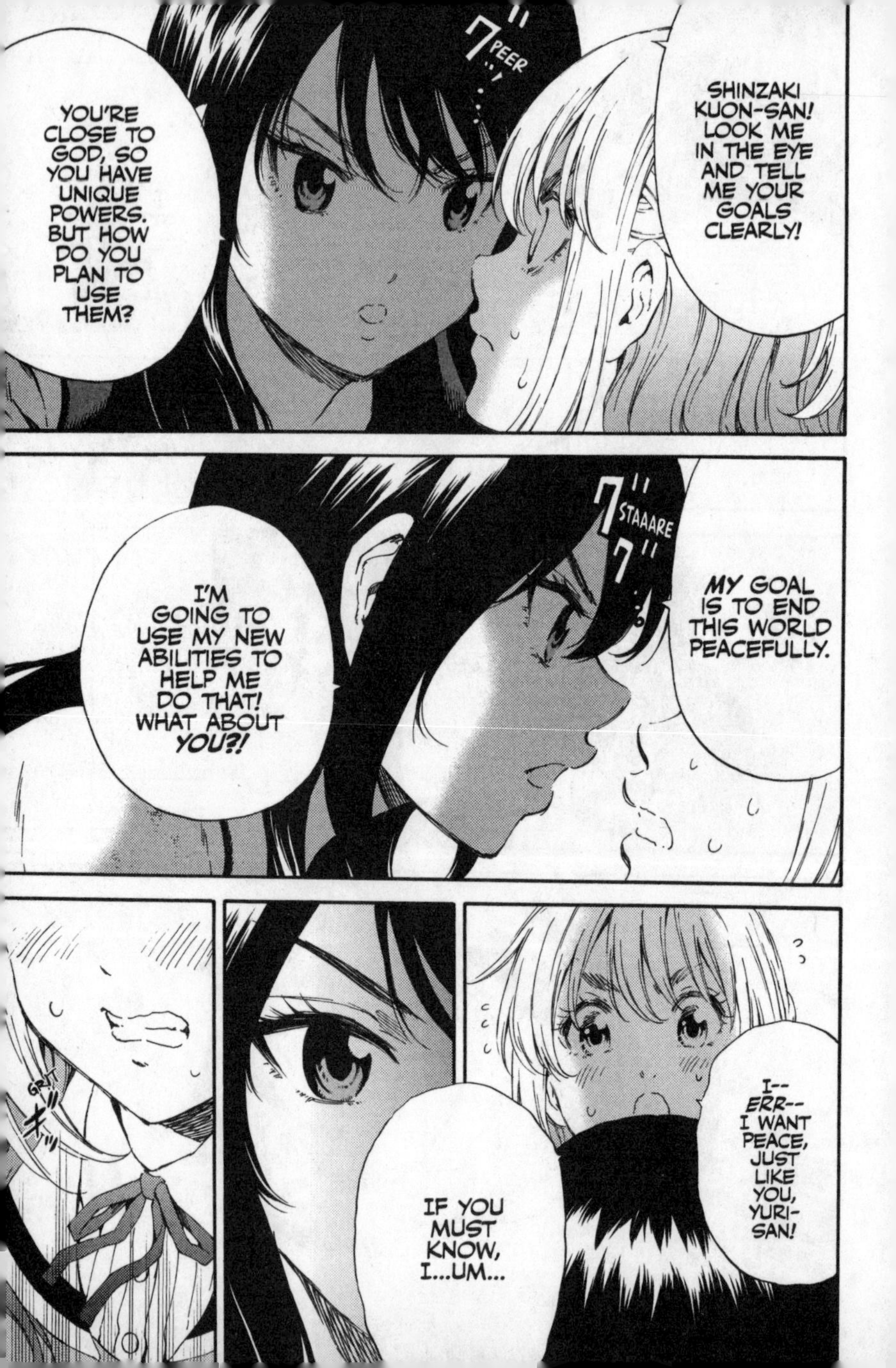
SHINZAKI KUON-SAN! LOOK ME IN THE EYE AND TELL ME YOUR GOALS CLEARLY!
PEER
YOU'RE CLOSE TO GOD, SO YOU HAVE UNIQUE POWERS. BUT HOW DO YOU PLAN TO USE THEM?
MY GOAL IS TO END THIS WORLD PEACEFULLY.
STAAARE
I'M GOING TO USE MY NEW ABILITIES TO HELP ME DO THAT! WHAT ABOUT YOU?!
I-- ERR-- I WANT PEACE, JUST LIKE YOU, YURI-SAN!
IF YOU MUST KNOW, I...UM...
GRIT

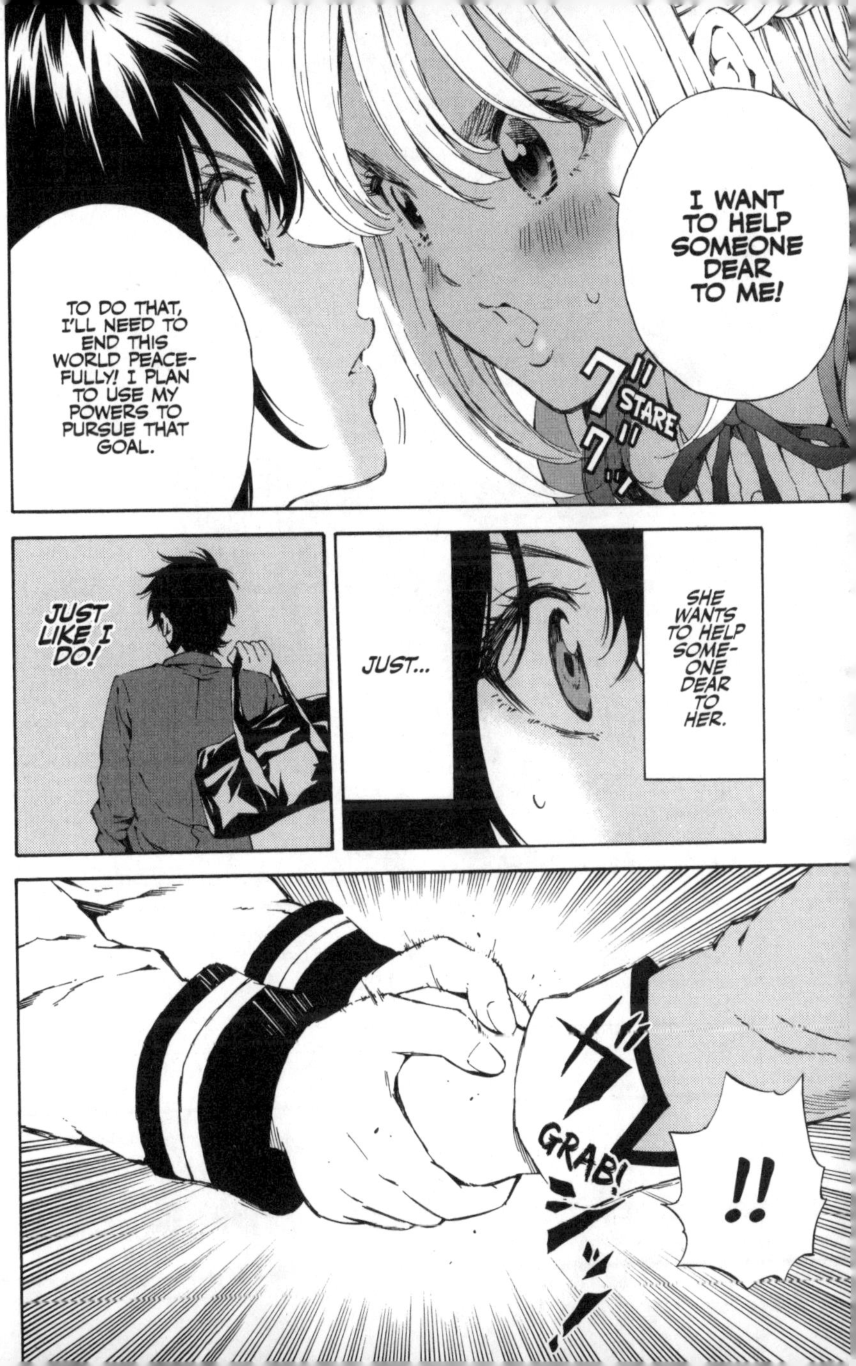
I WANT TO HELP SOMEONE DEAR TO ME!
STARE
TO DO THAT, I'LL NEED TO END THIS WORLD PEACE-FULLY! I PLAN TO USE MY POWERS TO PURSUE THAT GOAL.
SHE WANTS TO HELP SOME-ONE DEAR TO HER.
JUST...
JUST LIKE I DO!
!!
GRAB!

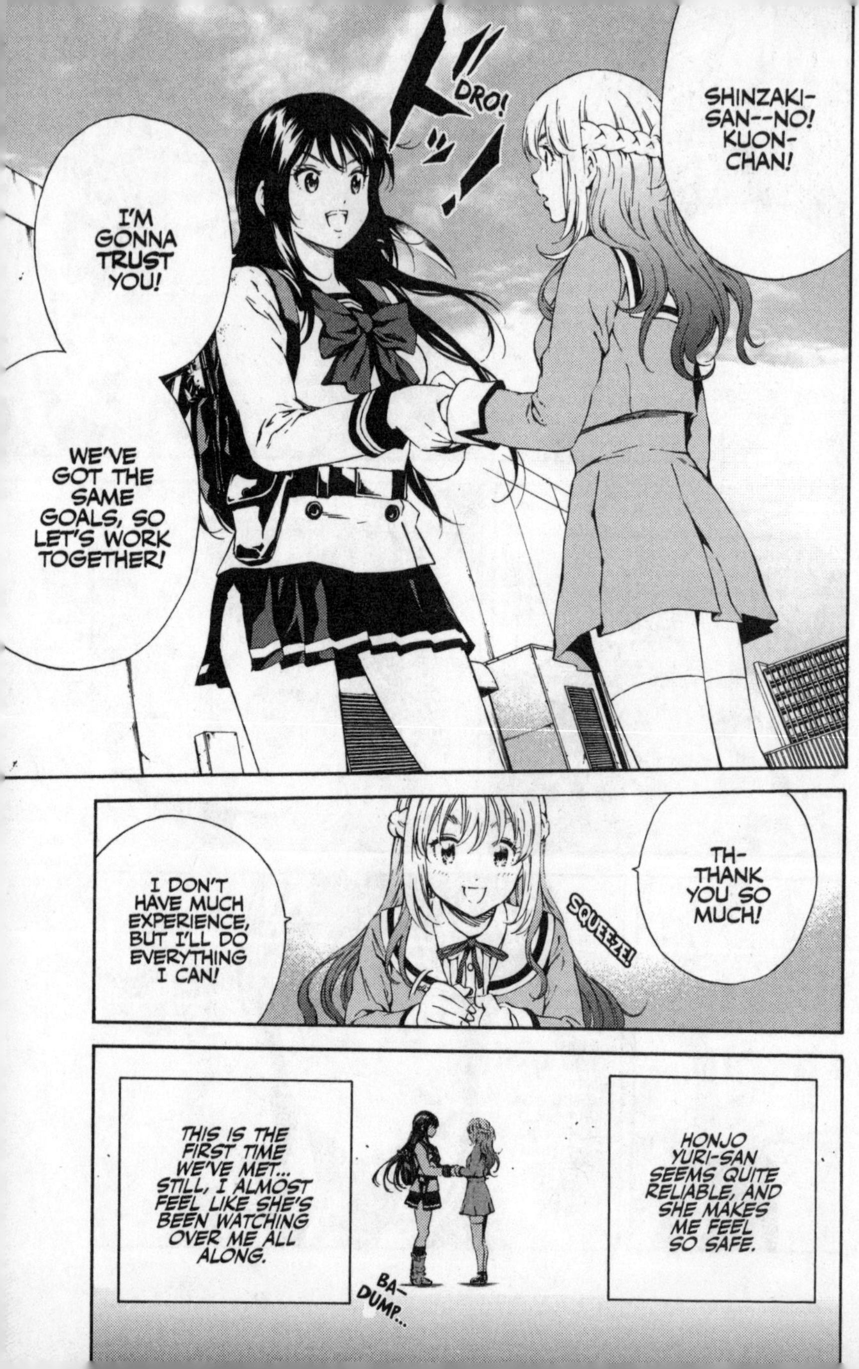
SHINZAKI-SAN--NO! KUON-CHAN!
DRO!
I'M GONNA TRUST YOU!
WE'VE GOT THE SAME GOALS, SO LET'S WORK TOGETHER!
TH-THANK YOU SO MUCH!
SQUEEEZE!
I DON'T HAVE MUCH EXPERIENCE, BUT I'LL DO EVERYTHING I CAN!
HONJO YURI-SAN SEEMS QUITE RELIABLE, AND SHE MAKES ME FEEL SO SAFE.
BA-DUMP...
THIS IS THE FIRST TIME WE'VE MET... STILL, I ALMOST FEEL LIKE SHE'S BEEN WATCHING OVER ME ALL ALONG.

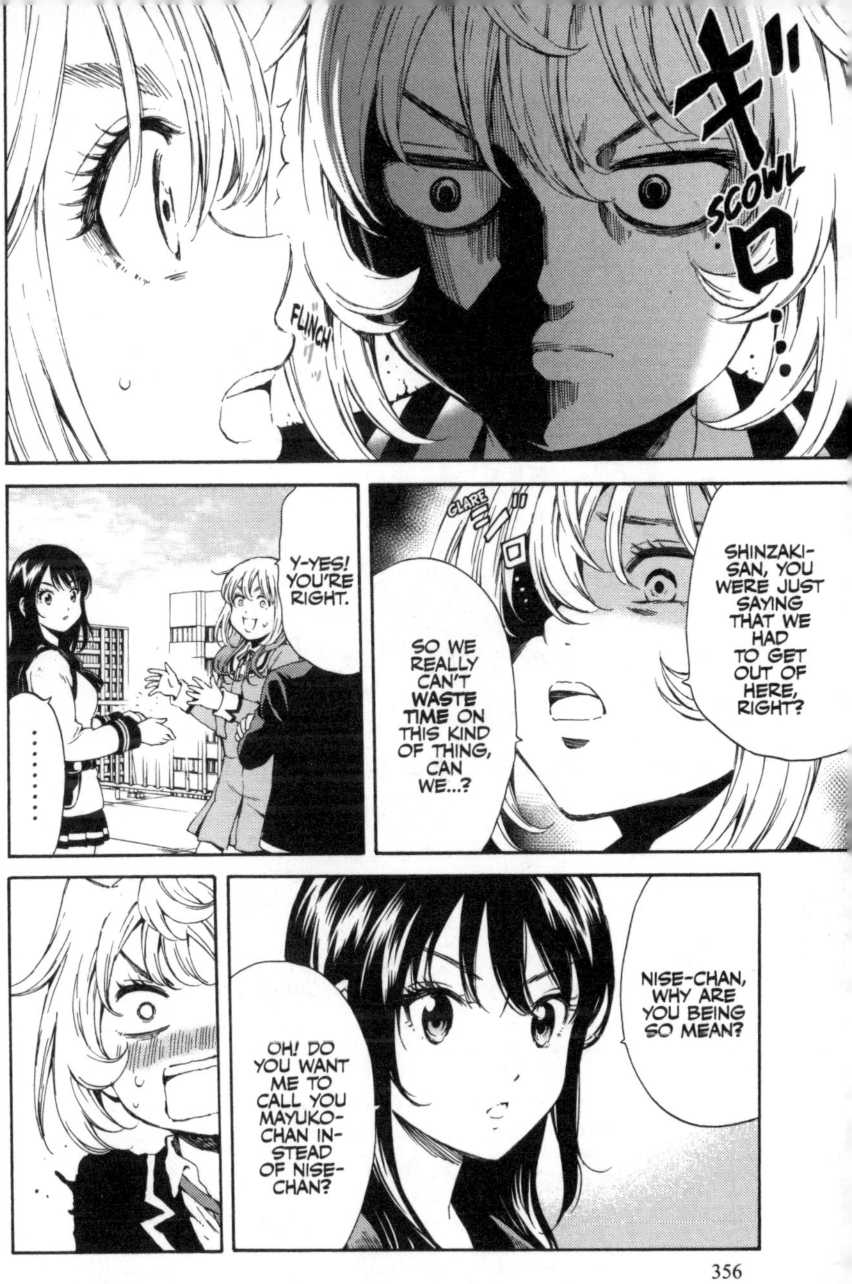
SCOWL
FLINCH
GLARE
SHINZAKI-SAN, YOU WERE JUST SAYING THAT WE HAD TO GET OUT OF HERE, RIGHT?
SO WE REALLY CAN'T WASTE TIME ON THIS KIND OF THING, CAN WE...?
Y-YES! YOU'RE RIGHT.
NISE-CHAN, WHY ARE YOU BEING SO MEAN?
OH! DO YOU WANT ME TO CALL YOU MAYUKO-CHAN INSTEAD OF NISE-CHAN?

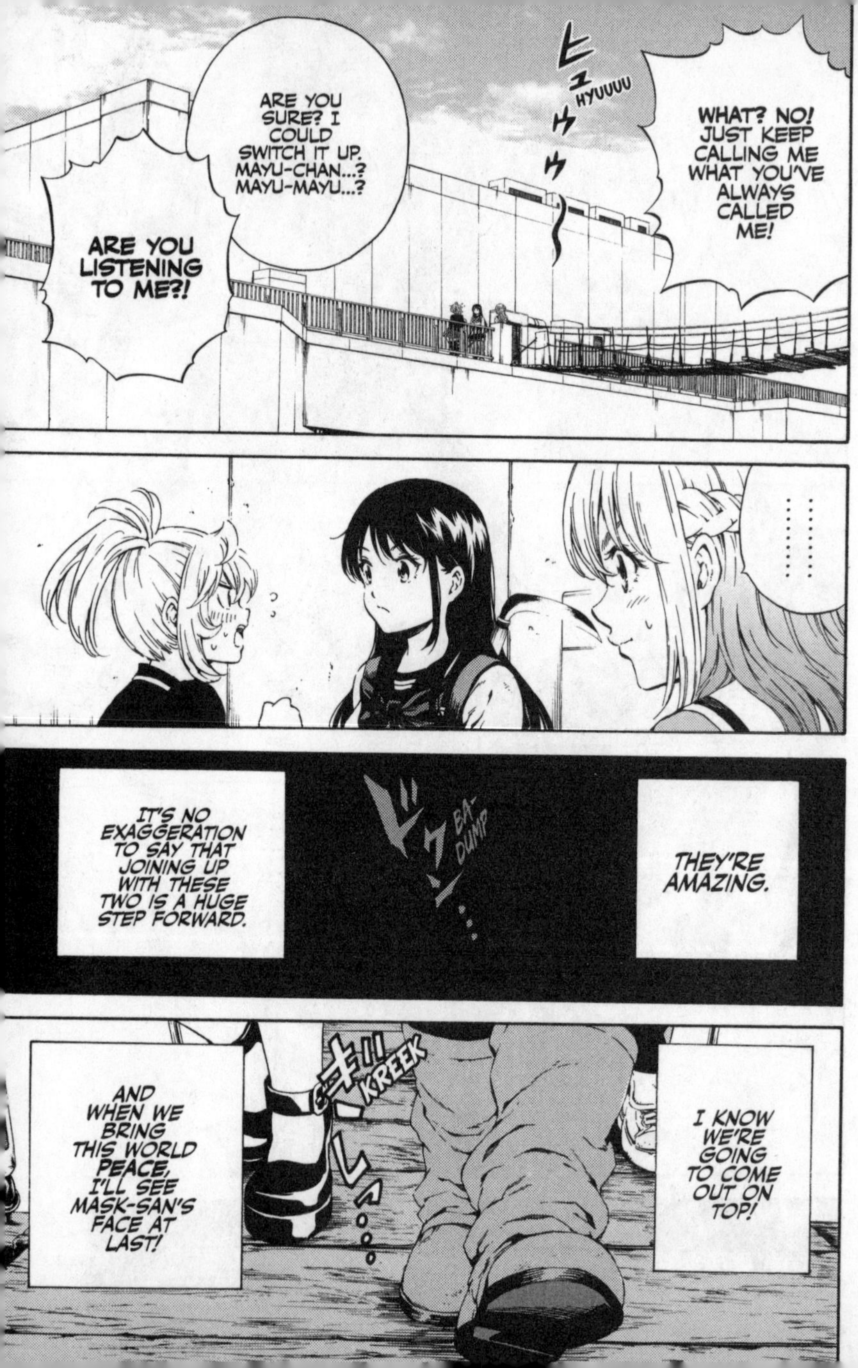
WHAT? NO! JUST KEEP CALLING ME WHAT YOU'VE ALWAYS CALLED ME!
HYUUUU
ARE YOU SURE? I COULD SWITCH IT UP. MAYU-CHAN...? MAYU-MAYU...?
ARE YOU LISTENING TO ME?!
......
THEY'RE AMAZING.
BA-DUMP
IT'S NO EXAGGERATION TO SAY THAT JOINING UP WITH THESE TWO IS A HUGE STEP FORWARD.
I KNOW WE'RE GOING TO COME OUT ON TOP!
KREEK
AND WHEN WE BRING THIS WORLD PEACE, I'LL SEE MASK-SAN'S FACE AT LAST!

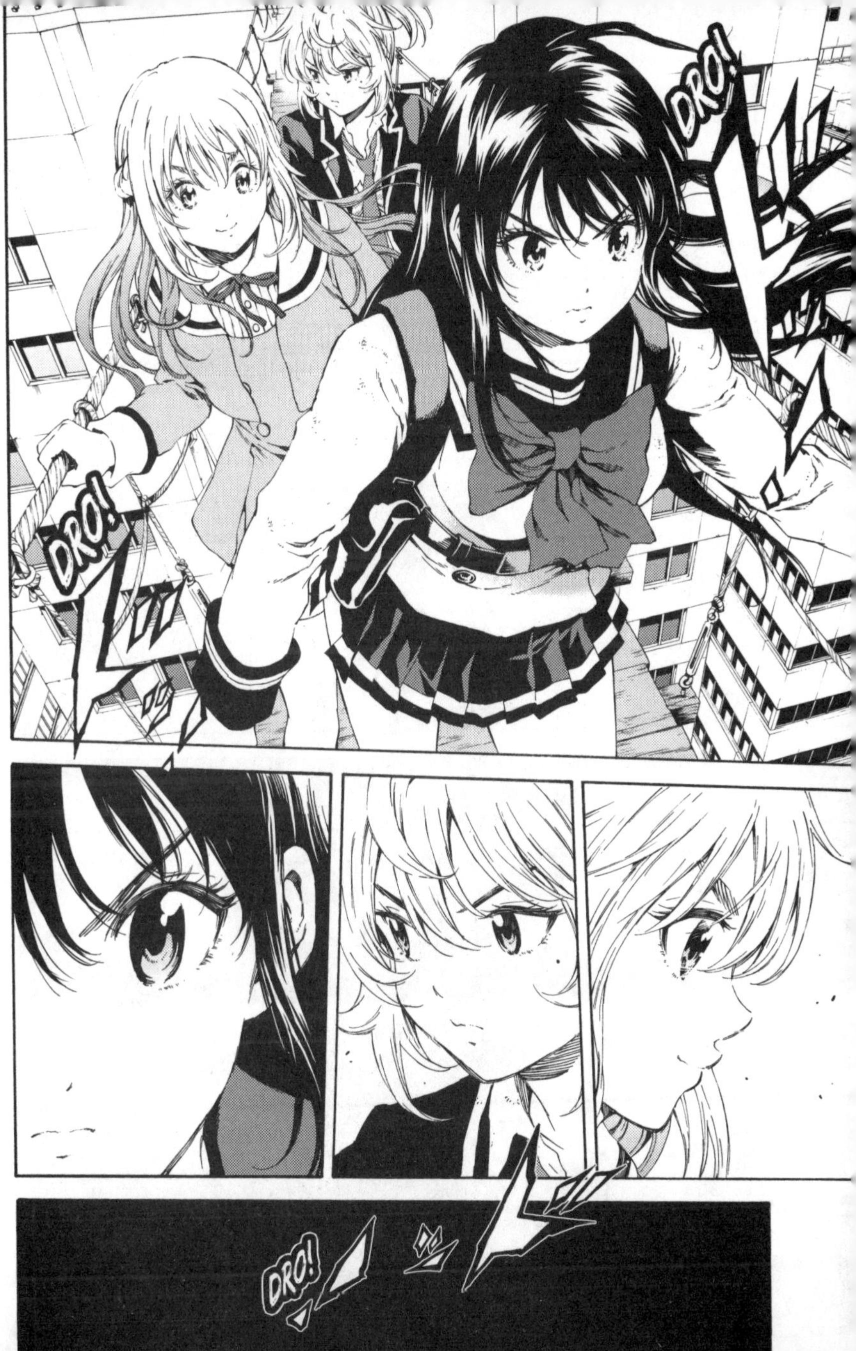
DRO!
DRO!
DRO!

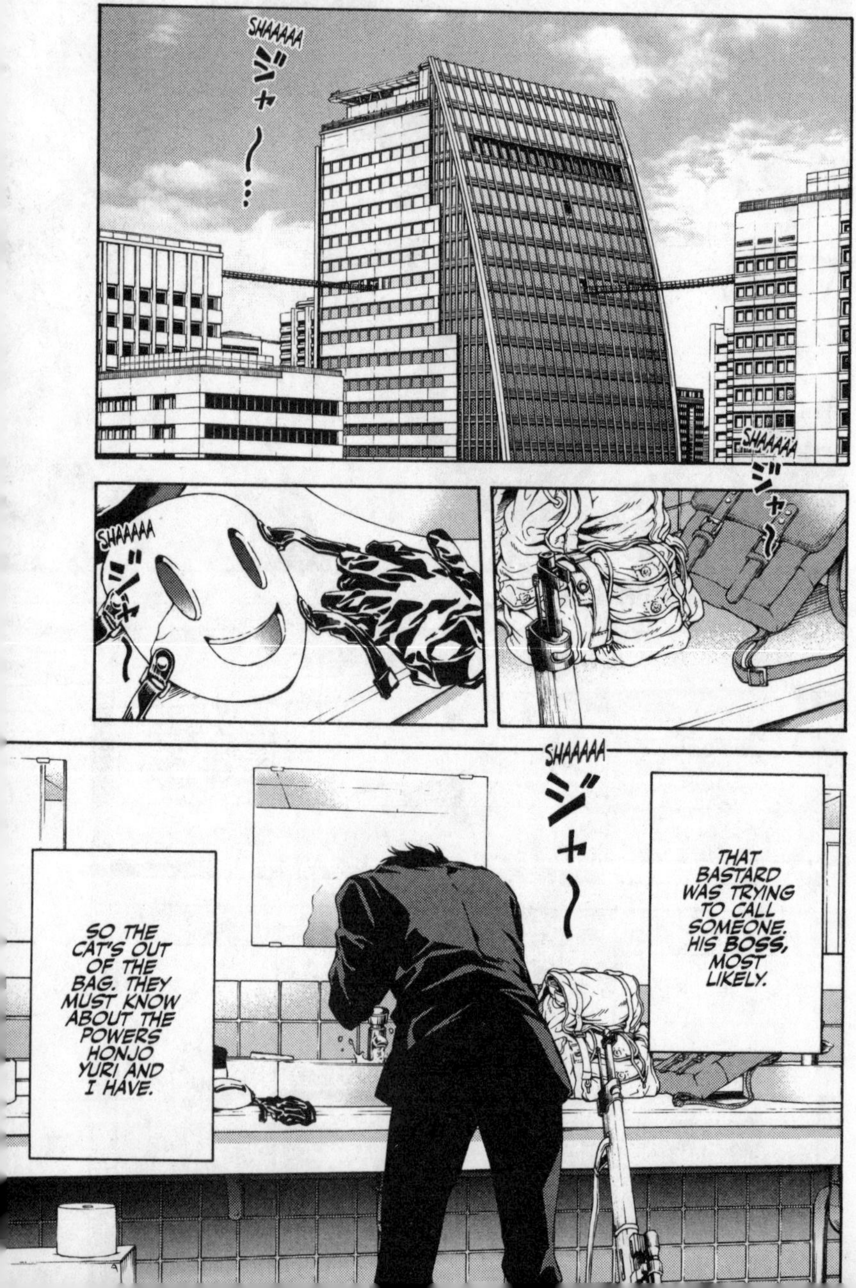
SHAAAAA
ジャ〜…
SHAAAAA
ジャ〜
SHAAAAA
ジャ〜
SHAAAAA
ジャ〜
THAT BASTARD WAS TRYING TO CALL SOMEONE. HIS BOSS, MOST LIKELY.
SO THE CAT'S OUT OF THE BAG. THEY MUST KNOW ABOUT THE POWERS HONJO YURI AND I HAVE.

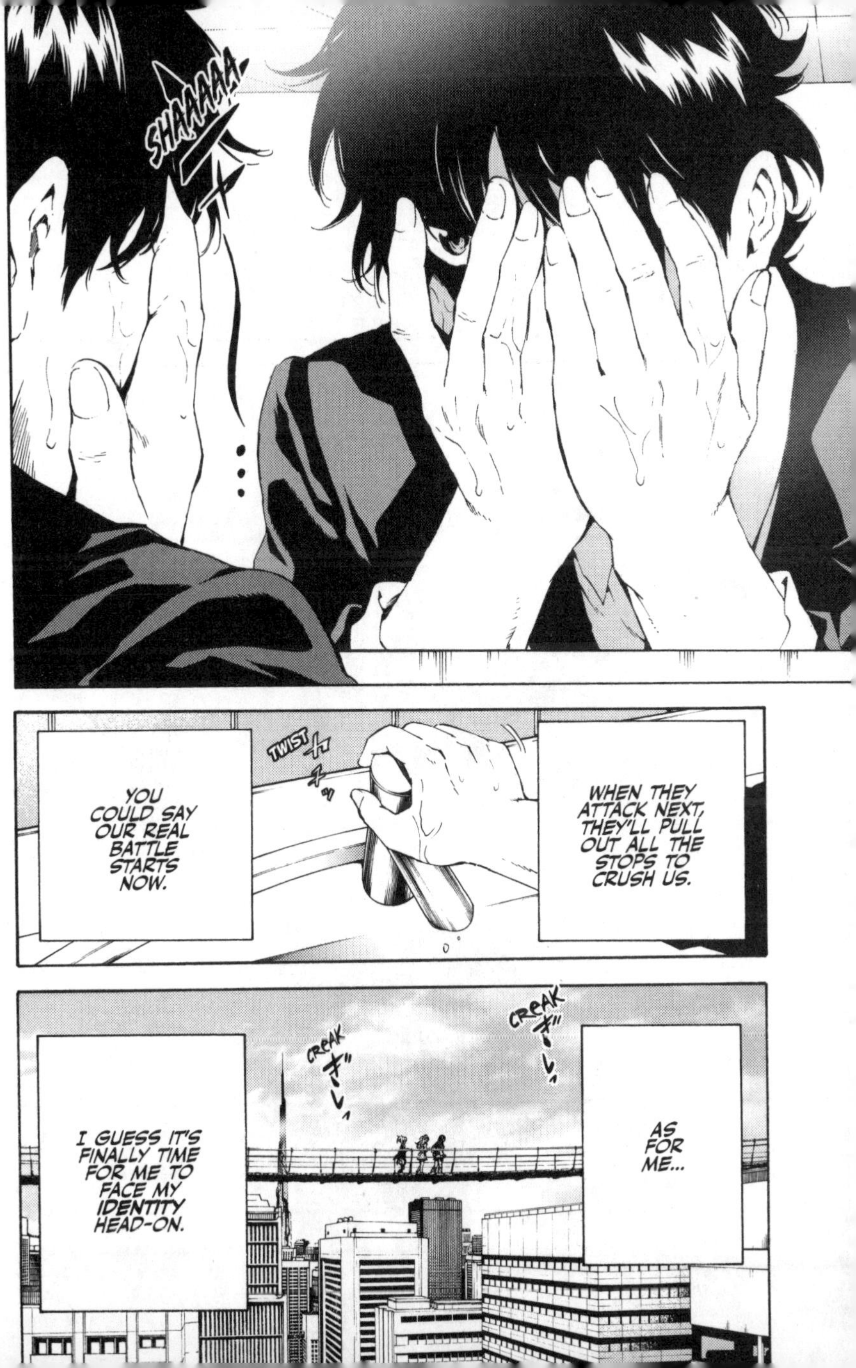
SHAAAAA
WHEN THEY ATTACK NEXT, THEY'LL PULL OUT ALL THE STOPS TO CRUSH US.
TWIST
YOU COULD SAY OUR REAL BATTLE STARTS NOW.
AS FOR ME...
CREAK
CREAK
I GUESS IT'S FINALLY TIME FOR ME TO FACE MY IDENTITY HEAD-ON.

CHAPTER 105: In Every World

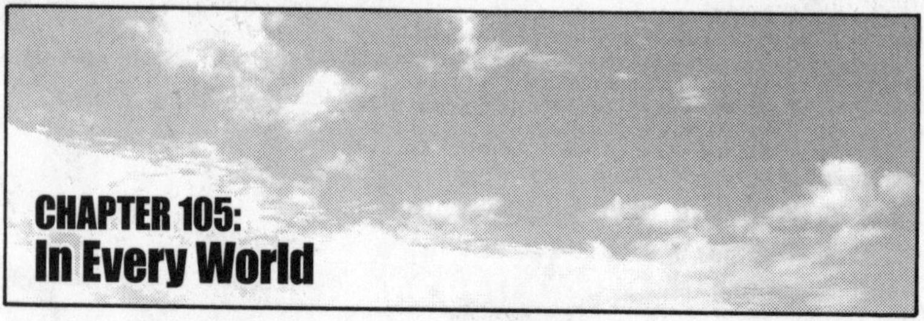

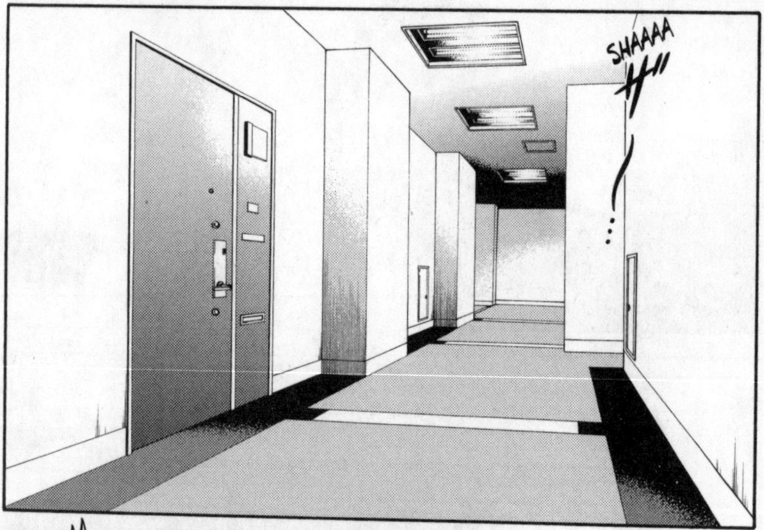
SHAAAA
...

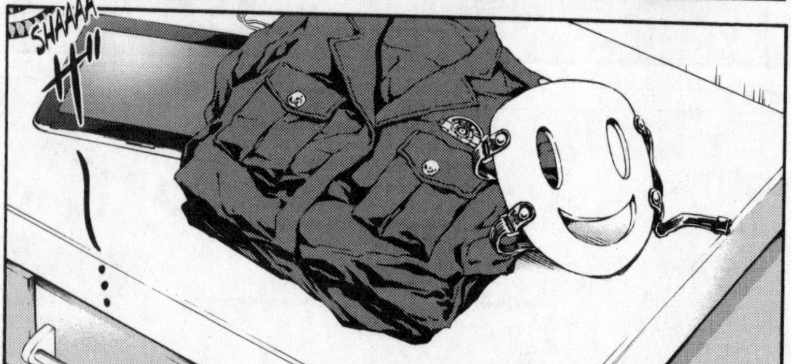
SHAAAA
...

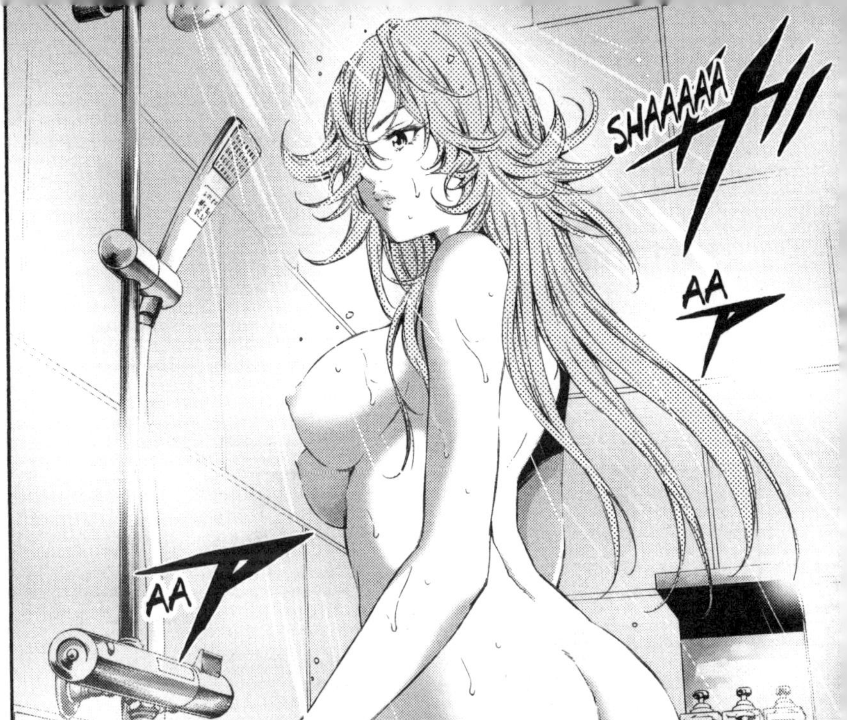
SHAAAAA
AA
AA
AAA
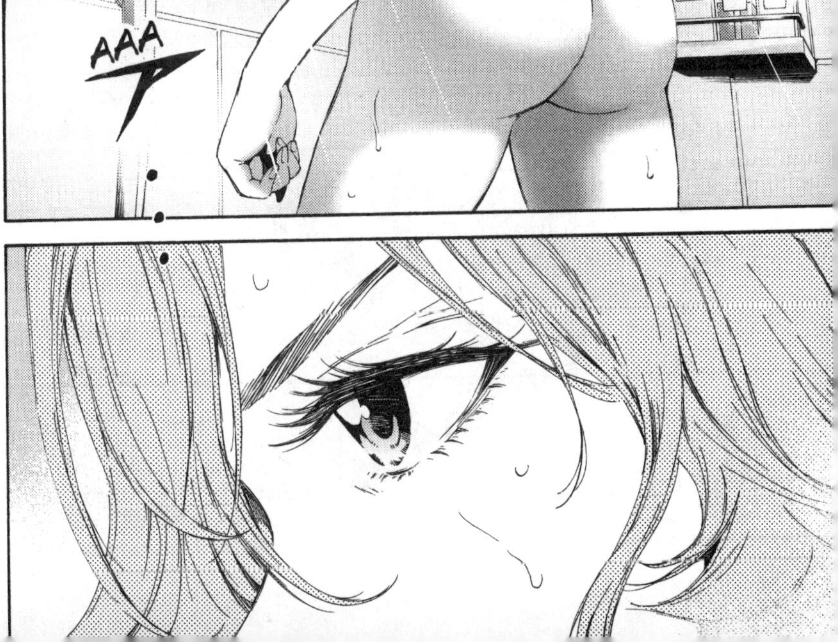

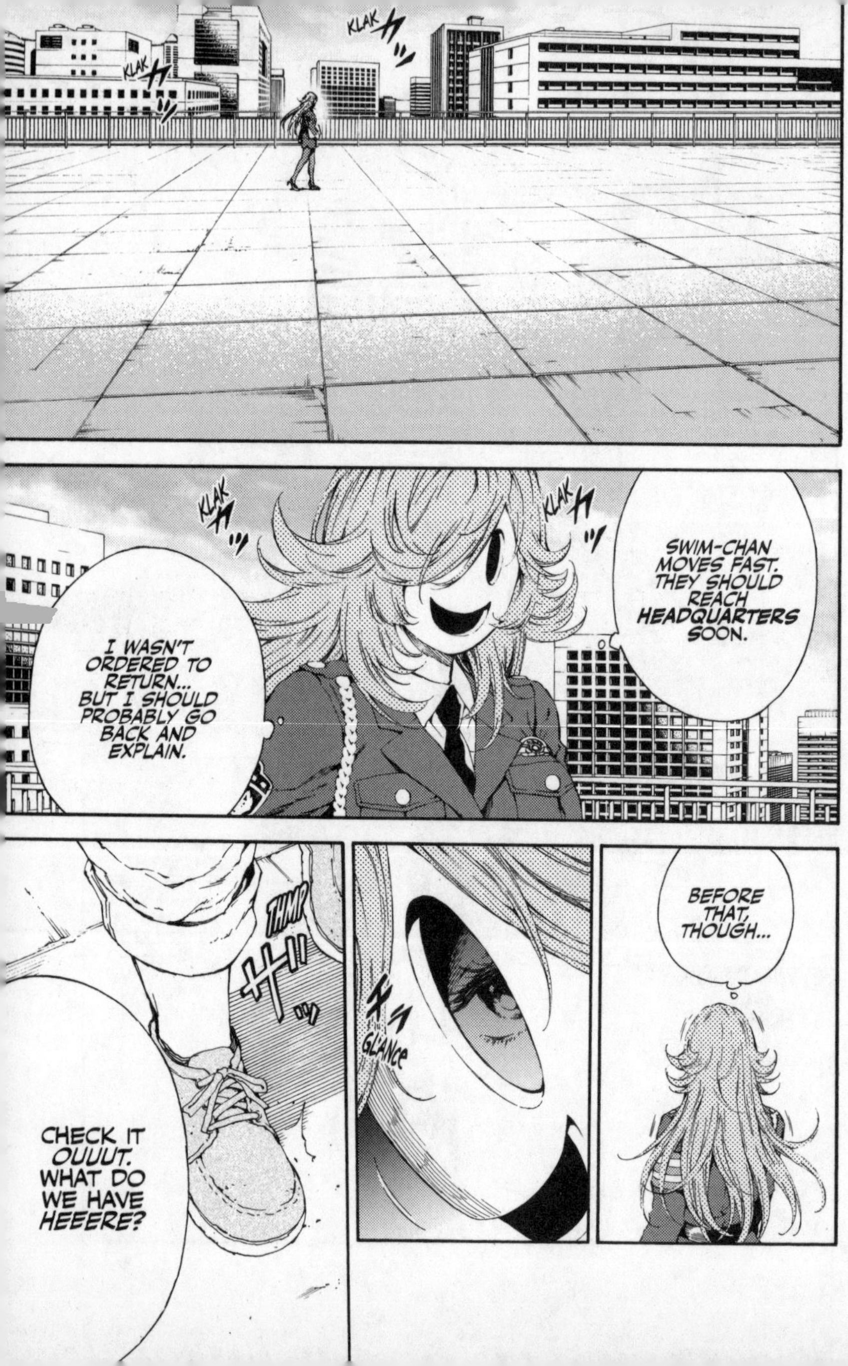
KLAK
KLAK
KLAK
SWIM-CHAN MOVES FAST. THEY SHOULD REACH **HEADQUARTERS** SOON.
KLAK
I WASN'T ORDERED TO RETURN... BUT I SHOULD PROBABLY GO BACK AND EXPLAIN.
BEFORE THAT, THOUGH...
GLANCE
THMP
CHECK IT OUUUT. WHAT DO WE HAVE HEEERE?

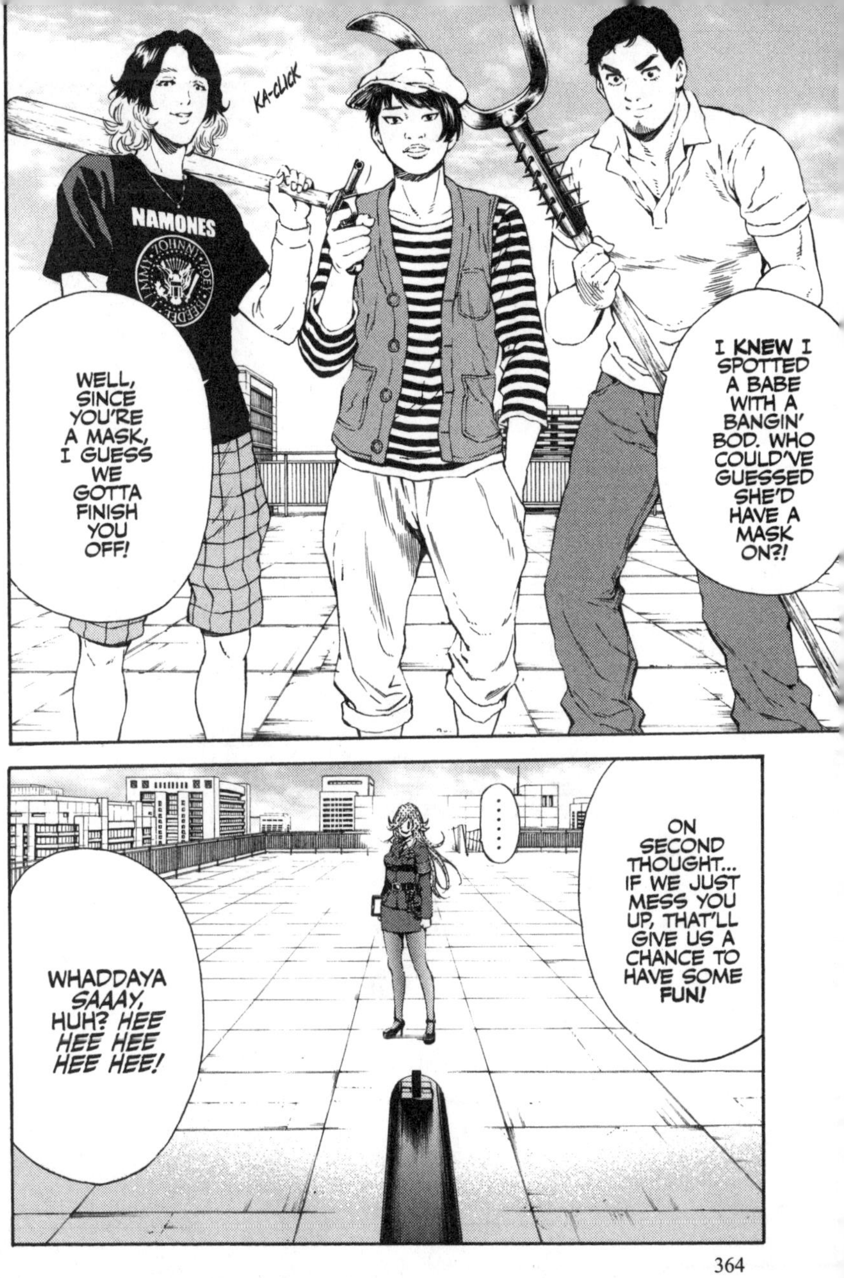
KA-CLICK
I KNEW I SPOTTED A BABE WITH A BANGIN' BOD. WHO COULD'VE GUESSED SHE'D HAVE A MASK ON?!
WELL, SINCE YOU'RE A MASK, I GUESS WE GOTTA FINISH YOU OFF!
......
ON SECOND THOUGHT... IF WE JUST MESS YOU UP, THAT'LL GIVE US A CHANCE TO HAVE SOME FUN!
WHADDAYA *SAAAY*, HUH? *HEE HEE HEE HEE HEE!*

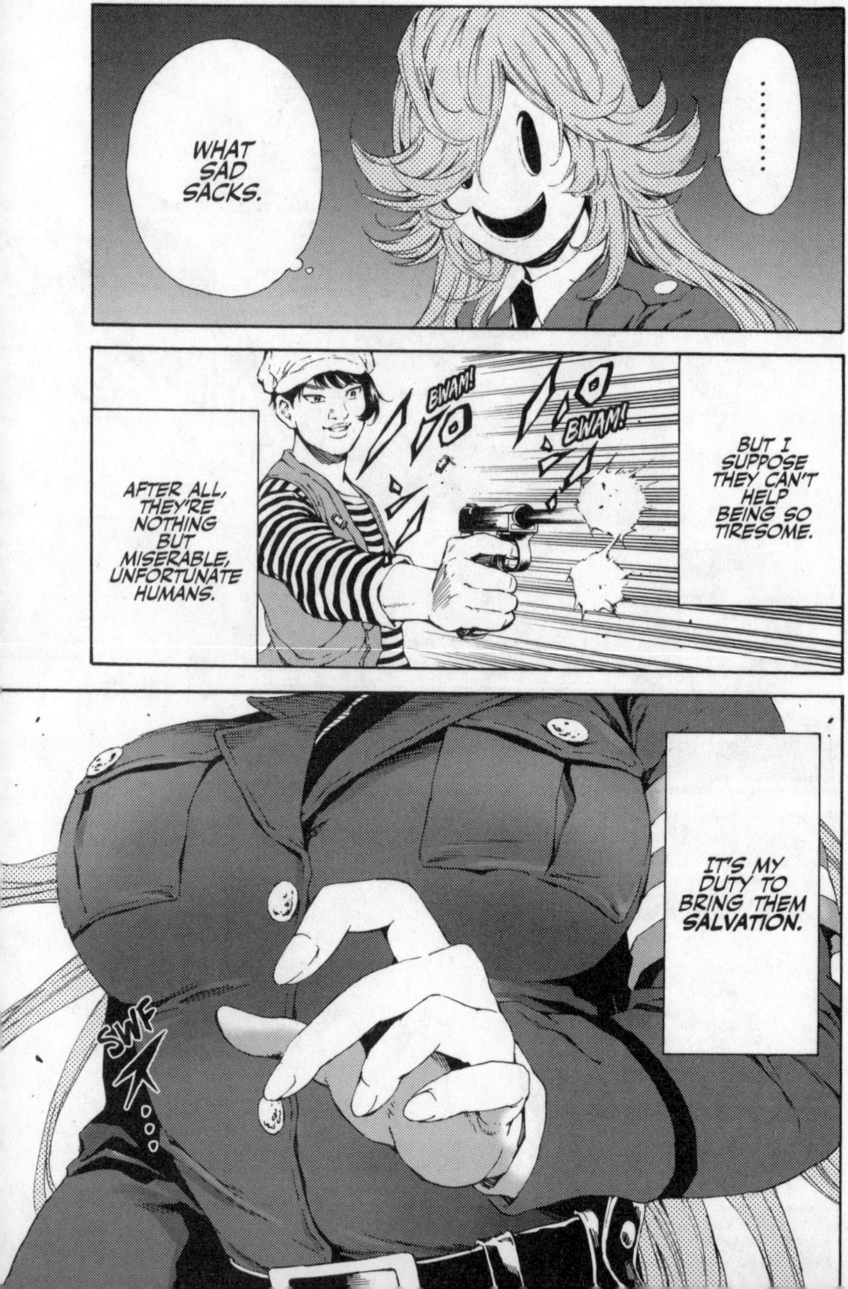
......
WHAT SAD SACKS.
BUT I SUPPOSE THEY CAN'T HELP BEING SO TIRESOME.
BWAM!
BWAM!
AFTER ALL, THEY'RE NOTHING BUT MISERABLE, UNFORTUNATE HUMANS.
IT'S MY DUTY TO BRING THEM SALVATION.
SWF

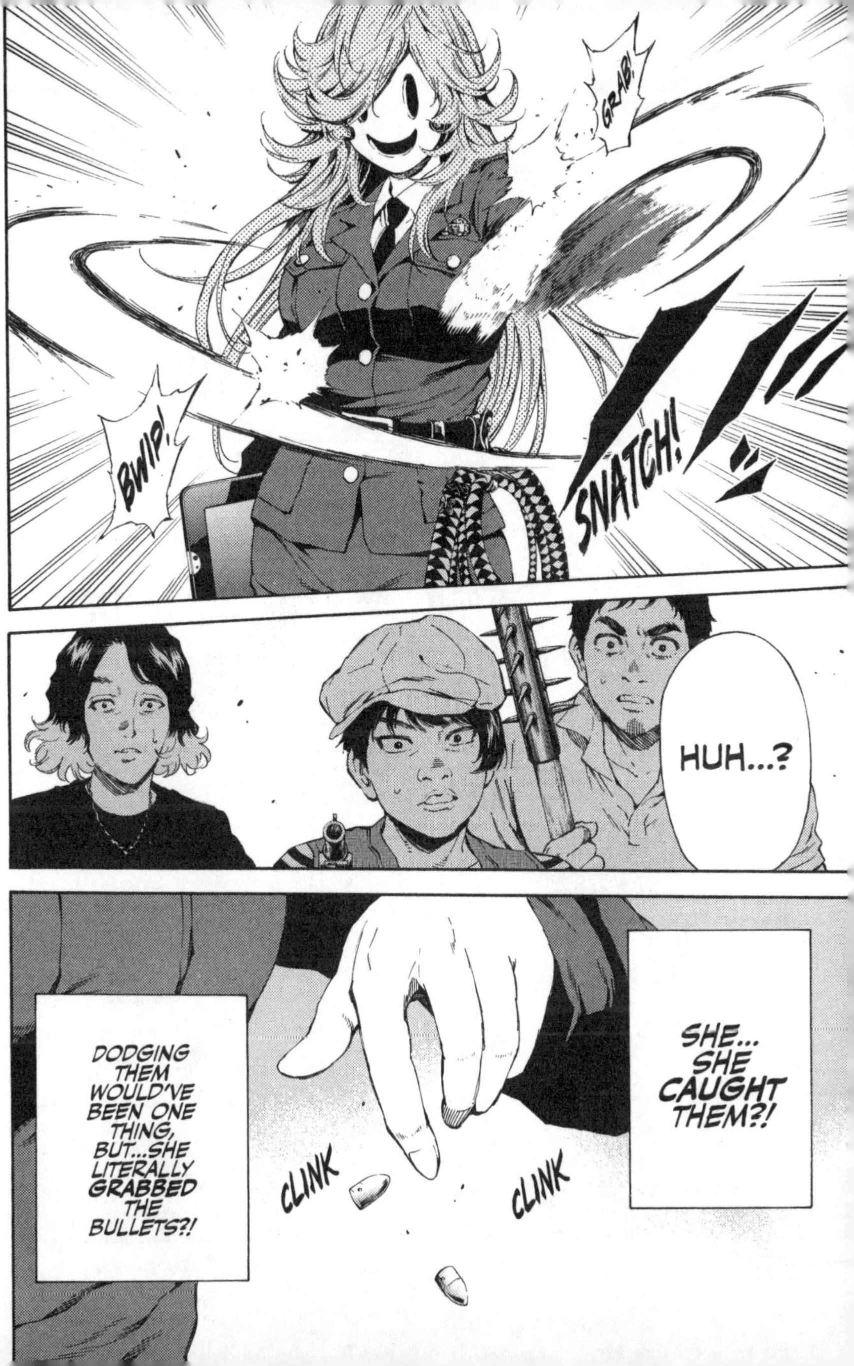
GRAB!
SNATCH!
BWIP!
HUH...?
SHE... SHE CAUGHT THEM?!
CLINK
CLINK
DODGING THEM WOULD'VE BEEN ONE THING, BUT...SHE LITERALLY GRABBED THE BULLETS?!

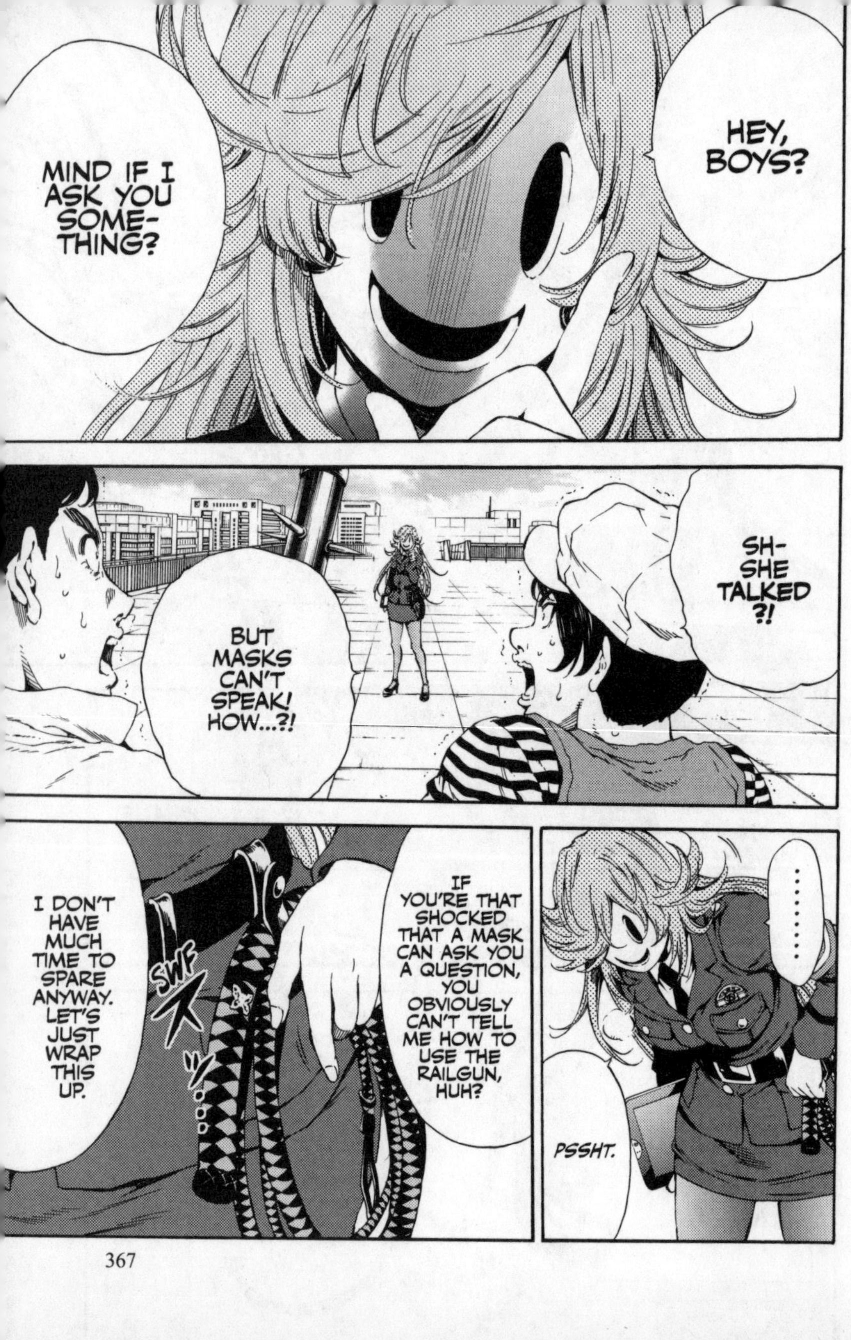
HEY, BOYS?
MIND IF I ASK YOU SOME-THING?
SH-SHE TALKED?!
BUT MASKS CAN'T SPEAK! HOW...?!
....
PSSHT.
IF YOU'RE THAT SHOCKED THAT A MASK CAN ASK YOU A QUESTION, YOU OBVIOUSLY CAN'T TELL ME HOW TO USE THE RAILGUN, HUH?
SWF
I DON'T HAVE MUCH TIME TO SPARE ANYWAY. LET'S JUST WRAP THIS UP.

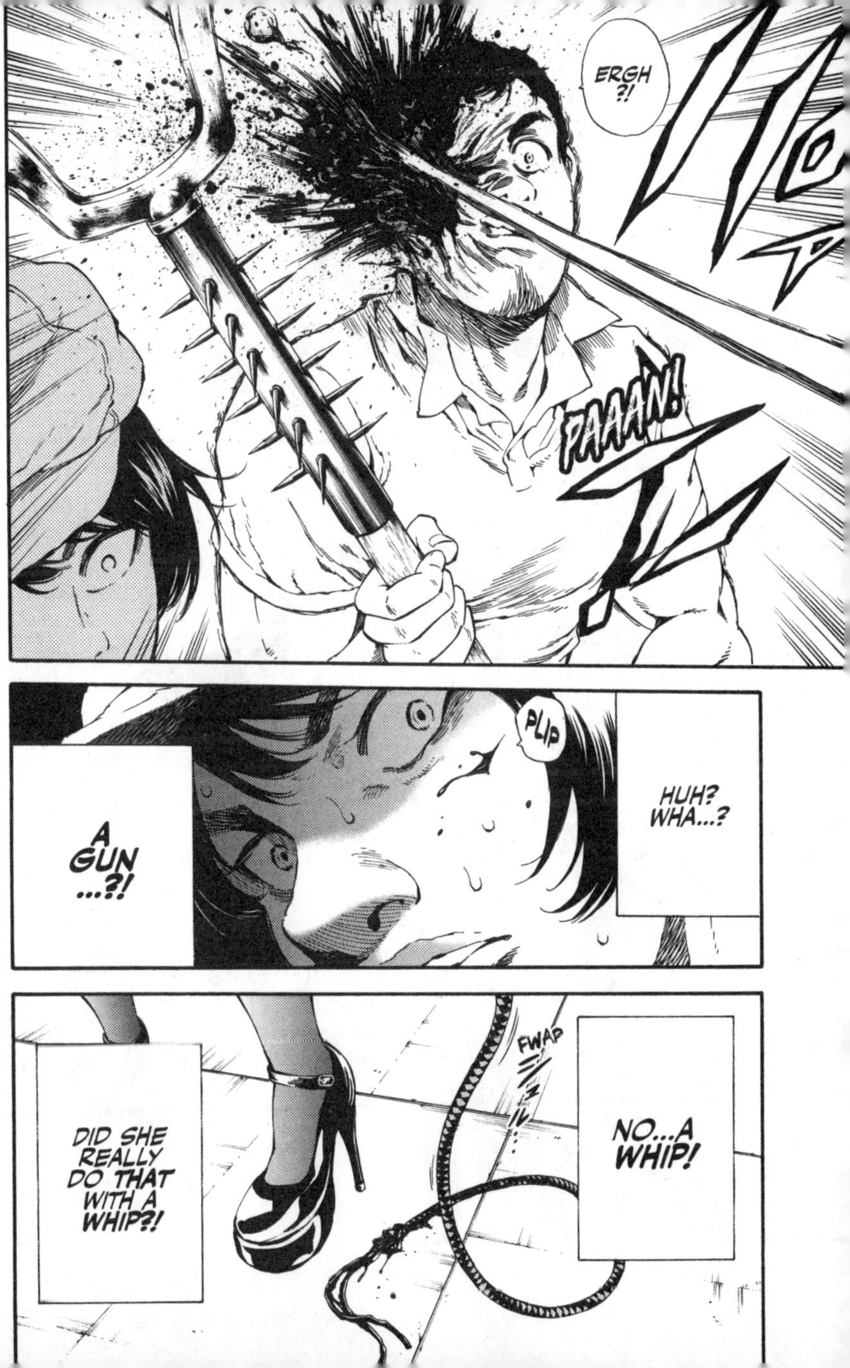
ERGH ?!
PAAAN!
HUH? WHA...?
PLIP
A GUN ...?!
NO...A WHIP!
FWAP
DID SHE REALLY DO THAT WITH A WHIP?!

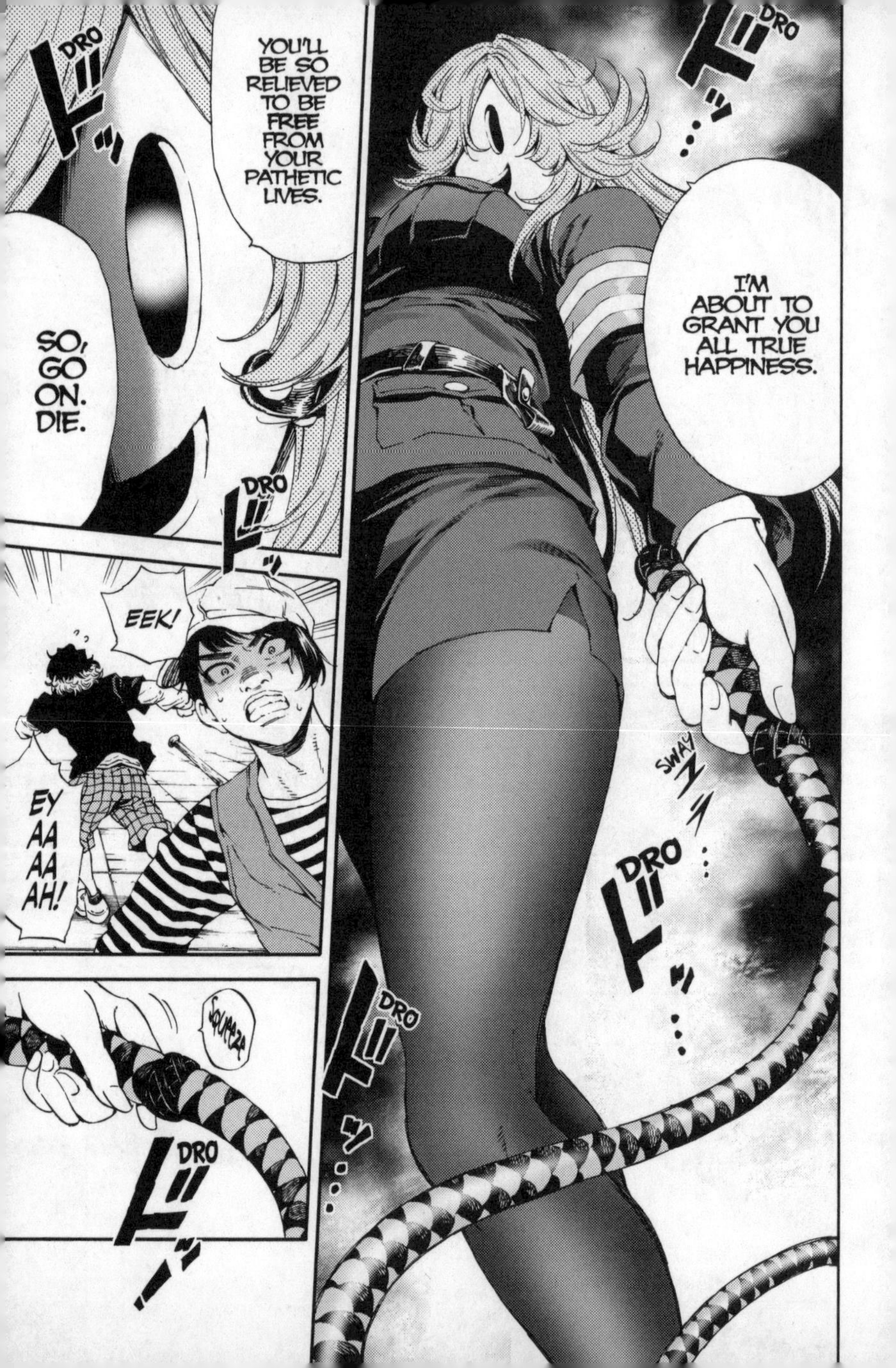

DRO
I'M ABOUT TO GRANT YOU ALL TRUE HAPPINESS.
SWAY
DRO
DRO
DRO
YOU'LL BE SO RELIEVED TO BE FREE FROM YOUR PATHETIC LIVES.
SO, GO ON. DIE.
DRO
EEK!
EYAAAAAAH!
Squeeze
DRO

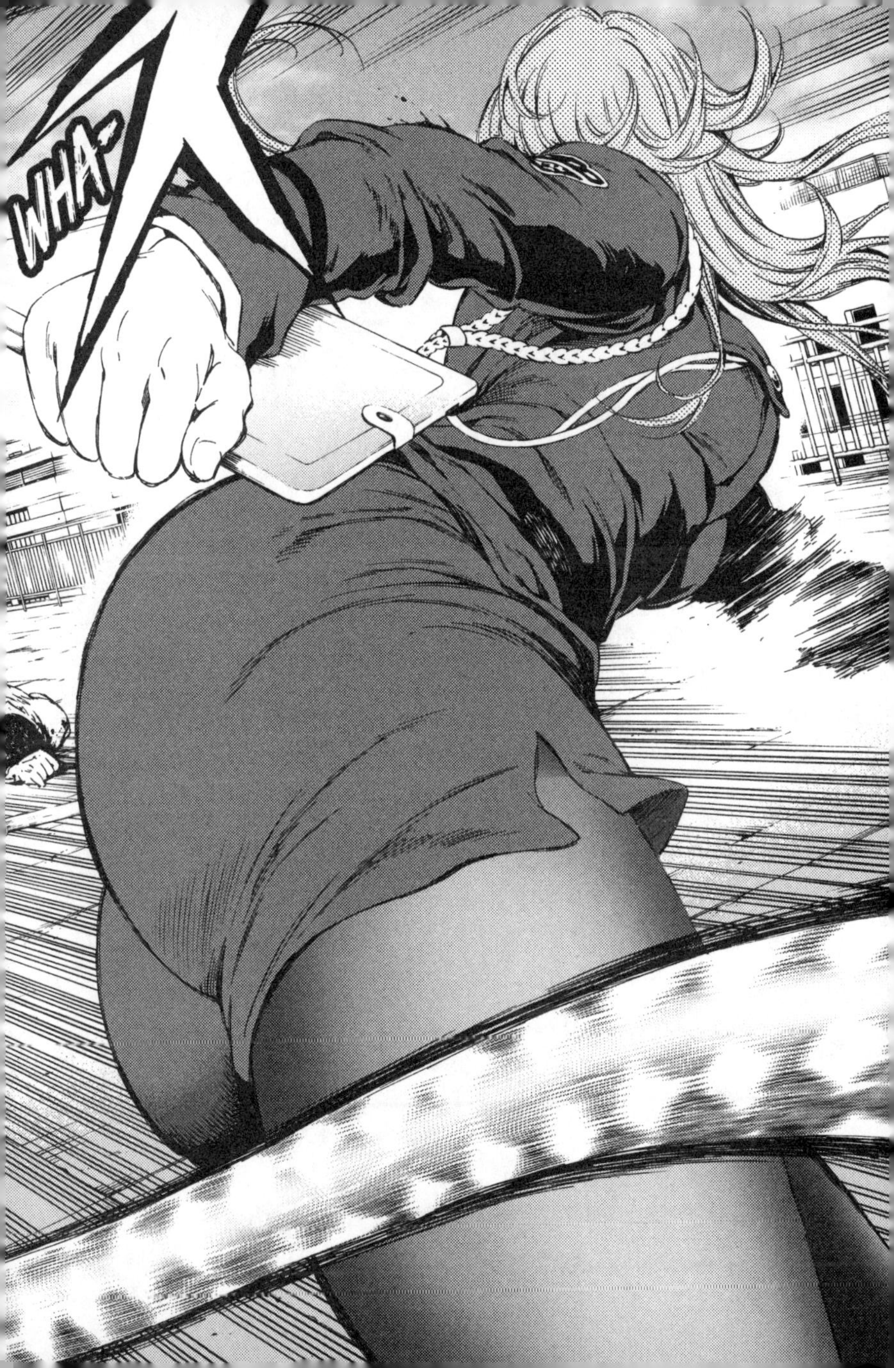
WHA-

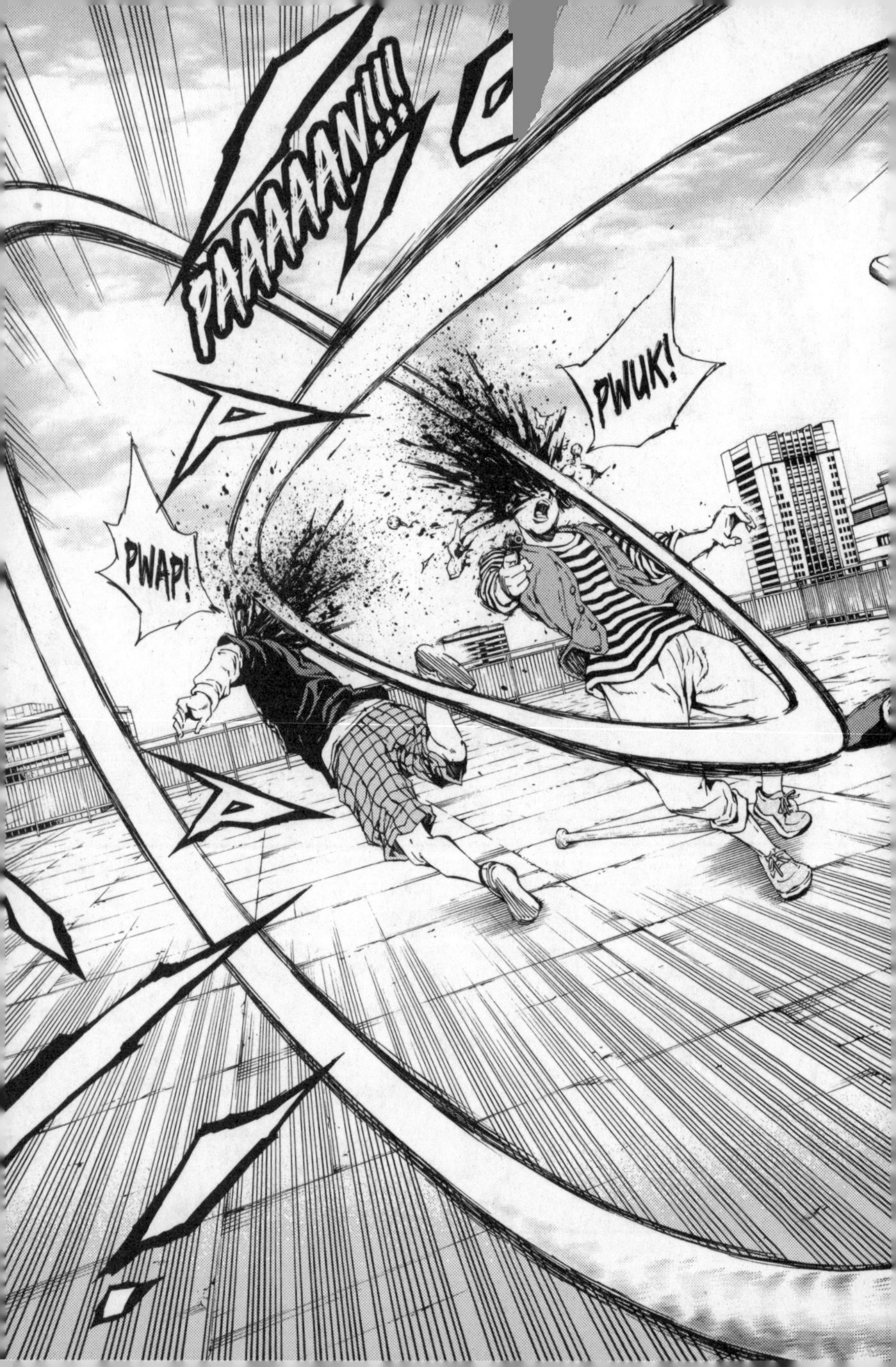
PAAAAAN!!!
PWUK!
PWAP!

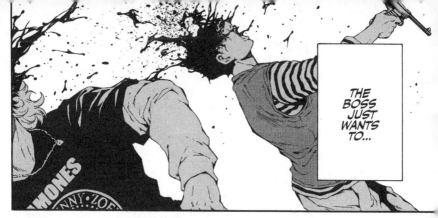

THE BOSS JUST WANTS TO...
MAKE HUMANKIND HAPPY.
NOT ONLY IN THIS REALM, EITHER. HUMANKIND IN EVERY WORLD.
HE'S TRYING TO OBTAIN GODHOOD SO THAT HE CAN MAKE THAT HAPPEN.
TO HELP MAKE THAT NOBLE DREAM COME TRUE, I'LL DESTROY ANYTHING IN HIS WAY!

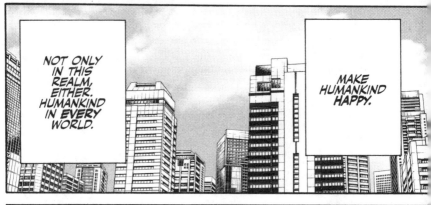

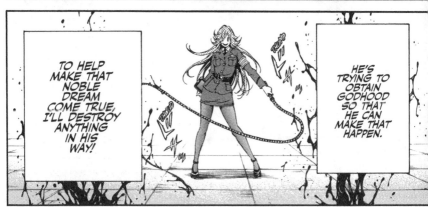

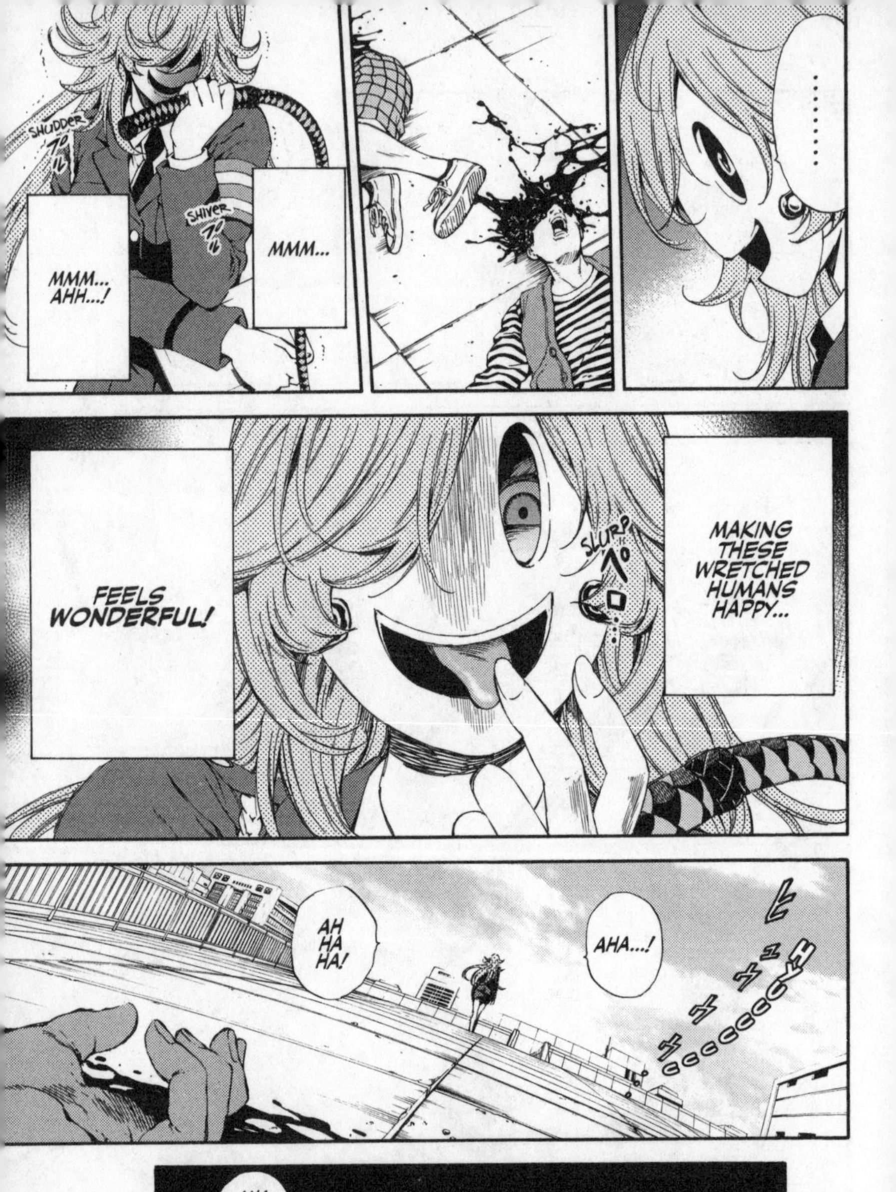

SHUDDER
フル
SHIVER
フル
MMM...
MMM... AHH...!
MAKING THESE WRETCHED HUMANS HAPPY...
SLURP
FEELS WONDERFUL!
ヒュククク
AHA...!
AH HA HA HA!
AHA HA HA HA!

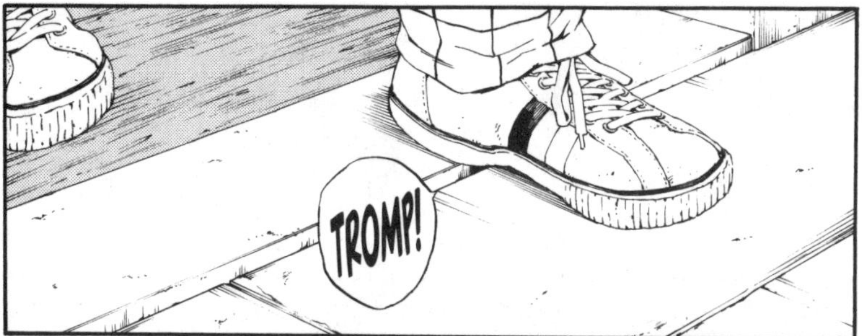
TROMP!

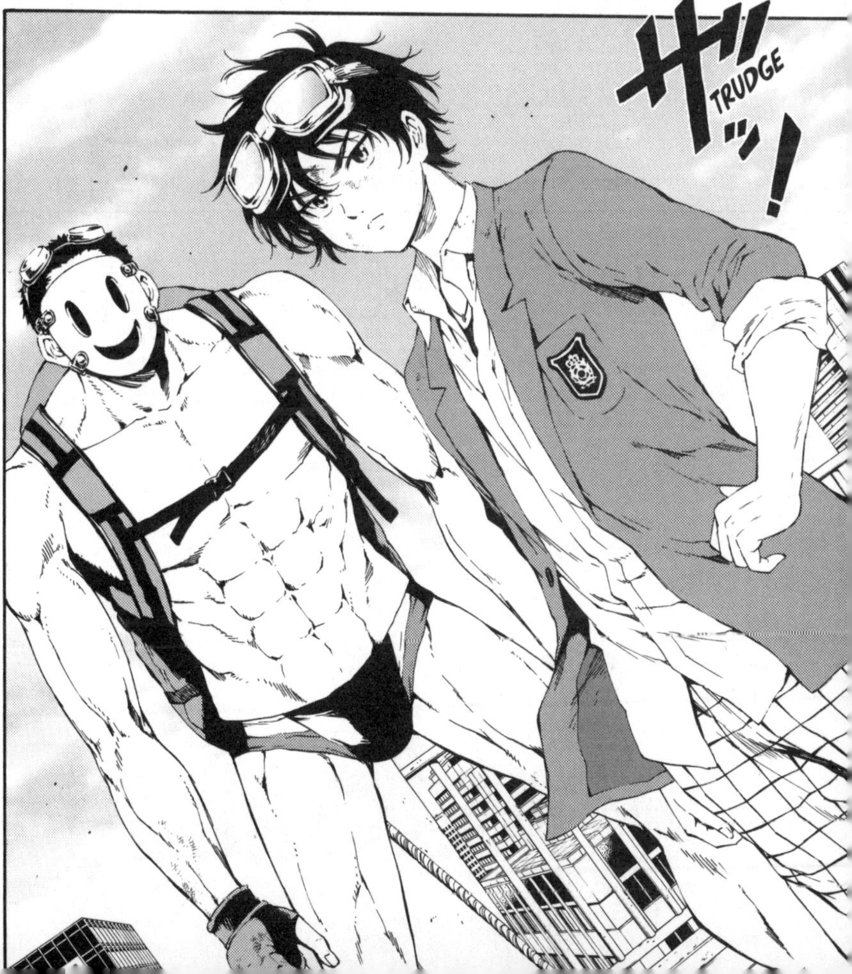
TRUDGE

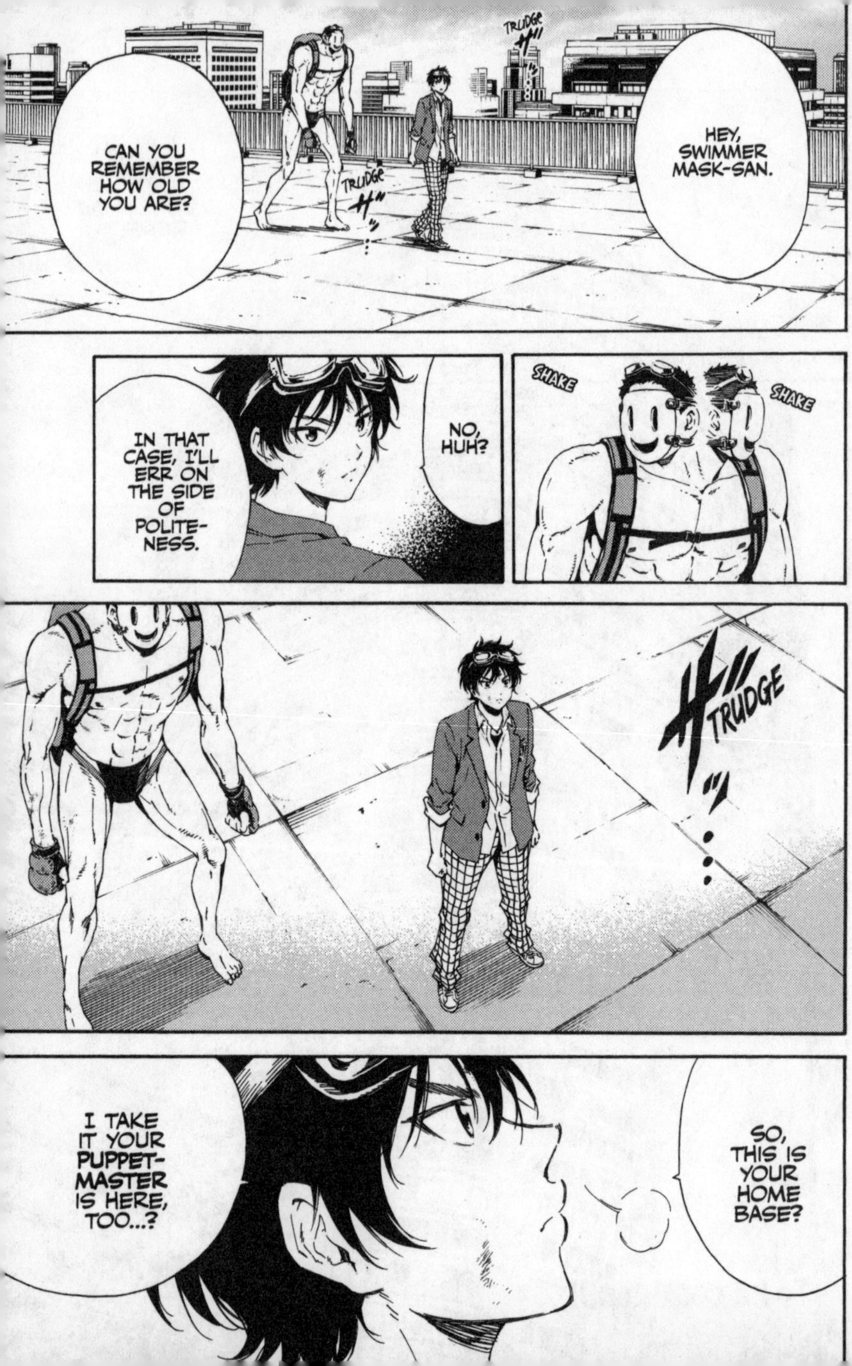
HEY, SWIMMER MASK-SAN.
TRUDGE
CAN YOU REMEMBER HOW OLD YOU ARE?
TRUDGE
SHAKE
SHAKE
NO, HUH?
IN THAT CASE, I'LL ERR ON THE SIDE OF POLITE-NESS.
TRUDGE
SO, THIS IS YOUR HOME BASE?
I TAKE IT YOUR PUPPET-MASTER IS HERE, TOO...?

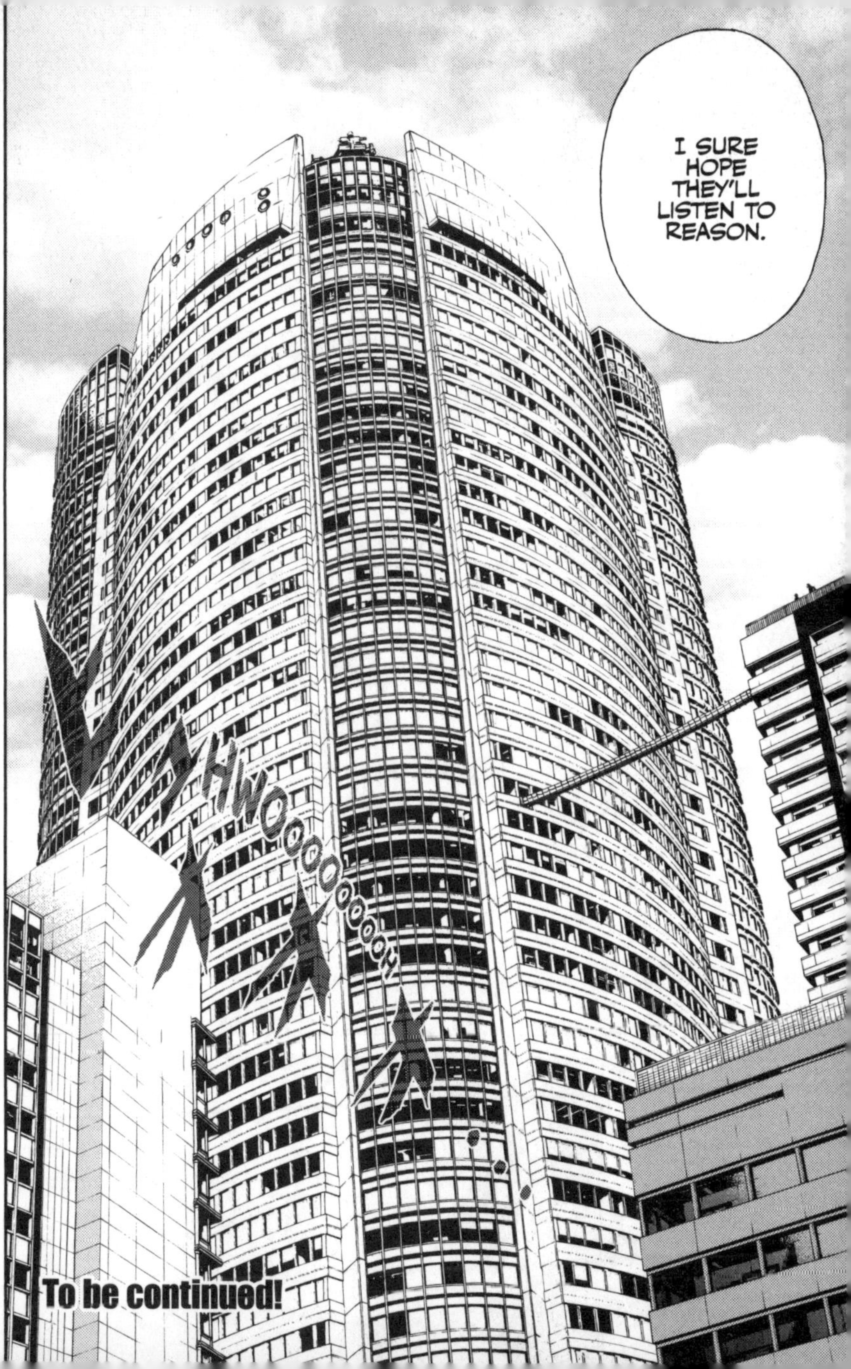
I SURE HOPE THEY'LL LISTEN TO REASON.
HWOOOOOOOOH
To be continued!

HIGH-RISE INVASION

STORY
Tsuina Miura

ART
Takahiro Oba

STAFF
Fukuen Kanako
Saito Yuusaku
Sakurai Hiroshi

EDITORS
Uchida Tomohiro
Kohori Ryuuichi

COMICS EDITOR
Nozawa Shinobu

COVER DESIGN
Inadome Ken

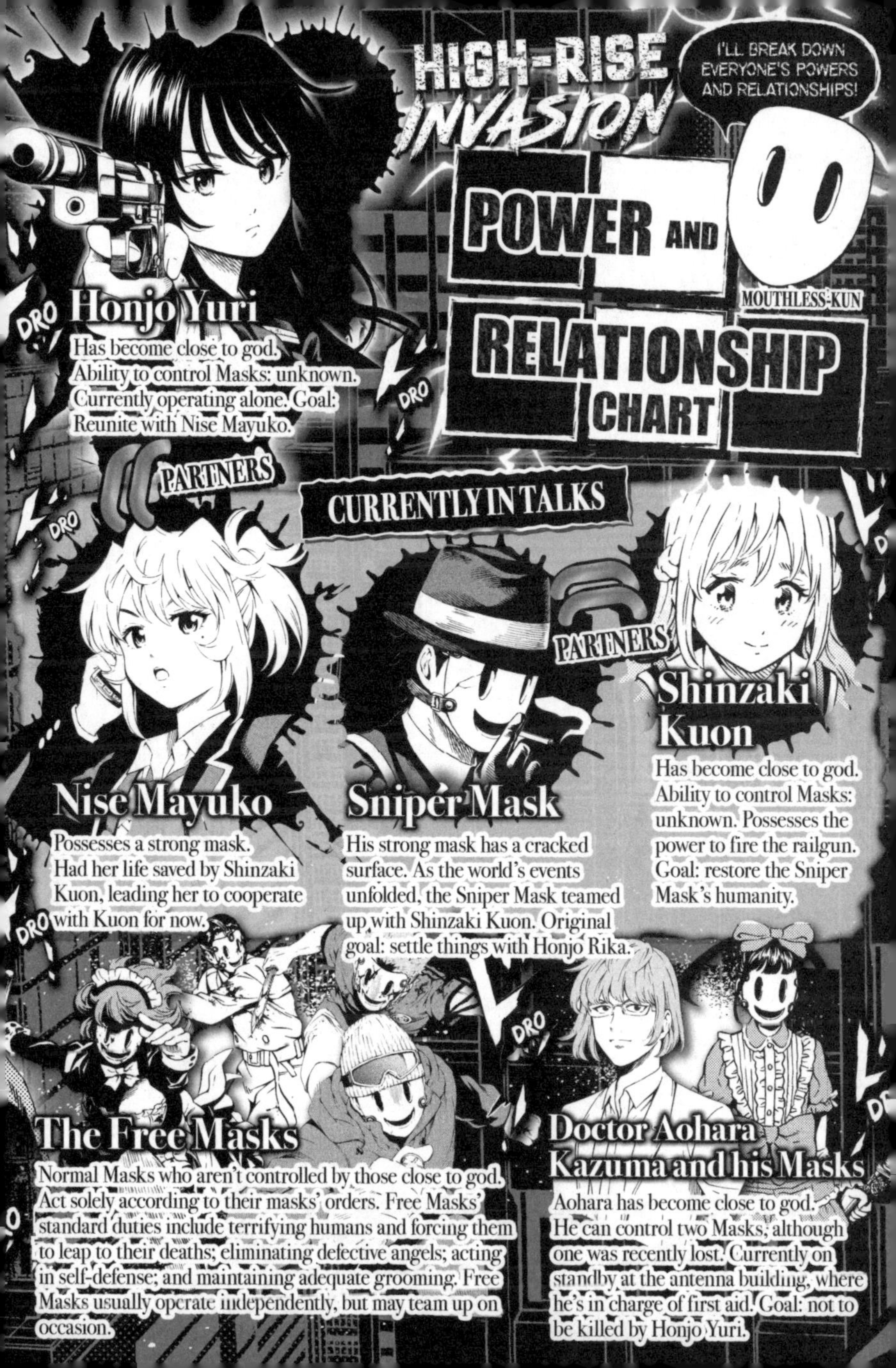

HIGH-RISE INVASION
I'LL BREAK DOWN EVERYONE'S POWERS AND RELATIONSHIPS!
POWER AND RELATIONSHIP CHART
MOUTHLESS-KUN
DRO
Honjo Yuri
Has become close to god. Ability to control Masks: unknown. Currently operating alone. Goal: Reunite with Nise Mayuko.
DRO
PARTNERS
CURRENTLY IN TALKS
DRO
PARTNERS
Nise Mayuko
Possesses a strong mask. Had her life saved by Shinzaki Kuon, leading her to cooperate with Kuon for now.
Sniper Mask
His strong mask has a cracked surface. As the world's events unfolded, the Sniper Mask teamed up with Shinzaki Kuon. Original goal: settle things with Honjo Rika.
Shinzaki Kuon
Has become close to god. Ability to control Masks: unknown. Possesses the power to fire the railgun. Goal: restore the Sniper Mask's humanity.
DRO
DRO
The Free Masks
Normal Masks who aren't controlled by those close to god. Act solely according to their masks' orders. Free Masks' standard duties include terrifying humans and forcing them to leap to their deaths; eliminating defective angels; acting in self-defense; and maintaining adequate grooming. Free Masks usually operate independently, but may team up on occasion.
Doctor Aohara Kazuma and his Masks
Aohara has become close to god. He can control two Masks, although one was recently lost. Currently on standby at the antenna building, where he's in charge of first aid. Goal: not to be killed by Honjo Yuri.

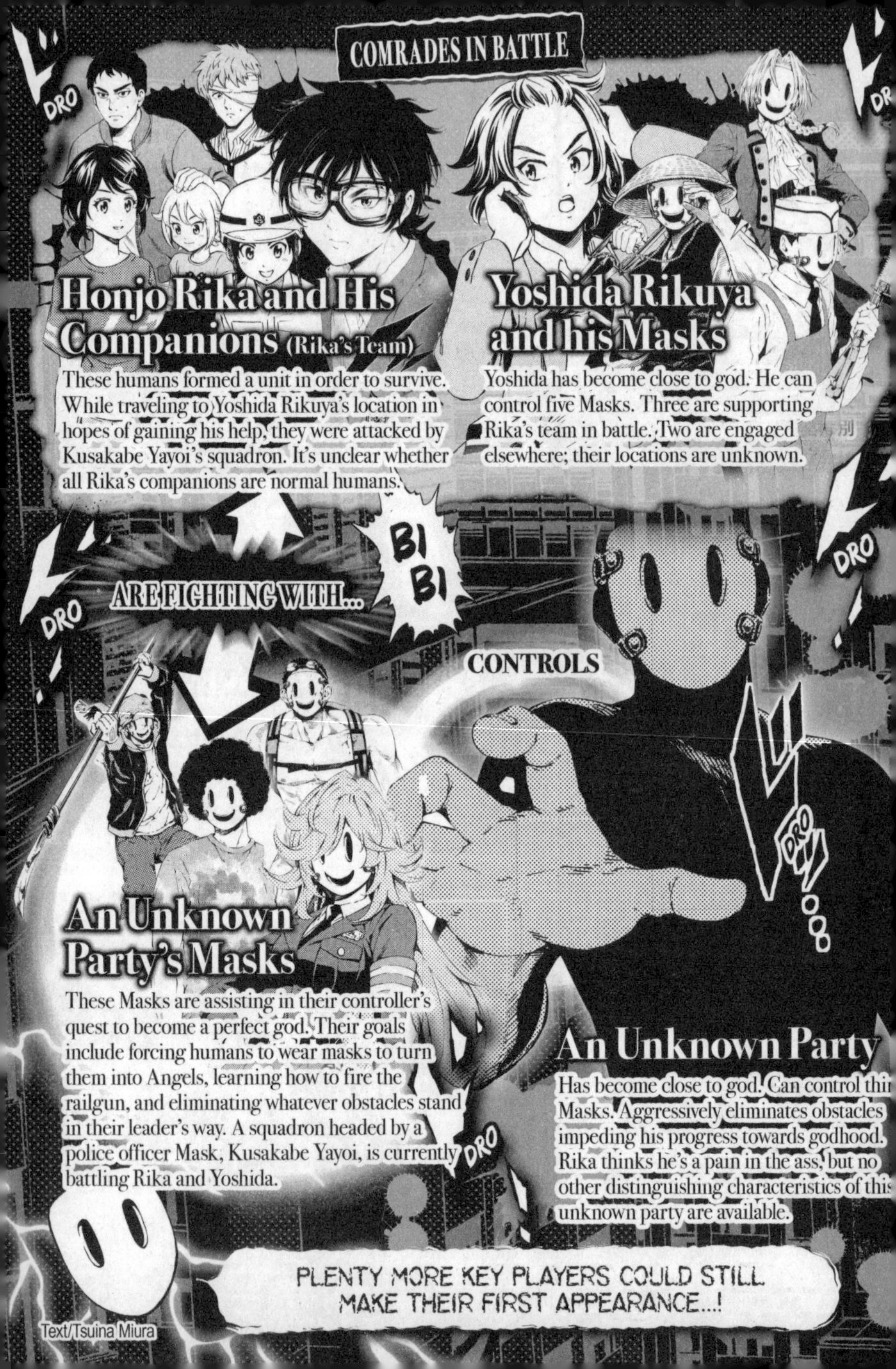

COMRADES IN BATTLE
DRO
DRO
Honjo Rika and His Companions (Rika's Team)
These humans formed a unit in order to survive. While traveling to Yoshida Rikuya's location in hopes of gaining his help, they were attacked by Kusakabe Yayoi's squadron. It's unclear whether all Rika's companions are normal humans.
Yoshida Rikuya and his Masks
Yoshida has become close to god. He can control five Masks. Three are supporting Rika's team in battle. Two are engaged elsewhere; their locations are unknown.
BI BI
DRO
ARE FIGHTING WITH...
DRO
CONTROLS
DRO
An Unknown Party's Masks
These Masks are assisting in their controller's quest to become a perfect god. Their goals include forcing humans to wear masks to turn them into Angels, learning how to fire the railgun, and eliminating whatever obstacles stand in their leader's way. A squadron headed by a police officer Mask, Kusakabe Yayoi, is currently battling Rika and Yoshida.
DRO
An Unknown Party
Has become close to god. Can control thi Masks. Aggressively eliminates obstacles impeding his progress towards godhood. Rika thinks he's a pain in the ass, but no other distinguishing characteristics of thi unknown party are available.
PLENTY MORE KEY PLAYERS COULD STILL MAKE THEIR FIRST APPEARANCE...!
Text/Tsuina Miura

To Celebrate the Schoolgirls Joining Forces...

Mouthless-kun will analyze the trio (kind of) thoroughly!

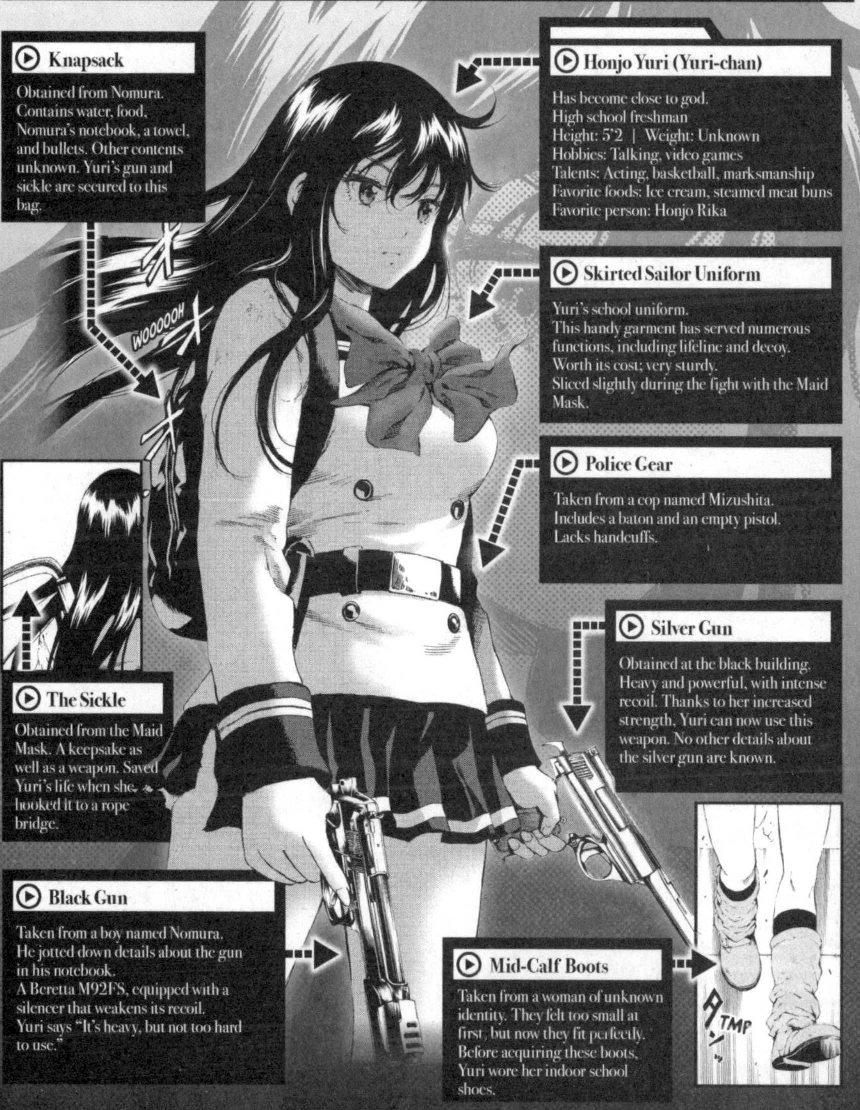
WOOOOOOH
TMP

Honjo Yuri (Yuri-chan)

Has become close to god.
High school freshman
Height: 5'2 | Weight: Unknown
Hobbies: Talking, video games
Talents: Acting, basketball, marksmanship
Favorite foods: Ice cream, steamed meat buns
Favorite person: Honjo Rika

Knapsack

Obtained from Nomura. Contains water, food, Nomura's notebook, a towel, and bullets. Other contents unknown. Yuri's gun and sickle are secured to this bag.

Skirted Sailor Uniform

Yuri's school uniform.
This handy garment has served numerous functions, including lifeline and decoy.
Worth its cost; very sturdy.
Sliced slightly during the fight with the Maid Mask.

Police Gear

Taken from a cop named Mizushita.
Includes a baton and an empty pistol.
Lacks handcuffs.

The Sickle

Obtained from the Maid Mask. A keepsake as well as a weapon. Saved Yuri's life when she hooked it to a rope bridge.

Silver Gun

Obtained at the black building. Heavy and powerful, with intense recoil. Thanks to her increased strength, Yuri can now use this weapon. No other details about the silver gun are known.

Black Gun

Taken from a boy named Nomura. He jotted down details about the gun in his notebook.
A Beretta M92FS, equipped with a silencer that weakens its recoil.
Yuri says "It's heavy, but not too hard to use."

Mid-Calf Boots

Taken from a woman of unknown identity. They felt too small at first, but now they fit perfectly. Before acquiring these boots, Yuri wore her indoor school shoes.

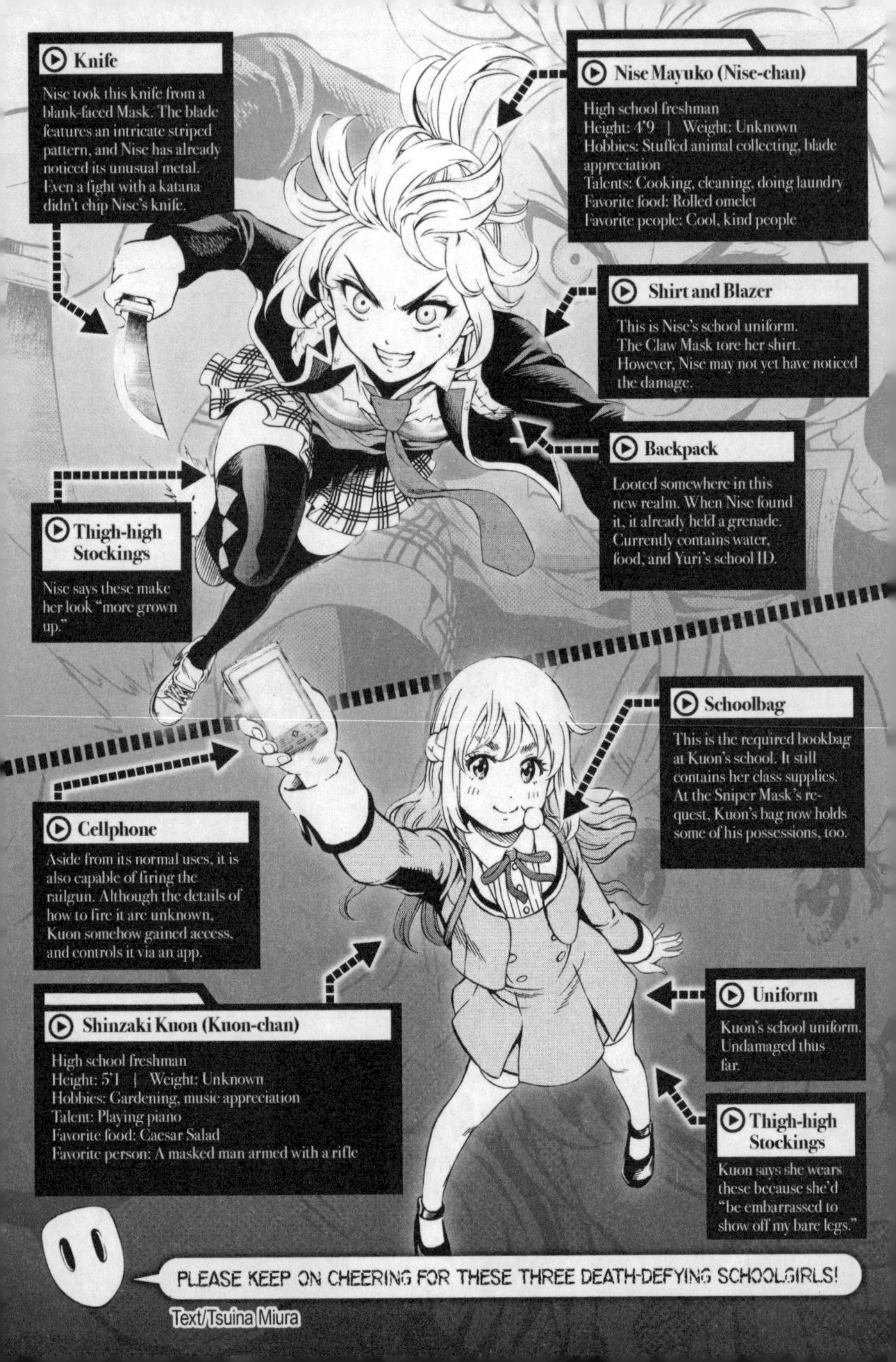

Nise Mayuko (Nise-chan)
High school freshman
Height: 4'9 | Weight: Unknown
Hobbies: Stuffed animal collecting, blade appreciation
Talents: Cooking, cleaning, doing laundry
Favorite food: Rolled omelet
Favorite people: Cool, kind people
Knife
Nise took this knife from a blank-faced Mask. The blade features an intricate striped pattern, and Nise has already noticed its unusual metal. Even a fight with a katana didn't chip Nise's knife.
Shirt and Blazer
This is Nise's school uniform. The Claw Mask tore her shirt. However, Nise may not yet have noticed the damage.
Backpack
Looted somewhere in this new realm. When Nise found it, it already held a grenade. Currently contains water, food, and Yuri's school ID.
Thigh-high Stockings
Nise says these make her look "more grown up."
Schoolbag
This is the required bookbag at Kuon's school. It still contains her class supplies. At the Sniper Mask's request, Kuon's bag now holds some of his possessions, too.
Cellphone
Aside from its normal uses, it is also capable of firing the railgun. Although the details of how to fire it are unknown, Kuon somehow gained access, and controls it via an app.
Uniform
Kuon's school uniform. Undamaged thus far.
Shinzaki Kuon (Kuon-chan)
High school freshman
Height: 5'1 | Weight: Unknown
Hobbies: Gardening, music appreciation
Talent: Playing piano
Favorite food: Caesar Salad
Favorite person: A masked man armed with a rifle
Thigh-high Stockings
Kuon says she wears these because she'd "be embarrassed to show off my bare legs."
PLEASE KEEP ON CHEERING FOR THESE THREE DEATH-DEFYING SCHOOLGIRLS!
Text/Tsuina Miura

HIGH-RISE INVASION

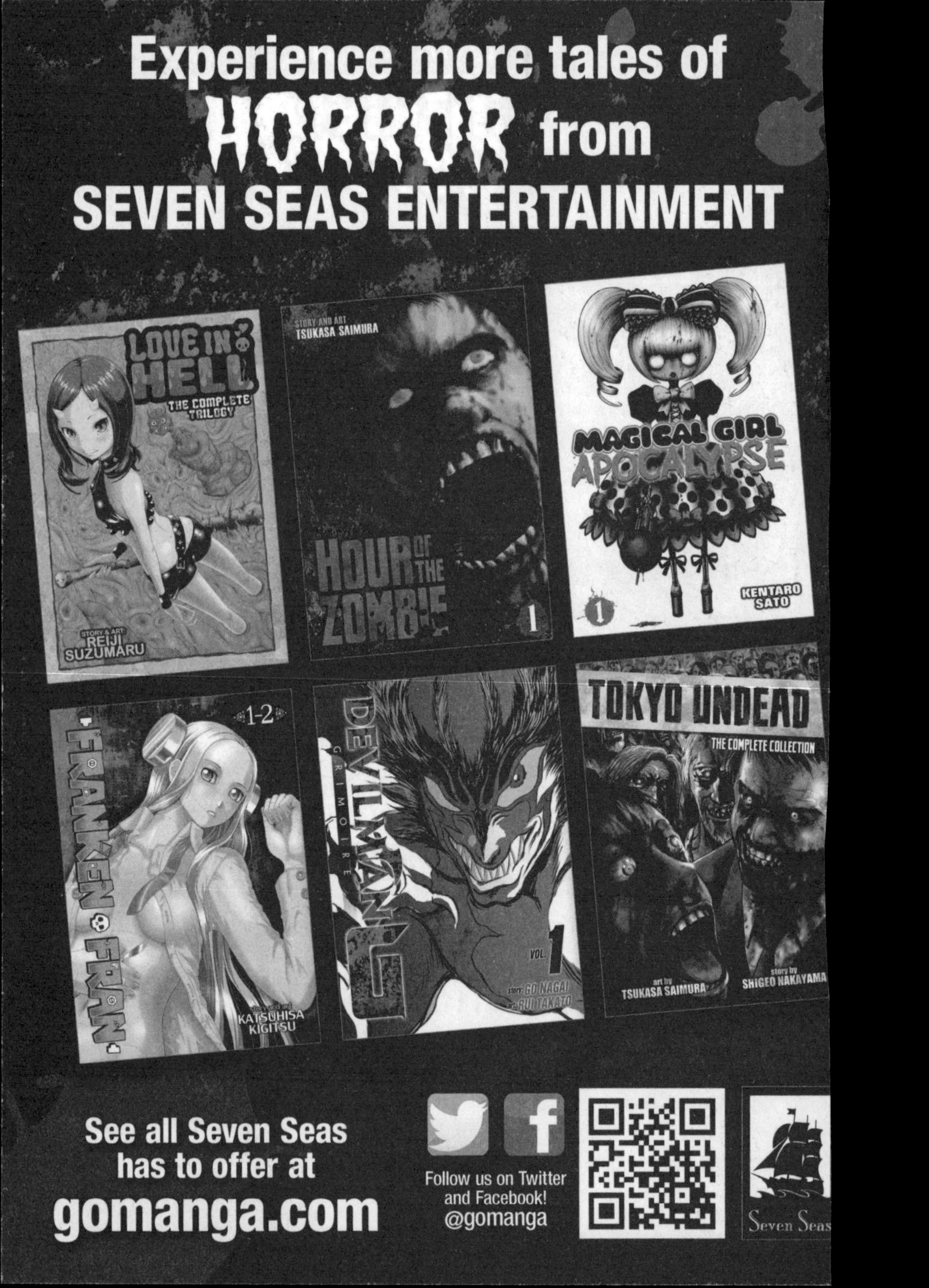

Experience more tales of
HORROR from
SEVEN SEAS ENTERTAINMENT
LOVE IN HELL
THE COMPLETE TRILOGY
STORY & ART: REIJI SUZUMARU
STORY AND ART TSUKASA SAIMURA
HOUR OF THE ZOMBIE
1
MAGICAL GIRL APOCALYPSE
1
KENTARO SATO
1-2
FRANKEN FRAN
KATSUHISA KIGITSU
DEVILMAN
GRIMOIRE
VOL. 1
story: GO NAGAI
RUI TAKATO
TOKYO UNDEAD
THE COMPLETE COLLECTION
art by TSUKASA SAIMURA
story by SHIGEO NAKAYAMA
See all Seven Seas
has to offer at
gomanga.com
Follow us on Twitter
and Facebook!
@gomanga
Seven Seas

SEVEN SEAS ENT...

vol. 7-8

story by **TSUINA MIURA** / art by **TAKAHIRO OBA**

TRANSLATION
Nan Rymer

ADAPTATION
Rebecca Schneidereit

LETTERING AND RETOUCH
Meaghan Tucker

COVER DESIGN
KC Fabellon

PROOFREADER
Janet Houck
Cae Hawksmoor

EDITOR
J.P. Sullivan

PRODUCTION MANAGER
Lissa Pattillo

MANAGING EDITOR
Julie Davis

EDITOR-IN-CHIEF
Adam Arnold

PUBLISHER
Jason DeAngelis

TENKUU SHINPAN VOLUME 7-8
© Tsuina Miura 2016, © Takahiro Oba 2016
All rights reserved.
First published in Japan in 2016 by Kodansha Ltd., Tokyo.
Publication rights for this English edition arranged through Kodansha Ltd.,
Tokyo.

Seven Seas press and purchase enquiries can be sent to Marketing Manager
Lianne Sentar at press@gomanga.com. Information regarding the distribution
and purchase of digital editions is available from Digital Manager CK Russell
at digital@gomanga.com.

Seven Seas and the Seven Seas logo are trademarks of
Seven Seas Entertainment. All rights reserved.

ISBN: 978-1-642750-77-5

Printed in Canada

First Printing: May 2019

10 9 8 7 6 5 4 3 2 1

FOLLOW US ONLINE: www.sevenseasentertainment.com

READING DIRECTIONS

This book reads from *right to left*, Japanese style.
If this is your first time reading manga, you start
reading from the top right panel on each page and
take it from there. If you get lost, just follow the
numbered diagram here. It may seem backwards at
first, but you'll get the hang of it! Have fun!!

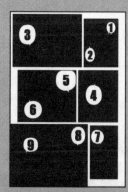